Western Broadcasting at the Dawn of the 21st Century

Communications Monograph
Vol. 4

Editors

Karsten Renckstorf
Department of Communication, University of Nijmegen
The Netherlands

Rolf T. Wigand
School of Information Studies, Syracuse University/NY
United States of America

Mouton de Gruyter
Berlin · New York

Western Broadcasting at the Dawn of the 21st Century

Edited by

Leen d'Haenens
Frieda Saeys

Mouton de Gruyter
Berlin · New York   2001

Mouton de Gruyter (formerly Mouton, The Hague)
is a Division of Walter de Gruyter GmbH & Co. KG, Berlin.

♾ Printed on acid-free paper which falls within the guidelines
of the ANSI to ensure permanence and durability.

Die Deutsche Bibliothek − *Cataloging-in-Publication Data*

> Western broadcasting at the dawn of the 21st century / ed. by Leen
> d'Haenens ; Frieda Saeys. − Berlin ; New York : Mouton de Gruy-
> ter, 2001
>   (Communications monograph ; 4)
>   ISBN 3-11-017363-8 brosch.
>   ISBN 3-11-017386-7 Gb.

Printing: WB-Druck, Rieden/Allgäu.
Binding: Lüderitz & Bauer, Berlin.
Cover design: Sigurd Wendland, Berlin.
Printed in Germany.

Acknowledgements

This book came to being thanks to the financial support of the *Action Jean Monnet*, European Commission, DG Education and Culture. We want to thank all the contributors for their time and expertise put in writing their chapters. To them we express our deepest gratitude and appreciation.

Nijmegen,   Ghent,

Leen d'Haenens   Frieda Saeys
Chair Jean Monnet "Europe's Media Policy"

Table of Contents

The National Level

Western Europe

Belgium

The Federal Republic of Germany
by Guido Ros   275

Italy
by Carlo Sorrentino   307

Non-Western Europe

Preface

You are holding a fully updated and enhanced version of the *Media Dynamics & Regulatory Concerns in the Digital Age* book first edited with Quintessenz in 1998. This book deals mainly with broadcast media in general, i.e. radio and television, leading to all kinds of forms of convergence with the new, interactive media. The publication maps out Western countries, belonging to the classical typologies of western democracies (Western Europe and North-America). Necessary attention is also paid to the developments within the European Union and the fading out of the East-West dichotomies within Europe. It is meant as a handbook for both undergraduate and graduate students in communication studies as well as their teachers, but can also be a useful tool for policy makers and media professionals and anyone with an interest in a comparative approach to recent developments on the broadcast media scene. The approach taken (i.e. theoretical framework followed by concrete media cases) is twofold. This also becomes clear in the accompanying CD-Rom in that:

- facts and figures are provided: data about the general developments in the western broadcasting arena and a few concrete, well-chosen broadcasting examples in order to clarify, illustrate, compare;
- a technique of analysis is offered: thanks to the systematic mapping out of certain aspects of developments in the broadcasting scene within a general theoretical framework and thanks to comparing concrete implementations in different countries, a critical analysis is drawn, allowing the reader to assess similarities and differences in great detail.

Some theoretical considerations behind this approach lie in the finding that broadcasting continues to be perceived as a barometer of the society in which it came to being. Broadcasting is an important indicator of its political, economical, social, cultural and geographical context. The last decades, however, the socio-economical conditions and societal organizational forms are becoming more and more uniform: diversity among countries is less and less the case than within each of the countries under scrutiny (e.g., economical, political, cultural, ethnic differences). The classical broadcasting typologies that used to be very useful tools for the analysis of broadcasting, are becoming less and less worth-wile in the current context. Notwithstanding, the organization of broadcasting in western countries continues to show a certain degree of variety, which can be ascribed to the contexts within which broadcasting came to being in each country. The societal diversity among the western countries which used to be more pronounced, has continued to bear its stamp to a certain degree on the further development of the broadcasting scene. An illustration is the ever important PSB concept in the United Kingdom, the impact of ideologically inspired pillarized broadcast organizations in the Netherlands, the influence of the unitary Belgium in Flemish and Walloon broadcasting respectively.

The first contact of a user of broadcast media is the program, the output. But, in order to be able to comprehend, to assess, and critically evaluate that output as a communication expert, one needs to be aware of the context within which these programs came to being: financial possibilities as well as limitations, often linked to the mission statement of a broadcaster, in its turn determined by the statute, that needs to fit within well-defined both national and international frames. In interaction with technical developments, all these factors are determining both the format and content of radio and television programs.

Within each of the broadcasting cases under scrutiny, attention is paid to the legal statute, the organization and operation, financing mechanisms, mission statement, programming policy, without neglecting the reaction of society. The latter are listeners, viewers, commissioners, and financers (government, advertizers, etc.) as well as the creative sector. Furthermore, within each media case, the following dimensions are taken into account:

1. A historical dimension: the description of the coming into existence and the development of the respective broadcasting organizations is deliberately kept short. Nevertheless, some historical perspective is deemed necessary in order to assess the intrinsicalities of each broadcasting situation.
2. The media production dimension: from the individual level of the broadcasting organization to and including international structures.

Each of the chapters illustrating a concrete broadcasting case in a given country looks at the following issues:

- *Short media history*, presenting the political and infrastructural context (including the main broadcasting laws and national regulatory bodies) until the 1980's (depending on the date of initial switch to mercantile goals on the national media scene).
- Emphasis on the *current situation* of the public and commercial broadcasting services in the 1990's (audience figures, market shares, appreciation figures, reach of radio and television).
- *Media content*: resisting Americanization, with figures and tables on supply of different program categories, including local fiction versus foreign imported (mostly American) fiction.
- *Media economics*: brief presentation of the local media mogul(s), current activities, shares in press, radio, television, new media, other.
- Special emphasis on national *anti-trust and cross-ownership media law initiatives*: brief presentation of anti-trust and cross-ownership laws (including cases with potential interest for an international audience); impact of lack thereof (referring to the high level of concentration); links with the European jurisdiction (and incompatibilities with the EU framework such as the Television Without Frontiers Directive).
- *The future*: convergence between the broadcasting and telecommunications industries. Attention is paid to the new, interactive media (digitization, video-on-demand,

Internet...) as well as various initiatives and investments on the part of the public and private radio and television sectors.

Structure wise, this book is divided into two sections: the first section examines the general theoretical framework; the second maps out eight Western European media cases and three non-Western European models. The first section of the book, which is a background study of the so-called European level, includes six chapters focusing at different aspects entailing European policy-making initiatives.

The first chapter (*Coppens, d'Haenens & Saeys*) deals with the regulatory framework, first seen from a general perspective, answering questions such as "Why regulate at all?" and "How to Regulate?" and summing up the different regulatory bodies in the countries under scrutiny in the book.

In the second chapter (*Castille*) follows then an illustration of the Commission's regulatory efforts put in the "Television Without Frontiers" Directive. Although the focus is on the European Commission, it is, nevertheless, important to realize that these European activities are undertaken by national governments working together.

The third chapter (*Pauwels & Cincera*) takes a close look at Europe's communication industry which has been in the process of restructuring itself through alliances, mergers and takeovers during the last decades. The margins of the EU competition and anti-trust policies are explored. This policy is wedged in between two well-nigh irreconcilable tasks: establishing an internal open market and striving not to hinder the activities of large-scale groups on the one hand, and ensuring diversity and pluralism on the other hand. After years of trying, simultaneously meeting both these objectives remains a difficult task.

The fourth chapter (*Biltereyst*) deals with one obvious consequence of trade liberalization and the new world order: the growing, world-wide success of American cultural products. Production centers from the USA systematically have extended their field of operation into the exploding audiovisual scene in Western Europe, the new liberal marketplaces in Eastern Europe and Asia, and they have embraced the new technologies. Special attention is given to fiction as a program category, as fiction production crystallizes all problems related to investment, financing, and profitability.

✓ The fifth chapter (*d'Haenens*) takes a pragmatic look at the future of public service television in a world of rampant commercialism. The primary concern here is the mission of public service television in the years ahead. Offering a model for public service television would be an impossible task since it has developed along partly converging and partly distinct lines in each European country, as can be seen in the second section of this book. No one-size-fits-all solution can be formulated. The focus is on what may be termed the two contextual conditions for public service television to fulfill a function without its program supply becoming redundant with respect to that of other channels (commercial, multi-genre TV, or single-format, pay-per-view or subscription TV): creative legislation and sufficient long-term public funding.

The sixth chapter (*d'Haenens & Bink*) takes a look at the current state of the new media market in the various EU countries, as the result of a process of convergence occurring between the formerly separate broadcasting, information and telecommunications sectors. Thanks to advances in digital technology it is now possible to send moving pictures, sound and text (data) over the same channel between any two points on the planet without any loss of clarity (bandwidth problems notwithstanding). This chapter explores the consequences from the point of view of the consumer (local or personalized services, open channels, channels for ethnic, religious, and sexual minorities, etc.), and formulates predictions regarding future developments in the media world.

The second section of the book maps out eight national broadcasting cases in Western Europe followed by three non-Western European cases. While currently at a crossroads, European broadcasting remains highly diverse due to the fragmentation of national policies. The broadcasting cases in the various countries within the European Union are selected on their intrinsic characteristics, and incompatibilities between media regulation at the national and European levels are systematically assessed. The summaries of the eleven chapters are as follows.

The chapter by *Antoine, d'Haenens & Saeys* shows that broadcasting in Belgium can be considered as a prototype of broadcasting in general in Western Europe, which was dominated for years by public broadcasting organizations that drew deeply for their inspiration upon the ideas of the British public services. This situation was to change profoundly, but this did not occur until the eighties. Moreover, Belgian broadcasting also provides a clear indication of the lines of social division in the country and the developments taking place within them, i.e. political and ideological divides, as well as those of language and region. Belgium's political structure is quite complex and has undergone significant changes over the last 25 years. At present, the country comprises three regions (the Flemish, Walloon and Brussels Capital regions) and three Communities (The Flemish, French-speaking and German-speaking Communities), each of which has its own legislative and executive institutions.

﹀ *Antoine* writes about Luxembourg, a tiny country at the heart of Europe, which has always understood the advantage which this strategic position affords it and the opportunity it provides for exploiting an inexhaustible, non-physical resource: radio and TV programs broadcast over electromagnetic waves and the concession systems associated with them. Lacking the means to fend for itself in public-sector radio broadcasting, the Grand Duchy decided, from the outset to concede its radio broadcasting rights to a private operator. Luxembourg was the first European country to have experience of private mass media and their logic, the Duchy's radio and TV broadcasting landscape being inseparable from the existence of the CLT, *Compagnie Luxembourgeoise de Télédiffusion* (Luxembourg TV-broadcasting Company), Luxembourg's main taxpayer.

The chapter on the Netherlands (*van der Haak & van Snippenburg*) illustrates that until recently, the Dutch government held on to a pluralistic public broadcasting system built along social and cultural lines, including in the eighties and early nineties, when international commercial broadcasting arose and national commercial broadcasting was legalized. Even today the government seems intent on keeping the public part of the whole broadcasting system as strong as possible in a context of national and international competition in commercial broadcasting. Social segmentation has lost important ground, but is still very present in the broadcasting system, as in Dutch society as a whole. Together with the relatively balanced program supply of NOS and NPS and the highly specific programs offered by the remaining small license holders, the programming of the large broadcasting associations representing the Netherlands' major social and cultural groupings make for a fairly pluralistic public broadcasting system. But in the near future, investments in content alone will not be enough. As a consequence of digitization the traditional radio and television programs can and will be distributed by alternative means. Digital cable, ADSL, DAB, DVB-T, DVB-satellite and broadband internet are the buzzwords. Leaving these areas to the telecom, cable, computer and internet operators would seriously threaten the impact of public broadcasting. The Dutch public broadcasters are therefore experimenting with most of these new distribution techniques. In particular two areas are being explored: Internet applications (electronic program guide, streaming audio, etc.) and the introduction of thematic TV-channels (news channel, culture channel and children's channel).

Ib Poulsen and Henrik Søndergaard argue that in Denmark radio and television were introduced in a period of strong political reluctance to any kind of commercialism within the electronic media, and as a consequence the consensus was that radio and television should be preserved as a public service institution. Another issue of particular importance in the development of Danish television are the special conditions governing the language and culture of such a small country as Denmark. On the one hand, due to this small size, these are very sensitive to foreign cultural influences, and their survival would be problematic in the absence of public support. On the other hand, a small cultural area means that the economic basis for an independent media culture is severely limited. It is not cheaper to produce radio and television in Denmark than elsewhere, but with a population of only about 5 million it is evident that the electronic media will have to operate with considerably restricted means, whether financed by license fees or run along business lines. When Danish radio and television were organized as a public monopoly, this was not only due to cultural, political, and ideological reasons, but also to the fact that the Danish market simply was too small to be economically attractive to commercial interests.

As in most European countries, the French broadcast media system (*Regourd*) was originally structured as a public monopoly. Until 1959, the beginning of the Vth Republic, the French Radio and Television (*RTF*) was in fact an integral part of the public administration: no more than a ministerial department devoid of any legal personality. Broadcast media must be 'the Voice of France' – in other words that of the government. Thus in France the legal monopoly resulted in political hegemony. The repercussions of this political subservience can still be felt today. In the last decade the French legislator seems to have tried to provide for two conflicting objectives: retaining an anti-trust legal framework to guarantee operator – and therefore program supply – diversity on the one hand, and conversely, favoring the creation of media groups strong enough to face international competition and the globalization of the communication market.

Until the middle of the eighties, the broadcasting system of the Federal Republic of Germany (*Ros*) consisted of a number of public corporations, to the exclusion of any other organizational form. Following the Second World War broadcasting policy in the Western occupation zones was shaped by the Western occupying powers, especially the United States, Great Britain and France. The broadcasting policy adopted by the occupying powers was based on two principles: the broadcasting system was to be free of state influence, and it was to be independent of commercial interests. To this end, the powers chose a system of independent public broadcasting institutes, in the image of the BBC. Owing to the division in occupation zones and to the Allies' wish for decentralization, a third characteristic was added, viz. the regional structure of the system. Germany's commercial channels emerged in the framework of a number of pilot projects for cable distribution. The Ludwigshafen pilot project was started up on January 1, 1984, and also provided for the possibility of private-sector radio and television broadcasts. A new phase of expansion began in 1992–93. Six new channels were set up, mainly based on specific target groups. All in all, in 1998 there were 17 supraregional German private channels in the Federal Republic.

At the very beginning of the third millennium, the passwords of the Italian media system (*Sorrentino*) are: diversification and internationalization. Alliances, mergers and acquisitions follow one upon another at a relentless pace. This process creates unexplored territory for the Italian media system, which is traditionally used to moving and defining its image on the national scene where conditions of monopoly or oligopoly, as in the case of television and telecommunications, or conditions of protected markets have barred access to foreign operators. Mediaset continues to be the only true commercial television group. Economic consolidation is an absolutely necessary condition for the group headed by the tycoon Berlusconi in order to set going a process of diversification made mandatory by the law of July 31, 1997 regulating the television sector.

Public service broadcasting in the United Kingdom (*Coppens & Downey*) is often cited as the basis for many similar broadcasting systems around the world. Yet in many ways it is different from those systems which are claimed to be modeled after the BBC. Competition was introduced in the British television market as early as the 1950's, while other public broadcasters continued to enjoy a monopoly position until the end of the 1980's. Competition has made PSB into an evolving concept with commercial broadcasters obliged to fulfil certain public service functions, the notion of PSB has not changed as dramatically in Britain as in many other countries. Britain's public service idea, although copied many times, still remains quite unique. But the seemingly inevitable drift towards an essentially commercial digital broadcast system raises the question of the future of public service broadcasting, particularly, but not solely, the license-fee funded BBC, in Britain. With the birth of the fifth terrestrial channel, the launch of digital satellite and terrestrial television, digital audio broadcasting, and further experimentation with video-on-demand and the fast growing Internet (one in three British homes is connected to the Net), the British media landscape promises to become very interesting and increasingly complex.

The question whether actual trends are merely a consequence of European and national legislation or also of intrinsic changes within the media themselves can only be answered by looking at some non-Western European cases. Therefore, and for the sake of comparison and completeness, the following three chapters critically assess one Eastern European broadcasting case (Russia) and two North-American cases: the US free-for-all versus Canada's cultural identity-building model.

The Soviet Union, as shown by *De Smaele and Romaschko*, had a centralized, monopolistic, State-owned media system under Party control, whose programming entirely consisted of propaganda. Societal changes led Russia to introduce a dual system, with State and private broadcasters operating along one another. The *Federal Service for Television and Radio Broadcasting* was established as the licensing agency of both State and non-State broadcasters. In July 1999 it was replaced by a new *Ministry for Press, Television and Radio Broadcasting, and Mass Communications*. A bill on broadcasting was prepared but, after several years, it still has not been made into law. Radio and television are still largely dependent (financially and organizationally) on the government, while corporate control (especially Russian banks) over the media is growing. The notion of public service television remains alien. ORT, the first and most popular channel, is a public broadcaster in name only, as it is partly owned by the State and by private shareholders. RTR and *Kultura* are State-owned nationwide broadcasters. Another 90 State broadcasters operate locally. Independent broadcasters are generally local stations; NTV can be considered nationwide, and Moscow-based TV6 broadcasts to large portions of the country. The growth of private channels has gone hand in hand with the development of the advertising market, the introduction of systematic audience research, and the commercialization of the media content.

The Canadian media system (*Taras & Klinkhammer*) was shaken by enormous changes in 2000. Indeed the geological plates on which the system has rested for the past twenty years have shifted dramatically. What we are seeing in effect is a transition from an older media model in which broadcasters focused only on broadcasting and newspaper owners were only concerned with newspapers to a new system in which multi-platform media groups dominate the landscape. During the 1990's the Canadian media skyline could be described as a series of low level buildings with the publicly financed Canadian Broadcasting Corporation (CBC) and its French language counterpart – Radio-Canada looming a little larger that the rest. Today, three immense skyscrapers dominate the horizon. BCE, Global and Quebecor all tower over a much smaller and more run down CBC.

The last chapter deals with the US electronic media system (*Ostroff*), which is large and highly complex, with over 10,500 commercial radio stations and almost 1,200 commercial television stations. There are also more than 2,000 noncommercial radio stations and almost 400 noncommercial television stations. More than 67% of the 100 million homes subscribe to cable television. Some 7 million homes receive programming directly by satellite or microwave-based *wireless cable*. Commercial television stations can choose to affiliate with one of six national networks, while more than 120 'basic' (primarily ad-supported) television services are delivered by multi-channel providers. Twenty-six pay channels as well as pay-per-view services are available to cable subscribers. Radio is even more complex. Since the rise of television, radio has been primarily a local medium. However, much of the programming, such as recorded music, is from centralized sources. Broadcasting, cable television and the other services are regulated by the federal government, but cable television systems are also regulated in part by municipal or other local governments. In 1997 the FCC (Federal Communications Commission) issued its rules for the new digital television service. The 'big four' network affiliates in the ten largest markets (which serve about 30% of the TV households in the US) had to begin digital transmissions by May 1999. Those affiliates in the remaining top 30 markets had to begin as of November 1999. At that point digital signals reached about 53% of US television households (although few had the receiving equipment to view the programs). All commercial stations must offer digital services by 2002, and public television stations by 2003.

As part of this book edition, a CD-Rom is enclosed in the back cover. Sections of the book are mentioned on the CD-Rom, after its content has been restructured, since the CD-Rom adopts a thematic approach as opposed to the country-by-country angle used in the book. The use of an index makes the CD-Rom easy to browse through. Other additional information such as bibliographic references are mentioned on the CD-Rom, including many hyperlinks to useful websites.

Leen d'Haenens
Frieda Saeys

Media Policy and Regulatory Concerns

by Tomas Coppens, Leen d'Haenens and Frieda Saeys

Chief among media policy instruments is some kind of regulatory framework – created by a given authority at whatever level – which defines and limits the activities of electronic media. The legal framework in which it operates determines to a great extent the nature of a broadcasting system. In Western Europe, for example, five major periods in broadcasting regulation can be distinguished:

1. The first broadcasting laws enacted in the early twentieth century had little to do with broadcasting as we know it. Broadcasting was then purely a technical issue, needing no regulating beyond some technical norms.
2. A second wave of broadcasting laws appeared in the 1920's. Between 1925 and 1935, most developed countries passed 'real' broadcasting legislation which included rules about content. State monopolies on broadcasting were established in several countries.
3. In the 1950's broadcasting regulation had to be adapted to the arrival of a new medium. Television changed broadcasting and the laws that governed it.
4. In the 1980's new technologies and a shift in political opinion in favor of private enterprise caused a major change in media policy, especially in Europe. State monopolies were abandoned; massive deregulation revolutionized broadcasting.
5. A fifth and – for now – final phase is going on now as broadcasting is becoming more and more international in nature and is converging with other media.

I   Models of Broadcasting Regulations

Many authors have tried to classify broadcasting systems according to the political and legal forces that affect them, since "each government has shaped its national broadcasting system in keeping with its own nature, especially its political nature" (Head, 1985: 57). Starting off with a simple bipolar axis with at one extreme the 'free' American model and at the other end the totalitarian (often Soviet) model, typologies have become increasingly complex, distinguishing among up to six or seven broadcasting models. In reality most broadcasting systems contain elements belonging to several broadcasting models. As Hedwig de Smaele will show in her chapter on the Russian media, even the Soviet model contained some 'Western' elements, such as advertising. McQuail (1983: 133) also writes: "Most national media institutions and practices and most relations between state and media display a mixture of several elements: libertarian, 'responsible,' and authoritarian." These nuances are often lost in even the most elaborate typology. In a later edition McQuail (2000) questions the relevance of such models in today's media society. Nowadays, with economic imperatives coming more and more to the fore and the media showing increasing complexity, the ideologies which inform the various broadcasting models have become secondary. But typologies remain useful inasmuch as they let us understand the differences in relations between government and media.

Summarizing some classic typologies, we can roughly extrapolate four major models:

1. *The authoritarian model.* As old as the media themselves (and worldwide still probably the most widespread model), the authoritarian concept aims to make broadcasting a part of the State. Radio and television are to support the government at any cost. In his classic work, *Four Theories of the Press*, Siebert (Siebert, 1956a: 18) states: "The units of communication should support and advance the politics of the government in power so that this government can achieve its objectives." Censorship is therefore a major regulatory tool. Although criticized by Nerone (1995), who claims that Siebert's authoritarian model is based on too many different ideological movements (Communism, Fascism, Roman Catholicism) to be compressed into one single model, the authoritarian model is present in most typologies. Lowenstein and Merrill (1990), Head (1985), and Hachten (1996) all describe this model, with the latter stressing its loathing of diversity: "To the authoritarian, diversity of views is wasteful and irresponsible, dissent is an annoying nuisance and often subversive, and consensus and standardization are logical and sensible goals for mass communication" (Hachten, 1996: 15–16).

2. *The Communist model.* Although often considered as a subcategory of the authoritarian model (Head, 1985; Lowenstein & Merrill, 1990), the Communist model does have some distinctive features. According to Lenin's theory of the press, broadcasting serves a threefold function, that of collective 'propagandist, agitator, and organizer' (Altschull, 1984). It differs from the authoritarian model inasmuch as it prohibits private media ownership. The media are owned by the working class, i.e., the Communist Party, and are used for socialization, education, information, motivation, and mobilization (McQuail, 1983: 93–94).

3. *The Western, Paternalistic model.* Broadcasting systems in Western Europe, and especially in the United Kingdom, are the best examples of this model – called 'paternalistic' because of its top-down approach: media policy is not a product of what the audience wants, but of what the authorities believe the audience needs and wants (Head, 1985). Peterson's social responsibility theory (Peterson, 1956) is similar inasmuch as it stresses that the media have duties towards society at large and that authorities need to make sure these duties are adhered to. Lowenstein and Merrill (1990) divide this model up into more specific ones, while McQuail's valuable democratic-participatory model (small-scale and two-way media – 1994) can be seen as amending the paternalistic model, which is in fact dominated by a monopolistic public broadcaster. Most European cases presented in this book are good examples of the paternalistic model, and they illustrate how it has been changing into a fourth model:

4. *The Western, Libertarian model*. Similar to the previous model – Hachten (1996) does not even see more than one Western model – the most important difference lies in the media's commercial function. Siebert (1956b: 51) emphasizes that besides providing information and entertainment, under this model the media have a third function: "developed as a necessary correlate to the others to provide a basis of economic support and thus to assure financial independence. This was the sales or advertising function." The American broadcasting system, as presented in this book by David Ostroff, is a textbook example of this model. It can also be argued that the European broadcasting systems are evolving into this libertarian model, despite the presence of a strong, and sometimes non-commercial, public broadcaster.

5. All the aforementioned models are based on the notion that broadcasting is a powerful medium, and they are to some extent inspired by the classic stimulus-response theory as well as a static vision of societal relations. Many authors, mainly from critical schools, have defined other models which include alternative broadcasting institutions (underground media, grassroots media, etc.). These alternative models can often be considered as slight variations on one of the major models./Hachten (1996: 27) defines his *revolutionary concept* as "a concept of illegal and subversive communication utilizing the press and broadcasting to overthrow a government or wrest control from alien or otherwise rejected rulers." It is a concept closely linked with forms of dictatorship, whether right-wing (authoritarian model) or left-wing (Communist model). Another model closely related to the authoritarian model is the **developmental concept** (Hachten, 1996; McQuail, 2000). This views in a more positive light the media models to be found in underdeveloped countries (lack of funding and infrastructure, etc.). As McQuail (2000: 155) writes: "In the circumstances it may be legitimate for governments to allocate resources selectively and to restrict journalistic freedom in some ways." In practice, the difference between this concept and the authoritarian model is marginal. A final model we would like to mention is McQuail's **democratic-participant theory** that can be seen as a variation on the western-paternalistic model. Key concepts include grassroots media, participation, and two-way communication. The best example of this concept is the wave of free radios that swept across Europe in the 1970's, partly as a protest against the monopolistic, bureaucratic, and centralist public broadcasting corporations.

II Why Regulate at all?

In today's democracies, one principle underlies all broadcasting regulations: that of freedom of speech. Europe's main reference in this field is Article 10 of the European Convention on Human Rights and Fundamental Freedoms (ECHR, 1958 – introduced three years after the International Declaration of Human Rights and its Article 19), which guarantees the freedom to have and spread any opinion without government intervention. That same Article does, on the other hand, also limit this fundamental right by stating that governments can subject the media to a system of licensing. In other words, although the principle of free speech is recognized, the principle of restricting media activities is equally acknowledged. The UN's International Telecommunications Union (ITU) even requires its Member States to license electronic media.

The initial motive behind broadcasting regulations was and remains *technical* considerations. To ensure interference-free broadcasting, some sort of frequency scheme was necessary, and not just at a national level. Technical issues dictated the first national broadcasting laws, dating back to the early twentieth century. And although some technical limitations are outdated and terrestrial broadcasting is being replaced by cable or satellite broadcasting, some technical regulations will always be needed. A subsequent factor in electronic media regulations was the shortage of frequencies. Choices had to be made about who could broadcast (hertzian beam transmissions, and later transmissions through cable or satellites) and who could not. A democracy requires clear and fair legal criteria to allocate access. Another regulatory motive follows as the government needs a control mechanism to establish whether those broadcasters granted access meet these criteria (Hoffman-Riem, 1996).

A second, important principle for regulation in a democracy is to ensure political and cultural *diversity* by safeguarding the free flow of ideas, or the position of different minorities. Most democracies have rules about access of political factions to radio and television, about minority programming, or, on a higher level, about media ownership as another element of diversity. Many examples of this can be found in this book. But, as Feintuck (1999) mentions, diversity has its own limits. Explicitly violent or pornographic scenes can, for instance, be justified in the name of diversity. But higher principles, such as the protection of children, can restrict diversity. Another example can be found in the tension between freedom of information and the right to privacy. While the diversity principle has been pursued differently in the US (libertarian model) and in Europe (paternalistic model), today diversity is less and less part of the political discourse and more and more defined in economic terms.

Thirdly, there is an *economic* ground for regulating the media. Governments can choose not to interfere with the free market if seen as providing society with what it needs while offering a range of economic benefits. But Gibbons (1998: 74) sees the deficiencies of the free market as the main arguments in favor of regulation. The free market is inadequate in several respects. A non-regulated free market can lead to media concentration, even monopolies, with the usual side effects: artificially high prices for consumers, and of course a decrease in diversity. Another part of economic media regulation can be inspired by attempts to unify a trade market. Integrating national and international law is a major drive for regulatory reforms in the EU Member States. The European Union provides us with the best example of how different legal frameworks have to be tuned into one another. In a (not so) distant future other economic alliances such as NAFTA or MERCOSUR may lead to similar moves. Although national broadcasting regulations remain in force in all countries, international regulations cannot be ignored, however insufficient they may be at the moment. The 'Television Without Frontiers' Directive, as discussed by Valérie Castille later on in this book, is still mostly focused on hardware and driven by economic considerations.

In the 1970's a tendency for deregulating broadcasting was noticeable, prompted by technical change and an increasing belief in the benefits of the free market. In the 1980's Europe was hit by a deregulatory wave: state monopolies were abandoned, the number of broadcasters grew spectacularly, as did commercial funding (Barker, 1997). But this also had less than desirable effects – extreme forms of commercialization, concentration, cross-ownership – which led to what has been described by Dahlgren (1995: 15) as a 're-regulation' "to counteract the negative aspects of market forces and to optimize the positive role [the media] can play." Examples of such re-regulation can be found in numerous cases presented in this book: limits on children's advertising in Belgium (which may be introduced in the whole of the EU), plans to limit commercial funding for the French public broadcaster, the creation of new public service channels in the United Kingdom and Germany (children's, cultural, educational channels).

But won't digital media make regulation obsolete? It may be argued that heavy regulation deters media companies from investing in new technologies, and that limits on cross-ownership are useless as media convergence is rapidly rising. And digital media hold the promise of a wide range of channels, 'something for everyone,' thus making 'diversity' less of a ground for regulation. The digital age, however, started with large-scale media mergers and alliances (e.g., Time-Warner and AOL, CLT and Bertelsmann, Canal Plus and Vivendi), raising questions about exactly how diverse this new digital media landscape will be. It seems that a decreasing number of companies are going to be in a position to decide who gets access to which technology and at what cost (Humphreys & Lang, 1998).

III   How to Regulate?

A central element of broadcasting regulation is a system of *licensing* which establishes who can broadcast and who cannot. The ITU actually requires its members to work out licensing criteria. This means that broadcasting can only be allowed provided that the broadcaster has obtained a license from the government that is responsible for the use of wavelengths and that can determine the exact nature of the licensing criteria. Authorities usually attach all kinds of conditions to the granting of a license. Nationality is often one such condition, since radio and television are linked to a nation's culture and can be important nation-building factors in times of crises. Economically, the nationality criteria can also be used to protect domestic media institutions against foreign control.

A second, central element in many licensing procedures is rules to prevent concentration and to *restrict cross-ownership*. Fixed quota or merger commissions are the main instruments to achieve these aims. As the chapter by Caroline Pauwels and Patrizia Cincera will demonstrate, the European Union is particularly active in that area and has intervened in national regulation on many occasions in order to prevent excessive concentration. There are doubts as to the actual effectiveness of this EU policy, however, especially given the conflicting nature of two of the EU's goals in the matter: limiting concentration and favoring competition with American and Asian conglomerates.

As a third element we could refer to Head's (1985) 'regulation of fairness' which results in a set of rules about *objectivity, impartiality,* and *accountability.* These rules are vital for the establishment of a healthy and balanced relationship between broadcaster, government, and audience.

Program regulation is often an essential element of licensing procedures as well. Governments may require broadcasters to offer a wide range of programming, or programming for a given minority or language group; they may also impose limits on some types of content (usually sex and violence), or set a watershed for certain programs; and they can restrict foreign programs for cultural or economic reasons (or both).

A final major element of regulation has to do with *funding* from different sources. Commercial funding is often limited in order to protect the consumer from excessive advertising or at least certain forms of advertising, or to prevent advertisers from having too much influence on programming.

Although the aforementioned elements are present in many regulatory frameworks, there can be *considerable national differences* in regulating the media, resulting in very diverse broadcasting systems, as was already shown when discussing the various media models. In the USA, for example, the authorities opted for a federally controlled system, dominated by private enterprise with minimal intervention by the State. Most European nations, however, still emphasize the *steering role of the government.* Such differences are becoming smaller, as economic rules take over. Authoritarian or Communist regimes take intervention even further and strive for complete control.

Another difference is the *geographical level* on which the main decisions concerning media policy are made. France and the United Kingdom are examples of very centralized regimes, in which the national governments define media policy. In Germany and Belgium, regional authorities are the most important media regulators; the role of the national government is limited to co-ordination. Other countries such as the USA and Russia have a mixed system whereby both the central and regional governments have a major say in broadcasting matters. In Europe supranational regulation is becoming more and more important. Organizations like the Council of Europe and the European Union play an increasing role in broadcast regulation. In most democratic States, at least part of the regulatory process has been withdrawn from the government and entrusted to more or less independent regulatory bodies.

Legislation itself, of course, remains the preserve of the parliamentary institutions – though some codes of conduct drawn by regulatory institutions can be seen as legislative documents – but the impact of regulatory bodies cannot be ignored as they can have numerous functions (Robillard, 1995):

- Most regulatory bodies play a crucial role in the organization of broadcasting by allocating licenses, mainly to commercial broadcasters.

√• Controlling and sanctioning broadcasters is another typical task for a regulatory body. If broadcasters fail to meet the criteria on which their license is based, they can be given penalties, ranging from a small fine to license withdrawal.

√• Nearly all regulatory bodies have an advisory function, which allows them to influence legislation.

√• Some act as a watchdog to safeguard broadcasters' independence from the government or from economic powers.

√• A rare function is that of appointing top media decision makers, such as the president or general managers of public broadcasters, as is the case in France.

√• Regulatory bodies can have some minor judicial powers as well, and serve as a complaints commission.

In this book many different examples of regulatory bodies will be presented. Table 1 enables the reader to get to know the various institutions involved in media regulation active in the different countries dealt with in this book.

Some are responsible for both private and public broadcasting (e.g., the American FCC or the French CSA), some only for private broadcasting (e.g., the British ITC). Some have authority over only one medium (e.g., the British Radio Authority), the scope of others stretches as far as other forms of telecommunications (e.g., the FCC). There can be a difference in degree of independence: British regulatory bodies are fairly independent, as opposed to the French CSA. The composition of the bodies is another dissimilarity. Regional German regulatory bodies can consist of dozens of members, while the Flemish *Commissariaat voor de Media* has only three members. A final, major difference lies in the actual power such institutions have.

Table 1. *Institutions Involved in Regulation and Thus Shaping Media Policy*

Country	Institutions involved in regulation	Function
GENERAL: EU	Court of Justice of the European Communities	The Court ensures that the law is observed in the process of Community integration.
	European Commission	The Commission proposes Community legislation, monitors compliance with legislation and with the Treaties, and administers common policies.
	European Parliament	The Parliament represents the peoples of the Community. It takes part in the lawmaking and budgetary processes and has limited, but increasing, powers of control.
	Council of Europe	The Council, composed of 15 members (one minister from each government), takes decisions and adopts Community legislation.
	Institute for European Media Law (EMR)	The EMR studies the latest developments in European media policy
	European Broadcasting Union (EBU)	The EBU represents the interests of public service broadcasters before the European institutions and provides a full range of other operational, commercial, technical, legal and strategic services.

BELGIUM	Flemish Media Council	The Council provides advice to the Flemish government on matters concerning media policy.
	Central Regulatory Body with regard to Broadcasting in the French Community	The CSA is a regulatory body on radio and television policy in French-speaking Belgium.
	Telecommunications Federal Regulatory and Supervisory Body (BIPT)	BIPT is responsible for strategic (it is competent to give opinions regarding post and telecommunications sector policies), regulatory (drafting of Belgian regulations and transposition into Belgian law of European directives), operational (management of licenses, approvals and frequencies), conciliation (between operators), and monitoring missions.
DENMARK	The Danish Ministry for Cultural Affairs	The Ministry is responsible for shaping the Danish culture policy
	TV-Byen	The Danish Broadcasting Corporation representing the TV-Broadcasting channels DR1 and DR2
	Radiohuset	The Danish Broadcasting Corporation representing the Radio-broadcasting channels P1, P2, P3 and P4
	Telestyrelsen	National Telecom Agency, in charge of administrative and regulatory functions based on the legislation governing telecommunications.
FRANCE	Ministry of Culture and Communication	The Ministry is responsible for shaping the French culture policy
	Higher Audiovisual Council (CSA)	The CSA is the independent administrative body in charge of protecting the independence of the media in France.
	Telecommunications Regulatory Authority (ART)	ART is an independent regulatory body on telecommunications in France
GERMANY	Association of German Public Service Broadcasters (ARD)	The ARD looks after the interests of the public broadcasters in Germany.
	Association of Private Broadcasters and Tele-communications (VPRT)	The VPRT looks after the interests of the private broadcasters and the telecommunications and multimedia companies in Germany.
	Association of Regulatory Authorities for Broadcasting	The ALM safeguards the interests of member regulatory authorities ('Landesmedienanstalten') in the broadcasting field at national and international level.
	Regulatory Authority for Telecommunications and Post (RegTP)	The Regulatory Authority is in charge of promoting the development of the postal and telecommunications markets through liberalization and deregulation.
ITALY	The Italian Regulatory Authority in the Communications Sector (AGCOM)	AGCOM was established to carry out the tasks assigned under EU directives, both in the field of the telecommunications market and of audiovisual de-regulation.
	The Ministry of Communications	The Ministry is responsible for shaping the Italian (tele-)communications policy.
LUXEMBOURG	Media and Audiovisual Department	Advisory body on media policy in Luxembourg.
	Luxembourg Telecommunications Institute	Regulatory body on telecommunications in Luxembourg.

THE NETHERLANDS	The Netherlands Broadcasting Corporation (NOS)	Corporation of the Dutch public broadcasters.
	The Dutch Media Authority	The Dutch Media Authority upholds the rules which are formulated in the Dutch Media Act as well as in the regulations based on this act.
	Ministry of Education, Culture and Science (OCW)	In charge of regulating education, culture and science policy in the Netherlands.
UNITED KINGDOM	Independent Television Commission (ITC)	The ITC licenses and regulates commercial television in the UK. It looks after viewers' interests by setting and maintaining the standards for programs, advertising and technical quality.
	British Broadcasting Corporation (BBC)	Corporation of UK public broadcasters.
	Office of Telecommunications (OFTEL)	OFTEL is the regulator – or "watchdog" – for the UK telecommunications industry. The main way OFTEL regulates is through monitoring and enforcing the conditions in all telecommunications licenses in the UK.
	Department for Culture, Media and Sport	The Department for Culture, Media and Sport aims to improve the quality of life for all through cultural and sporting activities and through the strengthening of the creative industries.
RUSSIA	State Committee of the Russian Federation on Communications and Computers	The State is the central body of the federal executive power, responsible for state management in the field of communications and development of all kinds of telecommunications and postal service.
CANADA	Canadian Broadcasting Corporation (CBC)	Canada's public broadcaster.
	Canadian Radio-Television and Telecommunications Commission (CRTC)	The CRTC is vested with the authority to regulate and supervise all aspects of the Canadian broadcasting system, as well as to regulate telecommunications service providers and common carriers that fall under federal jurisdiction.
UNITED STATES	Federal Communications Commission (FCC)	The FCC is charged with regulating interstate and international communications by radio, television, wire, satellite, and cable.
	National Telecommunications and Information Administration (NTIA)	The National Telecommunications and Information Administration (NTIA), an agency of the U.S. Department of Commerce, is the Executive Branch's principal voice on domestic and international telecommunications and information technology issues.
	National Association of Broadcasters	The National Association of Broadcasters is a full-service trade association that promotes and protects the interests of radio and television broadcasters.
	Corporation for Public Broadcasting	The corporation is public broadcasting's source of funds for analog and digital program development and production. CPB also funds more than 1,000 local public radio and television stations across the country.

References

Altschull, J. (1984). *Agents of Power. The Role of the News Media in Human Affairs.* New York: Longman.

Barker, C. (1997). *Global Television. An Introduction.* Oxford: Blackwell Publishers.

Castberg, F. (1974). *The European Convention on Human Rights.* Leiden: A.W. Sijthoff.

Dahlgren, P. (1995). *Television and the Public Sphere. Citizenship, Democracy and the Media.* London: Sage Publications.

Feintuck, M. (1999). *Media Regulation, Public Interest and the Law.* Edinburgh: Edinburgh University Press.

Gibbons, T. (1998). De/Re-regulating the system: The British experience. In J. Steemers (ed.), *Changing Channels. The Prospects for Television in a Digital World* (pp. 73–96). Luton: University of Luton Press.

Hachten, W. (1996). *The World News Prism. Changing Media of International Communication.* Ames, Iowa: Iowa State University Press (Fourth Edition).

Head, S. (1985). *World Broadcasting Systems. A Comparative Analysis.* Belmont, CA: Wadsworth Publishing Company.

Hoffmann-Riem, W. (1996). *Regulating Media. The Licensing and Supervision of Broadcasting in Six Countries.* London: Guilford Press.

Humphreys, P. & Lang, M. (1998). Digital television between the economy and pluralism. In J. Steemers (ed.), *Changing Channels. The Prospects for Television in a Digital World* (pp. 9–36). Luton: University of Luton Press.

Lowenstein, R. & Merrill, J. (1990). *Macromedia. Mission, Message and Morality.* New York: Longman.

McQuail, D. (1983). *Mass Comunication Theory: An Introduction.* London: Sage Publications.

McQuail, D. (2000). *McQuail's Mass Communication Theory.* London: Sage Publications (Fourth Edition).

Nerone, J. (1995) (ed.). *Last Rights. Revisiting Four Theories of the Press.* Urbana: University of Illinois Press.

Peterson, T. (1956). The social responsibility theory of the press. In F. Siebert, T. Peterson & W. Schramm (eds.), *Four Theories of the Press* (pp. 73–103). Urbana: University of Illinois Press.

Robillard, S. (1995). *Television in Europe: Regulatory Bodies. Status, Functions and Powers in 35 European Countries.* London: John Libbey.

Schramm, W. (1956). The Soviet communist theory of the press. In F. Siebert, T. Peterson & W. Schramm (eds.), *Four Theories of the Press* (pp. 105–146). Urbana: University of Illinois Press.

Siebert, F. (1956a). The authoritarian theory of the press. In F. Siebert, T. Peterson & W. Schramm (eds.), *Four Theories of the Press* (pp. 9–37). Urbana: University of Illinois Press.

Siebert, F. (1956b). The libertarian theory of the press. In F. Siebert, T. Peterson & W. Schramm (eds.), *Four Theories of the Press* (pp. 39–71). Urbana: University of Illinois Press.

The 'Television Without Frontiers' Directive Mainstream and Independent European Broadcasting in the Digital Age

by Valérie Castille

I   Introduction*

The television quotas must be viewed in the broader legal framework pertaining to the 'free circulation of services' laid down in Article 59 of the EC Treaty. Since broadcasting activities are described as services, the Member States are obliged to reckon with the construction of a single European audiovisual area (see chapter on media policy and regulatory concerns by Coppens, d'Haenens & Saeys). The most important community instrument which achieves this is the 'Television Without Frontiers' (TWF) Directive. This Directive aims to free broadcasting and reception of foreign European TV-programs within the European Community.

In this chapter, we emphasize the very flexible terms of the quotas phrasings of the 'Television Without Frontiers' Directive. Issues of lawfulness and desirability of television quotas are beyond the scope of this chapter. We therefore refer to other authors (De Witte, 1995: 29; Grosheide & Mochel, 1997: 18–24; Hitchens, 1996: 47; Pauwels, 2000: 40–45; Salvatore, 1992: 975–976; Waelbroeck, 1996: 13–22).

II   The Directive

2.1 Scope

The regulations making up the 'Television Without Frontiers' Directive (European Council, 1989) form the legal regulatory framework for the application of television broadcasting activities in the European Community.[1]

For the purpose of this Directive 'television broadcasting' means: "The initial transmission by wire or over the air, including that by satellite, in un-encoded or encoded form, of television programs intended for reception by the public. It includes the communication of programs between undertakings with a view to their being related to the public. It does not include communication services providing items of information or

---

* This paper is an update of a previous document concerning the flexibility of the television quotas (see Castille, 2000).

[1] The TWF Directive is also applicable in countries (although they do not belong to the European Community) which belong to the European Economic Space (e.g., Sweden).

other messages on individual demand such as facsimile, electronic data banks and other similar services."

This definition of 'television broadcasting' in Article 1a of the TWF Directive tells us that the new interactive services, such as video-on-demand, are not affected by the Directive, unlike pay-per-view services, which are offered simultaneously to a mass audience; in other words, they involve a point-to-multipoint connection rather than a point-to-point connection as is the case with interactive services.[2]

2.2 Implementation

The TWF Directive is based on two pillars, the 'minimum rules,' and a number of requirements applicable throughout the European audiovisual space.[3] The Directive contains 'minimal' coordination provisions[4] in the following fields: television quotas, advertising and sponsoring, protection of minors, and right of reply. In these different fields, the TWF Directive guarantees the same 'minimum rules' in each Member State of the European Community. Article 3 of the old TWF Directive explicitly states that Member States remain free to implement more detailed or stricter rules for the broadcasting organizations falling within their jurisdiction. This possibility can of course create problems as it can lead to different national stipulations within the European audiovisual space.

Besides the application of these minimum regulations in the national legislation, the TWF Directive requires each Member State to adhere to several crucial principles. The 'obligation of control' by the originating State means that all television programs originating from and meant for reception in the Community must meet the legal requirements of the broadcasting Member State. This system of exclusive control by the originating state means that the latter must – when a broadcasting license application is being submitted – check that the applicant meets the minimum requirements of the TWF Directive (Castille, 1996). After issuing the broadcasting license, the State must then see to it that the broadcasting organization still meets the minimum rules (Castille, 1996). When the originating state finds an irregularity, it must rebuke the broadcasting organization and impose any necessary penalty.

The State where a broadcast originates is required to guarantee freedom of transmission – and therefore the free circulation of programs – so that there is no need for the State of reception to intervene in any way (Castille, 1996). The control exerted by the

---

[2] For a definition of the difference between broadcasting and telecommunications, see among others Gay-Bellile, 1996: 19–20; Rony, 1996: 17–18; Uyttendaele, 1996: 47–95; Wangermee, 1996: 13–25.

[3] For a more exhaustive description of the TWF Directive, see Castille, 1998a: 37–42; Castille, 1998b: 1–15.

[4] In European law there was a choice between harmonization or a 'minimal' coordination of the stipulations.

originating state is enough to ensure freedom of broadcasting and reception (no limitations or obstacles[5]) in all other Member States.

With the TWF Directive providing for 'minimal coordination' in connection with the principle of national control, the logical conclusion is that it leads to the mutual recognition by Member States of one another's national legislation.

2.3 Television Quotas[6]

The television quotas aim to support the European audiovisual program industry, the reasoning behind this being that the stronger this industry becomes, the better it will be able to compete with the US program industry on the European market (De Witte, 1995).

Article 4 of the TWF Directive requires Member States to see to it that those broadcasters falling under their jurisdiction as broadcasting reserve a 'majority proportion' of their (total) transmission time for European works:

> "Member States shall ensure where practicable and by appropriate means, that broadcasters reserve for European works, within the meaning of Article 6, a majority proportion of their transmission time, excluding the time appointed to news, sports events, games, advertising and teletext services. This proportion, having regard to the broadcaster's informational, educational, cultural and entertainment responsibilities to its viewing public, should be achieved progressively, on the basis of suitable criteria."

As a matter of fact, Article 4 of the old TWF Directive made it compulsory for each channel to devote the majority part of its total transmission time to European works; the wording of the new Article 4 eases this requirement somewhat: "(...) should be achieved progressively, on the basis of suitable criteria."

The old TWF Directive does not give a definition of the basis that must be taken into account for the calculation of the proportion. However, by excluding explicitly 5 categories of programs, the Directive gives as it were a negative definition of this basis. The five excluded program categories are: news, sport events, games, advertising, and teletext services. There is no obligation as to broadcasting times (primetime/ late hours).

The definition of 'European production' is found in Article 6, based on 'country of establishment' for producers and 'country of residence' for authors and workers.

---

[5] The TWF Directive provides for the possibility of suspension in cases of clear and serious infringement of the stipulations regarding the protection of minors. Before the State of reception can suspend the transmission, a number of cumulative conditions must be met.

[6] The stipulations concerning television quotas and the waiting time for theatrical movies are not applicable to local television programs which are broadcast nationally.

'European works' means the following:
1. Works originating in EU Member States.
2. Works originating in European Third States party to the European Convention on Trans-frontier Television of the Council of Europe and meeting the conditions of paragraph 2.
3. Works originating in other European Third Countries made exclusively or in co-production with producers established in one or more Member States by producers established in one or more European third countries with which the Community will conclude agreements in accordance with the producers of the Treaty, if those works are mainly made with authors and workers residing in one or more European States.

In comparison with the 1986 version, the definition of European works has been broadened as a result of a double dispute:

1. An internal dispute within the European Community.[7]
2. An international dispute between the United States and the European Community.[8]

Article 5 provides for the compulsory broadcasting of or investment in European works created by independent producers:

"Member States shall ensure, where practicable and by appropriate means, that broadcasters reserve at least 10% of their transmission time, excluding the time appointed to news, sport events, games, advertising and teletext services, or alternately, at the discretion of the Member State, at least 10% of their programming budget, for European works created by producers who are independent of broadcasters. This proportion, having regard to broadcasters' informational, educational, cultural and entertainment responsibilities to its viewing public, should be achieved progressively, on the basis of suitable criteria; it must be achieved by earmarking an adequate proportion for recent works, that is to say works transmitted within five years of their production."

---

[7] "The political bargaining which took place between single-market supporters, who wanted the adoption of the Directive in order to liberalize the market of broadcasting, and cultural and industrial policy-makers, who made the quotas a condition for agreeing to the text of the Directive, led to the inclusion of European television program content requirements in the Directive which was eventually adopted in 1989" (De Witte, 1995: 104).

[8] "Largely as a result of United States pressures, the European Parliament significantly modified the Council's proposal, adding measures that allowed the Member States to exercise discretion in meeting the quotas and reducing the quotas for 'European works' to 50%" (Lupinacci, 1991: 119, Grosheide & Mochel, 1997: 18–24).

The aim is obviously to encourage investments in new European independent works. Unlike Article 4 (which pertains to broadcasting only), Article 5 gives channels a choice between a broadcasting obligation or an investment obligation.

If a channel chooses the broadcasting obligation, then it must devote 10% of broadcasting time to recent, independent European works. If it chooses the investment obligation, 10% of its programming budget must be earmarked for recent independent European works.

Due to the lack of a definition of the term 'independent producer' in the TWF Directive, Member States have been free to interpret any way they chose. Article 5 does however include one other requirement: part of these independent European works must be 'recent.' Recent means that these works must be broadcast within five years of their creation. How large the proportion of 'recent' works must be is indicated in Article 5 through the term 'adequate.'

At the end of 1994, Henry Ingberg (1991: 30) described the flexible system of the TV quotas as follows:

"What does this mean in practice? It means that one does what one can to achieve one's goal. Those texts paraphrasing or commenting on the directive, seem to indicate that it isn't possible to go below the quota that was in place before the implementation of the directive (the 1988 results). To go back to our TNT Cartoon example, the channel argued that it could not be in violation of the directive since it initially broadcast no European program whatsoever! I am of course overstating the facts (or am I?), but there is need to look closely at the real meaning of this statement: 'whenever achievable through appropriate means.' You may remember what I had to say about the initial political compromise, and this highly contentious wording is a direct reflection of it." [our translation]

The delicate nature of a system of minimal coordination linked with the obligation of mutual recognition cannot be over-emphasized. Furthermore, the wording of the TV quota provisions is quite noncommittal: "where practicable," "by appropriate means," "progressively", "on the basis of suitable criteria," etc. This can only lead to varying interpretations in national legislations and, logically, to a very flexible application of the quotas in practice.

This noncommittal wording is the result of a political[9] compromise[10] between advocates and opponents of the TV quotas.[11]

---

[9] "Pourtant, l'acheminement progressif vers une diffusion d'œuvres majoritairement européennes reste un objectif politique dénué d'obligation juridique, vœu pieux et à la discrétion des Etats" (Buffet-Tchakaloff, 1990: 373), "(...) eine politische Zielvorstellung" (Möwes & Schmitt-Vockenhausen, 1990: 123).

[10] "Le contenu de la Directive opère un compromis entre les pays d'Europe du Sud, France en tête, qui revendiquaient une harmonisation protectrice, et les pays hostiles au dirigisme culturel ou au protectionisme communautaire contre les œuvres étrangères, surtout américaines, c'est-à-dire la

Some kind of counterweight to this legal flexibility was therefore needed. We will limit ourselves to the compulsory two-year report of the Member States and the monitoring by the European Commission. In this two-year report the Member States have to give a statistic survey of the extent to which the channels have achieved the TV quotas. In all the cases where a channel has not achieved the required proportion (European works, European works of independent producers, recent works), the Member State has to give the reason for it. Finally, the Member States must indicate which measures they have taken against any channel having failed to comply with the requirements. The European Commission then processes all these national reports and makes the results public.

In 1990, Mr. Bangemann confirmed that the two-year monitoring system was to be seen as a legal counterweight:

> "While the Council failed to agree on a more restrictive wording, it made provisions for the weakness of the legal stipulations to be offset by political control, to be exerted, pursuant to Article 4, paragraph 3, by the Commission acting as the guarantor of actual commitments."[12] [our translation]

In total four reports have been drawn up and published by the European Commission (1994, 1996, 1998, and 2000). In this chapter we only pay attention to the last report, which pertains to the 1997–1998 period (for a discussion of the three previous reports, please see Castille, 2000).

III   The 'Television without Frontiers' Directive in 1997

In 1995, the European Commission announced a proposed amendment to 1989 TWF Directive.[13] The first round of monitoring of the application of the TV quotas by the Member States enabled the Commission to suggest amendments to Articles 4–6.

As regarded Article 4, the Commission narrowed down the basis for the calculation of the TV quotas by adding teleshopping[14] to the other explicitly excluded program categories. Both 'stock' and 'flux' programs remain eligible for inclusion in the quotas.

République fédérale d'Allemagne, les Pays-Bas, la Grande-Bretagne, le Danemark et le Luxembourg" (Buffet-Tchakaloff, 1990: 357).

[11] See Hitchens, 1996: 47: "The essentially economic motivation for the Directive became complicated by the inclusion of a quotas for European works. The quotas indicated a more confused response to the Directive's goals. The economic motivation for the TWF Directive became enmeshed with cultural goals."

[12] Answer (January 4, 1990) in the name of the Commission to a written question by Mr. Kenneth Collins, November 23, 1989: 646.

[13] For a more general situation: Defalque (1995): 193–198.

[14] About the growing importance of teleshopping see, among others, La lettre du CSA (1994): 1–11.

The European Commission also noted that while generalist channels had no trouble complying with the quotas, this proved much more difficult for the ever-increasing number of specialist channels. The Commission thus came up with the idea that these channels should be allowed to choose between the existing broadcasting obligation or an investment obligation of 25% of their programming budget. According to the Commission's proposal Member States would have to provide some leeway as regards specialist networks.

As regards newly created television networks, the Commission provided for a three-year period at the end of which they must meet the quota requirements. This period is necessary in order to let them reach financial stability. Moreover, this period of three years corresponds to the fact that the measures for the promotion of European works are only applicable for ten years.

Considering that the Commission's proposed amendment provided for differential treatment according to channel type (generalist or specialist channel), a logical inference would be that it was attempting to reduce the flexibility of the current Directive. Moreover, as made obvious in the national reports, the current wording had been a source of uncertainty and therefore of legal disputes resulting in both a distortion of competition and the disintegration of the internal market. Dropping the offending caveats would ensure a higher level of certainty from a legal point of view.

The Commission also wanted these measures to be no longer valid after a ten-year period, as a quota system in place for an indefinite time would only serve to keep the European production industry in a perennial state of fragility owing to the fact that rationalization and reinforcement would not be stimulated.

It appeared from that first round of monitoring that compliance with Article 5 was generally satisfactory on the part of broadcasters, which meant that it was a valid piece of legislation. Existing measures were therefore retained to a large extent. The only change proposed by the European Commission concerned the 'adequate proportion' of recent independent works, to become "at least 50%." As it has important implications with regard to corporate concentration, Article 5 will not be withdrawn after ten years.

The European Parliament[15] was largely in agreement with the amendments proposed by the European Commission – amendments directly based on the results of the First Communication. However, the Council saw things in a different light, choosing (1996) to maintain the quotas as set out in Articles 4 and 5 of the TWF Directive:

"The Council decided to retain the system for promoting European works introduced by Directive 89/552/EEC. Taking the view that this leaves Member States an advisable degree of flexibility, while ensuring the desired promotion of European audiovisual works. The Council also set up a Contact Committee to keep a very close watch on the implementation of the Directive, particularly as a forum for debate on matters relating to Articles 4 and 5. The clause in Article 4(4) and in Article 1 (32) of the com-

---

[15] For the response of the Social Economic Committee and the European Parliament on the proposed amendments of the television quotas, see Castille (2000).

mon position will enable Parliament and the Council to review such matters on the basis of a report from the Commission and taking into account an independent study on the impact of the measures in question at both Community and national level."

The Council only agreed to amendments broadening the excluded program categories as basis for the calculation of the TV quotas (adding teleshopping to the list). The notion of 'European work' was also broadened with a view to promoting more co-productions. The European Parliament (1996) and the European Commission agreed to this.

On July 30, 1997, the new TWF Directive was published in the Official Journal (European Parliament & Council, 1997); in particular, it was meant to bring clarifications in the field of jurisdiction disputes (Castille, 1998a: 38–39). As already abundantly clear from the July 1996 Common Position, the flexible quota system was maintained in the new Directive. There was no distinction made between specialist and generalist channels, and no time limit in the applicability of the quotas (Traimer, 1997: 127–129).

While the new TWF Directive does devote several considerations to TV quotas, these do not offer a lot to hold on to from a legal viewpoint. Consideration 30 emphasizes that a gradual system is necessary to account for economic realities. The notion of 'independent producer' is not even defined in a consideration. Consideration 31 only mentions that a number of criteria must be reckoned with: property of the production company, number of programs delivered to a given broadcasting organization, and ownership of the secondary rights.

The amended TWF Directive makes much of co-productions, especially in connection with a greater opening to former Eastern bloc countries. Article 6, paragraph 4:

"Works that are not European works within the meaning of paragraph 1 but that are produced within the framework of bilateral co-production treaties concluded between Member States and third countries shall be deemed to be European works provided that the Community co-producers supply a majority share of the total cost of the production and that the production is not controlled by one or more producers established outside the territory of the Member States."

The fourth report of the European Commission[16] (European Commission, 2000) reviews the implementation of Articles 4 and 5 in the application period of the amended TWF Directive (1997–1998).

So that the Member State reports would all be of a reasonably similar format the Commission drew up a number of guidelines (1999). These were in fact a second version incorporating changes made necessary by provisions of the 1997 Directive, amending the 1989 Directive (Suggested Guidelines, 1999: 1). These guidelines were drawn up at the Contact Committee meeting of November 9, 1999. The Contact Committee was created as part of the 1997 review of the TWF Directive. It includes representatives

---

[16] See europa.eu.int/comm/avpolicy/regul/twf/art45/art45_eng.htm.

of the relevant authorities of the Member States and is chaired by a representative of the Commission (art. 23a). One of his tasks consists of being "the forum for an exchange of views on what matters should be dealt with in the reports which Member States must submit pursuant to Article 4 (3), on the methodology of these, on the terms of reference for the independent study referred to in Article 25a, on the evaluation of tenders for this and on the study itself."

These guidelines are meant to harmonize the collection of the data used in the national reports, but are not legally binding (Suggested Guidelines, 1999: 1). Member States are only asked to state in their report the reason why, if such be the case, they use different definitions from those of the guidelines.

This fourth Communication consists of three Chapters and three Appendixes. In Chapter I the Commission gives its opinion regarding the application of Articles 4 and 5 for the reference period, as provided for in Article 4(3) of the Directive. Chapters II and III contain the summaries of the reports sent in by the Member States and by those EFTA States that are part of the European Economic Area (European Commission, 2000: 3).

The Commission's opinion on the application of Articles 4 and 5 for the period 1997/1998 is quite positive: "As regards the channels' compliance with the rules on the broadcasting of European works and independent productions, the results indicated by the national reports are generally satisfactory. (...) The aims of the Directive have broadly been met" (European Commission, 2000: 4). It remains to be seen to what extent this comparative optimism is justified, since it remains unclear whether 'broadcast European works' includes non-national European works.

IV   The Part of the Television Quotas in the Information Society

Since the scope of the new TWF Directive has not been changed – the result being that the new interactive services are not subject to the provisions of the Directive, therefore escaping the quota provisions – the following question arises: what is the place of the TV quotas in the emerging information society?

One of the features of the information society is increasing use of the same technology in various industries, such as telecommunications, media/broadcasting, and IT. According to the December 3, 1997 Green Paper, this is a major feature of the Information Society: "(...) increasing use by different sectors, notably the telecommunications, media and information technology (IT) sectors, of the same technologies. Evidence of such convergence has been mounting in recent years with the emergence of the Internet and with the increasing capability of existing networks to carry both telecommunications and broadcasting services" (European Commission, 1997).

At the end of 1998, the European commissioner in charge of media policy published a report entitled 'The Digital Age: European Audiovisual Policy' which was the result of conversations between 'a High Level Group on Audiovisual Policy' (Oreja, 1998). This report is very important because it states explicitly that the starting point of any audio-visual policy review must be the recognition of the special character of the media and the necessity to keep a balance between the 'market' on the one hand and the public interest on the other hand. In this report the special role of broadcasting is once more emphasized:

> "The audiovisual industry is not an industry like any other and does not simply pro-duce goods to be sold on the market like other goods. It is in fact a cultural industry par excellence, whose 'product' is unique and specific in nature. It has a major in-fluence on what citizens know, believe and feel. (..) namely, there has never been as-sumed in Europe that the broadcasting and audiovisual sector should be treated as an economic subject only or that the market would guarantee a pluralistic service" (Oreja, 1998).

In a recent Communication the Commission (1999b) sets out the principles and guide-lines for the EU's audiovisual policy in the digital age as well as the Commission's priorities for the next five years – including maximizing the competitiveness of the European audiovisual industry to ensure that digitization does not simply result in a flood of imported or archived (repeated) material. The Commission stresses "that the European audiovisual market remains overwhelmingly dominated by American pro-ductions":

> "Whilst the digital revolution poses new challenges to European Union audiovisual policy, the fundamental goals of this policy remain the same, namely: to encourage the production and distribution of European works, by establishing a secure and stable legal framework to guarantee the freedom to provide audiovisual services on the one hand, and through appropriate support mechanisms on the other" (European Commission, 1999b: 7).

In its last general report dated January 15, 2001 about the implementation of the TWF Directive, the European Commission once more emphasizes the importance of the TV quotas. We note the constant will of the European Commission to retain the quota prin-ciple as long as it is adapted to the 'digital' environment, in order to promote 'European' content in TV broadcasts and thus improve the competitiveness of the European pro-gram industry in general. In consideration of the total review of the TWF Directive in 2002, the Commission has ordered three different studies to be completed in early 2002. The first one – pursuant to Article 25a of the TWF Directive – pertains to the impact and implications of the TV quotas on the European program industry and aims to assess "the impact of measures to promote the distribution and production of European television programs. It will, in particular, evaluate the effectiveness of the quotas in the Directive as compared with other measures" (Third Report from the Commission: 17). The find-ings of this research are expected in the short term.

V Conclusion

Although, based on several recent documents, we can believe in the determination of the European Commission to maintain TV quotas in the information society, we cannot escape the impression that compliance on the part of European broadcasters in no way guarantees the development of a single European audiovisual area. Indeed, the European Commission needs to pay attention to the difference between national and not-national European programs. If we are to create a truly pan-European audiovisual area, we need to encourage the broadcasting of non-national European works.

References

Bangemann, M. (1990). *Revue trimestrielle du droit européen* 26(3): 646.

Bazzanella, S., Queck, R. & Willems, V. (1996). Le régime juridique de la fourniture de services multimédias en Belgique, *Auteurs & Media*: 94 and further.

Buffet-Tchakaloff, M.F. (1990). La réglementation communautaire de la communication audiovisuelle, D.P.C.I. 16(3): 373.

Castille, V. (1996). Libre réception et retransmission du program 'TNT & Cartoon Network' dans la télédistribution bruxelloise, I.R.D.I.: 46–47.

Castille, V. (1998a). De Europese Televisierichtlijn, *Gids Informatiesector 1998/1999* (pp. 37–42). The Hague/Rotterdam: NBLC/Media Business Press BV.

Castille, V. (1998b). De nieuwe televisierichtlijn. Enkele krachtlijnen van de omzetting in het Vlaamse Omroepdecreet, *Mediarecht, Radio en Televisie*: 1–15.

Castille, V. (2000). De Europese televisiequotas: flexibiliteit of compromis als rode draad? In D. Bittereyst & H. De Smaele (eds.), *Transformatie en continuïteit van de Europese televisie* (pp. 53–78). Ghent: Academia Press.

Defalque, L. (1995). Vers une nouvelle Directive 'Télévision sans frontières'?, J.T.D.E., 193–198.

De Witte, B. (1995a). Nieuwe controverse over de quota's, *Mediaforum* (3): 29.

De Witte, B. (1995b). The European content requirement in the EC Television Directive – Five years later. In E.M. Barendt (ed.), *The Yearbook of Media and Entertainment Law* (pp. 107–109). London: Clarendon Press.

European Commission (1994). *Communication from the Commission to the Council and the European Parliament on the Application of Articles 4 and 5 of 89/552/EEC Directive ('Television Without Frontiers')*, March 3, COM (94), 57 final.

European Commission (1995). *Proposal for a European Parliament and Council Directive amending Council Directive 89/552/EEC on the Coordination of certain Provisions laid down by Law, Regulation or Administrative Action in Member States concerning the Pursuit of Television Broadcasting Activities*, OJ, C n°. 85, July 19.

European Commission (1996a). *Communication from the Commission to the Council and the European Parliament on the Application of Articles 4 and 5 of 89/552/EEC Directive ('Television Without Frontiers')*. July 15, COM (96), 302 final.

European Commission (1996b). *Opinion of the Commission*, December 4, COM (96), 626 final.

European Commission (1997). *Green Paper on the Convergence of the Telecommunications, Media and Information Technology Sectors, and the Implications for Regulation towards an Information Society Approach*, December 3, COM (97), 623.

European Commission (1998). *Third Report from the Commission to the Council and the European Parliament on the Application of Articles 4 and 5 of 89/552/EEC Directive ("Television Without Frontiers") concerning the Calendar Years 1995 and 1996*. Available at [http://www.europa.eu.int/en/comm/dg10/avpolicy/twf/art45/3download_en.html].

European Commission (1999a). *Suggested Guidelines from the Monitoring of the Implementation of Articles 4 and 5 of the 'Television Without Frontiers' Directive*, June 11.

European Commission (1999b). *Communication from the Commission to the Council, the European Parliament, the Economic and Social Committee and the Committee of the Regions. Principles and Guidelines for the Community's Audiovisual Policy in the Digital Age*, Brussels, December 14, COM (99), 657 final.

European Commission (2000). *Fourth Communication from the Commission to the Council and the European Parliament on the Application of Articles 4 and 5 of Directive 89/552/EEC 'Television Without Frontiers' for the period 1997–8*, Brussels, COM (2000), 442 final.

European Commission (2001). *Third Report from the Commission to the Council, the European Parliament and the Economic and Social Committee on the application of Directive 89/552/EEC 'Television Without Frontiers,'* Brussels, COM (2001), 9 final.

European Parliament (1996). *Decision on the Common Position adopted by the Council with a view to the Adoption of a European Parliament and Council Directive amending*

Council Directive 89/552/EEC on the Coordination of certain Provisions laid down by Law, Regulation or Administrative Action in Member States concerning the Pursuit of Television Broadcasting Activities, OJ. C, n° 362, December 2.

European Parliament & European Council (1997). *Directive 97/36/EG of the European Parliament and of the Council of 30 June 1997 amending Council Directive 89/552/EEC on the Coordination of certain Provisions laid down by Law, Regulation or Administrative Action in Member States concerning the Pursuit of Television Broadcasting Activities*, OJ. L, July 30.

European Council, (1989). *Council Directive 89/552/EEC of 3 Octobre 1989 on the Coordination of certain Provisions laid down by Law, Regulation or Administrative Action in Member States concerning the Pursuit of Television Broadcasting Activities*, OJ. L, n°. 298, October 17.

European Council, (1996). *Common Position (EC) n°49/96 adopted by the Council on 8 July 1996 with a view to adopting Directive 97/36/EC of the European Parliament and of the Council amending Council Directive 89/552/EEC on the Coordination of certain Provisions laid down by Law, Regulation or Adminstrative Action in Member States concerning the Pursuit of Television Broadcasting Activities*, OJ. C, September 11.

Gay-Bellile, D. (1996). Audiovisuel/Télécommunications: un problème de définition, *Légipresse* 129 (II): 19–20.

Grosheide, W. & Mochel, P. (1997). Quotering van televisieprogramma's in de EU – de zaak Verenigde Staten contra Gemeenschap, *Mediaforum* (2): 18–24.

Hitchens, L.P. (1996). Identifying European Community Audiovisual Policy in the Dawn of the Information Society. In E.M. Barendt (ed.), *The Yearbook of Media and Entertainment Law* (pp. 47 & 69). London: Clarendon Press.

Ingberg, H. (1991). Le contrôle général de la Directive 'Télévision sans frontières'. In G. Vandersanden (ed.), *L'espace audiovisuel européen* (p. 30). Brussels: Editions de l'Université de Bruxelles.

La lettre du CSA (1994). *Le télé-achat dans le monde* 63: 1–11.

Lupinacci, T.M. (1991). The pursuit of television broadcasting activities in the European Community: Cultural preservation or economic protectionism?, *Vanderbilt Journal of Transnational Law* 24(1): 119.

Möwes, B. & Schmitt-Vockenhausen, M. (1990). Europäische Medienordnung im Lichte des Fernsehübereinkommens des Europas und der EG-Fernsehrichtlinie 1989, EuGRZ (6/7): 123.

Oreja, M. (1998). *The Digital Age: European Audiovisual Policy. Report from the High Level Group on Audiovisual Policy chaired by Commissioner Marcelino Oreja*, October 26. Available at [http//europa.eu.int/comm/dg10/avpolicy/key_doc/hlg1_en. html].

Pauwels, C. (2000). De creatie van een competitieve Europese audiovisuele programma-industrie: mission impossible? In D. Biltereyst & H. De Smaele (eds.), *Transformatie en continuïteit van de Europese televisie* (pp. 5–51). Ghent: Academia Press.

Salvatore, V. (1992). Quotas on TV programs and EEC law, *Common Market Law Review* 29(5): 967–990.

Rony, H. (1996). La notion de radiodiffusion: un besoin de clarification. *Légipresse*, 129(II): 17–18.

Traimer, M. (1997). Neufassung der EU-Richtlinie 'Fernsehen ohne Grenzen' verabschiedet. *Medien und Recht* (3): 127–129.

Uyttendaele, C. (1996). Convergentie, so what? In J. Dumortier (ed.), *Recente ontwikkelingen in media- en telecommunicatierecht. Juridische beschouwingen over liberalisering en convergentie* (pp. 47–95). Bruges: Die Keure.

Waelbroeck, D. (1996). Les modifications de la Directive télévision sans frontières. In C. Doutrelepont (ed.), *L'actualité du droit de l'audiovisuel européen* (p. 13–22). Brussels: Bruylant.

Wangermee, R. (1996). La notion de radiodiffusion dans les autoroutes de la communication. In C. Doutrelepont, P. Van Binst, & L. Wilkin (eds.), *Libertés, droits et réseaux dans la société de l'information* (pp. 13–25). Brussels: Bruylant.

Concentration and Competition Policies Towards a Precarious Balance within the Global Audiovisual Order

by Caroline Pauwels and Patrizia Cincera

"There is no bigness like show bigness" is how lead magazine *Variety* parodied the famous Hollywood slogan when referring to the remarkable merger between Time and Warner in March 1989 (Pilon, 1991: 282). It soon became obvious that this merger was only the first in a long series to follow. The communication industry, especially the audiovisual segment referred to in this chapter, has been in the process of restructuring itself through alliances, mergers and take-overs which have attracted varying amounts of attention. Concentration and transnationalisation were a key factor in the last decades. For the coming years a similar concentration activity is foreseeable, under the influence, among other things, of the expected convergence between the telecommunications, media and information technology industries. The beginning of the 21st century thus witnessed the birth of two media titans. In January 2000, media giant Time Warner merged with America Online (AOL), the world's largest internet access and service provider. A few months later, French telecommunications and media company Vivendi and its subsidiary, French pay-TV company Canal Plus, acquired Seagram, which owns a major portfolio of music and film assets through its take-over of Polygram (1998) and Universal Studios (1995).

This chapter is an attempt to delineate such concentration movements. It also explores the margins of the competition and anti-trust policies of the European Union. Such policies are meant to achieve two conflicting, almost irreconcilable objectives: establishing an internal open market without hindering the activities of large groups, and ensuring diversity and pluralism. Year after year, this has proved difficult at best.

I   Some Methodological Remarks

Anyone looking at media concentration has to deal with four built-in problems. First and foremost, the lack of standardized and permanently updated information makes it supremely hard to attain a realistic overall picture of ownership ratios, alliances, mergers, and ultimate hard facts about media concentration. Deregulation and the concomitant, ever-changing national, European or even global ownership entanglements have continued to increase the complexity and non-transparency of the audiovisual industry. Because of this, the researcher can rely only on incomplete and heterogeneously compiled statistical overviews (Screen Digest, Idate, Council of Europe, European Union, European Audio-visual Observatory), and a miscellany of press cuttings. These sources are not sufficient, however, to present the phenomenon of media concentration in a coherent, scientific manner. At best, they are relevant in pointing out a number of global trends. This recognized lack of reliable statistical material led the Commission and Council to set up a Community statistical information structure relating to the industry and markets of audiovisual and related industries[1] (April 1999).

The second problem is analytical and pertains to the choice of criteria, definitions and approaches that enable the researcher to analyze the theoretical concept of media concentration. Defining the concept and acquiring a sense of measurability regarding media concentration entails a number of analytical and methodological problems. In this respect, approaches are as varied as they are controversial (McQuail, 1992; Hoffmann-Riem, 1987; Knoche, 1980; Sanchez-Tabernero, 1993). This also has to do with the fact that a debate or inquiry into media concentration invariably involves the use of such debatable, vague and ambiguous concepts as *pluriformity* (internal and/or external), *pluralism* and *diversity*. In more general terms, a purely economic-industrial and legal analysis of concentration phenomena involves a series of disputable items such as dominant position, abuse of dominant position, relevant market (product or service-linked, geographic, time coverage) or again 'collective dominance,' a concept that recently gained acceptance in EU competition policy (Lensen, 1991; Van Loon & Schuijt, 1989; Cini & McGowan, 2000; Kiessling & Johnson, 1998). Differing approaches are bound to shed a varying light on concentration, resulting in diverging policy recommendations. As Van Cuilenburg (1992) points out, it should be clear that market failure in the media industry is evidence of a lack of ideas rather than a lack of suppliers. Therefore any meaningful discussion of media concentration needs to assume that there is a difference between the two, with a potentially negative correlation. This implies that research into content difference is in fact the only possible approach, involving in turn painstaking and historically staggered research.

The third problem, linked to the analytical and methodological complications mentioned above, is constituted by the fact that certain normative preconceptions either subvert or block a level-headed media concentration debate, not to mention effective research. This results in the media concentration debate being bogged down in the usual and unending controversies between free market, free enterprise advocates on the one hand, and proponents of state intervention to guarantee freedom of expression, diversity, and economic efficiency on the other hand (Bonnell, 1989; Negrine & Papathanassopoulos, 1990; Sanchez-Tabernero, 1993). And while it was generally assumed in Europe until the mid-1980's that pluralism and cultural diversity could only be achieved through a public broadcasting philosophy, more and more voices are saying today that it is in fact the market that does this. Community policy documents, in particular the 1997 Green Paper on convergence, are departing ever more explicitly from this assumption. Only very recently EU Commissioner Viviane Reding argued that, in the coming digital age, where a scarcity of frequencies and other distribution channels will no longer be a prob-

---

[1] See Council decision of April 26, 1999 establishing a Community statistical information infrastructure pertaining to the activities and markets of the audiovisual and related industries (1999/297/EC), Official Journal, L117, May 5, 1999:39.

lem, "... some public interest objectives, such as pluralism, will increasingly be met by the market itself" (Reding, 30 November 2000; Tongue, 1999; CEC COM(97)623 December 3, 1997).

In more general terms, finally, the concentration debate is being influenced by an unresolved fight between schools of economics, inspired by Schumpeterian theories about competition and the formation of monopolies. With respect to industrial economics, Schumpeter hypothesized that large firms can be more conducive to innovation because their market power allows them to set higher prices for the resulting product and thus realize a higher return from the innovation (Humphreys & Lang, 1998; Kiessling & Johnson, 1998).

II   Media Concentration as an Economic Reality

Keeping in mind these methodological assumptions, it comes as no surprise that certain researchers should minimize the impact of multimedia conglomerates and the cultural dangers they may represent, while others are tempted to stress the importance of these very factors (Guillou, 1985, 1986a, 1986b; Schiller, 1991; Miège, 1993; Negrine & Papathanassopoulos, 1990; Conso, 1991; Murdock, 1990; Mansell, 1993; Mosco, 1996; Rutten, 2000). There is nothing surprising, then, in the fact that contradictory research findings should have given birth to an ambivalent policy.

It is certain, however, that concentration, integration, and ownership entanglement between industrial/economic conglomerates and media corporations are neither explicitly recent phenomena nor strictly linear evolution processes (Mattelart, 1991a; Pilon, 1991; Conso, 1991; Crookes, 1996). In Europe, for instance, state-owned broadcasting corporations have mostly been vertically integrated (production, programming and broadcasting monopolies), radio and television stations were sometimes set up in different locations at the behest of powerful electronics companies, whereas in America certain industrial and financial conglomerates have been interested in the Hollywood studio system ever since the 1960's· The 1980's and 1990's, however, have been characterized by an increasing number of take-overs, mergers and alliances, as is illustrated, among other things, by the rising number of cases which the European Union is having to process under its merger regulation (see table 1). It is worth noting that these alliances have not only been spectacular in size – the largest merger of all times is the one between AOL and Time Warner (January 2000), with a combined value of US$ 18.7 billion. Other figures confirm this trend: in 2000 alone, five out of the ten largest mergers were related to the telecom and media industry. At the same time these mergers have led to a fundamental strategic reorganization of the audiovisual industry (Idate, 1992: 7; Luyken, 1990: 621; Pilon, 1991; Hancock, 1993; Booz Allen & Hamilton, 1989, 1992). An overview of these rearrangements and alliances is given in table 2. It also offers the reader an idea of the growing economic clout of the global audiovisual industry.

The most spectacular mergers and take-overs so far took place in 1989, 1990, 1993 and 1995, 1998 and 2000. But such transactions do not take place only in times of particular turbulence. Alliances are continually being forged and broken. Industrial-financial groups buy up stock in media companies. Often enough these transactions or alliances are aimed at the consolidation or creation of national media champions. These aim to ward off external take-over threats by foreign groups, while in other instances they are meant to secure a firm position on the national markets, as a launch pad for transnational expansion. Most corporations strive to achieve both purposes.

These restructuring moves have set the stage for a new era. Back in 1988 American networks were the world's largest audiovisual concerns, but from 1989 on they were overtaken by corporations pursuing horizontal and mostly vertical integration strategies in the production, distribution, hardware, and software (programs) areas (see table 2). Since the 1989 merger *Time Warner* has consistently achieved top positions in the list of major audiovisual companies. This position was recently confirmed when Time Warner was itself taken over by internet provider America Online (AOL). Equally dramatic were the take-overs by foreign companies of a majority of Hollywood studios at the end of the 1980's[2]. While in those years, along with a trend towards integration of soft and hardware companies, such sales of major American companies kept the headlines buzzing, since the middle of 1990 the emphasis has been on convergence between telecommunications groups, computing, and audiovisual corporations[3]. Intra-

---

[2] Hardware manufacturer Sony took over Columbia in 1989 for US$ 3.4 billion. In 1990 Matsushita, another Japanese hardware company, took over MCA/Universal for US$ 6.5 billion. In 1990, Paretti acquired MGM/UA for US$ 1.3 billion, and was in turn taken over by Crédit Lyonnais. In 1990, Murdoch took over 20th Century Fox for US$ 375 million. Since then, new restructuring moves have occurred, such as Viacom/Paramount/Blockbuster (1994). MCA/ Universal was subjected to another take-over in April 1995. This time it became the property of Canadian beverage conglomerate Seagram for US$ 5.7 billion (Le Monde, April 11, 1995: 20). This triggered a new spate of take-overs. In July 1995, Walt Disney acquired Capital Cities/ABC for US$ 19 billion (Le Monde, August 5, 1995: 10). On August 1, CBS was swallowed by the Westinghouse electricity company for US$ 5.4 billion. In another merger, the largest ever, Time Warner took over Turner Broadcasting System (TBS) for US$ 7.5 billion (Le Monde, September 1, 1995: 17). The resulting concern generates a turnover of about US$ 18.7 billion (De Morgen, August 3, 1995: 3)

[3] Testimony to the convergent interests and cooperative mergers between telecommunications operators and broadcasters is the abortive negotiations for a mega-merger between Bell Atlantic, one of the Baby Bells, and TCI, America's foremost cable operator. TCI is also linked to Time Warner, which in May 1993 entered into an alliance with US West, another telecommunications operator (Le Monde, October 15, 1993). Furthermore, TCI was, through its participation in teleshopping channel QVC, involved in a take-over struggle over Paramount, with Disney the only surviving American major. TCI's competitor in this take-over struggle was Viacom, another important cable and television operator, which in turn is related to AT&T and Nynex (Le Monde, November 9, 1993: 29&ff. and Le Monde, September 15, 1993: 28). QVC in turn has been trying to find broader financial support with Bell South, another Baby Bell (De Morgen, November 9, 1993). Similar arrangements also occurred in the United Kingdom, where cable operators are allowed to offer telephone services. In order to remain competitive, rival telecommunications operators British Telecom and Mercury have also requested permission to operate cable services (Le

sectoral or horizontal alliances, which point to an initial trend towards consolidation of core activities, continue, admittedly, to represent the large majority (57.9%) of the 181 alliances which were concluded in 1995/1996 within the communications industry (telecom/media/IT) in the broadest sense of the term. However, a quarter of these alliances can already be placed under the heading of convergence alliances. The difference in financial clout between the telecommunications and audiovisual industry is expressed in the fact that while both enter each other's terrain to almost the same extent, the telecom industry tends to favor take-over scenarios while the audiovisual industry seems more intent of convergence. The telecom operators' strategy here is, as a former BT chairman remarked, "to become (CP) retailers of anything that can be converted into digital form" (IMO working paper 95/5). These alliances, whatever form they take, point to what the Green Paper on convergence refers to as a trend towards diversification as a response to the economic and technological opportunities being created in the EU and the global market. And even though some alliances tend to misfire[4], usually leading to a renewed focus on core activities, further integration of telecommunications, cable, film industry, program packaging, and consumer electronics seems inevitable (Mansell, 1993; Noam & Kramer, 1994; Noam, 1996), especially because the communications industry is one in which corporate interests seem prepared to lose money for a long time. This tendency is further illustrated by strategic alliances paving the way for digital (pay-)television, as has been the case in the mergers – planned, cancelled or effective – between Kirch/Richemont/Telepiù, Canal Plus and Nethold[5] (September 1996), Bertelsmann/UFA and CLT, British Digital Broadcasting (BDB), BT and BSkyB (BIB), MSG (Bertelsmann/Kirch/Deutsche Telekom), Bertelsmann/Kirch/ Deutsche Telekom (Betaresearch), Bertelsmann/Kirch, TPS, BSkyB and KirchPayTV (Idate, 2000). These alliances can also be interpreted within the general framework of American and European plans for the establishment of *information highways* (Burgel-

---

Monde, November 9, 1993 and December 21, 1993). Negotiations regarding the launching of Cablevision, a potential alliance between Spanish telecommunications operator Telefonica, cable company Sogecable, and Canal Plus further illustrate the convergence trends (TechEurope, July 1996: III.3). The European Commission has started an inquiry into the acceptability of this alliance. Similar agreements exist between Microsoft Corporation, NBC TV Network, Dream Works Studio (Spielberg), and cable companies such as TCI, Comcast (USA), and Compagnie Générale des Eaux (France). American telecommunications operator MCI in turn has entered into agreements with News Corp (Murdoch). Additionally, three regional Baby Bells (Ameritech, Bellsouth, and SBC) made a deal with Walt Disney. A further three Baby Bells (Bell Atlantic, Nynex and Pacific Telesis) entered into an agreement with talent agency Creative Artists Agency (Crookes, 1996).

[4] The many different agents in this field, from all kinds of network operators to consumer electronics companies and software distributors, seem not to be driven so much by rational, long-term strategies, but rather by a possibly short-sighted compulsion not to miss out on current developments and state-of-the-art technology (Burgelman, 1994).

[5] Nethold has been built on Swiss and South African capital (Richemont) and it operates, among others, M-net – South Africa's leading pay-television channel – and Filmnet, a pay television channel on the Scandinavian and Benelux markets.

man, Punie & Verhoest, 1995)[6]. And of course, the latest rash of take-overs and mergers (AOL and Time Warner, Vivendi, Canal Plus and Seagram[7], etc.) show how pivotal the internet has become. With this integration of the old and the new economies, the 'megalization' within the cultural industry has clearly taken on a new dimension. At the same time the economic value of the newly created companies is climbing to previously unseen heights: to acquire the 'old-fashioned' American media conglomerate Time Warner, AOL, the biggest player in the new media economy, is ready to pay five times as much as Viacom did five years ago for CBS (Rutten, 2000). The strategy underlying the entire process aims to create synergies between various pools of competencies in order to coordinate the production and distribution/marketing of information and entertainment products.

These latest integration developments illustrate very clearly the way in which the 'content' industry has over the years become a strategic take-over target (Tongue, 1999; Rutten, 2000). The more distribution channels are added through technological development and deregulation[8], the greater the demand for content, whether for traditional culture industry products like films, music, novels, magazines, and television programs, or more recent forms of electronic services. In the audiovisual industry this need to secure the rights to profitable programs – especially sports and fiction – has given rise to a ruthless bidding war between the richest media conglomerates such as News Corp/ BSkyB and Kirch. As mentioned in official European Commission reports, between 1993 and 1996 these developments pushed up the cost of broadcasting rights by 20 to 25% (CEC/DG X, October 23, 1997). TV rights for Sydney 2000 totaled over US$ 1.3 billion, more than twice as much as what the world's TV stations paid for Barcelona '92. Because of these exorbitant figures companies are once again forced to

---

[6] See also the 1994 Bangemann report (May 26, by the EU's high-level group on the information society).

[7] The Vivendi, Canal Plus and Seagram merger, following the same logic as the AOL-Time Warner's marriage, is a striking example of what could be the concrete outcome of the convergence phenomenon between the media, telecommunications, and the computing sectors. Vivendi Universal is present along the whole media value chain from the production of content to its delivery. Vivendi has used the cash flow from the water and waste-treatment business to acquire 49% of Canal Plus, Europe's largest pay-TV company (and a major player in European film production) and a 24.5% stake in Britain's Sky Broadcasting Group, Rupert Murdoch's lucrative satellite broadcaster in the UK. Vivendi also owns Havas, a major publisher of books, magazines, software and video games. Additionally, Vivendi has created France's second largest cellular phone company, Cegetel, and has launched, in partnership with Vodafone Airtouch PLC, the world's number one cell-phone operator, a new European portal named *Vizzavi*. Vizzavi is intended as Europe's answer to AOL, a portal for the 80 million subscribers of Vodafone, Canal Plus and Cegetel. Finally, the US$ 34 billion Vivendi take-over of Seagram brings with it two main entertainment assets, musical content with Universal Music, and cinema with Universal Studios.

[8] According to Screen digest, continental Europe had over 650 TV channels at the end of 1998. With regard to the growth of digital TV, Idate calculated that as of June 1999, there were 35 digital TV platforms in the EU, compared with 20 at the end of 1998. At the end of 1999 Idate therefore estimates that there are around 400 digitally broadcast TV channels in the EU (Idate, 2000).

enter strategic alliances. The exclusivity deals arising from this have in the meantime drawn the attention of the European Commission.

In conclusion one can read two fundamental trends in the concentration and integration movements of the 1980's and 1990's (Pilon, 1991; Mosco, 1996). Most significant is the presence of a limited number of outsize multinational conglomerates which are active in a number of media and entertainment related industries, which show decidedly oligopolistic tendencies and, moreover, which conduct their activities worldwide. Comments by the corporation's Director General following the 1989 Time Warner merger were eloquent in this respect: "The media and entertainment industry will consist of a limited number of global giants. These companies will be vertically integrated (...). They will be large enough to produce, commercialize, and broadcast over the whole world and be flexible enough to take on the costs of such activities by way of a vast and ever growing network of distribution facilities. Time Inc. is determined to be one of these companies" (as quoted in Schiller 1989: 10–11).

AOL's recent take-over of Time Warner should undoubtedly be seen in the light of these comments. Noticeable within this movement towards integration is the small clout of Europe's audiovisual industry (see also table 1). As the Audiovisual Observatory notes, among the 50 top-ranking companies there are more European (24) than American (14) or Japanese (8) corporations. On the other hand, these are on average much smaller than their American competitors, with the total audiovisual turnover of the Europeans amounting in 1997 to under half that of the Americans (US$ 2.3 billion as compared to US$ 4.8 billion). In addition, European corporations are growing more slowly (−0.1%) than their US counterparts (+13.6%), and several are actually confronted with falling revenue (Audiovisual Observatory, Statistical Yearbook 1999: 63). These developments are also generating a growing audiovisual trade deficit between Europe and America – a deficit that in 1997 amounted to US$ 5.89 billion, rising to US$ 6.6 billion in 1998, and approaching €7 billion today (CEC COM(1999) 657final). According to the Commission's communication on 'Principles and guidelines for the Community's audiovisual policy in the digital age' (CEC COM(1999) 657final), "American productions account for between 60 and 90% of Member States' audiovisual markets (receipts from cinema ticket sales, video cassette sales and rentals and from sales of television fiction programs), while the respective European share of the American market is of the order of 1 or 2%." In terms of content this is visible in the overwhelming presence of American movies on European TV and television screens. Of the top 50 box office successes in 1998, just 10 were of European origin, including two British-American co-productions. As Tongue argues "This deficit has a cultural, social and political impact on the UK and Europe" (Tongue, 1999: 108).

A second fundamental feature lies in the paradox of what has recently been called the post-Fordist economy. Alongside a clearly visible tendency toward integration, we are now witnessing a process of decentralization and differentiation in which small and medium-sized companies are being born and developed in the shadow of the major TNMCs (transnational media corporations). In political economics, however, this evolution is interpreted more as a strengthening of the power of the major concerns than as the emergence of a counterweight (Galbraith, 1977; Mosco, 1996). While it is the small and medium-sized enterprises which (temporarily) bear the risks and high costs of innovation and experimentation, the major conglomerates' control of capital and distribution remains untouched. This in turn makes the small and medium-sized companies very vulnerable to take-over by the TNMCs.

III   EU Competition and Anti-Trust Policies

3.1 Three Levels of Intervention

Existing tendencies towards excessive concentration evoke queries regarding pluralism, diversity and fair competition. Insofar as market mechanisms seem in themselves to engender a tendency towards concentration (Schumpeter, 1962; Mansell, 1993; Burgelman, Punie & Verhoest, 1995; Collins, 1990; Pauwels, 1995), reference could be made to the potential role of regulatory authorities as guarantors of pluralism, diversity, and fair competition. Given the global ambitions of media corporations, the competition policies of a transnational authority such as the European Union would seem crucial. But of course this institution, pursuant to EU legislation, judges alliances on the basis of industrial strategy objectives rather than out of cultural policy considerations.

EU competition policies are meant to reconcile two conflicting objectives (Pauwels, 1995). On the one hand, sizeable corporations are essential for achieving internal market objectives and strengthening European competitiveness. Improving technical efficiency, referring to the production and introduction of a given set of (new) services at the lowest possible cost and the overcoming of fragmentation are important criteria in the industrial economic analysis of alliances. On the other hand these holdings should be deterred from taking advantage of their increased market power to undermine competition: any anti-competitive behavior towards both competitors and suppliers as well as abuse of dominant position over a user base must be rooted out (Kiessling & Johnson, 1998; Cini & McGowan, 2000).

Contrary to other domains of intervention, the European Commission is vested with special power in the field of competition policy: it can act independently from the Council of Ministers and the European Parliament and make decisions concerning the legitimacy and desirability of certain agreements, mergers, powerful positions, state aids, etc. In this way it becomes not only the executive, but also the supervisory and even legislative authority. In case of a dispute regarding a decision by the Commission, the sole competent body is the European Court of Justice.

As regards the media, Community competition policies add an extra dimension stemming from the added cultural value of a software product. Here, while decisions regarding competition may have an impact on media pluralism and diversity, as such these policy principles (which in Europe are traditionally associated with a public service mission) do not fall within the scope of EU competition policy, which is concerned solely with fair competition. The Commission has nevertheless been seeking a specific media approach, but in this it has always been hindered by member states, which consider the media very much a national matter.

In the Commission's actions regarding concentration trends and market distortions in the media industry, three levels of intervention can be discerned:

- First level: the direct enforcement of competition rulings under the EC Treaty (articles 81 (restrictive practices policy – former art. 85), 82 (monopoly policy/abuse of dominant position – former art. 86), 86 (public sector – former art. 90) and 87 (state aid – former art. 92);
- Second level: the general 1989 merger regulation, as revised in 1997. In the context of alliances, a cooperative agreement falls under article 81, whereas a concentration agreement falls under the merger guidelines. An important difference between the treatment of cases under merger guidelines and under competition rules is that the decision of compliance under the merger regulation has to be taken within a clearly defined time frame, while treatment of cooperative agreement under the competition rules implies a more open-ended investigation (Kiessling & Johnson, 1998; Cini & McGowan, 2000).
- The third level of intervention, finally, was the Green Paper on pluralism and media concentration (1992) and the resulting (but subsequently derailed) proposal for a directive.

3.2 Direct Enforcement of the Competition Provisions

As for the direct implementation of competition provisions as set out in the EU Treaty (art. 81, 82, 86 and 87), the rule is that state aid as well as the creation of cartels and monopolies that undermine competition and the workings of the free internal market, are all totally unacceptable and therefore prohibited. Under certain circumstances, when they are for example in the interest of the internal market and the consumer, such subsidies and alliances may be approved, however (Pauwels, 1995; Defalque, 1991; Cini & McGowan, 2000). Article 82 in turn forbids the abuse of dominant positions. This implies that it is not the holding of a position of power as such that is forbidden, but the misuse of such a position. In this case it is therefore up to the Commission, and in many cases also the Court of Justice, to specify where a dominant position exists, and where this dominant position is being abused. As Cini and McGowan stipulate "The focus of the Commission's investigation rests on the notion of an *abuse*, that is on the conduct of the firm and not just on its structure" (Cini & McGowan, 2000: 18). Before the Commission can decide whether a firm holds a position of dominance, it must first of all define the relevant market and more specifically the relevant product market (do various competitive or substitution products exist?), the relevant geographical market and the time dimension (Pauwels, 1995; Gunther, 1998). This means assessing market power, for example based on market share. Only then will the Commission set out to assess the abuse of a position of dominance[9] (Cini & McGowan, 2000).

3.2.1 Securing Access to Content

When it comes to the enforcement of articles 81 and 82 (former articles 85 and 86) to media and audiovisual matters, the common factor in several decisions taken so far is a concern to secure better distribution of and access to software and program rights (content) for both broadcasters and individuals. Direct and indirect illustrations of this include the following cases: ARD-Degetofilm (a subsidiary of the MGM/MA Hollywood major), UIP (United International Pictures, a joint distribution channel for MGM/UA, Paramount and MCA/Universal)[10], Eurosport and the general approval of the EBU/Eurovision exchange system[11], and UIP-Pay-TV. As pay-television comes to the fore and strengthens the trend towards exclusivity rights, two lines of Community competition policy appear to be fundamental. The first one is the limitation of exclusivity rights in time, the second is the requirement to provide access to program rights to third parties as well (ARD/Degetofilm; Eurovision exchange system), and in the case of UIP, the requirement to help distribute third party production, in this particular case European productions (Van Miert, January 1997). The problem of distribution and access is handled, in a supplementary fashion, through secondary Community law. Evidence of this is provided by the quotas set by the 'Television without Frontiers' Directive (89/552/EEC) and, more importantly, Article 3a, introduced as part of the revision of this directive, which seeks to secure free-to-air access to individual (particularly sports) events which are considered to be of major importance[12]. Industry-specific regulation for digital television conditional access should, to some extent, also be seen in this framework (Nikolinakos, 2000).

The decisions which have been made on the basis of articles 81 and 82 (former 85 and 86) are of course not free from criticism. Especially noteworthy, for example, is the

---

[9] These include unfair pricing, discriminatory pricing, unfair trading conditions, tying agreements, refusal to supply, etc. (Cini & McGowan, 1998: 88).

[10] In September 1999 the European Commission renewed the exemption under article 81.3 of the agreements establishing UIP BV. The Commission also announced a review in five years time.

[11] On April 3, 1989 the EBU had applied for negative clearance or for an exemption pursuant to article 81.3 in respect of the Eurovision system. The Commission adopted an exemption decision on June 11, 1993, but this was later overturned by the Court of First Instance. After changing its internal rules, the EBU/Eurovision's joint acquisition and sharing of broadcasting rights for sports events was granted an exemption from normal antitrust law on May 11, 2000. The exemption is valid until 2005.

[12] Indirectly the Television Standards Directive (95/47/EC O.J. L281/51 of November 23, 1995), as well as the cable directive (95/51/EC O.J. L 256 of November 26, 1995) and the proposed revision thereof (structural distinction between telecom and cable networks) can be seen as ways of facilitating access to the networks, and hence to content.

fact that the ARD and UIP decisions are largely directed at the distribution of American films[13]. This comes at a time when there is still no large-scale project for supporting the distribution of European films and, as already emphasized above, the domination of American films on the European continent is a generally recognized problem (local productions barely hold 15% of the European market, while Hollywood majors enjoy a comfortable 85% share). The antitrust authorities' policy in the audiovisual industry – based on Articles 81 and 82 – recently drew fundamental criticism from the EFCA (European Film Companies Alliance). Concern among the European audiovisual industry and national and regional policy-makers is made even more acute by the Competition Directorate-General's interpretation of Article 87 (state aid) and its intended measures.

3.2.2 State Aid

With regard to the enforcement of the rules concerning state aid, an area that is traditionally not regarded as 'anti-trust', it is the general belief of the Commission, as stated by former Commissioner Van Miert, that state aid does not contribute to economic efficiency. Its only benefit is to remedy market imperfection (Van Miert, November 10, 1997). It is owing to this belief that state aid cases have been adjudicated. With the Commission constantly stressing the structural weaknesses of the European audiovisual industry, and also wishing to remedy them, it also seemed until recently that the enforcement of the state aid rules in the audiovisual area could be positively evaluated (CEC, COM(96)160 final of April 17, 1996), in particular since the EC Treaty made provision for a new exception to the enforcement of state aid rules in order to support culture (art. 87.3.d). In this context it should, however, be emphasized that the Commission and the Court seldom deviate from the legal essence of European unification, i.e. broad rules and no exceptions. Discriminatory and non-proportional provisions included in German, French, Danish, Spanish, Italian, Dutch and Greek support mechanisms for the film industry have had to give way under pressure from the Commission. Since 1998, however, the Commission has been seeking to lay down a more general policy line with regard to state aid to cinema and television programming. In its decision of June 9, 1998 on the French system of support to film production, the Commission set out a list of 4 specific criteria on the basis of which it intended to assess state aid to cinema and TV program production under the cultural exception clause (Article 87.3.d.). In particular the provisions that aid to the audiovisual industry should be limited to 50% of the production budget and that producers receiving such support must be free to spend at least 20% of the film budget in another member state led to an uproar in professional and

---

[13] The internal inconsistency of the Community's audiovisual policy is taken to task by former MEP Tongue: "We could point to the cartel that the European Commission itself allowed UIP to conduct from 1989 to 1997. When this arrangement was first allowed, the US had a 56% share of EU box office receipts; that share is now well over 80%" (Tongue, 1999: 125).

political circles, especially as the DG Competition had omitted to consult with national governments and the culture industry. Declarations from DG Competition representatives such as "culture should not serve as an alibi for subsidizing an industry" have, however, recently been neutralized by the adoption in November 2000 of a resolution stating that the audiovisual industry is an "exceptional cultural industry." Assistance to film and media is, according to the resolution "one of the most important means of maintaining cultural diversity, which is precisely the objective of government assistance." Whether this marks a watershed remains to be seen. A resolution is a weak legal tool, and it is looking very likely that DG Competition has other forms of direct or indirect state aid to the audiovisual industry in its sights, such as must-carry rules, or the specifications imposed by national policy-makers on private and public broadcasters. In other words, the limits of what in the eyes of DG Competition represents camouflaged forms of state aid are being clearly explored. This has also been the case for some time now when it comes to the enforcement of the competition rules, including those concerning state support to public broadcasting.

3.2.3 State Aid – Public Service

Insofar as the Treaty recognizes the importance of the concept of public service and provides guarantees for its existence and maintenance (arts. 7d, 86, 87.3.d), the decisions of the Commission is evidence of a certain amount of good will. In the audiovisual industry member states have gone so far as to emphasize the importance of public broadcasting by endorsing the Protocol on public service broadcasting which was appended to the Amsterdam Treaty[14]. One illustration of this positive stance towards public service broadcasting is the aforementioned approval of the Eurovision exchange system. According to the Commission, this exemption would preserve the interests of small broadcasters and their access to program rights. Of more fundamental importance, however, are the proceedings that the Commission has initiated concerning state support to public broadcasting (see the chapter on the future of European public television further in this book). Various private broadcasters have indeed complained that the license fee system distorts competition, especially when coupled with advertising on public service broadcasters. Several complaints have been brought before the Commission on this basis by private broadcasters (Spain, Portugal, Italy, France, Germany) (Oreja, 1998). The Portuguese RTP case was the first one which the Commission has adjudicated (decision of

---

[14] The protocol states that as "the public broadcasting system in Member States is directly connected with the democratic, social and cultural needs of every society and the need to maintain media diversity", (…) "the provisions of this treaty (…) do not detract from the rights of member states to provide financial resources for public broadcasting, insofar as such resources are provided to broadcasting organizations for the fulfillment of the defined and organized missions entrusted to them in the public service area, and providing that these resources do not influence trading and competition conditions in the Community to such an extent that, taking into account the demands of public service, they are opposed to the public interest."

November 7, 1996). The Commission concluded that the public financing which the RTP enjoys is not a form of government support because, in return, the RTP is required to fulfil public service tasks which are clearly defined by law. Whether this created a precedent is, however, another matter, as the Commission's decision was recently (May 2000) cancelled by the Court of First Instance, that found that the Commission had reached a decision too quickly and should conduct a more thorough enquiry. Commission decisions were also found wanting by the Court of First Instance in the case of TF1 versus France 2 and 3. It is clear that, in the eyes of the Commission (Oreja, 1998) and the Court of Justice, support measures have always to be tested against principles such as transparency, proportionality, objective necessity, and the like, which are arbitrary in that they have never been precisely defined. This raises the question as to whether, in what form, and in what way license fees can be maintained: 1) are they indeed proportional (meaning that the funding of public broadcasting does not exceed what is strictly necessary) and 2) are they objectively necessary to fulfil the public service mission? Insofar as 1) the added cost is almost impossible to calculate – a fact recognized by the Commission itself – and 2) criteria such as proportionality and the like are interpreted restrictively, public service broadcasters remain in a situation of legal uncertainty[15]. In this way public service institutions may become the victims of the 'Community fundamentalism', a good example of which is to be found within the Court of First Instance (Cini & McGowan, 2000: 155). The Commission, just as in other state aid cases, is no longer able to resist the pressure from the Court in audiovisual matters[16]. As EU Commissioner Viviane Reding recently remarked, the Commission must now yield to this pressure in all the pending files concerning state aid to public broadcasting (Le Monde, July 22, 2000). Still, past attempts to introduce general directives or a framework with regard to (un)acceptable state aid to public broadcasting, have run into massive resistance from member states, who want to keep their hands free when it comes to the mission, financing and organization of their public broadcasters, as was also confirmed in a resolution of November 17, 1998. But any idea that the above-mentioned resolution has checked the Commission's zeal is illusory, as is shown by the newly opened proceeding against France, Italy, Portugal and others. In fact, the latest EU cases are assuming ever more explicitly that public objectives are not automatically

---

[15] The concern of EBU members was again confirmed at a symposium organized on July 22, 2000 in a joint declaration in which they emphasize "the need for a secure legal and financial basis for carrying out their public service mission, including with regard to Community legislation" and also complain about "the lack of a common interpretation of the competition rules and the Amsterdam protocol" (Le Monde, July 22, 2000: 14).

[16] Generally speaking, policy on state aid has become tougher, especially since state aid appeals became the preserve of the Court of First Instance. The bias of the Commissioners and hence the ambivalence of state aid policy, continues to be denounced on a regular basis: "(...) most Commissioners, being career politicians and viewing themselves as national representatives, tend to side with the home government. In state aid matters the Commissioners can be expected to prostitute themselves to political interests unless and until the Court requires otherwise" (Bishop, 1995: 331).

secured by public broadcasting, but can be achieved just as well – in other words, perhaps better – by the market (Oreja, 1998; Tongue, 1999). The deregulation of public broadcasting within the EU therefore remains a process of giving with one hand and taking with another (Vandersanden, 1992; Tongue, 1999). There remains however one inalienable and unassailable privilege: as 'guardian of the Treaties', the "Commission must ensure that the funding of public television by Member States does not distort competition in the common market to the detriment of the common interest" (Oreja, 1998, CEC, COM(1999)657 final, December 14, 1999).

IV   The merger regulation (1989)

In spite of the Commission being granted a decisive role on competition issues, its efficiency was limited by the fact that it can only act a posteriori concerning corporate concentrations. As a result the Commission has striven since 1972 to obtain a priori control over concentrations. This went against the grain for a number of Member States which considered it an instance of extravagant tampering and interference with national competition policies. They felt their national champions were being threatened. A priori control became a fact in 1989, however, with the adoption of a merger regulation. Ever since the regulation came into force (September 21, 1990), the Commission – through the Task Force it established as part of Directorate General Competition – has had the exclusive prerogative of ruling on proposed mergers with a view to pronouncing beforehand on mergers with a 'Community dimension' and investigating whether they can be deemed compatible with the internal market (one-stop-shop system).

According to this regulation, and especially its revised and extended 1997 version, mergers with a Community dimension are those that create entities with worldwide sales above €5 billion. Furthermore, internal market sales of at least two participating companies should be above €250 million separately. In addition to this, the revised version of 1997 provides for a priori control by the Commission for merger cases which do not meet these thresholds but which nevertheless have a significant cross-border effect (in the case of three or more national notifications). A new combination of criteria, amongst them a combined worldwide turnover of more than €2.5 billion and €100 million for EU turnover, will thus apply to such merger cases (Harcourt, 1998a & 1998b). There can be exceptions to this rule, however. Member States can back mergers worth more than the thresholds imposed by the directive when so-called 'licit (or legitimate) interests' are at stake. Article 21 section 3 explicitly mentions licit interests as regards media pluralism. This clause under article 21 section 3 means that, with respect to media concentrations with a Community dimension, the EU regulation does not apply exclusively. National legislation can be invoked. If the Commission allows a certain merger, a Member State can have it rendered null and void under the protective ruling of media plurality. The reverse is not possible however: a merger forbidden by the Commission cannot be approved by the Member States. By introducing this ruling, the Commission effectively acquiesces to the principle of subsidiarity (Lensen, 1991: 25). While the onus of guaranteeing fair competition is on EU institutions, preserving pluralism is up to Member States (Green Paper on pluralism and media concentration in the internal market COM (92) 480 final of December 23, 1992: 91).

Since the regulation came into effect a number of mergers involving audiovisual media and allied services have been reported. Statistics on the merger regulation enforcement moreover show increased merger activity in the telecommunications and media industry since 1996 (Cini & McGowan, 2000: 124). Of the 1,158 decisions which have been taken until now on the basis of the merger regulation[17], about 45 decisions are related to the media industry and 142 to the telecommunications industry[18]. More importantly, however, six of the twelve negative decisions made until now under the merger regulation directly affect the media industry: MSG Media Service (1994), Nordic Satellite Distribution (1995), HMG (RTL/Veronica/Endemol (1995), Bertelsmann/Kirch/Première (1997), Deutsche Telekom/Betaresearch (1997) and MCI Worldcom/Sprint (2000). Other negative decisions such as Telefonica/Sogecable and Time Warner/EMI were avoided at the very last minute by the withdrawal of the alliance (Gunther, 1998; Kiessling & Johnson, 1998; Motta & Polo, 1997). But just as important are of course those alliances – including two recent and headline-grabbing ones, those of Warner/AOL (2000) and Vivendi/Canal Plus/Seagram (2000) – that were approved, albeit with strings attached. Increased decision making in the media industry under the merger regulation, as well as the procedures under which the decisions were finally taken, can be seen in table 2.

Aware that the audiovisual media section is one "with a high growth potential, where entry barriers can be very substantial (costs of broadcasting rights, equipment and marketing investments, infrastructures), the Commission is seeking in its decisions to ensure that the market is not closed nor competition falsified by certain alliances or concentrations, or by a problem of access to programs" (CEC, 1996, SEC(97)628 final: 32). As noted by Gunther, the overall line taken by the Commission in the matter of competition policy in the media industry is characterized by a twofold concern: favoring alliances between European corporations, while at the same time ensuring that the market remains open to competition (Gunther, 1998). This means that access to the existing or emerging market, access to infrastructures or networks, and access to programming rights must be guaranteed at all times by anti-trust policy. The Commission is also looking very closely at all horizontal and vertical media alliances that could have a potential gate-keeping effect, or which could bring about a situation of collective or oligopolistic dominance in the media industry. The EU's negative decisions in the media industry (MSG Media Service (1994), Nordic Satellite Distribution (1995), HMG (RTL/Veroni-

---

[17] As the Commission remarks in its 1999 Annual Report on Competition: "There has been a fivefold increase in the number of cases notified under the merger regulation since 1990."

[18] This count is based on the NACE codes. Double-counting of telecommunication/media is, however, possible in the context of convergence trends.

ca/Endemol (1995), Bertelsmann/Kirch/Première (1997), Deutsche Telekom/Betare-search (1997) and MCI Worldcom/Sprint (2000), should all be seen in the light of these criteria, either individually or in their mutual combinations (Gunther, 1998; Motta & Polo, 1997; Kiessling & Johnson, 1998).

As EU Competition Commissioner Monti himself recently commented: "a certain pattern is emerging from all the (media and telecommunication merger) decisions. First, the Commission has taken action each time that it has identified that a gatekeeper concern was likely to arise in the short or medium term. In most cases, however, the problems could be limited in time or scope and solutions have been found through granting access to competitors. When, however, the problem could not be resolved (...) prohibition was the only possible outcome. Moreover, the Commission has also insisted in eliminating minority shareholdings or links among competitors that could prevent effective competition in certain markets" (Monti, 2000).

The recent approval of the AOL/Time Warner and Vivendi/Canal Plus/Seagram mergers need to be seen in light of these comments:

• On October 11, 2000, the European Commission approved the proposed merger between AOL and Time Warner (TW) after AOL offered to sever all structural links with German media group Bertelsmann. In this case, the Commission was concerned that AOL, because of the merger with Time Warner, which in turn had planned to merge its music recording and publishing activities with EMI, and because of its joint ventures with Bertelsmann, would have controlled the leading source of music publishing rights in Europe. In Europe, Time Warner, EMI and Bertelsmann together would have held approximately 50% of all music publishing rights. Against this background, AOL could have emerged as the gatekeeper in the emerging market for Internet music delivery on-line. The proposed undertakings, and the fact that the EMI/Time Warner deal did not take place, will prevent AOL from having access to Europe's leading sources of music publishing rights. In view of this, the Commission could approve the operation (Monti, 2000).

• On October 13, 2000, the European Commission also approved the take-over by French telecommunications and media company Vivendi and its subsidiary Canal Plus of Canada's Seagram. The Commission had been concerned that the deal would have allowed Vivendi/Canal Plus to have preferential or even exclusive access to Universal film rights and, therefore, would have created or strengthened its existing dominant position in pay-television in a substantial number of countries. The parties, however, agreed not to grant Canal Plus first window rights for more than a certain percentage of Universal production. But most notably, they also agreed to divest their stake in British pay-television company BSkyB. This will enable BSkyB to be an independent competitor to Canal Plus and at the same time will sever any links between Universal and Fox Studios, another major film producer that is controlled by the BSkyB group (Monti, 2000).

In connection with future EU policies on the information society, these decisions have all become highly significant. While some people had tended to believe EU plans regarding the information society had in fact been fashioned to please large private companies, the negative decisions give the impression that the Commission is indeed taking its basic premise regarding fair competition to heart[19]. We should, however, join Galbraith (1977: 241) in wondering whether these are not merely token decisions, 'superficial pinpricks.' For him the existence of harmless anti-trust laws is a general phenomenon within today's present capitalistic planning system[20]. They could be viewed as aiming to diminish the distrust that is prevalent in some circles regarding EU decisions, and confirm the integrity and consistency of the EU's approach, while at the same time diverting attention away from other restructuring moves.

In general the Commission is also accused of being too lenient in its treatment of merger cases. Critics refer to the overwhelming majority of cases that have been approved, and the very small number that have been rejected (only 12 negative decisions until now, amongst which 6 are media-related). In addition, reference to subsidiarity is particularly ambiguous in the context of merger regulation (Art. 21, section 3), with anything under the thresholds, and possibly even above them, being referred to national legislation if it pertains to media concentrations[21]. Referring to national legislation presupposes that this legislation effectively exists, that it is being implemented and that it is indeed meant to enhance and protect media pluralism. But decisions made at the national level often serve an economic rather than a cultural objective (Lensen, 1991; Motta & Polo, 1997), a fact of which the Commission and the Court are not unaware, as is shown by the jurisprudence relating to the Flemish cable legislation. Referral of such matters to the national anti-trust authorities is equally problematic, however, as shown by the Belgian situation. The Belgian institution in charge of anti-trust policy has been operating for years within an inadequate legal framework and with insufficient resources (12 persons). It may be that the supervisory authorities can operate better in other countries – the Dutch institution has 70 full-time employees – but then the problem arises of cooperation between national and Community policy institutions. The

---

[19] Commissioner Karel Van Miert (in charge of competition matters) declared in this respect: "Certain members of the Bangemann think-tank which focuses on the information highway, proffered opinions regarding the abolition of all legislation regarding matters of competition in order to further promote joint action. I strongly object to this, and most members of the Commission shared my rebuttal. We must at all cost ensure that competition in matters of new telecom services is not effectively rooted out" (De Standaard, November 10, 1994: 23).

[20] "(...) seen from the viewpoint of the technostructure and the planning system the anti-trust laws are remarkably harmless (...) A government cannot declare half of the economic system to be illegal (...) The only thing which the planning system has to fear from the anti-trust laws are superficial pinpricks. The most important consequence is that the public is convinced that something serious is happening" (Galbraith, 1977: 241).

[21] According to article 22, the opposite is also possible: Member States can ask the Commission to step in regarding mergers below the thresholds, for instance if there is no applicable national legislation. This was the case for RTL-Veronica.

transfer of control to the national level only has the effect of making Member States into both judge and jury, a situation which does little to promote the effectiveness and consistency of competition policy. Insofar as competition and anti-trust policy is used as a means of taking care of national interests, there can be no easy flow of information between the various levels (local, national, Community, global).

The fact that the Commission has long been unsuccessful in its attempts to gain more control – among others things through lower intervention thresholds[22], shows that it does not have objective allies in the Member States. As a consequence, competition policies are, if not primarily, then certainly to a high degree, the result of political compromise. The political pressure exerted by Member States makes implementation of a truly independent supranational competition policy very difficult indeed (Pauwels, 1995).

Efficiency in control moreover presupposes a well-staffed department, a condition which has not been met so far. The evident and ever increasing complexity of the issues under scrutiny, their high political content, and the short period of time in which they must be processed (five months at the most), mean a lot of pressure for Task Force members to bear. It is therefore highly doubtful that every issue can be handled with the necessary thoroughness[23]. Increasing case load and understaffing make the regulation more an instrument for economic efficiency and rationalization than for the preservation of fair competition. Its (positive) impact on media pluralism is just as questionable.

V   The Green Paper on Pluralism and Media Concentration (1992)

The acknowledged gaps in its policy enforcement have pushed the Commission to seek a media-specific concentration approach. Ever since the beginning of the 1980's it has to a large extent been encouraged to do so by the Economic and Social Committee, and most of all by the European Parliament (Lensen, 1991; Van Loon, 1993; Harcourt,

---

[22] This request pertaining lower intervention thresholds was the subject of the Commission's new Green Paper, published on January 31, 1996 (COM(96)19 final. Community Merger Control: Green Paper on the review of the merger regulation). The effective revision of the thresholds became a fact with the approval of the amended regulation in June 1997.

[23] Significant in this respect is the following declaration by Gareth Locksley, a former DGIV official (G. Locksley was not part of the Task Force but of DGIV, department A4. This department looks after the implementation of the competition rules, including the significant article 86 regarding public institutions and state monopolies): "There are more people counting paper clips in the Commission than there are dealing with competition matters in telecomm. The whole of DGIV is under-resourced. The least resourced, given its importance, is telecomm. There are cases getting away that should be tackled. There is legislation in place that is not being implemented by the member states. But it (the Commission) does not have the resources to act as an effective policeman" (quoted in EuroInfoTech November 17, 1994; see also EuroInfoTech April 6, 1995: 16).

1998a & 1998b). The EP did not see media concentration as a problem of market inefficiency. Rather it was viewed politically as a threat to democracy, freedom of speech, and pluralist representation (Harcourt, 1998b). The long awaited Green Paper on pluralism and media concentration within the internal market was only published in December 1992, however, at the behest of the Commission, more specifically Directorate-General III/XV (internal market) (Com(92)480def.; Harcourt, 1998a & 1998b). The Green Paper, through a process of negotiations with the parties involved, purports to inquire into the potential need for a Community policy on media concentration and pluralism in radio, TV and print media (Van Loon, 1993).

Anyone who might have thought that the publication of the Green Paper would lead to accelerated problem-solving in the field of media concentration was to be disappointed. As with every other Green Paper, it provided for a very long period of reflection and consultation. To date, it has not resulted in one single directive. Moreover, both its content and that of a proposed directive were a disappointment in many respects.

From the outset the favored option was a limited approach. The Green Paper covers only TV, radio and the print media. It takes no notice of aspects relevant to policy, such as vertical integration (production through distribution), the role played by advertising agencies, or convergence between telecommunications and broadcasting corporations[24].

The same restrictive approach can be read in the way the concept of pluralism was tackled. The content criterion, deemed to best reflect information pluralism, was eschewed for methodological reasons. The Green Paper also revealed fundamentally biased notions. On the basis of the EU's objectives and competence which, as stressed by the Commission, comprise the internal market but not pluralism as such, the only object of investigation remained the question whether national ownership regulations hamper the internal market. The question as to what degree the internal market jeopardizes pluralism, was never at issue. This relates to the Green Paper's questionable assumption that internal market and competition would automatically produce pluralism and diversity (Harcourt, 1998a & 1998b)[25]. The Green Paper could therefore in no way be interpreted as an impartial consultation document.

This one-sided analysis has led the Commission to the equally questionable conclusion that pluralism can be achieved primarily by harmonizing ownership regulations. Other initiatives, such as guaranteeing independent editorial status or media transparency, were swept under the carpet of subsidiarity. Transparency and pluralism concerns were left to the national authorities, while items of vital necessity to the internal market, business interests and, increasingly, the information society, were viewed as matters to be dealt with by the EU.

---

[24] A significant indication of this half-hearted approach is the fact that the current state of affairs regarding media concentration within the various member states is deftly expedited in a mere 10-page brief, despite the obvious complexity of the problems (Green Paper on pluralism and media concentration in the internal market Com(92) 480 final of December 23, 1992: 23).

[25] As stated by theories on political agenda-setting: "agenda-setting is not just about having an issue considered actively by the government; it is also about how this issue will be defined once it makes it to the agenda" (Harcourt, 1998a: 370).

Community policy-makers, however, seemed unable to come up with satisfactory answers. In October 1994 the consultation period was extended once again (Communication from the Commission to the Council and EP – follow-up to the consultation process relating to the Green Paper on "pluralism and media concentration in the internal market – an assessment of the need for Community action" COM(94)353 final October 5, 1994). In this Paper the Commission reiterated the internal market argument. This document differed from the first, however, in that it focused on the information society. In response to the Bangemann report, it argued that national restrictions on media companies constrict the growth of the information society within the single market (Harcourt, 1998b). Subsequently, the department in charge of internal market affairs, led by Commissioner Mario Monti, drew up a draft directive aimed at the harmonization of national media ownership laws. Too liberal for some, too interventionist for others, it is clear that the compromise which has been arrived at was convincing neither from an economic nor a cultural point of view. Its political feasibility was therefore also in doubt. Since 1997 no single resubmission of a draft directive on media concentration has been scheduled (Harcourt, 1998a & 1998b). With the Green Paper on convergence, on the other hand, a more market-oriented approach towards media concentration appears to have gained the upper hand over a more *dirigiste* approach. More generally, the Green Paper carries the message that convergence must lead to deregulation of the audiovisual industry (CEC COM(97)623 December 3, 1997; Tongue, 1999). In this context the onus for guaranteeing pluralism is again placed on member states themselves. Which again raises the danger of the Commission viewing forms of 'over-regulation' of the media industry as harmful to the operation of the internal market, the creation of the information society, and the convergence of telecommunications and the media. In short, EU policy in the media industry appears to be caught in a vicious (policy) circle.

VI   Conclusion

> "The market is a jungle. It is nonsense to believe that the companies are going to stick to the rules on their own initiative (…) the more liberal the market, the more government control is necessary" (EU Commissioner for Competition Van Miert, quoted in De Morgen February 4, 1998: 14).

It is all very well for former EU Commissioner Karel Van Miert (who was in charge of competition matters from 1993 till 1998) to spell out the need for an anti-trust policy. But the effectiveness of EU competition policy in this respect is another matter entirely.

The first problem lies in the speed with which alliances are created and undone, and the administrative and bureaucratic slowness in reacting to them. On top of this, effective *ex ante*, *in itinere,* and *ex post* control is obviously also a question of internal manpower availability, a condition which is not met, and which has a paralyzing effect in a situation in which the case load is constantly increasing. There is no doubt that in this way a number of concentrating moves slip through the Community net.

The second problem is more fundamental. Although the Commission has far-reaching powers in these areas, its competition policy mostly exists by the grace of the Member States. It is the Member States which establish the powers of the Commission in the Treaties and it is they who subsequently define the scope of its action, among other things through the choice of form and content of secondary Community law. As long as EU competition law enforces arbitrary concepts, as long as it is subject to varying interpretations and long procedures, and as long as Member States are able to play fast and loose with its provisions, the EU's anti-trust policy cannot be said to be effective or consistent (Pauwels 1995; Cini & McGowan, 2000).

Finally, it is currently unclear how EU antitrust authorities will manage to reconcile criteria of economic efficiency with more democratic and cultural policy principles such as pluralism, cultural diversity, freedom of expression, etc. The notion that guaranteeing economic efficiency will automatically preserve cultural policy and democratic principles is laughable, to say the least. There is no historical example of a free market delivering all that society needs. When asked if he was in favor of a draft harmonizing media concentration, EU former commissioner Van Miert did not beat around the bush (quoted in Harcourt, 1998b: 447): "I am convinced of a need for European legislation on media concentration. From a democratic point of view, it is necessary. When we said no to the Nordic satellite case, the ruling was considered difficult. We cannot use competition rules to govern democratic issues."

Table 1. *Media Cases under the EU Merger Regulation*

Nb	Date of notification	Companies	Decisions	NACE	Merger procedures	A	AWC	Proh.
1	03.12.1990	Matsushita/MCA	M.37	0.92.10	Art.6(1) b 10.01.1991	X		
2	07.08.1991	ABC/Générale des Eaux/Canal+/WHSmith	M.110	0.92.20	Art.6(1) b 10.09.1991	X		
3	27.11.1991	Sunrise	M.176	0.92.20	Art.6(1) a 13.01.1992	/		
4	06.06.1994	MSG Media ServiceJO C 225 P.3	M.469	I.64.20 K.74	Art.6(1) c 18.07.1994 Art.8(3) 09.11.1994			X
5	01.07.1994	Kirch/Richemont/Telepiù	M.410	0.92.20	Art.6(1) b 2.08.1994	X		
6	04.08.1994	Bertelsmann/NewsInternational/VOX	M.489	0.92.20	Art.6(1) b 6.09.1994	X		
7	21.11.1994	VOX (II)	M.525	0.92.20	Art.6(1) b 21.12.1994	X		
8	23.02.1995	Nordic Satellite Distribution (NSD)	M.490	0.92.20	Art.6(1) c 24.03.1995 Art.8(3) 19.07.1995			X
9	23.03.1995	Blockbuster/Burda	M.579	0.92.10	Art.6(1) b 27.04.1995	X		
10	28.03.1995	Kirch/Richemont/Multichoice/Telepiù	M.584	0.92.20	Art.6(1) b 05.05.1995	X		
11	07.04.1995	CLT/Disney/SuperRTL	M.566	0.92.20	Art.6(1) b 17.05.1995	X		
12	21.04.1995	RTL/Veronica/Endemol Holland Media Group (HMG)	M.553	0.92.20	Art.22(4)&art.6(1)c 2.05.1995 Art.22(4)&art.8(3) 20.09.1995			X
			M.553	0.92.20	Art.22(4)&art.8(2)with cond. 17.07.96		X	

No.	Date	Name	M.No.	Code	Decision			
13	21.04.1995	Seagram/MCA	M.589	0.92.10	Art.6(1) b 29.05.1995	X		
14	09.10.1995	Canal+/UFA/MDO	M.655	0.92.20 DE.22	Art.6(1) b 13.11.1995	X		
15	21.11.1995	Channel Five	M.673	0.92.20	Art.6(1) a 22.12.95	/		
16	22.02.1996	Viacom/BearStearns	M.717	0.92.20	Art.6(1) b 25.03.96	X		
17	12.08.1996	N-TV	M.810	0.92.20	Art.6(1) b 16.09.1996	X		
18	04.09.1996	Bertelsmann/CLT	M.779	0.92.20	Art.6(1) b 07.10.1996	X		
19	08.11.1996	BellCablemedia/C&W/Videotron	M.853	I.64.20 0.92.20	Art.6(1) b 11.12.1996	X		
20	13.11.1996	Cable&Wireless/Nynex/Bell Canada	M.865	0.92.20 I.64.20	Art.6(1) b 11.12.1996	X		
21	16.01.1997	RTL 7	M.878	0.92.20	Art.6(1) b 14.02.1997	X		
22	24.01.1997	Castle Tower/TDF/Candover/Berkshire	M.887	0.92.20	Art.6(1) b 27.02.1997	X		
23	01.12.1997	Bertelsmann/Kirch/Premiere	M.993	0.92.20	Art.6(1) c 22.01.98 Art.8(3) 25.05.1998		X	
24	08.12.1997	Deutsche Telekom/Betaresearch	M.1027	0.92.20	Art.6(1) c 29.01.98 Art.8(3) 27.05.1998		X	
25	11.12.1997	DowJones/NBC- CNBC Europe	M.1081	0.92.20	Art.6(1) b 22.01.1998.	X		
26	01.07.1998	Cegetel/Canal+/AOL/Bertelsmann	JV.5	I.64.20	Art.6(1) and 81(3) without conditions 04.08.1998	X		
27	18.08.1998	Seagram/Polygram	M.1219	0.92.10 0.92.30	Art.6(1) b 21.09.1998	X		
28	28.04.1999	Telia/Telenor	M.1439	0.92.20 I.64.20	Art.6(1) c - 15.06.99 Art.8(2) with cond. 13.10.99			X

						A	AW C	Proh
29	30.06.1999	Kirch/Mediaset	M.1574	0.90.20	Art.6(1) b 03.08.1999	X		
30	22.12.1999	BVI Television/SPE Euromovies Investments/Europe Movieco Partners	JV.30	0.92.20	Art.6(1) b 03.02.2000	X		
31	11.01.2000	MCI Worldcom/Sprint	M.1741	I.64.20	Art.6(1) c 21.02.2000 Art.8(3) 28.06.2000			X
32	07.02.2000	BskyB/KirchPayTV	JV.37	0.92.20	Art.6(1) b & art.6(2) with cond. 21.3.2000		X	
33	18.02.2000	CLT-UFA/Canal+/VOX	M.1889	0.90.20	Art.6(1) b 21.03.2000	X		
34	28.04.2000	AOL/Time Warner	M.1845	I.64.20	Art.6(1) c 19.06.2000 Art.8(2) with conditions 11.10.2000		X	
35	05.05.2000	Time Warner/EMI	M.1852	0.92.30	Art.6(1) c 14.06.2000			Aborted or Withdrawn 05.10.2000
36	05.05.2000	VIAG Interkom/Telenor Media	M.1957	I.64.20 0.93	Art.6(1) b 14.06.2000	X		
37	16.05.2000	Canal+/Lagardère/LibertyMedia/Multichoice	JV. 47	0.92.20	Art.6(1) b 22.06.2000	X		
38	16.05.2000	Canal+/Lagardère/CanalSatellite	JV.40	0.92.20	Art.6(1) b 22.06.2000	X		
39	16.05.2000	Canal+/Lagardère/Liberty Media/Multithématique	JV.47	0.92.20	Art.6(1) b 22.06.2000	X		
40	24.05.2000	Bertelsmann/GBL/Pearson TV	M.1958	0.92.20	Art.6(1) b 29.06.2000	X		
41	25.05.2000	Telecom Italia/News Television/Stream	M.1978	0.92.20	Art.6(1) b 29.06.2000	X		
42	06.06.2000	Vodafone/Vivendi/Canal+	JV.48	I.64.20	Art.6(1)b; art.6(2) with conditions 20.07.2000		X	
43	08.06.2000	Telefónica/Endemol	M.1943	0.92.20	Art.6(1) b 11.07.2000	X		
44	31.08.2000	Vivendi/Canal+/Seagram	M.2050	I.64.20 0.92	Art.6(1)b; art.6(2) with conditions 13.10.2000		X	

Source: http://europa.eu.int/comm/competition/mergers/cases/index/by_nace_o_html#o_91_20
A: Accepted
AW C: Accepted with corrections
Proh: Prohibited

Table 2. *15 Largest Audiovisual Concerns (million US$)*

1988			1989		
Group	**Origin**	**Sales**	**Group**	**Origin**	**Sales**
1. Capital Cities/ABC	USA	3,749.00	1. Time Warner	USA	4,863.00
2. General Electric/NBC	USA	3,638.00	2. Sony (+ Columbia)	Japan	3,970.00
3. ARD	Germany	3,053.80	3. Capital Cities/ABC	USA	3,900.00
4. Fujisankei	Japan	2,970.00	4. General Electric/NBC	USA	3,392.00
5. CBS	USA	2,780.00	5. Fujisankei	Japan	3,046.00
6. NHK	Japan	2,752.90	6. CBS	USA	2961.50
7. Sony	Japan	2,655.70	7. ARD	Germany	2,896.00
8. BBC	UK	2,562.30	8. NHK	Japan	2,848.70
9. MCA	USA	2,290.00	9. MCA	USA	2,675.00
10. Fininvest	Italy	2,152.00	10. Fininvest	Italy	2,662.00
11. Warner	USA	2,027.00	11. BBC	UK	2,533.70
12. RAI	Italy	1,871.00	12. Polygram	Netherlands	2,297.00
13. Paramount	USA	1,862.00	13. Paramount	USA	2,071.80
14. Polygram	Netherlands	1,711.00	14. RAI	Italy	2,041.80
15. Columbia	USA	1,616.00	15. Bertelsmann	Germany	1,843.90

Table 2. cont.

1994			1995		
Group	**Origin**	**Sales**	**Group**	**Origin**	**Sales**
1. Sony	Japan	7,945.00	1. Viacom	USA	9,121.00
2. Viacom	USA	7,733.00	2. Sony	Japan	8,619.00
3. Time Warner Ent.	USA	6,267.00	3. ARD	Germany	6,746.00
4. ARD	Germany	5,757.00	4. Time Warner Ent.	USA	6,308.00
5. NHK	Japan	5,744.00	5. NHK	Japan	6,043.00
6. Capital Cities/ABC	USA	5,277.00	6. Walt Disney	USA	6,002.00
7. Walt Disney	USA	4,793.00	7. Capital Cities/ABC	USA	5,728.00
8. MCA	USA	4,606.00	8. Polygram	Netherlands	5,479.00
9. Polygram	Netherlands	4,525.00	9. Kirch	Germany	5,250.00
10. Kirch	Germany	4,200.00	10. Bertelsmann	Germany	5,127.00
11. Nintendo	Japan	4,183.00	11. Thorn EMI	GB	4,773.00
12. Time Warner	USA	3,986.00	12. MCA	USA	4,744.00
13. Bertelsmann	Germany	3,863.00	13. News Corp	Australia	4,246.00
14. News Corp	Australia	3,802.00	14. Time Warner	USA	4,196.00
15. CBS	USA	3,712.00	15. General Electric/NBC	USA	3,919.00

Source: European Audiovisual Observatory, *Statistical Yearbook 1996–1997*

2000 Top 15 media companies ranked by latest annual turnover (million US$)					
Group	Origin	1997	1998	1999	2000
1. Time Warner Inc	USA	24,371	26,244	27,333	-
2. Walt Disney	USA	22,473	22,976	23,402	-
3. Sony	Japan	11,560	15,734	18,119	16,438
4. News Corporation	Australia	9,252	12,185	14,001	-
5. Time Warner Ent.	USA	11,318	12,246	13,164	-
6. Viacom	USA	10,685	12,096	12,858	-
7. AT&T Broadband (ex TCI)	USA	-	-	4,871	-
8. Fox Ent. Group	USA	5,847	7,023	8,057	-
9. Seagram/ Universal	USA	5,593	5,044	7,500	-
10. CBS Corp.	USA	5,371	6,812	7,398	-
11. Comcast	USA	4,468	5,145	6,209	-
12. NBC	USA	5,153	5,269	5,790	-
13. Hughes Electronics	USA	2,838	3,481	5,560	-
14. Pearson	UK	-	3,867	5,380	-
15. AOL	USA	2,197	3,091	4,777	-

Source: *Screen Digest* from company reports, June 2000

References

Bazzanella, S. & Gerard, P. (1997). *Télécommunications et Audiovisuel: Convergence de vues?* Brussels: Centre de Recherches Informatique et Droit.

Biltereyst, D. (1993). *Televisiekijkers tussen culturele identiteit en imperialisme: een geïntegreerde receptie-analyse benadering van de cross-culturele impact van VS televisiefictie.* Brussels: Free University of Brussels (Unpublished Doctoral Dissertation).

Bishop, S. (1995). State aids: Europe's spreading cancer, *European Competition Law Review* 16(6): 331–333.

Bonnell, R. (1989). *La vingt-cinquième image. Une économie de l'audiovisuel.* Paris: Gallimard/Femis.

Booz Allen & Hamilton (1989). *Strategic Partnership as a Way Forward in European Broadcasting.* Media Viewpoint.

Booz Allen & Hamilton (1992). *Study to Establish a Methodology for the Implementation of Article 4 Paragraph 2 and 4 of Council Directive 89/532/EEC. Television without Frontiers.* Final report. Brussels, February 4.

Bourg, J.F. (1991). Sport et télévision. Entre éthique de la compétition et ordre économique. In J.M. Charon (ed.), *L'état des médias* (pp. 67–70). Paris: La Découverte/ Médiaspouvoirs.

Burgelman, J.-C. (1994). *Convergence in Europe: State of the Art.* Paper prepared for *Impact* (EC/DGXIII/E). Brussels: Free University of Brussels (CSNMIT).

Burgelman, J.-C., Punie, Y. & Verhoest, P. (1995). *Van telegraaf tot telenet. Naar een nieuw communicatiebeleid in België en Vlaanderen.* Brussels: VUBPress.

Cini, M. & McGowan, L. (2000). *Competition Policy in the European Union.* London: Macmillan Press.

Collins, R. (1990a). Broadcasting policy: competition and public service. In S. Thomas & W.A. Evans (eds.), *Communication and Culture. Language, Performance, Technology and Media* (pp. 305–317). Norwoord, New Jersey: Ablex Publishing Corporation.

Commission of the European Communities (1992). *Green Paper on Pluralism and Media Concentration in the Internal Market – An Assessment of the Need for Community Action.* Brussels COM (92) 480 final, December 23.

Commission of the European Communities (1996). *Community Merger Control. Green Paper on the Review of the Merger Regulation.* Brussels, COM (96) 19 final, January 31.

Commission of the European Communities (1997). *XXVIth Report on Competition Policy.* Brussels, Sec(97) 628 final.

Commission of the European Communities (1999). *Communication from the Commission to the Council, the European Parliament, the Economic and Social Committee and the Committee of the Regions. Principles and Guidelines for the Community's Audiovisual Policy in the Digital Age.* Brussels, COM(1999) 657 final, December 14.

Conseil de l'Europe. Comité directeur sur les moyens de communication de masse (CDMM) (1991). *Evaluation définitive des résultats des études de cas nationales sur les concentrations des médias.* Strasbourg.

Conso, C. (1991). Comment s'explique la montée en puissance des groupes multimédias dans le monde. In J.M. Charon (ed.), *L'Etat des médias* (pp. 290–293). Paris: La Découverte/Médiaspouvoirs.

Council of the European Union (1997). Council Regulation (EEC) No 4064/89 of December 21, 1989 on the control of concentrations between undertakings with amendments introduced by Council regulation (EC) N° 1310/97 of June 30, 1997, OJ L 180.

Crookes, P. (1996). Convergences and alliances: the shape of things to come, *The Bulletin* (European Institute for the Media) 13 (2): 1–4.

Defalque, L. (1991). L'audiovisuel et la politique de la concurrence. In G. Vandersanden (ed.), *L'espace audiovisuel européen* (pp. 17–32). Brussels: Editions de l'Université de Bruxelles.

Eurocommunication Research Group (1990). *Convergence of Telecom-munications and Broadcasting in the European Community.* Liège: Lentic.

Frohlinger, M. (1993). EG-Wettbewerbsrecht und Fernsehen, *Rundfunk und Fernsehen* 41 (1): 59–65.

Galbraith, J.K. (1977). *Economics and the Public Purpose.* Harmondsworth: Penguin.

Garnham, N. (1990). *Capitalism and Communication. Global Culture and the Economics of Information.* London: Sage Publications.

Gunther, J-Ph. (1998). Politique communautaire de concurrence et audiovisuel: état des lieux, *Revue trimestrielle de droit européen* 34 (1): 1–33.

High-Level Group on the Information Society (1994). *Europe and the Global Information Society. Recommendations to the European Council.* Brussels, May 26.

Guillou, B. (1985). Les stratégies multimédias des groupes de communication, *Dossiers de l'audiovisuel* 19: 18–21.

Guilllou, B. (1986a). Télévision du futur, télévisions sans contraintes, *Revue de l'Idate* 25: 659–680.

Guillou, B. (1986b). L'Europe à l'heure des groupes multimédias, *Association politique aujourd'hui en Europe* 1: 46–51.

Hall, S. (1973). *Encoding and Decoding in the Television Discourse.* Birmingham: University of Birmingham.

Hancock, D. (1993). The world's top AV companies: The IDATE 100, *Screen Digest*, August: 181–184.

Harcourt, A.J. (1998a). EU media ownership regulation: Conflict over the definition of alternatives, *Journal of Common Market Studies* 36(3): 369–390.

Harcourt, A.J. (1998b). The European Commission and Regulation of the Media Industry, *Cardozo Arts & Entertainment Law Journal* 16(2): 425–449.

Hoffmann-Riem, W. (1987). National identity and cultural values. Broadcasting safeguards, *Journal of broadcasting* 31 (1): 57–72.

IDATE (1990). *Marché mondial du cinéma et de l'audiovisuel. Analyses industrielles.* Montpellier: Idate (Institut de l'audiovisuel et des télécommunications en Europe).

IDATE (1991). *La stratégie internationale des principales chaînes de télévision de service public en Europe.* Montpellier: Idate.

IDATE (1992). *Marché mondial du cinéma et de l'audiovisuel. Analyses industrielles.* Montpellier: Idate.

IDATE (2000). *Development of digital television in the European Union, reference report/1999.* Montpellier: Idate.

Kiessling, T. & Johnson, G. (1998). Strategic alliances in telecommunications and media: An economic analysis of recent European Commission decisions. In S. MacDonald & G. Madden (eds.), *Telecommunications and Socio-Economic Development* (pp. 155–176). Amsterdam: North-Holland Publishers.

Knoche, M. (1980). Die Messbarkeit publizistischer Vielfalt. In S. Klaue, A. Zerdick & M. Knoche (eds.), *Probleme der Pressekonzentrationsforshung*. Baden-Baden: Nomos Verlaggesellschaft.

Lensen, A. (1991). *Concentration in the Media Industry. The European Community and Mass Media Regulation.* Northwestern University: The Annenberg Washington Program Communications Policy Studies.

Luyken, G.M. (1990). Das Medienwirtschaftgefüge der 90er Jahre, *Media Perspektiven* 10: 621–641.

Mansell, R.E. (1993). *The New Telecommunications. A Political Economy of Network Evolution.* London: Sage Publications.

Mattelart, A. (1991a). Communication et médias, matière à risque. In J.M. Charon (ed.), *L'Etat des médias* (pp. 19–25). Paris: La Découverte/Médiaspouvoirs.

Mattelart, A. (1991b). Mythes et réalités de l'homogénéisation des contenus culturels. In J.M. Charon (ed.), *L'Etat des médias* (pp. 33–36). Paris: La Découverte/Médiaspouvoirs.

McQuail, D. (1992). *Media Performance. Mass Communication and the Public Interest.* London: Sage Publications.

Miège, B. (1993). Les mouvements de longue durée de la communication en Europe de l'Ouest, *Quaderni* 19: 45–58.

Monti, M. (2000). Speech/00/389, *Twenty-eighth Annual Conference on International Antitrust Law and Policy – The Fordham Corporate Law Institute.* New York October 20.

Morley, D. (1992). *Television, Audiences and Cultural Studies.* London: Routledge.

Morley, D. (1993). Active audience theory: Pendulums and pitfalls, *Journal of Communication* 4: 13–19.

Mosco, V. (1996). *The Political Economy of Communications. Rethinking and Renewal.* London: Sage Publications.

Motta, M. & Polo, M. (1997). Concentration and public policies in the broadcasting industry, *Economic Policy* 25: 295–334.

Murdock, G. (1990). Redrawing the map of the communications industries: Concentration and ownership in the era of privatization. In M. Ferguson (ed.), *Public Communication. The New Imperatives. Future Directions for Media Research* (pp. 1–16). London: Sage Publications.

Nikolinakos, N. (2000). The new legal framework for digital gateways – the complementary nature of competition law and industry-specific regulation, *ECIR* 9: 408–414.

Negrine, R. & Papathanassopoulos, S. (1990). *The Internationalisation of Television*. London: Pinter Publishers.

Noam, E. & Kramer, R. (1994). Telecommunications strategies in the developed world: A hundred flowers blooming or old wine in new bottles. In C. Steinfield, J.M. Bauer & L. Caby (eds.), *Telecommunications in Transition. Policies, Services and Technologies in the European Community* (pp. 272–286). London: Sage Publications.

Noam, E. (1996). Media concentration in the United States: Industry trends and regulatory responses, *Communications et Stratégies* 24: 11–23.

Oreja, M. (1998). *Financing and Regulation of Public Service Broadcasting*. Address of EU Commissioner Oreja before the Subcommittee on the RTVE, December 11.

Paracuellos, J.C. (1993). *La télévision. Clefs d'une économie invisible*. Paris: La Documentation française.

Pauwels, C. (1995). *Cultuur en economie: de spanningsvelden van het communautair audiovisueel beleid. Een onderzoek naar de grenzen en mogelijkheden van een kwalitatief cultuur- en communicatiebeleid in een economisch geïntegreerd Europa. Een kritische analyse en prospectieve evaluatie aan de hand van het gevoerde Europees audiovisueel beleid*. Brussels: Free University of Brussels (Unpublished Doctoral Dissertation).

Pilon, R. (1991). Groupes et stratégies. L'industrie mondiale des médias et de divertissement. In J.M. Charon (ed.), *L'Etat des médias* (pp. 282–290). Paris: La Découverte/ Médiaspouvoirs.

Porter, V. (1991). *Film and Television in the Single European Market. Dreams and Delusions*. Inaugural Professoral Lecture, Westminster University, October 17.

Porter, V. (1994). Public service broadcasting in the European Union – states aids, competition policy and subsidiarity, *Journal of Media Law and Practice* 15 (2).

Council of the European Communities (1990). Council regulation No 4064/89 of December 21, 1989 on the control of concentrations between undertakings, *Official Journal*, September 21, L 257: 13.

Reding, V. (2000). *Community Audiovisual Policy in the 21st Century. Content without Frontiers?* Speech delivered at the British Screen Advisory Council, London, November 30.

Rutten, P. (2000). De toekomst van de verbeeldingsmachine. De culturele industrie in de eenentwintigste eeuw, *Boekmancahier* 43(12): 7–25.

Schumpeter, R. (1962). *Capitalism, Socialism and Democracy*. New York.

Sanchez-Tabernero, A. (1993). *Media Concentration in Europe. Commercial Enterprise and the Public Interest*. Düsseldorf: European Institute for the Media, Media Monograph 16.

Schiller, H.I. (1989). Faut-il dire adieu à la souveraineté culturelle? *Le Monde Diplomatique*, August: 10–11.

Schiller, H.I. (1991). Not yet the post-imperialist era, *Critical Studies in Mass Communication* 8: 13–28.

S.R. (1993). *Politique de la concurrence et mutation du secteur de la fusion audiovisuelle*. Paris: OCDE.

Tongue, C. (1999). Culture or monoculture? The European audiovisual challenge. In Ch. Marsden (ed.), *Convergence in European Digital TV Regulation* (pp. 99–140). London: Blackstone Press.

Tracey, M. (1987). European viewers: what will they really watch, *Columbia Journal of World Business* 22 (3): 77–86.

Tunstall, J. & Palmer, M. (1991). *Media Moguls*. London: Routledge.

Van Cuilenburg, J.J. (1992). Over de mogelijkheden en onmogelijkheden van persfusieonderzoek. In H. D'Ancona, J.J. Van Cuilenburg, H.W. De Jong, W.G. Klinkenburg, J.J. Nouwen, A.P. Poels, & J. De Vries (eds.), *Persfusies: mogelijkheden en onmogelijkheden van een persfusieregeling* (pp. 9–15). Amsterdam: Otto Cramwinkel.

Van Loon, A. (1993). EG-Groenboek Pluralisme en mediaconcentratie in de interne markt, *Informatie en informatiebeleid* 2: 32–41.

Van Loon, A.P.J.M. & Schuijt, G.A.I. (1989). *Cross Media Ownership. Een inventarisatie van buitenlandse en Europese regelgeving voor multimedia integratie*. Amsterdam: Instituut voor informatierecht.

Van Loon, A.P.J.M. & Schuijt, G.A.I. (1990). Uit Nederlands onderzoek Cross-ownership blijkt machteloze rol overheden, *Telecombrief*, June 29: 143.

Verstraeten, H. (1991). Transnationale satelliettelevisie en culturele identiteit. In L. Heinsman & J. Servaes (eds.), *Televisie na 1992. Perspectieven van de Vlaamse en Nederlandse omroep* (pp. 119–131). Louvain: Acco.

Reappraising European Policies
to Protect Local Television Content against US Imports

by Daniel Biltereyst

I   Introduction: Europe and the Debate on US Television Dominance

"We must remind the reader of the obvious, namely that this whole global, yet American postmodern culture is the internal and superstructural expression of a whole new wave of American military and economic domination throughout the world."

This quotation from Frederic Jameson's (1984) seminal essay – 'Postmodernism, or the Cultural Logic of Late Capitalism' – can be seen both as a synthesis and revitalization of a central claim in the 1960's and 1970's critical discourse on international mass media and popular culture. In these decades many critical scholars frequently used concepts such as 'American cultural imperialism' and 'conspiracy' as metaphors for the idea that the huge imports of cheap US movies, television programs and other products would lead to a global cultural erosion – and that this cultural invasion was only part of a global US strategy to dominate the world based on a conservative, ultra-capitalist ideology[1].

In the 1980's and 1990's this critical analytical and conceptual apparatus on international media and communication seemed to be made obsolete by the changing world order – politically characterized by the collapse of communism, the victory of the capitalist system, and the partial dismantling of national boundaries. In economic terms all this resulted in trade deregulation, increased (inter)national competition, and a decreased role of the state as an active participant or provider of services and goods. These changes were strongly reflected in the area of culture and communication. One obvious consequence of trade deregulation and the new world order was the growing, worldwide success of US cultural products. US production centers systematically entered the exploding Western European audiovisual scene as well as Eastern Europe and Asia's newly deregulated marketplaces, and they embraced the new technologies. In the 1980's and 1990's the US cultural industry was more than ever recognized as the center of transnational popular culture.

In these 'postmodern' times however new ideas and concepts on global culture and communication power were introduced. The dominant academic and policy discourse no longer used concepts such as 'American cultural dominance' or 'media dependency,' but thought in terms of the wealth of the market system, of opportunities for local power and resistance, and of international cultural exchange. The most enigmatic concept in

---

[1] I would like to thank Jay G. Blumler for his enormously helpful comments on this article.

this respect has been 'globalization', indicating that on a cultural level there is a constant exchange of styles, talents and views (world music, etc.). The 1980's also saw the emergence of new exporting centers besides Hollywood, such as Australia's and Brazil's strong television production companies (Sinclair, Jacka & Cunningham, 1996). As a result, speaking of a conscious strategy of domination organized from one (US) center no longer seemed a valid approach.

Such relativist accounts were not universally accepted, however. In addition to critical academic scholars continuously deconstructing the use of these concepts (e.g., Schiller, 1996), there were also forums where the issue of American cultural dominance and resistance to it was more alive than ever, even leading to renewed rivalry and concrete political action. The most significant example has been Western Europe, where the arrival of American mass media products has been seen by cultural and political elites as an invasion and a threat.

Crucially, by the end of the 1980's, EC policy-makers realized that the deregulation of the media industries on the old continent did not result in the expected growth in production, cross-border distribution and employment within the local audiovisual sector. Above all, they had to admit that this mostly benefited the US cultural industry. The growing number of channels and the fact that all existing channels increased their program output due to ever fiercer competition led to an exploding demand for cheap and popular programming in the international television market. And of course, the most obvious providers, with their impressive program catalogues, were the Americans. Sales of US programs grew more than tenfold, from $330 million in 1984 to $3.6 billion eight years later. European exports to the USA accounted for only $288 million, leading to a trade deficit of some $3.5 billion by the end of the 1990's (Wasko, 1994). And the gap has continued to widen. In the broader context of the audiovisual and digital media, the European Commission recently forecast a $6 billion trade deficit, amounting to some 250,000 jobs (EC, 1998). In other words, in the 1990's, Western Europe became the largest and fastest growing export market for US programs.

It is hardly surprising that the issue of the American dominance in such a strategic economic domain as the audiovisual industry should have soon become a major topic both on the European policy agenda and on public forums. In 1989 the approval of the EC's 'Television Without Frontiers' (TWF) Directive started a virulent debate which was fuelled further when the directive came into force in EC Member States (October 1991). This milestone directive stated the "de-regulatory principle of mutual recognition" of channels within the Community (Humphreys, 1996), but it also included some protectionist quotas reserving a majority of broadcasting time for European material. This was of course interpreted as a clear move against US products. In 1993 the issue again became so urgent that the European Union blocked the crucial GATT free trade negotiations – not on issues regarding traditionally important sectors such as agriculture or textiles, but on a cultural issue. Of all problems holding up the talks, concerns over the protection of the European movies and television industry against US products was the biggest. Europe welcomed as a major victory the exclusion of the audiovisual issue from the agreement. Such a plea for a 'cultural exception' regarding movies and television was clearly a desperate move induced by the severe crisis in the European television industry, the moribund state of the national film sectors and the huge dominance of US audiovisual products.

In the 1990's EU policy-makers also finally set aside their traditionally euphoric tone on the growth prospects of the audiovisual sector. In their 1994 Green Paper on the 'Audiovisual Policy of the European Union' they made a rather crude diagnosis of the key structural shortcomings and malfunctions of the European program industry (EC, 1994). In this Green Paper the European Commission pointed to a long list of structural problems: weak production structures, catalogue shortage, market share decline, inability to attract large financial investments, and fragmentation into national markets. This diagnosis was based on an even more critical report by a group of European audiovisual professionals, commissioned by the European Union and presented in March 1994. This Think-Tank (1994) openly stated that the "transnational dissemination of European audiovisual products is extremely weak and the trend is downwards" and that "the single EU market only operates effectively for the non-European, specifically US industry."

The most problematic category in all this is fiction (movies, series, serials, TV movies). As a popular, highly expensive and labor-intensive category, fiction accounts for a very large share of the global television output – ranging from 25% to 40% and more, depending on the different types of television channels. The demand for popular fictional material, estimated some years ago at more than 160,000 hours in the EU Member States only, increased exponentially as a result of the increasingly competitive nature of the European audiovisual scene. The EU trade deficit for fictional material alone stood at about € 1.3 billion in favor of the USA in 1994 according to Eurostat. This deficit is apparent in Europe, where US production and distribution companies control some 80% of the motion picture market, a state of affairs clearly reflected in their significant share in European television programming. Recent figures from the Motion Pictures Association of America (MPAA) continue to underline the growth of Western European broadcasters. In 1994–97 the MPAA's sales of films and television fiction grew from $ 1.8 to 2.6 billion (EAO, 1999; see also Pauwels, 2000).

In this respect it is not surprising that European audiovisual policy often focused on the production and distribution of fictional material in the hope of stimulating local content and protecting it against US imports. However, as will become clear, this focus is probably less rooted in cultural concerns than in economic ones, because it fully complies with the EU's more general policy purposes of global industrial growth and massive job creation, as defined in the EC's 1993 White Paper[2], for instance.

For European policy-makers fiction is definitely a field of potential economic growth, and since the second half of the 1980's several policy lines have been developed in this area. A central question is of course whether and to what degree these and other policy measures have been effective in protecting European content against the influx of

---

[2] This was optimistically estimated at some 2 million new jobs by the year 2000 (see EC, 1994b: 18–19).

US programming. In this chapter we address this difficult question by confronting the changing patterns of programming on European television with international audiovisual policies. As far as comparative and longitudinal programming analyses are available, we first focus on the basic historical shifts in the global program offer and in the importance of American fictional programming, before and after the paradigmatic changes in European broadcasting in the 1980's. In this respect an historical approach of the programming strategies can be very instructive inasmuch as it places major discussion points (such as the growing *addiction* to US programs) in correct perspective. We then look at the importance of fictional material: why has fiction – that is to say, mostly US imports – become so important for European broadcasters, and how effective have policy mechanisms been on a national and supranational level? Our thesis is that the failure to create a strong single audiovisual European space and to protect local production is due to more than just structural economic, political and technological factors. We claim that many policy lines are often contradictory and technocratic, thus neglecting or underestimating cultural factors such as the needs of audiences in terms of language and cultural proximity.

II   European Trends in Program Genres and Imports before and after the Advent of Multichannel Competition

2.1 Programming Dynamics under the Public Service Monopoly

The most recurrent thesis in studies on European television is that the deregulation policies implemented from the mid-1980's onwards turned it into a more market-oriented, not to say crassly commercial, activity. The 'new television marketplace' (Blumler, 1991) tends to drive all channels into new programming strategies – with more interest in audience maximizing categories, with an expanding output, with little money to finance program production, and with a large reliance on cheap (US) imports. It is also often suggested that the new competitive media environment instigated a process of adaptation or convergence between public and private stations, with even public service broadcasting organizations (PSB) aping their commercial counterparts – which ultimately led to a crisis with respect to their traditional philosophy and practice.

Although this line of analysis may be correct in emphasizing the challenge of late 1980's commercialism to European PSBs, it may also be simplistic in that it implies that programming had been relatively stable under the 'older model,' which held sway until the early 1980's (McQuail, 1995). This tends to ignore the dynamics of programming change that operated even within a monopolistic system. It might then be interesting to look at what happened before the 1980s. In fact, some longitudinal programming analyses show that more "commercial" types of programming, and especially an increased dose of US fiction imports, were far from new.

Massive imports of US TV products began in the 1960's, when the international flow of television programs began to intensify (Browne, 1968; Fortner, 1993). In the Western hemisphere the international trade of television programs soon came to be dominated by those products made for the US commercial networks. In the second half of the 1960's, and especially in the 1970's, US production centers became the single largest exporter to Western Europe, Latin and South America. Kaarle Nordenstreng and Tapio Varis's famous UNESCO report on the international flow of programs (published in 1974) already spoke of a 'one-way street' from the big exporting countries to the rest of the world. The USA soon became the main (Western) purveyor of audiovisual imports, the main category being none other than entertainment (fiction). In Western Europe, TV stations (mostly PSB) relied on imports for about one quarter of their programming, with a significantly higher import rate for fiction.

These findings were strengthened in the next years, shown by a follow-up study by Tapio Varis (1985), also commissioned by UNESCO and focusing on television output during two weeks of 1983. Above all, this pointed to a significant increase of imported material, up to nearly one-third. It also indicated those categories that were affected the most. Thus it was clear that Western European stations were highly dependent on fiction imports: actual figures were 72% for movies and 70% for television fiction such as series and serials. As table 1 indicates these were also the categories where the dominance of one single country – the USA – was felt the most. Smaller European countries were especially dependent on fiction imports (82%), much more so than larger countries such as France, Britain and Germany (an average of 45%).

Table 1. *Import Rate for Several Program Categories in Western Europe, 1983*

Program Category	Import Rate (%) Importing Country	Most Important (Import Rate in %)
Information, news	0	-
Other information	5	UK (38)
Documentary	18	USA (19)
Education	4	UK (30)
Other educational programming	27	UK (53)
Cultural programming	12	France (29)
Religious programming	11	Italy (60)
Children's programming	36	USA (46)
Movies	72	USA (62)
Television fiction	70	USA (51)
Sports	36	UK (12)
Other entertainment	17	UK (37)
Other	5	Finland (56)

Source: Varis (1986: 53)

Thus, according to these well-known studies the prevalence of US fiction dates back to well before the changes of the mid-1980's. In this respect it is important to look more closely at the programming dynamics even within a so-called monopolistic PSB environment. First of all there has never been a single type of public broadcasting programming. In countries with a strong traditional vision of PSB, such as Scandinavia, a very different public broadcasting philosophy was brought into practice than in countries such as Spain, whose public corporation largely relied on advertising revenue and commercial programming strategies (McQuail, 1995). The old public broadcasting model – with its proclaimed high standards of programming and its regulatory framework requiring it to inform, educate and entertain – was theoretically dominant, but its practical organization and output strategies were far from unequivocal.

Another aspect of the programming dynamics in this period is the fact that public broadcasters did significantly change their schedules over time (in the 1960's, 1970's, and 1980's), owing to changing economic constraints (such as dwindling financial resources), new types of internal/external competition (the runaway success of cable in some countries during the 1960's and 1970's, new transnational satellite services, etc.), the products on offer in the international television markets, and so on. However, one of the most important factors behind programming dynamics in this monopolistic environment was growing public pressure and audience dissatisfaction with the paternalistic, cultural-educational bent of many PSB corporations in the 1950's and 1960's. It is quite difficult to trace the concrete programming strategies and policies developed by the PSB's in these periods as there is a general lack of research on former scheduling dynamics. An interesting longitudinal and comparative research was conducted some years ago by Ben Manschot (1988), who systematically analyzed the programming schedules of Belgian, British, Dutch, and German stations in the 1965–86 period. Manschot's study shows that the share of the major categories hardly changed throughout this long period: most PSB stations evidenced a similar pattern, with a ratio of entertainment (mainly fiction and shows), light (sports, service and youth programs) and serious current affairs programs (news, documentaries, education and arts programming) of respectively 4:2:4. But, most interestingly, Manschot's study shows how, within the category of entertainment itself, fiction increasingly became more important at the expense of categories. This increase in fiction output was made possible by the massive growth of imported fictional, serialized material from the USA, especially in smaller countries. In the 1965–86 period, imported fiction doubled or even tripled in most stations, while domestic drama production heavily decreased. Other studies have yielded very similar results: for instance, one such study carried out by the European Television Task Force (1988) on the programming pattern in the years 1975–85 indicates that in this period public (monopolistic) stations in most European countries increased their total broadcasting time by more than one quarter, while the local drama output tended to shrink.

Manschot's and similar studies basically say that in the so-called monopolistic area with strong national regulation of content inspired by a PSB philosophy, European public broadcasters tried on the one hand to stay loyal to their mandate (with lots of information, etc.), while on the other hand significantly altering their output. An important category in these changing programming dynamics was entertainment, which slowly incorporated more and more fiction and imported US material in a serialized format. These findings can be supplemented by many longitudinal national programming analyses from other parts of Europe, such as the Scandinavian countries.

In summary, we can conclude that the flood of US serialized fictional material observed in the second half of the 1980's was far from new in most Western European countries, actually going back to the 1960's. In those years when PSB's still were in a monopoly situation, dependency on US material was already established and growing for financial and strategic reasons – one being that such material was what the audiences wanted to see. Of course this did not prevent this over-reliance on US audiovisual material from becoming a major issue in many countries in this period. In the second half of the 1980's, however, the issue somewhat outgrew these traditional cultural and critical forums and started to circulate within broader circles, including the established European audiovisual industry and policy-makers.

2.2 Deregulation, Competition, and more US Imports

By the mid-1980's the old model of television had undergone significant changes in virtually all countries, mainly as a result of the key policy line deregulation on a national and a EC level. To varying degree, the opening up of the audiovisual sector to market forces was in progress: advent of commercial television, private funding (mostly through advertising), gradual abolition of the local broadcasting monopolies, introduction of new technologies. Such free-market policies were strongly reinforced at the EC level through a process intended to create a single European audiovisual space with advertising as the driving force for the commercial sector (Humphreys, 1996; McQuail, 1990). Both the 1984 European Green Paper and the 1989 'Television Without Frontiers' Directive were mostly based on this notion of removing internal barriers to television services. Since the second half of the 1980's, television markets had been dominated by the growing number of commercial stations and the resulting atmosphere of abundance, competition and fragmentation. In the 1980's the number of channels in Western Europe more than doubled, from 90 in 1988 to 136 in 1991 (EBU, 1993). In response to this, all existing channels increased their program output by approximately one third during the 1980's (McQuail, 1990). Deregulation also led to a quantitative explosion in the form of a wider diversity and typology of broadcasters. Most Western European countries went from a nationally oriented, state-owned broadcasting monopoly to a mixed, heterogeneous, and multi-channel environment with wildly different types of channels. This led to a significant increase in viewing time[3], a wealth of viewing options, and the (cultural) fragmentation of audiences.

---

[3] McQuail (1990: 309) found that the average amount of TV viewing rose by 22% in the 1980's, from 129 to 167 minutes per day.

Unsurprisingly, such paradigmatic shifts had a strong impact on program purchase, production, financing, scheduling strategies, etc. In recent years a wide range of studies have described and analyzed these 'new' strategies, with often very similar conclusions (for an overview, see Hellman & Sauri, 1994). These generally claim that the arrival of many new channels – combined with the extension of broadcasting volume per channel and the further exploitation of the afternoon and weekend morning slots – resulted in skyrocketing demand for audiovisual material, especially of a cheap and commercially proven nature. The major shift in programming has then been the growing provision of entertainment programs in a multiplicity of forms[4]. Indeed, this period can be viewed as that of the final break-up of Manschot's 'stable proportion' of entertainment and light and serious information (4:2:4). Entertainment has become ever more important in the private and public sectors, sparking controversies on commercialization and standardization as well as on the convergence between public and private strategies. Many studies indicate that entertainment became the prime strategic tool for all stations, especially during primetime (De Bens et al., 1992; McQuail, 1990). An analysis by Horizons Media International on the changing programming schedules in the 1985–87 period showed that the share of entertainment during primetime went up from 43 to 54% on public stations and from 78 to 81% on private ones (HMI, 1988).

Within this broad strategic program category, fiction has been – again – a steady grower, especially in serialized forms. In the second half of the 1980's the total hourly volume of TV fiction in the EC actually tripled, from 58,000 to 162,000 hours (Eurostat, 1994). In 1994 the global fiction output of 88 EC stations was in excess of 250,000 hours according to the European Audiovisual Observatory (EAO, 1995). The cause for this is mostly the extreme popularity of fiction programming with audiences as well as the scheduling convenience of serialized fiction (filling air time, binding audiences through horizontal programming, etc.). Just as important was the high availability of cheap American fictional material in the international markets. In the early years especially, most (new) channels were confronted with high start-up costs and the fragmentation of audiences and resources, so that they strove to keep production and purchase costs low.

Given their structural weaknesses (e.g., lack of broad program catalogues, undercapitalized production centers) the European production industries could not keep up with this hunger for programs. Hence the large share of repeats and soaring imports from the European market. In the beginning there was a heavy dependency on imports from several regions, such as the growing Australian, Japanese, Canadian and Brazilian industries, and of course the USA. The extent and causes of the European dependency on American production centers has been well-documented. An analysis of the programming of 53 European channels in 1988 and 1991 (Euromedia) showed that the share of US serial fiction had grown from 36 to 56%, while home-made fiction had fallen from 37 to 17% (De Bens et al., 1992). In 1994 some 69% of all fictional imports

---

[4] According to the Euromonitor research group (Baldi, 1994), the increase of "infotainment" is a "megatrend" in European television.

in the EU were American (175,190 hours). The circulation of European fiction within the EU is marginal; Great-Britain is the largest European fiction provider (6%), followed by France (3%), Germany (2%), and Italy (2%). Other non-European importing countries are Australia (3%), Canada (2%) and Japan (0.4%) (EAO, 1995). More recent data for 1997 (see table 6) seem to indicate that US imports are now in excess of 71% (EAO, 1999).

The European dependency and the international success of US fictional material in international markets are based on different causes, as many authors have shown. According to Toby Miller (1998) "Hollywood's success has been explained mainly in terms of 'a flexible managerial culture and an open and innovative financial system' that has adapted to changing economic and social conditions." The most obvious factors to explain US dominance pertain to classical economics: notions such as economies of scale, advantage of the home market size, and other comparative or competitive advantages.

Compared to the highly fragmented European television market, the USA is a largely homogenous market in terms of language. Hollywood not only relies upon the largest English-language domestic market in the world. It can also be seen as the perfect testing ground for products intended for international market domination: Colin Hoskins and Rolf Mirus (1990) wrote in this sense that in the USA "programming that can be appreciated by a broad spectrum of the polyglot American population is necessary," and they introduced concepts such as 'common-denominator programming' and 'cultural discount.' By the latter concept they mean that European products are strongly rooted in their own culture, and that they "will have a diminished appeal elsewhere as viewers find it difficult to identify with the style, values and behavior patterns of the material in question." A related economic advantage is that in the US the average production, marketing and distribution budgets are much higher than in the small European markets.

A distinctive indicator in this respect has been the different levels of investment in film production in Europe and the USA. In the 1990's, the average US film budget grew from about $9 million in 1990 to some $14.5 million seven years later. European budgets are about $3 million (1997), even taking into account the relatively high average investments noted in major countries such as France ($5.5 million), Germany ($5.7 million) and the UK ($8.34 million). In small European countries film budgets do not exceed $2.25 million (Pauwels, 2000).

Such economic factors cannot be viewed in isolation from broader cultural and historical factors, as acknowledged in a report from a 1998 Birmingham conference on the *'Challenges and Opportunities of the Digital Age'* (Tessier & Woodward, 1998):

"The cultural and historical factors which define the European industry hardly permit any useful comparison with the so-called 'US model' when considering potential solutions to the European problem: whereas the US studios and TV networks have access to a unified market area of 270 million consumers, Europe (...) remains linguistically and culturally divided in 15 blocs, where citizens' tastes and interests extend to other European countries only in a very limited way. In the US entertainment companies have perfected the art of creating entertainment product for a 'melting pot' of socially and culturally diverse North American consumers and this quality has served them well in Europe (...). European entertainment companies on the other hand remain constrained by the size of their individual domestic markets and the sheer diversity of the European cultural identity."

There also lies one of the main economic advantages of US programs, namely export pricing in the international market. Hirsch and Peterson (1992) wrote that "by the time American series go on sale in Europe, the bulk of their production costs have been written off in their home market." This mechanism is especially relevant for fiction, which is by far the most expensive program category. A comparative analysis of the average purchase and production costs for fiction at the beginning of the 1990's (Biltereyst, 1995a) showed that in Western Europe the ratio between the cost of US fiction and the production costs for local fiction is about 1:9:7. In small countries the ratio is even higher (1:22). It is hardly surprising then that stations with low production capacities and meager resources should be more dependent on imports than their wealthier counterparts. Table 2 shows that in small countries such as Austria, Belgium, or Portugal – fiction accounts for almost one third of the overall output, and import figures are very high. Local products account for less than 10% (8.8%). Nearly one-half is of US origin, while over one-third of imports come from other European countries. In larger countries such as France, Germany, Italy and the UK there is a clear bi-polarization, where fiction output is dominated by local products (average of 42.5%) and US imports (36.4%).

Table 2. *Average Fiction Output per Channel in Large and Small European Countries, 1990*

	Channels in Small Countries*	Channels in Large Countries**
Fiction Output:		
- broadcasting hours	1,058	2,131
- share (%)	30.6	25.9
Domestic Fiction:		
- broadcasting hours	88.5	905.3
- share (%)	8.4	42.5
US Fiction:		
- broadcasting hours	499	776
- share (%)	47.2	36.4

Source: Biltereyst (1992, 1995a, 1995b)
Notes:
(*): Channels included are: ORF (Austria), BRTN, VTM, RTBF, RTL (Belgium), DR (Denmark), MTV, YLE (Finland), ERT (Greece), NOS, RTL4 (Netherlands), NRK (Norway), RTP (Portugal), SRG (Switzerland).
(**): Channels included are: TF1, Antenne 2, FR3 (France), ZDF (Germany), BBC (UK), RAI (Italy).

Beyond economics, many other factors also explain US dominance. American political economist media historian Janet Wasko (1994) thus points to the long history of success for US companies in film and television markets, especially in the periods following both world wars, which left the European film industries in shambles. Other factors she mentions include significant support from the US government, strong worldwide distribution cartels, the use of specific content and textual strategies, etc. In the 1980's and 1990's another strand of literature emerged in this context, referring to reception and other audience related perspectives. They looked at the use and cross-cultural interpretation of US drama by foreign audiences, leading to the recognition of the high appeal and the openness of US productions for an active interpretation by different types of viewers all over the world.

2.3 Was There a 'Magical Programming Formula'?

We have seen that the flood of US serialized fictional material starting in the second half of the 1980's was far from a new phenomenon, but that the basic policy line of deregulation strongly reinforced it. Most stations developed a strategy of audience maximization based on extended air time and cheap popular programs (American imports on the rise, falling local production figures). The main economic beneficiary of this approach has been the USA.

Unsurprisingly, this view of programming dynamics within Western European broadcasters since the mid-1980's gave rise to vehement debates on the impending eradication of the European audiovisual sector, causing protective policies to be implemented. However, this analysis does not take into account many other strategies which have been more positive in the development of the local audiovisual sector. The focus on fiction is important indeed, but may tend to overshadow other strategies. First of all, it is really necessary to differentiate between the programming strategies developed by very different stations. Given the high diversity and the explosion of the broadcasting typology since the mid-1980's, it is no longer possible to speak of one single programming strategy based on the 'magical' formula of "more entertainment, more imports, more US fiction imports." Even within the group of former monopolistic PSB stations, there have been quite diverse strategies. Research on the issue of the so-called convergence between public and private stations concluded that most European PSB stations ultimately relied on a mixed programming system – based on a certain fidelity to traditional programming policy, but also with inexorable signs of adaptation to commercial strategies (Hellman & Sauri, 1994; Hultén, 1995; Krüger, 1991). But not all public stations reacted in the same mixed way, given the different local television cultures, the financial resources, the political and social background. An interesting comparative analysis by Yves Achille and Bernard Miège (1994) on the programming strategies in six European countries clearly shows that different strategies have been developed by PSB stations since then – from a strategy of adaptation or identification (entertainment, low-cost fiction) to one of opposition (stressing information and maintaining the educational mission), to one of differentiation and partial confrontation (mixed strategies). This means that not all stations fell for the 'magical' formula.

Another fact worthy of note is that fiction is not the only growing category. In fact, as shown in table 3, the output of just about all categories has been increasing in nominal figures. The only – very significant however – exception has been education, whose global broadcasting time decreased (–32%), while its share went from 5 to 3%. What did happen is that the global extension of broadcasting time (+26% in this period) went hand in hand with a nominal increase in all categories: fiction (+57%), music (+11%), sports (+3%), and even religion (+1%). While the largest nominal grower has been fiction, other categories have made great strides as well: news (+45%) and current affairs (+20%), and art, humanities and science(+29%). In real terms, however, only fiction (+7%) and news (+2%) actually grew.

Table 3. *Television Output by Genre for 17 European Public Stations, 1988–92*

Program Categories	1988		1992		1988/92	
	Output (hours)	Share (%)	Output (hours)	Share (%)	Nominal Growth (%)	Real Growth (%)
Fiction	34,429	(27)	53,890	(34)	+57	(+7)
Light Entertainment	13,739	(11)	15,152	(10)	+10	(-1)
Music	4,681	(4)	5,190	(3)	+11	(-1)
Sports	17,580	(14)	18,089	(11)	+3	(-3)
News	12,743	(10)	18,451	(12)	+45	(+2)
Information	13,895	(11)	16,624	(10)	+20	(-1)
Art/Humanities/ Science	9,519	(8)	12,269	(8)	+29	(0)
Education	6,418	(5)	4,365	(3)	-32	(-2)
Religion	1,776	(1)	1,801	(1)	+1	(0)
Other	11,292	(9)	12,971	(8)	+15	(-1)
Total	126,072	(100)	158,802	(100)	+26	

Source: EBU

So looking at fiction alone may be an exceedingly limiting approach. Since the mid-1980's the European broadcasting sector has not stood still: it did invest in other, often less expensive categories. Confronted with heavy start-up costs and working in a highly competitive, fragmented and uncertain environment, it was quite safe for many financially fragile broadcasters to rely on cheap programming.

But, broadcasters did sometimes invest in expensive programming, even local fiction, which may serve to qualify the purported constant use of the 'magical' formula. Many stations clearly used cheap US imports as a tool to fill the gaps in their schedule, while they reserved local fiction for primetime. This is well illustrated in table 4, which refers to the origin of fiction on 36 channels in six European countries[5] (De Bens & de Smaele, 2000). This one-month survey (1997) indicated that US imports are significantly (and unsurprisingly) more present on commercial channels than on public service ones (71.7 versus 40.3%). On the other hand, domestic fiction seems largely reserved for primetime, both on private and public channels (20.6 and 40.9%). These figures reaffirm the so-called 'Polyfilla' function of US fiction, formulated more than ten years ago by Tracey (off-peak time slots). Domestic fiction programs, especially soaps and other serialized material, are widely reserved for primetime.

Table 4. *Origin of Imported Fiction (in %, January 1997)*

	Public Channels	Private Channels	Total
Domestic			
General output	28	13.4	17.3
Primetime	40.9	20.6	26.5
Non-domestic European			
General output	25.1	9.4	13.5
Primetime	26.6	10.1	14.9
USA			
General output	40.3	71.7	63.4
Primetime	30.8	67.5	56.8
Other			
General output	6.6	5.5	5.8
Primetime	1.7	1.8	1.8

Source: De Bens & de Smaele (2000)

An important difference is also visible between channels in large and small countries. While in Germany, France and the UK local fiction accounts for more than half of primetime fiction output, its share is almost negligible in small countries such as the Netherlands and Belgium. But even in these European countries with weak production capacities, there has been a tendency to increase local fiction. This has been particularly the case since the introduction of broadcasting competition at the end of the 1980's. A study on the fiction output in small European countries in the 1990–93 period (Biltereyst, 1995a, 1995b) showed that fictional products were clearly growing strongly (+37.6%) within an exploding global television output (+13%) – two natural offshoots of the increasingly competitive character of the European television landscape. More importantly, this growth of fiction does not benefit non-national European programs.

---

[5] The countries/regions and broadcasters included in this study were: the Flemish- (BRTN, VTM, etc.) and French-speaking parts of Belgium (RTBF, RTL, etc.), the Netherlands, the U.K. (BBC, ITV, Channel 4, etc.), Germany (ARD, ZDF, etc.), France (TF1, France 2, etc.) and Italy (RAI, Rete 4, etc.).

While there was a nominal increase in imports from most major exporting European countries (+22.8%), the share of non-national European imports fell (–3.4%). US imports continued to increase (+21.7%) and to dominate the output (40.1% in 1993). The most significant shift however is that in small European countries/regions with limited production capacities there is a significant growth in domestic fiction: in this period it nearly doubled (+88%) and its share within the fiction output grew to 10.5%. This can again be viewed as a clear and growing bipolarization between domestic and US programming – a strategy which so strongly characterized the fictional program structure of channels in the major exporting countries.

Table 5. *Average Fiction Output per Channel in Large and Small European Countries, 1990*

	1990	1993	1990-93 (%)
Fiction Output:			
- broadcasting hours	1,028	1,414	+37.6
- share (%)	26.4	32.1	+5.7
Domestic Fiction:			
- broadcasting hours	79	148	+88
- share (%)	7.7	10.5	+2.8
Non-domestic European Fiction:			
- broadcasting hours	331	407	+22.8
- share (%)	32.2	28.8	-3.4
US Fiction:			
- broadcasting hours	465	567	+21.7
- share (%)	45.2	40.1	-5.1

Source: Biltereyst (1995a, 1995b)
Notes:
(*): Channels included are: ORF (Austria), BRTN, VTM, RTBF, RTL (Belgium), DR (Denmark), MTV, YLE (Finland), ERT (Greece), NOS, RTL4 (Netherlands), NRK (Norway), RTP (Portugal), SRG (Switzerland).

The main reason for the increase in local programming is its tremendous popularity, owing to the need for cultural proximity programming with local audiences. Often however these programs are based on transnational (US) formulas in serial forms, and made with very limited budgets. Even in countries such as France local fiction more that ever has to respond to 'the profit imperative': given the ethos of financial rationalization and management efficiency within (private) television companies, even low budget local fiction is often considered as too expensive in relation to the directly generated advertising income (Jézéquel, 1993; see also Buonnano, 1998a, 1998b).

What seems to be happening with the provision of fictional material in Western Europe is that on the one hand local broadcasters try to increase the local production rate as an important tool for competition, however with very limited money so that both quality and export possibilities tend to diminish. On the other hand non-domestic European fiction seems to be losing further appeal. And this is possibly the real tragedy of the European audiovisual sector: the lowering standards of domestic production are undermining the appeal of European fiction in general as well as its internal circulation, leaving the doors wide open for attractive US production.

The most recent data from the Council of Europe's European Audiovisual Observatory (EAO, 1999) tend to confirm these trends. Based on the programming schedules of broadcasters in sixteen (Western) European countries, table 6 indicates the relative stability and even slow decrease of most types of European imports. On the other hand, US imports continued to grow, reinforcing the trend to bipolarization. The increasing demand for attractive fiction is more than ever met by local products and US imports.

Table 6. *Origin of Imported Fiction Programs in 16 European Countries (1994–97, in %)*

	1994	**1997**
German imports	1.7	1.6
French	2.9	2.3
British	6	5
Italian	1.6	1
European co-productions	2.7	4
Mixed co-productions	1.8	2
Non-European co-productions	0.4	0.4
Canadian imports	1.5	1.7
Australian + New Zealand imports	3.4	3.1
US imports	69.8	71.3

Source: EAO (1999)

2.4 Digital Revolution

On a policy level this trend to bipolarization has also been recognized as highly problematic, as the following quote from Tessier and Woodward (1998) indicates:

> "European consumers' experience of audiovisual entertainment is essentially polarized between very domestic television programming on the one hand and US films on the other, whilst films and TV programs drawn from the rest of Europe generally fulfill the needs and interests of a small audience. (...) As a result of these factors, Europe is entering the new electronic media revolution with a severe handicap. As in-

ternet commerce and other forms of on-line interactive delivery gradually extend their hold on audiovisual consumers over the next decade, European content suppliers are not making any significant contribution to the product distributed through these consumer-led delivery systems."

In the 1990's, the European program industry did not succeed in creating a strong integrated European market. The question then is, whether it will reach "the critical mass required to remain competitive in the global marketplace of the future" (Tessier & Woodward, 1998). It is feared that the digital revolution will only reinforce existing structural weaknesses. In a recent policy document on Media Plus (COM (1999)658def) the European Commission tries to illustrate the opportunities of the digital technologies, although it also recognizes the ill-prepared state of the European program industry. According to this document, the number of television channels will continue to grow, as it did in the 1990's: between 1990 and 1998 there was an increase from 104 to 659 broadcasters, but in the year 2000 there should be more than a thousand of these. This could well increase the financial fragmentation and under-capitalization of the European production sector. This is why the Commission plans to support more international production strategies.

III   A Policy to Protect and Stimulate Local Fiction

3.1 Policy Initiatives

It comes as no surprise that what happened after deregulation should have given rise to new policy concerns to protect and stimulate the production and distribution of fictional material in both the broadcasting and motion picture sectors. In fact, very similar tendencies were seen in the film production and exhibition sector, where the share of US films grew from 35% in 1968 to more than 40% at the end of the 1970's and then went up to 70% at the end of the 1980's (Think Tank, 1994). In the 1990's these figures ranged from 70% to 80%. Another contributing factor was the opening up of Eastern Europe in 1989 and Hollywood's ensuing *Conquest of the East* (Wasko, 1994).

In the end of the 1980's, some policy-makers evidenced a growing awareness that Europe could not afford to neglect its own 'software,' certainly not in an era of accelerated audiovisual expansion owing to the advent of new markets in the East, the digitization of television, and the creation of ever more channels. In order to compete with US and other rivals, strong supranational European actors had to be nurtured in the field of production, distribution and broadcasting.

In fact, Europe has a long tradition of regional and national support to the production of local fictional material, mainly movies – a tradition that in most countries goes back to the 1950's. But at the end of the 1980's there was a need for aid at a supranational level, mainly promoted by the European Community/EC (now: European Union/EU) and the Council of Europe/CofE. Both supranational organizations have been working closely together in order to protect the audiovisual heritage. A good example has been the European Convention on the trans-border television, adopted by the CofE in March 1989, which is highly compatible with the EC's TWF Directive.

This important directive of October 1989 can be seen as a milestone in the establishment of a common legal framework and for regulating the trans-border flow of television services within the (then) 12 member states (Council, 1989). The directive also contained a highly discussed article which stipulates that "where practicable," Member States should ensure that broadcasters "reserve for European works (...) a majority proportion of their transmission time, excluding the time appointed to news, sport events, games, advertising and teletext services" (art. 4). This article has been interpreted by many observers – including all US production companies – as a way to curb the growth of fiction imports and to stimulate the internal circulation of European drama. Even within Europe the directive has been highly controversial. The 'quota'-article can be seen as a perfect example of the policy of consensus and compromises between 'liberals' and 'dirigistes,' to use Collins's terminology (1994). On the one hand, free-marketers argued against quotas and in favor of programming freedom and the abolishment of television frontiers. The state-control school (dirigiste), strongly promoted by the French socialists and the film industry, pleaded for a more culturally inspired policy, including protectionist quotas requiring broadcasters to reserve more air time for local and European material and to invest more in the latter. The directive first looked as a compromise between both schools of thought, but finally turned out to be a victory for the free-marketers and the industrial audiovisual forces. In particular, the applicability of article 4 has been considered as very weak, given the presence of the phrase "where practicable." Proposals and amendments to strengthen the quota requirements and to drop this phrase – such as those made in 1996 by the European Parliament and the Commission – were never adopted by the Council. The TWF directive was reissued with minor changes in 1997 (Castille, 2000).

Besides this broad regulatory framework there have also been a number of more direct financial support mechanisms, both from the EC/EU and the CofE. And some of these initiatives are strongly directed towards promoting the production and cross-border distribution of fictional material. A good example has been the CofE's Eurimages, the first pan-European support fund for the co-production and the distribution of feature films and creative documentaries. Strongly supported by France, Eurimages is designed first as a production fund, mainly by encouraging and financing the co-production of films and documentaries involving independent producers from at least three different member states. Eurimages also wants to intensify the exchange of European audio-visual works, mainly by supporting their distribution. Although Eurimages is an important tool for the production and cross-border circulation of Euro-fiction (mainly feature films), it is handicapped by its very limited financial resources.

In addition, the EC/EU developed important direct financial support tools. The MEDIA program (1994c, 1996) is an large-scale initiative providing for several projects or funds available to the European audiovisual industry. This EC/EU initiative is considered complementary to the CofE's Eurimages production fund, as it specializes in the pre- and post-production phase of audiovisual works. The MEDIA program has already gone through several generations. After a pilot phase of a couple of years in the second part of the 1980's, the European Commission succeeded in turning MEDIA into a regular action program at the end of 1990. MEDIA I (1991–95) became a well-known and widely solicited program covering 19 very diverse projects: distribution, promotion and exhibition of movies, development of scenarios, training in financial management, etc. MEDIA I has been a very important, wide-ranging and courageous initiative, but it suffered from fragmentation and some lack of co-ordination. The most important problem however, has been a financial one: MEDIA I was allocated the relatively small budget of € 230 million over five years (Pauwels, 2000).

In the first half of the 1990's it became clear that the European audiovisual policy was not really a success, given the growing dependency on US production and distribution firms in both film and broadcasting. These difficulties were neatly expressed during the 1993 GATT talks, and again in the 1994 Green Paper and the Think-Tank report commissioned by the EU. In this period it also looked as if Central and Eastern European markets were once again in the grip of the US audiovisual industry. All these prospects encouraged the EU policy-makers to slowly change their policy. The Commission managed to launch MEDIA II with a higher budget (€ 310 million) over the 1996–2000 period. Rather than continuing to support single projects, MEDIA II emphasized the establishment of stronger local audiovisual actors by giving "priority to strengthen the base of companies with potential for a number of programs, thereby helping them to spread the inherent risks" (EC, 1994b). The main objectives of MEDIA II are to improve the competitiveness of the European industry and to create a favorable environment for companies in the sector (MEDIA, 1996). Its main thrusts pertain to the development and distribution of European audiovisual works (€ 265 million) as well as various training programs (€ 34 million).

In the meantime, the European Commission is preparing a follow-up plan entitled Media Plus (EC, 1999), which will run from January 2001 to the end of 2005. Media Plus will continue to stress training, production, distribution and promotion of European works, with a strong emphasis on digital technologies. An important objective will be further diversification: digital broadcasting, Internet, DVD, etc. According to a Commission document (EC, 1999) it will be necessary to follow a more industrial and structural policy. This means that the European Union will give priority to companies based on their market results, in order to strengthen the sector in a more structural manner. The central question however is whether the proposed budget will be large enough. Compared to the skyrocketing corporate budgets in the field of digital media, the € 400 million proposed budget for 2001–2005 (Media Deskkrant, February 2000) may be no more than a drop in the ocean...

Another important European initiative in the field of the audiovisual media is Audiovisual Eureka – another project promoted by France. First launched in 1989 with the aim of contributing to the creation of a European audiovisual market, it has become a platform for innovative initiatives in the audiovisual field. At the end of 1995 its mission was readjusted. Since January 1996 the new Audiovisual Eureka acts as an intermediary between the EU audiovisual legislation and programs (such as MEDIA) and 'Greater Europe.' Its main purpose is to build a bridge between the EU and associated countries from Central and Eastern Europe, that is, to prepare their integration in the AV field (TEI, 1996).

3.2 Evaluating Policy Effectiveness

Many authors have cast a critical eye on the credibility (enforceability and effectiveness) of the EU's audiovisual policy initiatives aiming to stimulate the production and cross-border circulation of European works (e.g., Burgelman & Pauwels, 1992; Castille, 2000; Collins, 1994; Humphreys, 1996; Pauwels, 2000; Think-Tank, 1994). As already indicated much has been said about the weakly formulated quota regulation and its applicability. There are also major doubts about the effectiveness of the various support mechanisms, given their small budgets, their fragmentation and lack of co-ordination. Even official European sources such as the Green Paper and the Think-Tank report openly indicate some 'perverse effects' of the current audiovisual policy: creation of 'lame-duck' mentalities, lack of coordination between the support mechanisms on a regional, national and supranational level, etc. (Think-Tank, 1994; EC, 1994a).

Another way of evaluating the policy's effectiveness has consisted in interviewing professionals. Such a procedure was followed in 1992–93 in the context of a commissioned evaluation of the MEDIA I program, where "audiovisual professionals, members of the advisory committees and those responsible for MEDIA and its projects" were interviewed (EC, 1993a). Although such an approach can be useful, its appropriateness for policy evaluation is highly questionable. In this context it was not surprising that the evaluation report should reach positive conclusions on the impact of the MEDIA program.

The ultimate test of such a clear policy effort aiming to stimulate the cross-border circulation would simply be to look at what actually happened in the field, as well as the pattern changes in the circulation and distribution of audiovisual works. That a first step in this direction has been taken is evidenced in the monitoring reports released by the Commission regarding the implementation of article 4 of the TWF directive. In the report (which covers 148 channels for the 1993–94 period), the Commission came to the (highly positive) conclusion that "91 broadcast a majority proportion of European works" (EC, 1996). The report further indicated that "by and large, general-interest terrestrial channels, and in particular the public ones which have been in existence for many years now, have no difficulty in attaining a majority proportion of European works, and that home-produced works account for a fairly large share." On the other side of the spectrum there are the satellite channels, which find it very difficult to reach the 50% mark. Although these results turned out to be relatively positive, the Commission's report is fairly honest in stating that the data have to be interpreted with great care. The Commission writes that they "should not be interpreted as either proving the effectiveness or the economic impact of article 4 and 5 on the development of the European television industry." In the 1994 Green Paper on the EU audiovisual policy (EC, 1994b), the Commission openly referred to the clear lack of 'essential indicators' and basic 'reliable data' in relation to the question "What is the proportion of European works that would not have been broadcast if there had been no legal obligation?"

This is of course a question which can not be answered in a simple manner, given the many different contextual factors, the global international television tendencies, and the programming dynamics within the different types of broadcasters. If one concentrates on fiction, however, some of the empirical results presented in the section on programming trends are quite relevant. Thus the 'bipolarization' trend in the fiction output, both in large and small countries, can be considered as conflicting with EU audiovisual purposes. The data on the small European countries indicate that the cross-border dissemination of European audiovisual productions is characterized by a relatively downward trend. The quota rules have been flouted by most stations in EU member states as far as this program category is concerned. Intensifying competition in most countries seems to incite the channels to concentrate on national strategies and US products. This bipolarization trend, which has been defined as "one of the most negative symptoms of the change in the audiovisual market in the EU" (Think-Tank, 1994), is now visible in smaller countries/regions. In this context it is remarkable that even the report of the professional think-tank should acknowledge that these tendencies have been intensified by the policy of deregulation of television and the fierce competition between stations. These critical remarks however, which indirectly point to one of the contradictions in EU policy lines – deregulation and the growing dependency on US imports versus stimulation of European content distribution – were not included in the final Green Paper.

IV   Discussion

In this chapter on the relationship between television content and basic policy lines in Western Europe, we mainly concentrated on the 'fiction' program category. This clearly lies at the intersection of the major problems encountered by attempts to create and police a pan-European cultural industry, such as the addiction to US cultural products and the political and economic imperatives governing the culture field. Besides structural causes this article also pointed to many policy problems. A closer look at this category highlights the most recurrent policy hesitations, contradictions and conflicts – between the economic and cultural logics, between the national and supranational levels, between various countries or schools of thought (free-marketers vs. protectionists, etc.), between various players within the audiovisual industry itself, and so on.

A major problem, which seems to have been underestimated by EU policy-makers, is the strength of the linguistic and cultural factor. This factor is quite evident in the consumption and popularity of locally produced drama, but it also has a strongly impact on the origin of imports. According to the Green Paper (EC, 1994a) these barriers can and should be overcome by developing high quality dubbing and subtitling in order to promote the distribution of European programs. In this context one can indeed question whether cultural proximity can be reduced to the language aspect.

Another major barrier to the creation of a strong pan-European audiovisual space is a number of conflicting policy lines (culture vs. economics, etc.). In this respect, "political policies designed to guarantee programs reinforcing national cultural values became embroiled with economic policies designed to ensure free competition in the delivery of audiences to advertisers and sponsors" (Porter, 1990). Since the 1980's, according to André Lange (1990) four types of policy logics have emerged to create a common European space. Some years ago he spoke of a continual confrontation between what he calls a commercial logic (against regulation and in favor of free trade), a constitutional one (referring to the importance of television in the public sphere), a cultural one (audiovisual products as a means of cultural and creative expression) and an industrial one. If one follows this line of reasoning, it seems clear that since the mid-1990's the latter is by far the dominant force. And this will only be reinforced by the new Media Plus project, which is trying to bring policy answers to the digital challenges of the information society. The industrial logic aims at developing major media groups in Europe in order to resist the US transnational competition.

This logic also permeates the 1994 Green Paper, the MEDIA II and Media Plus objectives. This option, which is increasingly gaining ground among EU policy-makers, can be criticized for rewarding intensive lobbying, favoring companies in the (large) countries with high production facilities, and for advancing the monopolizing process in the audiovisual sector. In this context it is unclear how these policy lines – strengthening production companies, stressing the global and pan-European dimension over an intra-European one, underestimating language and cultural factors – can be reconciled with the rhetorical call for cultural diversity (EC, 1994b).

In this context it would be advisable that the existing policy lines take into account both the structural inequalities and the cultural barriers within Europe. The strong emphasis on a genuine pan-European dimension could then be left aside for an approach designed to stimulate both co-production and distribution between nations and regions on the basis of cultural proximity. In particular, the (co-)production of high quality programs must be encouraged, since the tendency to produce more cheap domestic drama in the respective national markets often results in products with low export possibilities. And finally, in this perspective it would be wise to formally reaffirm the vital role of the PSB tradition – which could be essential in (re-)establishing production quality and diversity and lessening the impact of bottom line considerations (Curran, 1998).

References

Achille, Y. & Miège, B. (1994). The limits to the adaptation strategies of European public service television, *Media, Culture & Society* 16(1): 31–46.

Bastiansen, H. & Syvertsen, T. (1996). Towards a Norwegian television history. In I. Bondebjerg & F. Bono (eds.), *Television in Scandinavia* (pp. 127–155). London: UPL.

Biltereyst, D. (1992). Language and culture as ultimate barriers? An analysis of the circulation, consumption and popularity of fiction in small European countries, *European Journal of Communication* 7(4): 517–540.

Biltereyst, D. (1995a). *Hollywood in het Avondland. Over de afhankelijkheid en de impact van VS-fictie in Europa.* Brussels: VUB Press.

Biltereyst, D. (1995b). European audiovisual policy and the cross-border circulation of fiction: A follow-up flow study, *European Journal of Cultural Policy* 2(1): 3–24.

Blumler, J. (1991). The new television marketplace: Imperatives, implications, issues. In J. Curran & M. Gurevitch (eds.), *Mass Media and Society.* London: Edward Arnold.

Blumler, J. (1992) (ed.) *Television and the Public Interest. Vulnerable Values in West European Broadcasting.* London: Sage Publications.

Browne, D.R. (1968). The American image as presented abroad by US television, *Journalism Quarterly* 45(2): 307–316.

Buonanno, M. (1998a) (ed.). *Imaginary Dreamscapes. Television Fiction in Europe.* Luton: ULP.

Buonanno, M. (1998b) (ed.). *Eurofiction 1998.* Rome: RAI-ERI.

Burgelman, J.C. & Pauwels, C. (1992). Audiovisual policy and cultural identity in small European states: The challenge of a unified market, *Media, Culture and Society* (14): 169–183.

Castille, V. (2000). De Europese televisiequota: flexibiliteit of compromis als rode draad? In D. Biltereyst & H. de Smaele (eds.), *Transformatie en continuïteit van de Europese televisie* (pp. 51–76). Ghent: Academia Press.

Collins, R. (1994). *Broadcasting and Audiovisual Policy in the European Single Market.* London: John Libbey.

Council (1989). *Council Directive 'Television Without Frontiers'*, Council of the European Communities, October 3.

Curran, J. (1998). Crisis in public communication: A reappraisal. In T. Liebes & J. Curran (eds.), *Media, Ritual and Identity* (pp. 175–202). London: Routledge.

De Bens, E., Kelly, M. & Bakke, M. (1992). Television content: Dallasification of culture? In K. Siune & W. Truetzschler (eds.), *Dynamics of Media Politics. Broadcasting and Electronic Media in Western Europe* (pp. 75–100). London: Sage Publications.

De Bens, E. & de Smaele, H. (2000). De instroom van Amerikaanse televisiefictie op de Europese zenders herbekeken. In D. Biltereyst & H. de Smaele (eds.), *Transformatie en continuïteit van de Europese televisie* (pp. 108–138). Ghent: Academia Press.

Dyson, K. & Humphreys, P. (1990) (eds.). *The Political Economy of Communications. International and European Dimensions*. London: Routledge.

EAO (1995). *Statistical Yearbook*. Strasbourg: Council of Europe, European Audiovisual Observatory.

EAO (1999). *Statistical Yearbook*. Strasbourg: Council of Europe, European Audiovisual Observatory.

EBU (1993). *EBU Diffusion*, Spring.

European Commission (1984). *Television Without Frontiers. Green Paper on the Establishment of the Common Market for Broadcasting, especially by Satellite and Cable*. Brussels, EC.

European Commission (1993a). *Commission Communication on the Evaluation of the Action Programme to Promote the Development of the European Audiovisual Industry*. Luxemburg, July 23.

European Commission (1993b). *White Paper. Growth, Competitiveness and Employment – The Challenges and Ways Forward into the 21st Century*. Brussels, December 5.

European Commission (1994a). *Communication from the Commission to the Council ad the European Parliament on the Application of Articles 4 and 5 of Directive 89/552/EEC 'Television Without Frontiers'*. Brussels, March 3.

European Commission (1994b). *Green Paper. Strategy Options to Strengthen the European Programme Industry in the Context of the Audiovisual Policy of the European Union*. Brussels, April 7.

European Commission (1996). *Communication from the Commission to the Council and the European Parliament on the Application of Articles 4 and 5 of Directive 89/552/EEC 'Television Without Frontiers'*. Brussels, July 15.

European Commission (1998). *Politique Audiovisuelle de l'Union Européenne*. Brussels.

European Commission (1999). *Mededeling van de Commissie over een voorstel voor een programma ter ondersteuning van de Europese audiovisuele sector (Media Plus – 2001–2005)*. Brussels, Commission. COM (1999) 658 def.

European Television Task Force (1988). *Europe 2000: What Kind of Television?* Manchester: European Cultural Foundation, EIM.

Eurostat (1994). Audiovisual services, *Panorama 1994*. Brussels.

Fortner, R.S. (1993). *International Communication*. Belmont: Wadsworth.

Hellman, H. & Sauri, T. (1994). Public service television and the tendency towards convergence: Trends in prime-time programme structure in Finland, 1970–92, *Media, Culture & Society* 16(1): 47–71.

Hirsch, M. & Petersen, V.G. (1992). Public broadcasting in the state of flux. In K. Siune & W. Treutzschler (eds.), *Dynamics of Media Politics* (pp. 42–56). London: Sage Publications.

Hoskins, C. & Mirus, R. (1990). Television fiction made in the USA. In P. Larsen (ed.), *Import/Export: International Flow of Television Fiction* (pp. 83–90). Paris: Unesco.

Hultèn, O. (1995). Diversity or conformity? Television programming in competitive situations, *Nordicom Review* 1: 7–22.

IIC (1988). *Stories Come First: Television Fiction in Europe*. London: International Institute of Communications.

Jameson, F. (1984). Postmodernism, or the cultural logic of late capitalism, *New Left Review* 165: 53–92.

Jézéquel, J.-P. (1993) (ed.). *La Production de fiction en Europe*. Paris: La Documentation Française.

Krüger, U.M. (1991). Zur Konvergenz öffentlich-rechtlicher und privater Fernsehprogramme im dualen System: Programmanalyse 1990, *Media Perspektiven* 5: 303–332.

Lange, A. (1990). *L'Europe à la recherche d'une politique audiovisuelle*. Paper for the ARCQ Conference, Montreal.

Manschot, B. (1988). Publieke omroep en programmastrategie. In L. Heinsman & J. Servaes (eds.), *Hoe zijn de nieuwe media?* (pp. 39–57). Leuven: Acco.

Heinsman, L. & Servaes, J. (1988) (eds.). *Hoe nieuw zijn de nieuwe media?* Leuven: Acco.

McQuail, D. (1990). *Electronic Media Policy in Western Europe.* Amsterdam: Report for ERG, September.

McQuail, D. (1995). Western European media. In J. Downing, A. Mohammadi & A. Sreberny-Mohammadi (eds.), *Questioning the Media* (pp. 147–164). London: Sage Publications.

MEDIA (1994). *Media. Guide for the Audiovisual Industry.* Brussels: European Commission.

MEDIA (1996). *Media. Instruction Manual.* Brussels: European Commission.

Media Deskkrant (2000). Media Plus in de startblokken, *Media Deskkrant* 6(1): 1–2.

Media Salles (1999). *European Cinema Yearbook.* Milan: Media Salles.

Miller, T. (1998). Hollywood and the world. In J. Hill & P. Church Gibson (eds.), *The Oxford Guide to Film Studies* (pp. 371–381). Oxford: Oxford University Press.

Nordenstreng, K. & Varis, T. (1974). *Television Traffic – A One-Way Street?* Paris: Unesco.

Pauwels, C. (2000). De creatie van een competitieve Europese audiovisuele programma-industrie: mission impossible? In D. Biltereyst & H. de Smaele (eds.), *Transformatie en continuïteit van de Europese televisie* (pp. 24–50). Ghent: Academia Press.

Porter, V. (1990). The EC: Broadcasting, competition policies and national sovereignty, *Intermedia* 18(3): 22.

Schiller, H. (1996). *Information Inequality. The Deepening Social Crisis in America.* New York: Routledge.

Schou, S. (1992). Postwar Americanization and the revitalization of European culture. In M. Skovmand & K.Ch. Schroeder (eds.), *Media Cultures. Reappraising Transnational Media* (pp. 142–60). London: Routledge.

Sinclair, J., Jacka, E. & Cunningham, S. (1996). *New Patterns in Global Television. Peripheral Vision.* Oxford: Oxford University Press.

Sondergaard, H. (1996). Fundamentals in the history of Danish television. In I. Bondebjerg & F. Bono (eds.), *Television in Scandinavia* (pp. 11–41). London: UPL.

Tessier, M. & Woodward, J. (1998). *European Support for the Audiovisual Industry. European Audiovisual Conference: Challenges and Opportunities of the Digital Age.* Available at [http://europa.eu.int/eac/engwg2.htm].

Think-Tank (1994). *Report by the Think-Tank on the Audiovisual Policy in the European Union.* Luxembourg: EC-Publications.

TEI (1996). *Trans-Europe Images. The Audiovisual Eureka Newsletter.* Brussels.

Tracey, M. (1988). Popular Culture and the Economics of Global Television, *Intermedia* 16: 8–25.

Varis, T. (1985). *International Flow of Television Programs.* Paris: Unesco.

Wasko, J. (1994). Hollywood goes east. In K. Jakubowicz & P. Jeanray (eds.), *Central and Eastern Europe: Audiovisual landscape and copyright legislation* (pp. 75–88). Antwerp: Maklu, Audiovisual Eureka.

European Public Television in Search of a Mission in an Era of Economic and Technological Change

by Leen d'Haenens

This chapter takes a pragmatic look at a highly topical issue: based on its current circumstances – legal and structural/financial constraints and technological change, audience figures and market shares, and the information society's uncertainties and opportunities – where is public service television to go from here? Or to put it differently, what is the future of public service television (be it funded through license fee or public subsidies, or advertising and sponsoring, or a mix of both) in a world of rampant commercialism? Our primary concern here is the mission of public service television in the years ahead. Offering a model for public service television would be an impossible task since it has developed along partly converging and partly distinct lines in each European country, as can be seen in this book. No one-size-fits-all solution can be formulated. We only touch on a number of ingredients which we believe are necessary to strike a healthy and durable balance between the mission attributed to public service television (diversity, pluralism, quality, education, culture, etc.) and financial health.

We focus on what may be termed the two 'contextual' conditions for public service television to fulfil a function without its program supply becoming redundant with respect to that of other channels (commercial, multi-genre TV, or single-format, pay-per-view or subscription TV): creative legislation and sufficient long-term public funding (spanning several years). Within the legal field, the most important instrument applying to any broadcaster is the EU's 'Television Without Frontiers' Directive (for more details, we refer the reader to this book's chapter by Valérie Castille). Moreover, according to the subsidiarity principle, the Member States entrust their public services with tasks defined based on their national needs. Further, they are free to decide how their public service broadcasters should be financed. Nevertheless, the issue of mixed funding (a combination of public subsidies and advertising revenue) has become particularly contentious owing to the competition rules established under the Treaty of Amsterdam, and has been subject of several complaints by commercial stations to the European Commission. The central issue here is that of the 'elbow-room' the EU Member States may or may not have with respect to the funding of their own public service: public monies granted public service broadcasters can be construed as State aid. The European Commission is therefore bound to look into the matter in the light of the Protocol to Amsterdam Treaty, which clarifies how competition rules should be applied and sets out the responsibilities and obligations of the Member States and the Commission.

I   Commercialization and Forced Changes of Course

The 1950's and 1960's saw the birth of traditional public television, the so-called 'generalist' or 'primitive' channels: a mix of entertainment, information and education, with emphasis on homemade programs. In the 1980's public service broadcasting in Western Europe (except for the UK, where this had been the case since 1955) faced the sudden and massive emergence of commercial broadcasters (Avery, 1993; Raboy, 1996). Since then, public broadcasting channels have had to live in a constant state of crisis. According to Achille (1994), the origin of this crisis was threefold: identity, financing, and operating problems. Public channels had to revise their program strategies in many European countries. Moreover, there was (and still is) an urgent need to tighten the bond with viewers (d'Haenens & Heuvelman, 1996; d'Haenens, 1996a, 1996b). In most EU countries public television is left with the lowest audience share. In this respect, Greece (lowest market share) and Denmark (highest market share) mark both ends of the spectrum. Table 1 provides an overview of the audience shares of both public and commercial television channels in the EU.

Table 1. *Audience Shares and Financing of EU Public TV Channels*

Audience Shares in % (1999)			Financing of Public Channels (1999)		
Country	Public Channels	Private Channels	License Fee/ Public in %	Advertising in %	Other in %
Austria	59	41	48	42	10
Belgium Flemish	31	69	60	33	7
French	20	80	71	20	9
Denmark	68	32	65	25	10
Finland	44	56	74	12	14
France	44	56	61	32	7
Germany	41	59	78	10	12
Greece	10	90	83	3	14
Ireland	51	49	34	41	25
Italy	48	52	50	35	15
Netherlands	37	63	66	22	12
Portugal	34	66	43*	41	16
Spain	49	51	12*	73	15
Sweden	47	53	93	0	7
United Kingdom	50	50	76	6**	18

* In Portugal and Spain public subsidies amount to 43% (no license fee).
** In the United Kingdom public subsidies amount to 6% (no advertising).
Sources: *Legal and Financial Data* prepared for the 'European Public Sector Television at a Time of Economic and Technological Change' Symposium, held in Lille, July 19 & 20, 2000, by the *Direction du développement des médias* (SJTIC, Paris) in collaboration with the European Audiovisual Observatory (EAO, Strasbourg).

Due to accelerated commercialization in the 1980's and 1990's, public stations have tended to model their program strategy after those of commercial channels, which only served to make competition worse. Based on analysis of program supply, channel typologies can be identified. While table 2 looks into the audience shares and program supply of the EU public television stations, table 3 provides an overview of the market shares of the main private competitors. Analysis of program supply reveals trends concerning the (re)positioning of European public channels which are either geared towards entertainment (e.g., RAI1 or TVE1) or culture and education (e.g., NED3, La Sept/Arte, La Cinquième). In other words, a contradictory, schizophrenic evolution has been taking place, dictated by mutual 'infection' or differentiation. The original program model was disrupted by the arrival of commercial stations in the 1980's and 1990's, leaving public service broadcasting with a dilemma: should it offer a 'commercial' program supply, or should it refine even further its public service logic? Repositioning of the public service was the answer given to accelerated change in the television landscape: depending upon financial strength (see table 2), the program supply selected and the associated costs, each public television channel attempted to maximize its audience or audience segment. Channels were forced to rationalize at the expense of diversity: the massive re-broadcasting of American programs, at least as 'filling material' was both the simplest and safest solution to the imbalance between supply and demand. Moreover, the general trend towards longer broadcasting times meant that less money could be spent per broadcast hour. The bidding wars for key elements of the broadcasting schedule (e.g., reliance on the 'star system' or fighting for transmission rights of sports events) have further upset the television market, making it ever more difficult for public broadcasters to retain an identity of their own.

Table 1 shows the varying configurations of financing sources which public broadcasters can rely on. We differentiate between countries in which at least three fourths of the budget of public television comes from license fees or public subsidies (Sweden (93%), Greece (83%), United Kingdom (76%) and Finland (74%), as opposed to countries where public revenue is the smallest part of a channel's income – Spain (12%) and Ireland (34%). Table 2 illustrates the financial position of EU public television channels. Their comparative 'poverty'or 'wealth' is of course intimately related to the size of the population (read market) to be served. Table 3 completes the financial picture, providing an overview of the main private television competitors and their main shareholders (media multinational corporations operating in several EU countries, or smaller-scale, national media concerns). This book's other chapters deal with the national perspectives in much greater detail.

The funding of European public television stations remains a highly controversial issue. Public broadcasters supported by both license fees and advertising money have drawn a considerable amount of flak from their commercial competitors, several of which even filed formal complaints (see for instance TF1's March 10, 1993 complaint respecting the public funding of France 2 and France 3). In 1996 complaints were filed in no less than five Member States (France, Greece, Italy, Portugal, Spain). The European Commission responded with a communication on the services of general interest

Table 2. *Audience Shares, Program Supply and Income of EU Public TV Channels (1999)*

Country	Channel	Audience Shares	Program Supply	Income in 1998 (in € million)
Austria	ORF1	24.9	Generalist	76
	ORF2	34.4	Generalist	
Belgium Flemish	TV1	22.7	Generalist	226
	TV2 Canvas		Gen./Cult./Sport	
	Ketnet	8.1	Children	
	La Une	17.1	Generalist	224
French	La Deux	2.9	Generalist	
Denmark	DKR1	29.3	Generalist	372
	DKR2	2.6	General./Drama	
	TV2	36	8 reg. stations.	
Finland	TV1	23	Gen./News/Edu News/Edu	351
	TV2	21	General./Drama	
France	France 2	22.5	Generalist	777
	France 3	17	Generalist Region-based*	853
	La Sept/Arte	1.6	Cult./European	176
	La Cinquième	1.9	Educational	119
Germany	ARD1	14.6	General./News	5,600
	ARD3	12.5	9 reg. stations	
	ZDF	13.4	General./News	1,400
Greece	ET1	5.7	General./Drama	214
	ET2	4.2	News	
	ET3			
Ireland	RTE1	33	Generalist	283
	Network 2	17	Generalist	
	Teilfis Na		In Gaelic	
	Gaelilge	1	Language	
Italy	RAI Uno	22.9	Gen./Entertain.	2,500
	RAI Due	16.3	Generalist	
	RAI Tre	8.9	Gen./Drama/ Sport	
Netherlands	Ned 1	14	Generalist	859
	Ned 2	13	Family/Sport/ Documentaries	
	Ned 3	10	Cult./Info	
Portugal	Canal 1	28.1	Gen./Entertain.	161
	TV2	5.6	Gen./Sport	
Spain	TVE-1	24.9	Gen./News	641
	La 2	8	Gen./Drama	
	11 channels**	16.5	Generalist	
Sweden	SVT1	21.4	Generalist	391
	SVT2	25.8	Generalist	
United Kingdom	BBC1	28.3	General./News	4,400
	BBC2	11.1	Gen./Cult./Edu	
	Channel 4	10.1	Gen./Drama/ Multicultural	914

* France 3 has 19 switchovers and 13 region-based stations.
** The 11 channels belong to the so-called Autonomous Communities.

in Europe (September 26, 1996). Sections 51 and 52 were dedicated to radio and television (for full text, see Documentation Section). The Commission re-emphasized the general interest dimension and referred to program content, the expression of moral and ethical values such as plurality of content, information ethics and protection of the individual. A series of new, vehement complaints[1] led to the adoption of the Protocol to the Treaty of Amsterdam on public broadcasting systems in the Member States (October 2, 1997; for full text, see Documentation Section). The Protocol stipulates that funding for public service broadcasting is a Member State preserve provided this funding does not affect competition throughout the Community. In September 1998 the Commission's Directorate General for competition unsuccessfully attempted to draw up a deliberation document with guidelines on State aids to public sector broadcasters. Instead the Member States opted for a case-by-case approach (Michalis, 1999).

In December 1998 the Directorate General for competition held a hearing to gather information on the state of competition in the market. The Council prepared a Resolution concerning public broadcasting (January 25, 1999; for full text, see Documentation Section). This brought fresh support to the notion that public service broadcasting is a vital factor in advancing democracy, pluralism, social cohesion, and cultural and linguistic diversity. It stated that the comprehensive nature of public service broadcasting remains crucial given the increased diversification of programs on offer, and reaffirms the competence of the Member States concerning public remit and funding, as set out in the Protocol to the Treaty of Amsterdam. The Resolution focuses on the benefits of technological progress, quality programming, broad access and equal opportunities. In addition, striving to enlarge audience figures and providing a wide range of programs is considered perfectly legitimate. Decisions on pending issues were made in 1999. The Commission authorized State aid to Germany's Phoenix and Kinderkanal channels, for instance. It also issued an injunction concerning the financing of Spain's RTVE and regional television stations. The French case remains unclear: following an injunction from the Commission and a Court ruling against the financing of France 2 and France 3, France filed an appeal before the Court. This led to a formal hearing on the part of the Commission to examine subsidies (other than fees) granted to France 2 and France 3. Finally, the Commission authorized State subsidies in favor of the Britain's BBC News 24 channel. In 2000 the Communication on the services of public interest was revised.

---

[1] From the German Association of Private Broadcasters (VPRT) (allocation of public monies to the Phoenix and Kinderkanal channels), from BSkyB (creation by the BBC of its News 24 channel using public funds), and from Spain's CanalSatellite (involvement of RTVE and the regional TV channels in digital pay-television).

Table 3. *Audience Share, Main Shareholders, Program Supply of the Main Private TV Competitors in the EU*

Country	Channel	Audience in 1999 in %	Main Shareholders in %	Program Supply
Austria	ATV	Launch in Jan. 2000	UPC (26); Alegro (H. Kloiber) (14); Tele München (26); Erste Bank (8)	Supra-regional
	RTL Öst.*	6.2	CLT-UFA (89); BW TV und Film (11)	Generalist/Entertainment
	Sat1 Öst.*	5.1	PKS (Kirch Media GmbH) (44); Axel Springer Verlag (20); Aktuelle Presse-Fernsehen (20); AV Euromedia (15)	Generalist/Drama
	Pro7 Öst.	5.3	Kirch Media GmbH; Rewe-Beteiligung	Generalist/Films
Belgium Flemish	VTM	27.2	Vlaamse Televisie Maatschappij (regional press groups)	Generalist
	Kanaal 2	5.7	Vlaamse Televisie Maatschappij (regional press groups)	Entertainment
	VT4**	8.4	Scandinavian Broadcasting System	Entertainment
French	RTL-TV1	19	CLT-UFA (66); Press groups	Generalist
	Club RTL	4.9	CLT-UFA (66); Press groups	Entertainment
	Canal+ Belgique	2	Canal+ (73); RTBf-RMB (26)	Films/Sport
Denmark	TV Danemark	7.8	Scandinavian Broadcasting System	Entertainment
	TV3**	10.3	MTG (Kinnevik)	Entertainment
Finland	MTV 3	42	Alma Media	Generalist/Entertainment
	Nelonen	9	Helsinki Media Company (61); Egmont (25); TS-Group (14)	Entertainment
France	TF1	35.3	Bouygues (40); François Pinault (16); Société Générale (3)	Generalist
	M6	12.9	CLT-UFA (42); Suez-Lyonnaise (35)	General./Music/11 switchovers
	Canal+	4.6	Vivendi (49); Caisse des Dépôts (3.9); Société Générale (1.6)	General./Film/Coded
Germany	RTL	14.9	CLT-UFA (89); BW TV und Film (11)	Generalist/Entertainment
	Sat1	11.8	PKS (Kirch Media GmbH) (44); Axel Springer Verlag (20); Aktuelle Presse-Fernsehen (20); AV Euromedia (15)	Generalist/Drama
	Pro7	8.5	Kirch Media GmbH (58.4); Rewe-Beteiligung Holding (41.6)	Generalist/Films
	Kabel 1	4.4	ProSieben Media AG	Entertainment
	RTL2	3.6	CLT-UFA (35.9); Tele München (32.2); Heinrich Bauer Verlag (32.2)	Generalist
	VOX	2.8	CLT-UFA (99.7); DCTP (0.3)	Entertainment
Greece	Antenna 1	23.6	Broadcasting enterprises	Generalist
	Megachannel	20.7	Teletypos SA	Generalist
	Star Channel	13.4	New-Television Star; Channel SA	Generalist
	Skai	16.3	Greek Satellite TV SA	Generalist/News
Ireland	TV3	5	CanWest Global Com. (45); Paul McGuinness, O. Kilkenny, James Morris (20); Ulster Television	Entertainment

Country	Channel	Audience in 1999 in %	Main Shareholders in %	Program Supply
Italy	Canale 5	20.5	Mediaset (Fininvest, KirchGruppe, AlWeleed)	Generalist/Entertainment
	Rete 4	10.2	Mediaset (Fininvest, KirchGruppe, AlWeleed)	Generalist/Drama
	Italia 1	11.3	Mediaset (Fininvest, KirchGruppe, AlWeleed)	Generalist
	TMC	2.2	Cecchi Gori	Generalist
Luxembourg	RTL Tele Lëtzebuerg	15.5	CLT-UFA (100)	Generalist
Netherlands	RTL4	17.5	CLT-UFA (65)	Generalist
	RTL5	3.8	CLT-UFA (65)	Youth
	Veronica	10.4	HMG (100)	Youth
	SBS6	10.9	Scandinavian Broadcasting System	Generalist
Portugal	SIC	45.9	Impreger (Pinto Balsemão)	Generalist
	TVI	15.8	Media Capital	Generalist
Spain	Antena 3	22.7	Telefonica (49); Recoletos (Pearson) (10); BSCH (29.6)	Generalist
	Tele 5	20.4	Mediaset (49); KirchMedia (25); Correo (25)	Generalist
	Canal+ España	2.7	Prisa (21.27); Canal + (21.7)	Films/Sport
Sweden	TV4	27.1	MTG (Kinnevik)	Generalist
	Kanal 5	5.8	Scandinavian Broadcasting System	Entertainment
	TV3 Sweden**	10.8	MTG (Kinnevik)	Entertainment
United Kingdom	ITV	31.8	Granada Group; Carlton Comm.; United News & Media	Generalist/Regional
	Channel 5	5	CLT-UFA (35.7); United News & Media (35.37); Pearson (29.26)	Generalist/Drama
	Sky One		BskyB	Generalist

* RTL Österreichischer, SAT 1 Österreichischer and PRO7 Österreichischer are Austrian windows of the German channels.

** VT4 (Flanders), TV3 (Denmark) and TV3 (Sweden) operate with a British license.

II   Digitization

With the rapid growth of specialized cable and direct-to-home satellite channels, public television will continue to face aggressive competition. Even with a 'must-carry' provision, guaranteed by the regulator, public television will find it much harder to become visible in such a crowded marketplace. Digitization, interactive new technology, and two-way communication will become more and more important features of the so-called 'transactional television,' be it the relatively successful asymmetric, interactive two-way services or the still elusive 500 satellite channels. Another important development is the building of interconnected superhighways in cyberspace for all kinds of information transmission. Undoubtedly the most significant consequence of digitization, technological convergence between formerly separate industries (telephone, radio, television, computers, and print media) is in favor of television's rivals. On top of it all, it seems that high definition television (HDTV) and broadscreen television – with the emphasis on image quality rather than technical flexibility – will not be able to counter these tendencies in the long run. Digital industries such as telephone and computer are claiming part of television's territory. Still, while television has been losing ground to computers – the Internet is competing for people's leisure time; people also spend more and more time in front of their computer screen playing games, instead of watching their one-way television set – television programs remain in high demand, and television viewing remains the most popular leisure activity (in terms of time spent).

In this respect, Dries & Woldt (1996: 19) seriously question the broadcasters' presumed lack of flexibility in connection with the ambivalence of recent developments in the information and communication sector: "(...) obviously broadcasting (i.e., radio and television) will be by far the most important element of the various services on offer for the foreseeable future. No other medium has the same appeal to the audiences nor the same creative potential." Elkabbach (1996: 49) also believes public television must not be rooted out by the digital changes now underway. Moreover, he sees access to the information highway as critically important for public television: "To exclude public service television from the digital and multimedia worlds is to weaken it and condemn it to decline for short-term political reasons."

Obviously, the Internet can provide alternative ways for packaging and distributing program content and as such fulfil the public service remit: from web-based weekly program listings and on-line news programs to specific on-line programming aimed at targeted user groups, or stock images offered as background material. The EU public broadcasters' strategies have varied accordingly – from developing yet another web-based program guide to planning to become an Internet service provider via the television set, or even using their brand name to create a "portal" from which users can navigate the Internet (Winsbury, 1999). Such moves are viewed as a threat by commercial broadcasters, Internet service providers and cable TV companies planning interactive television services (Hills, 2000), since the Internet activities of public service broadcasters may be an objectionable mix of public and commercial services. In fact the European Commission (1997) itself challenged use of the Internet as an additional means of reaching out to audiences. In October 1999, the British Internet Publishers' Alliance (BIPA) filed a complaint with the Commission concerning the BBC's on-line activities. BIPA seriously questioned the British government's decision that the Internet should be the so-called third arm of broadcasting, next to radio and television (for more details, we refer the reader to the chapter on the United Kingdom in this book).

Table 4. *'Added Value' on Public Television Sites*

Public TV Sites	Hyperlinks	Discussion Groups	Feedback	News/ Archives	Multimedia	Updates
BBC *United* *Kingdom* www.bbc.co.uk	Many; linked to sources in- and outside BBC site; Portal to other web-sites	Chat rooms, forums, voting platform	General e-mail Addresses	News, weather, football, educa-tion, entertain-ment; archive. With search option	Video & audio services	Day of last update
NOS *The Netherlands* www.omroep.nl	Many; linked to sources in- and outside the general PSB site	None	E-mail addresses of all public broadcasting Organizations	Archive of NOS' TV & radio newscasts of past week	Video & audio services	Time and day of last update
VRT *Flanders, Belgium* www.vrt.be	Few; linked to sources inside VRT	None Chat rooms on different site: www.tv1.be	E-mail addresses of all broadcas-ting stations & general e-mail address	Archive available for texts (press reports)	None (only on www.tv1.be)	Not indicated
RTBf *Wallonia,* *Belgium* www.rtbf.be	Few; linked to sources inside RTBf	None	Standardized letter to the webmaster	Archive of TV & radio newscasts	Audio services	Day of last update
ARD-ZDF *Germany* www.ard.de www.zdf.de	Many; linked to sources in- and outside ARD (e.g., travel, finance)	Forum: guest-room	General e-mail addresses	News & archive with search option (e.g., overseas, stocks)	Video & audio services	Day of last update
DR *Denmark* www.dr.dk	Many; linked to sources inside DR	Forum (on-line debates)	General e-mail addresses	Archive with search option	Video & audio services	Time and day of last update
France 2 *France* www.francetv.fr www.france2.fr	Many; linked to sources inside France 2/3 Portal to other web-sites	Chat clubs, forums and voting platform	Standardized letter to the editor	News (e.g., sports, stocks, weather), archive With search option	Video & audio services	Day of last update
RAI *Italy* www.rai.it	Many; linked to sources inside RAI	Forum and chat room	General e-mail address	Multimedia archive with search option	Video and audio services	Day of last update

To illustrate the presence of public broadcasters on the Internet, we conducted a small survey of eight EU public service websites and drew a list of so-called added values such as hyperlinks, archives, and multimedia services (see also Jankowski & van Selm, 2000) offered based on on-line content as opposed to 'linear' broadcast material. The latter added values may enable the broadcaster to tighten its bonds with the audience. In terms of richness of content development (hyperlinks, archival material, multimedia) and interactivity (discussion groups, feedback and updates), the comparison revealed more differences than similarities. Some broadcasters are most concerned with merely providing schedules of their programs, with or without program background content. Others make fuller use of the Internet's specific nature, such as allowing users to send e-mails from their site or designing new, interactive content aimed at a variety of user groups. In terms of news, the bulk of the information pertains to sports and stock listings. The French sites tend to focus more on culture and films than other sites. Not surprisingly, the BBC and the France 2 and 3 sites are among the most attractive, offering the richest content and the highest interactivity. As for the smaller public broadcasters, such as Belgium's VRT and RTBF, they still have a long way to go.

III   What about the Ideological Arguments?

In addition to market and technological changes, public service broadcasting in Western Europe has had to endure fundamental ideological shifts throughout the years. The – often esoteric – arguments used over and over again in debates on its relevance or redundancy, its necessity or obsolescence, have changed significantly over time. When public service broadcasting still enjoyed a monopoly position, it was criticized for being a bulwark of the ruling elite. Moreover, it was seen as somehow linked to the political and economic imperatives ruling capitalism in Western Europe. Yet, with the arrival of commercial stations and new technologies, media critics began to defend the concept of public service broadcasting from an ideological point of view. Structural criticisms were now only leveled at commercial stations. Therefore, in a period characterized by ever-increasing consumer choice, public service broadcasting has become – in a remarkable reversal of its former role as described in the critical media discourse – a paragon of national integration. What used to be criticized as *bourgeois* public television culture was now called 'our' culture, with public channels expected to provide all audience segments with open and equal access to high-quality cultural and information programs. In other words, public service broadcasting was being defended because of its unique integrative function and its ability to operate somehow independently from market imperatives. This vision is somewhat unrealistic: all audience segments cannot be reached if no account is taken of market mechanisms. Moreover, independence has been no more than a pipe dream for public broadcasters, due to, among other things, political interference with personnel management, and programs made by so-called *third parties* to be broadcast during primetime. A market-oriented reflex is absolutely necessary as a minimum audience share is crucial to achieving the aim of open and equal access. Thus audience figures (share and, more recently, reach) and appreciation scores do play a significant role. Voorhoof (1992: 63) considers public service broadcasting as the only efficient means of defense against commercial broadcasting which, because of tight production conditions, is unable to creatively play with the medium: "If one wants to formulate an answer to this reality, one needs to choose a broadcasting service, an audiovisual production context wherein this economic logic is not dominant, a context wherein commercial logic and the aim at maximum profit are absent. (...) The only organization in the audiovisual sector able to realize this is a well-established public service broadcasting (...). A public service, not as a bureaucratic Moloch organizing political interference and severely limiting audiovisual creativity and critical journalism, but a public audiovisual sector which develops a dynamic of its own, which plays an innovative role, creating a space for culture and information."

Nevertheless, a defense of public service broadcasting based on traditional arguments – one monopolistic national medium broadcasting programs for a monolithic, national audience, etc. – has become completely irrelevant, for economic reasons (since the market, at the production and consumption levels, is now both global and local), but also for more political and philosophical ones (since the beginning of the 1980's, media policy has entered the sphere of the European Union; it is no longer the sole preserve of the nation state). Moreover, audience behavior leaves no room for doubt: commercialization and the new media have clearly resulted in a general fragmentation of the market. Ever more suppliers want to reach the same audience. As a result, there is no longer such a thing as a 'general' audience: this is the era of target audience television (a news channel, a sports channel, etc.). Therefore, we believe there is still room for a public service designed to compete in this new, single-genre oriented market. However, the notion of a public service specializing in high-quality information and current affairs and exclusively aimed at certain audience segments (modeled after high-brow newspapers, for instance) seems far too limiting to us.

Translated into a concrete *program supply* for public service broadcasting – even though audience research has often proven the universal appeal of Hollywood's products and most viewers enjoy movies and most men enjoy sports programs – research also shows that there is a lot of variation in people's secondary viewing preferences. This is a huge opportunity for public service broadcasting to avoid the danger of 'erosion' by one-genre channels as predicted by Clemens (1996: 6–7). Audience-wise, public service broadcasting must make sure it does not alienate specific audience groups by pushing them into the arms of the commercial channels. Furthermore, the make-up of a public station's audience needs to reflect as accurately as possible that of the population as a whole, in connection with the profile of the station: a first, second or even a third channel (as is the case in Italy and in the Netherlands).

3.1 In Search of Performance Indicators

As Raboy (1996: 22) points out, "there is no shortage of goodwill or good ideas" with regard to public service broadcasting. Among these were the nine requirements or mandates for public service broadcasting as these were formulated by the fourth European Ministerial Conference on Mass Policy (Council of Europe, 1994). Summarized, the nine mandates include: (1) providing a reference point for all audience members and a factor for social cohesion; (2) providing a forum for public discussion; (3) broadcasting impartial and independent information; (4) developing pluralistic, innovative, and varied, high quality programming; (5) developing programs both for broad audiences and minority groups; (6) reflecting different ideas and beliefs, aiming at mutual understanding; (7) contributing to a greater appreciation of the national and European cultural heritage; (8) scheduling a significant proportion of original productions, especially fiction; (9) offering a program supply which is complementary to that of commercial broadcasters. The problem with these mission statements is that they often bear no relation to reality. In an attempt to break away from ambiguity, Menneer (1996: 16) argues in favor of "cogent, clear and practical criteria on which public broadcasting can be judged (...). Accountability and transparency are, and will remain, the order of the day." Corner (1995: 161–162) makes it clear that the notion of *quality* has always been hotly debated ever since television emerged as a force in public life. Corner (1995) also sketches the evolution of the concept of quality from a purely aesthetic matter (television as a popular art institution) to a way of countering harsh criticism aimed at television (as a "time waster, a cultural invader, a taste debasement, an attitudinal influence and a cognitive impairment"). Over time, quality has come to refer to the notion of taste and lack thereof (e.g., violence and sex, bad language). *Quality* also refers to ways of remedying this by uplifting people's spirits. Finally, another school of thought views quality as a factor enhancing the quality of life of the audience (from a paternalistic vision – giving the people what they need – to a purely mercantile one – giving the people what they want). An eminently relative notion, quality is primarily assessed by the audience (since viewers can switch channels at any time) and it varies according to program genres – which is not to say that the role of public service broadcasting is merely to supply those programs wanted by the audience and to package them to taste. Public service broadcasting must also be a driving force, one which creates space for the experimental and quality programming the entertainment industry is not inclined to offer. Again, such experiments should not be too unusual in order not to scare viewers away: public service broadcasting is at its best when it manages to 'push the envelope' while meeting well-targeted viewer expectations.

IV   Conclusion

Apart from shifts in the media supply, changes in audience composition are also apparent. Distribution channels for media content are increasing in number, boosting the overall supply in the process. Owing to the heterogeneous audience composition and the increase in both distribution channels and media supply, media use is becoming increasingly fragmented. The digitization of cable will free up capacity for theme and target-group channels and pay-per-view services, as a result of which the supply of television, and also that of public television, can only continue to grow. Many households in Europe devote a substantial amount of their viewing time to channels available via satellite. Internet use is also advancing by leaps and bounds. Broadband Internet became available recently via cable or ADSL, allowing moving pictures of (admittedly still low) quality to be carried on-line. The web sites of (public) broadcasters are among the most frequently visited; such sites will probably play a more and more important role as portals and gateways to the information and entertainment sources available on the Internet.

The above-mentioned technological and economic developments are making for ever more intertwined media and telecommunications industries. It logically follows that an overall communications policy is required to integrate these two poles. And such a policy must be implemented throughout Europe, to replace the current and totally inefficient – because they are fragmented – terrestrial, cable and satellite policies. Such an integrated, Europe-wide communication policy would require a forward-looking attitude and appropriate research instruments, with as their driving force one central question: what should be the mission of public broadcasting in a democracy? Technological convergence and the policy debates that go with it can be extremely helpful in trying to establish a workable definition of public service broadcasting: the notion of open/universal access in telecommunications is especially straightforward. What is so different about public service broadcasting is the fact that it tends to consider its audience as a sum of thinking individuals rather than a brain-dead consumer market.

An inescapable conclusion is that public service entails one essential concept which will remain as relevant as ever in an increasingly commercial and digital context: that of *performance*, which goes hand in hand with the notion of *quality*. Quality can be achieved through complementarity with the commercial stations' program supply on the one hand, and open access for all audience groups (not excluding those who cannot afford to buy a decoder or pay a subscription fee) on the other. Complementary research methods will play an ever more decisive role in indicating performance. The various chapters in this book focus on the respective options and resulting performance of the national public broadcasters under scrutiny. But to assess a broadcaster's performance one needs to look at the stability, consistency, and overall reliability of its financing mechanisms. In this respect, a look at the European broadcasting landscape clearly shows (except for Sweden) that the ideal model of a public service funded exclusively by the state no longer exists. Another question has to do with the extent to which broadcasting legislation is *creative*. By creative we mean a consistent, predictable, forward-looking, professional, and responsible media policy characterized by improved, three-way coordination between the regional, national, and European levels.

References

Achille, Y. (1994). *Les télévisions publiques en quête d'avenir.* Grenoble: Presses universitaires de Grenoble.

Avery, R.K. (1993). *Public Service Broadcasting in a Multichannel Environment.* New York: Longman.

British Broadcasting Corporation (1998). *BBC's Response to the Green Paper on Convergence of Telecoms, Media and IT. The Implications for Regulation.* London: BBC.

Clemens, J. (1996). The forces shaping the future, *Diffusion: Quarterly Journal of the European Broadcasting Union*, Summer: 38–41.

Corner, J. (1995). *Television Form and Public Address.* London: Edward Arnold.

Council of Europe (1994). *The Media in a Democratic Society.* Political Declaration, Resolutions and Statement, 4th European Ministerial Conference on Mass Media Policy. Prague, December 7–8, MCM(94)20.

Dries, J. & Woldt, R. (1996). *The Role of Public Service Broadcasting in the Information Society. A Contribution to the EBU Conference 'An Information Society for All.'* Düsseldorf: The European Institute for the Media.

Elkabbach, J.-P. (1996). French public television – a total commitment, *Diffusion: Quarterly Journal of the European Broadcasting Union*, Summer: 49–52.

European Commission (1997). *Green Paper on the Convergence of the Telecommunications, Media and Information Technology Sectors, and the Implications for Regulation. Towards an Information Society Approach.* Brussels: COM (1997) 623 final, December 3.

d'Haenens, L. (1996a). Arts programmes on public television. An analysis of cognitive and emotional viewer reactions, *European Journal of Communication* 11 (2): 147–172.

d'Haenens, L. (1996b). Réalisation, réception et recherche. Optimiser le dialogue communicateur-téléspectateur: un rôle pour le chercheur, *Réseaux* 77: 117–141.

d'Haenens, L. & Heuvelman, A. (1996). The researcher as a mediator between public broadcaster and audience. Some European experiences, *Communications. The European Journal of Communication Research* 21 (1): 297–315.

Hills, J. (2000). The Internet: A challenge to public service broadcasting?, *Gazette. The International Journal for Communication Studies* 62 (6): 477–494.

Jankowski, N.W. & van Selm, M. (2000). Traditional news media online: An examination of added values, *Communications. The European Journal of Communication Research* 25 (1): 85–101.

Menneer, P. (1996). Performance indicators: A candidate top 20, *Diffusion: Quarterly Journal of the European Broadcasting Union*, Spring: 16–20.

Michalis, M. (1999). European Union broadcasting and telecoms: Towards a convergent regulatory regime?, *European Journal of Communication* 14 (2): 147–171.

Raboy, M. (1994). The role of the public in broadcasting policymaking and regulation: Lesson for Europe from Canada, *European Journal of Communication* 9 (1): 5–23.

Raboy, M. (1996). Public service broadcasting in the context of globalization. In M. Raboy (ed.), *Public Broadcasting for the 21ˢᵗ Century.* Luton: University of Luton Press (Acamedia Monograph 17).

Voorhoof, D. (1992). Mediarecht, omroep en business: deregulering en schijnregulering [Media law, broadcasting and business: Deregulation and pseudo-regulation]. In S. Gutwirth (ed.), *Recht: Schijn en Werkelijkheid [Law: Appearances and Reality].* Ghent: Mys & Breesch.

Winsbury, R. (1999). Public space on the Internet: An on-line search for a PSB portal into the twenty-first century, *Intermedia* 27(3): 14–20.

Digital Convergence
The Development of a New Media Market in Europe

by Leen d'Haenens and Susan Bink

I Introduction

We are currently witnessing a phenomenon of *convergence*. This means that old media systems such as radio, television and the telephone will eventually melt together as one single infrastructure. In future we will only be using one appliance, instead of several. In other words, a process of convergence is occurring between the formerly separate broadcasting, information, and telecommunication sectors. This is due to two central factors: technological advances in transmission techniques and the process of market deregulation. For the first time digital technology is making it possible for moving pictures, sound and text (data) to be transmitted worldwide over one single medium, without any loss of clarity (McKenna, 2000). This development is bound to bring about huge complications: consumers must be prepared for and get used to various pieces of equipment, physical connections need to be changed from analogue to digital (*decoding*), regulations will need adjustment to the new situation – in other words, the whole market will change completely. The deregulation of national communication markets is leading to individual national markets becoming part of a global market. This will be oligopolistic in nature, where corporations tend not to find it in their interest to compete on price, opting instead for cunning service packages making comparisons with rival services difficult. While this will not happen overnight, the pace of technological change is speeding up so that new digital developments will be entering our living room within a few years.

The Human Development Report (1999) cites the time new technologies have taken from inception to achieve fifty million users (defined as widespread acceptance). Radio reached this number of users in thirty-eight years, the personal computer in sixteen years, television in thirteen years, while it has taken only four years for the World Wide Web to attract fifty million people worldwide. Nowadays, NUA Internet surveys reports that there are 407.1 million users throughout the world, as of November 2000. In other words, the Internet is undoubtedly the fastest-growing communication tool we have known so far.

The Internet can be considered as the forerunner of these new developments. Already it has begun to merge with older services: radio (web-radio), television (web-TV), and cellular phones (WAP). Another major development is the switch from analogue to digital transmissions. A channel that is used to carry a single analogue service can carry up to seven higher quality digital services by satellite or cable or four terrestrially broadcast programs. Digital television has a lot of benefits for viewers: increased program choice, new services (pay-per-view, video-on-demand, electronic program guides, interface with the Internet, etc.) and better picture quality. But there is also the burden of costs: new equipment, subscriptions, increase in license fees to finance the construction of new networks.

These new technological developments bring with them new possibilities. The new media technologies are better suited to meet the personal needs of consumers, as shown by the emergence of local services, open channels, and channels for ethnic, religious and sexual minorities. One inevitable consequence of this is of course increased audience fragmentation, since consumers can now thoroughly customize their 'viewing menu.'

This chapter takes a look at recent developments in the various EU countries and their impact on the European media market, including consumers, and attempts to predict future orientations in the media world.

II   Comparative Research in Europe: Different Countries, Different Environments

In conducting comparative research, facts and figures referring to the amount of time people spend with particular media need to be carefully interpreted in the context of the available media and the policies which regulate them. They also need to be interpreted in the context of a wide range of cultural factors which frame the everyday lives of Europeans in different countries. For while European countries differ in media provision, these differences are in turn partly explained by national wealth or socio-economic indicators and partly by differing 'lifestyles' at all levels, from individual domestic practices to national policy matters (Livingstone, d'Haenens & Hasebrink, 2001).

2.1 Demographic Context

Population-wise (table 1), Europe includes five largish countries (France, Germany, the United Kingdom, Italy, and Spain), the largest being Germany with some 82 million inhabitants. Looking at population density, the Netherlands is the most crowded, followed closely by Belgium (with a population density equal to that of Japan) and then by three of the big five: the United Kingdom, Germany, and Italy. The least crowded countries are Sweden and Finland.

In terms of Gross Domestic Product (GDP) per capita in purchasing power (table 1), Greek, Portuguese, and Spanish families rank among the poorest, followed by Swedish, Finnish, Italian, and British households (lower than average income levels). Conversely, Danish, Austrian, Belgian and Luxembourg households are among the wealthiest (Livingstone, d'Haenens & Hasebrink, 2001).

Table 1. *Population Characteristics and National Wealth*

	Total Population (000s)	Urban Pop. as % of total	Population Density (Inhabitants/sq. km)	Real GDP per Capita in PPP$
Austria	8,140	65	97	23,166
Belgium	1,014	97	332	22,223
Denmark	5,270	86	122	24,218
Finland	5,154	64	15	20,847
France	58,683	75	106	21,175
Germany	82,133	87	230	22,169
Great Britain	58,649	89	240	20,336
Greece	10,600	60	80	13,943
Ireland	3,681	58	52	21,482
Italy	57,369	67	190	20,585
Luxembourg	422	90	163	33,505
Netherlands	15,678	89	384	22,176
Portugal	9,869	37	107	14,701
Spain	39,628	77	79	16,212
Sweden	8,875	83	20	20,659

Source Population: http://www.unicef.org (last update, 01/12/99, United Nations Population Division).
Source Urbanization: Human Development Report 2000, data from 1998.
Source Population Density: http://www.undp.org/popin/wdtrends/p98/fp98.htm, United Nations, Department of Economic and Social Affairs.
Note: GDP = Gross domestic product; PPP$ = purchasing power parities in US$, based on comparisons among prices of consumer goods.
Source: Human Development Report 2000, data from 1998.

2.2 Media Environments Across Europe

One important commonality of European broadcasting systems – and one in marked contrast with the United States – is that European broadcasting landscapes are organized as 'dual systems' with public service broadcasters not just being a supplement to commercial, but a major (and until recently, the only) pillar of the broadcasting system. However, this is also the only great similarity between European countries, as the overall picture is one of diversity. European media environments are shaped by the characteristics of the respective media markets. We can group countries according to three criteria: the size of the language markets, technical infrastructure, and the distribution of new technologies.

For media products language plays a significant role: the greater the number of native speakers of a given language, the bigger the potential market for media products in this language. As a result one may expect media environments serving larger language communities to provide more options than those serving smaller communities. In addition, and for the same reasons, imported television programs in countries with large language markets are usually dubbed, while in other countries they are usually subtitled. In each of the five major countries (Germany, Spain, France, United Kingdom and Italy) the vast majority of television channels available are thus broadcast in the national language. As shown by other studies (e.g., Eurobarometer 1994), in these countries knowledge of foreign languages is lower than in the other group, with smaller language communities (Belgium-Flanders, Denmark, Finland, the Netherlands and Sweden).

In the 1980's and early 1990's the development of television in European countries was influenced by the technical infrastructure, the main factor in that period being cable distribution. Due to marked differences in cable policies, the quantity of television channels available differs considerably across Europe. For example, in Belgium and the Netherlands – small countries with the highest population density in Europe – cable technology has represented an appropriate means of broadcast distribution; almost 100% of the television households in these countries are connected to cable. Switzerland and Germany also have high cable density. In these four countries most viewers live in a multi-channel environment with more than 23 channels available on average (IP, 1998). The key difference between Belgium and the Netherlands on the one hand and Germany and Switzerland on the other is that in the latter the majority of channels available are in the national language. More channels means more variation, but also possibly more inequality across households within countries with many channels. Scandinavian countries have experienced a rapid growth of channel availability by cable and especially by satellite over the last few years. But there are significant differences between those countries with a high number of channels available. For instance, in Belgium and the Netherlands fewer than half of the channels available are national channels. This contrasts with the situation in Sweden and Finland, where there are fewer channels available and a stronger focus on national channels. In Italy and Spain, cable and satellite reception is relatively rare. The United Kingdom and France are experiencing a rapid growth of satellite as well as cable distribution, but nevertheless their figures are far below those of the other countries we discuss here (Livingstone, d'Haenens & Hasebrink, 2001).

2.2.1 Distribution of New Technologies

In order to assess the preparedness of different countries for the demands of a networked society, the World Economic Forum (2000) published a ranking of countries (the *Current Competitiveness Index Ranking*) based on number of phone lines, mobile phones, television density, cable and satellite connections, PC penetration and the overall maturity of business use of new technologies. Seven European countries are in the top ten: Finland (*1st*), Germany (*3rd*), the Netherlands (*4th*), Switzerland (*5th*), Denmark (*6th*), Sweden (*7th*), and the United Kingdom (*8th*). An intermediate group includes Belgium (*12th*), Austria (*13th*), and France (*15th*), while Spain (*23rd*), Italy (*24th*), and Portugal (*28th*) seem to be less well prepared for the information society.

Rogers (1995) provides us with a model of the diffusion process which helps to make sense of these differences. His model focuses on the relative speed with which an innovation is adopted, measured in terms of the length of time required for a certain percentage of potential users to adopt. Most adoption rates are S-shaped. However, variations occur in the slope of the 'S.' When the diffusion takes place relatively rapidly, then the S-curve is quite steep. Conversely, a more gradual S-curve is indicative of a slower diffusion process. The S-shaped diffusion curve 'takes off' at between 10 to 25% adoption, when interpersonal networks become activated so that a critical mass of users starts to develop. This critical mass is achieved when a sufficient number of individuals have become users, ensuring that the innovation's further rate of adoption becomes self-sustaining. Before this happens, the rate of adoption is slow. Afterwards it starts to accelerate.

The model identifies five adopter categories, which map on to the diffusion of innovation curve, depending on how late or early individuals become users. First to take up the new medium are the 'innovators,' those few venturesome individuals who are able to cope with uncertainty and willing to accept early setbacks. They represent the first 2.5% of adopters in Rogers's system. Next come the 'early adopters:' this group consists of respected opinion leaders, and represents the addition of a further 13.5% of users in Rogers's model. At a later stage still the 'early majority' become users. Such individuals are not opinion leaders, but represent an important stage in the adoption process, as they make up a third of the total system. Next come the 'late majority,' skeptical individuals who require convincing and who constitute a further third of the total system. Finally we are left with the 'laggards,' the recalcitrant sixth of the total system who are traditionalists, suspicious of innovations.

The fact that old and new media emerged in very different policy climates may explain why such unequal access to computers and advanced telecommunications infrastructure has occurred across the various European countries. The diffusion of old media was supported by universal and public service policies, whereas the new media have been emerging in times of privatization, with heavily indebted governments leaving the development of the necessary infrastructure almost entirely to the market (see e.g., Van Dijk, 1999). However the new, interactive media are considerably more expensive than older media, since, among other things, they become obsolete at a much faster rate and constantly require ever more powerful equipment and software (see Van Dijk, 1999; Loader, 1998). As a result, Mike Holderness (1995), amongst many others, has identified a direct link between nations' ability to become connected and to gather and disseminate information on the one hand, and their material position on the other hand (expressed in GNP per capita, for instance). "For the vast majority of the world's population, the possibility of constructing virtual identities is entirely dependent upon their material situation. Clearly most people are not free to choose but instead are subject to a variety of social and economic conditions which act to structure and articulate their opportunities for action" (Loader, 1998: 10).

III   The Development of the Information Society

The development of the Information Society, or Knowledge Economy, has been an economic and political priority for EU Member States during the last years. The emergence of the Internet as a new economic and cultural paradigm signals the arrival of a 'new economy' as a source of economic growth and societal development. Across Europe, economists, industrialists, and politicians alike are recognizing that if Europe is to take full advantage of this development it needs to be globally competitive in Information and Communication Technology (ICT) markets and industries.

But Europe is falling behind the US and Japan in most ICT sectors. It is lagging in the field of productivity/efficiency software and IT services. In communication and network services, Europe still has problems in broadband local access, and in switching and transmission equipment, European providers are losing ground to more agile and fast growing US competitors. At the same time, the experience with mobile communications has shown that Europe can build global leadership positions. Early and open competition, industry wide standardization (GSM) and other factors have made mobile communications services in Europe into the world's largest and fastest growing market. But then again, European Internet penetration stands at one fourth of US levels and Europe still accounts for only a small portion of the world's e-commerce market. Even more worrying is the emergence of a digital divide within Europe: while Scandinavian countries approach US penetration and spending levels, markets in Southern Europe are much less developed and are growing slower – in other words, the gap is widening (Ministry of Economic Affairs, 2000).

3.1 Mobile Communications

Europe has a world-leading position in mobile communications. But as in so many ICT sectors, European averages conceal a wide disparity across Europe, with 65% of Finns using a mobile phone compared to just 26% of Germans. These penetration differences are often explained by a relative lack of competitiveness and therefore high prices. In the case of telecommunications, things have changed since 1998. The deregulation of much of the European telecommunications services sector since then opened the way for interconnect agreements between incumbent operators and the entry of new players building pan-European, data-optimized networks of huge capacity. But with so much progress in the long distance market, local access has now become the crucial bottleneck to development. The next generation of telecommunications and internet services – including multimedia, streaming video and interactive television – all require broadband connections to the business or residential user. To date, just five countries have deregulated the local loop (home connection). While cable operators are beginning to make their presence felt in the market, too many are still owned by the state incumbent. The US is forging ahead, but Europe is still in the starting blocks (Ministry of Economic Affairs, 2000).

3.2 Internet

While always lagging far behind those in the US, European Internet penetration figures show that Europe has now definitely taken to the Net. In July 2000, 94 million people were connected in Europe (NUA Internet Survey, 2000). Owing to the high growth of Internet adoption in Europe, any research soon becomes out of date and estimates of the numbers on-line are inevitably inexact as surveys abound and very different measures are used. Table 2 shows that Internet use differs widely between European countries: Scandinavia, the Netherlands and the United Kingdom are 'early adopters.' Northern European countries are clearly the leaders in the field, at a more advanced stage in the diffusion process both for the Internet and computers in general. The Netherlands, and the United Kingdom are following at close range, but Spain and Portugal (the 'late majority') have a lot of catching up to do. The gap between leaders such as Sweden and Finland, with levels of penetration approaching those in the US, and the Southern European countries with less than 10% Internet penetration, is widening. The specter of a 'two speed' Europe in terms of Internet access appears to be fast becoming a reality (Ministry of Economic Affairs, 2000).

Table 2. *Number of Internet Users*

Country	Date of Survey	Users (000s)	% Population	Source
Austria	03/2000	1,850	22.7	AIM
Belgium	03/2000	2,000	19.6	InSites
Denmark	10/1999	1,900	35.5	CyberScan
Finland	02/2000	2,150	41.6	Taloustukimus Oy
France	03/2000	9,000	15.3	AFA
Germany	03/2000	15,900	19.4	GfK
Greece	10/1999	1,330	12.4	IDC Research
Ireland	07/2000	819	21.6	Nielsen NetRatings
Italy	07/2000	11,160	20.1	Between ICT Brokers
Luxembourg	02/1999	86	19.7	ILReS
Netherlands	02/2000	4,500	28.5	ProActive
Portugal	07/2000	700	7.0	ITU
Spain	12/1999	3,625	9.3	AIMC
Sweden	12/1999	3,950	44.3	Computer Industry Almanac
United Kingdom	07/2000	1,947	32.7	Nielsen NetRatings

Overall sources: NUA Internet Surveys – *How many on-line?* (www.nua.ie)
European Audiovisual Observatory – *Statistical Yearbook 2000*

The Internet opens up a lot of new possibilities, mainly due to the rapid rise of e-mail and the World Wide Web. People can get in touch in seconds with friends located on the other side of the globe, purchasing goods through the Internet is an increasingly practical proposition, the information accessible on the World Wide Web is more than plentiful, and the downloading of music is the order of the day. Consumers make use of the Internet under different circumstances and with different purposes. Internet users can be divided into two categories:

- *Recreation seekers*: users looking for games, recreational sites and other forms of entertainment – and who view the Internet itself as a form of entertainment per se, and
- *Information seekers*: users looking for information (usually for professional purposes) – engineers, students, journalists, advisors, researchers, managers, salespeople, etc.

Recreation seekers and information seekers will often be the same person, but under different circumstances: at home, looking for relaxation, versus at work, looking for relevant information. This distinction is related to the original difference between television and the PC (entertainment versus information). Although this distinction is fading, television can be considered as a 'ten foot space,' which implies a passive attitude on the part of the user, while the PC would be a 'three foot space' which implies active involvement (Van den Hooff & Schoenman, 1997).

A look at the penetration rates shows that things are changing very fast. Scandinavian countries are obviously the forerunners in the Internet race, but Southern countries are attempting to catch up. According to a recent NetValue survey, Spanish Internet users are the most active in Europe. Recent key Internet results (November 2000), covering the UK, Spain, Denmark, France, and Germany showed that the average Spanish Internet user spends 8.1 hours per month on-line (as compared with Denmark, the leading country in terms of Internet penetration, where the average user stays on-line for only 4.5 hours per month). The survey indicates that Spain is a rapidly developing Internet market. Currently, 12% of the Spanish population have access to the Internet, half of which (46.2%) have been connected to the Net for less than a year. As for Italy, it has now 12 million Internet users (21% of the population), up from 8.6 million a year ago, and according *Between ICT Brokers*, an Italian Internet research company, the figure will be 16 million by September 2001. The majority of new users in 2000 were women, although there are still 2.6 Italian men on-line for every female user.

So, it is almost impossible to keep up with the growth of Internet users. As for the Web itself, there are many estimates of how many new sites are appearing. Some claim they double every few months while others come up with at least one site every minute. The truth is, no one really knows how quickly the Web is growing. The only certainty is that it is growing fast (Feldman, 1997). With more people on-line, more platforms for on-line access, and increased use, the Internet in Europe is quickly becoming an integral part of everyday life.

IV   From Analogue to Digital Transmission: Digitization in Europe

The electronic superhighway consists of three subdivisions: *transport infrastructure* (cable, telephone-system, satellite, etc.), *services* (pay-TV, Internet, electronic pay-services, etc.) and *peripheral equipment* (PC, television, telephone, modem, etc.), by which providers and consumers of these electronic facilities communicate with each other. The last few years the different technologies are entering one another's territory. This *convergence* of technologies is expected to increase in the future. Various systems will provide us with the same services. New services will include features formerly thought of as belonging to the telecommunications or the information sectors (multimedia). These services can be offered via different channels: telephone cables, cable television networks, broadcasting networks, or electronic networks. The uses to which TV and the personal computer can be put are overlapping more and more.

Markets are subject to convergence too. Cooperation, mergers, alliances and takeovers between different companies in telecommunications and multimedia are the order of the day. Only a few companies are strong enough and have the knowledge and finances to be successful on their own in this changing technological environment. Other companies decide to join forces and face the new market possibilities together. Vertical integration can accomplish the desirable parallelism in the development of infrastructures and services.

4.1 Digital Broadcasting

Digital broadcasting for radio and television is a new transmission system which uses computer technology instead of standard (analogue) signals. It converts sounds and pictures in computerized digits, which are transmitted through the air by modified transmitters. The digits can be received on standard aerials, on satellite dishes, or via cable, but have to be decoded back into analogue signals. This is done by a special device which is either standalone (set-top box) or built-in the TV or radio (an 'integrated' set). Digital broadcasting means that many more TV and radio channels can be transmitted than before, each with high quality pictures and crystal clear sound. With the right equipment it also becomes possible to use interactive services such as on-screen shopping, banking, internet access, and e-mail. Interactive television can change the way some programs are watched – for example, sports coverage can be viewed from different camera angles and customized action replays can be created by using the remote control. Digital technology is already a part of people's every day lives – e-mails can be sent and the weekly shopping done via the TV, TV programs can be watched on the PC, interactive TV programs are a fact, and the new WAP (Wireless Application Protocol) technology now brings the internet to the mobile phone.

Since early 1996 the EU's digital TV market has, on the whole, enjoyed a relatively high growth rate. In Europe digital television is based on a series of standards laid down by the Digital Video Group (DVB). One of the DVB Group's pivotal choices was to adopt the MPEG-2 standard for audio and video coding. The DVB Group also set out the standards for digital satellite broadcasting (DVB-S) (December 1993), digital cable broadcasting (DVB-C) (March 1994) and digital terrestrial broadcasting (DVB-T) (December 1995). The main specifications were normalized by the ETSI (European Telecommunications Standards Institute), while European Directive 95/47 on the transmission of signals by cable and satellite made their use compulsory within the European Union. This Directive set up a light regulatory framework to support the launch of digital television services, providing certainty for investors, and ensuring that public interests requirements were met (Lange, 1999).

On December 9, 1998, the European Commission launched a new consultation process, publishing *The Green Paper on Policy on the radio-electric spectrum, taken within the context of Community Policies on telecommunications, broadcasting, transport and research and development.* The report contains the following observations on digital terrestrial broadcasting:

> The digitization of terrestrial broadcasting would potentially allow for reduced radio spectrum occupancy for existing broadcast services, thereby freeing up radio spectrum. However, it is very likely that in many countries, a lengthy transition period to digital will be needed. Consumers will need time to replace their radio sets. They will also need to purchase one or more decoders to upgrade their analogue TV sets or to buy one or more new integrated digital TV sets. A period of 'simulcasting' will therefore be necessary (of anything up to 15 years) and this will in fact put additional strains on the availability of radio spectrum. Moreover, the range of broadcast services is already increasing rapidly, with more Near-Video-On-Demand (NVOD), thematic channels and interactive TV becoming available. On the other hand, as TV and transactional, retail style delivery of programs 'on demand,' and wireless communications evolve towards multimedia, the terms for access to spectrum which terrestrial broadcasters currently enjoy are increasingly being called into question by economic actors in other sectors (...) (COM(98)596: Annex I: III).

The digitization of TV services available via satellite is now approaching 100%, that is to say that:

- almost all TV channels available in Europe via satellite are broadcast in digital standard. In Germany, only ten TV stations continued to broadcast exclusively in analogue standard in 1999.
- dual illumination (analogue/digital simulcast) is nevertheless still the dominant approach for satellite services.

What constitutes a significant change since the end of 1997 is the distinct trend toward digitization of cable and terrestrial networks (Meyer & Fontaine, 2000).

4.1.1 The Introduction of Digital Terrestrial Broadcasting in the EU Member States

Current reception systems in the various European Member States are highly heterogeneous and this, naturally enough, affects the way in which digital television is beginning to be introduced. An overview can be given by splitting the market up into four categories according to state of development:

- Countries where cable is the main form of television reception (> 80% of TV households with cable subscriptions): Belgium, the Netherlands.
- Countries where, as well as cable reception, there is also a significant growth in satellite reception (> 50% of multi-channel households): Austria, Germany, Denmark, Ireland, Sweden.
- Countries where cable and satellite reception are still in the development stage (between 15 and 50 households are 'multi-channel') and where terrestrial reception is the only television reception system for 50 to 85% of households: Spain, Finland, France, the United Kingdom, Luxembourg, Portugal.
- Countries where growth in cable and satellite reception remains insignificant (> 5%) and where terrestrial reception is the only form of reception: Greece, Italy.

In theory, it can be supposed that consumer interest, and therefore operator interest, for digital terrestrial television (DTT) should show where cable/satellite reception is at its lowest, in other words the two latter categories (Lange, 1999).

With the significant and notable exception of the UK, digital terrestrial television got off to a disappointing start worldwide more than a year after launches in North America and Europe in November 1998. DTT was overshadowed by the phenomenal growth of digital satellite, the aggressive launch of digital cable, ambitious interactive and e-commerce services (primarily on other digital TV platforms), the promise of imminent, true video-on-demand over cable and DSL, growth of more attractive consumer products such as hard-disk storage set-top boxes and DVD players, as well as the seemingly unstoppable rise of the Internet. Were it not for the UK, it would be all too easy to write off DTT as a non-starter. With 552,000 subscribers just over a year after launch, UK commercial operator Ondigital is the only unqualified success story in DTT's brief history. Yet despite these initial setbacks, the future for DTT still bodes reasonably well. DTT operators are gearing up in the Netherlands (Digitenne) and Ireland (Digico), whilst concessions have been or are likely to be made to commercial broadcasters in Finland, Germany, Italy and Belgium. France alone has indicated that DTT will primarily be used for free-to-air transmissions, as a tool for giving the French population access to the 'information society,' whilst countries with high cable penetration (Germany and the Netherlands) stress future mobile and data DTT services (Screen Digest, 2000).

The introduction of digital television depends on the competitive environment of the market. If the market is quite stable, then it is easier to introduce rational strategies for the introduction of digital television. This is the case in the United Kingdom, Ireland

and Finland, where the development of digital television is working out quite smoothly. In the UK, there has been a tradition of fair competition between terrestrial broadcasting channels, and the frequencies for digital broadcasting has been divided between the BBC, ITV, ON-digital, Channel 4, Channel 5 and the Welsh channel S4C. The BBC controls a multiplex channel on its own, ITV and Channel 4 own a multiplex channel together, and Channel 5 as well as S4C have access to another multiplex channel. In Finland the competition has always been fair between the public channel YLE and the biggest private channel (now MTV3). Both broadcasters have been involved in plans concerning the introduction of digital television in the year 2000. Digital television in Ireland has been the subject of controversy between 1998–99. But the overall opinion is to speed up the introduction of digital television to face the increasing influence of British digital programs broadcast by satellite.

Table 3. *Launch of Digital Terrestrial Television (DTT) in Europe 2000–2003*

Country	Launch Date	Initial Coverage	Initial DTT Operators	DTT Transmitters in Operation	
				Early 2000	At End Year 1
Austria	2002<	-	-	3 (tests)	-
Belgium	2000-2001	-	RTBF/VRT/Canal+	-	2
Denmark	2001	-	-	2 (tests)	3
Finland	27/08/2001	50%	YLE/MTV/Canal+/ City TV/Helsinki Media	4	15
France	2001	60-80%	TDF, France Télévision	4	9
Germany	2000-2001	Urban areas	NDR, Deutsche Telekom	15 (tests)	58 (tests)
Ireland	2001	75-95%	Digico	-	-
Italy	2000-2003	60%	RAI, TELE+, Elettronica Industriale	3	8
Netherlands	2000-2001	-	Digitenne	2	28
Portugal	2000-2001	-	Portugal Telecom	3	-
Spain	05/2000	52%	Quiero	44	180
Sweden	1/04/1999	50%	Canal+, MTG	51	90-110
United Kingdom	15/11/1998	70-90%	ONDigital	378	492

Source: European Audiovisual Observatory – *Statistical Yearbook 2000*

In those Member States where digital television is now well established, development of the range of digital television services has depended on a strong pay-television market. The range of services has developed rapidly towards transactional services and new services, including Internet and home banking in particular where there were competing pay-television platforms. Table 3 shows that in Sweden and Spain a relatively high number of DTT transmitters are in operation. France has been conducting some of the most extensive tests for DTT in Europe, and Germany is also conducting tests in its urban areas. But regional responsibility for broadcasting regulation complicates the situation in Germany. In the Netherlands and Belgium, the launch of digital terrestrial television is seen as a possible way of putting an end to the cable distributors' monopoly. Such a decision, however, is liable to run up against opposition not only from the cable distributors, but also from other local interests involved in the cable industry. In the case of Belgium, further complications arise due to its linguistic/cultural division that sees the French-language public broadcaster (RTBF) participating in DTT trials with Canal Plus, but not the Flemish one (VRT). Austria remains one of the most backward DTT countries in Europe, with no frequency plan, spectrum overcrowding, and plans to launch new analogue channels. Limited technical DTT trials have been launched, however (Lange, 1999; Screen Digest, 2000).

Some countries have already set 2010 as the year of the 'switch-off' of the analogue terrestrial transmission: France, Germany, Italy, the Netherlands, Spain and Sweden. But according to experts, this date is over-optimistic, because it takes a long time for a country's whole population to switch to DTT equipment, especially among the under-privileged. Unless broadcasters are willing to abandon free over-the-air television in favor of satellite, cable and DSL platforms, analogue television is set to remain a fact around the globe for at least another 10 to 25 years.

4.1.2 Financing

Financing issues with respect to the switch to digital TV are of prime importance. Digital technology provides new opportunities for the whole of the television system to benefit from new sources of revenue (pay-TV, pay-per-view, prospective revenue from new services, etc.), but it also brings with it fresh costs:

- increased transmission costs (dual – analogue/digital – broadcasting, either terrestrial or by satellite);
- launch of new services (new TV channels, pay-per-view, Internet, etc.);
- increase in programming budgets.

Traditional television revenue sources (public money, especially the license fee, advertising) have only increased slightly over the last few years and they may well soon reach their upper limits. As for pay-TV revenues, they have been the main source of growth in the last few years, but that growth could stop at any moment.

Growth of the television sector in the European Union in 1993–1997 was around 40%. This is not equally divided according to years and types of broadcasters. The biggest earners are Pay-TV channels, but their performance flagged in 1996. 1997 is the year of highest growth for the overall industry (+11%) due to a increased public service revenue (mainly explained by the substantial growth of Channel 4 and TV2 Denmark advertising revenue, as well as increased license fee revenue for BBC and ZDF) (see table 4).

Table 4. *Evolution of Television Revenue in Europe – 1993–1997 (€million)*

	1993	1994	1995	1996	1997	1997/1993
Public service (incl. radio)	18,394	19,270 5%	19,550 1%	20,389 4%	22,459 9%	22%
Traditional commercial channels	10,153	11,580 14%	13,040 13%	13,852 6%	14,899 8%	47%
Pay-TV channels	2,255	2,951 31%	3,731 26%	4,559 22%	5,740 26%	155%
Total EUR 15	30,802	33,801 10%	36,321 7%	38,801 7%	43,098 11%	40%

Source: Lange (1999)

By cross-comparing the size of the TV channel editing and distribution market with the extent of advertising-based financing of the sector, it is possible to break down the Member States into four categories:

- 'Big' countries, where there is diversity in the methods of financing and where subscription plays an important role, pointing to a degree of 'maturity' of the market. These are France, the United Kingdom, and Germany.
- 'Medium-sized' countries where financing methods are gradually diversifying: Spain and Italy.
- 'Small' countries where financing is also fairly diversified but usually based more on license fees than on direct financing through subscriptions: Belgium, the Netherlands, Scandinavian countries, Austria, and Ireland.
- 'Small' countries where 75% of TV funding is derived from advertising revenues: Luxembourg, Portugal, and Greece.

Throughout Europe, the economic model chosen for digital TV is the same as for Pay-TV. Platform operators view subscriptions and rented or subsidized decoders as the business model that is the best suited to the rapid extension of their services and the growing number of new digital thematic channels. Therefore, subscription to a digital TV service is still the main source of funding for digital TV in Europe (Meyer & Fontaine, 2000).

4.1.3 European Satellite System Operators

Since 1996, Digital Satellite Broadcasting covers the whole EU territory, mainly thanks to the Astra and Eutelsat satellite systems. SES-Astra's satellite system appears to be the

European leader in the provision of digital satellite broadcasting capabilities for TV channels and Pay-TV platform providers. Astra supplies satellite broadcasting capacities to six European digital Pay-TV operators and three free-to-air digital TV platform operators. The number of DTV services broadcast through Astra has risen to more than 400 (85 of which are digital free-to-air services). To meet the rising demand for digital satellite services, SES/Astra has scheduled the launch of two additional satellites (Astra 2C and 2D) between the end of 2000 and the first half of 2001. Eutelsat – which is in charge of signal transport for six European digital Pay-TV operators and one free-to-air digital TV platform operator – comes in a close second. Eutelsat delivers more than 450 DTV channels to Europe, North Africa and the Middle East. The Hispasat (Spain, Portugal), Thor and Intelsat (both Scandinavian countries) satellite systems play a marginal role in digital satellite TV broadcasting in the European Union (Meyer & Fontaine, 2000).

4.1.4 Interactive Television

Interactive television (i-TV) is the coming together of television and new interactive technology. It is domestic television with interactive features usually funneled in through a 'back channel' and/or advanced terminal. In other words, it provides added value to content by making it possible for viewers to interact with it, empowering them to use television in new ways. There are many delivery systems and technical standards, and potential uses and content are plentiful. These range from the WWW to home shopping, Digital Video Broadcasting to Internet, on-demand movies to video telephony. The unifying factor is the TV set that is central to the entertainment, education, information, leisure and social life of millions of homes all over the world.

The first port of call for i-TV users is the Electronic Program Guide (EPG), an electronic directory for advanced multi-channel television and interactive TV. It is a sophisticated interface program installed in the set top box (STB) or television set that will enable users to search and select programs interactively. It can be considered an essential part of new digital TV services and an important tool for developing and testing mass market interfaces for interactive TV. This remains a controversial matter in commercial and regulatory terms, as it acts as a gateway for the TV services, causing some broadcasters to worry that the company that controls (e.g., subsidizes) the STB will develop an EPG that favors particular programs.

V   The Shift from Regulation to open Competition

At a December 1993 meeting the European Council requested a panel of experts to report into the specific measures to be taken into consideration by the Community and the Member States regarding the necessary infrastructure needed in the sphere of information. The minutes of this meeting state that the main risk of the widespread availability of new information tools and services lies in the creation of a two-tier society of have and have-nots. Ways must be found to minimize risks and maximize benefits. This places responsibilities on public authorities to establish safeguards and ensure the cohesion of the 'new' society. Fair access to the infrastructure must be guaranteed for all. The key issue regarding the emergence of new markets is the need for a new regulatory environment allowing full competition (McKenna, 2000).

With digital technology altering transmission systems in fundamental ways and resulting in a compulsion to build a Global Information Infrastructure, the regulatory framework – once considered nothing short of crucial – is now viewed as mostly outdated and unnecessary. The new 'philosophical' approach is to leave free rein to so-called 'free and fair' competition in open markets – the main control mechanism being general legislation on competition. But there is a very real danger that a few transnational corporations (broadcasting, telecommunications, IT) will extend their influence in converging sectors, nipping in the bud any potential competition. Future corporations will be able to control the transmission of all basic communication products: voice, data and video. Therefore, several proposed mergers and joint ventures within the broadcasting industry (MSG, HMG and NSD cases) were prohibited under the Merger Control Regulation (1997), on grounds that they were incompatible with the common market and in particular would have created or strengthened dominant positions in upstream, downstream or related markets. Rachel Oldroyd (1999: 3) argues: "At stake is the prize of controlling all the electronic information and entertainment, including telephone, television, Internet access and interactive digital services such as home shopping and on-line computer games. The winners will be the companies that pull in the most consumers by putting together the most attractive offers – whether the services arrive via satellite, cable or the TV aerial." Another concern is the risk that diverse national legislation would lead to further fragmentation in a market which increasingly depends on global reach for its success – because globalization and deregulation are the keywords in this new, quickly developing information society.

5.1 Consequences of Deregulation

It is foreseeable that services will become bundled together with the possibility that Internet access and telephone services may be used as 'free' inducements to take up digital television packages. If this were to occur, then companies providing internet only access or telephone only services may find that a serious loss of customers could jeopardize their viability. People who cannot afford such packages may find that Internet access is available on a subscription only basis and lack of competition in the telephone only business will have forced call charges up. Therefore in a deregulated world, open competition may actually reduce choice and diversity for poorer people. Even for those who can afford communication services, there are doubts as to what 'open, unregulated' competition might ultimately mean. The converging industry is rapidly consolidating, a practice we have already seen encouraged in Europe as a means to help European corporations reach the size they needed to compete globally. Such consolidation may quickly reduce available choices even for those able to pay. The danger must be that as convergence occurs within the communications industry, and regulation is rapidly discarded in favor of competition controls, any subsequent attempt to re-impose regulatory structures will simply not be possible due to the political and financial power of the corporations that will dominate the sector. Gillwald (1998) argues that rather than deregulating or even maintaining the current regulatory levels "that as markets increasingly open up, in order to ensure a fair competitive environment for new entrants, so the need for regulation increases, rather than decreases" (McKenna, 2000).

VI   Consuming New Media

Owing to the rapid pace of change in the media world, consumers are faced with a huge amount of new offerings. With the rise of digital television, the offer of TV channels is building up fast and the choice is widening. In most cases, consumers need extra equipment (*set top boxes*), or they must pay a subscription fee (pay-TV). Another possibility lies in interactivity (dating services, real estate, banking, home shopping, etc.). This takes effort and money, which makes the access threshold rather high. Unsurprisingly, younger people are usually the most willing to make this effort and are open-minded about the new media. For example, in its place of origin, the USA, home shopping has not been 'widely profitable' and is largely limited to trinkets and non-essential goods. Media analysts argue that for interactivity channels to succeed "improved programming, interactivity and changes in consumer attitudes will be required" (Mullan, 1997).

The inevitable result of increasing choice in television usage is that different people want to make different use of television. This means that audience fragmentation will be the keyword in future. Video-on-demand (selecting a program from a catalogue in order to watch it whenever convenient) and the EPG (which helps users find the programs of their choice by giving information about content and broadcast times) are examples of new technologies that cause such fragmentation by placing the consumer in control of the media content. The offer of information, communication and entertainment will not be adjusted to the collective taste of the public, but to the individual preferences of the consumer (van Kaam, 1996).

6.1 Consumers of Digital Television

Since the end of 1999, most European households have been provided with an increasing choice of digital TV offers thanks to competing digital networks and platforms. Most of them can have access to digital TV provided they subscribe to a digital TV service and/or purchase the necessary equipment. Digital free-to-air TV packages are gradually emerging. Yet these can often be argued to be 'conditional' free-to-air services, since in most cases the DTV signal is encrypted, as it is the case in Sweden, France or in the UK (in connection with license fees or programs rights). In Italy, public broadcaster RAI has been offering a new free-to-air digital package based on the Eutelsat/Hotbird II satellites since July 1999. In Germany, besides the free-to-air satellite digital packages of public service broadcasters ZDF and ARD, most of the commercial programs are transmitted via satellite both in analogue and digital form (Meyer & Fontaine, 2000).

Audiences for TV channels broadcast *exclusively* in digital form are still small, for this new broadcasting method involves transmission via cable or satellite and most often the use of a special – and expensive – encryption system. This small number of digital subscribers to digital services makes the gathering of accurate information about households difficult. France and the UK are thus the only two markets where this kind of information seems to be easily found and reliable enough. In France, TPS's and CanalSatellite's subscribers profiles show that French digital pay-TV households are younger than the national average and originate from families with at least one child aged between 0 and 14 years old. They generally live in a small town of less than 20,000 inhabitants and are over-equipped with TV, PC and video terminals. In the UK the demographic profiles of digital terrestrial vs. satellite customers are quite different. *Ondigital*'s customers tend to be middle-class, include young married couples and many over 50 years of age. A NOP survey conducted in April 1999 found that the typical early adopter was male (57%), young (half were in the 15–34 age range), and part of a more affluent socio-economic group. A third of these 'early adopters' were subscribing to both SkyDigital and Ondigital (Meyer & Fontaine, 2000). Here as well, the early adopters fit the above description. Consumers of new media seem to be mostly young, male, and highly educated. Yet, according to Dutch market research office *Trendbox*, women are catching up especially in Internet use. Trendbox's quarterly *Internet Update* (July 2000) shows that 40% of all Internet users are female, a 25% increase in only six months. In addition, children start using computers, the Internet, virtual games, etc. at an increasingly younger age, in school, but also at home. They are the new generation who cannot even imagine a computerless age. Times are changing and more and more consumers are embracing the new media.

VII   Conclusion

In a world characterized by incessant and rapid-fire changes in communication technology, Europe is doing its best to catch up with the world leader, the USA. Scandinavian countries were the first to seize on the new developments, resulting in a leading position in Europe. Southern European countries have been lagging behind for years, but Spain and Italy now seem intent on bridging the gap.

Besides the Internet, another important development is the rise of digital television. Digital TV in Europe has grown in terms of both supply and demand. In June 1999, Europe numbered 6.5 million DTV households (compared with 2 million at the end of 1997). In European terms, digital TV take-up remains limited, however, since less than 5% of TV households are subscribed to a digital TV package. This installed base is still concentrated in the larger Member States: France, Spain, UK – and a high proportion (80%) of digital TV households are subscribers to satellite, digital pay-TV. But digital TV platforms are emerging and the overall picture in Europe is of a huge increase in digital TV channels. The latest trend in digital television is the launch of digital terrestrial television (DTTV), first in the UK (November 1998), then in Sweden (April 1999). The launch of DTTV services was also scheduled for the year 2000 in Ireland, Spain and Finland. In the short term, the European DTV market should experience a rapidly growing penetration of digital cable and terrestrial networks which will contribute to a higher penetration of digital households. Also, 1998 and 1999 have witnessed a rapid development of i-TV services. An increasing number of projects are announced while almost each of the DTV platforms in the major EU markets now includes new i-TV services.

The level of competition in the digital TV market is undoubtedly on the increase. The first cause of this was the changeover of cable and terrestrial networks from analogue to digital. In a significant number of cases, this increased competition between delivery mechanisms and/or DTV platforms has led to a very dynamic market, thanks to a decrease in services and hardware prices (directly, through aggressive marketing strategies, and indirectly, with subsidized digital set-top boxes). Second, together with an increased number of digital pay-TV services, a new generation of TV channels has appeared, mostly operated by the latter (Meyer & Fontaine, 2000).

What will all these new developments mean for the average media consumer? This seems hard to predict because it depends on country, individual needs, income levels, occupations, etc. Consumers will need time to get used to this new world of possibilities. But digitization is now an inescapable fact of life. While most users of the new technologies are currently male, with high income and high education, this will change gradually towards a more balanced situation.

In future the consumer will be the center of the digital communication revolution, because any company with an interest in the electronic superhighway will want to focus on his/her individual needs. Only then will new investments be profitable. A new trend is the willingness of public broadcasters to invest in new media through alliances with commercial partners. It is likely that a lot of actors in the media market will end up joining forces in order to attract consumers. On the consumer's side, fragmentation is on the rise through self-customization of content, with the media offer focused on individuals rather than mass audiences. Conversely, from the point of view of the industry, alliances and mergers are the future. One thing is certain: the whole of the media market is being turned upside-down, and researchers will be hard put to keep abreast of the new developments because the media environment is changing every day.

References

Brosens, M. (1996). Consumenten en acceptatie van nieuwe media. In M. Brosens, K. van Kaam & T. Schotgerrits (eds.), *De Nieuwe Media Consument*. Alphen aan den Rijn: Samson BedrijfsInformatie.

Calvert, S. (1999). *Children's Journeys Through the Information Age*. Boston: McGraw-Hill College.

Carey, J. (1989). Consumer adoption of new communication technologies, IEEE *Communication Magazine* 27(8): 28–32.

Commission of the European Communities (1998). *Green Paper on Radio Spectrum Policy*. Brussels, COM(98)596 final.

European Audiovisual Observatory (2000). *Statistical Yearbook 2000: Film, Television, Video and New Media in Europe*. Strasbourg: European Audiovisual Observatory.

Feldman, T. (1997). *An Introduction to Digital Media*. London/New York: Routledge.

Gillwald, A. (1998). Convergence, regulation and the public interest, *Intermedia* 3: 36.

d'Haenens, L. (2001). Old and new media: Access and ownership in the home. In S. Livingstone & M. Bovill (eds.), *Children and their Changing Media Environment: A European Comparative Study* (pp. 53–84). Hillsdale, NJ: Lawrence Erlbaum Associates.

Hooff, B. van den & Schoenman, H. (1997) (eds.). *Internet. Adfo DM&SP Dossier*. Alphen aan den Rijn: Samson BedrijfsInformatie.

IP (1998). *Television 1998: European Key Facts*. Brussels: IP-Group.

Jong, A. de & Bouwman, H. (1994). *Consumenten en nieuwe media: 1990–1993*. Amsterdam: Het Persinstituut.

Kaam, K. van (1996). Nieuwe media en de betekenis voor marktpartijen en overheden. In M. Brosens, K. van Kaam & T. Schotgerrits (eds.), *De Nieuwe Media Consument*. Alphen aan den Rijn: Samson BedrijfsInformatie.

Lange, A. (1999). *Developments in Digital Television in the European Union*. Strasbourg: European Audiovisual Observatory.

Lange, A. (2000). Die Entwicklung des digitalen Fernsehens in der Europäischen Union. In C. Matzen, A. Herzog & F. Reimann (eds.), *Internationales Handbuch für Hörfunk und Fernsehen 2000/2001*. Baden-Baden: Nomos Verlagsgesellschaft.

Livingstone, S., d'Haenens, L. & Hasebrink, U. (2001). Childhood in Europe: Contexts for comparison. In S. Livingstone & M. Bovill (eds.), *Children and their Changing Media Environment: A European Comparative Study* (pp. 3–30). Hillsdale, NJ: Lawrence Erlbaum Associates.

McKenna, A. (2000). Emerging issues surrounding the convergence of the telecommunications, broadcasting and information technology sectors, *Information & Communications Technology Law* 9(2): 93–127.

Meyer, L. & Fontaine, G. (2000). *Development of Digital Television in the European Union*. Montpellier: IDATE.

Ministry of Economic Affairs (2000). *The Competitiveness of Europe's ICT Markets: The Crisis Amid the Growth*. Noordwijk: Ministerial Conference, March 9–10.

Mullan, B. (1997). *Consuming Television: Television and its Audiences*. Oxford: Blackwell Publishers.

NFO Trendbox (2000). *Internet Update juli 2000*. Amsterdam. Available at [http://www.trendbox.nl/eye/docs/nieuwemedia.doc].

NUA Internet Surveys (2000). *How Many On-line?* Dublin. Available at [www.nua.ie/surveys/how_many_online/index.html].

Oldroyd, R. (1999). Grabiners stars in the new digital dance, *Financial Mail on Sunday*, July 18: 3.

Rogers, E.M. (1983). *Diffusion of Innovations*. New York: The Free Press.

Screen Digest (2000). *Digital Terrestrial Television. A slow start to global roll-out* (pp. 85–95). London: Screen Digest Limited.

Belgium

by Frédéric Antoine, Leen d'Haenens and Frieda Saeys

I   Introduction

Broadcasting in Belgium can be considered as a prototype of broadcasting in general in Western Europe, which was dominated for years by public broadcasting organizations that drew deeply for their inspiration upon the ideas of the British public service. The situation was to change profoundly, but this did not occur until the 1980's, the very moment when European regulations became dominant. Moreover, Belgian broadcasting also provides a clear indication of the lines of social division in the country and the related developments (political and ideological, linguistic and regional divides). Belgium's political structure is quite complex and has undergone significant changes over the past 25 years.

At present, the country comprises three regions (the Flemish, Walloon and Brussels Capital regions) and three Communities (The Flemish, French-speaking and German-speaking Communities), each of which has its own legislative and executive institutions. Above them is the federal government, which exercises power in national affairs.

As the country has almost always been governed by a coalition, the development of public broadcasting policy is invariably the result of compromise and seldom reflects a straightforward vision. Besides this, public broadcasting structures reflect the evolution within Belgian state structures: the movement from a unitary to a fully federalized model. In the meantime, the three Communities have also developed their own separate policies on private broadcasting companies, each fitting into the framework of its own policies on the media. So strictly speaking, we can only speak of a 'Belgian' public broadcasting until about 1970 and no later. From then on, each Community began writing its own history in this respect. Federal affairs are regulated by laws and royal decrees, while at community level we speak of decrees of the Flemish as opposed to French-speaking or German-speaking community. As the broadcasting activities of the small German-speaking Community are very limited, we will not deal with them in a separate paragraph.

II   A Unitary History of Belgium

As in most West European countries, radio began to develop in Belgium shortly after the First World War and was the result of private initiative. The first national private radio, *Radio Belgique*, dates from 1923. It was French-speaking and was set up by the *Société Belge de Radio-Electricité* (SBR), a supplier of electrical equipment. Flanders followed in 1928 with *De Vlaamsche Radiovereniging* (VRV). These politically neutral initiatives, which were mainly motivated by technological and financial concerns, were soon followed by more politically and ideologically based broadcasting associations both in Flanders and in Wallonia. This gave rise to a landscape of private broadcasting companies that represented the most prominent – or should we say the most powerful? – movements in society (Bertels, 1972: 31–53). Fearing that it might lose control of the airwaves, the government followed the example of Great Britain in setting up a national public broadcasting company (1930) called the NIR/INR (National Institute for Radio Broadcasting). This unitary organization provided programs both in French and in Dutch and was financed by government funding which consisted of 90% of the revenue from radio licenses. Advertising was prohibited. During the 1930's, pluralism was guaranteed in different ways. The NIR/INR did not have a broadcasting monopoly; moreover, part of its programs had to be made in cooperation with existing or newly-founded private broadcasting and production companies (Bertels, 1972: 11–12).

In 1937, a separate director was appointed for French and for Dutch-speaking programs within the NIR/INR. A third director was appointed to run the administrative and technical department, as well as all services common to both language groups. This was the first step to what later would lead to a complete division of the broadcasting system.

In the immediate post-war period, when serious crises were destabilizing Belgian society, the authorities intervened on several occasions in the running of public broadcasting. First of all, a *de facto* monopoly was brought about for the NIR/INR. The former independent broadcasting associations were limited to showing 'guest' programs, which provided a platform for the major political parties, management and trade unions and religious or philosophical groups. The second move was to incorporate the private regional stations into a national system. To restore NIR/INR's credibility, its statute needed to be revised but this would not happen until 1960. In the meantime, the operating rights of television in Belgium were assigned to the NIR/INR. The first public television broadcast took place on October 31, 1953. However, broadcasting would no longer be a reflection of a unitary country. The French and Flemish language television stations would be completely different, not only in their programs, but even in the number of display lines on the screen, influenced as they were by their larger neighbors to the north and south: The Netherlands and France.

In 1959 the NIR/INR was finally taken out of the hands of the Ministry for Post, Telegraph and Telephone and merged with the Ministry of Cultural Affairs. In 1960, a law abolished the INR/NIR and public broadcasting was given a new statute as a result of which its *de facto* monopoly and further decentralization was ratified (Herroelen, 1982: 15 and further). The NIR/INR was split into two separate organizations (*Belgische Radio en Televisie, Nederlandse Uitzendingen* – BRT – for Flanders, and the *Radiodiffusion-Télévision Belge, Emissions françaises* – RTB – for French-speaking Belgium). From then on, each service would make its own programming decisions and each would have its own budget. News programs were to be made without prior government censorship but in a spirit of rigorous objectivity. Both bodies were financed by yearly appropriations and advertising remained forbidden. Government intervention was limited in theory, but in practice the Government exerted a lot of influence through its appointment procedures. This resulted in the Board of Directors being composed of members of the three main political parties. The autonomy of both the BRT and the RTBF with respect to the government, which was guaranteed by law, was limited to programming policy (Voorhoof, 1982: 96 and further). The 1960 Law on Radio and Television was one of the first steps taken on the path towards a community-based broadcasting policy.

From the 1970's onwards, following consecutive reforms of the Belgian State, radio and television gradually had to deal with two different levels of the legislature. Broadcasting policy would gradually be removed from the ambit of national law and handed over to the Communities (who rule by decrees). On the one hand, public broadcasting became part of cultural affairs as a result of the law of July 21, 1971 and was therefore under the power of the Communities. On the other hand, four issues still remained in the hands of the national government, i.e., technical matters, revenue from radio and TV licenses, government announcements and advertising. The phases of state reform that followed further undermined the power of the central government by transferring these areas one after another to the competence to the Communities. Between 1971 and 1976, most of the activities of the Institute for Common Services were divided up between the French and Dutch sections. The law of February 18, 1977 completed the separation of the public broadcasting companies. Then a separate public broadcasting company was founded for the German-speaking Community in Belgium and called the BRF (*Belgisches Rundfunk- und Fernsehnzentrum der Deutschsprachigen Gemeinschaft*).

The law of July 16, 1973, better known as the *Culture Pact*, had far-reaching consequences for public broadcasting, its intention being to ensure the protection of the variety of ideological and philosophical movements in the country. The boards of directors of public broadcasting companies had to reflect the proportion of seats held by the political parties within the Community Assemblies. This system consolidated the politicization of public broadcasting.

In the late 1970's, French-speaking Belgium and Flanders issued their first decrees on broadcasting, in 1977 and 1979, respectively. During the 1980's they developed sep-

Table 1. *Evolution of Cable Penetration in Belgium*

Year	Number of Cable Subscriptions	Cable Penetration (%)
1976	725,000	47.2
1981	1,206,584	72.0
1993	2,065,295	96.5
2000	3,788,650	94.6

Sources:
1976–1993: Biltereyst & Burgelman (1995)
2000: IP (2000a), *Television 2000, European Key Facts*
VRT Research Department
Belgian National Institute for Statistics (NIS)

arate broadcasting policies. Meanwhile, due to economic, geographic and demographic factors, Belgium became one of the most densely cabled countries in the world (see table 1). Though the number of Belgian broadcasting companies was limited, Belgian viewers were soon supplied with a wide range of foreign stations. This formed a threat, not only as far as the viewers market was concerned but also for national advertising. As long as commercial radio and TV advertising remained banned in Belgium, advertisers could only reach their audience through foreign stations. The pressure exerted by this phenomenon was felt much more strongly in French-speaking Belgium than in Flanders. In the course of the 1980's, it was to become an important argument in both Communities in favor of lifting the monopoly of public broadcasting companies.

III   Flanders

3.1 1977–1987: Emergence of a New Broadcasting Scene

Following regionalization, the Flemish government focused on adapting the legal framework of existing public broadcasting. The first Flemish decree on public broadcasting dates from December 28, 1979. The BRT was thereby attributed a fourfold task, i.e., education, information, training and entertainment. As was the case in the past, particular attention was paid to newscasting, which had to be carried out in a "spirit of strict objectivity and without the slightest measure of censorship from the government." The decree was amended a couple of times during the 1980's, but it was only in the 1990's, as a result of pressure from commercial channels, that public broadcasting was to undergo a profound change. As far as radio was concerned, the monopoly of public broadcasting came to an end in 1981 (Herroelen, 1991). The Royal Decree of August 20 legalized local radio stations, but under strict conditions. Besides the technical conditions they had to fulfil, their broadcasting range was limited and they were forbidden to advertise. In practice, this ban on advertising was totally ignored and in 1985 advertising was legalized for all non-public local radio stations. The conditions for recognition were laid down in a Decree dated May 6, 1982 (Govaerts & Lentzen, 1986: 7–14). The small scale status of 'non-public' radios was confirmed by a Decree dated November 7, 1991 (Herroelen, 1991). Given their limited size during the 1980's and 1990's, these local radio stations were not considered as posing a real competitive threat to public radio, whose market share however diminished temporarily to as little as 65% in 1982. Public television, on the other hand, did indeed experience the loss of its monopoly position in the late 1980's. As early as 1981, the then center-right government declared its intention to substitute the monopoly of public television with a system of open competition. Because of the strong opposition and many practical problems involved however, this intention did not reach fruition until 1987 (Drijvers, 1990). The Law on Radio and Television Advertising of February 6, 1987 made it possible for broadcasters to derive revenue from advertising. In the meantime, the Flemish government had already passed its so-called Cable Decree (Decree of January 28, 1987), which laid down the legal basis for ending the monopoly of the public broadcasting company.

According to the national 1987 law, the 1987 Cable Decree confirmed that only one commercial TV company could be set up and allowed to broadcast via the cable network and address as such the whole Flemish population. The *Vlaamse Televisie Maatschappij* (VTM) was issued a license for no less than 18 years and soon gained a larger market share than public television. One point of interest here is the 'must and may carry' regulation for cable distributors. Each cable network operator is required to broadcast programs from the Belgian public broadcasting companies as well as those from VTM and the local station in its area (Decree of October 23, 1991). The showing of all other programs is subject to prior agreement by the Flemish government and to other conditions it may see fit to stipulate. In 1985 the Flemish Media Board (*Vlaamse Mediaraad*) was created, whose task it was to provide advice to the Flemish government and to the Flemish Council on matters concerning media policy. The Board was inaugurated as late as 1987, at a time when a number of important political decisions had already been taken. Following the passing of the 1987 Cable Decree and a number of other executive decisions, the powers of the media board were extended and consolidated. A number of decisions and authorizations made by the Flemish government and the Minister for Culture on matters concerning broadcasting were made subject to a request for prior advice from the media board. This advice was not binding however and was often required to be delivered in too short a time. In the beginning, the impact of the media board on media policy was therefore limited (Voorhoof, 1994).

A Decree dated December 17, 1997 altered the function and composition of the Media Board. From then on it would clearly have an advisory and supportive role in outlining policy. The say of the groups forming the media lobby was further limited. Of the 21 board's members, 11 were representatives of various sectors of the media, 5 were experts and 5 were representatives of consumer associations.

Next to the Flemish Media Board, the Flemish Directorate for the Media was also founded. The Directorate mainly replaced the former Board for Advertising and Sponsorship and the Local Radio Board. The Directorate had far reaching powers covering the issuing of official recognition and licenses, the supervision of compliance with the regulations and the drawing up of sanctions. It comprises three magistrates and began its work on January 15, 1998. Initially the activities of the Directorate were rather limited and mainly involved the handling of complaints. In addition it also issued a number of licenses.

3.2 The End of the Monopoly

Up until 1988, the public broadcasting company had a comfortable monopoly, which was only broken by the legalization of 'non-public' radio stations. Following an all-time low in 1982, public radio did regain a market share of about 85%, however. Despite its official monopoly, public television did experience real competition, particularly from

Dutch television, which acquired a 25% market share in Flanders during the 1980's (Saeys, 1991; NOS Research Department). Nevertheless, the increasing density of cable networks did not result in a further segmentation of available viewers.

Table 2. *Market Share of TV in Flanders, 1985–1989*

	1985	1986	1987	1988	1989
BRT-TV 1	51.4	45.8	41.0	41.1	22.5
BRT-TV 2	7.9	13.4	14.9	16.2	9.0
Netherl.	24.0	24.5	27.1	25.2	17.1
RTBF	3.0	2.8	2.3	1.9	1.3
RTL (Luxemb.)	3.3	3.0	2.9	3.1	1.9
France	4.2	4.5	5.1	6.2	3.7
Other	6.2	6.0	6.7	6.3	44.5

Source: VRT Research Department

Only from 1987 on, when competition from national companies began to be felt, did the public broadcasting company begin to worry about its aims in this new context as well as about the number of its viewers, its tasks and its finances. According to the *1973 Culture Pact*, the public broadcasting company was to be managed by a Board of Directors and a Permanent Committee whose members were selected to match political divisions within the Flemish Cultural Council. Daily business was placed in the hands of a General Administrator. Under him was an extremely hierarchical and highly politicized organization, at all levels of management. The number of personnel rose over the years from 1,900 in 1975 to more than 2,700 in 1990.

Its most important source of income was a yearly grant from the government. Initially this was directly earmarked for radio and television from the national budget. In 1982, a system of rebates was developed for the Communities, which allowed them to determine the amount of the grant themselves. Since the late 1980's, the amount of the grant for Flemish public broadcasting amounted to nearly half the revenue from radio and TV licenses in Flanders.

Table 3. *Grants for Public Broadcasting in Flanders in Proportion to License Revenue (1975–1990)*

Year	Grants (in €)	License Revenue (in €)
1975	64,410,472	85,303,731
1980	94,761,811	155,238,510
1985	127,399,919	232,279,851
1990	156,076,242	303,696,910

Source: VRT Research Department

Increasing sponsorship of radio and television programs became an additional source of income. Commercial advertising, however, was only permitted from 1990 on and solely for radio. The public broadcasting company used these funds to finance five radio stations and two TV channels. During the 1980's, much attention was paid to propagating the distinct images of the various public radio stations: BRT1, the current affairs station; BRT2, the most popular station, which focused alternately on light entertainment and regional news; BRT3, the culture station for art lovers, particularly classical music buffs. In 1983, a new popular station called *Studio Brussel* was created and targeted at young people. And finally, BRT provided overseas services for Belgians abroad as well as programs about Belgium in a number of languages. There were two TV channels, but they hardly ever differed in their approaches.

3.3 The Rise of VTM

The 1987 national law on radio and TV advertising specified that only one company could advertise via the cable network per language Community, for the whole of that Community. The 1987 Flemish Cable Decree was drawn up along the same lines, and when competence in matters of advertising was transferred to the Communities in 1988, the Flemish government decided to comply with this principle – while the French-speaking government did not. Only one commercial station (VTM) was granted a license to broadcast to the whole of Flanders and was given a monopoly on advertising for no less than 18 years. VTM was launched in February 1989. In order to anticipate foreign stations targeting the Flemish market from abroad, a number of limitations were built into the Cable Decree. Foreign television stations would only be allowed access to the cable if they broadcast in one of the languages of their country of origin. This limitation was explained and justified from a cultural point of view. In 1992 however, the European Court of Justice ruled that these limitations were in conflict with art. 59 of the EC Treaty, because they were in fact measures of economic protection. As a result, the language stipulation was removed from the Cable Decree.

VTM was required to provide a balanced and diversified set of programs that should consist of information, education and entertainment. At first, it mainly focused on entertainment but gradually invested more and more in information. In compliance with European regulations, VTM had to reserve part of its viewing time for European productions. Moreover, the 1988 Performance Decree stipulated that, following a period of five years, half of VTM's programs should consist of Flemish cultural productions. No clear definition had been given of what this meant precisely, so in 1994 a quota regulation was put in place. From then on, news, games, sport, ads and teletext could no longer be considered as Flemish cultural programs. The Flemish government would determine which quotas were to be respected. This decree also required VTM to allot 1/10 of its viewing time to independent producers.

The *Vlaamse Televisie Maatschappij* (VTM) is a private company whose shares have been held equally by nine publishers of Flemish dailies and weeklies, ever since its foundation. According to the Cable Decree at least 51% of its shares should be owned by Flemish publishers. In this way, the government tried to anticipate possible problems that might arise from the loss of advertising returns for the press. It was also a means of ending direct subsidization of the press by the government, which was initiated in order to ensure diversity among the daily newspapers. This resulted however in a very strange situation in which the government propagated cross-ownership in the media instead of limiting it, as was the case in most other countries. The clause that made the participation of the Flemish press compulsory would later be deleted following pressure from the European Commission. In the meantime, VNU (a Dutch publishing company) gradually acquired more control over VTM, i.e., 44.26% of the shares in 1996. To combat this, a number of Flemish shareholders set up the *Vlaamse Media Holding* together with BMH (Maes Brewers) and gained control of 55.55% or the majority of the shares. BMH withdrew from the holding in 1996; so once again VTM was completely in the hands of publishers, though not all of them were from Flanders anymore. In 1998 the VNU sold its shares and as a result VTM again became fully owned by the Flemish publisher groups Roularta and the Persgroep (each owned 50%). The name of the company (VTM) was changed in VMM (Vlaamse Media Maatschappij). The television station belonging to VMM kept its old name, VTM.

Table 4. *Shareholders in VTM, 1989–1998*

Year	Shareholders	Share in VTM (in %)
1989	IUM/TUM	11.11
	TVV	11.11
	Perexma	11.11
	Roularta Media Group	11.11
	De Vlijt	11.11
	Het Volk	11.11
	Concentra	11.11
	De Persgroep	11.11
	Almaspar	11.11
1996	VNU (Neth.)	44.26
	VMH:	55.55
	De Persgroep	22.22
	Roularta Media Group	19.44
	Concentra	13.89
	De Vlijt	0.19
1997	VNU (Neth.)	44.26
	VMH:	55.55
	De Persgroep	27.78
	Roularta Media Group	27.78
1998	VMH:	100
	De Persgroep	50
	Roularta Media Group	50

When it was launched in February 1989, VTM immediately gained 27% of the viewers market. This rose to 37% by the end of the year, the price being paid by the Dutch stations and the BRT (TV1 and TV2). Despite the fact that the average Flemish viewer already had a wide range of programs on the cable network, it was only in the 1990's that the viewers market became really fragmented.

Table 5. *Television Market Shares in Flanders since 1989*

	1989	1990	1991	1992	1993	1994	1995	1996	1997	1998	1999
TV1	22.5	21.8	25.7	25.5	25.0	22.5	17.5	19.3	21.3	24.3	25.3
TV2/ Canvas	9.0	7.0	4.1	4.6	4.5	6.4	5.1	5.7	6.5	8.9	7.9
VTM	27.4	35.6	38.1	37.3	38.3	36.4	37.1	32.8	28.9	30.6	30.1
Ka2							3.9	6.5	6.5	6.6	6.6
VT4							6.1	7.9	8.7	9.1	8.5
Netherl.	17.1	11.5	9.4	9.1	9.0	8.7	6.4	5.3	5.0	4.5	4.5

Source: VRT Research Department

The VTM monopoly on advertising was ended *de facto* in February 1995 by the setting up of VT4. VT4, a subsidiary of SBS, is officially a British station that nonetheless targets Flemish viewers and Flemish advertising. By broadcasting from Great Britain, it can get around VTM's monopoly on advertising. As a British station moreover, it is not required to comply with the Flemish government stipulations on advertising, which are much more restrictive than those laid down for commercial stations in Great Britain. Nor is it required to present daily news programs. Because of the competition created by VT4 from 1995 on, VTM's turnover and profits dropped and figures for 1996 seem to indicate that they were heading for a loss. VT4 not only creamed off part of the advertising market, it also forced VTM to make investments to counter competition. One of the measures it took was to set up a second channel (Ka2). Both stations initially hoped to reach a new audience by showing prestigious programs, but soon had to adapt their policy because they failed to reach the number of viewers they expected.

In December 1996, the European Commission declared that VTM's monopoly was in conflict with European Community regulations. Flemish legislation on the matter would therefore have to be amended and stations such as VT4 would also have to be allowed to be shown on the Flemish cable network. But even though the Advertising Decree of April 28, 1998 effectively put an end to VTM's monopoly, VT4 still chose to remain British. VT4's owners, SBS also applied for licenses for two Flemish television stations. These licenses were granted in January 2001 by the Flemish Commissariat for the Media, which of course means that SBS's new channels will have to operate according to Flemish regulations.

3.4 Programming in a Competitive Environment

All Flemish broadcasting companies are subject to a number of programming regulations. In the first place there are the constraints issuing from the 'Television Without Frontiers' Directive. The stipulations of these guidelines are rather flexible and subject to interpretation, both with regard to the quotas laid down for programming European productions and to those for purchasing independent productions (Castille, 2000). On the other hand, licenses issued by the Flemish Commissariat for the Media do contain quotas on the programming of Flemish cultural productions. In addition to the quotas laid down by the European institutions and the Flemish government, Flemish broadcasting companies were also required to provide a diversity of programs consisting of information (news, current affairs), education and entertainment. There is a clear distinction between public and private television stations as far as the origin of programs is concerned (De Bens & De Smaele, 2000):

Table 6. *Origin of Fictional Programs on Flemish Public and Private Television (1989–1998, in %)*

	Series and Serials				Movies			
	Public		Private		Public		Private	
	1989	1998	1989	1998	1989	1998	1989	1998
Flanders	4.6	17.2	2.7	15.5	10.2	5.7	2	0.9
Europe	17	20.2	3.7	4.9	23.8	23.7	7.9	7.8
USA	17	31.5	74.6	75.3	50.8	60.1	86.3	87.4
Australia	45.4	28.6	12.8	3.7	3.4	1.6	0	0.4
Other	16	2.5	6.2	0.6	11.8	8.9	3.8	3.5

Source: De Bens (2000: 214–215)

All radio and television companies operating under Flemish law are required to broadcast a number of news programs daily. When VTM began broadcasting there was a fear they would not take news seriously and moreover that the programming of public television would as a result veer far too strongly towards that of a 'fun' station. What actually happened was much more complex. Commercial station VTM set about building up its image as an entertainment and fiction station, especially in the beginning, but nevertheless it did fulfil its obligations as a newscaster. In fact, with time it began diversifying its current affairs and news programs. The arrival of VTM did not bring about an immediate shift towards entertainment and fiction programming in public television. What it did bring about was a reshuffling of the various program categories on both stations (Van Poucke & Van der Biesen, 1991).

3.5 Smaller Players

The 1987 Cable Decree not only provided for the setting up of a commercial station for the whole of Flanders but also for a number of local stations and for stations that addressed special target groups. So much attention was paid to getting VTM off the ground as quickly as possible that very few real conditions were worked out for the other stations. It was only in 1990–1991 that this problem was really addressed. Since then a regional station has been set up in each of the 11 viewing regions.

Target group TV initiatives initially remained limited to Kinder-Atelier (Children's Workshop), which had little success. In 1997, Phoenix Vision, the company responsible for Kinder-Atelier, launched Senior-TV, a station which targeted viewers over 50 years of age and which was completely financed by sponsorship. The 'narrowcasting' Company TNCC was also launched in 1997, its target being mainly the medical sector. TNCC took over the target TV channel Senior-TV in 1998 and then launched Agrion, a program that addressed the farming and market gardening community. TNCC closed down the very same year, however.

One of the problems facing all these channels was that they had applied for a target-group TV license and therefore fell under the so-called 'may carry' regulation. This meant that cable companies were free to choose whether they would carry such channels or not. Those stations which had applied for the statute of generalist TV channel were more successful in this respect, for they fell under the so-called 'must carry' regulation. As a result, in February 1999, the publishing company Roularta and the Financieel-Economische Tijd newspaper joined forces to launch Kanaal Z, a channel which mainly provides economic news, stock market reports, etc. In addition there is Event-TV, which cannot be considered a target-group channel, but rather a specialist channel, as its programs are built around specific events. This channel was gradually acquired by Liberty Networks, a French concern, and was renamed Libertytv.com in 2000. And finally, there is Vitaya, which was officially launched in 2000 as a generalist channel and which largely addresses a female audience. The most successful of all these channels is youth channel The Music Factory (TMF), the Flemish equivalent of the same channel in the Netherlands. Set up in 1998, its gross weekly viewing figures amount to virtually 60% of the target group. In April 2001, TMF was sold to pan-European company MTV.

Pay-TV acquired a market share rather early on, albeit a modest one. FilmNet did not even wait for the 1987 Cable Decree to begin operations. They had already begun in 1985 with a number of cable network companies and a pay-TV network, having first received authorization from then Culture Minister Poma. The pay-TV station was officially recognized in 1989. FilmNet was originally a subsidiary of the Swedish concern *Esselte*, but was then taken over by Canal Plus-Nethold. Initially, FilmNet only showed movies, but gradually it diversified into two and finally three stations. The first station still mainly showed movies, but programming was interrupted twice daily for children's program K-TV. Since August 1, 1995, the second station has been showing sports programs (*SuperSport*) in the evening on weekdays and all day on the weekend, the rest of the time being filled by movies. Some cable network companies also carry the group's third station, i.e., Hallmark Entertainment Network (HEN), which mainly shows TV movies and short serials. One can subscribe to the whole network or to each station separately.

FilmNet's success remained below expectations, perhaps because of the wide range of programs already available to cable subscribers on the network at no extra charge. With nearly 200,000 subscribers in 1995, it still did not manage to break even. Super-Sport also failed to achieve the expected results, despite large investments in exclusive contracts, and folded in 1997. FilmNet also adjusted its programming in the same year and finally changed its name to Canal+. Its station networks revised their image in 1998. The first station, Canal+ still mainly shows sport and movies. The second, Canal+ Blue, addresses a younger audience and is more 'adventurous' in its programming. The third station, *Canal+ Jaune* is reserved for events and children's programs. Their Canaldigital also provides a range of digital items in cooperation with NBC Europe. This new formula appears successful for the moment as there has been a slight rise in the number of subscribers (see IP, 2000a). The new Advertising Decree definitely dealt a blow to Canal+'s revenue. Like its French owners, this pay-TV station had hoped to broadcast unscrambled programs during prime time, which would have allowed it to show ads at the same time. The new Advertising Decree does not allow this, however.

3.6 Public Broadcasting since 1989

All these rapid and profound changes in the media landscape made a review of the judicial framework of public broadcasting necessary (Voorhoof, 1995). The fact that the March 27, 1991 Decree changed the name 'BRT' into 'BRTN' was symbolic of the whole enterprise. The intention of the decree, among other things, was to give public broadcasting more autonomy and more scope not only to face the recent increase in competition at home, but also to meet the new developments in technology, economics and law at an international level. The 1991 Decree completed the reform of public broadcasting, which had already been set in motion by the Mini-Decree of 1990. It would soon become apparent that an even more drastic approach was needed if the BRTN wished to remain a strong contender and worthy partner in the field of broadcasting in the final years of the century.

3.6.1 Programming

Although the arrival of a commercial competitor had been talked about for years, public broadcasting was not really prepared for this. Only in 1990 did the BRT decide to re-style itself completely, not only for television but also for radio. It strengthened the image of its radio stations, which were now called Radio 1, 2 and 3. It also launched umbrella projects like all-night radio. Its World Service was renamed *Radio Flanders International*. And finally in 1992, it launched *Radio Donna* whose image was that of a trendy, relaxed, romantic and creative station. This new station would be completely funded by advertising, which had just been allowed. The arrival of VTM initially caused panic in public television – something that did not help the growth of the specific image of its two channels. In competing with VTM, public television did not react immediately by increasing the number of its entertainment programs, but adjusted its program policy instead. Entertainment was increased within prime time and on TV1 in general, whereas it was reduced on TV2 (Van Poucke & Van der Biesen, 1991). No consistent programming policy was pursued for the two channels in the years that followed. When the strategy of making TV2 a channel for 'a specialized niche of passionate viewers' failed to deliver the expected result right away, the two channels were once again re-examined in order to create a specific image for each (d'Haenens, 1994). In the meantime, VTM gained a record market share of 38.3% in 1993 (Aspemar, 1995) and a prime time share of 42.9% (VTM Research Department, 1994).

All these changes had to be made in keeping with BRTN's legally outlined tasks both for radio and television, i.e., to provide a balanced set of programs which consisted of information, education and entertainment. Particular attention had to be paid to information (news, current affairs, etc.), which had to be truthful and impartial. Moreover, since 1994 all programs had to be free of discrimination. Furthermore, particular care had to be taken in projecting and promoting the cultural identity of the Flemish Community. Besides showing its own information programs, which had to be strictly objective, public broadcasting also allowed for certain 'guest' programs which leave room for a variety of political and ideological opinions. The 1991 Decree did not bring about any important changes to this situation. Broadcasting time was reserved for political, ideological and professional associations. For radio, this range of associations has been extended to include those of social importance. This system of 'guest' programs had been a source of controversy for years. The positioning of these 'third parties' weighed upon the programming of public radio and television and cost the broadcasting company some of its yearly grants (Saeys, 1992; Coppens, 1995).

3.6.2 Financing

The financing of public broadcasting was also a delicate matter. For years, the public broadcasting grant consisted of sums attributed by the national government to the organizations concerned. In 1982, following federalization, a system of rebates was adopted: 71.9% of the net returns from radio and TV licenses were allocated to the Communities. Out of this amount, 64% was reserved for the Flemish Community and 36% for the French-speaking Community. Each Community then determined the amount of the grant it wished to attribute to its public broadcasting company. In fact, the net returns increased from year to year, but increasing amounts remained in the treasury. In compliance with the law of January 16, 1989, radio and TV licenses became part of Community taxation: the amounts were still collected at a national level, but net revenue was transferred in its entirety to the Communities. The percentage of revenue on licenses that returned to public broadcasting was not laid down by law until 1990. The so-called Mini-Decree of June 13, 1990, which was issued in anticipation of a total reform of public broadcasting, attributed the BRTN a fixed percentage for the first time, i.e., 51.5%. This was considerably less than the 70% the company had hoped for! At the same time however, advertising was permitted on public radio stations, which was a thorn in VTM's side. This meant a loss of advertising profits for VTM, who had continued to believe that public broadcasting should be wholly financed by the government and not through advertising. The 1991 Decree further reduced the yearly grant to 49.5% of the revenue on radio and TV licenses collected in Flanders. Shortly afterwards however, a Decree dated July 1, 1992 severed the link between the BRTN's yearly grant and increases in radio and TV fees. The new point of departure was a basic sum, i.e., 169 million for 1993 which was linked to a double index, i.e., increases in wage costs (for 53%) and the index of consumer prices (for 47%). An additional grant of 4% was also permissible if and when certain conditions had been filled.

Table 7. *Evolution of Grants for Public Broadcasting in Proportion to Radio and TV License Revenue since 1991*

Year	Grants (x €1,000)	License Revenue (x €1,000)
1991	171,914	319,128
1992	167,241	337,361
1993	175,543	351,379
1994	178,399	369,042
1995	184,567	394,151
1996	185,796	404,066
1997	188,697	409,024
1998	196,232	426,377
1999	198,364	436,293
2000	206,297	446,208

Sources: VRT Research Office/Flemish Ministry of Finance/Flemish Ministry for the Media

In order to supplement its annual grant, BRTN can use program sponsorship, both on radio and on television. Ever since the issuance of the Mini-Decree of June 13, 1990 commercial advertising has been allowed on public radio. Advertising on BRTN radio began on October 1, 1990. The conditions required for advertising and sponsorship were further stipulated in a Decree dated June 6, 1991. BRTN Television was not allowed to advertise but could broadcast certain items of public interest or import. Those who had access to these slots were humanitarian organizations, public institutions or associations, or corporations the majority of whose Boards of Directors were members of the government. Both sponsoring and advertising for the public broadcaster are managed by the VAR (*Vlaamse Audiovisuele Regie/Flemish Audiovisual Board*) a form of cooperation between the BRTN, the most important partner, and the VUM, the only group of Flemish daily newspapers that was not initially connected either directly or indirectly to commercial channel VTM. Sixty-five percent of the profits realized through VAR were attributed to BRTN. Initially VAR was involved in radio advertising but in December 1991 its sphere of competence was enlarged to include the sale of broadcasting rights outside Europe, books, CDs, videos, etc. As a result the VAR grew to become the commercial arm of the VRT. In 1995 the VAR realized an annual turnover of €47 million (a net profit of €3.3 million).

3.6.3 Structure and Organization

The changes to its structure brought about by the 1991 Decree were not very drastic. The public broadcasting company was still managed by a Board of Directors, but the board was no longer constituted to match the spectrum of political representation in the Flemish Council. In practice however, the presence of the various Flemish political families was still very clearly visible in the profiles of those in management. The Permanent Committee and the Board of Advisors formed from viewers and listeners were still required to respect the spectrum of political representation. The position of General Administrator at the head of the organization was kept, along with those of the directors general. What was new was that the company had to submit a five-year plan to the Flemish council. The Flemish government exercised control over the budget. Its tutelage was limited to supervising so-called third-party broadcasts as well as ensuring that the laws, decrees and decisions were applied and complied with.

3.7 Major Changes in Public Broadcasting since 1995

3.7.1 The Transition Period

The various decrees and decisions passed at the beginning of the 1990's certainly did not solve all the problems. A Decree dated March 8, 1995 coordinated all previous decrees concerning public radio and television (Voorhoof, 1995). Those who thought that this decree would finally establish peace and stability in public broadcasting were soon disappointed. In the very same year (1995), E. Van Rompuy, the Minister for the Economy, SME's, Agriculture and the Media, commissioned research agency McKinsey to conduct a detailed review of the BRTN. The agency proposed a number of profound measures of change to its structure and content. In anticipation of a total reform, the Flemish Parliament passed a decree on December 22, 1995 that would have serious consequences for BRTN's managerial structure. The Board of Directors would remain, but the Permanent Committee was dropped along with the post of General Administrator. Instead, an Executive Director was to be put in charge of administration and finances. Daily business would be carried out by a managerial committee composed of the Executive Director and a number of general managers – those currently in charge of radio and TV. This move was the first step in the depoliticization of BRTN management. One of the most painful points in this reform plan was undoubtedly personnel policy. The first to go were 15 senior management members who were forced to retire at 60 (Goossens, 1998). An overall agreement for the staff was put off till the issuance of the so-called *Maxi-Decree*, the most important articles of which were passed by the Flemish government in October 1996. Though the majority of the staff employed at the BRTN occupies statutory positions, the intention was to employ more people on a contractual basis in the future.

Moreover, a Decree dated December 22, 1995 clearly took the McKinsey report into consideration as far as programming was concerned. The general task now presented was "to reach the largest possible number of Flemish people by supplying a diverse number of programs." Information and culture were priorities here, as well as providing a sufficient number of sports, contemporary education, Flemish drama and tasteful entertainment programs. Youth and children's programs would also have to be on offer. Quality was the key word in programming, in addition to universality and complementarity. What was new was its resulting obligation: the company was required to clarify its tasks in a mid-term plan (several years) and set measurable objectives for itself. In 1996, a policy plan was drawn up for the television in cooperation with research agency Censydiam. One of its points of departure was the division of Flemish viewers into six more or less homogeneous groups based on their expectations: *TV addicts* (15%), *family viewers* (15%), *seekers of added value* (22%), *active discoverers* (17%), *spontaneous enjoyers* (22%), and *the restless* (9%). According to Censydiam, the needs of two of these sections did not match the tasks set for a public broadcasting company by the Decree, i.e., the *restless* (mainly VT4 viewers) and the *TV addicts* (mainly VTM viewers). The BRTN therefore decided to tune its programs to the four remaining groups. In doing so, it opted for an integral mixture of serious programming and entertainment, but also created a clear differentiation between TV1 (broader programming) and TV2 (in-depth programming). Regarding their commitment to quality, they drew up a number of parameters in keeping with the Decree which did not only involve quantities: they not only included conventional viewer numbers and market shares but also range, ratings, the number of viewers of informative programs, and programs meant for specific target groups. In the meantime, radio was given a complete facelift and its programs were restructured. The role of public radio had never been as hotly disputed as that of television, not to mention its funding sources – at least not for the present.

3.7.2 The 'Maxi-Decree' of 1997

The so-called 'Maxi-Decree' was passed by the Flemish Parliament on April 29, 1997. This completed the reform of the BRTN that had been initiated by the 'Mini-Decree' of December 1995. The changes made to public broadcasting were quite considerable. On January 1, 1998, the BRTN became a limited company (LtdCo) under public law and was given a new name: *Vlaamse Radio en Televisie* (VRT/Flemish Radio and Television). Older employees could benefit from a more beneficial early retirement scheme instead of compulsory retirement at 60. The most striking change consisted in the new relationship between the public broadcasting company and the government: from now on it would take the form of an executive agreement between both parties. The first agreement of this type between the Flemish government and the BRTN had already been signed in May 1997 for a period of five years (1997–2001). This agreement mainly consisted of a number of measurable objectives for public broadcasting and also stipulated the grant required to achieve these objectives (see table 8). If public broadcasting did achieve its objectives, then the grant (which was set at a basic 188 million in 1997) would be increased annually by 4%. Next to its yearly grant, the VRT could still rely on income resulting from program sponsorship[1] on radio and television and from commercial advertising on the radio. Radio and television could also broadcast programs 'of general import.'

Revenue from television sponsorship amounted to € 6,693 million in 1998. That year public broadcasting changed its policy on sponsorship at the beginning of the new season. From then on, within the new system 17 sponsors were given an integral package that included one program with top ratings, one with lesser ratings and a number of other programs. Fourteen sponsors would pay € 371,840 each per annum for TV1 and 3 sponsors would € 173,525 each for Canvas. The children's channel would remain without sponsors. In 1999, the VRT held 93.2% of the market share for radio advertising. Radio Donna posted a record turnover of € 37.2 million in radio advertising, with Radio 2 posting € 21.6 million and Studio Brussel and Radio 1 € 10.4 and € 34.6 million, respectively. There was no advertising on Radio 3. Together, the VRT's sponsoring and advertising returns rose steadily from € 37.2 million in 1997 to more than € 57 million in 2000.

3.7.3 Measurable Objectives in Programming

As far as radio is concerned, the VRT is committed to reaching 55% of the population with its five national stations and to achieve an average daily listening time of 3 hours and 15 minutes. To reach these goals the images of the various stations were to be developed through time, particularly following listener research, etc. The images of the various stations were set out in the managerial agreement: Radio 1's image would be competent, informative and exciting, Radio 2 would mainly cover entertainment and regional information, while *Klara* (the former Radio 3), which was launched on December 2, 2000, would play mostly classical music, but also cover other music genres and provide in-depth cultural information. Studio Brussel was the youth-orientated pop and rock station, and Radio Donna would play mainstream pop and cover lifestyle and

---

[1] Sponsorship = any amount provided by a government-owned company or any other company which is not involved in broadcasting activities or in the making of audio-visual productions towards the financing of programs, the goal of which is to heighten public awareness or knowledge of the said company's name, brand name, image, activities or achievements (art. 2 of the coordinated Broadcasting Decree of January 25, 1995).

culture, relaxation and entertainment, and current affairs. Radio Vlaanderen Internationaal was given a dual task: to provide information and services for Flemish people abroad and to promote Flanders among foreigners both at home and abroad. All stations had to broadcast at least 50 minutes of news daily and reach 80% of listeners in doing so.

The managerial agreement also contained a number of well-defined goals for television. The VRT would develop two separate stations: a general station and an in-depth station. The former, TV1 had to be a lively, accessible channel with plenty of family entertainment. It also had to be a leader in newscasting. Culture and education would be provided for within a mixed set of programs. The entertainment value of TV1 had to be high, but all form of sensationalism and voyeurism had to be avoided. The in-depth channel had to be reliably informative, educational and expert. It had to complement the other channel's newscasting by providing in-depth news and current affairs programs. It also had to offer programs for children and teenagers. In real terms it had to produce two yearly drama series of 13 weeks each, two yearly Flemish comedy series of 13 weeks each, midday news and a slot for the young, including a daily news program. As far as viewers were concerned VRT would try to reach 76% of the population, ranging from 1,5 million viewers for news and current affairs, to an average of 75% in ratings for entertainment and fiction, to a weekly average of 15% for cultural programs and 10% for educational programs and up to a 50% share of Flemish prime-time productions (6:00 p.m. till 10:00 p.m.). Most of these objectives were already achieved by 1997: ratings for entertainment and fiction reached 77% and 78% respectively, the average weekly viewing level was 78.1%, while weekly levels for educational and cultural programs were 21.2% and 16.8% respectively. The expected goal of 1.5 million viewers for the various news programs together was not achieved however, with public newscasting reaching only 1,413,900 viewers per day. The other stipulations of the managerial agreement concern, among other things, general editing policy (like drawing up an editors statute, for example), general financial and personnel policy and the research and implementation of technical developments.

For the public at large, the first visible result of this managerial agreement was the reshaping of the images of the two stations. The new TV1 was launched with a new logo, 16 new programs, a midday news program. In addition the evening news program was moved to the 7:00 p.m. slot in order to compete directly with VTM News. Viewing on the second TV station was split up into two blocks: until 8:00 p.m., KETNET targets children between 4 and 16 years old and broadcasts a daily news program, which holds center stage in its programming. Then Canvas takes over from 8:00 p.m. – a station for those in search of added value and high quality programs ranging from documentaries and current affairs to fiction, especially of British origin. Both KETNET and Canvas proved a success. The market share of the second public channel rose from 5.6% in November 1997 to 6.6% in December 1997. By December of the same year KETNET had already gained a market share of 28% of all viewers between 4 and 12 years old. Ratings also prove that children's and youth programs shown by the public broadcasting company are extremely popular.

3.7.4 Personnel Policy

Despite the fact that no compulsory retirement scheme had been provided for, many of the staff took advantage of the favorable early retirement arrangements. The idea was to reduce overall staff numbers and to gradually replace permanent statutory staff by contractors. All these profound measures of change and the incertitude they brought with them caused unrest among the staff. In fact talks between the trade unions and management on the new labor agreement broke down, which resulted in viewers being shown the test card for a full day – for the first time in 18 years. Yet, there seems to be a certain dynamism in the programming that has at least prevented the number of viewers from dropping. The position of the radio is less clear however; a change to a new research system has made comparison between listener ratings difficult.

3.8 Radio: The End of the Last Monopoly

In 1998, it was the turn of public radio to see its comfortable position threatened. A Decree dated July 7, 1998 brought about profound changes to radio in Flanders. Till then there was only public radio and a few other relatively small-scale initiatives. Most local radio stations began illegally in the 1970's as politically committed or purely commercial ventures. They were only legalized at the beginning of the 1980's, the intention then being to limit their numbers and keep them small. In practice, the larger networks began to dominate the scene, the result being a leveling off in program quality. In 1990, a new decree was drawn up on non-public radio stations which once again put the stress on the regional: these radio stations could only operate in a limited area (max. 8 km) and their transmitters could not exceed 100 Watts; at least 50% of the information they broadcast had to pertain directly to their area; and advertising had to be strictly regional. Local radio stations were permitted to cooperate with each other but had to remain structurally independent. The ban on syndication was much challenged and often circumvented in practice. Nor were advertising limits respected and, as was the case with regional television, this was carried out in close cooperation with printed-media companies like the Roularta Media Group or VUM. The IPB, the advertising board of the RTL, also managed advertising for about 140 of the more than 350 local radio stations, among which was *Radio Contact*, a sizable station.

The July 7, 1998 Decree on local radio stations lifted the ban on syndication. From then on, local radios would only have to fill 20% of their airtime with their own programs (instead of 80%) and furthermore each station would no longer have to have its own name. Another change stemmed from the Advertising Decree that contained a number of stipulations concerning local radios. From then on local radios could also broadcast national advertising. This merely meant the regularization of an existing situation, as had been the case with the law on regional television. The two flexible changes to regulation, i.e., the possibility to syndicate and broadcast national advertising were in part informed by the lack of clarity regarding the VRT's monopoly on radio advertising and its compliance with European regulations. Following a query from Media Minister Eric Van Rompuy, the then European Commissioner for Competition Policy, Karel Van Miert declared that he could no longer guarantee that the monopoly could be maintained. In fact, the new law had already put an end to the monopoly. The allowance of syndication, large-scale radios and national advertising put small-scale radios under considerable pressure. These enlargements of scale also posed a threat to public broadcasting, which until then had held the monopoly for national radio broadcasts and national radio advertising (Saeys & Coppens, 2000: 156–157). Moreover, an amendment to the 1998 Decree created space for two new commercial nationwide radio stations. A new plan for the allocation of radio frequencies must be developed in consultation with the French-speaking Community.

Table 8. *Radio Market Shares 1996–1998 (all day, in %)*

Station	Radioscan									
	1996 (1)	1996 (2)	1997 (1)	1997 (2)	1998 (1)	1998 (2)	1999 (1)	1999 (2)	2000 (1)	2000 (2)
Radio 1	8.3	7.6	7.9	7.5	8.1	8.8	8.2	9.0	7.4	8.1
Radio 2	35.3	36.1	35.2	36.6	34.4	35.2	33.6	33.6	32.1	32.8
Radio 3	1.6	1.3	1.2	1.4	1.7	1.6	1.2	1.0	1.7	1.1
Studio Brussel	10.1	9.9	10.7	8.7	8.3	7.5	7.4	7.0	7.4	7.6
Radio Donna	22.5	22.7	24.4	25.0	26.7	29.1	30.3	32.0	36.0	34.2
VRT Total	77.7	77.6	79.5	79.2	79.1	82.1	80.7	82.6	84.6	83.9

Source: VRT Research Department
(1) first measurement
(2) second measurement

3.9 Recent Evolutions

The repositioning of public broadcasting with respect to commercial stations both in terms of financing and in terms of objectives and programming still lies at the center of broadcasting policy in Flanders. Negotiations between the VRT and the Flemish government eventually resulted in a new management agreement (May 2001) for the period 2002 to 2007. In 2002, public broadcasting will receive a grant of €221 million, i.e., €6 million more than the present grant. These additional funds are mainly intended to boost the quality of news programs. The principle that the grant would be increased by 4% each year was a point of contention for a considerable period but has been ultimately upheld. On the other hand, revenue from advertising and sponsorship will be limited from now on to a maximum of € 50 million, which means € 10 million less than present returns from the sector. A separate agreement is to be concluded with e-VRT, a subsidiary founded to develop new electronic media services. An extra budget of 10 million has already been earmarked for this new venture. This agreement is clearly a compromise which, following drawn-out negotiations, has managed to satisfy the fiercely contradictory interests of VRT and VTM. And yet this does not mean that the discussion on the financing of these broadcasting companies has reached a definitive conclusion. Moreover, the viability of the regional broadcasting companies still remains problematic. Furthermore, the rise in the number of players in the field will certainly have to be taken into account in the near future. The issuing of two new nation television licenses to SBS and the prospect of a national commercial radio station are undoubtedly important new developments.

IV   French-Speaking Belgium

If one had to point to an area in continental Europe that has served as an experimenting ground for the deregulation of radio and television, one would look to French-speaking Belgium. Largely because of its geographical proximity to the Grand-Duchy of Luxembourg but also because of its situation of endemic cultural dependence on France, it was the first region in continental Europe to put the phenomenon of multi-choice television to the test on a large scale, to experience on a daily basis inter-station competition and to subject its television viewers to aggressive competition between public and private broadcasters. While most European countries have only experienced competitive systems since the early 1980's, French-speaking Belgium has lived with the influence of foreign French-language radio programs since the 1930's and has experienced a *de facto* internal private/public television duopoly system since the early 1970's. This long history has created a complex radio and television system in which the public authorities have themselves encouraged private businesses and public companies to cooperate, in an effort to protect the cultural identity of this small community in the face of the globalization of media systems, and to make this small area a model that is truly unique, even differentiating it from the economic, social or legal framework which has accompanied the development of the media in the Flemish part of the country.

4.1 A Public Service Subject to Competition

4.1.1 Competition from Outside

In radio the first foreign competition the Belgian public radio service had to face can be traced back to the years preceding World War II and came from Luxembourg. Founded in 1932 by the *Compagnie Luxembourgeoise de Radiodiffusion* (CLR – Luxembourg Radio Broadcasting Corporation). 'Radio Luxembourg,' a popular station, started attracting Belgian listeners who were tired of the INR's austere pre-war program supply.

At the end of the 1940's, at a time when television did not yet exist in Belgium, the owners of the first TV-sets were receiving programs from a French transmitter located in Lille. When Belgian television did finally begin, the habit of consuming programs transmitted from abroad was already entrenched. The public television service found itself immediately in a situation of competition with French television, some of whose programs it even relayed.

Subsequently this subordinate role to the French media world remained a feature of the RTBF, which opted for a policy of complementarity with the French channels rather than attempting to compete with them, not realizing that the competition which would affect it most directly would in fact come from Luxembourg. While Europe was dominated by monopolistic public television services, it was from that tiny state East of the border that competition was to come, supported in its targeting of Belgian audiences by cable television. Born in 1961 in Namur, the first European city to benefit from this new technology, cable television was at first only used to supply deep valleys with the images which otherwise they had great difficulty in receiving. But very soon aerials and cable television distribution companies enabled Walloons to receive TV broadcasts from all neighboring countries: France, Great Britain, the Netherlands, Germany and Luxembourg. Suddenly Luxembourg television – intended until then only for viewers in France's Lorraine region – also reached several 100,000 Belgians. For *Télé-Luxembourg*, this arrival on the Belgian market was something of a life-saver as, from its foundation in 1955 by the CLT (Compagnie Luxembourgeoise de Télédiffusion), it had been limited in its Hertzian transmission range and had never succeeded in reaching 'critical mass' from an economic point of view. As for the cable distribution companies, the inclusion of this channel among the programs on offer (the only means for almost all French-speakers to tune in to this station) became an indisputable commercial advantage as the television of the Grand-Duchy was characterized by the attractive nature of its range of drama programs. As a result the rest of the country was quickly equipped with cable infrastructure. As early as 1966 the Belgian government found it had to regulate cable distribution through a royal decree defining the mission of the cable distribution company and specifying that the programs relayed could not be exempt from the Belgian legislation banning any advertising on radio or television.

For several months cable companies complied with this act. The CLT then notified them that it considered advertising an integral part of its program supply and that suppressing it was not an option. In the end cable companies gave in to the CLT's threats.

The resulting situation was thus legally impossible and the royal decree was never enforced. Deregulation had officially taken root in French-speaking Belgium. Subsequently radio and television legislation was to become increasingly ignored in French-speaking Belgium. And it was because it had heard of the possibility of pirate television stations broadcasting through cable that the French Community authorized the first experiments in Community television by cable in Wallonia, and then in Brussels, starting in 1976. It was also as pirates that the first free radio stations came on the air in French-speaking Belgium (1977–1988) before being authorized by laws laying down prerequisites of a social-cultural nature, which most of these stations then blithely ignored as they had become private commercial-type stations in the meantime. Thus the divorce between the letter of the law and the spirit of tolerance of the time was consummated.

4.1.2 Competition from Inside

These early deregulation symptoms were accentuated in the early 1980's when the politicians then in power (Christian Democrats and conservative Liberals) began to perceive differently the future of radio and television within the French Community. Accusing the public service of being too politically committed to the left and too influenced by the unions, some parties challenged the internal pluralism system in force at the RTBF, favoring a kind of 'external pluralism,' including private media, which it was asserted would better guarantee a balanced representation of the range of political opinions. This occurred at a time when the RTBF was beginning to be aware of the competition it was facing from the Luxembourg channel, a time also when the legitimacy of the public service found itself increasingly under fire. Despite the authorization it received in 1983 to broadcast 'non-commercial advertising,' the public sector was slow to react and lost significant audience shares to its increasingly aggressive Luxembourg competitor.

Realizing that it could only conquer the French-language market by giving a 'Belgian' content to its program supply, the CLT created a specific channel for Belgian audiences in the late 1970's and then, in 1983, secured from the Belgian government a Hertzian beam enabling it to broadcast to Luxembourg programs produced live in Brussels. If it were not for the fact that Hertzian transmission of the RTL signal originated in Luxembourg rather than in Belgium and that the revenue from Belgian advertising on this channel ended up in Luxembourg hands, French-speaking Belgium could be said to have had from then on a true private channel competing directly with public television. At any rate everything was now in place that would lead to the deregulation of the existing media system.

4.1.3 Official Deregulation

This official deregulation took place under another government made up of Christian Democrats and Liberals, both at the central ('federal') level and at the level of the French Community. In February 1987 the 'federal' government introduced an act authorizing advertising on radio and television, something which in theory had been forbidden until then. In July of the same year, by means of an ambitious decree embracing all radio and television related issues, the government of the French Community redefined the radio-television scene to the benefit of new private operators. Allowing the creation of private television stations within the French Community, it awarded them a monopoly for advertising revenue. In practice this recognition was granted to RTL-TVI, a company incorporated in Belgium and controlled by the CLT and most of the daily press groups in French-speaking Belgium.

However, a few months after this act had been passed, elections sent home the current government and brought to power a Christian Democratic/Socialist coalition whose credo was a so-called 'return of the heart.' Legislation adopted by the preceding government was therefore amended by several new laws (mainly in 1989 and 1991) intended to balance resources and influences between the public and private sectors as part of what can be termed a 'Belgian-style compromise,' that is a method of governing which seeks a common denominator in the expectations of the various parties, while always making sure to satisfy, at least to some extent, each of the players taking part in the negotiations. The different components of the media scene laid out at the time of the deregulation were therefore preserved, but the positions established were modified. This compromise remains the key feature of the radio and television sector in the French Community even though changes have been made with respect to advertising.

4.2 The Advertising Question

4.2.1 The Advertising Agreement

Following the federal act of February 1987 permitting advertising both on radio and television, the government granted RTL-TVI a monopoly on advertising for French-language television. Although five years earlier it had been opposed to this in the name of the independence of the public service, the RTBF would apparently have been only too happy then to avail itself of such resources in order to cope with the growing operating expenditure caused by its overabundant staff, increased TV and radio production costs, and the sheer number of its regional services. From the mid-1980's these factors led the first financial audits (McKinsey) to make pessimistic forecasts for the future of the public Institute. These were confirmed in 1988 when the RTBF – still deprived of advertising revenue – showed a €2.01 million deficit. The following year the deficit had grown to €5.68 million.

As a result the Socialist/Christian Democratic majority that succeeded the government which had granted exclusive advertising rights to RTL-TVI decided to review this position in 1989, the year in which competence in the area of advertising was handed from the Federal State to the Communities. Owing to the threat of private French channel TF1 entering the Belgian advertising market, something which would terminally destabilize the media within the French Community, top-level negotiations took place in 1989 between the government and representatives of the public and private television sectors. These talks resulted in a Belgian-style national union solution (March 20, 1989), unthinkable in another country[2]: a compulsory system of sharing advertising income between the public and private television sectors under the auspices of a common company, called TVB, which was given the task of managing the sale of advertising space on the two channels on behalf of their respective authorities and of redistributing the resulting income. Although they were in a situation of competition, public and private TV stations were thus constrained to work together since most sales of advertising space on the channels had to take place through a grouped purchase system (called the 'nome system'). In many cases this required a would-be purchaser of an advertising slot on the RTBF to simultaneously purchase another two on the private channel. A minimum net-income threshold for each channel was prescribed: € 16.9 million for the public channel, € 57.0 million for the private channel. Above this threshold TVB redistributed the income in a proportion of 40% for the public channel and 60% for the private channel. Advertising on the public channel thus guaranteed the revenue of the private channel, as the decree which authorized advertising on the RTBF (July 4, 1989) also stipulated that the RTBF's advertising revenue could not exceed 25% of its budget. In 1990 the TVB agreement was extended to pay-channel Canal+ TVCF, when the latter also became allowed to generate revenue through advertising. In 1991, the French Community also authorized advertising on public sector radio. This agreement, challenged even within the RTBF, remained in force until the end of September 1996. It was then cancelled, and since that date, the radio and television channels have been in head-to-head competition, not only in attracting advertisers, but also viewers. But the ceiling for the RTBF advertising revenue was maintained at 25% of its budget.

Since the beginning of the 1990's, in compliance with the relevant European directives, the introduction of advertising into television programs is subject to certain conditions. Program breaks may only occur once every 45 minutes in the case of movies and TV movies and once every 20 minutes for variety shows and television series. There may only be 12 minutes of advertising per hour (20% of hourly transmission time) and advertising may only account for a maximum of 15% of the daily transmission time of each channel. The television channels may only transmit one hour of teleshopping per day, but can obtain exemption to transmit more. Advertising is forbidden in certain specific programs lasting for less than 30 minutes, among which children's programs. At the RTBF, sponsoring is forbidden in subsidized programs. On the television side the RTBF is not allowed to intersperse advertising breaks within programs, except when it

---

[2] Executive Decree of September 10, 1989.

intersperses advertisements into natural program breaks. Although RTL-TVI challenged its right to interrupt the transmission of American series with advertising, the courts found for the RTBF, reckoning that these series contained a narrative structure that naturally separated their various parts. On the radio, it may not break up its news programs with advertising.

4.2.2 Compensation

Even before the Community decided to grant RTL-TVI the concession intended for private television, the latter had taken the precaution of establishing an alliance with the majority of Belgian French-language daily newspaper publishers, grouped together in the association Audiopresse (1985). Realizing that its 'official' position on the Belgian market would harm newspapers, the CLT undertook to compensate the press by guaranteeing it an annual income of €3.0 million if they became partners, which they did. But this equilibrium was again called into question by the TVB agreement, which also significantly increased the number of advertising slots offered to advertisers.

Aware of the effects that this growth would have on the financial position of the press, the 'TVB agreement' set up a system for redistributing a part of the profits made by the broadcasters to a 'Press Development Fund.' This fund's purpose was to redistribute the money between the publishers of daily papers in the French Community in proportion to circulation. The sum was €3.3 million on the creation of the fund in 1989, of which 75% was payable by the RTBF. Since then this amount has been around €2.7 million. When the RTBF also became allowed to broadcast advertising on radio, the government of the French Community decided to increase this subsidy by obliging the RTBF – and the RTBF alone – to pay 3% of gross radio and television advertising proceeds to the fund. This money was to be given out by the Community as part of special aids to certain comment-and-analysis daily newspapers or weeklies. In 1999, a new radio and television minister decided to allocate this sum to daily newspapers in difficulty, no matter to which press group they belonged. Furthermore, 2% of net radio advertising resources on RTBF had to be paid to an aid fund for radio production. A new decree on private radio stations (July 24, 1997), adopted later, will soon oblige (2001 or 2002) the private radio networks to contribute to this development fund to the extent of 1.5% of their gross advertising revenue.

The introduction of advertising on RTBF channels did not take place without a number of concessions. Initially, in the early 1990's, this increased financial inflow helped the station return to a – slightly – profitable situation. But from 1992 the RTBF found itself into the red once again, with a deficit of more than €6.7 million and projections for the following years indicated that the worse was still to come. Consequently the public service had no choice but to agree to further restrictions. It thus introduced a new austerity plan and asked for the re-examination of the TVB agreement; this it obtained in 1996. Belgium-wide advertising investments are divided up as follows: 42.2%

in the south of the country, 57.8% in the north[3]. Between 1993 and 1994 investment in television advertising in the south of Belgium grew by 16%, 32% of which was television's advertising market-share in 1994. This proportion fell somewhat in 1995 but reached 32% again in 1996[4]. Between 1993 and 1994 revenue from radio advertising grew by 3%, but the radio advertising market share remained unchanged at 8.7% for a long time. In early 1996 it rose slightly (10.5%).

4.3 The Players on the Media Scene

4.3.1 Looking for a New Lease of Life

As has just been mentioned, the introduction of advertising at the RTBF did not result in balancing the station's book, with projections for the 1990's pointing to chronic deficits in excess of €9.9 million annually. The profit ceiling imposed by the logic of the TVB system, which favored private television, had clearly something to do with this. But the politicians, by deciding at the same time not to increase nor to index the amount of public funds paid to the RTBF, were also responsible. In 1991, the allocation made to the RTBF by the State was €144 million. In 1993 it was €2.5 million below this amount and in 1994 €2.0 million above it. In 1987 the allocation accounted for 87% of the RTBF budget. In 1991 it was only 74%. And in 1994 out of a €208 million the funding from the French Community still made up 70% (€146 million) of its budget, with advertising proceeds rising from ±15% in 1991 to 19% (€39.7 million) in 1994.

Table 9: *RTBF Budget Development*

(Thousands of €)	1992	1993	1994
Revenue	199,453	220,476	208,487
Expenditure	206,257	218,648	215,390

To remedy this situation the public service embarked in 1993 upon a restructuring plan called 'Horizon '97,' intended to balance the budget by 1997. As financial costs relating to salaries accounted for 54% of the station's expenditure, it was agreed that the firmest action had to be taken on this item. It was thus decided that 20% of the staff of the RTBF, first among whom the General Administrator and Directors of the television and the radio, would be asked to take early retirement (at the end of January 1990, the RTBF had 2,854 management positions. This number had already dropped to 2,578 in January 1995, two years before the end of the 'Horizon '97' plan). To back up the plan, the

---

[3] Source: MDB, year 1994.
[4] Figures for the first four months of 1996, source Mediamark/Carat Crystal.

RTBF also called into question the mechanism of the TVB agreement, which it considered unfairly advantaged the RTL-TVI. As proof, the advertising department of RTBF admitted having had to think up ways of providing the station with resources, by having recourse to financing methods which were not subject to the TVB agreement, through the broadcasting of sponsored programs of very short duration (±1 minute) devoted to cultural and linguistic topics.

In July 1996 the RTBF's message finally got through, as demonstrated by the political decision to abandon the TVB agreement and grant each channel a comparative degree of autonomy with regard to advertising, provided that an overall balance was maintained. New laws concerning advertising wcrc to arise out of this transformation of the advertising scene. Since 1994, in application of the 'Horizon '97' plan, the deficit of the RTBF budget has tended to decrease. The RTBF expected a € 8.8 million deficit for 1994. The actual figure was € 6.9 million. The year 1995 ended with a € 5.0 million deficit, that is to say € 1.7 million less than expected. And for 1996 the deficit is expected to be near € 6.4 million.

4.3.2 Still Financially Unstable

If the 'Horizon Plan '97' was theoretically to have allowed the RTBF to recover its financial equilibrium in 1997, in practice the Institute's situation remained precarious. The 1997 financial year ended with a small loss. And furthermore, all things being equal, the budget for 1998 envisaged a deficit of € 3.2 million at 1999 rates). Despite the profit gained from abandoning the 'TVB system' and from establishing direct competition between the channels on the advertising front, the limits imposed by law on the financing of the public service radio and television media through advertising continued in effect to perpetuate RTBF's heavy dependency on the annual public grants from the French Community, for which there was no legal guarantee either as to the amount or to the continuity. In order to avoid new cost-saving plans and reduction in the public service, it was a question of ensuring the Institute's public funding and of stabilizing it. This is what the RTBF's new statute allowed, defined by a Decree dated July 14, 1997, which transformed the semi-public corporation into an independent cultural company responsible for the public service radio and television mission in the French-speaking part of Belgium.

While this new statute did not fundamentally change the institution's mission or internal workings, it enabled relations between the public service radio and television and the State to become formalized by contract, by defining on the one hand the nature of the financial undertakings conceded by the authorities, and, on the other, the requirements and constraints that this funding imposed on the RTBF. These elements were settled in a 'Management Contract' concluded, on October 14, 1997, between the RTBF and the French Community for an initial period of four years.

In order for to be able to carry out its public service mission, the contract stipulated that the RTBF was to receive an annual grant from the French Community that could not be less than € 153 million, a sum completed by the financial support of the State for the RTBF's participation in international television events and the amortization of some borrowings. In 1998, the total of the RTBF's revenue amounted to € 216 million. Alongside a little more than € 49.6 million coming from advertising revenue and other direct income, this sum comprised € 164 million of subsidy from the French Community, including € 3.9 million allocated for TV5.

4.3.3 An Independent Company Under Contract

In return, the management contract defined the RTBF's obligations. The independent cultural company thus undertook "to produce, co-produce, acquire, program and transmit federal radio and television transmissions," to provide access for everything that is eventful, "whether in particular it be important live current affairs, major sporting encounters, cinematographic works and significant cultural events," "to contribute to the strengthening of social values, especially by a code of ethics based on respect for the human being and for the citizen" and "to provoke, whenever possible, debate in its programs and to clarify the democratic imperatives of society."

The management contract stipulates that the company is to broadcast at least five radio and two television channels. In radio: one original general-interest chain, two original general-interest channels offering programs intended for the Brussels Region and the Walloon Region, including a program "reserved for every kind of ancient, classical or contemporary music." In television: one general-interest program and one general-interest or specialized program.

The RTBF television channels must broadcast an average of more than seven hours of own production or co-production transmissions, including a regional news program and two general news programs. The television channels are to ensure that an annual average of 3,000 minutes in current affairs debate and dialogue are broadcast. In application of the European legislation, at least 51% of the airtime, apart from the exceptions envisaged in the directive, is to be devoted to European works. Thirty-three percent of the airtime (excluding news, sporting events, games, advertising, teletext and test card services) is to be reserved for works for which the shooting, direction or production were carried out by French-language professionals. In radio, the RTBF is to offer 18 general news bulletins or sequences by day on a general-interest channel, 5 general news bulletins or sequences, and 5 regional news bulletins on the other channels. An annual average of 6,000 minutes of current affairs debate and dialogue is also imposed. Less precise requirements concern the cultural, scientific and continuing education transmissions, magazines and documentaries, of which the annual volume is decided upon by the company's Board of Directors. However, in television, the annual number of those musical, lyrical, choreographic and dramatic shows, with priority given to those produced in the French Community, could not be less than 12 per year. Transmissions such as 'Cine Club' are also to be screened at least 40 times a year. In radio, a minimum of 200 concerts or musical/lyrical shows are to be broadcast each year. Both in radio and in television, in variety transmissions, the RTBF has to endeavor to give pride of place to French-language songs and to present and promote the artistes of the French Community. In radio, it is to broadcast at least 30% of music with French texts. At least 15% of this percentage is to concern musical works of composers, musicians or producers from the French Community. Finally, a sum of money that is not to be less than BF 100 million (indexed on an annual basis) is reserved each year for contracts for co-production, acquisition and/or purchasing of television rights concluded with independent producers from European radio and television bodies.

The Management Contract confirmed that the RTBF was authorized to broadcast advertising and marketing material. In television, the time devoted to advertising was not to exceed a daily average period of 6 minutes per hour of transmission, nor 12 minutes in any one-hour. Between 7:00 p.m. and 10:00 p.m., this period generally was not to exceed 21 minutes, unless there were special cases as foreseen in the contract. The advertising was not to interrupt the programs, especially movies, or the various sequences of the same program, nor the news bulletins or the dramatic or lyrical art transmissions "except during natural breaks." In television, commercial advertising was prohibited for certain drugs, disinfectants and antiseptics, tobacco products, alcoholic drinks with an alcohol content higher than 20%, weapons, imitation weapons, or products likely to provoke violent, racist or xenophobic behavior, matrimonial agencies and singles clubs, including those using e-mail. Advertising for confectionery containing sugar is allowed provided a warning is included. For automobiles, it cannot be based on the promotion of speed. The Management Contract elsewhere lays down the nature of the collaboration between the RTBF and the Community television stations, the Press, cinema and private radio stations and in particular defines the amount of the financial contributions that the company must make in this context to certain development funds, in accordance with the amount of its annual advertising revenue. Should the RTBF fail to fulfil all of these requirements, the contract envisages a series of sanctions by payment of an indemnity "that could on no account be more than 1% of the total subsidy" paid by the French Community.

As the contract demands, at the present time, the station manages two television channels (a generalist channel, *La Une* and a supplementary channel, *La Deux*), as well as five radio stations (geographical diversification, according to age groups and the nature of the programs). As the law has authorized it to do since 1985, the RTBF has holdings in several subsidiaries and external companies. Another peculiarity of the Belgian system, the public television service accordingly owns some of the capital of the private company, which manages French-speaking Belgium's Pay-TV channel (*Canal+ Belgique*). The act, whose initial draft allowed the public-sector radio and television company to offer this service all by itself, finally authorized it to hold no more than 26% of the capital required to set up a Pay-TV channel. Because Canal+ Belgique has already had to be recapitalized several times and given the RTBF's financial position, this stake is currently held by the RTBF (7,9%) and its advertising authority, RMB (15,6%). Since 1988, Canal+ and the RTBF jointly own the CCT (Cinema-TV Center), with the public service holding 51% of the capital. This company's role is to purchase broadcasting rights on behalf of both stations.

The RTBF is also a shareholder in French-language satellite television chain *TV5* (11% of capital) as well as in *Euronews* (0,7%). Previously the RTBF was also a shareholder in *Arte*, at a time when the band ascribed to the public service's second channel was used both by the latter and the French version of the Arte program supply. In March 1994 this formula was abandoned in the context of the reorientation of the activities of public sector radio and television. But the RTBF remains an associate member of the channel, with which it does a number of co-productions. On the other hand, the RTBF concluded a contract from March 1997 to March 1999 with the Eurosport company to transform one of its channels into a sports channel consisting both of its own productions and sporting events covered by Eurosport. This channel, which was only accessible by cable, did not achieve the expected success and on many occasions prevented the premium public service channel from broadcasting important sporting events. Eurosport 21 was therefore finally suspended, and the specific programs offered on that channel re-incorporated into RTBF 1 or 2.

4.3.4 A Private Sector no longer in Deficit

Although the CLT had for a long time targeted Belgian audiences, the conversion of this 'foreign' channel into an officially Belgian one – RTL-TVI (official opening: September 1987), with 66% of the capital being held by CLT and 34% by the major daily newspaper publishers grouped together in the Audiopresse company – did not immediately bring the expected benefits. At first the 'Belgicized' channel had even worse audience ratings than the Luxembourg station from which it was taking over. This situation did not last long, however, with RTL-TVI eventually garnering larger audiences than public television. Financial results were another matter, however. It quickly became apparent to the CLT that setting up a specific television channel for an audience as small as that of French-speaking Belgium cost proportionally more than it could bring in. RTL-TVI being part of a foreign multinational group which sometimes paid some of the costs incumbent upon the station, the latter's own financial results were not always easy to interpret. On examination it nonetheless appears that the initial years of the channel in Belgium resulted in a loss of € 166,089 in 1989, a situation serious enough that the question was raised of discontinuing the operation and converting the station into a regional bridgehead for a centralized European network based in Luxembourg. This possibility, whose appropriateness was not agreed upon by the whole CLT board, became more distant when the station's balance sheet became slightly positive in the early 1990's, and has not been a real one since 1994, after the financial position of RTL-TVI really improved.

The financing of RTL-TVI is based essentially on advertising proceeds. Unlike the RTBF, its staff is not very large: 102 in 1992, 174 in 1994, 212 in 1997 and 432 in 1998 (but this figure includes the staff of the IPB advertising agency, bought by TVI SA in

1998). In order to increase its audience, in February 1995 the channel began broadcasting a second general program mainly intended for young city-dwelling adults. While it has not achieved impressive audience ratings (its programming changed therefore in December 1996, and since then a daytime largely centered on children's and young people's programming that is very popular with these age groups), this station completes the range of the market share already in the hands of RTL-TVI.

In an effort to complete its television coverage with a radio presence in French-speaking Belgium (where RTL Paris has enjoyed great popularity for a long time) the CLT took over a private radio station (RFM), initially created by a print media group, and turned it into a network of private radio stations under the *Bel-RTL* name (gross advertising revenue in 1995 was €11.5 million). The CLT owns 43% of the network's capital, the other partner being the Radio Contact SA corporation, which also directly manages another radio network (*Radio Contact*), and indirectly two other radio networks: Fun Belgique (25%) and BFM Belgique (21%). The CLT itself owns 35% of the capital of Contact SA (1998's gross advertising revenue was €16.2 million).

Table 10: *RTL TVI + Club RTL Revenue*

€ million	1997	1998
Consolidated Turnover	96.1	101.2
Operating Profit, Group Share	5.4	7.1
Net Profit, Group Share	2.9	4.7

4.3.5 A Mixed Pay-TV System

Another peculiarity of Belgium's French-language media scene is its Pay-TV channel, the common property of the Canal+ France corporation and the RTBF, as well as of a number of various Belgian shareholders (Strateurop/Canal+ France, 45%; Deficom (Benelux Pay-TV), 28.03%; RTBF, 23.6%; Réalia, 4.05%, Brutélé 4.0%). In the world-wide constellation of Pay-TV channels, French-speaking Belgium provides one of the few examples where a public radio/television broadcaster has formed a structural association with a private company in order to produce a program of this type. This solution is the result of long political discussions, which started in 1983. The idea was to make the pay-channel into a partner of the public television service rather than a competitor. The creation of a purchasing group common to the two organizations is an illustration of this intention. It also sought to ensure political control over the pay-channel, through the RTBF. The successive recapitalization operations carried out on the channel, which required the RTBF to sell off some of its assets to its advertising subsidiary RMB, show the limitations of such a system.

Canal+ TVCF (*Télévision de la Communauté Française* – Television of the French Community), which was to become *Canal+ Belgique*, was authorized in February 1989.

It first came on air in September 1989. The pay-channel was allowed access to advertising in 1990. Transmitted by Hertzian beam and cable, the channel reported 187,911 subscribers in July 1999, with a re-subscription rate of 92%; 95% of its revenue come from subscriptions and 5% from advertising. In 1994, the profits of Canal+ Belgique were € 1.8 million, i.e., double the figure for 1993, for a turnover of € 40.0 million. A twin of Canal+ France, Canal+ Belgique has long dreamt of extending the range of pay-programs it can offer Belgian viewers. For a long time cable distributors were reticent regarding this multiplication of specialist channels which would take up many of their bands without any guarantee of profitability. With digital transmission solving the problem, Canal+ undertook in March 1998 to broadcast its mother-program in multiplex (C+ red, yellow and blue) and then started to market a multichannel package of programs in January 1999. This digital package of some twenty channels contains much of the offer available on the multichannel package of CanalSatellite (C+ France), except essentially the cinema channels. It is made up of channels for music, children, sport, several documentaries, classical movies and one containing erotic material. None of these channels is produced in Belgium. It is simply a relay of foreign programs, mainly French.

This package is available by cable only from the majority of Walloon cable companies and in part of the Brussels Region. Certain private cable operators have in effect refused to reach agreement with Canal + on this subject. The Pay-TV reacted by bringing various court actions against them, claiming that its programs should benefit from a 'must-carry.' Concerning the obligation to broadcast its mother-program in multiplex, the court found in favor of Canal +. The court's decision concerning the obligation to broadcast the multichannel package is still pending, however.

4.4 Content: The Cultural Identity Struggle

Table 11. *RTBF and RTL-TVI Program Structures, in % (1997)*

	RTBF	**RTL-TVI**
News	48.81	11.72
Drama	23.26	54.54
Continuing education	13.74	–
Variety shows and games	4.14	11.1
Children's programs	–	0.6
Music programs	2.35	–
Advertising	4.41	8.59
Other	3.28	13.45

Source: RTBF, RTL-TVI. The categories used by the stations preclude any item-per-item comparison.

The cultural models carried by the public and private television channels within the French Community are not similar, which may be explained by the share of home production in each of these channels: less than 24% for the two private channels in 1997, 69% for the RTBF (counting repeats). Public television also differs from its private counterpart in its ability to offer high-level magazine and educational entertainment programs at the beginning of prime time. A sign of the permanence of the public service (but also of its ossification) is the fact that some RTBF programs are unusually long-lived. With lesser means than the RTBF, RTL-TVI frequently proves more audacious than its public competitor. While the RTBF only began to come on the air at midday in the fall of 1996, RTL had been doing this since 1977, and broadcasting without a break from 12 midday to midnight since 1987. RTL-TVI was the first (before the French channels) to start early in the morning on the weekend (1983) with children's programs.

4.4.1 Fiction

The broadcasting of fiction constitutes the major characteristic of the private channels and pay-TV of the French Community in Belgium. In 1977, on these two channels, the RTBF devoted 23% of its airtime to broadcasting fiction (11% in series and serials, 7.5% in movies, and 4% in television movies). But, at the same time, fiction represented 54.5% of the RTL-TVI programming (35.5% in series and cartoons and 19% in movies), and 78% of Club-RTL (of which 64% in series and cartoons). On Canal+, movies make up 60% of the programming.

Since the deregulation of the radio and television scene, the share of fictional programs has noticeably increased on public television, particularly during prime time. A TV movie or movie is thus programmed during the first or second part of every evening on the leading public channel. Like the majority of general-interest channels, the RTBF also fills part of its daytime grid with fictional items. But numerous repeats of own-production transmissions also appear there, which markedly reduces the relative importance of fiction in the whole of public channel broadcasting as compared with the situation in the private channels.

On RTL-TVI, programming has always been conceived with reference to the broadcasting of fiction, and firstly in the prime-time slots. The presence of programming types other than movies, TV-movies and series throughout the whole of prime time and nighttime is an extremely rare occurrence on this channel, even contradicting the image that it has forged for itself. Following the example of the majority of private channels, RTL furthermore fills its essential daytime programming with series. The second private channel, Club-RTL, fulfils a complementary function in this regard. During the day, it concentrates on series and cartoons for children and then for teenagers. The audience age increases until prime time, which mostly consists of old movies. Every evening, Club-RTL shows the same movie twice, interspersed with a popular infotainment magazine.

4.4.2 Americanization

In 1997, 46% of the total volume of RTBF airtime was composed of own and co-productions, and 24% of first-showing purchase and exchange. In this second category, non-European production accounted for 48% of the time for broadcasting movies, 75% of the time for broadcasting series and serials and 15% for television movies. Just about the whole of these percentages concern products of American origin. In comparison with 1996, the share taken by North American productions increased significantly for movies and series, but decreased for TV-movies.

On RTL-TVI and Club-RTL, the number of own-production hours in 1997 represented 44% of airtime excluding repeats, as against 31% in 1996. In 1997, American productions occupied 77% of airtime for movies and TV-movies on TVI and 75% on Club-RTL. No accurate figure is available concerning the share occupied by the transmission of American series, but it can be estimated at 80% of the total airtime reserved for series on TVI and at 95% on Club-RTL. There is no complete set of statistical data available for Canal+. According to the reports submitted by the channels to the controlling authorities, it would appear however that Canal+ had transmitted only 41% of movies of European origin in 1997 as against 48% in 1996, the proportion of TV-movies being 30%, as against 29% the previous year. For RTL-TVI, the proportion of European works for 1997 is estimated at 49.6%, which is slightly less than the recommendation of the EU's 'Television Without Frontiers' Directive. TVI is however progressing on this point since the beginning of the decade.

4.5 Production and Cultural Protection

A small community surrounded by large countries and dominated by its French neighbor, the French Community of Belgium has for a long time sought to protect its cultural identity and its radio and television market from foreign appetites. Which is why, especially, French-speaking Belgium has always been active within international bodies (especially GATT, and then WTO) in favor of a cultural exception clause for radio and television products.

Where possible, the Belgian French-speaking radio and television product has always been the subject of protectionist measures in order to enable the survival of the national television channels, both public and private, under threat from the arrival of foreign channels, and in particular TF1, which planned on several occasions to set out to conquer the Belgian advertising market by broadcasting into this country a specific satellite signal intended for the heads of the cable networks. The purpose of the TVB advertising management system (see above) was to counter these initiatives, which were also controlled via a mechanism of entry conditions determined by the government of the French Community.

The European directives guaranteeing free circulation of pictures among members of the Union and encouraging the emergence of a European (and non-national) radio and television sector, delivered a fatal blow to these protectionist aspirations. On September 10, 1996 the French Community of Belgium was found guilty on this count by the European Court of Justice, finding the system of prior Authorization in violation of the 'Television Without Frontiers' Directive.

In order to maintain a degree of protection for the national territory, various systems of taxation based on audience share were later concocted and even reached draft legislation. But their implementation was consistently always been challenged so that such measures were never implemented. As recommended by the European Directive, the Belgian television market is today totally open to European operators and there is no longer any obstruction to the cable distribution of their programs. Being unable to legislate in the domain of Hertzian and satellite reception, the current lawmakers determine the operating conditions of the radio-TV distribution networks, still subject to government authorization. The 'must carry' and 'may carry' principles are still in force. But the conditions imposing the retransmission of certain programs have been considerably relaxed.

No longer being able to condition foreign channel access to its market, the French Community chose, following the example of other European laws, to encourage the development of a programming and production industry for its own radio and television content. In this domain as well, however, the conditions envisaged in the past, intended for the exclusive support of the Belgian French-speaking market, have today been replaced by much more relaxed standards. The promotion of Europe is often more encouraged there than the promotion of the French language or culture in the widest sense and the culture of the French Community of Belgium in the strictest sense. So, apart from the direct application of the quotas recommended by the 'Television Without Frontiers' Directive, the law will ultimately require the TV stations of the French Community television stations to meet a quota of original French-language works reaching 1/3 of the airtime allocated to European works.

Although many requirements concerning the promotion of the radio and television industry as well as the culture of the French-language Community are to be found in the Management Contract between the RTBF and the government, similar requirements also exist in the legal texts and the agreements concerning private and pay-TV television stations. Thus the private television stations have to ensure that 20% of their programming is own-production, and spend a set amount on recourse to external services. For at least 5% of their programming time, the private television stations have to enter into French-language co-production agreements or external service contracts with individuals or companies "established in the French language region, in the bilingual region of Brussels-Capital, or elsewhere in the European Community."

According to other legal obligations, these same channels must also enter in co-production agreements or external service contracts for at least 2% of their programming, with individuals or companies established in the same geographical area as the one mentioned above. By agreement, RTL-TVI undertook to allocate a sum set at 2.2% of its previous year's gross turnover to co-production (for 1997: €2.6 million). The channel also undertook to allocate an annual sum of €1 million for programming. Finally, the channel is to acquire the broadcasting rights for programs produced in the French Community "as a priority and whenever possible" from an independent producer or distributor of the French Community.

The pay-TV stations have to ensure that 5% of their programming is own-production, or €3.3 million, of which 80% is to be from external services. Ten percent of the total of external services are to be realized by companies with no direct link to with the organism (namely a participation of the organism or of one of its shareholders in the service provider's capital). The channels must also undertake to promote the French Community heritage, and to devote to this task promotional transmissions or screenings, for the amounts laid down in the agreements.

4.5.1 Anti-Concentration Measures

Because of its size, and the difficulties encountered by media companies in reaching critical mass, there are few anti-concentration measures in French-speaking Belgium. For instance there is no legislation controlling the cash flow of the press or television groups. Only a few checks on cross-media concentration exist in law. The owner of more than 24% of a private television station cannot own more than 24% of the capital of another television station, or more than five private radio stations. Until the adoption of the last decree on private radio stations, one operator could not own more than five stations. The recognition of the radio networks has eliminated this condition. Another measure concerns cable companies that cannot hold more than 24% of a private radio broadcasting body nor have a participation of more than one-third or be the manager of a private radio station or community television station.

4.6 New Controls

4.6.1 To Control and to Sanction

In contrast with the laxity that characterized the way of working of the Belgian media system in its initial stage of deregulation, in the end of the 1990's it was sought to introduce a more voluntary control policy, by setting up a body in charge of authorizing, supervising if necessary sanctioning the radio and television companies. This control, which developed little by little, does not concern the players on the radio and television scene. It does not preoccupy itself with cross-media problems, and especially not with the economic problems relating to the phenomena of media concentration and mergers.

Modeled after its French counterpart, the Higher Radio and Television Council (CSA) of the French Community of Belgium was established by a Decree dated July 24, 1997. It is made up of three Colleges, with very varied powers and missions, and of an 'Executive Committee' of four members (1 President and 3 Vice-Presidents, members of the three colleges). Some of these colleges have genuine power of initiative and sanction, others are more consultative in nature, close to the configuration of the former CSA functioning in French-speaking Belgium until the adoption of the new regulations.

The Authorization and Control College, composed of nine members, fulfils the most important role. A veritable management 'Executive' of radio and television policy, this College exercises two types of power: on the one hand, authorization, on the other hand, control. The latter includes the power to sanction operators in the event of their failing to meet their legal or contractual obligations. This College is thus responsible for rendering a prior, reasoned opinion for each authorization (or authorization renewal) for the government of the French Community of Belgium for every private radio, private television, pay-TV organization or local or community television service.

It is required to render an opinion each year on compliance with the specification or the agreements passed with the said bodies, and with the requirements contained in the RTBF's specification. It has to report any infringement of law, decree or regulation in radio and television matters and any breach of contractual requirement. Finally, it is responsible for sanctioning operators in the event of infringement. In comparison with the Authorization and Control College, the Opinion College, made up of 24 members, is a kind of assembly where debates are conducted and opinions exchanged. The main mission of this College is in effect to render opinions on all questions relating to radio and television, whether on its own initiative or at the request of the government or of the French Community Parliament. More precisely, this College is responsible for reaching decisions on statutory modifications called for, in its view, by technological, economic, social, cultural development or amendments to radio and television law. It can reach decisions on the respect for the democratic rules guaranteed by the Constitution and especially on the principle of non-discrimination and on the protection of children and teenagers in radio and television programs.

The Advertising College (18 members) is the most specific. It replaces an authority specializing in the study of advertising questions, established following the general introduction of advertising into the Belgian French-speaking radio and television media. This College has three main missions: to draft an advertising code of ethics and to render an opinion on any deficiency in this area; to come to decisions on any issue relating to the advertising content broadcast in the radio and television media; to report to the Authorization and Control College on the evidence of infringement of laws, decrees and regulations in advertising matters in the French Community radio and television media. Since its creation, the CSA has had the opportunity of assessing the specifications and the requirements with which the recognized operators are deemed to comply. In general its appreciations have been rather benevolent. If an operator fulfils the major part of his contractual obligations, the CSA is content to draw attention to the non-respect of certain particular clauses. Even, for example, in the area of transmission of European works, where pay-TV Canal+ does not achieve 50% of the required airtime, while RTL-TVI is left alone as long as it gets a little nearer each year.

So far, one of the most significant decisions of the CSA concerned RTL-TVI, which on January 20, 1999 (based on the transposition into internal law of Clause 22 of the amended 89/552/EEC Directive) was fined €2,500 for showing scenes of gratuitous violence within one of its news bulletins. This sentencing presages a desire on the part of the CSA to intervene directly as a player on the media scene. A strategy that it surely intends to develop – if it is granted the time and means.

4.7 At the Dawn of Forced Competition

In June 1999, a new political coalition bringing together Liberals, Socialists and Ecologists dispatched the Catholic party, in power for forty years without interruption, to the opposition benches. The coalition, strongly led by the liberals, has not decided to call into question the current balances, nor to destabilize the public radio and television sector for the benefit of the private sector, as was the case at the time of their coming to power during the 1980's. However, despite its official independence, public service broadcasting does not yet enjoy complete autonomy. Even after the signing of its Management Contract, the radio and television ministers still intervened to impose on the RTBF some of their choices (resuming international transmissions to Africa, creating a news bulletin for children, etc.). The new minister also decided to re-examine the entire procedure for allocating frequencies and the recognition of private radio stations, despite the previous governments' commitment to it. Furthermore, questions remain concerning the real independence of the CSA (Higher Radio and Television Council) vis-à-vis the political world.

At the same time, the multiplication of the supply of channels is on a collision course, in French-speaking Belgium, with the *de facto* monopoly in the hands of the cable companies. For as long as virtually the entire Belgian population is dependent on cable for its radio and television consumption, the 'national' equilibrium between private and public television will be maintained. But there is no guarantee that things will stay the same if the Belgians were to abandon this system that they pioneered, or if, through the development of fiber optic networks, the supply of French-language TV programs, or international programs dubbed into French, were to grow in a substantial manner.

V   Conclusion

Although the media landscapes of Flanders and Wallonia are similar in many ways, particularly as far as their general structures are concerned, one can notice increasing differences of focus between them. The end of the public broadcaster's monopoly and the taboo on advertising was more abrupt in Wallonia at the end of the 1980's. The impact of foreign financial concerns on commercial broadcasting is greater than in Flanders. There is also more diversity and experimentation in Wallonia as well as more decentralization in the creation of local cultural programs. Walloon media policy is more realistic in dealing with European regulations, which means that less adjustment is needed over time.

Flanders was much more thoroughgoing than Wallonia in its public broadcasting reforms of the late 1990's. One striking development is the drive towards depoliticization within the VRT. Its objectives in the fields of personnel and programming policy are much more clearly outlined than those of the RTBF. Whereas traditionally speaking Wallonia sought to maintain contacts with other French-speaking communities and cultures, this is much less the case in Flanders. In both parts of the country however the audiovisual landscape will become further fragmented in the very near future. A far-reaching deregulation of the communications market, which has been stimulated both by the regional and federal governments as well as by the European institutions, is no stranger to this process. One important question also remains: how and to which extent, if at all, will the cultural identities of the respective communities be reflected by their public broadcasting companies? Moreover, will such identities be at all recognizable in the new multimedia landscape? The development of on-line multimedia services will hinge on the availability of the necessary infrastructure, which has to be both high quality and affordable. In such a volatile context, the specific tasks and possibilities of public broadcasting will have to be re-examined very closely in the near future. It is already clear today that it can be much more than a mere provider of radio and television programs.

References

Annual Reports (Several Issues). Brussels: Banque Nationale de Belgique.

Annuaire de l'audiovisuel (1995). Brussels: Edimedia.

Antoine, F. (1987). *On nous a changé la télé*. Brussels: Beuc-Coface.

Antoine, F. (1989). Panorama de l'audiovisuel en Belgique, *Guide des médias* 1. Brussels: Kluwer.

Antoine, F. (1991a). Le service de tv de Belgique francophone face à l'invasion télévisuelle luxembourgeoise et la reconnaissance de RTL-TVi, *Referaten van het 13e Vlaams congres voor communicatiewetenschap. Strategieën van openbare omroepen versus commerciële omroepen* (pp. 59–70) (Proceedings of the 13 th Flemish Conference on Communication Science: Strategies of Public versus Commercial Broadcasting Services). Ghent: University of Ghent, February 28.

Antoine, F. (1991b). La télévision, de l'idéal-type au produit marchand. Une analyse de l'évolution des modèles télévisuels à travers vingt ans de programmation, *Etudes de radio-télévision* 41: 125–185.

Antoine, F. (1991c). La programmation sur RTL-TVI, *Guide des médias* 7. Brussels: Kluwer.

Antoine, F. (1992). L'audience de la télévision, *Guide des médias* 12. Brussels: Kluwer.

Antoine, F. (1993). La programmation télévision à la RTBF, *Guide des médias* 15. Brussels: Kluwer.

Antoine, F. (1995). *La Belgique. Les télévisions du monde.* Paris: Corlet-Télérama-Centre national du cinéma-Procirep.

AVBB (1994). *Aanbevelingen voor de berichtgeving over allochtonen.* Brussels: AVBB.

Bertels, W. (1972). *Die dingen behoren allemaal tot het verleden. Geschiedenis van de omroep in België.* Brussels: BRTN.

Biltereyst, D. & Burgelman, J.C. (1995). Belgium. In Bertelsmann Foundation & European Institute for the Media (eds.), *Television Requires Responsibility.* Volume 2: International Studies (pp. 69–102). Gütersloh: Bertelsmann Foundation Publishers.

Blocry, P. (1989). Canal+, Télévision de la Communauté Française de Belgique, *Guide des médias* 1. Brussels: Kluwer.

BRTN Research Department. *Het continu kijkersonderzoek (Several Issues).* Brussels: BRTN.

BRTN Research Department. *Het continu luisteronderzoek (Several Issues).* Brussels: BRTN.

Burgelman, J.C. (1990). *Omroep en politiek.* Brussels: BRTN.

Castille, V. (2000). De Europese televisiequota: flexibiliteit of compromis als rode draad? In D. Biltereyst & H. De Smaele (eds.), *Transformatie en continuïteit van de Europese televisie* (pp. 53–78). Ghent: Academia Press.

Caufriez, P. (1990). La politique des programmes radio à la RTBF, *Guide des médias* 3. Brussels: Kluwer.

CLT Annual Reports (Several Issues). Luxembourg: CLT.

Collard, S. (1990). Les télévisions communautaires et locales en Communauté Française de Belgique, *Guide des médias* 4. Brussels: Kluwer.

Collard, S. & Martens, F. (1992). Programmation et production propres des télévisions locales, *Guide des médias* 10. Brussels: Kluwer.

Coppens, T. (1995). *Politieke 'derden' op BRTN-televisie.* Ghent: University of Ghent (non-published MD thesis).

Coppens, T. & Saeys, F. (1997). Omroep. In Stichting Speurwerk & NBLC (eds.), *Gids Informatiesector 1997/1998* (pp. 81–86). The Hague: NBLC/Boekblad BV.

Coppens, T. & Saeys, F. (1998). Omroep. In *Gids Informatiesector 1998/1999* (pp. 107–113). The Hague: NBLC/Boekblad BV.

De Bens, E. (2000). Tien jaar TV-zenderrivaliteit in Vlaanderen: meer of minder diversiteit van het aanbod? In D. Biltereyst & H. De Smaele (eds.), *Transformatie en continuïteit van de Europese televisie* (pp. 185–217). Ghent: Academia Press.

De Bens, E. & De Smaele, H. (2000). De instroom van Amerikaanse televisiefictie op Europese zenders herbekeken. In D. Biltereyst & H. De Smaele (eds.), *Transformatie en continuïteit van de Europese televisie* (pp. 111–141). Ghent: Academia Press.

De Bens, E., Janssens, H. & Van Landuyt, D. (1997). *Regionale Televisie in Vlaanderen: toetsing aan de praktijk van de decretale bepalingen inzake programmatie, reclame en sponsoring.* Unpublished paper. Ghent: University of Ghent.

De Bens, E. & Raeymaeckers, K. (1998) (eds.). *Regionale Media in Vlaanderen. Een doorlichting.* Ghent: Academia Press.

d'Haenens, L. (1994). *Kijkers in de kijker.* Ghent: Mijs & Breesch.

d'Haenens, L. & Saeys, F. (1996a) (eds.). *Media en Multiculturalisme.* Ghent: Academia Press.

d'Haenens, L. & Saeys, F. (1996b). Media and multiculturalism in Flanders. In S. Lodge (ed.), *Alliances and Alignments: Communication in the New Europe. The Scottish Communiation Association Journal* 2: 71–102.

d'Haenens, L. & Saeys, F. (1998) (eds.). *Media Dynamics & Regulatory Concerns in the Digital Age.* Berlin: Quintessenz Verlag.

De Coster, S.P. (1990). Les procédures de contrôle de la RTBF, *Guide des médias* 4. Brussels: Kluwer.

Drijvers, J. (1990). De private televisie in Vlaanderen, *Kluwer Media gids* 14. Brussels: Kluwer.

Gerard, Y. (1989). Télévision et publicité, *Guide des médias* 22. Brussels: Kluwer.

Goossens, C. (1998). *Radio en Televisie in Vlaanderen. Een Geschiedenis.* Louvain: Davidsfonds.

Govaert, S. & Lentzen, E. (1986). *Les médias en Flandres.* Brussels: Crisp 1108.

Govaert, S. & Lentzen, E. (1989). Les radios privées dans la Communauté française de Belgique, *Guide des médias* 2. Brussels: Kluwer.

Govaert, S. & Lentzen, E. (1996). La télévision privée de la Communauté française de Belgique: RTL-TVI, *Guide des médias* 23. Brussels: Kluwer.

Herroelen, P. (1982). *Eén, twee, ... veel? Kroniek van 20 jaar Belgische radio en televisiebestel.* Louvain: Acco.

Herroelen, P. (1991). De private radio's in Vlaanderen van nabij bekeken, *Kluwer Media Gids* 18. Brussels: Kluwer.

IP (1995). *Television 95, European Key Facts.* Cologne: IP/CLT-UFA.

IP (2000a). *Television 2000, European Key Facts.* Cologne: IP/CLT-UFA.

IP (2000b). *Radio 2000, European Key Facts.* Cologne: IP/CLT-UFA.

Jacobs, J. (1989). Volumes de production propre de la télévision RTBF, *Guide des médias* 2. Brussels: Kluwer.

Jongen, F. (1989). *Le droit de la radio et de la télévision.* Brussels: De Boeck.

Jongen, F. & Stephany, P. (1990). *Audiovisuel: les révolutions de '89.* Brussels: Pol-His.

Jongen, F. (1991). Le Conseil Supérieur de l'Audiovisuel, *Guide des médias* 6. Brussels: Kluwer.

Jongen, F. (1994). *Medialex.* Brussels: Kluwer.

Leroy, P. (1995). Le paysage audiovisuel belge francophone (PAFB) face à la concurrence étrangère, *Recherches en communication* 3: 189–208.

The Media Market in the Netherlands & Flanders. A Statistical Guide 1993–1994 (1993). The Hague: NBLC & Rotterdam: Boekblad BV.

Merry Hermanus, A. (1990). *Tempêtes sur l'audiovisuel.* Liège: Editions du Perron.

Michielsens, M., Celis, K. & Delhaye, C. (1995). *Vrouwen in media en reclame.* Brussels: Ministry of Employment and Labor and Equal Opportunities.

Navadic, J. (1975). *Télé Luxembourg a vingt ans.* Paris: France-Empire.

NIS. *Several Issues.* Belgian National Institute for Statistics.

NOS Research Department. *NOS-Jaarverslag (Several Issues).* Hilversum: NOS.

190   *Frédéric Antoine, Leen d'Haenens and Frieda Saeys*

De Pers-La Presse. *Several Issues*. Brussels: Belgische Vereniging van de Dagbladuitgevers.

Poesmans, D. (1989). Het kijkgedrag automatisch gemeten, *Ratel* 19(2): 6–8.

RTBF. *Annual Reports (Several Issues)*. Brussels: RTBF.

Saeys, F. (1991). Kijkcijfers. Het belang van het getal. In *Strategieën van openbare versus commerciële omroepen. Referaten van het 13e Vlaams Congres voor Communicatie-wetenschap* (pp. 48–58). Ghent: University of Ghent.

Saeys, F. (1992). De BRT en zijn levensbeschouwelijke derden, *Kultuurleven* 59(2): 28–29.

Saeys, F. (1994). Vlaanderen. Omroep. In *Gids Informatiesector 1994* (pp. 258–264). The Hague/Rotterdam: NBLC/Boekblad BV.

Saeys, F. & Coppens, T. (2000). Omroep. In *De mediamarkt in Nederland en Vlaanderen 2000* (pp. 259–264). The Hague/Rotterdam: Biblion/Media Business Press.

Saeys, F. & Coppens, T. (2001). Omroep. In *De mediamarkt in Nederland en Vlaanderen, editie 2001* (pp. 159–165). Rotterdam: Media Business Press.

Santy, H. (1993). Kijk- en luisteronderzoek, *Argus-nieuwsbrief voor Media en Communicatie* 3(4): 1–12.

Sobemap (1996). *Studie Regionale Televisie*. Brussels: Sobemap Marketing.

Vanneuville, B. (1996). Telecommunicatie-infrastructuur, *Kluwer Mediarecht* 7(111): 1–14.

Van Pelt, H. (1974). *De omroep in revisie. Ontwikkeling van het radio- en televisiebestel in Nederland en België*. Louvain: Acco.

Van Poucke, L. & Van der Biesen, W. (1991). Programma- en nieuwsaanbod op BRT en VTM. Een onderzoeksverslag. In *Strategieën van openbare versus commerciële omroepen. Referaten van het 13e Vlaams Congres voor Communicatiewetenschap* (pp. 24–47). Ghent: University of Ghent.

Van Rhijn, P. (1995). Le système TVB, *Guide des médias* 21. Brussels: Kluwer.

Voorhoof, D. (1982). Vergelijkend onderzoek mediarecht. In *De Gemeenschapsproblematiek in de massamedia. Referaten van het 10e Vlaams Congres voor Communicatiewetenschap* (pp. 96–134). Ghent: University of Ghent.

Voorhoof, D. (1994). De Vlaamse mediaraad, *Kluwer Mediarecht* 1(25): 1–8.

Voorhoof, D. (1995). Openbare omroep, *Kluwer Mediarecht* 4(35): 1–14.

VTM Research Department (1990–1996). *VTM Jaaroverzicht*. Vilvoorde: VTM.

Vuylsteke, C. (1994). Les réseaux de radios privées de la Communauté Française de Belgique, *Guide des médias* 19. Brussels: Kluwer.

Luxembourg

by Frédéric Antoine

A tiny country at the heart of Europe, Luxembourg[1] has always understood the advantage which this strategic position affords it and the opportunity it provides for exploiting an inexhaustible, non-physical resource: radio and TV programs broadcast over electromagnetic waves and the concession systems associated with them. Lacking the means to fend for itself in public-sector radio broadcasting, the Grand Duchy decided from the outset to concede its radio broadcasting rights to a private operator. Luxembourg was the first European country to have experience of private mass media and their logic, the Duchy's radio and TV broadcasting landscape being inseparable from the existence of the *Compagnie Luxembourgeoise de Télédiffusion* (CLT, Luxembourg TV-broadcasting Company), Luxembourg's main taxpayer. Defined in a 1929 act governing 'radio stations established in the Grand Duchy,' the principle of 'concession of a public service' was renewed several times to the benefit of the CLR (*Compagnie Luxembourgeoise de Radiodiffusion* – Luxembourg Radio-broadcasting Company, founded on May 30, 1931), then of the CLT. The CLT succeeded it on July 1, 1954, when the supremacy of radio was being displaced by TV as the dominant medium. The last concession renewal took place on January 1, 1996.

I   Historical And Political Context

This concession is governed by contractual terms and conditions whose foundation was laid in 1930. These initially stipulated that a majority of the regular artistic, administrative and technical staff had to be Luxembourg nationals, as had also a majority of the members of the Board of Directors, its chairman, and its executive director. According to the terms of the agreements establishing the concession, the Luxembourg government also appointed a commissioner for the CLR whose duty it was to attend to the interests of the Luxembourg government, and created two committees to assist him, one technical, the other artistic, composed of a majority of Luxembourg nationals. The technical committee had responsibility for matters regarding the smooth running of the station. The artistic committee, also called 'program committee,' had as its explicit function the supervising of the quality, objectivity and uniformity of the programs proposed.

This precaution, which allowed the idea of a certain impartiality in program content to take root, was not without its usefulness in 1933, the year when *Radio Luxembourg*

---

[1] Some key figures (IP, 1995; 1996): total population: 413,000; total number of TV set-owning households: 155,000 (99%); single color TV set ownership: 99%; multiset ownership: 42%; VCR ownership: 77%; private satellite dish ownership: 1.5%; total number of cabled households: 130,531 (89%).

was born: presented as a multilingual European station, it nonetheless had a significant part of its audience in France and the other French-speaking countries. This made perfect sense as the capital of the CLR was then dominated by French interests and, according to its first director, the function of the station could have been to broadcast "the voice of France from behind a neutral mask" to an international public (Maréchal, 1994: 46). This intention never materialized, as the young station always remained neutral *vis-à-vis* Germany (Sabbagh, 1995: 49), but it explains why a little over twenty years later, in 1954, an act was introduced imposing strict political neutrality on the CLT. Since then and at least up until the international break-up of the group, this preoccupation has remained a constant one for the company[2].

From the beginning, the concession also allowed the Luxembourg government to control to some extent the flow of share transfers within the company. This prerogative, as well as the vague national independence concerns evidenced in the concession contract, can be explained by the international character of the ownership of the company's capital. It proved useful on several occasions when the presence of certain foreign groups in the company's capital was strengthened to the extent that Luxembourg was in danger of losing any influence over the station. The Luxembourg government accordingly experienced a period of very difficult relations with France when, in 1965, the French government tried to muzzle *Radio Luxembourg*, the only station broadcasting from its periphery which it did not control, by attempting to acquire a substantial share of its capital through SOFIRAD, a company managing the interests of the French government in private radio and television. Luxembourg blocked the move. This did not entirely have the expected effect, however, because at the end of the crisis the French government succeeded in securing a – modest – interest in the capital of the CLT through Havas, another state-owned company.

This relative failure incited the Luxembourg government to define the terms of its control over the CLT during the renegotiation of the concession granted the company in 1975. In future, 70% of the capital of the CLT would be represented by registered 'Class A' shares. These shares could not be transferred without prior consultation with the Luxembourg government, which could veto the transfer in three cases: if the political neutrality of the company was endangered or its private character called into question by a foreign power or a political organization; if the purchaser was a competitor of the CLT; or if there was a risk of a shift in balance between the holders of at least 1% of the shares of the company. The same provisions stipulate that, should it find it impossible to exercise its veto, the Luxembourg government reserves the right to repurchase the Company's facilities.

---

[2] "There was a time," former RTL-radio (Paris) news editor Jean-Pierre Farkas explains in an interview, "when we did not have the right to say 'our Prime Minister.' We had to speak of the 'French Prime Minister.' In 1968, when 'RTL Longues Ondes' was accused of serving the cause of the barricades, it was to the Luxembourg Ambassador in Paris that the French government protested about 'the excessive coverage devoted by RTL to the events in the Quartier latin'" (Presse Actualités, 1974 (95): 5).

However more closely the State's means of control over the CLT may have been defined, it was never honed to perfection. While Luxembourg political circles and CLT management were always close, to the extent that former ministers of council presidents sometimes turned up at the helm of the company, the government has never managed to exercise real control over an organization created and long dominated by French economic and political interests, and which later found itself under Belgian influence (until the Spring of 1996). This shift was bound to please Luxembourg, which economically, financially, socially and politically is closer to Belgium than to France. But it took place in an economic and political context extrinsic to the State of Luxembourg. The first stage of the process occured just as the company experienced financial difficulties in the wake of World War II, when the *Banque de Bruxelles*, a private Belgian bank, facilitated the recapitalization of the firm and would have taken over its management if the French authorities had not used their veto in the matter. A second step took place during the first crisis within the European iron and steel industry, which did not spare Luxembourg. On this occasion Belgian interests in Luxembourg iron and steel were reinvested in the broadcasting sector and added to the shares already owned by the *Banque de Bruxelles*, giving birth to the Audiofina holding company, a Luxembourg corporation bringing together Belgian interests (37% of the capital) in the CLT. The third stage of the process was an offshoot of French domestic politics. Afraid that the left would win the 1973 parliamentary elections, the French government tried to 'protect' *Radio Luxembourg* from an expected political take-over. While in 1965 the authorities had wanted to muzzle the freedom of expression of this station broadcasting from its periphery, eight years later they wished on the contrary to ensure that it remained the mouthpiece of the political opposition. To this end they decided that French control over the CLT would have to be loosened, something which could be achieved by associating a French partner with the Audiofina group. From then on the company's center of gravity shifted from France to Luxembourg, that is, to all intents and purposes, to Belgium. Havas was given this task and Audiofina became the majority operator in the CLT, with control over the company passing into the hands of Belgian group Bruxelles-Lambert (GBL) of Albert Frère, who became the *Belgian mogul* of a Luxembourg company. This state of affairs endured until the events of 1996, giving rise episodically to strained relations with its French Audiofina partner, the Havas group, until a new player appeared within the capital of the company: Germany's Bertelsmann group.

Bertelsmann's interest in the CLT dated back to the group's first investments in private television in Germany, in 1984. Over the years the group changed from being a shareholder in a television channel to a shareholding partner in Fratel, a company representing Luxembourg's interests in the CLT, before taking a direct interest in the capital of the company. In 1996, the arrival of digital television led Bertelsmann to take a 50–50 share with Audiofina in the capital of the company, renamed CLT-UFA.

II   The CLT-UFA and RTL-Group

In 1995 the CLT signed a new concession agreement with the State of Luxembourg (valid until 2010). As part of the agreement the company undertook to develop its activities in the Grand Duchy, where it had been asked to set up the necessary technical infrastructure for digital television. In order to be ready for the digital revolution, the company had repositioned itself strategically in 1994–1995 by giving up many of its investments outside the broadcasting sector, and had restructured its capital through a public exchange offer (two CLT shares for one Audiofina share) centering around CLMM (*Compagnie Luxembourgeoise Multi-Media*), a Luxembourg holding company controlled by GBL/Electrafina and Havas which had become Audiofina's reference group (with 54% of its capital).

Faced with the financial cost of the changeover to digital technology and despite the release of internal liquid assets, the CLT knew that it would not be able to go it alone in this new battle in France and Germany. In France, the company found itself in direct competition with Canal+ and gave up the fight in December 1995. In Germany, after several attempts to form a partnership with the Murdoch group (BSkyB), the Bertelsmann group said it was interested, before dropping CLT in favor of a common digital platform which included Bertelsmann itself, Murdoch, Canal+ and Havas, to compete with CLT. Bertelsmann, Canal+ and Havas, which shared direct and indirect interests in pay-TV in Germany, turned their back on CLT although two of them were associated with the group, with which they had already launched several joint companies in television (with Bertelsmann in Germany) and advertising (the IP group with Havas). While Bertelsmann deserved a good part of the blame for this desertion, it was presented essentially as a desertion of the CLT by Havas. On April 2, 1996, a project to divide CLT shares between Audiofina and Bertelsmann was made public, while the CLT was also starting negotiations with TF1 in order to enter TPS, the cluster of French digital channels in competition with that of Canal+. On July 3, the CLT-UFA agreement was finalized.

In this set up, the CLT-UFA was 98% owned by the CLT-UFA holding company. This was owned equally by BW TV (Bertelsmann-WAZ TV), a German company bringing together the interests of the Bertelsmann Group (80%) and of the regional press group, WAZ (20%) and by Audiofina, itself controlled both directly and indirectly by GBL. As a result Belgian influence within the Luxembourg company was at least offset by that of the German publisher, which has forced Belgium's Bruxelles-Lambert group to restructure its presence in Audiofina.

On the other hand, the advent of Bertelsmann forced the CLT to revise its strategy and to withdraw from the development of digital broadcasting in Germany, although its exclusion from the digital platform of Bertelsmann, Murdoch, Canal+ and Havas had been the cause of its forced reconciliation with Bertelsmann. With the CLT having lost €90 million in this unsuccessful venture, Bertelsmann announced, on September 17, 1996, its intention to withdraw from digital TV. Nine days after this decision the new CLT management agreed to reposition itself in more traditional market segments: 'toll-free TV' and pay-TV.

Throughout the months that were to follow this decision, the CLT-UFA position on pay-TV and digital multi-channel packages developed somewhat erratically. In France, CLT-UFA sided with private station TF1 and its public partners in the TPS package. In June 1997 in Germany, CLT-UFA and the Kirch group announced their decision to combine the activities of Première and DF1. The related contracts were finalized in November and included provisions relating to the joint control of Premiere by CLT-UFA and the Kirch group, following the purchase of shares held by Canal+. Furthermore, to put an end to a conflict that was poisoning relations with the Havas Group concerning the management of the IP advertising agencies, Havas International/IP was to be bought by CLT-UFA on December 24, 1997.

These operations, in addition to inroads in Great Britain (Channel 5) and Eastern Europe, were to prove extremely expensive for the company. Experiencing constant growth since its successful penetration of the German market, the CLT-UFA group recorded consolidated sales of €3.09 billion in 1998, which represented €793 million more than in 1996. However, despite an increasing turnover, in 1997 CLT lost its legendary profitable situation. In 1998, the Group ended the period with a loss of €14.03 million. Its loss of the previous year had been significantly greater: €71.44 million.

In order to stem the hemorrhage, the company management decided to change strategies. Betting on the German market and its agreement with Kirch, it abandoned its participation in TPS at the beginning of 1998, selling it to French company M6 (5%) and to the Lyonnaise des Eaux (15%). Thus CLT-UFA was only indirectly involved in digital television in France. Similarly, CLT-UFA was to sell in March 1988 65% of its holding in French-language channel RTL9 to the French AB Group. This operation, which brought the chain together with the major distributor of programs broadcast in France, nevertheless maintained this channel within the bosom of Luxembourg, which enabled it to take advantage of more 'favorable' legislation in terms of advertising transmissions.

As an epilogue to the story of digital television in Germany, a decision of the European authorities concerning the CLT-UFA/Kirch joint venture was delivered at the end of May 1998. Contrary to the hopes of the partners, it was negative based on the risks of abuse of dominant position. Following this decision, the company completely revised its growth strategy. On March 25, 1999, CLT-UFA sold 45% of the Première capital to Kirch. This transaction had been authorized by the Federal Cartel Office, and CLT-UFA thereafter owned only 5% of the channel's capital, and chose to focus once and for all on free television. This remaining 5% furthermore will be transferred to Kirch on January 11, 2001.

In December 1999, the long hesitation of the French Vivendi (ex-Havas) Group concerning its interest in CLT also came to an end. As operator of the Canal+ Group, Vivendi had been worrying for some time about its pursuit of an investment in the Audiofina company, CLT's Franco-Belgian leg. Vivendi finally pulled out, leaving the way clear for Albert Frère and his associate, the Canadian Desmarais Group.

The story, however, was not to end there. It had been known for a long time that the Belgian financier, Albert Frère, was wondering about maintaining his presence in CLT, and, in view of his age, he was said to be ready to transfer his holdings in Audiofina. Furthermore, although present in numerous European countries, the CLT-UFA was not managing to impose itself as the leading European audio-visual company. Its presence in the United Kingdom, in particular, remained too restricted. Further reshaping of the company was required. This occurred in two time frames. In April 2000, CLT-UFA's capital was opened to the British company, Pearson PLC, an audiovisual specialist in Great Britain and the United States (catalogue proprietor, program designer and television operator [Thames TV, Channel 5 UK]). CLT-UFA and Pearson were already associated in the capital of the British channel, Channel 5.

Officially, Pearson would allow CLT-UFA access to its catalogues and its know-how in television matters. Unofficially, the association finally allowed the 'continental' CLT-UFA business to set its sights on the Anglo-Saxon world. Furthermore, by opening itself to the capital market, the new structure departed from the 'family' capitalism by which it had been constituted until then.

Following the advent of Pearson, the company was renamed as the RTL Group. Even if the importance of its British wing were to continue to grow, it was agreed that its head office would remain in Luxembourg. The weight of the partners within the company was presented as follows: BW-TV 37%, Audiofina 30%, Pearson 22%. The balance, 11%, was intended to be quoted on the London and Brussels stock markets. This occurred in July 2000, with RTL Group SA being officially created on July 24, 2000.

Less than a year after Pearson's entry, on February 5, 2001, Bertelsmann AG and the Groupe Bruxelles Lambert S.A. (GBL) announced that Bertelsmann was going to acquire the 30% interest held in the RTL Group by GBL and its majority company, Electrafina. In exchange, GBL would become a 25.1% shareholder of Bertelsmann. For the first time, the German family group opened itself up to a minority partner. Following this transaction, Bertelsmann and its partner, WAZ, would now control 67% of the RTL Group. The other RTL Group shareholders were not affected by the transaction. Since that date, the RTL Group shareholding has been presented as follows: Bertelsmann 67% (37% of which with WAZ), Pearson 22%, the public 10.3%, the Group's cash flow .7%. The European Commission sanctioned the company's new structure on May 11, 2001. The RTL Group wholly owns the CLT-UFA holding company, which owns 99.6% of CLT-UFA. The Group also wholly owns Pearson Television and its programming company, Grundy, and holds 28% of the Groupe Jean-Claude Darmon, the specialist in audio-visual rebroadcasting rights.

Adapting its strategy to technological development, the CLT was always careful to take full advantage of its central position in Europe. In the radio era, this meant a very large broadcasting area (France, United Kingdom, Germany, Benelux). While beneficial for radio, this location was more of a hindrance for the CLT in the early days of television, its physical Hertzian coverage area being limited to sparsely populated regions. New technology (cable, then satellite) would allow the CLT television signals to overcome these natural barriers and reach heavily populated areas, first of all in Belgium, and then in Germany. This strategy (pan-European broadcasting from Luxembourg) prevailed in the CLT until the early 1980's. Then, the company opted for a policy of decentralization based on the creation of national channels, established in and, if possible, transmitting directly from the geographical zones concerned (Belgium, then France and Germany, then the Netherlands and the United Kingdom). While Luxembourg remained the hub of its business activities, the company thus became a true multinational corporation, both with respect to target audiences and capital ownership.

Table 1. *CLT Key Figures, in €million (€100 = LUF 4,034)*

Description	1997	1998	%
Turnover (1)	2,800	3,086	+9
Operating result (1)	139	278	+100
Net result (2)	-72	-15	+80
Shareholders' equity (3)	476	464	-3
Balance sheet total	2,752	3,004	+9
Traditional operations	84	156	+88
Projects & developments	-136	-121	+11
Non-operating result	-20	-50	-150
Net result (2)	-72	-15	+80

(1) Consolidated
(2) Group share
(3) Excluding minority interests
Source: CLT-UFA Annual Report 1998

Table 2. *CLT Key figures 1999–2000, in €million (1999 = before merging, 2000 = after merging)*

Description	December 2000	December 1999	Change
Revenue	2,854	1,383	+ 106%
EBITA (1)	358	157	+ 128%
Amortization of goodwill	(172)	(69)	+ 149%
Profit before taxes	238	301	- 21%
Profit from ordinary activities	96	118	- 19%
Net profit for the year	77	110	- 30%
Earnings per share (basic and diluted) in EUR	0.76	1.82	- 58

(1) EBITA represents earnings before interest and taxes excluding amortization of goodwill and gain from sale of subsidiaries, joint ventures and other investments.

This is the context in which CLT established its initial contacts with the Bertelsmann group. In 1998, 74% of the CLT-UFA consolidated turnover came from television, 16%

from production rights and 8% from radio. Sixty-three percent of these sales figures were achieved in Germany, 16% in France, and 12% in Benelux countries. CLT-UFA is active in 11 European countries.

In 2000, the RTL Group's turnover, taking Pearson's contribution into account, was up 14.3% on the previous year. Television accounted for 71% of this, the programming business 27%, and radio 6%. Fifty-six percent of the radio and television turnover was achieved in Germany, 19% in France, 11% in The Netherlands, 10% in the United Kingdom, and 4% in the other territories where the RTL Group was developing its activities.

III   Legal Framework

In the Grand Duchy of Luxembourg, the single concession system (which views the CLT as the private sector equivalent of a state monopoly) was revised in 1991 as part of an act drawn up in the general European context of radio and television deregulation. The content of this law needed to be brought up to date, taking account of the necessity of incorporating into Grand Ducal law the elements of the European 'Television Without Frontiers' Directive and in order to avoid, at least in the wording, the manifest appearance of the principle of priority of concession de facto granted to CLT. A draft text was drawn up with this in mind.

The principle of the law is that of an individual and non-transferable concession or license for broadcasting, which is of limited duration but renewable, and which may at any time be withdrawn in the event of non-compliance with the conditions on which it was granted or the obligations of the contractual terms and conditions. The act makes a distinction between various types of programs: programs broadcast internationally, programs aimed at a small audience, and 'other broadcasting modes.' In many respects it would seem to have been tailor-made to satisfy those players already in the Luxembourg broadcasting system, namely the CLT (mainly in local and international television) and the SES corporation (the owner of Luxembourg's Astra satellite system) in its provisions concerning satellite transmission. The Luxembourg legislation would therefore seem above all to ratify the *de facto* monopoly situations previously seen in the radio- and television sector, enabling the government to be the sole decision maker in most matters.

In adapting the new European directive to Grand Duchy realities, the draft text defines the qualities expected from a Luxembourg television broadcasting body and by extension those of a radio broadcasting body. It defines non-Luxembourg television and radio programs as emanating from a radio or television body that does not fall within Luxembourg jurisdiction, but which uses a Luxembourg frequency. The text also mentions Luxembourg programs that are not 'broadcast' (satellite programs) and Luxembourg cable programs. The commentary on the draft amendment to the law thus stipulates that the law applies when there is transmission of a program intended for public consumption. In this case, one must first establish which broadcasting body is responsible. In the case of a television program, it is the criteria coming from the directive that will enable later determination of whether it comes from a Luxembourg television broadcasting body. In the case of a radio program, the definition of the Luxembourg radio broadcasting body will be decisive. If the broadcasting body is from Luxembourg, then the program also is from Luxembourg. This would be either a broadcast program, a satellite program, or a cable program, according to the transmission mode employed. In the case of Luxembourg broadcast programs, a further distinction is drawn between the various types of programs. In the case of a non-Luxembourg broadcasting body, the program is considered a non-Luxembourg program. Even though it was transmitted on a Luxembourg terrestrial broadcasting frequency, it would have the status of a non-Luxembourg broadcast program.

Luxembourg places particular emphasis on the official location of radio and television activity. Thus the law defines television broadcasting bodies established in Luxembourg as those having their real head-office in the Grand Duchy of Luxembourg, with all relating to programming there. In the commentary on the text, it is stipulated that the location of a significant part of its staff employed in television broadcasting activity in Luxembourg does not mean that the broadcasting body has to have the majority of its personnel in Luxembourg. This provision aims rather to make it clear that the presence in Luxembourg cannot be merely theoretical or symbolic. A letterbox and an office will not do. The head-office has to be effectively located in Luxembourg and part of the operational personnel must be there as well. On the other hand, the location of part of the personnel, even a majority part, in a country other than Luxembourg in no way precludes the body from being considered as being established in Luxembourg.

An Independent Broadcasting Commission (CIR) and a National Program Council (CNP) have official powers of opinion and supervision in programming matters. The CIR also fulfils a function regarding the appointment of all radio and television media operators. In practice, this mostly concerns local media, as the ultimate decisions are always made by the government. The CIR is made up of five members appointed for four years, including a judge as president and one member who is proposed by the Press Council. The CNP includes a maximum of 25 members, delegated for five years by the most representative organizations of social and cultural life of the country, including recognized churches, parliamentary political parties, unions and employer organizations, and various federations of associations. The act offers some possibilities for opening up the field to new players in local radio as well as in the radio network sector, where it gives some attention to anti-trust questions: no natural person or legal entity may hold shares in more than one network nor may they hold more than 25% of the shares in the network to which they belong.

The 1991 act, which was drawn up to suit the international situation of the CLT, sets out the general contents of the licensee's terms and conditions, stipulating in particular that the licensee's activity is to be monitored by government commissioners. In line with the precautions taken previously regarding the shareholding structure of radio and TV broadcasting companies operating in the Grand Duchy, the act specifically provides for a governmental right of supervision regarding the articles of association, the shareholders and the various departments of the licensee and all companies participating in the concession. With regard to social and cultural programs, the act specifies that one high-frequency band must be – entirely or partially – reserved for this type of programs. The act also takes other broadcasting methods into consideration. It specifies that any operation of a Luxembourg satellite system is subject to the granting of a concession by the government.

IV   Radio and Television Broadcasting for Luxembourg Citizens

Unlike local legislation, Luxembourg's broadcasting scene remains underdeveloped. The only *national* broadcast, representing the local identity of the Grand Duchy, is a daily hour-long program in the Luxembourg language (*Letzeburgesch*) called *RTL Télé Letzebuerg*, since 1999 preceded by a half-hour children's program. Only composed of local and regional news plus a complement of special service and entertainment features of interest to Luxembourg, this program is broadcast every day at 7:00 p.m. and runs three times in a continuous loop. Alongside this daily broadcasting, RTL Luxembourg also broadcasts one hour of cultural programs per week, and one hour of sports. CLT-UFA may also broadcast on this channel half-a-dozen repeats of exceptional events.

The station's maximum amount of advertising revenue is set out each year by the government (11% of the total advertising revenue of the Luxembourg media in 2000). In radio, the CLT transmits *RTL Radio Letzebuerg*. For 30 years this was the only 'national' radio station in Luxembourg before the new act governing broadcasting opened up new opportunities. The radio station collects 13% of the advertising expenditure in the Luxembourg media and 78% of the advertising investment in the radio sector.

The Grand Duchy also has two local cable television stations: Uelzechtkanal and Nordliicht. Run by non-profit organizations, they broadcast weekly or monthly.

Since the new media law of 1991 which formally abolished the monopoly of CLT, four new radio broadcasting franchises were allocated in 1992 to consortia involving the written press. *Eldoradio*, the most successful, is indirectly controlled by CLT/RTL. Other shareholders are the *Tageblatt*, the *Letzebuerger Journal*, *Revue* and the *d'Letzebuerger Land*. The reference shareholder of *Den Neie Radio* (DNR) is *Imprimerie Saint-Paul*, Luxembourg's leading press group, supplemented by some Catholic associations and some business interests. Imprimerie Saint-Paul also finances *Radio Latina*, which addresses itself primarily to 32% of the foreigners residing in Luxembourg. *Radio Ara* is owned by organizations belonging to the so-called associative movement.

Table 3. *The CLT Empire in Europe (excluding production, service and rights management companies)* (2001)*

	Interests in Radio	Interests in Television
Belgium	36% of *Radio Contact. SA* 47% of *Bel-RTL (SA INADI)*	66% of *RTL-TVI* 66% of *CLUB RTL*
Germany	100% of *RTL Radio+* 100% of *RTL 104.6+* 16% of *Antenne Bayern+* 29% of *Radio Hamburg+* 8.1% of *Klassik Radio+* 9.8% of *Radio 21+* 51% of *FM Radio Network* 16.1% of *Radio NRW+* 30% of *Berliner Rundfunk+*	100% of *RTL-Télévision* 35.9% of *RTL2* 50% of *Super RTL* 99.7% of *Vox*
France	100% of *RTL Paris* 100% of *RTL2* 100% of *Fun Radio*	35% of *RTL9* 43.8% of *M6* (*Métropole Télévision*) (+ participations via *M6*) 23.8% of *TMC*
Luxembourg	100% of *RTL Radio Letzebuerg*	100% of *RTL Télé Letzebuerg*
The Netherlands	100% of *Veronica FM*	100% of *RTL4* 100% of *RTL5 Nieuws & weer* 100% of *Veronica*
Sweden	100% of *WOW 105.5* 49% of *104,7 RTL*	
UK and Ireland	80% of *Atlantic 252*	64.6% of *Channel 5* (UK)
Hungary		49% of *RTL Klub*
Poland		100% of *RTL 7*
Spain		17% of *Antena 3* 5% of *Via Digital*

*In order to depict the RTL Group's activities as a whole, one would need to add to this table all the
Group's companies involved in audiovisual content production, which considerably grew in number
as a result of the merger with Pearson, as well as its new developments in multimedia.

According to the law, 40 local radio stations could also be licensed. But only a dozen
make regular broadcasts. Finally, in 1993 the State created a public socio-cultural radio
station. Funded by taxpayers' money (€ 2.9 million in 1999) it is called RSC (*établisse-
ment public de radio socio-culturelle*) or 100.7 or 'Honnert 7.' This radio had initially to
share its national FM frequency with RTL. But, since 1998, it transmits a 24-hour program and has the exclusive use of its frequencies.

Table 4. *Television Programs under Luxembourg Concession (Hertzian or satellite transmission) (2000)*

RTL Télé Letzebuerg	CLT-UFA S.A.
RTL 9	CLT-UFA S.A.
RTL TVi	CLT-UFA S.A.
Club RTL	CLT-UFA S.A.
RTL 4	CLT-UFA S.A.
RTL 5	CLT-UFA S.A
RTL 7	CLT-UFA S.A.
RTL Television	CLT-UFA S.A.
Uelzechtkanal	Uelzechtkanal a.s.b.l.
Nordliicht	Nordliicht TV s.a.r.l.
Grand Tourisme	Canal Europe Audiovisuel S.A
No ZAP TV	Canal Europe Audiovisuel S.A.
ALICE	Sitcom International S.A.
NUVOLARI	Sitcom International S.A.
LEONARDO	Sitcom International S.A.
LIBERTY TV.COM	Maastricht Multimedia S.A.
WHISHLINE	Multithématiques Luxembourg S.A.

RTL Télé Letzebuerg	CLT-UFA S.A.
RTL 9	CLT-UFA S.A.
RTL TVi	CLT-UFA S.A.
Club RTL	CLT-UFA S.A.
RTL 4	CLT-UFA S.A.
RTL 5	CLT-UFA S.A
RTL 7	CLT-UFA S.A.
RTL Television	CLT-UFA S.A.
Uelzechtkanal	Uelzechtkanal a.s.b.l.
Nordliicht	Nordliicht TV s.a.r.l.
Grand Tourisme	Canal Europe Audiovisuel S.A
No ZAP TV	Canal Europe Audiovisuel S.A.
ALICE	Sitcom International S.A.
NUVOLARI	Sitcom International S.A.
LEONARDO	Sitcom International S.A.
LIBERTY TV.COM	Maastricht Multimedia S.A.
WHISHLINE	Multithématiques Luxembourg S.A.

V   Television from Abroad and Audience Figures

Even though only *RTL Letzebuerg* broadcasts in the Luxembourg language, the local population can watch every day more than 40 foreign languages channels, some belonging to the CLT and originating in Luxembourg, others broadcast from abroad and provided via cable. The density of the cable network in Luxembourg is among the highest in Europe. But unlike their neighbors, the Luxembourgers are not overcharged as a result: the yearly subscription fee ranges from € 37 to 124 depending on the cable company.

Following various reorganizations, seven companies are currently sharing the cable market. Cable coverage in the Grand Duchy is 96%, while the estimated number of satellite dishes is a mere 20,000. Due to the size of the Duchy and the volume of revenues, no other domestic television service has arisen to compete with *RTL Télé Letzebuerg*. There are no pay-TV and no pay-per-view services. But viewers can subscribe to Canal+ or Première.

Table 5. *TV Audience Shares in Luxembourg (7:00–24:00, 1998 – Viewers aged 12+)*

Television Channel	Audience Share (in %)
RTL Tele Letzebuerg	15.5
RTL (Germany)	11.0
TF1 (France)	9.4
PRO 7 (Germany)	9.4
ARD (Germany	7.6
SAT 1	6.2
ZDF (Germany)	6.1
RTPI (Portugal)	5.4
M6	4.0
France 2	2.9
RTL II	2.9

Unlike a majority of European countries, Luxembourg's limited television market has not lent itself to the introduction of an automated audience measurement system. There is only a daily telephone survey consisting of 1,000 interviews among a panel of 3,522 individuals representative of the population aged 12 and over. Its aim is to measure TV viewing using the 'day-after recall' method. Its results only pertain to the 7:30–8:30 p.m. time slot, which does not allow comparisons with other countries. In this slot, the Luxembourg program is the leader. Hot on its heels are a number of mainly German-language programs (Letzeburgesch being very similar to German). The 5% audience share of Portuguese TV station RTPI owes to the large numbers of Portuguese immigrants living in the country.

VI   The Future of CLT

The reconfiguration of CLT that occurred in 2000–2001 enshrined the company in a pan-European perspective simultaneously combining development rationales, vertical integration (bringing together all the stages of audio-visual production and transmission) and horizontal integration (installation in a large number of countries). The association with Pearson, which enabled it to develop its presence in the Anglo-Saxon countries and gave it access to program catalogues that had been unavailable to it, also conferred a new bipolarity on the RTL Group (Germany-Great Britain), from which the European Latin (French-speaking) orbit was absent. This, however, had previously occupied an essential role in CLT's identity.

Because of the fresh capital that the company intended to acquire from its entry into the stock market, the growth of its activities internationally should not be problematical. A development of the RTL Group's projects in the area of multimedia is currently on the agenda. In the end, the company could be looking to integrate beneath a single umbrella all its media activities, whether relating to the classical media (radio and television) or multimedia (the Internet).

VII   New Media

The future of television in Luxembourg hinges on the development of the SES corporation (*Société Européenne des Satellites*). This company, in whose capital the CLT does not have any share, operates under a franchise agreement with the State of Luxembourg; the latter holds 20% of the company's capital through two state-owned financial institutions and can be considered as the company's reference shareholder. Incorporated in Luxembourg, SES was founded in 1985. Since 1989, it has been operating the Astra Satellite System which transmits television and radio channels throughout Europe. Its franchise, that was to expire in 2015, has been extended to 2021 at the time of the company's merger with General Electric. SES's revenue is generated by leasing channels on the Astra satellites to television and radio broadcasts. The latest satellites launched by Astra are completely designed for digital television.

After being first done by Arianespace, the launches of the American-made Astra satellite, were entrusted to the Russians at Baikonour. These satellites occupy two key orbital positions (19,211° East and 28,21° East). Very well established in Europe, where it shares with Eutelsat virtually the whole of the satellite transmission market, SES took a 34% interest in Chinese satellite operator, AsiaSat (Hong Kong) in 1998.

On March 28, 2001, SES merged with GE American Communications Inc (GE Americom), a subsidiary of America's General Electric. This association between the European company and its transatlantic equivalent spawned the world's largest satellite operator. Directly or indirectly, the two companies in 2001 were managing 41 telecommunication satellites. In exchange for consenting to this merger, the Luxembourg State received €6.4 billion from the company, an advance on the license fees payable from 2001 to 2021. This sum will be reinvested in SES, but the Luxembourg State is maintaining 33% of the company's voting rights. Nearly 80% of the SES voting rights are still European, with the balance falling into American hands.

While it has historically focused on broadcasting only, the Grand Duchy later decided to encourage production. To this end, a tax-shelter system was set up at the end of the 1980's, enabling investors, including foreigners, to benefit from tax cuts on money invested in finance companies involved in radio and television production in Luxembourg.

References

Antoine, F. (1996). La CLT, un petit prince marié pour un empire, *Guide des médias*, 25:1–29. Brussels: Kluwer.

Benasi, S. (1995). Luxembourg, *Les télévisions du monde* (pp. 238–245). Paris: Corlet-Télérama-CNC-Procirep.

CLT Annual Report 1990, 1991, 1992, 1993, 1994, 1995. Luxembourg: CLT.

Hirsch, M. (2000) *The Luxembourg Media Landscape*, European Journalism Center, Maastricht. Available at [http://www.ejc.nl/jr/emland/luxembourg.html].

Lentzen, E. (1976). La Compagnie Luxembourgeoise de Télédiffusion (CLT), *Courrier hebdomadaire du CRISP* 721: 2–35.

Lentzen, E. (1985). La Compagnie Luxembourgeoise de Télédiffusion (CLT), *Courrier hebdomadaire du CRISP* 1066: 3–47.

Marechal, D. (1994). *Radio Luxembourg, 1933–1993*, Presses universitaires de Nancy/ Editions serpenoises.

RTL Group Annual Report (2000). Luxembourg: CLT.

Sabbagh, A. (1995). *La radio, rendez-vous sur les ondes*. Paris: Gallimard.

Television 1995. European Key Facts. Paris: IP.

Television 1996. European Key Facts. Paris: IP.

The Netherlands

by Kees van der Haak and Leo van Snippenburg

I   Broadcasting in the Netherlands: The Rise and Decline of Segmentation

1.1 The Early Years – When Radio Was King

Radio broadcasting in the Netherlands started in 1919 with the transmission of the program *Soirée Musicale* by engineer H. Steringa Idzerda, who owned an electronics company. In the beginning, he financed the venture himself, not only for business reasons, but also due to the appeal of the new technology and the opportunities afforded by the new medium. Later on he asked his listeners to contribute to the financing of the station. It was probably the world's first continuously scheduled radio service for the public, at least according to some (Dutch) historians. This initiative was soon followed up by many other radio stations. Among these pioneers were hobbyists as well as businessmen intent on promoting electronic products.

As early as the 1920's, the government tried to prevent things from becoming too chaotic by requiring broadcasters to apply for a license. In order to secure a broadcasting license the many applicants were advised to merge into larger units and to apply formally (Browne, 1989: 135). The government soon turned to a policy giving the highest priority to the cultural interests of the various cultural groups that made up Dutch society. This is how broadcasting policy came to contribute to the segmentation of society in the Netherlands.

Some five organizations arose in those years. These were voluntary membership associations including members of one of five of the country's major social and cultural segments. The first to emerge was *NCRV* (Dutch Christian Radio Association), an association regrouping (moderate to orthodox) members of the Protestant church that received a license in 1924. In 1925 this was followed by *KRO* (Catholic Radio Association), representing the Catholic segment, as well as *VARA* (Association of Radio Enthusiasts), a broadcasting association targeting blue collar workers. In 1926 *VPRO* (Modern Protestant Radio) was allowed into the system as the 'voice' of the more liberal Protestants. In 1928 *AVRO* (General Association of Radio Broadcasting) was born of a merger between a number of associations of radio broadcasting hobbyists often related to producers of electronic equipment (Wijfjes, 1994: 48–49 & 393–400). AVRO was, and still is, less tied to a particular social and cultural segment than the other four associations. However, it can be characterized as having a rather middle-class, bourgeois cultural identity.

Conflicts arose between the different associations as to the proper allocation of total available air time on the two transmission installations in operation at that time. In 1930 the government solved the problem through the so-called *air time decree* allocating

20% of total air time to each of the four larger associations (NCRV, KRO, VARA and AVRO) and 5% to the smaller one (VPRO). The remaining 15% of available air time was reserved for services to be broadcast under the responsibility of some smaller specific institutions. Among them were services for small religious groups, educational services, and general knowledge services that would otherwise be neglected (educational programs for barge dwellers and general educational programs for adults).

This decree supported the further development of the broadcasting system based on existing social and cultural segments. Using arms-length regulation it maintained a measure of order amongst broadcasting interests and guaranteed pluralism in a public service system based on private (non-profit) associations with voluntary membership. Until recently, the Dutch government held on to this policy of support to a pluralistic public broadcasting system built along social and cultural lines, including in the 1980's and early 1990's, when international commercial broadcasting arose and national commercial broadcasting was legalized. Even today the government seems intent on keeping the public part of the whole broadcasting system as strong as possible in a context of national and international competition in commercial broadcasting.

Already in the 1920's and 1930's the government sometimes chose to interfere with programming content, sometimes even going so far as banning programs considered offensive to public morality or friendly nation states, for instance. Broadcasters disregarding government censorship were punished. This often happened to VARA. In addition, starting in the 1930's, supporters of a national public broadcasting corporation and trade and industry interest, all of which opposed the segmented system, tried to attack the powerful alliance of the broadcasting associations and the government. They called for the system to be accessible to other agents, in addition to the five associations. At first they did not succeed. The government, itself always a coalition of representatives of an equally segmented political system, continued to favor the existing, exclusively public broadcasting system.

In the 1920's and 1930's the broadcasting associations had to raise the necessary funds from their members and related organizations. Advertising and sponsoring were not allowed. License fees for all radio equipment owners were not imposed before 1941, when Nazi Germany occupied the Netherlands (Bakker, 1991: 125). After the 1940 invasion, the existing broadcasting system was replaced by a centralized system which many people chose to ignore, illegally tuning in to radio stations outside German-controlled territory. When all radio receivers had to be surrendered to the occupying forces, some people kept on listening secretly in spite of the danger. The actual proportion of the population who kept listening to the foreign stations and to *Radio Oranje* (a station set up by the Dutch government in exile in London) is not known (Wijfjes, 1994: 51–58).

In 1945 the old public broadcasting structure was restored in the Netherlands. Some new licenses were granted to smaller institutions for the use of part of the 15% slot not allocated to the five larger broadcasting associations. The associations and the newly installed government also agreed to pool resources and to cooperate more than before in order to achieve better efficiency, as members of the *Nederlandse Radio Unie* (*NRU*), an umbrella association whose board included a representative of the minister for education, culture and science. This representative held a right of veto in all board decisions, but never used it.

1.2 The Arrival of Television

In 1951, when radio had found its way in just about every Dutch household, television was introduced. The broadcasting associations and some of the small license holders were immediately granted TV broadcasting licenses. A joint body for television (NTS) was established. Trade and industry, as well as other potential broadcasters, were excluded from the system. Advertising and sponsoring remained forbidden. In the first years TV air time was restricted to a few hours and a few days per week, and a comparatively large proportion of it was to be filled by the NTS.

In the 1950's the population proved slow to adopt television (things went much quicker after 1960). There were four major causes for this:

1. low incomes among large parts of the population together with the relatively high prices of television sets;
2. restricted reach – only one TV transmitting facility was available, and this did not even cover the whole of the Dutch territory;
3. air time restricted to only a few hours and a few days a week;
4. religious views among parts of the population – television being seen as potentially harmful for the minds of believers (Stappers, Reijnders & Möller, 1990: 24).

From the beginning television attracted viewers from all segments of society, regardless of the particular broadcasting association filling the air waves at that particular moment. This was not the case with radio programs, which had mostly attracted members of the specific segment being catered for. Television's relatively all-inclusive nature in this sense probably contributed to softening the sharp distinctions between the various components of Dutch society in the 1960's.

Trade and industry renewed their efforts to gain access to the broadcasting system, but to no avail until the mid-1960's. But pirate radio stations (such as *Radio Veronica*), not to mention one commercial radio and television station (*Radio/TV Noordzee*) had already started broadcasting from outside Dutch territorial waters in the North Sea. In general, no special government measures were taken to prevent pirate radio stations from airing their programs (mostly popular music laced with commercials). However, the illegal television broadcasts were stopped by the military, which stormed TV Noordzee's oil rig after Parliament had passed a specific law allowing the Dutch government to take such an action (Browne, 1989: 14; Sterk, 1991: 33).

From 1964 a second TV broadcasting facility was made available to the established television associations. Political pressure to open up the broadcasting system to commercial interests and new public license holders increased. In 1965 the Dutch government coalition fell after failing to reach an agreement on the distribution of advertising revenue. The new government soon came up with the *Nota Open Bestel* (White Paper on an Open System) in which it unveiled its plans for a renewal of the broadcasting system, including new broadcast regulations as part of a specific broadcasting act. This would give the Netherlands its first broadcasting legislation since radio's emergence back in 1919.

1.3 The Broadcasting Act

The new system eventually came into effect in May 1969, after the arrival of color television (1967). The new act was a compromise between commercial and public interests, attempting to preserve the old segmented structure while acknowledging the existence of a number of new public players. The commercial/public broadcasting compromise was that commercial broadcasting remained prohibited while advertising was introduced, under strict regulation, into the public system. In order for the public broadcasters to remain independent of commercial interests, a broadcasting advertising corporation (*STER*) was founded in 1967. Commercials were only allowed in between – and never during – complete programs, making up only a small portion of daily air time. Most of the profits were divided among the public broadcasters, to be spent on programming. Part of the profits had to be handed over to the print media to make up for subsequent advertising revenue losses.

While traditional broadcasting associations kept their protected positions, some newcomers were allowed entrance in the system provided: (1) they had a valid claim as representatives of distinctive social and cultural parts of the Dutch population, (2) they were able to meet the latter's needs and (3) they had the support of at least 40,000 registered members. The first newcomer was *TROS* (Television and Radio Broadcasting Corporation). It had had a foot in the door since 1967, when it had been granted the status of aspiring broadcasting association. Soon to follow were *EO* (Evangelical Broadcasting Corporation) and *VOO* (Veronica Broadcasting Organization, also the offspring of a former pirate station), respectively in 1970 and 1975 (Sterk, 1991: 35–36).

Under the new broadcasting act the air time allocated to the various broadcasting associations – and therefore their share of the TV programming budget – were related to the number of registered members. The associations fell into four categories: a so-called 'aspiring broadcasting association' category, and C, B, and A categories, based on membership (40,000, 100,000, 300,000 or 450,000 members respectively). Members were, and still are, subscribers to the magazine of a particular broadcasting association or people paying a regular subscription fee to the association – a small annual fee such as €7 is enough to qualify as a member.

A fourth important regulation merged the umbrella radio broadcasting organization (NRU) with the umbrella organization of television broadcasters (NTS). The resulting organization was named *NOS* (Netherlands Broadcasting Corporation). It became responsible for more centralized program making (such as regular news releases on television and high quality cultural programs), and more coordination and representative tasks than had been performed before by the two separate organizations. It also would receive a guaranteed share of air time, license fees and advertising revenue. In addition NOS was granted increased autonomy. Another of its tasks was the management of all television and radio facilities to be used by the associations and NOS itself for the production of programs. The NOS was to be governed by a board of representatives of the broadcasting associations and the government (Browne, 1989: 143).

1.4 Competition and *'Vertrossing'*

Competition for popularity and members among the broadcasting associations was stimulated by the arrival in the public broadcasting system of new broadcasting associations, especially TROS and VOO – two organizations without a clear foundation in specific social and cultural groups – as well as the fact that air time and budget share were now based on actual membership 'status.' As a consequence the program supply of several associations gradually lost depth and quality. More and more talk shows, sitcoms and other foreign – especially American – series came to be shown on TV. These imported programs were much cheaper than those made for the small Dutch home market, and they proved very popular with a large cross-section of the Dutch population (Manschot, 1993).

Simultaneously, the associations (especially TROS and VOO) indulged in thinly veiled commercial activities such as surreptitious advertising, product placement and merchandising. Such trends – superficiality of programming, competition for members seen as a market-share strategy, and a more commercial attitude – have been dubbed *vertrossing*, after the name of the TROS broadcasting association, which was the first to take on such a stance as early as the 1960's.

When, in the early 1980's, satellite and cable television began to gain ground, the public system found itself under a growing outside threat. External competition from foreign commercial stations, and later on from stations broadcasting from abroad but targeting Dutch viewers directly, in their own language (Luxembourg-based *RTL*), as well as the *vertrossing* of the system forced the government to take action.

1.5 A New Act

To make the system more defensible against increased internal and external competition while evading new demands that the system be opened up to private initiative, the government came up with new, stricter criteria for entrance in the system and admission in a higher category. This measure clearly aimed to keep out new potential public broadcasters. For example, under the new rule an association had to have 60,000 members, instead of the former 40,000 to be eligible for *aspirant* status. This requirement became effective as early as 1980.

Second, and more significant, in 1983 the Christian/Right Wing government coalition of the time came up with a completely new White Paper on the future of the mass media in the Netherlands. This was followed by a new law coming into force in 1988, called *Mediawet* (Media Act). The new law did not target the broadcasting system only, as had been the case with the 1969 *Broadcasting Act*, but included regulations for all mass media. And, like the *Broadcasting Act*, the new act was again "a compromise rather than a wholesale revamping of the broadcast structure" (Browne, 1989: 149).

With respect to the actual media developments nowadays, four regulations of this act are especially relevant. These are the following:

1. According to the 1988 Act, only public broadcasters could make use of the available terrestrial frequencies. Dutch commercial stations remained forbidden, including on cable. Even foreign stations were not allowed on the cable systems if they carried advertising in the Dutch language or otherwise mainly directed at a Dutch audience. However, the operation of infrastructure services via satellite and cable was left to private enterprise.
2. NOS had to give up its production facilities, which from then on would be handled by a limited liability company, the NOB (Dutch Broadcast Production Company) (Browne, 1989: 149). From then on, NOS would stick to its broadcasting, coordination and representative tasks.
3. A so-called *Media Commission* was established. This institution was independent both from the government and broadcasters and was supposed to take over part of the government and NOS's tasks regarding supervision, discipline, and air time allocation. This pertained not only to radio and television services at the national level, but also to their local and regional counterparts. Later on, in the 1990's, when commercial broadcasting finally became legal in the Netherlands, its jurisdiction would be extended to commercial stations.
4. The following general requirements were set out regarding public TV programming: 20% of total air time had to consist of cultural programs, 25% of information oriented programs, 5% of educational programs, 25% of entertainment. The balance was left to the initiative of the broadcasters themselves. However, 50% of total air time had to be allocated to programs made by the broadcasters themselves or specially commissioned by them (cf. Sterk, 1991: 41).

The government's manifest intention with the enforcement of the *Media Act* was to protect the public broadcasting system against increasing internal and external threats and thus secure its social and cultural pluralism together with its informational, educational and cultural functions. Further aims were to make the system more efficient and to keep commercial broadcasting out of the Netherlands. The latter intention showed the *Media Act* as being clearly out of step with international media developments.

Concurrent to the preparation of the Media Act the government decided, on request from Parliament, to allow the public broadcasters to take possession of the third television network, whose frequencies – covering the whole territory – had been allocated to the Netherlands but had remained unused. The third channel was to be run by NOS and the minor (educational or religious) public broadcasters, in order to make room for the eight broadcasting associations on the two existing channels. So the third channel would have a specific mandate to complement that of the two other channels whose air time would be shared by the eight broadcasting associations. Thus the third channel started broadcasting in April 1988. However, this arrangement was soon abandoned. In 1991, the NOS board, following the advice of consultants *McKinsey & Company*, decided that the three public channels should become equally attractive, both to audiences and to advertisers. So programming on each channel was to be done by a fixed combination of three major public broadcasters and a number of minor broadcasters. To arrive at nine major public broadcasters, part of NOS was transformed into an independent organization, called NPS (Netherlands Program Corporation), and granted the same amount of air time as the associations had. As this required a review of the Media Act, it took several years before NPS, as a partner of VARA and VPRO on the third channel, could start operating (January 1995). Ironically, in the same year VOO (Veronica Broadcasting Organization) left the public broadcasting system. So in the arithmetic of public broadcasting, eight plus one still made eight.

Such is, roughly sketched, the history of the Dutch broadcasting system. Social segmentation has lost important ground, but is still visible in the broadcasting system, as in the schools system. Together with the relatively balanced program supply of NOS and NPS and the highly specific programs offered by the remaining small license holders, the programming of the large broadcasting associations representing the Netherlands' major social and cultural groupings make for a fairly pluralistic public broadcasting system. Public broadcasters achieved a television audience share of 39% in the year 2000 (population of six years and over; 6:00 p.m.–12:00 p.m.). The open door system is still working. In September 2000 a new broadcasting association joined the existing seven: BNN, targeting at a young audience.

II   The Rise of Commercial Broadcasting

2.1 Current Stations

RTL 4 and RTL 5
As mentioned above, the Media Act which came into force in January 1988 created a new supervisory body that would play an important role in the take-off phase of commercial broadcasting: the Media Commission. The wisdom of the Media Commission was put to a test in September 1989, when the Commission had to rule on two initiatives in relation with commercial broadcasting. Both initiatives originated from within the country, but as the Media Act did not allow commercial broadcasting, both had to be disguised as foreign broadcasters and use a satellite uplink from another European country. The signal would reach the Dutch population mainly by cable, which at the

time had 77% penetration. One of the would-be broadcasters was *RTL-Véronique*, a venture of Luxembourg company CLT that hardly tried to conceal the participation of Dutch public broadcaster Veronica. The other one was *TV 10*, set up by a consortium dominated by the Netherlands' biggest independent producer of television programs, Joop van den Ende. Both were ready to start broadcasting in October 1989. A few weeks before the newcomers were scheduled to come on the air, the Media Commission allowed RTL-Véronique's programs to be relayed by the Dutch cable operators, but banned TV 10. The Commission judged that CLT had a long standing tradition of providing radio and television programs to other countries, whereas TV 10 was obviously attempting to bypass Dutch law and could not be regarded as a genuine foreign broadcaster. Both rulings of the Media Commission were upheld in appeal procedures to the Council of State. Public broadcaster Veronica had to pay a fine of €7 million for its unlawful involvement in starting up a commercial station. TV 10 never went on the air and Joop van den Ende, who was boycotted by his former clients, the public broadcasters, had to sell off his star-studded shows to his rival RTL in order to avoid bankruptcy. RTL-Véronique (which changed its name to RTL-V first and then to RTL 4) gave up its initial low-budget programming in February 1990 and became very successful with Joop van den Ende as its main program supplier.

This success induced RTL to start a second channel, RTL 5 in 1992. This station's program supply included fewer original productions than RTL 4 and relied heavily on American series.

Yorin
In September 1995 Veronica, after 19 years as a public broadcaster, returned to its commercial roots and joined RTL 4 and RTL 5 to form the *Holland Media Group* (*HMG*). Veronica's target group was the *young and wild*. Veronica's first year as a commercial TV station was disappointing. Young people tend to be light television viewers and apparently seven days a week of Veronica programming was too much for them to digest. After broadening its target group Veronica did better in the following years. In 2000 Veronica decided to leave the HMG and to concentrate on internet. The Veronica association sold its 35% shares in HMG to the now only shareholder CLT-UFA. It was agreed that the HMG would continue the former Veronica station under a new name. From April 2001, the station is renamed *Yorin – the movement*.

SBS 6 and Net 5
Another commercial television station to be launched in 1995 was *SBS 6*, a joint venture of *Scandinavian Broadcasting System S.A.* (largely owned by American investor Harry Sloan, cable company UPC and Viacom/Paramount) which has a 70% share, and the Netherlands' largest newspaper, *De Telegraaf* (30%). Starting off as a true outsider, four days before Veronica, and competing with the latter to occupy the sixth position on the viewers' remote control, SBS 6 gained popularity presenting a mixture of reality-TV, eroticism, and feature films. In 1999, the year in which SBS 6 was reported to break

even, SBS launched a second channel, Net 5, positioning itself as a quality station and intending to lure viewers away from the three public channels.

V8 and The Music Factory

The year 1995 saw two more commercial television stations starting. They were launched as low budget stations by the Dutch record company Arcade. One station was called TV10 although it had nothing to do with Joop van den Ende's doomed venture of the same name. Its initial ambitions were limited to re-broadcasting old American series. Several changes of format, name and ownership later, the station was acquired by SBS Broadcasting S.A. in 2001. SBS now had three stations in the Dutch market (SBS 6, Net 5 and V8), just like its main rival, the Holland Media Group.

The second Arcade station, The Music Factory (TMF), was meant as a Dutch substitute to MTV, presenting more Dutch video clips than did MTV. Within two years, its popularity compared well to that of MTV. In 2000 the owners, who needed cash to finance the purchase of regional newspapers, sold the station to its rival MTV.

An overview of all national public and commercial television stations specifically geared to the Dutch market is presented in table 1. Public broadcasters are grouped under the channel on which they broadcast at least two-thirds of their programs. NOS broadcasts on all three channels but primarily uses 'Nederland 2' for its sports coverage and live reporting of special events. Teleac/NOT and RVU are educational broadcasters. The numerous religious and spiritual broadcasters are not mentioned individually.

Table 1. *Television Broadcasters in the Netherlands (June 2001)*

Public Television		Commercial Television	
Nederland 1	AVRO	*HMG*	RTL4
	KRO		RTL5
	NCRV		Yorin
	Teleac/NOT		
	Religious/spiritual broad-	*SBS*	SBS 6
	casters		Net 5
			V8
Nederland 2	EO		
	TROS		Cartoon Network
	NOS*		Discovery Channel
			Eurosport
Nederland 3	NPS		Fox Kids
	VARA		Kindernet
	VPRO		National Geographic Channel
	RVU		The Music Factory

* NOS broadcasts on all three channels but primarily uses Nederland 2 for its sports coverage and live reporting of special events

2.2 International Stations and Audience Shares

In addition to all the aforementioned stations, which were specifically designed for the Dutch market, *Eurosport, National Geographic Channel, Discovery Channel, Kindernet* and *Cartoon Network* subtitle their programs in the Dutch language. The commercial television stations that matter, however, are the three stations of the Holland Media Group and SBS 6. The Dutch television audience is divided up as shown in table 2. In 1999 the three public television channels commanded a combined audience share of 37%, the Holland Media Group stations shared a 32% figure between them, and SBS 6 had 11%. Market leader RTL 4 earned a disproportionate share of advertising revenue. Fortunately for the public broadcasters, net advertising expenditure on television doubled between 1989 (€227 million) and 1995 (€487 million) (VEA, 1996: 13). So the public broadcasting system could afford to lose half of its audience without facing immediate financial problems.

Table 2. *Market Shares (%) – Television Stations (6:00 p.m. – 12:00 p.m.)*

TV Station	1990	1991	1992	1993	1994	1995	1996	1997	1998	1999	2000
Ned. 1	24	20	17	17	16	15	13	13	13	14	13
TV 2	25	22	21	18	17	17	15	14	17	14	17
Ned. 3	13	12	17	16	18	13	11	11	10	10	9
Public Service	62	54	55	51	51	45	39	38	40	38	39
RTL 4	21	27	27	29	26	24	22	20	18	17	15
RTL 5	-	-	-	2	6	8	6	4	4	4	4
Veronica	-	-	-	-	-	3	8	10	10	11	8
Net 5	-	-	-	-	-	-	-	-	-	3	4
SBS 6	-	-	-	-	-	1	6	9	10	11	10
Fox 8 (TV 10)	-	-	-	-	-	0	1	2	2	1	2
The Music Factory	-	-	-	-	-	0	0	1	1	1	1
Cartoon Network	-	-	-	-	-	-	-	0	0	0	1
Other*	17	19	18	18	17	17	17	16	16	16	16

* Foreign stations and VCR use included

Source: CKO, by Intomart, commissioned by NOS and STER

Unless otherwise indicated, the source of all program and audience statistics presented in this contribution is the NOS Audience Research Department (NOS/KLO). This unit reports on the basis of continuous television and radio audience measurement, carried out by market researcher INTOMART on behalf of all public and commercial broadcasters. Percentages apply to the population of six years and over.

2.3 Analysis

The willingness of advertisers to spend more money on television is one of the factors explaining the rapid rise of commercial television in the Netherlands. The public broadcasting system always had little leeway regarding advertising. Under the Media Decree they cannot devote more than 6.5% of air time to advertising, while commercial broadcasters, pursuant to the 'Television Without Frontiers' Directive (October 3, 1989), can broadcast commercials for up to 15% of their air time. Public broadcasters, unlike commercial broadcasters, cannot have commercial breaks within programs, only in between. Finally, public broadcasters are more restricted in accepting program sponsorship offers and in undertaking merchandising activities.

The Dutch government has been slow in recognizing the attractiveness of a – then – 77% cabled nation, that was under-served in market-oriented programming, to audiovisual entrepreneurs. Reluctantly it introduced domestic commercial broadcasting more than three years after the start of the first Luxembourg-based Dutch commercial TV station. The main reason for this reluctance may have been the wish of the government and the parliamentary majority to protect the national broadcasting system as it had developed over 65 years. Because this system had been meant as a reflection of society's structure, allowing in a type of broadcasting that was alien to the system's very nature may have been anathema to the politicians. Economic considerations concerning the development of a national audiovisual industry were subordinated to culturally oriented motives.

The public broadcasters, whose resistance against legalizing commercial broadcasting comes as no surprise, made the major error of maintaining the boycott against Joop van den Ende as soon as his ambition to become a broadcaster himself had been thwarted by the Media Commission. This left him with only one survival option: selling his popular programs to RTL 4. This certainly accelerated the growth of commercial television in the Netherlands.

III   The Strategy of Public Service Broadcasting

3.1 McKinsey's Advice

When it became apparent that RTL 4, newly armed with the full complement of Joop van den Ende's programs, would become a competitor to be reckoned with (1990), the public broadcasters, with the full support of the government, hired consultancy firm *McKinsey & Company* to advise them on the best strategy to counter commercial competition. McKinsey's final report provided the basis for the public broadcasters and the government's policy in the next decade. The most important recommendations were as follows.

- The public broadcasters should not imitate their commercial competitors, but concentrate instead on high quality programs that commercial broadcasters were not likely to offer, such as excellent news and information programs, expensive drama and original children's programs. In genres that were provided by both commercial and public broadcasters, the latter should offer superior quality.
- The public broadcasting system should coordinate its three television channels to maximize choice. Ideally, at any moment in primetime there should be a program for a large audience, one for a substantial audience and one for a small audience. The proportion of programs for small audiences in primetime should be reduced from 50% to 35% by improving existing programs and by moving educational programs and programs for ethnic minorities to day-time. Information should not take up more than 40% of air time.
- The individual public broadcasters should cooperate intensely in permanent combinations per channel, not even excluding an eventual merger. The three channels should be equally strong and attract the same size of audience.

Most of these recommendations were adopted by the public broadcasters and the government. The Media Act was reviewed to encourage cooperation between broadcasters, both at the channel level and at the level of the public broadcasting system as a whole. All of the (about 30) existing public broadcasters obtained a license valid from 1995 to 2000.

In 1994, however, a new government coalition prepared a more thorough restructuring of the public broadcasting system, resulting in reviews of the Media Act that concentrated power in the hands of an independent three-person Board of Management of the NOS. The old Board of 15, on which all the broadcasters are represented, was restricted to a supervisory role. The responsibilities of the new Board of Management include channel branding and scheduling, allocation of substantial parts of the budgets and accountability for the compliance of individual broadcasters with all statutory obligations.

From September 2000 the NOS is the only licensee, with the authorized individual broadcasters being regarded as participants in the NOS license. To compensate for the loss of status and to mitigate competition for members, broadcasting associations now only need to have 300,000 members. So the system based on the A, B and C broadcaster categories is no longer in force.

On the last day of 1999 the license fee was abolished. It was replaced by a small income tax increase yielding the same revenue. Starting in 2000 public broadcasting is financed by a government subsidy (about 75%) and by advertising (about 25%). To safeguard public broadcasting's independence from the government of the day the budget is fixed in the law at the level of 1998, pegged on inflation and the increase in the number of households.

3.2 Philosophy of Public Broadcasting

Until 1989 the existence of public broadcasting had been self-evident. Under discussion was the legitimacy or the desirability of adding commercial broadcasting to the existing public service. The introduction of commercial television on a relatively large scale reversed the issue. Now the legitimacy of public broadcasting had to be demonstrated to satisfy those who argued that the market could provide for most, if not all, program categories that the public wanted. Most of the time it was not the existence of public broadcasting as such that was questioned but its mandate. Should a public broadcaster compete with commercial broadcasters for audience and advertising revenue by offering entertainment and sports? Or should public broadcasting be complementary to commercial broadcasting, offering only those program categories that commercial broadcasters will gladly leave to the public service because there is no money in them?

Subsequent governments in the 1990's – while of different political stripes – held the view that public broadcasting should offer a comprehensive program supply comprising all program categories, and should seek to reach the vast majority of the population. The key concept in this philosophy of public broadcasting is *public functions*, that is the roles which broadcasting can play in the functioning of parliamentary democracy, in the integration of society, in consensus-making regarding social, political and ethical issues, in the advancement of culture, and in the education of individual citizens. Although the performing of such functions is by no means the exclusive domain of public broadcasters, the presence of a public broadcasting system guarantees that these functions are implemented. One cannot expect this from commercial broadcasters who have no other responsibility than making a profit and ensuring the continuity of their enterprise.

Guaranteeing the performance of public functions is the first argument in favor of a broad mandate for public broadcasting. A second argument can be derived from the way television is used by the public. If public broadcasting only offered highbrow information and culture, its audience would soon be restricted to a small academic and cultural elite, leaving the public at large to the commercial broadcasters. In so doing, public broadcasting would have little impact on social processes and the implementation of public functions would be merely theoretical. Third, it can be argued that such elitist programming would be inconsistent with the compulsory payment of the license fee by every household using a television set. License fee (or tax) payers should get some value for their money (*Publieke omroep in Nederland*, 1991: 5). It is obvious that advertising, public broadcasting's second source of income, hinges very much on audience size. So this constitutes a fourth argument underlining the necessity of serving large audiences. Unlike Blumler (1993: 411) we believe that the goals of the advertiser and those of the public broadcaster can coincide. Blumler, criticizing van Cuilenburg & Slaa (1993), adds a fifth argument for not limiting public broadcasting's tasks to information: the forum role of television is not only performed by news and current affairs programs. Entertainment television, including soap operas, drama and sitcoms, also serves as a *cultural forum* for the exploration of social and moral issues (Blumler,

1993: 409). Summarizing most of the arguments presented above, it could be stated that, if public broadcasting is to be expected to play a significant role in society – which it is – it needs significant audiences and cannot avoid competing with commercial broadcasters for audience figures.

3.3 Maintaining Program Quality

The goals of (broadcast) media policy, as distinct from economic policy, can be summarized as follows: to reach as large an audience as possible for the best possible programs. There are a number of instruments to promote program quality, including statutory requirements, financial incentives, institutional arrangements and government supervision.

The *requirements* concerning program quality are specified in the Media Act and in the Media Decree (which elaborates on the provisions of the Media Act). Broadcasting associations are required to present a comprehensive program and to devote at least:

* 35% of air time to information and educational programs;
* 25% to cultural programs, including 12.5% to arts programs;
* 50% to Dutch language programs.

Overlapping between the percentages for information and culture is allowed.

NPS (an independent broadcaster created through the Media Act to supplement the program supply of broadcasting associations as of January 1995) is required to devote 40% of air time to cultural programs, including at least 20% of arts programs. 20% of its television broadcasts and 25% of its radio broadcasts must target or pertain to ethnic minorities. Furthermore NPS's programming must include background information on political and social developments related to economics, science, or technology. Consumer information and educational programs for children are also required.

As a broadcaster in its own right (apart from its tasks as an umbrella organization for all of the public broadcasters), NOS is required to perform the following tasks:

* daily news coverage;
* Parliament activity reporting;
* reporting on national events and celebrations;
* sports reporting, including national leagues and international events;
* provision of news for children and for the deaf and hard-of-hearing;
* service information for persons involved in agriculture, fisheries, navigation, and road traffic (radio only);
* a daily fitness program (radio only).

Apart from these requirements specifying what should be broadcast, there is a requirement *not* to schedule feature films and other program material that are unsuited for children under the age of 12 or 16 before 8:00 or 10:00 p.m. respectively. This requirement applies both to public and commercial broadcasters operating under a Dutch license. The 'Television Without Frontiers' Directive contains some other quota requirements regarding European content and independent productions, which apply to all European broadcasters.

Enough said concerning program requirements as an instrument for media policy to ensure a certain kind of program quality. A *second* category of measures, serving the same goal, consists of *financial incentives*. Examples of these are a statutory fund for Dutch productions of outstanding cultural quality (€14 million available annually) and another fund for joint productions with Flemish television, with the Dutch film sector and the performing arts (€9 million available annually).

A *third* way to create conditions which favor (a certain kind of) program quality pertains to *institutional arrangements*. To qualify as a public broadcaster, broadcasting associations have to be strictly noncommercial and to represent certain currents among the population. New associations have to demonstrate that their admission in the system will increase diversity in programming. It should be reminded that there are separate institutions for religious and educational programs. Churches and spiritual societies (including Humanists, Jews, Muslims and Hindus) as well as political parties have their own share of air time. So has the government for government information purposes. The broadcasting associations, NPS, NOS, and the educational broadcasters are all required to set out the rights and duties of their journalists in a program charter. This obligation equally applies to commercial broadcasters operating with a Dutch license.

Finally, a very effective way of maintaining program quality on behalf of the government is supervision by the Media Commission. In principle, the observance of all statutory obligations and restrictions is monitored. The Media Commission pays special attention, however, to surreptitious advertising within programs, which is strictly forbidden. Owing to the many requirements which they must comply with, public broadcasters receive more attention from the Media Commission than do commercial broadcasters. Regional and local broadcasters are reminded by the Media Commission that half of their air time should be spent on regional or local information.

Together, these measures tend to stimulate a kind of program quality that best suits the needs of society. The question could be asked whether incentives to promote program quality (in the sense outlined above) should be restricted to public service broadcasting or be extended to commercial broadcasters as well (Blumler & Hoffmann-Riem, 1992: 227). Traditionally, the United Kingdom has chosen to impose public service obligations on its independent terrestrial broadcasters, to the effect that Channel Four and – to a lesser extent – ITV can be regarded as public service broadcasters. In the Netherlands a different approach has been chosen. Of the above-mentioned requirements, only those pertaining to the percentage of Dutch language programs and to the scheduling of programs that are unsuitable for children and the obligation to have a program charter apply to commercial broadcasters operating with a Dutch license. The remarkable difference between the two countries can easily be explained by the time and the way commercial television entered the scene. In the UK commercial television was introduced by the government in 1954, before any competition from abroad through cable and satellite was around. In the Netherlands commercial television made its entry in 1989 by satellite from Luxembourg much against the wish of the Dutch government and well beyond its jurisdiction. It was only after RTL 4 had become popular that domestic commercial television and radio were provided for in the Dutch legislation (1992).

Imposing on commercial broadcasters program requirements that go beyond the requirements embodied in the 'Television Without Frontiers' Directive would either be ineffective (in the case of foreign-based satellite broadcasters) or induce commercial broadcasters to move abroad. There is another argument for not saddling commercial broadcasters with programming obligations, an argument that also derives from European law. In order to justify the financing by the license fee and the granting of the best frequencies to the public broadcasters, the difference between public and commercial broadcasters as to the burden imposed upon them should be substantial. Any blurring of this difference either by imposing obligations on commercial broadcasters or by weakening the obligations of public broadcasters would make the privileges awarded to the public broadcasters, more difficult to justify. This is especially true in countries (like the Netherlands) where public and commercial broadcasters compete for advertising revenue (*Commissie Donner*, 1992: 19). Last but not least, a clear difference in the way the two categories of broadcasters are treated nicely fits the European concept of freedom of information. This concept includes government non-interference on the one hand and government intervention to establish or maintain pluralism on the other.

IV   Radio Broadcasting

4.1 Public and Commercial Radio

So far we have been dealing implicitly with television only in this section and in the previous one. This adequately reflects the small amount of attention policy makers tend to pay to radio. There are a number of reasons that account for this lack of interest. Television is the newer medium. It offers sound and image, demanding exclusive attention from the user. Its impact on the individual and society is generally supposed to be much larger. Television is much more expensive and attracts three times as much advertising money (television, net expenditure €633 million; radio, €201 million – VEA, 1999: 13). Radio has become a background medium, accompanying other activities mainly in the daytime. This function calls for stations with a homogeneous programming, which can be listened to continuously. Station identity is more important than program identity and certainly more than broadcaster identity, when, as in the Dutch public broadcasting system, several broadcasters share a station.

The public broadcasters hesitantly introduced a pop music station (in 1965) and a classical music station (in 1975) under political pressure. The streamlining of the public radio stations was accepted as a principle by the NOS board in 1980, but is still not complete. Meanwhile, the character of each of the five public radio stations has been defined in the Media Act (until 2000, when it was left to the broadcasters themselves again).

Table 3. *Radio Broadcasters in the Netherlands (June 2001)*

Public Radio*		Commercial Radio	
Radio 1	news and sports	Radio 10 FM	golden oldies
Radio 2	light entertainment	Sky Radio	light pop music
3FM**	pop music	Radio 538	pop music
Radio 4	classical music	Yorin FM	pop music
747FM**	debate, opinion, and	Noordzee FM	popular Dutch music
	special target audiences	Love Radio	romantic pop music
		Arrow Classic	rock music
Regional	13 regional stations	Rock	
		Classic FM	classical music
Local	328 local stations	Kink FM	alternative pop music
		Colorful Radio	world music

*Both radio and television programs are broadcast by associations such as AVRO, TROS or VPRO.
** For marketing reasons, Radio 3 is renamed 3FM and Radio5 has become 747AM.

Adapting the formats of the public radio stations to the listening habits of the population became a necessity when, beginning in the late 1980's, commercial radio stations, each offering one sort of music, ate in the audience share of public radio and conquered the advertising market. Between 1987 and 1997 about 25 commercial radio stations emerged, 15 of which survived. The first stations used foreign uplinks and were distributed by satellite and cable only. Licensing for domestic commercial broadcasting became possible in 1992 and terrestrial broadcasting frequencies (lacking national coverage) were allotted to seven commercial broadcasters in 1994, 1995 and 1997. Table 3 is an overview of the most important public and commercial radio stations. Audience shares are given in table 4. In 2000, the largest shares were held by Sky Radio (15%) and the combined regional public stations (15%).

The discussion on the legitimacy of public broadcasting, which has been referred to above, concerns both television and radio. There is a difference, however, between the two media when downsizing the public sector is being considered. Reducing the number of TV channels from three to two would diminish the audience share of public television, but the latter would still be able to offer a comprehensive program, as can be seen in most neighboring countries, where public television only has two channels. Taking away one or more public radio stations would involve, however, a decision on which type of program will be left to the market. Put in a positive way: which strand of programming is considered too important to be left to market forces? Radio 3 has been suggested most often as a candidate for privatization, notably by its commercial competitors. This would mean that pop music would be exempted from cultural policy. An additional consideration could be that Radio 3 is the only public radio station that reaches young people. In the review of the media act which entered into force in April 2000 three television channels and five radio stations are guaranteed for public broadcasting at the national level until September 2010.

Table 4. *Market Shares (%) – Radio stations (7:00 p.m. – 12:00 p.m.)*

	R_1	R_2	R_3	R_4	R_5	Reg.*	R_{10}	Sky	R_{538}	Yorin FM	Noord-zee FM	Other	Tot.
1988	13	21	46	3	2	4	-	-	-	-	-	8	100
1989	12	19	40	3	1	8	3	4	-	-	-	8	100
1990	11	16	36	3	2	11	5	9	-	-	-	7	100
1991	10	15	30	2	1	17	7	9	1	-	-	8	100
1992	12	9	27	3	1	15	10	11	1	-	-	11	100
1993	10	7	26	3	1	17	8	8	4	2	2	12	100
1994	9	6	24	2	1	16	10	8	3	1	7	13	100
1995	9	7	17	2	1	16	8	10	7	3	9	11	100
1996	8	8	15	2	1	15	8	14	7	3	9	11	100
1997	9	9	14	2	1	15	8	16	6	3	8	11	100
1998	7	9	14	2	1	14	9	18	6	4	6	11	100
1999	7	10	14	1	1	15	7	16	6	5	5	13	100
2000**	8	9	12	2	1	15	8	15	8	5	5	13	100

* Regional stations ** 1988–1999: listeners over 13 years, 2000: listeners over 10 years

Since about half of radio listening concerns receivers that are not connected to cable, terrestrial broadcasting frequencies are of the utmost importance. These frequencies are still scarce and 90% of them have been allotted to national, regional, and local public radio, as well as the military. So there is a serious problem for commercial radio broadcasters. In the long run digital audio broadcasting may solve this problem, but the government has to take action earlier. An independent study showed that additional frequencies could be made available, resulting in eight packages, each with a reach of about 70% of the population. The government decided to auction these frequencies before September 2001. One of these five packages will be reserved for a commercial news station.

V   Cable and Pay-TV

5.1 Cable: From Community Antenna to Program Provider

The Netherlands may be called a wired nation: 93% of the 6.5 million homes are passed by cable, with 87% actually connected. The average cable system delivers about 25 television stations and 50 radio stations for less than €9 a month. Large scale construction of cable networks started in the first half of the 1970's. Cable was promoted as an alternative to the individual antenna, providing a better picture and more (foreign) programs. The local governments, under whose authority cable systems were built, had an additional motive: getting rid of the ugly forests of antennas on the roofs of houses. In most communities, the local government or the regional gas and electricity company took up the management of the cable system. The cable system was not considered as a source of revenue, but as a public utility that had to be provided to the citizens at the lowest possible price. In the early 1990's cable systems began to look quite different. Fiber optics, digitization, and signal compression made it possible to offer a multiplicity of channels. The development of decoders paved the way for conditional access. Not only did subscription to premium channels or plus-packets become feasible, but so did pay-per-view and near-video-on-demand. The possibilities of interactive television were explored in local experiments. And, last but not least, the telecommunications landscape was deregulated, both at the European level and the national level (with the introduction of competition in the formerly monopolistic post office and telephone market). Cable operators were encouraged to set up competing telephony services. As it became clear that the development of these new applications of cable would require expert knowledge and huge investments, and would involve high risks, many local governments decided to sell their cable system to private enterprises that considered cable as their core business. The city of Amsterdam sold its 525,000-strong subscriber network in 1995 for € 66 per subscriber. The buyer was *A 2000*, a consortium of *United and Philips Communications* and *US West*. One year later, The Hague received € 70 per subscriber when it sold its cable network to the largest Dutch cable operator, *Casema*. Part of the agreement in these cases, as in most other comparable deals, was a freeze on the price of the basic cable packet for the next five or more years.

The liberalization of the Media Act in 1997, aimed to increase the freedom of the cable operators. They were allowed to insert commercials in programs and to run their own program services in addition to those of other program providers. At the same time restrictions were being imposed on the cable operator concerning the composition and the price of the basic packet and the prices they may ask other providers for relaying their programs. The act requires every cable operator to offer a basic packet of at least 15 TV channels and 25 radio stations. The TV channels include the must-carry channels (Nederland 1,2,3, the regional public television station, the local public station, if any, and the two Belgian Dutch-language public stations). The remaining stations in the basic packet are to be selected by local or regional program councils. Access of program providers to cable systems is guaranteed by an anti-trust authority, operating under the ministry of economic affairs, which may prescribe a model to determine a reasonable price for access. This also applies to access for providers of broadband internet services.

5.2 Pay-TV for Spoilt Viewers

The pioneer of pay-TV in the Netherlands has been FilmNet. It started in 1985 as a joint venture of Esselte (Swedish media company), VNU (Dutch publisher) and Rob Houwer (Dutch film producer). FilmNet changed formats and shareholders several times, tried pay-per-view and developed its own digital decoder (for which it won the support of

German tycoon Leo Kirch), but never attracted enough subscribers to make a profit. The combined number of subscribers for FilmNet and sister channel SuperSport is about 300,000. FilmNet is part of an international company, NetHold, that operates pay-TV channels in Scandinavia, the Benelux, Greece, the Middle-East, and Africa. In September 1996 its two owners – South Africa's Rupert family, through Richemont, its Swiss luxury goods company, and South African pay-TV operator MIH – sold their shares to Canal Plus in exchange for 15% (Richemont) and 5% (MIH) shares in Canal Plus respectively.

A few months earlier, Philips and KPN (the post office and telephone service) had agreed to take over NetHold's pay-TV daughter company TeleSelect, FilmNet's only competitor in the Dutch market. A setback for pay-TV as such was the failure of Sport 7, a station which started broadcasting in August 1996 and had to close down in December of the same year. Its shareholders included (again!) Philips Electronics and KPN, but also ING Bank, independent program production company Endemol, a number of cable operators, and the largest national newspaper, *De Telegraaf*. This consortium had secured from the national soccer association a seven-year license to broadcast all soccer games, outbidding NOS and the Holland Media Group in the process. But the end came within four months, after a series of miscalculations and misfortunes. The initial idea of having every cabled household pay €1 a month was opposed by the cable operators, who wanted to include the sports channel in a multi-channel packet that would only be accessible to subscribers who would install a decoder and pay a monthly fee of about €11. Sport 7 agreed to be offered for free to all households until enough digital decoders were available, which was expected to be the case by mid-1997. But even as a basic cable program, Sport 7 failed to attract audiences large enough to please would-be advertisers and to prompt cable operators to invest in decoders. Most cable operators decided to postpone the introduction of decoders until 1998. This meant a considerable extension of the loss-making period for Sport 7, which eventually went into receivership in December 1996.

One cause of the failure of Sport 7 to attract viewers seems to have been the ongoing popularity of the free sports programs of public broadcaster NOS, which negotiated generous sub-licenses from Sport 7. In the same way the very slow start of pay-TV in the Netherlands in general can be explained by the simultaneous growth of the basic cable packet. Pay-TV operators have complained that the public has been spoiled by being offered 25 television stations for a subscription fee of €7 to 9 only. The future of pay-TV is indeed bleak as far as soccer and erotic programs are concerned: while they are often thought of as trigger applications, their wide availability on unscrambled TV channels precludes such a role.

VI Broadcasting and Program Production: An Emerging Industry

6.1 A High Volume of National Production

A considerable part of the TV program output is specifically produced for the Dutch market. In 1995 the three public TV stations produced or commissioned 74% of their total output, which represents 4,685 hours of Dutch production. The four main commercial TV stations (RTL4, RTL5, Veronica, and SBS6) produced or commissioned nearly half of their total output, which amounts to 2,847 hours of national production. As shown in table 5, the percentage of home-produced programs as compared with imported programs not only serves to distinguish public from commercial broadcasters, but also varies with program categories. Information is generally home produced, whereas a large part of entertainment is imported. Most of the imports come from the US. This is especially true for feature films and TV series. Imports by public broadcasters are more diversified (including British, German and French productions) than imports by commercial broadcasters, who heavily rely on American fare. From 1995 to 2000 the volume of air-time and of Dutch productions has increased, but the tendencies did not change significantly.

Table 5. *Program Categories – Share of Total Broadcasting Time as of 2000*

	Public Television		Commercial Television	
Total minutes	1,085,324		2,076,548	
Information	54%	95% Dutch	26%	73% Dutch
		1% American		16% American
Education	12%	75% Dutch	2%	28% Dutch
		1% American		22% American
Entertainment	27%	41% Dutch	59%	31% Dutch
		18% American		42% American
Remaining	7%	100% Dutch	13%	93% Dutch
		0%		5% American

Example: 95% of all information programs (51% in total time) on public television was produced in the Netherlands.

6.2 Public Service Broadcasting in 2000–2010

Several reviews of the Media Act brought about a new structure for the public broadcasting system (at the national level). Instead of a five-year license for every broadcasting association, one ten-year license was awarded to NOS, from September 2000 onwards. The associations obtained an acknowledgement as participants in the NOS license, valid for five years. The responsibility for scheduling was put in the hands of the NOS, as were allocation of 25% of the budget and the responsibility for the observance of the program requirements. Within NOS the executive power was entrusted to an independent board of management. The representation of the associations was confined to a supervisory board. Every five years an external committee is to judge the quality of the performance of the public broadcasting system as a whole as well as that of each individual broadcaster's contribution.

The first significant change in programming policy was channel branding. For each of the three public TV channels and each of the five public radio stations an editorial board was formed, on which all broadcasters that contributed programs to that channel or station are represented. Each board is led by a channel coordinator, appointed by the NOS. The character of the radio stations did not change a lot. The first TV channel, called *Nederland 1*, is an in-depth channel inspired by familiar cultural values. *Nederland 2* aims to be the most accessible public channel, the one most likely to pinch viewers from the commercial channels. *Nederland 3* is an in-depth channel again, but guided by culturally progressive values and tastes. All programming for children under twelve will be broadcast in dedicated time-slots on *Nederland 3* carrying one name: *Z@ppelin*. Through such channel branding as well as horizontal programming on both radio and television the public broadcasters hope to create lasting relationships between audiences and specific channels, stations or programs. For each TV channel a target audience share was indicated: *Nederland 1*: 13%, *Nederland 2*: 17% and *Nederland 3*: 10%.

A spearhead in the TV programming policy of the new NOS board is an increase in fiction programming. According to the 1999–2002 plan, Dutch drama should grow from 3% in the season 1997/98 to 5% in 2002/03. The percentage of imported drama should rise from 13% to 20% in the same period (September to May, 4:00 p.m.–12:00 p.m.). To raise the level of Dutch fiction, substantial additional investments are being made in the co-productions of feature films with independent film producers.

In the near future investments in content alone will not be enough. As a consequence of digitization the traditional radio and television programs can and will be distributed by alternative means. Digital cable, ADSL, DAB, DVB-T, DVB-satellite and broadband internet are the buzzwords. Leaving these areas to the telecom, cable, computer and internet operators would seriously threaten the impact of public broadcasting. The Dutch public broadcasters are therefore experimenting with most of these new distribution techniques. In particular two areas are being explored: Internet applications (electronic program guide, streaming audio, etc.) and the introduction of thematic TV-channels (news channel, culture channel and children's channel).

6.3 New Business Opportunities

To a small country within a deregulated European market the 'Television Without Frontiers' slogan means impending invasion by media groups operating on a European or even a global scale. As has been seen earlier in this chapter, the main *Dutch* commercial television stations are controlled by foreign industrial groups. Luxembourg-based CLT owns 100% of the Holland Media Group, which operates three commercial television channels in the Netherlands. Two other commercial TV channels, SBS6, NET5 and V8, are controlled by SBS S.A., a subsidiary of US media companies Walt Disney/ABC and Viacom/Paramount. The only pay-TV operator is part of French company Canal Plus.

The business opportunities offered by the aforementioned explosion of distribution capacity have led (and still lead) to horizontal and vertical integration in and across the audiovisual, telecommunications and computer industries. Taking into account the small size of the Dutch market this means inevitably further internationalization of the Dutch media scene.

There are two clear examples of these concentration processes. One is the concentration of nearly all cable systems in the hands of three cable operators: UPC, Casema and Essent. UPC (renamed United Pan-European Communications after Philips left the company) is an American company owning cable systems throughout Europe. Casema is owned by France Telecom. Essent is still a Dutch company but it has announced its intention to sell all its cable activities. So a further concentration is possible.

The cable company that is most aggressive in developing new services is UPC. It negotiated a deal with the Amsterdam local government to introduce a very unattractive basic cable packet (public service channels only), thereby 'forcing' most citizens to pay extra for an extended packet. It acquired the cable system of Haarlem (city near Amsterdam) under the condition that it would provide all inhabitants with a free digital decoder. In March 2000 UPC agreed to buy SBS Broadcasting S.A. comprising TV channels in 15 European countries. After a sharp decline of UPC shares at the Amsterdam exchange UPC had to cancel the deal. UPC announced it would compete for transmission rights of soccer games (which it did not win). In July 2000 its daughter company (Chello) intended to merge with American company Excite@home to form the first broadband internet provider operating on both sides of the Atlantic. UPC/Chello and Excite@home are both controlled by AT&T. The newly formed company, to be called Excite Chello, would have potentially access to 30 million European homes, but this deal was also cancelled. In the first half of the year 2001 UPC featured in the news mainly because of its huge debt and continuing decline of stock value.

The second example of concentration is the acquisition of Dutch television production company Endemol by Spanish telecom operator Telefonica in 2000. The take-over came after Endemol had developed into a transnational producer with subsidiaries in 15 European countries.

The vertical integration of cable operators and telecom companies with producers of content is apparently needed to make sure that the infrastructures become profitable by carrying services ranging from extended television packets to broadband internet access. At the same time horizontal integration offers economies of scale. The same services can be offered on all cable systems within one market (Dutch model) or in different markets (other European countries). Since the Dutch market is too small to support new services on its own, this country cannot expect anything else than being served along with wealthier nations.

In June 1999 a committee created by request of Parliament advised the Dutch government on media concentration and cross-ownership. It recommended no additional measures, arguing that both from a competition and from a pluralistic point of view there was no reason to worry. The existing policy instruments – a competition watchdog (NMA), a telecommunications watchdog (OPTA) and a broadcasting watchdog (*Commissariaat voor de Media*) – were sufficient to maintain competition and pluralism at the same time. However difficult to accept it may be (while the concentration in the press is also continuing), this conclusion may also be true since the market as a whole is expanding at an even faster pace than does concentration.

References

Aldershoff, L. (1997). Bestedingen TV-reclame in '96 met 3 procent gedaald, *Adformatie* 3: 42.

Bakker, P. (1991). *Mediageschiedenis, een introductie* [*Media History, An Introduction*]. Groningen: Wolters-Noordhoff.

BBC/VEA (2000). *Reclamebestedingen in Nederland 1999*. Amsterdam: VEA.

Bekkers, W. (1996). Audience research in the Netherlands, *Communications. The European Journal of Communication Research* 21 (3): 317–330.

Blumler, J.G. (1993). Meshing money with mission: Purity versus pragmatism in public broadcasting, *European Journal of Communication* 8: 403–424.

Blumler, J.G. & Hoffmann-Riem, W. (1992). Toward renewed public accountability. In J.G. Blumler (ed.), *Television and the Public Interest: Vulnerable Values in West European Broadcasting* (pp. 218–228). London: Sage Publications.

Browne, D.R. (1989). *Comparing Broadcasting Systems: The Experience of Six Industrialized Nations*. Ames Iowa: Iowa State University Press.

Commissie-Donner *(1992). Verdeelde frequenties, veranderde omroep.* [*Allocated Frequencies, Changed Broadcasting System*]. Advies van de Commissie etherfrequenties en commerciële omroep (Commissie-Donner). Rijswijk: Ministerie van WVC.

Cuilenburg, J. van & Slaa, P. (1993). From media policy towards a national communications policy: Broadening the scope, *European Journal of Communication* 8: 149–176.

d'Haenens, L. & Heuvelman, A. (1996). The researcher as a mediator between public broadcaster and audience. Some European experiences, *Communications. The European Journal of Communication Research* 21 (3): 297–315.

Manschot, B.J.A.M. (1993). *Het zijn de programma's die het 'm doen: normen en feiten over de televisieprogrammering in Nederland 1972–1992. [It Are the Programs that Matter: Norms and Facts on Television Programming in the Netherlands 1972–1992].* Amsterdam: Otto Cramwinckel.

McKinsey & Company (December 19, 1990). *Herwinnen van aantrekkingskracht door versterking van televisieprogrammering. Hoofdelementen voor een meerjarenplan van de Nederlandse publieke omroep. [Regaining Attractivenenss by Reinforcing Television Programming. Main Elements for a Four-Year Plan of the Dutch Public Broadcasting System].* Final Report to the NOS Board.

Publieke omroep in Nederland (June 6, 1991). Tweede Kamer 1990–1991, 22 147 (2). [*Public Broadcasting in the Netherlands*]. Government White Paper.

Sterk, R. (1991). Het wervende woord: de bewogen geschiedenis van de Vaderlandse omroep. [The canvassing word: The stirring history of the Dutch broadcasting system]. In J. Bardoel & J. Bierhoff (eds.), *Media feiten, structuren* [*Media Facts, Structures*] (pp. 25–47). Groningen: Wolters-Noordhoff.

Stappers, J.G., Reijnders, A.D. & Möller, W.A.J. (1990). *De Werking van Massamedia: Een Overzicht van Inzichten [The Working of Mass Media: An Overview of Insights].* Amsterdam: Uitgeverij De Arbeiderspers.

Wijfjes, H. (1994). Het Radiotijdperk, 1919–1960 [The Radio Era, 1919–1960]. In H. Wijfjes (ed.), *Omroep in Nederland [Broadcasting in the Netherlands]*. Zwolle: Waanders Uitgeverij.

Denmark

by Ib Poulsen and Henrik Søndergaard

I   Some Basic Features

While radio and television are generally viewed as two different media, they have so many features in common that it seems reasonable to treat them from the same perspective. Such an approach is eminently suited to Denmark, where they were initially established within the same institution. In addition, they shared the same program policy objectives, and in several other aspects they were regarded as a single unit. If one disregards for a moment the technological and expressive aspects, the main difference between radio and TV is that they emerged in different historical periods. In Denmark both radio and television are strongly linked to a broader social and cultural context, and this relationship is in many ways of greater importance than the way in which these media were organized (Søndergaard, 1994).

At first radio and then television were the objects of rather extensive political and cultural power struggles. The political struggle was primarily a clash between the Social Democrats and, on the other, right-wingers wanting the media to be ruled by the market. While the cultural struggle about radio and television is admittedly a byproduct of political oppositions, it also has an independent aspect. Its background is first and foremost a profound conflict between elite and mass culture which generally plays an important part within Danish cultural policy and within the field of media it primarily revolves around the question as to whether the electronic media should be used for enlightenment or entertainment purposes (Bondebjerg, 1990). The starting point was the standards of the elitist culture governing Danish radio and television, but in recent years popular culture has been gaining in influence along with a growing market awareness.

Radio developed in the 1920's, and remained the dominant medium right up to the 1950's, while television was first established in the 1950's and made its breakthrough in the 1960's. The history of radio is marked by a strong political polarization which characterized the inter-war period and was expressed first and foremost through a battle between representation and influence on the new medium. Television is, on the other hand, a product of post-war welfare society, in which many previous political and class oppositions of the preceding periods faded as a consequence of widespread social cultural reforms. As a result, television was perceived, to a larger extent than radio, as a useful tool in a social and cultural modernization process which caught on in a big way in the 1960's.

Seen from a historical and institutional perspective, the development of radio and television in Denmark can be divided into three main phases which are fundamentally the same for the two media, but take place at different times. The first phase is the *monopoly phase* covering the period in which radio and television were a public monopoly run by the Danish Broadcasting Corporation (DR). In the case of radio this phase runs from 1925 until 1983. In the case of television it is somewhat shorter, namely from 1954 until 1984, a period where only one TV channel existed in Denmark. The next phase – the *transition phase* – includes most of the 1980's and represents a period in which the monopoly of the DR was challenged by a range of experiments with community radio and local television. These were part of a sweeping process of media policy change and announced the deregulation and commercialization of the electronic media which were to take place later on. In the case of television, the last phase – the *competitive phase* – began by the end of the 1980's when TV2 was established as a competitor to the DR. This phase is characterized by the existence of a multi-channel system consisting of Danish as well as foreign television channels. Radio has barely reached an equivalent state of competition. Until March 1, 1997 there was a monopoly. From then on there has been only one national commercial channel (R2). On the other hand radio has been in constantly increasing competition with the dominant television medium since the 1960's.

This basic pattern of development has been witnessed in most other Western European countries, where a monopoly was gradually replaced by a multi-channel system. However, in Denmark and the rest of Scandinavia the process has been slower. In Denmark radio and television were introduced in a period of strong political reluctance to any kind of commercialism within the electronic media, and as a consequence the consensus was that radio and television should be preserved as a public service institution.

The background for this is a widespread consensus about the founding of the welfare state. As a result the Social Democrats enjoyed a dominant position as the governing party in most of the inter-war and post-war period, a position which was first challenged in the 1980's with the implementation of a right-wing agenda. Still, radio and television have been a public monopoly for a considerably longer period than in several other countries, and even today there is a relatively high degree of State control over the electronic media despite the deregulation drive of the 1980's.

Furthermore, the Social Democratic dominance implied that radio and television were primarily regarded as a cultural political issue while the economic aspects had a modest influence compared to their impact in other countries. Thus Danish radio and television were also, in an ideological and cultural sense, strongly influenced by the Social Democrats, whose political ideals about cultural democratization went hand in hand with a more traditional notion of enlightenment of the people

Another issue of particular importance in the development of Danish television is the special conditions governing the language and culture of such a small country as Denmark. On the one hand, due to its small size, these are very sensitive to foreign cultural influences, and their survival would be problematic in the absence of public support. On the other hand, a small cultural area means that the economic basis for an independent media culture is severely limited. It is not cheaper to produce radio and television in Denmark than elsewhere, but with a population of only about five million it is evident that the electronic media will have to operate with considerably restricted means, whether financed by license fees or run along business lines. When Danish radio and television were organized as a public monopoly, this was not only due to cultural, political, and ideological reasons, but also to the fact that the Danish market simply was too small to be economically attractive to commercial interests (Søndergaard, 1996). The economic limitations are of course of greater significance for television than for radio, as radio broadcasting is essentially cheaper.

II   The Monopoly Phase

In Denmark the government took over radio broadcasting in 1925 and established a governing board to monitor the program supply. The takeover was presented as temporary and intended to last only a year, but on March 12, 1926, it was confirmed through legislation whose basic principles remained the same until 1983. Up to this point radio programs had been produced by a number of private radio clubs, with both commercials and sponsors being quite acceptable. The legislators chose to take over radio broadcasting to make sure they had control over the new medium and that it was functioning for the benefit of the people. Legislative provisions set out that radio broadcasting was to be financed solely through license fees and that the program supply should be "of a diverse, cultural and enlightening nature." The supreme authority was the Radio Board whose task it was to ensure that the media complied with radio legislation

In 1951 the only existing radio channel was supplemented with Program 2 (P2), a cultural channel which only broadcast in the evening hours. This expansion in radio channels occurred at the same time as television was introduced. But the introduction of a two-channel system for radio was not accompanied by any changes in the way the purpose of radio was viewed. On the contrary, renewed emphasis was placed on the desire to provide the population with enlightening programs and elevated cultural experiences. In the 1930's the program policy battle was a question of who should be permitted access to the microphone. The program framework was dominated entirely by music, mostly classical, as well as informative lectures and radiocasts of public events. After WW II and in the 1950's – the golden age of radio – the medium became 'the dangerous radio,' as it led to the cultural hegemony being challenged by statements from ordinary Danes and their matter-of-fact and materialistic reflections on life and sharp critique of society. However, the paternalistic concept of public service radio itself was not seriously challenged until the late 1950's when Radio Mercur began broadcasting popular music, entertainment and commercials in Denmark and Sweden (1958–1962). Radio Mercur was killed off through legislation, but it was one of the main reasons for starting the more youth-oriented P3, which even employed several people from Radio Mercur. It was necessary for radio to acknowledge the need for entertainment and especially popular music among the population at large and particularly among young people. The political struggle regarding radio reached new heights in the 1970's with accusations that employees were biasing the program supply with their personal (left-wing) views, and the Radio board gradually developed into a political battlefield, with the monopoly being increasingly questioned, especially by the right-wing. At this point, however, the public had lost much of its interest for radio, to the advantage of television.

From 1963 to 1975 the radio program structure was as follows: P1 broadcast from 6:00 a.m. to 12:00 p.m., P2 from 7:00 p.m. to midnight, P3 from noon to 2:00 a.m. In other words, coverage was roughly equal to that of television in terms of broadcasting hours. In the meantime, radio's primetime had changed from evening to daytime hours, and the program structure was reorganized, with regional radio programming being established in recognition of the diverse needs of the population. The reorganization must be characterized as both a strategic retreat with respect to television and an offensive maneuver in the hours when there was no television. From 1975 the structure of radio programs looked as follows: P1 still broadcast from 6:00 a.m. to midnight but now offered a range of programs; P2 broadcast from 6:00 a.m. to midnight, and offered regional and educational programs, and P3 broadcast from 5:00 a.m. to 2:00 a.m., with its program supply including music, news and public service announcements.

In the monopoly phase television was governed according to the same principles as radio (Lund, 1976; Engberg, 1986). However, while radio was eventually to broadcast on three channels, television remained a one-channel proposition throughout the whole monopoly phase. This structure was mostly a matter of economy, and it heightened several of the conflicts from which the monopoly system already suffered. In many ways, television found itself at the center of the political and cultural power struggles previously taking place within radio. For this reason the Radio Board had a growing influence on television, implementing increasingly restrictive policies that added to the widespread discontent with the DR. Nevertheless, television grew steadily in the monopoly phase, primarily through a constant expansion of broadcasting hours but also with new program genres focusing more on popular culture.

III   Deregulation

Deregulation of the electronic media took place in Denmark in the 1980's, as was the case in most other Western European countries. However, this did not happen all at once, but through the gradual displacement of the DR's monopoly and a limited opening to commercial forces. The starting point of the deregulation was a careful relaxation of monopoly rules making it possible to establish local radio and television channels on an experimental basis. This alone could hardly be called deregulation, but it had a significant impact because many of those who invested in the local media helped bring about a more general restructuring of the media system (Jauert, 1990).

In 1983 the radio monopoly was breached. In 1981 the Danish parliament passed a law permitting experiments with local radio and television, and two years later the first experiments began. The intention was to create diversity, to stimulate the democratic process and to make it possible for more people to have a voice in the media. But in 1988 the law was altered to allow commercials, to a limited extent (no more than 10% of total broadcasting time), while sponsored programs became permissible later. Later networking in the news was allowed as well.

The next major change in radio came in 1989 when national radio changed from *block* radio to *framework* radio. Prior to 1989 programs were produced by a series of local departments (among others the Dept. of Theater and Literature, the Dept. of Culture and Society, the Dept. of Music). Each department produced a number of programs of a given length which were placed in blocks in the program framework without any connection with one another. In 1989 almost all these departments were replaced with a number of programming groups (early morning, morning, early afternoon, late afternoon, evening, and weekend) with programming responsibility for the three channels.

This new type of 'framework' radio can be viewed as the first step in the direction of *format* radio which was introduced on January 1, 1992 when the number of channels was expanded to four. Format radio is characterized by a program framework which can be adjusted according to the needs and preferences of specific target groups (young people, seniors, city residents, country people, etc.); the program framework can also be dominated by a specific type of content (news, talk shows, culture, religion – or a particular kind of music). In Denmark two of the four public service radio channels are geared to a specific target group (P3: young people up to the age of 40; the Danish Channel: adults from the age of 30). Two channels are formatted by specific content (P1: information, culture and debate, and P2 Music: classical and other kinds of 'demanding' music).

Deregulation has been more extensive in the case of television than of radio, because the television monopoly raised serious problems and was the object of considerable discontent. Already by the end of the 1960's a strong political desire prevailed to establish yet another channel and thus create greater diversity while remedying part of the negative effects of the monopoly. However, no agreement could be reached on the way a new television channel should be organized and financed.

In the early 1980's, with foreign satellite television a reality, it became plain that the DR's monopoly could not be sustained much longer. The Danish media system had to adapt to the new conditions. For industrial policy reasons, among others, Denmark wished to be part of future developments in media technology; however, there was also deep concern as to the impact which the use of foreign commercial media by the Danes would be having on Danish television and culture.

The first steps of the deregulation process clearly reflected this ambivalence. On the one hand it was decided to give the telephone companies permission to build a national cable system which should provide the industry with a new data service and distribute foreign satellite television to the Danish population (Qvortrup, 1988). On the other hand, a decision was made that experiments with local television should be permitted in order to form a Danish counterpart to the foreign threat.

In the beginning the national cable operator had a monopoly on foreign television distribution; the cable network is still not fully established, however, with coverage centering primarily on densely populated areas. Later private persons and community antenna televisions were allowed to put up their own satellite dishes, slowing down the expansion rate of the cable system. Nevertheless the proportion of the population able to receive satellite television has been growing; in 1999 the figure was 69%.

Local television experiments had a slow start in the mid-1980's as most of the 30 channels thus established operated on minimal budgets, mostly due to the ban on commercials. Only in Denmark's capital city area, where a greater audience could be found, did local television become a serious competitor to the DR. Meanwhile, more of the players (private business people, film industry types, trade unions members) began to see local television as an investment in the future television market (Hjarvard & Søndergaard, 1988). As a result, the ban on commercials in local television was removed in the early 1990's. Even so, however, making money on this market has proved difficult. Nevertheless, Danish local television has been the focus of considerable foreign investments in the past years, as the American-owned Scandinavian Broadcast System (SBS) has become the main shareholder of large commercial TV stations at the local level.

However, the real break with the DR's television monopoly did not happen because of private investors, but as a consequence of yet another public television channel being established. Through a change in legislation introduced in 1986, TV2 was established as an independent public television channel which started broadcasting in 1988. As an old monopoly institution the DR was entirely license-financed and its programming was based on its own productions, while TV2 is mostly financed through advertising revenue and is run as a private company whose own production only includes news and sports programs. Moreover, TV2 is linked to eight regional television stations broadcasting within the national broadcasting time frame. Still, TV2 is subject to a number of fairly restrictive rules for advertising which aim to limit the influence the means of financing may have on program policy. While most of the DR's program policy commitments have been imposed on TV2 as well, both channels enjoy extensive freedom in matters of program policy. They are run by their respective, politically appointed supervisory boards, which make sure that they comply with the legislation.

The establishment of TV2 was not only meant to break the DR's monopoly, which had become fairly outdated. It was also intended to help Danish television compete with foreign satellite channels. The idea was that two Danish public channels would have to compete with each other, raising the quality level of Danish television and stave off foreign competition (Media Commission, 1985). These goals have been largely achieved since together the two channels hold 69% of the market. Still, it is worth noting that the Danes do not as a matter of course prefer the Danish public service channels. The DR and TV2 are not in a situation of free competition since they continue to have sole and exclusive broadcasting rights on a national level; it can be said that they enjoy a fairly dominant position. Such regulation of the market can be explained by a desire to ensure TV2's financing through advertising revenue, a crucial economic precondition for the current television system.

Even so, in the last five or six years the DR and TV2 have been confronted with growing competition. First and foremost there are two commercial Danish television channels: On the one hand the Swedish-owned TV3 which runs two Danish-language channels both of them broadcasting to Denmark from London via satellite: TV3 (mainstream) and TV3+, caters to younger people and sports aficionados. On the other hand TvDanmark which is owned by SBS and consists of two channels: TvDanmark 1 broadcasting via satellite from London and TvDanmark 2 which is a network of private local channels. The commercial channels are in competition with TV2, especially from an economic point of view, not least because TV3 and TvDanmark 1 clearly benefits from not being subject to restrictive rules TV2 has to adhere to regarding commercials. Broadcasting time for commercials is limited on TV2, and advertising for tobacco, alcohol and medicines is prohibited; furthermore, commercials must be broadcast in blocks between programs. On the other hand, TV3 and TvDanmark 2's economic prospects are limited by the fact that the channel only reaches that part of the population which can receive satellite television.

IV   The Present Situation

In the last years the electronic media field has been marked by increased competition caused by its rapid development. This is the case for both radio and television, but the impact of competition is far more distinct in television, where the changes have been the greatest. This is the reason why the following takes a separate look at the two media.

4.1 Radio

The current public service radio system in Denmark consists of one independent broadcaster: DR (Danmarks Radio). DR runs 3 national channels: P1, is a 'serious' talk channel with a daily reach of 11% (2001), P2, a classical music channel with a daily reach of 8%, and P3, a music and entertainment channel for younger people, with a daily reach of 30%. DR also runs 9 regional stations sharing a fourth channel, P4, and on average the regional channels have a daily reach of 39%. Besides DR runs two AM-channels, a short wave channel and three internet-channels (DR Classic and two youth-channels: Skum 1 and 2) and January 2001 DR got a fourth FM-frequency for public service radiobroadcast. In total, public service radio in Denmark has a marked share of 67% of the listeners.

The commercial radio system in Denmark includes over 100 local and regional stations, an increasing number of which are associated as part of networking agreements. In 1997 a national commercial music and news channel was launched (R2). However, this channel has had a limited success with a market share of only 2%, partly due to the fact that it is distributed by satellite. In total commercial radio in Denmark has a market share of around 29% (2001).

As it appears, radio in Denmark is still primarily the Danish Broadcasting Corporation (DR). The latter broadcasts a total of about 55,000 hours of radio a year (1999), with 6,400 hours on P1, 4,500 hours of music on P2, 8,700 hours on P3, a solid

29,000 hours of regional radio broadcasts on P4, 3,600 hours on short waves, 1,800 hours classic radio, and 1,200 hours of AM Broadcasts. 67% of all radio listening concerns one of these four channels according to Gallup polls (1st quarter). However, among the four main channels there are great differences: P3's daily reach is 30%, and P4's 39%, while those of P1 and P2 are only 11% and 8%, respectively.

P4 with its regional programs, is the most listened to in the morning (between 6:00 and 9:00 a.m.). While figures taper off in the early afternoon, P4 takes up to more than 50% of the DR's total share. Similarly, P1's share is above 10% from 7:00–8:00 a.m., hitting its peak listening rate at 11:00 p.m. with more than 30%.

Table 1. *Percentage Distribution by Program Type*

News	Current affairs	Culture/ Education	Fiction	Music*	Entertain- ment	Sports	Services
8	33	7	2	27	10	4	9

The remaining 33% of the time spent listening to the radio mainly goes to the 228 local and regional (outside DR) radio stations found in Denmark (distributed over 150 broadcasting areas). A 1998 Ministry of Culture report on local radio estimates that the total annual broadcasting time for all 228 local radio stations is about 500,000 hours. This works out to an average of about 2,000 hours per station per year. Since 1994 the share of these local and regional stations has increased by 13% (from 20% to 33%).

The Danes do not listen much to foreign radio, including that of neighboring countries, despite the fact that the cable networks provide a number of interesting program choices. Daily foreign radio listening figures are 4% for the whole country, but 11% in the southern part of the country. Even though the local radios' overall listening figure does not exceed 33% during the day, it is worth noting that this figure reaches about 40% between 8:00 and 9:00 p.m. Their share is also significant in the late morning and early afternoon.

Table 2. *Denmark's 10 Most Listened-to Local Radio Stations, 1st quarter 2001**

Station	Listeners in Primary Area (in %)	Daily Listeners
Radio Charlie, Varde	45	15,000
The Victor, Esbjerg	42	38,000
Radio Viborg, Viborg	38	98,000
Radio Horsens, Horsens	35	34,000
ANR Hit, Aalborg	34	88,000
Radio SLR, Slagelse	34	43,000
ANR, Hjørring	32	22,000
Radio Holsted	32	52,000
ANR, Frederikshavn	31	22,000
Radio Køge, Køge	30	17,000

But as we know, numbers can be calculated in various ways. If one begins by looking at the larger local, commercial radio stations, as was done for the DBR Index (2001 Gallup polls), daily reach is 39%. This number is arrived at based on 54 local radio stations covering 76% of the population.

Except from two stations, all the most dominant stations are located in Jutland, and none of the stations come from the two biggest cities in Denmark: Copenhagen and Aarhus. Local loyalty in listening to radio plays an important role in the areas outside the big cities in Denmark. Some of the local radio stations clearly enjoy significant audience figures, in two cases exceeding 40% of daily reach. Of course, this does not mean that people only listen to local radio. But if one looks at them in a competitive perspective, these figures show that the battle for the listeners can be extremely fierce, especially in some of the larger province towns. On the other hand, the local radio stations have comparatively low audience figures in the greater Copenhagen area.

4.1.1 Use of Radio

In Denmark people listen to the radio about 3½ hours a day on average. This is as much as in Sweden and half an hour more than in Norway. The Finns spend a little more time listening to the radio (3 3/4 hours). Within the rest of Europe the Italians and Belgians are the heaviest radio users, with 4½ hours and 4 1/4 hours respectively, while England is at the bottom of the list with 2 hours. One may wonder whether or not 3½ hours a day is a lot, but on a European scale the time the average Danish spends listening to the radio is comparatively small, and the amount of time spent listening to the radio seems to decrease in proportion to the degree of governmental regulation. It should be remembered, however, that in this purely quantitative appraisal, no consideration is given as to how people listen to the radio – intently to a debate program, or absently to its muted sound in the background, for instance.

When it comes to radio reach, on the other hand, Denmark seems to place itself nicely in relation to the rest of Europe. The accumulated weekly reach is about 90% according to the latest listener surveys (DR, 1998) while it is 89% in England and 87% in Germany (Kagan, 1993). As for daily reach, Denmark's yearly average is 75%. In Sweden the reach percentage is approximately the same, whereas in Norway it is 72%. Even if the Danes do not really listen a lot to the radio, radio is, on the whole, in contact with over 3/4 of the Danish population for at least 15 minutes every single day. By way of comparison, television's daily reach in Denmark in 1994 was 74% (with a minimum of 5 minutes of television daily), and the accumulated weekly reach was 95%. Thus, a greater cumulative reach, but still a significantly lower daily reach. In other words, the Danes are at least as much in contact with radio as they are with television, and this is true for the time spent using the two media as well. While the Danes listen to the radio for 3½ hours on average, as already mentioned, the figure for television is 2½ hours.

Finally, it could be interesting to take a look at the demographic analysis undertaken in connection with the Danish Broadcasting Corporation's listener survey, based on listening diaries from 2,500 persons, selected representatively. This analysis provides only a relatively rough indication of the listeners' profile and the extent to which they listen to the public service channels. Unsurprisingly, the most devoted listeners are adults between the ages of 40 and 69. The Danish Broadcasting Corporation reaches about 80% of this group daily, whereas it only reaches 40% of the teenagers. For the latter group, the local radio stations are an attractive alternative. And this is also the case for the 20 to 29 age group, although here the tendency is not as pronounced. A good 60% of those between 20 and 29 years of age are in contact with the Danish Broadcasting Corporation every day. The other side of the coin is that almost 60% of the country's teenagers are not in contact with public service radio on a daily basis, while among those between the 20 and 29 years of age the figure is close to 40%. It has not been possible to trace the exact extent to which these percentages change with age, but in any case this is certainly a trend public service radio should be aware of.

The Danish Broadcasting Corporation's listener survey also explores the issue of educational level. Reach is highest (76%) among the least educated segment of the population (primary school level), while it is only 67% for younger people having attended school for another 1–2 years. For people with a secondary school diploma the average figure is 71%. Of course, different segments of the population obviously listen to different parts of the program framework and listening environments and situations vary. However, it is a fact that the least educated people are over-represented among listeners of public service radio. No matter what other consideration this may give rise to, it creates a special demand for easily accessible and comprehensive ways of communicating news items, debates and cultural issues.

4.2 Television

The television system offers a decidedly more complex picture due to the gradual establishment of the multi-channel system to provide international, national and local channels (Mortensen, 1992). The following table describes the situation at the end of 1999. This is no more than a 'snapshot' of the situation as the conditions are constantly changing.

It should be noted that households cannot normally receive more than a small number of the 80 international channels because the cable network can only carry 10 to 24 channels. Satellite channels have generally a very modest audience in Denmark, but the Swedish-owned, London-based TV3 and TvDanmark2 run by SVS are special cases as they broadcast programs intended for a Danish audience.

In most cases, individual channels in the television system work independently of one another. However, in reality there is a high degree of interconnection because they compete for the same audience and to some extent for the same economic resources as well. The commercial element in the television system has primarily increased the competition already going on due to the increase in the program supply.

Table 3. *Danish Television, 2001*

	Channels	Types of Institutions
	8 neighboring channels About 80 satellite channels	Public service institutions Mostly private commercial channels
National	DR1 & TV2/Denmark DR2 & T2 Zulu TV3, TV3+, TvDanmark1 TvDanmark FilmNet TV1000 DK4	Public service channels Public satellite channels Private commercial satellite channels Private commercial network channel Private, pay-channel Private, pay-channel Private, sponsored cable-channel
Regional	TV2 system, 8 regional stations	Public channels
Local	About 40 channels plus some 50 small information channels for community antenna television	Private, commercial channels as well as service-minded television

The current public television system in Denmark consists of two independent broadcasters, DR and TV2. DR is the former monopoly and is funded by license fees. DR runs two coordinated channels: DR1, which is distributed on the terrestrial net, and DR2, which is transmitted by satellite. DR1 is the main channel with an audience share of 29% in 2000, while DR2 is a kind of minority channel and has a marked share of only 3%.

TV2 runs one channel, which is funded by a mix of advertising income (80%) and license fees, which gives it a more 'commercial' or 'popular' profile, though TV2 has to fulfil more or less the same public service obligations as DR. However, TV2 is organized as a national channel with 8 regional TV2 stations affiliated, so that part of the TV2 schedule is regional television. Moreover, TV2 only produces news, sports programs and current affairs, while the rest of its output is based on independent producers. TV2's audience share amounted to 36% in 2000 which makes it Denmark's most popular channel, whereas TV2 Zulu still has a very small market share (between 1 and 2%).

In Denmark there are only two commercial television stations: TV3, a satellite channel based in England, and TvDanmark, a network of 7 local channels. While TV3 is owned by Swedish company Kinnevik, TvDanmark is owned by SBS. Neither TV3 nor TvDanmark has national reach, but they are nevertheless strong competitors to TV2, as they attract a substantial part of advertising expenditure. TV3 runs two channels, the main channel (TV3) has a market share of 9%, while TV3+ has only 3%. TvDanmark has been relatively successful in the last few years, reaching a market share of 7% in 2000, as TvDanmark 1 has a market share of 2% whereas TvDanmark 2 has 5%.

4.2.1 Programs on Offer

The major players on the television market are the DR, TV2, TV3 and TvDanmark, and each of them has a distinctive programming profile. The DR has a traditional public service profile, focusing heavily on news, information, and Danish drama. While in many ways TV2 has a profile similar to that of the DR, it offers far more entertainment in addition to its regional programs. Unlike the public channels, TV3 and TvDanmark have a purely commercial program supply, mostly consisting of entertainment programs and foreign fiction.

Table 4. *Broadcasting Time by Program Type (in percentage of broadcasting time) at the DR1, DR2, TV2, TV3 and TvDanmark, 1999.*

	DR1	DR2	TV2	TV3	TvDanmark
News	9	7	9	1	5
Current affairs	13	16	17	2	1
Information and Culture	26	40	7	3	4
Education	3	6	0	0	0
Music	2	3	4	1	0
Entertainment	8	6	8	13	33
Drama and Fiction	31	17	42	78	57
Sport	7	5	10	2	0
Regional TV	0	0	3	0	0
Broadcasting time (hrs.)	4.472	2.1769	5.493	7.049	7.039

Source: Gallup (2000)

Imported programs have always been a major constituent of Danish television, as it is much cheaper to buy programs than to produce them. In the DR's program supply the share of Danish produced programs was 62% in 1993; out of the imported programs 17% were from North America, 15% were from the EU and 4% from Scandinavia. On TV2 50% of the programs were Danish while among the imported programs no less than 27% were of American origin. There are no figures for TV3; however, the proportion of foreign programs is considerably smaller. As for fiction the ratio foreign/own productions is very high, although not so high on the DR (75%) as on TV2 (92%) (Søndergaard, 1995).

4.2.2 Market Share and Reach

Since 1993 daily viewing results have been published based on a television meter panel, and detailed information is available about the four main channels (DR, TV2, TV3, TvDanmark). TV2 is the most popular television channel in terms of audience share with an average of 36%. Even though the DR has lost ground every year since the break-up of the monopoly, DR1 is the second most popular channel with 29%, while TV3 has a 12% market share and TVDanmark a share of 7%. These figures give a somewhat distorted picture of the actual power relationship since only 69% of the population are capable of receiving TV3 and TvDanmark 1. When one only focuses on the viewers who are able to receive TV3, that is satellite television, the conclusion is that both TV2 and DR are in a weaker position compared to TV3. Nevertheless, it is obvious that together DR and TV2 are very strong, even though it is worth noting that to a certain extent DR and TV2 appeal to different audiences, which also partially explains why their market shares are so different. TV2 mostly attracts the traditional, heavy TV viewers, that is, older people and the less educated, while DR is primarily watched by well-educated adults whose TV use is more sporadic (Bentzon et al., 1991).

Table 5. *Market Shares, 1998–2000 (%)*

	1998	1999	2000
TV2/Zulu	38	36	36
DR1	29	28	29
DR2	2	3	3
TV3	10	11	9
TV3+	2	3	3
TvDanmark	7	8	7
Others	12	12	12

Source: Gallup poll index (2000)

Table 6. *Average Weekly Reach, 1997–1999 (%)*

	1997	1998	1999
TV2	88	89	85
DR1	86	87	85
DR2	15	18	23
TV3	42	42	42
TV3+	12	15	19
TvDanmark	30	39	39
Local television	10	8	8
Others	44	43	42
Total	94	95	93

Source: Gallup poll index (1999)

As far as reach is concerned TV2 and DR are in a strong position, while TvDanmark's and TV3's reach is relatively small. Reach figures show that TV2 and DR are the Danes' primary channels while both TvDanmark and TV3 are used as complementary channels (cf. Svendsen, 1996).

4.2.3 Economic Conditions

In economic terms DR and TV2 are also Danish television's center of gravity since they claim by far the largest part of the resources. There are no public records of the economic conditions in commercial television, but in the case of DR and TV2 the budget looks as follows:

Table 7. *DR and TV2, turn over*

€ million	1997	1998	1999
DR	345	361	376
TV2	205	210	204

As shown in table 7, DR is more expensive to run than TV2, among other things because it handles more projects. Another reason is that DR has an expensive production machine.

License fees are apportioned between DR and TV2, and TV2 currently receives only a smaller share amounting to 15% of TV2's total revenue. The annual license fee was a good € 376 in 1996 for both television and radio, while the annual license fee for radio alone is € 39.

4.3 Media Concentration and Anti-Trust Legislation

Due to the strong position of the public television channels, until now there has been no need for the legislator to limit the possibilities of owning television channels in Denmark. Only within the field of local television has there been a real potential for concentrated power and capital. Consequently various legal restrictions have been in force to preserve the local media's grassroots nature and prevent the industry from gaining a dominant influence. Defining 'dominant influence' is an impossible task, however, and in fact a large foreign media company, SBS, has already been able to buy a Danish local TV station.

At a hearing about media concentration by the European Commission (1995) the Danish ministry of culture rejected the notion of specific legislation against media concentration: "It does not seem appropriate to lay down specific rules regarding media concentration in a small country such as Denmark, which is dominated by strong national public service channels, especially not if the number of viewers must be used as the criteria for market dominance" (The Media Committee, 1996: 113). Another reason for this answer, however, is that no local players are to be found in Denmark that are strong enough to dominate the market. Nevertheless, recently government had begun to reconsider if more control of ownership would be appropriate, since the media convergence seems to pave the way for media concentration. In the report *Konvergens i netværkssamfundet [Convergence in Network Society]* published by the Ministry of Culture and the Ministry of Research in 2001, it is stated that media concentration is not in itself a threat against cultural diversity and pluralism, and it is recommended that we should wait and see if media concentration legislation is needed in the future.

4.4 Danish Attitude Towards European Media Policy

As a Member State of the EU Denmark has adjusted its media legislation in order to harmonize with the EU directives. Major legislation revisions were done in 1992 with regard to the 'Television Without Frontiers' Directive, which implemented a program quota system for European programs and a number of rules concerning commercials and sponsorship. However, Denmark is against the quota system, which it views as intervention in cultural politics, a purely national matter. When it comes to the regulation of commercials and sponsorship Denmark has invented its own, more restrictive legislation in order to protect consumers and to restrict further commercialization of the media. In general Denmark has an ambivalent attitude towards EU regulations, which make it possible to regulate non-national broadcasting but could also turn out to pose problems for Danish media policy. In particular, the Commission's proposed restrictive measures regarding public service broadcasting are seen as very problematic in Denmark as they could make it difficult for Danish public broadcasters to maintain their strong position.

V   Future Developments

In recent years in Denmark the debate has focused on the potential extension of public service radio through the introduction of a fourth frequency. However, in the light of impending developments in radio technology, such a discussion may be rather shortsighted. Within the next few years new technology will open up a multitude of possibilities via digitizing, compression of radio signals, co-transmission, telecommunication and computer technology. Thus in the near future European listeners will be able to receive 700 radio channels via satellite. Already a British company (Music Choice Europe) is planning to move its radio cable network to the ASTRA satellite, which would enable it to offer 64 full-time radio channels to 16 million European households. In addition new forms of distribution will emerge. Pay-radio is already a reality, while audio-on-demand will be soon. Radio has been introduced on the Internet and is expected to be followed by subscription radio, radio home shopping, and other interactive radio services (Løns-mann, 1995).

In March 2000 the Danish Parliament passed a resolution about the working out of DAB-radio. According to this resolution DR has been put forward as the most promi-nent developer of DAB. However, commercial stations will be allowed to use digital channels in a second phase as well when a national DAB transmission network has been established. In the resolution it is foreseen that within a period of 10–15 years all ana-logue radio transmission has been substituted by digital transmission.

No answer has yet been found to the question of the consequences which this huge choice may have on the daily use of the radio medium. Will traditional radio become ob-solete? Whether or not this is going to happen does not solely depend on the new tech-nology. More important is the question of how and to what extent the everyday lives of ordinary people are going to change, which will not necessarily coincide with the tech-nological developments. In a not too distant future many people are going to have a job which lets them listen to the radio while they work. Many people are going to use means of transport where only radio listening is allowed. And many people will be working at home and listening to the radio. Radio will remain an attractive medium as it can be lis-tened to while doing something else. In addition, the aging of the population is likely to lead to increased interest in radio as experience has shown that older people are more as-siduous radio users. So radio as we know it today is likely to exist for many years to come.

However, some of the conditions of radio are fundamentally changing. The future challenge of *public service radio* lies in its ability to reflect and serve a multicultural so-ciety with a population whose self-awareness will gradually become heterogeneous (so-cially, culturally and ethnically), while acting as a common cultural denominator at a local, regional, national and, to some extent, international level. This is no easy task: while television is seen as a communal medium, radio has become more and more in-dividualized as a medium, and if public service radio is to remain the radio of the *entire* population, it needs to take this conclusion seriously.

Compared to radio, television faces significantly larger changes, not least because the competition has a different character and involves considerably more actors. It is a fact that digitizing will enlarge the playing field and thus subject the DR and TV2 to in-creased competition; this prospect led to an extensive analysis being made by a govern-mental media committee. In the spring of 1996 a range of considerations were pub-lished; the committee presented proposals to slightly adjust the television system, but characteristically most proposals aim to maintain and protect the current system (The Media Committee, 1996).

Nevertheless the deregulation drive has been intensified, with a number of legis-lative changes in the end of the 1990's. The most important aspect of this is the fact that the local, commercial television stations have been given the opportunity to join a proper network in order to broadcast programs nationally. This legislation made TvDanmark possible, and for TV2 this had lead to a significantly increased competi-tive pressure, while simultaneously making local television an attractive investment proposition for foreign capital. To compensate for this effect TV2 has reorganized through the closure of the currently independent advertising company (TVR). Thus TV2 is now able to make use of its advertising revenue as it sees fit; furthermore TV2 has been permitted to extend the time devoted to commercials from 10% to 15% of total broadcasting time. The DR's license financing will be maintained but in return the DR was given permission to launch a supplementary channel, DR2, broadcasting via satellite.

Future developments in the Danish television system will no doubt be influenced by investment from a number of big companies. Although DR and TV2 together are very strong, the Danish market is viewed as potentially very lucrative, hence the current flurry of investment there. Meanwhile, it is significant that a number of large Scandinavian media companies have been investing in all of the Scandinavian market through various forms of cross-ownership as well as attempts to gain control over production, distribution and sale of programs and commercials. The main players in this field are Sweden's Kinnevik and Bonniers, Denmark's Egmont and Norway's Schipstedt, as well as SBS, whose primary interest is local television.

Digitization will most certainly lead to an increase in the TV supply, especially in subscription television, near-video-on-demand and various kinds of interactive services. The Norwegian-French company Canal Digital have launched a digital service based on satellite distribution, MTG, the company that owns TV3, also offers satellite based digital television, while the former national telecom company TDC has for more that three years offered digital television in their cable net. Plans for building a terrestrial digital net have passed parliament in 2001, and considerable funds have been allocated for the digitization of both DR and TV2. It seems clear that the public channels will come to play an important role in the new terrestrial net, but so far it is not decided which other channels that are going to use the net. The net will be able to carry 16 channels which leaves room for a number of new actors, but as long as the conditions for private channels to use the net are not decided it is difficult to say how the future development of Danish television will look like.

References

Andersen, O.E. (1995). *Medieudbud og medieforbrug i Danmarks 1983–1994 [Media Supply and Media Consumption in Denmark 1983–1994]*. Copenhagen: Rapport udarbejdet for Statsministeriets Medieudvalg [Report prepared for the Media Committee of the Prime Minister's Dept.].

Bentzon, K.-H., Nielsen, N.A. & Svendsen, E.N. (1991). Ligheder og forskelle [Similarities and Differences]. In E. Nordahl Svendsen (ed.), *Medieforskning i Danmarks Radio 1990 [Media Research within the Danish Broadcasting Corporation]* (pp. 16–59). Copenhagen.

Bondebjerg, I. (1990). Opbuddet fra monopolkulturen [Departure from the Culture of Monopoly], *Sekvens 89*: 91–136.

Danmarks Radios Lytterundersøgelser [The Danish Broadcasting Corporation's Listener Survey] (1998). Copenhagen: Radioens Udviklingsenhed [Dept. of Radio Development].

Engberg, M. (1986). Før det hele begyndte – hvordan fjernsynet kom til Danmark [Before It All Began – How Television Came to Denmark], *Sekvens 86*: 5–24.

Gallup (1999). *Årsrapport for 1998. TV-meter undersøgelsen i Danmark.*

Gallup Polls Index 2001, 1st quarter. Available at [http://gallup.dk/radio_tal.html].

Giersing, M. (1982). *Nordic TV – Between Paternalism and Commercialism.* Copenhagen: University of Copenhagen (Department of Comparative Literature).

Hjarvard, S. & Søndergaard, H. (1988). *Nærsyn på fjernsyn: Kanal 2og Weekend TV [A Close Look at Television: Channel 2 and Weekend TV].* Copenhagen: C.A. Reitzel.

Jauert, P. (1990). Massemedier, kultur og lokalsamfund [Mass Media, Culture and Local Community]. In H. Hortstbøll & H.K. Nielsen (eds.), *Delkulturer [Part Cultures]* (pp. 101–126). Aarhus: University of Aarhus.

Kagan's European Radio (1993). London: Kagan World Media.

Lund, A. B. (1976). *Magten over Danmarks Radio [Power over the Danish Broadcasting Corporation].* Aarhus.

Lønsmann, L. (1995). *The Changing Radio Landscape and the Need for Research.* Paper presented at the *Nordic Seminar on Radio Research.* Tampere (Finland), October 26–29.

Mandags News, Aabenraa (1994). Week 35.

Mediekommissionen (The Media Commission) (1985). *Betænkning om dansk mediepolitik [Report on Danish Media Policy].* Copenhagen: The Prime Minister's Department.

Medieudvalget (The Media Commitee) (1996). *Betænkning om medierne i demokratiet [Report on Mass Media and Democracy].* Copenhagen: The Prime Minister's Department.

Mortensen, F. (1992). *De elektroniske massemedier i Danmark år 2005 [The Broadcast Media in Denmark year 2005].* Copenhagen: Undervisningsministeriets Forlag.

Nielsen, S.H. (ed.) (1995). *Lokalradio og lokal-tv [Local Radio and Local Television]*. Copenhagen.

Poulsen, I. (1995). *Radioen som public service medie [Radio as a Public Service Media]*. Rapport udarbejdet for Statsministeriets Medieudvalg [Report to the Media Commission of the Prime Minister's Office]. Copenhagen.

Poulsen, I. (1997). Public service radio in Denmark today. In U. Carlsson (ed.), *Radio Research in Denmark, Finland, Norway and Sweden*. Nordicom Review 1/1997, Göteborg.

Qvortrup, L. (1988). *Et spil om hybridnettet [A Game on the Hybrid Cable Net]*. Copenhagen.

Skovmand, R. (1975). *DR 50*. Copenhagen: Danmarks Radio.

Svendsen, E.N. (ed.) (1996). *TV-medieforskning i Danmarks Radio 1994–95 [Research on Television in DR 1994–95]*. Copenhagen: Danmarks Radio.

Søndergaard, H. (1994). *DR i tv-konkurrencens tidsalder [DR in the Age of Competition]*. Copenhagen: Samfundslitteratur.

Søndergaard, H. (1995). *Public service i dansk fjernsyn: Begreber, status og scenarier [Public Service in Danish Television: Concepts, Status and Scenarios]*. Rapport udarbejdet for Statsministeriets Medieudvalg [Report to the Media Commission of the Prime Minister's Office]. Copenhagen.

Søndergaard, H. (1996). Fundamentals in the history of Danish television. In I. Bondebjerg & F. Bono (eds.), *Television in Scandinavia. History, Politics and Aesthetics* (pp. 11–40). London: University of Luton Press.

France

by Serge Regourd

I   A Series of Distinctive Features Rooted in History

As in most European countries, the French broadcast media system was originally structured as a public monopoly. This 'public service' monopoly status was itself a consequence of the status previously applied to other media: the post-office, then the telegraph and the telephone, then radio – whose initial name was *wireless telegraph*, and
finally television. Every time a new technical breakthrough or invention emerged, the
Government replicated the legal status applied to earlier supports: thus the monopoly
status spread from telephone to radio to television. Until 1959, the beginning of the Vth
Republic, the French Radio and Television (*RTF*) was in fact an integral part of the public administration: no more than a ministerial department devoid of any legal personality. In 1959 the *RTF* was granted a measure of institutional autonomy, becoming an 'industrial and commercial public institution.' But this new-found legal and financial freedom did not extend to independence from the political authorities: for many years radio
and television remained subject to stringent political control from the executive power, a
situation that reached its highest pitch under the successive presidencies of General de
Gaulle and his former prime minister, Georges Pompidou. The official justification for
this was that broadcast media must be 'the Voice of France' – in other words that of the
Government. Thus in France the legal monopoly resulted in political hegemony. The repercussions of this political subservience can still be felt today...

After Giscard d'Estaing became president of the Republic in 1974, France's broadcast media – especially television – took on another special characteristic: a 1974 Act
broke up the *ORTF* (French Radio and Television Agency), the single organization
which had been in charge of managing the various operations of the public broadcasting
system. The *ORTF* was broken down into seven distinct organizations: three television
'program corporations' (*TF1*, *Antenne 2*, and *FR3*) each using one of the three existing
TV channels, one radio program corporation (*Radio-France*), one production corporation (*Société française de production, SFP*), one public broadcasting agency (*Télédiffusion de France, TDF*), and one public institution for archives, training, and research
(*Institut National de l'Audiovisuel, INA*).

The five corporations' legal status was that of limited companies, but the state held
on to 100 percent of their capital. The public service monopoly remained, but operations
were now carried out through distinct organizations. As for television, three public
channels were set up as competitors both for audience share and advertising revenue.
The Act failed to provide for any structure or procedure for consultation or complementing strategies concerning the three channels' program supply. This meant that a
system of commercial competition logic was being implemented even within France's
public monopoly. The only thing the various public organizations had in common was a

system requiring the programming corporations to order programs from the production corporation (*SFP*).

The monopoly was repealed in 1981, after François Mitterrand had become France's new president. An Act dated July 29, 1982 proclaims in its very first section that "broadcast communication is free." The first broadcasting licenses granted to private operators were for radio, then television was opened to private initiative as well. The first private TV station to be created, in December 1984, was *Canal Plus*, an encrypted, pay-TV channel. This was followed in 1985 by two new private channels transmitted nationwide through a terrestrial broadcasting system: *La Cinq* (whose first operator was Berlusconi) and *TV6*, partly designed as music channel. The 1982 Act which abolished the public monopoly also created an independent regulatory authority so as to cut off the political umbilical cord between the broadcasting system and the Government. This *Haute Autorité de la Communication audiovisuelle* (the *Haute Autorité*) was meant to guarantee the independence of broadcast media from the Government. (It included nine key public figures appointed by the State's highest-ranking officials: three by the president of the Republic, three by the president of the Senate, and three by the president of the National Assembly). The persistence of this political umbilical cord was to become plain as soon as the political pendulum swung the other way, however, with right-wing parties winning the 1986 parliamentary election and their leader, Mr. Chirac, becoming prime minister. A new Act was passed on September 30, 1986. Among other things, it provided for the following:

* The *Haute Autorité* was replaced with a new controlling body, the *CNCL* (*Commission Nationale pour la Communication et les Libertés*), with a majority of whose members' political allegiance ensuring that the new government had total control over it (in 1989, following the Left's return to power, this body was in turn replaced with the current *CSA – Conseil Supérieur de l'Audiovisuel* – modeled on the former *Haute Autorité*, but with more regulatory powers).
* The licenses granted to the private operators of the fifth and sixth TV stations were revoked and awarded to new operators closer to the new majority.
* But the 1986 Act's main provision had a different purpose, constituting another distinctive feature of the French system: the privatization of one of the three public channels, *TF1*, which then enjoyed a 40 percent audience share and 55 percent of total advertising revenue, and was the premier European medium in terms of commercial resources. The dominance of the privatized *TF1* had serious repercussions on the overall regulation of the French TV system, including the elimination of the second private channel (*La Cinq*), which went bankrupt due to insufficient advertising revenue (its 11 percent audience share prevented it from negotiating high enough rates in the face of *TF1*'s 40 percent share). Several major operators had successively tried their hand at running this station, but to no avail: after Berlusconi and Hersant (France's largest daily print media group), even the Hachette group had to give up its television venture…

The void left by *La Cinq*'s demise was then filled by the French-German cultural channel *Arte* (in the evening slot from 7:00 p.m.) as well as a new public, education-oriented channel created in 1994: *La Cinquième* (in the day-time slot until 7:00 p.m.).

In 1994 a new Act accelerated the changes favoring private operators, both through a significant relaxation of media concentration rules (the maximum interest a shareholder could hold was raised from 25 percent to 49 percent of stock, for instance) and the establishment of an automatic broadcasting license renewal procedure for two five-year periods. Thus, while *TF1* and *M6*, the two private general interest channels, had been initially granted a ten-year license, the 1994 Act granted them two additional five-year periods, which amounted to a doubling of the original license. As for radio, the original five-year license's duration was thus trebled...

A new law was passed on August 1, 2000 after drawn-out negotiations begun in the wake of the 1997 parliamentary election upset. Its initial purpose was to strengthen antitrust provisions concerning the private sector, with a view to preventing large industrial corporations (Bouygues, Vivendi, Lyonnaise des eaux, etc.) from grabbing the lion's share of public procurement contracts. But determined opposition from these corporations soon derailed this attempt at reform, and the new law ended being mostly concerned with public sector restructuring.

The most publicized change was the cut in allowed advertising times on public channels, previously a regulatory concern rather than a legislative one. Another change was the reorganization of the public sector as part of a newly created holding company (France-Télévision) which included the France 2, France 3 and La Cinquième channels, while its president's term of office was conveniently increased from three to five years. The establishment of France-Télévision was the culmination of an institutional process initiated in an Act dated August 2, 1989 which provided for a common president for France 2 and France 3 with a view – already – to the "revitalization of the public audiovisual sector." This structural reorganization of the public sector is paralleled by a relegitimization of the activities of the public sector: Article 3 of the August 1, 2000 Act clearly states that the public corporations "carry out public service missions."

Rather belatedly, this Act provides for the implementation in domestic law of the EU "Television Without Frontiers" Directive as revised in 1997. Thus the Act includes several crucial provisions pertaining to various fields such as broadcasts of "major events," which must be available to the public on an unscrambled channel despite any exclusivity rights, or the criteria regarding the definition of the official place of business of TV operators and the ensuing considerations of domestic jurisdiction.

The considerable technical changes that have occurred since the February 1, 1994 Act required new legal provisions regarding the Internet, even though these remain highly fragmentary. In the hope of preventing existing legislation from being superseded by new technical developments, Parliament chose to establish a much broader legal framework for digital terrestrial (hertzian) television. In addition, the new legislation closes down a long standing loophole concerning satellite broadcasting, by treating it like cable broadcasting.

II   Diversity and Concentration: Legal Framework and Economic Positions

In the last decade the French legislator seems to have tried to provide for two conflicting objectives: retaining an anti-trust legal framework to guarantee operator – and therefore program supply – diversity on the one hand, and conversely, favoring the creation of media groups strong enough to face international competition and the globalization of the communication market.

2.1 Single Medium Restrictions

The first shareholding restrictions pertain to the ownership of TV stations. Until the February 1, 1994 Act any natural person or legal entity could not hold more than 25 percent of the capital of a national TV station. This has now been raised to 49 percent. This stake may be held directly or indirectly. This limit is lowered to 15 percent when the shareholder already owns more than 15 percent of the capital or voting rights in another corporation in possession of such a license, and to five percent when the shareholder owns more than five percent in two corporations holding such a license.

For satellite television, this limit is 50 percent ownership per company; it is lowered to one third of stock or voting rights for any shareholder already owning more than one third of the capital of another corporation in possession of such a license, and to five percent when the natural person or legal entity already owns more than five of the capital or voting rights in two corporations holding such a license. Satellite radio is subject to the same restrictions. There is a similar 50 percent shareholding limit (stock or voting rights) for any local, terrestrial broadcasting TV station covering an area whose population totals 200,000 to six million individuals.

In addition to such shareholding restrictions, there are limitations to the number of licenses one can hold: an operator holding a national TV broadcasting license cannot hold another license of the same type, even for a local station. More than one cable TV license may be held provided the overall coverage area of the networks owned does not exceed eight million individuals. No more than two satellite TV licenses are permissible.

Unlike television, and except for the very special case of satellite broadcasting, no shareholding restrictions are enforced on radio operators. Radio ownership restrictions pertain only to broadcasting areas. Since the introduction of the 1994 Act the maximum coverage for one operator has been extended to 150 million individuals, which means one operator can own up to the equivalent of three national radio networks. Such 'single medium' restrictions are supplemented with 'multimedia' restrictions simultaneously applying to television, radio, cable transmission and print media.

2.2 'Multimedia' Restrictions

At the national level no natural person or legal entity is entitled to more than two of the following four situations:

1. Holding terrestrial TV broadcasting licenses covering more than four million individuals.
2. Holding local radio licenses covering more than 30 million individuals.
3. Holding cable TV licenses covering more than six million individuals.
4. Controlling at least one daily political and general information publication equivalent to more than 20 percent of the total circulation of similar publications.

Similarly, at the regional and local levels ownership restrictions apply beyond two of the following four situations:

1. Licenses for TV services (national or otherwise).
2. Licenses for a radio broadcasting service equivalent to more than ten percent of maximum potential coverage in the area in question.
3. Licenses for the operation of cable distribution networks in a given area.
4. Control over daily, political and general information print media in a given area.

More specific restrictions apply to foreign stock ownership of the program corporations.

2.3 Foreign Ownership Restrictions

Unlike common law on foreign investments, broadcast media law does not recognize the notions of 'resident' or 'non-resident.' It applies indiscriminately to all 'foreigners' – European Union nationals being the only exception to this rule. Companies considered foreign are those whose capital is mostly owned by foreigners and associations whose management team is entirely or mostly composed of foreigners. Thus the Act restricts foreign ownership to 20 percent of stock or voting rights. However this only applies to French-language terrestrial TV and radio broadcasting. It does not apply to foreign-language channels nor to satellite and cable channels. Hardly anybody takes exception to this legal framework in France as it does not hinder major operators: those private groups doing business respectively in television, radio, and the print media are distinct and each specializes in a specific domain.

2.4 Major Groups

In this respect, an economic characteristic of the French media system has been the inability of the major print media groups to enter the TV field. The most powerful among them (*Hachette* and *Hersant*) have made the attempt but failed. Hachette's failure as operator of *La Cinq* was especially dramatic as it led to the demise of the second national private TV channel (whose audience share was about 11 percent). The major regional print media groups are also absent from the TV field. One reason is the almost complete nonexistence of local and regional TV. The only such TV stations (in Toulouse and in Lyon) have been facing serious financial difficulties. Their operator – and majority shareholder – comes from the major urban utility companies in charge of water distribution and purification, Vivendi (the former Compagnie générale des eaux), Canal Plus's main shareholder.

Another major feature of private TV in France is precisely the dominant role played by those groups which were dubbed 'the newcomers' a few years ago to emphasize the fact that they were major industrial groups which until then had had nothing to do with the communication and television fields. First among these is the *Bouygues* group, the largest European construction and public works contractor, which bought *TF1* and remains the station's operator and majority shareholder. Such is also the case of two multinational urban utility corporations: the abovementioned *Compagnie générale des Eaux* (now Vivendi), which owns part of *Canal Plus*, and the *Société Lyonnaise des Eaux*, a shareholder of the other national private channel, *M6*, on an equal footing with Luxembourg's *CLT* (*Compagnie Luxembourgeoise de Télévision*). The *Société Lyonnaise des Eaux* is also France's main cable operator.

These major industrial groups whose operations are diversified in many fields and countries have a lot more economic power than those companies which have long specialized in the media business. The *Canal Plus* group is one of Europe's leading TV operators having successfully diversified in several countries (Belgium, Germany, Spain…). Right from its creation Canal Plus had become a major European communications group, and one of the most profitable, owing to international diversification based on the various formats (hertzian, cable, satellite, movie production and distribution, etc.). Main shareholder Vivendi, which held 49% of its capital (the maximum share allowed by anti-trust provisions), launched a takeover bid on both Canal Plus and Canadian group Seagram (owner of Universal Pictures and Universal Music, among others). This resulted in the creation of the world's second largest communications group (the first being AOL/Time-Warner, itself the product of the largest merger in the history of the media). These mergers stem from the convergence of technological and economic processes, which sees operators belonging to highly diverse industries (telecommunications, IT, radio and television) acting together on all of these communications platforms. They implement a vertical integration process for control of contents (movie, TV/radio and music copyrights), subscribers/consumers, and distribution channels/platforms/formats. Such mergers highlight the drastic changes currently upsetting the traditional means of regulating audiovisual communication through the prevalence of direct funding by the subscriber ou spot payment (pay per view, video on demand). In the case of the Vivendi/Seagram/Canal Plus merger, the Canadian group brought Universal's audiovisual rights (5,700 movies, 27,000 TV-movies and series episodes) as well as the copyrights of the world's largest music publisher (over 20% of the world market), which from then on could be exploited in connection with Canal Plus's 14 million subscribers (in eleven countries), SFR, Cegetel and Vodaphone's telephone subscribers (50 million in Europe), through the concurrent use of all platforms (music, cinema and TV, publishing, telephone as well as the Internet through the Vivendi's Vizzavi portal).

The merger took place just when the CSA was expected to grant Canal Plus a five year extension of its license (2001). This hinged on the approval of substantial changes to be done in the station's organization. The economic strategy behind the merger thus had to take into account the legal and institutional aspects imposed by the current legislation, in their letter if not in their spirit. Canal Plus was thus split in two companies, Canal Plus Distribution (fully controlled by new company Vivendi-Universal) and Canal Plus S.A., in whose capital Vivendi cannot hold more than a 49% share (legal limit), although it retains ownership of the subscriber files which represent the channel's market. Use of these files is conceded to Canal Plus Distribution, which pursues Vivendi's strategic objectives. It is also in charge of marketing the subscriber base. This legal arrangement is meant to ensure the independence of Canal Plus (the sole holder of the broadcasting license) with respect to the new Vivendi-Universal multimedia group. The CSA thus conditioned the extension of Canal Plus S.A.'s license on the implementation of a number of contract provisions between the latter and Canal Plus Distribution (that is, the Vivendi-Universal group), aiming to guarantee Canal Plus S.A.'s independence.

At the same time, the CSA made sure that the financial commitments in favor of French movie production remained in place (amounts higher than the legal requirements through contracts with professional cinema organizations – that is, FRF 20.5 per subscriber). Vivendi Universal also promised not to create a new movie channel that could compete with Canal Plus.

Since the 1982 deregulation move radio has seen the emergence of a new class of operators, most of whom have no ties whatsoever with the print media and television. Apart from the major exception that is the *CLT*, a shareholder of the *M6* TV channel and the *RTL* radio station, the new so-called 'specialist' (that is, primarily music oriented) radio networks have successfully carried out development strategies centering almost exclusively on radio.

In the field of radio the nature of the concentration and diversity issue is not the same: while initially deregulation worked to the advantage of local and non-profit radios (some 1,800 stations had been licensed), a few large commercial networks structured around four advertising agencies currently make up the larger part of the 'radio market.' These large specialist networks (*NRJ*, *Skyrock*, *Fun Radio*...) gradually became dominant, at the expense of non-profit radio stations and above all the independent, local commercial stations, which the networks gradually 'absorbed.' These specialist networks' main competitors are two general interest private networks (formerly called 'peripheral networks' as they broadcast from the periphery of the French territory): *RTL* and *Europe 1*. Public radio (*Radio-France*) includes several channels: a general-interest channel (*France Inter*), a 24-hour news channel (*France-Info*) and two cultural channels with a marginal audience share (*France-Culture* and *France-Musique*).

III   Public/Private Competition: Program Supply and Funding

The public service monopoly ended with the aforementioned July 29, 1982 Act which provided for the creation of private channels. The legal framework set out by the 1982 Act for private operators in national, terrestrial TV broadcasting was the 'public service concession' system. *Canal Plus* was initially created as part of this legal framework, based on a contract between the French State and *Canal Plus*'s operator (originally, the Havas agency). This contract remained in force until 1994. Since then *Canal Plus* has been for the most part subject to the same legal framework as the other private stations: license delivered by the *CSA*, and regulatory power of the latter over the former (which had not been the case until 1989).

The other private terrestrial broadcasting stations (*TF1* and *M6*) come under the legal framework instituted by the September 30, 1986 Act which replaced the 1982 Act. This framework is a purely license-based system whose procedures and content do not bear any relationship to the notion of public service mandate. *Canal Plus*'s TV programming debut took place under very special conditions, without any call for tender nor competitive bids. The French Government simply chose an operator it liked and proceeded to make available to it a free of charge nation-wide terrestrial transmission system – the system used formerly by the first public channel. Since this encrypted, (subscriber-oriented) pay-channel has a specific orientation in two program supply areas – films and sports –, some of the conditions listed in its charter differ from the regulatory provisions applicable to other channels.

As far as broadcasting licenses are concerned, both for television and for radio, a number of legal and regulatory constraints have been unilaterally imposed on applicants, but since 1989 any license granted includes a convention between the *CSA* and the licensed operator listing all requirements. *TF1*'s license was a special case owing to its situation as newly privatized station. The first difference with other licensed channels was financial. While licenses are granted free of charge, *TF1* was only granted a license after it had been sold (for an estimated total price of FRF 4.5 billion or USD760 million). The invitation to tender pertained to 50 percent of its capital (with the share of the operator and shareholder being at that time limited to 25 percent). Otherwise *TF1* comes under common law provisions, including for the duration of its license. The dual nature of the French TV system still bears the stamp of *TF1*'s privatization.

3.1   'Audimat' and Regulations

A few years ago the French system was described as a 'free-wheeling competition' system (like its Italian counterpart), as opposed to better balanced systems such as those of Germany or Great Britain. One characteristic of this competition is the fact that, unlike the previous 'public service' logic, the program supply is no longer driven by production; now production is driven by programming requirements. Program makers develop schedules based on targets pre-identified using marketing techniques with a view to maximizing audience figures.

The system's main regulating factor is a purely quantitative one: the *audimat* (people-meter monitoring), which measures the rating of each program on a daily basis and generates the amount of advertising revenue. For private operators, the sway of the *audimat* is absolute: insufficient audience figures mean a quick death for many a program. In the last few years, several shows have thus been 'canned' after just a few weeks, or even days, because their profitability was low.

Public channels, on the other hand, must reconcile audience maximization requirements with the specific public service mandates listed in their content requirements to air programs which the private sector cannot afford to touch due to their insufficient profitability. In such a context the research policies implemented within the channels or externally are not a determinant factor. Research is one of the main purposes of the aforementioned INA, but its influence on programming policy is very indirect at best.

The only restrictions to this audience regulation situation are a consequence of regulatory provisions concerning programming policy. But the program supply is hardly regulated in terms of quality or content, based on journalistic ethics or the protection of young people, for instance. Quantitative regulations are much more present, taking the form of broadcasting and production quotas. This is one of the consequences of France taking a leading role in the protection of the national cultural production, as illustrated by its fight for 'cultural exemption' during the GATT talks or its call for more stringent quotas in the Television Without Frontiers Directive. In this respect French law is a lot more strict and demanding than the directive: on the one hand broadcasting quotas are set at 60 percent of European-made programs, including 40 percent of French-language (not dubbed or subtitled) programs. On the other hand the very definition of the works deemed acceptable under the quota system is more restrictive, as it only includes works of fiction, creative documentary films, animated motion pictures, but not variety or talk shows. These broadcasting requirements are complemented with production requirements of French programs determined as a percentage of a channel's sales figures. In radio such provisions meant to counteract 'the invasion of US products' are more recent: all operators must broadcast at least 40 percent of French songs (before this quota was implemented some music stations would broadcast almost nothing but English-language recordings). On the other hand, neither the legislation nor program making practices evidence a specific concern with respect to ethnic or sexual minorities. 'French culture' remains, both historically and politically, determined by the Republic's values of Equality which prohibit giving a distinct status to a particular community, or even to women.

Broadcast programs are only required to comply with the general provisions of penal law which forbid racist slurs or attacks on the dignity of human beings, for instance. The sole requirement for all operators, both private and public, is the constitutional principle of the diversity of currents of expression which is set out in the very first section of the 1986 Act. For public channels this diversity principle is more onerous as it involves socalled 'direct expression' programs for major political parties, trade unions and national associations. The length of such programs is prescribed by the *CSA*. More significant, the major monotheistic religions (Catholics, Protestants, Jews, Moslems) have special Sunday morning programs on *France 2*.

3.2 Weaknesses and Strengths of the Public Sector

In recent years competition between the private and public sectors helped the latter restore a situation which was initially very unfavorable. The position of the public service – that is, *France-Télévision* (which includes *France 2* and *France 3*) – can be summarized in a few statements:

- overall audience rating which is now satisfactory since it is in excess of 40 percent (*France 2* regularly exceeds 23 percent, while *France 3* is doing better than before, with 17 percent).
- financial and identity problems due to the generalized practice in recent years of subcontracting production to private companies owned by *France 2* program hosts, which revealed serious management mistakes.

These problems were made even more visible by the severe crisis which *France-Télévision* faced during 1996 – one of the most serious in the history of public television. By the time the crisis was over, *France-Télévision* CEO Jean-Pierre Elkabbach had been forced to resign his position, six months before the normal end of his term. The crisis was a consequence of the extravagant contracts signed by the *France-Télévision* CEO with a number of 'host-producers' to whom had been subcontracted the production of many entertainment programs and talk-shows to be aired on *France 2*. For the first time in the history of French television, a parliamentary report revealed the amounts of these 'star' contracts which bore no relationship to the actual cost of the programs.

Out of a FRF 4.8 billion (€ 732 million) budget, six hosts shared a yearly sales figure of about FRF 650 million (€ 99 million) – a figure which had trebled in less than two years. The very terms of the contracts caused a resounding, widely publicized scandal as they were in violation of the public service ethos: total lack of openness, non-notification of the boards of directors and *France-Télévision*'s legal services. Some contracts had even been entered into on behalf of *France 3* without its executive director ever being told about it. In addition, one host's company had been created thanks to a capital advance from *France-Télévision* and the contract's clauses were unilaterally favorable for the host (including an exclusivity clause); there was no guarantee clause for the public channels (no 'exit clause' and no 'audience clause,' among other omissions). Thus the role of public television in France was once again called into question in a dramatic manner, in the face of potentially conflicting requirements: targeting a wide audience to compete directly with private channel *TF1*, on the one hand, and the requirement of 'quality' programming justifying its public financing through the licensing fee, on the other hand.

The *host-producers* scandal is indicative of a twofold problem in the station's management: a financial one (which led to a tightening of budgetary stringency requirements), but also one concerning program quality, as the host-producers' shows were mostly entertainment fare with little to differentiate them from the commercial programs on offer on the private channels. Despite such similarities with private television the program supply of the public channels has retained a specific character which explains both overall viewer satisfaction as expressed in opinion polls and, above all, their good ratings. Indeed, *France-Télévision*'s audience share in the last few years was above 40 percent.

In recent years TF1 remained the leader in terms of audience (or market) share, but it lost a good part of its lead: while its market share reached 40% in the early 1990's, it is only 33 to 34% in 2000/200, while the public channels' collective share is slightly above 40% (22% for France 2, 18% for France 3, and about 3% for La Cinquième (educational channel) in daytime (slightly less for Arte in prime-time). However these figures were rendered meaningless by the programming in May/June 2001 by private channel M6 of Loft Story (the French version of Dutch production house Endemol's Big Brother). M6's traditional weekly market share (13 to 14%) reached 20%, with record highs on Thursday nights, when the program aired: M6's audience share then exceeded that of all other channels, including popular private channel TF1, with a share over 35%. Regardless of the impact such a success has had on M6's advertising revenue, Loft Story has proved a far-reaching societal event, raising national controversies in the field of ethics and transfixing the whole media landscape for several weeks. The CSA even had to intervene, imposing a number of limits to the broadcasting of the program (suspension of broadcasts in certain time slots, audit of the contracts entered into by the participants – itself controversial – with respect to the treatment of the program by a radio station (Skyrock). Previously dismissed as an 'upcoming station,' M6 has thus managed to upset both traditional audience shares and programming schedules. Called 'trash TV' by private channel TF1's CEO, Loft Story may influence the nature of future programs aired by private channels.

3.3 Program Supply in the Private and Public Sectors

A number of recent studies agree on the fact that, despite *France 2*'s aforementioned management problems, *France 2* and *France 3*'s program supply by program genre is better balanced than that of private channels, with a stronger proportion of current affairs, documentary, and information programs as opposed to programs designed as pure entertainment. Such is the case both in the primetime and 'access to primetime' (between 7:00 and 11:00 p.m.) slots. Private operators (*TF1* and *M6*) only broadcast such programs after 11:00 p.m. Even in the primetime slot (at 8:45 p.m.) public channels air current affairs programs such as *Envoyé spécial* (*France 2*), *Des racines et des ailes* or *Ce qui fait débat* (France 3), *Thalassa* (*France 3*). In recent years this type of program made up about 28 percent of *France 2*'s program supply (between 7:00 and 11:00 p.m.)

and 44 percent of *France 3*'s (equivalent figures for *TF1* and *M6* are about ten percent 25 percent). M6 broadcasts a business-oriented program (Capital) in primetime on Sunday night, however, to compete with TF1 and France 2's movie nights.

Conversely, there are fewer game-shows on the public channels, whose quality in this respect is different as well: *Questions pour un champion* (*France 3*), the public service's star game, is a game of knowledge and 'general culture,' while *TF1*'s games are entirely based on the lure of money (*Le juste prix*, *La roue de la fortune*). Cultural programs (theater, classical music) are almost exclusively found on public channels. Finally, there is of course less advertising. The August 1, 2000 Act reduced from 12 to 8 minutes per hour the advertising times allowed on public channels (France 2 and France 3). On the public channels commercials cannot be aired during fiction programs (films and telefilms). In addition private (*TF1* and *Canal Plus*) and public channels are in head-on competition for sports broadcasts. Just like everywhere else, sports are an important audience magnet. In this area the public channels have done quite well, even though broadcasting costs have shot up in the last few years.

In 1990 a single sports division was created for *France-Télévision*; this division has since conducted an active policy of contract negotiating and renegotiating with the main broadcasting rights holders. This policy let it retain the broadcasting rights for high-profile events such as the *Tour de France* bicycle race or the Roland Garros and Bercy tennis championships. Public channels also retained broadcasting rights for rugby, a highly popular sport in France (French Championship and Six-Nation Championship). They also managed to reclaim the Paris-Dakar automobile and motorcycle rally, formerly in the hands of *TF1*. Only soccer, the most popular of all sports, has eluded them (the rights are held by the *TF1/Canal Plus* duopoly).

As a result, in order to retain the *Tour de France*, the year's most popular sports event in France, *France-Télévision* had to pay FRF 64 million (€ 9.75 million) in broadcasting rights in 1994, while these were only FRF 12 million (€ 1.82 million) in 1990. The contract provides for a FRF 5 million (€ 762,245) annual increase, which means that it will be worth FRF 90 million (€ 13.27 million) in 1999... Such inflationary practices, added to the aforementioned financial mistakes in associate production glaringly emphasized the budgetary constraints under which the public channels now find themselves.

But apart from major sports events such as soccer championship finals, French television has had its best viewing figures with fiction and serial fiction works, mostly those of TF1: *Navarro*; *Julie Lescaut*; *Les Cordier, juge et flic*; *Commissaire Moulin*; *Une femme d'honneur* are all police series which have been drawing viewers in record numbers for years.

3.4 Public and Private Financing

In France TV financing is based on three major sources: the licensing fee paid by TV set owners, which goes to the public channels, advertising revenue, which flows both to the public and private channels, and subscriptions, which are *Canal Plus*'s main source of income. The licenses granted to the private channels are free. They do not bring in any money to the public treasury. The licensing fee paid to the public channels' benefit is among the lowest in Europe (FRF 740 or € 113 for a color TV set in 2000); furthermore, four million households are not required to pay it on account of their low incomes (over 20 percent of exempt households). This insufficient public funding helps explain why advertising revenue became so crucial at certain times (over 60 percent of *Antenne 2*'s resources in the early eighties). When the competition of private channels – especially *TF1*'s – brought the public channels' advertising revenue down, they found themselves in severe financial straits and sometimes asked the State for one-time assistance packages to see them through the financial year.

Indeed, one of the major problems currently faced by public television in France is of a financial nature.

The financing structures of public and private channels are not the same, however: private channels are mostly financed through advertising, while for their public counterparts advertising only brings a supplementary income, as their primary source of revenue is the licensing fee.

The 1999 figures (released 2000) in million € are as follows:

Private Channels:	TF1 – Turnover:	1,286
	Share of advertising (and sponsoring):	1,261
	M6 – Turnover:	451
	Share of advertising (and sponsoring):	440
Public Channels:	France 2 – Turnover:	870
	Share of advertising (and sponsoring):	431
	France 3 – Turnover:	904
	Share of advertising (and sponsoring):	272

The financing structures of the two public channels are rather dissimilar: France 2 derives more money from advertising than from public subsidies, which explains the programming 'slip-ups' which make it much like TF1, while France 3 is more in tune with its public service mandate.

This steady downward trend in the public channels' financial endowment makes them more vulnerable to advertising market pressure. In the last few years *France 2* and *France 3*'s share of advertising revenue increased markedly, proportionally more so in fact than that of the private channels (especially since their joint advertising agency, *France-Espace*, was able to sell the two channels' overall market share, which is higher than that of *TF1*).

IV   New Perspectives: Technological Underdevelopment and Institutional Mutations

Until today, however, the technological mutations stemming from the 'digital revolution' have not caused any upheaval in the French TV system. The public debate in France remains quite removed from the conclusions which prevail at the EU level, as expressed, for instance, in the Bangemann Report on the 'Global Information Society' or in the latest EU Green Paper on audiovisual policy.

4.1 Modest Penetration of Computers and Cable and Satellite Transmission

France proved slower than other major European countries in its move into the information society, but in recent years (1999–2000) it has made up part of lost ground: Internet access has soared both among households and as part of government policy. Over 4 million people are Internet subscriber, which remains less than 10% of the whole population. This figure is comparable to that of Canal Plus's subscribers (4,5 million). Only 150,000 subscribers had a broadband connection in 2001, which means that there is currently no such thing as a Web-TV, with the exception of a few experiments of video broadcasting via the Internet. The general implementation of broadband connections and Web-TV will not happen before 2003/2004 at the earliest. One legal problem in recent years (2000–2001) pertained to TV advertising on Internet sites. This had been allowed by the CSA, including for sites dedicated to fields for which TV advertising is against the law (direct marketing, cinema, publishing, alcohol, tobacco, etc.). But an administrative court rescinded this interpretation of the law: Internet sites cannot be advertised on TV when they are about subjects for which TV advertising is forbidden. The August 1, 2000 Act is the first piece of legislation to include a number of provisions regarding the Internet, mostly to regulate the liability of service providers and Web hosting companies. But French law in the field of audiovisual media remains highly ambiguous as to the nature of the Internet, which may or may not be viewed as an audiovisual communication medium, and whose contents may or may not fall under the sway of audiovisual communication rules. A new bill on 'the information society' is in the works, but the upcoming elections (2001) make it impossible to predict what will come of it.

Cable's penetration rate is still low, but satellite broadcasting has skyrocketed thanks to two digital packages: Canal-Satellite and TPS (see below).

France's main specialist channels are transmitted on the cable networks and via satellite. These are LCI, an all-news channel and a TF1 subsidiary; Canal J (children's channel) and Canal Jimmy, two Canal Plus subsidiaries; movie channels such as Ciné-Cinémas and Ciné-Cinéfil; the Eurosport sports channel, the Planète documentary channel... But of course the audience share of such channels remains very low, almost negligibly so.

The reasons for this are manifold: 'cultural' blocks towards new technology, lack of French products and sufficiently attractive programming on cable-only channels, financial obstacles... At the time of the 1986 Act the decisions to privatize TF1 and deregulate the audiovisual system had been primarily justified by the priority being given to direct broadcast satellite as a replacement for general-interest, terrestrial transmission television. However, one can only note that in 1996 satellite television only had a 3.5 percent overall audience share. Thus it appears that television in France remains primarily a general-interest medium transmitted using terrestrial systems. Experts consider that at least ten years will have to elapse before the new digital programs start to create a mass demand, which itself could be the direct cause of adjustment problems for general-interest channels. And yet technological mutation is one of the motives behind the current public TV restructuring plans.

4.2 Restructuring and Growth Plans

Currently the only proposed privatization move pertains to the production sector, in other words the Société Française de Production, which serves the public channels but at times also TF1 for 'heavy production' purposes (TV movies and fiction series, coverage of major sports events). Since it has been 'in the red' for several years in an ultra-competitive market where the public channels have been farming out most of their production work to private companies, privatizing the SFP is a fairly old concern. Several times already the European Commission has called on France to go ahead with this privatization. The project has been delayed due to the initial lack of financially credible purchasers as well as trade union opposition, supported by part of the left-wing political opposition. Privatization is expected to take place in late 2001, even though the left-wing politicians currently in power had long supported SFP unions when privatization plans were being mooted by right-wing governments.

The successive creation of the Arte French-German cultural channel pursuant to a treaty signed on October 2, 1990, and then of educational channel La Cinquième (the 'knowledge, training, and employment' channel as set out by the February 1, 1994 Act which established it) took place in an empirical and overlapping manner due to the liquidation of the fifth terrestrial transmission system's private operator (La Cinq). Thus two state-owned stations were entrusted to two distinct corporations which have been airing two successive program schedules on the same terrestrial system, one of an educational nature until 7:00 p.m., and a cultural, French-German one after 7:00 p.m. This led to problems of coherence or harmonization with respect to program content as well as some duplication of activities and budget inconsistencies.

Both channels' audience shares remain modest (3 to 4 percent), which underscores the importance of the financial stakes, given the fact terrestrial transmission is used (which is explained by these aforementioned reasons: the demise of private station La Cinq, which freed the fifth terrestrial system, and the famously insufficient penetration rate of the cable networks).

The planned amalgamation of La Cinquième and Arte was finally abandoned, with the August 1, 2000 Act incorporating La Cinquième in the France-Télévision group along France 2 and France 3. France-Télévision thus has become a holding company comprised of three distinct subsidiaries.

The main hub is obviously France-Télévision, with the public service's historical, general-purpose channels: France 2 and France 3. As mentioned earlier, the 1974 Act had broken up the original, monolithic structure (the ORTF) into several distinct bodies, including three national programming corporations for television: TF1, Antenne 2, and FR3. After TF1 was privatized, it was deemed necessary to bring Antenne 2 and FR3 closer to each other; they were given a joint president as well as new names, as part of France-Télévision: France 2 and France 3, respectively.

Several public organizations are still part of the group: not just Arte, but those components of the 'external public audiovisual system' (EPAS) such as TV5 Europe, and the radio stations: Radio-France, Radio-France-Internationale (RFI), which is also part of the EPAS, and Réseau France-Outre-Mer (RFO), which fulfils a twofold function (TV and radio). Another innovation in the August 1, 2000 Act concerning public operators is that their funding is now conditioned on a 'objectives and means contract' entered into with the State.

But the future of television – both public and private – also has a direct impact on the new digital channels. There is in France one private TV station which has enjoyed a huge lead in encrypted, pay-TV: Canal Plus. This station did the sensible thing by moving into digital television, creating (in April 1996), its own programming cluster: Canalsatellite, which includes most of the aforementioned French specialist channels.

A second 'digital cluster' has also emerged to compete with Canalsatellite: TPS (Télévision par satellite). One original feature of this cluster is the fact that it includes public and private operators, even though the public channels' stock ownership is now lower than initially intended.

Table 1. *Stock Distribution*

Private Operators	*TF1*	*M6*	*CLT*	Lyonnaise Communication*
	25 %	20 %	20 %	10 %
Public Sector	*France-Télévision* + **Télévision Entreprises**		*France-Télécom* =	**France**
	8 % +		*17 %* =	**25 %**

* (main cable network operator and *M6* shareholder)

Such a partnership between *France-Télévision* and its private competitors (*TF1* and *M6*) is both an original and a fairly new situation. It makes it possible for the public service to be part of the mutations brought about by digital transmission technology. Two distinct, even conflicting, criticisms have been directed at this initiative:

- this partnership obviously creates new financial charges for public television at a time when it is facing budget cuts;
- because the partnership is based on a minority interest, *France-Télévision* may find itself overshadowed by the *TF1* and the *M6*, *CLT*, and *Lyonnaise Communication* group, already partners within *M6*.

TPS was launched on December 16, 1996; its program supply included three subscription levels (and two pricing levels). France's main specialist channels, whose transmission had mostly been done via cable, now become available either as part of *Canal-satellite*'s program cluster (*Canal Plus*' aforementioned subsidiary channels, but also *Eurosport* or *LCI* or that of *TPS*.

On *TPS* the first level of programming (terrestrial transmission channels plus the specialist channels) will be offered for less than FRF100 (€ 15.24) (a lower rate than for most cable networks, and lower than the *Canal Plus* subscription).

A specialist channel on 'History' will be offered by the public sector (*France-Télévision*, *Arte*, *INA*), as well as a region-oriented channel called *France 3 Régions*. The other existing specialist channels in which *France-Télévision* has a stake (*Festival*, *TV5*, and *France-Supervision*) are also part of the program cluster, which may also include *Euronews* (9 percent of whose capital is owned by *France 2* and *France 3*). Along these will be new private specialist channels, mostly created by *TF1*: *Odyssée* (documentary channel), *Tele-Toon* (cartoons and animated movies)…

The second programming level is based on movie broadcasting. *TPS* has already signed agreements with several US 'majors' and French copyright holders; these will ensure a steady supply of products for three new movie channels as well as the pay-per-view system, which will initially be implemented over some fifteen channels.

Finally, an all-in-one package will include both levels. *TPS*, just like *Canalsatellite*, also includes digital radio and interactive services. Beyond the criticisms already mentioned concerning *France-Télévision*'s participation in the *TPS* digital cluster, the sweeping contracts ('output deals') signed with Hollywood may be a problem for the public channels: *TPS*' private shareholders (*TF1*, *M6*, *CLT*) have an equal controlling interest in a joint company (*TCM*) which in the meantime purchased the unencrypted broadcasting rights for the whole Paramount catalogue. This means that *France-Télévision* no longer has access to this catalogue.

A more fundamental concern is the long-term future of two competing 'digital clusters' (*Canalsatellite* and *TPS*). Many experts have been doubting the economic viability of these two, directly competing program offers.

Pursuant to the August 1, 2000 Act the operators of the various satellite packages must be able to include the programs of the hertzian public channels (France 2, France 3, etc.) even though these were previously the sole preserve of TPS.

The other major innovation in the August 1, 2000 Act is the launch of Digital Terrestrial Television, one of the main questions to be tackled by the CSA in 2002. Owing to the very high cost of setting up such channels and the attendant economic difficulties, the Government has already decided to cut down to three the number of new digital terrestrial channels from the six that were originally planned. In the meantime private operators have been questioning the anti-trust ceilings (49% of capital), demanding that they be allowed to fully own the new channels as long as their audience does not exceed a given level...

V   Conclusion

The French media system has a number of peculiar features which give a rather paradoxical character to its public sector component, among others. France is the country which most adamantly defended the notion of 'cultural exception' in the GATT talks to oppose the United States' purely mercantile approach. However the French television system itself seems to be quite thoroughly permeated with such an approach. This is due to several consecutive reforms of a highly 'deregulatory' nature (first among which is the privatization of *TF1*, dating back to 1986). Today the future of public television seems determined by a series of conflicting factors. Public services are important to the French, which may preclude new reforms which would undermine them. France's underdevelopment in new communications technologies also strengthens the position of general-interest channels, including public channels. But France is also characterized by close ties between governmental circles and television: the budget cuts faced by the public channels may have harmful consequences, forcing the latter to increase advertising revenue at the expense of program quality as defined by their public service mandate. Thus financial and political pressure remain public television's main handicap.

References

Brocard, V. (1994). *La télévision – Enquête sur un univers impitoyable.* Paris: Lieu Commun.

Brochand, C. (1994). *Histoire générale de la radio et de la télévision en France.* Paris: La Documentation Française.

Chamard, M.E. & Kieffer, Ph. (1992). *La télé, dix ans d'histoire secrète.* Paris: Flammarion.

Cluzel, J. (1992–1994). *Regards sur l'audiovisuel.* Paris: L.G.D.J.

Conseil Supérieur de l'Audiovisuel. *Rapport annuel* (Several Issues).

Dossiers de l'Audiovisuel (Several Issues).

European Commission (1994). *Strategy Options to Strengthen the European Program Industry in the Context of the Audiovisual Policy of the European Union*, COM (94)96, final.

Franceschini, L. (1995). *La régulation audiovisuelle en France*. Paris: P.U.F.

Griotteray, A. (1996). *L'argent de la télévision*. Paris: Ed. Du Rocher.

High Level Group on the Information Society (1994). *Recommendations to the European Council. Europe and the Global Information Society* (Bangemann Report). Brussels: High Level Group on the Information Society.

Regourd, S. (1992). *La télévision des Européens*. Paris: La Documentation Française.

Regourd, S. (1995). France. In Bertelsmann Foundation & European Institute for the Media (eds.), *Television Requires Responsibility*. Volume 2: International Studies (pp. 139–176). Gütersloh: Bertelsmann Foundation Publishers.

The Federal Republic of Germany

by Guido Ros

I   A Public Corporation Monopoly

1.1 The *Land*-Based Corporations and ARD

Until the middle of the 1980's, the broadcasting system of the Federal Republic of Germany consisted of a number of public corporations, to the exclusion of any other organizational form. The system had remained the same for nearly forty years, a consequence of the allied occupation of Germany between 1945 and 1949. Following the Second World War broadcasting policy in the Western occupation zones was shaped by the Western occupying powers, especially the United States, Great Britain and France. This situation lasted until 1955, and in West Berlin even until the reunification of October 3, 1990.

The broadcasting policy adopted by the occupying powers was based on two principles: the broadcasting system was to be free of state influence, and it was to be independent of commercial interests. To this end, the powers chose a system of independent public broadcasting institutes, in the image of the BBC. Owing to the division in occupation zones and to the Allies' wish for decentralization, a third characteristic was added, viz. the regional structure of the system. The Americans set up one system in each *Land* of their zone: *Radio Frankfurt* (to be renamed *Hessischer Rundfunk*, HR, in 1948), *Radio Stuttgart* (from 1949 *Süddeutscher Rundfunk*, SDR), *Radio München* (renamed *Bayerischer Rundfunk*, BR, in 1948), and *Radio Bremen*. The British followed the example of the BBC and set up one big organization, the *Nordwestdeutscher Rundfunk* (NWDR), which in 1954–55 was split up into *Norddeutscher Rundfunk*, NDR, with its office in Hamburg, and *Westdeutscher Rundfunk*, WDR, based in Cologne. The French created the *Südwestfunk* (SWF) in Baden-Baden and *Radio Saarbrücken* in Saarland, to be renamed *Saarländischer Rundfunk* (SR) in 1952. In West Berlin the United States Information Agency set up RIAS in 1946 (*Rundfunk im amerikanischen Sektor*), which was joined by the *Sender Freies Berlin* (SFB) in 1953 (Frei, 1983: 319–326; Donsbach & Mathes, 2000: 482–485; Hickethier, 1998: 94; Meyn, 1999: 177).

In the Soviet zone the reconstruction of the broadcasting system had initially been supervised by the SMAD, the Soviet Military Administration. In late 1945 it was taken over by the German Central Administration for the Education of the People, but for the duration control and censorship remained with the Soviet occupiers. From the end of 1946 on, the broadcasting system of the Soviet zone was given the responsibility of contributing to the education of 'Socialist Man' (Wilke, 2000: 227–228). In 1952 the independent regional stations which had emerged after 1945 were abolished, and the radio was supervised by the *Staatliches Rundfunkkomitee* (State Broadcasting Committee), itself dependent on the Ministerial Council, the government of the German Democratic

Republic. In 1968 the *Staatliches Komitee für Fernsehen* (State Committee for Television) was created. As far as their organization was concerned, radio and television in the German Democratic Republic were two separate entities, but the system as a whole was centralized to a high degree and very much the affair of the state. Until the 'changes' of 1989 there were five radio stations and two television channels (Holzweißig, 1989: 101–115, 114–115; Schuler-Harms, 2000: 141).

The West German Basic Law of 1949, more particularly article 5, section 1, subsection 2, guarantees freedom of radio news broadcasts. This entails two criteria which the public broadcasting organization must meet: it must be free of state influence (*Staatsferne*) and it must not be entrusted to any particular social group (pluralism). In the Federal Republic of Germany cultural affairs (which include broadcasting) fall within the competence of the *Länder*. The powers of the central authority, notably the *Regulierungsbehörde für Telekommunikation und Post* (until early 1998 the Federal Ministry of Post and Telecommunications), do not go beyond the technical aspects of broadcasting. The Federation's legislative power is restricted to the organizations which broadcast to foreign countries (Rundfunkrecht, 1990: V).

Until 1991 there were nine *Land*-based broadcasting corporations, which had been set up through legislative work of the *Länder* or through treaties between the *Länder*. After the 'changes' and the reunification, the German Democratic Republic's broadcasting corporations disappeared[1], and it took a lengthy political debate before two new public corporations could be set up: the *Mitteldeutscher Rundfunk* (MDR) for the new *Länder* of Saxony, Saxony-Anhalt and Thuringia, and the *Ostdeutscher Rundfunk Brandenburg* (ORB). The *Land* of Mecklenburg-Pomerania acceded to the inter-state treaty on NDR. On May 31, 1997, the prime ministers of the *Länder* of Rheinland-Pfalz and Baden-Württemberg signed a state treaty about the foundation of the *Südwestrundfunk* (SWR), a merger of the *Südwestfunk* (SWF) and the *Süddeutscher Rundfunk* (SDR). The SWR started broadcasting on August 30, 1998 (Matzen, 1998: 135; ARD-Jahrbuch, 1999: 148). As a result, there are now ten public broadcasting corporations. They are all self-governing, and the authorities have no editorial control (*Fachaufsicht*) over them, although they do have legislative control over most of the corporations (*Rechtsaufsicht*).[2] In addition, they must fulfil a number of requirements: their broadcasts must be philosophically and ideologically diversified, and apart from their duty to provide news and entertainment they also have a cultural and educational task.

Initially the broadcasting corporations were solely funded by license fees. Very soon, however, they could also resort to advertising revenue: radio since 1948, television since 1956 (Matzen, 1996: 186; Chronik, 1994: 15). The collection of the license

---

[1] Article 36 of the reunification treaty provided that *Rundfunk der DDR* and *Deutscher Fernsehfunk* would continue to exist until December 31, 1991, as a joint organization of the five Eastern *Länder*. By that date, a treaty between the new *Länder* was to discontinue the *Einrichtung* or to replace it with public corporations of the individual *Länder* or of several *Länder* jointly (Vertrag, 1990: 82–84).

[2] This issue has not been settled for SFB, and for HR all forms of state supervision are banned (Schuler-Harms, 2000: 155).

fees was entrusted to a center set up for this very purpose in 1976: the *Gebühreneinzugs-zentrale* in Cologne is run by the public corporations and ZDF. The amount of the fee is set through an agreement between the *Länder*. Any increase is to be approved by the *Land* parliaments, after being prepared by a special commission (*Kommission zur Er-mittlung des Finanzbedarfs*, KEF) (Ricker, 2000: 264–265).

The rules on advertising which the public corporations must observe are very strict. Advertising on television is allowed only before 8:00 p.m. on working days. On an annual basis, no more than 20 minutes of advertising per day is allowed, with a maximum of 25 minutes. The commercials are grouped in blocks, around which early-evening serials are scheduled. In 1987 it was decided that programs of more than 60 minutes could be interrupted for advertising, and in 1991 that length was reduced to 45 minutes. Special arrangements apply to sports programs. Since 1991 sponsoring has been allowed. On radio, advertising spots are allowed on working days, with a maximum of 90 minutes per day on average (Staatsvertrag, 1991: 560–563).

All the public broadcasting corporations have at least three governing bodies. The broadcasting council (*Rundfunkrat*) looks after the interests of the community at large and checks if the corporation concerned carries out its duties as far as programming is concerned. It advises the *Intendant* as to general programming issues and makes sure that no infringement is committed in this area. Overall financial supervision is another of the council's powers (Schuler-Harms, 2000: 152–153). On the broadcasting council normally sit representatives of socially relevant groups: churches, universities, trade unions, associations of employers, towns, political parties, artistic and cultural organizations (Rundfunkrecht, 1990: XIII). Which groups are represented and how their delegates are elected, is set out in different ways in the legislation applying to the different broadcasting organizations. Although the members of the councils are supposed to represent diverse social groups, there is strong political party influence (Kepplinger, 2000: 122–123; Ricker, 2000: 262; Donsbach & Mathes, 2000: 484, 492). The administrative council (*Verwaltungsrat*) supervises the policy adopted by the *Intendant*, with the exception of those aspects which bear on the content of the programs, and draws up the budget, which is subsequently to be approved by the broadcasting council. As the power to nominate the *Intendant* rests with the administrative council, the latter does have an indirect influence on programming (Schuler-Harms, 2000: 152). At the head of the public broadcasting corporations is the *Intendant*. This director general is in charge of programming (though not for broadcasts produced by third parties) and he represents the organization towards the outside world. As a rule his/her term of office is six years.[3]

In addition to the *Land*-based public corporations, two federal broadcasting corporations – *Deutsche Welle* and *Deutschlandfunk* – have been in place since 1960. Until 1992 Deutsche Welle had only radio broadcasts, and aimed to acquaint listeners abroad with political, cultural and economic life in Germany and to explain how the German public felt about major issues. It broadcasts in German as well as 29 foreign languages

---

[3] Until 1998 Radio Bremen was led by a *Direktorium*, chaired by the *Intendant*. An amendment dated October 22, 1998 ended this exceptional situation (Matzen, 1999: 322).

and is financed entirely from federal funds (*Bundeshaushalt*). Since April 1992 Deut-sche Welle has also had a television program for foreign countries, transmitted via sat-ellite. It broadcasts 24 hours a day since July 1995 (currently 12 hours in German and 12 hours in English).[4]

Deutschlandfunk was a radio broadcaster only. It was set up as a counterpart of the East German *Deutschlandsender*, which had been renamed *Stimme der DDR* in 1971. Deutschlandfunk was to present a comprehensive picture of Germany to listeners in the two Germanies. The bulk of the station's funds came from the federal government, and some from listeners' contributions. In early 1994 Deutschlandfunk was merged with the first channel of RIAS Berlin and with *DS-Kultur*, a station which had emerged in the former German Democratic Republic after the 'changes.' The new combination was called *DeutschlandRadio*, and it offers radio broadcasts for the whole of Germany, on two channels, one based in Cologne and one in Berlin. DeutschlandRadio is financed exclusively from listeners' contributions.

The ten *Länder* broadcasting corporations and the two federal stations (as associated members) are grouped into *ARD*, the *Arbeitsgemeinschaft der öffentlich-rechtlichen Rundfunkanstalten der Bundesrepublik Deutschland*. ARD was set up in 1950, at a time when television broadcasts were being prepared. As ARD corporations vary widely in size, ARD is in charge of a redistribution of financial resources (*Finanzausgleich*), in which the largest institutes (WDR, NDR, BR, HR, SWR) part with some of their money to the benefit of the smaller ones (Radio Bremen, SR, SFB).[5]

Since 1954, the ARD members have jointly produced the programs of *Deutsches Fernsehen*, the first channel, which was renamed *Erstes Deutsches Fernsehen* in 1984. Each corporation produces a given part of the program, according to its size. In 1998, for example, WDR accounted for 21.25%, Radio Bremen for 2.50% (ARD-Jahrbuch, 1999: 481). Until 1992, the ARD corporations used to produce regional programs of their own, which were scheduled between 6:00 and 8:00 p.m., and included advertising messages. However, as of January 1, 1993, the early-evening program of ARD was har-monized in order to improve the channel's competitive position with regard to advertis-ing. Regional news time was slashed to 15 minutes, later even to 10 minutes (Frank-furter Rundschau, 1993, March 19; Frankfurter Rundschau, 1993, March 31), and the regional magazines were integrated in the Third Programs. In 1986 ARD launched a cultural channel, *Eins Plus*, the programs of which were transmitted via cable and sat-ellite. But the channel was discontinued on December 1, 1993, and ARD joined *3sat*.

Since the 1960's the ARD members have produced Third Programs, most of which are also transmitted via satellite. In the north (NDR and Radio Bremen)[6] and the south-west (SWR, SR) the ARD corporations cooperate in the production of these programs. Initially these broadcasts were intended as programs for minority groups and mainly

---

[4] Eleven hours in German and English as well as two hours in Spanish for Europe and the Americas.

[5] ORB and MDR are outside the *Finanzausgleich*, but they were given a special initial grant.

[6] Until early October 1992, SFB also contributed programs to N3. On October 1, 1992 SFB and MDR began producing a joint Third Program B1 (Chronik, 1994: 80–81).

had an educational and cultural character. However, they have gradually grown into fully-fledged channels (Stuiber, 1998: 1015). Each of the ARD broadcasters has four or five (Schuler-Harms, 1998: 144) radio stations, each with a clearly marked character of its own. Overall, the ten public broadcasting corporations of ARD have 56 programs (ARD-Jahrbuch, 1999: 212).

Table 1. *Share of ARD Corporations in First Channel's Programming (in %)*

Bayerischer Rundfunk	14.70
Hessischer Rundfunk	7.20
Mitteldeutscher Rundfunk	11.45
Norddeutscher Rundfunk	16.45
Ostdeutscher Rundfunk Brandenburg	2.75
Radio Bremen	2.50
Saarländischer Rundfunk	2.50
Sender Freies Berlin	4.25
Südwestrundfunk	16.95
Westdeutscher Rundfunk	21.25

Source: ARD-Jahrbuch (1999: 481)

1.2 ZDF

As early as 1958 ARD began making preparations for a second channel. In the same year the publishing companies launched attempts to start up a private-sector television channel (*Freies Fernsehen GmbH*). In 1960, urged by the then Federal Chancellor Konrad Adenauer, the *Deutschland Fernsehen GmbH* was founded. In the Chancellor's view, it was to be a federal organization and had to offset the influence of the first channel of the *Länder* corporations, which he thought was not friendly enough towards the government. However, the Federal Constitutional Court deemed the creation of a private broadcasting company unconstitutional, since broadcasting is a cultural matter and therefore within the competence of the *Länder*, and because the federal government would have had too great an influence on the proposed channel.

Following this ruling the *Länder* decided to set up a second public television channel themselves. A treaty between the *Länder* created the *Zweites Deutsches Fernsehen* (ZDF). It has been on the air since 1963, and in contrast with the *Land*-based ARD it is managed centrally, in the sense that all broadcasts are transmitted from central location, namely Mainz. ZDF is funded from viewing fees and from advertising revenue. Until 1996 ARD members had to transfer 30% of their income from viewing fees to ZDF. Regarding advertising, ZDF has to abide by the same rules as ARD. ZDF is managed by a television council (*Fernsehrat*), an administrative council (*Verwaltungsrat*) and a director general (*Intendant*).

Together with the *Österreichischer Rundfunk* (ORF), the *Schweizerische Radio- und Fernsehgesellschaft* (SRG) and ARD (after the discontinuation of Eins Plus), ZDF produces the satellite program *3sat*. In 1992 ZDF and ARD began to contribute programs to the French-German cultural channel *Arte*. The two networks are members of the European Broadcasting Union (EBU).

II   From Public-Sector Monopoly to a Dual System

2.1 The Rulings of the Federal Constitutional Court

In its first ruling on television broadcasting, in 1961, the Federal Constitutional Court had decided against private-sector television for the time being, basing its ruling on two arguments: the lack of available frequencies and the steep costs involved in television making. The forbidding cost price could have meant that television was controlled by wealthy groups, which would violate the principle of ideological diversity. However, in the same ruling the Court admitted that other organizational forms than the public-sector system were possible. From the second half of the 1970's, pressure mounted to allow private enterprise to engage in broadcasting side by side with the public corporations. The pressure was exerted by conservative politicians and supported by, among others, the not quite unchallenged theories formulated by Noelle-Neumann (*Schweigespirale*, double climate of opinion). Another argument was that the quality of the public broadcasters' programs would be enhanced thanks to competition with the private sector (Donsbach & Mathes, 2000: 498–499).

The Federal Constitutional Court's ruling of June 16, 1981 (the *FRAG-Urteil*) took into account the fact that the issue of frequencies had changed since 1961. The problem had virtually been solved by the new techniques of distribution such as cable and satellite. The Court did point out that the legislator, when giving permission to private-sector operators, must take measures to prevent broadcasting from being controlled by one single social group. The Court was of the opinion, however, that it was for the legislator to decide whether each prospective broadcaster was to let a variety of opinions be heard in his programs (*binnenpluralistische Struktur*) or whether it would suffice if the totality of the programs of all prospective broadcasters together reflected the full range of opinions (*außenpluralistische Struktur*). In its 1981 ruling the Court emphasized that the admission of private enterprise to broadcasting was to be subject to certain conditions: the private-sector channels were to comply with the same conditions as the public-sector channels, more specifically with regard to balance and diversity, both in the programs and in the opinions expressed in the programs.

The 1981 ruling was modified by a new one of November 4, 1986 (*Niedersachsen-Urteil*), which reiterated the principle that the broadcasting system was to be free of state control and that all opinions were to be heard. The Court added that these objectives could also be achieved in a dual system. In such a system the public corporations are responsible for the basic supply of programs (*Grundversorgung*), i.e., the conventional tasks of a broadcasting system (news, entertainment, cultural programs, minority programs), and to this end they are to be given adequate technical, organizational, financial and staff facilities (*Bestandsgarantie*)[7]. As long as the public corporations assume these tasks, and do so adequately, it is not necessary that the same strict requirements with regard to programming and ideological diversity should be imposed on the private operators as on the public corporations. This implies that the 1986 ruling virtually accepted the 'deficiencies' of a private-sector broadcasting system. It did point out, however, that there should be legislative measures to provide a forum for the greatest possible number of opinions and to prevent individual operators or channels from acquiring too much power (Rundfunkrecht, 1990: IX–X; Schuler-Harms, 1996: 91).

2.2 The *Länder*-treaties of 1987, 1991 and 1996

The 1986 ruling ended four years of debate, and in March 1987 agreement was reached on a treaty between the *Länder* on the new organization of broadcasting in Germany. The treaty of April 3, 1987 also emphasized that the existence and the further development of the public corporations must be guaranteed. In other words, the public corporations must be in a position to use all the new technical facilities for the transmission of programs, and their financial resources must be guaranteed. In addition, the private operators must also be given the chance of further development, among others through sufficient transmission capacity and adequate revenue (Rundfunkrecht, 1990: 3).

The treaty between the *Länder* provided that private stations need a license, which is granted by their respective *Landesmedienanstalt*[8]. Revenue from license fees cannot be used for the financing of programs made by the private operators, but 2% of that revenue is used for funding the bodies set up to supervise the private broadcasters.

With regard to advertising, the 1987 treaty included the following provisions. Advertising time on private channels was not allowed to be more than 20% of daily broadcasting time, and it must be clearly separated from the rest of the program and clearly marked as such. Commercials could only be scheduled in groups. The 1987 treaty also said that programs longer than 60 minutes could be interrupted for commercials once. Private channels were allowed to broadcast sponsored programs.[9]

---

[7] The fifth ruling on broadcasting (June 1987), the Baden-Württemberg-Urteil, of the Federal Constitutional Court explained the concept of Grundversorgung in greater detail. The public corporations are to make sure that the population as a whole is offered programs in which news, entertainment and culture are represented and in which a variety of opinions is voiced (Schuler- Harms, 1998: 144). The ruling also emphasized that the existence and the further development of the public broadcasting system was to be guaranteed (Bestands- und Entwicklungsgarantie) (Donsbach & Mathes, 2000: 503).

[8] The general name *Landesmedienanstalten* will be used throughout the present text, although the official names of the supervisory bodies differ from one *Land* to the next.

[9] The inter-*Länder* treaty of 1987 was not very clear on sponsored broadcasts in the public corporations (see Rundfunkrecht, 1990: 6; Witt, 1992: 26–27).

In order to make sure that the private operators were also open to a wide variety of opinions, the *Länder* treaty provided for the following as long as the whole of German territory is not covered by at least three complete commercial channels operated by different broadcasters, these channels must give a forum to a wide range of opinions in the totality of their programs. If the *Landesmedienanstalten* find that there is no guarantee of a broad range of opinions, each channel is under the obligation to ensure pluralism.

To counter the danger that private-sector broadcasting might suffer from one-sided domination by one group or several groups, the treaty provided that nobody was to control more than two channels, a provision which applied both to radio and to television. Of those two channels, only one was to be a 'complete' channel (i.e., offering news, entertainment and cultural items), and the other one a channel for specific target groups. The operators were to make sure, for example by setting up an advisory council for programming, that no single opinion could ever gain a dominating position. Only when no single operator had more than 50% of the shares or the voting rights were special measures deemed unnecessary (Rundfunkrecht, 1990: 7–9).

At the end of August 1991 a new treaty between the *Länder* was signed, a necessity after the reunification. The treaty guaranteed anew the existence and further development of the public broadcasting system (*Bestands- und Entwicklungsgarantie*). In addition, it emphasized that private-enterprise broadcasting was also to be given the opportunity of further development. The public corporations too were given the permission to air sponsored programs. Rules on advertising applying to commercial channels were made more precise as well as more flexible: more precise, in the sense that commercials can only constitute 15% of daily broadcasting time and they cannot take up more than 20% per hour of broadcasting time, and more flexible inasmuch as movies longer than 45 minutes can be interrupted for commercials and that *Dauerwerbung* (advertising in game shows) is allowed (Donsbach & Mathes, 2000: 511).

Furthermore, the new treaty included clauses intended to prevent monopolies or oligopolies. The number of channels that one operator was allowed to control remained limited to two, but the explicit provision was made that one single operator could only own one complete channel *or* one news channel. No single shareholder was to have 50% or more of the shares in such a network. A shareholder with a stake larger than 25% and smaller than 50% was not allowed to participate in more than two other channels, and only with a stake smaller than 25% (Staatsvertrag, 1991: 565). This structural model (*Anbietergemeinschaftsmodell*, Kübler, 1999: 379) repeatedly gave rise to controversy, since the ownership structure of the channels was not always very clear and could even be deliberately made obscure.

The 1991 treaty also adapted the national regulations to the demands of European legislation. As early as the preamble it was stated that the creation of new European television programs must be stimulated. Section 5 laid an obligation on the television channels to reserve the bulk of their broadcasting time for European productions and to make sure that their programming had a substantial share of home-made and contracted-out productions as well as co-productions between German-language and other European countries. Section 35 stipulated that the *Länder* must give permission for the distribution of European television programs which can be received in the whole of the Federal Republic, within the limits of the existing technical facilities (Staatsvertrag, 1991: 570).

In the normal course of events, the 1991 *Länder* treaty on broadcasting was to have been reviewed by early 1999. At the beginning of July 1996, however, the Prime Ministers of the *Länder* reached an agreement on a new treaty, taking effect on January 1, 1997. Since 1997, private companies are allowed to be the sole owner of an unlimited number of channels. Only if a company controls more than 30% of the market will steps be taken. At the last moment it was agreed that stakes smaller than 25% would not be taken into account (*Bagatellgrenze*), although the initial provision had been that all stakes larger than 10% would be included (Die Zeit, 1996, July 12). A provision which did go through was that all channels with a permanent market share larger than 10% must insert window programs produced by third parties for at least 260 minutes per week. Of those 260 minutes, at least 75 must be broadcast in primetime between 7:00 and 11:30 p.m (Dritter Staatsvertrag zur Änderung rundfunkrechtlicher Staatsverträge, 1996: 9, 11–12). In view of the commercial channels' aversion to such 'window' programs, they are allowed to take regional window programs outside primetime into partial account. Moreover, they can make proposals to the *Landesmedienanstalten* regarding the third parties to whom they are willing to give a window program (Frankfurter Rundschau, 1996, August 21; Frankfurter Rundschau, 1996, August 22).

A commission was set up to examine the evolution of concentration movements (*Kommission zur Ermittlung der Konzentration*, KEK). The prime ministers of the *Länder* have appointed as members of the Commission six specialists in the areas of the media, economics and constitutional law (Frankfurter Rundschau, 1996, October 18).

In order to make all this more palatable for the public corporations, the license fees were raised by €2.28 on January 1, 1997. ZDF's share in the revenue from viewing fees is no longer 30%, but is fixed according to the channel's requirements. Since 1997, ARD no longer has 70% of the viewing fees, but about 64% as the most (Frankfurter Rundschau, 1996, August 21).

ARD and ZDF were allowed to create one children's channel (*Kinderkanal*) and one channel offering special events coverage and documentaries (*Ereignis- und Dokumentationskanal*) (Frankfurter Rundschau, 1996, July 8). The former has been on the air since January 1, 1997, while the latter (*Phoenix*) was launched on April 7, 1997 (Matzen, 1998: 121, 139; De Coninck, 2000: 34, 50).

III   Organization and Development of Private Broadcasting

3.1 Organization

After the 1981 ruling of the Constitutional Court, several *Länder* passed broadcasting or media laws from 1984 onward, thus making it possible for private operators to enter the broadcasting market. Lower Saxony was the first *Land* to pass a law accepting private broadcasting (Rundfunkrecht, 1990: XVIII; Schuler-Harms, 1996: 96). The other West German *Länder* followed suit in the period from 1984 to 1989, and the new *Länder* of former East Germany introduced such legislation from 1991 (Matzen, 1996: 200–201; Van Eyghen, 1996: 22).

The licensing and control of the private operators is entrusted to *Landesmedienanstalten*. The *Landesmedienanstalten* are public corporations, totally independent from the authorities. They usually have two governing bodies: one with a fairly large number of members, composed of representatives of relevant social groups[10] and a director or, as is the case in a few *Länder*, a *Direktorium* consisting of three or four directors (Rundfunkrecht, 1990: XX; Schuler-Harms, 2000: 154).

The main responsibility of the *Landesmedienanstalten* is the granting of licenses. They have to guarantee that a wide range of opinions is represented and that there is no concentration of opinion-making power. The duration of the licenses is different from one *Land* to another, but it is ten years at most, although a number of *Länder* provide for its extension (Schuler-Harms, 1998: 150).

The license-holders are subject to constant supervision from the *Landesmedienanstalten* for compliance with legal provisions, but actual interference with the programs as such is not allowed (Schuler-Harms, 2000: 154). Finally, the *Landesmedienanstalten* are also in charge of the distribution of private programs (frequency allocation, access to the cable) (Donsbach & Mathes, 2000: 505). Some of the *Landesmedienanstalten* are also responsible for so-called open channels, on which citizens can produce their own radio and television broadcasts (Schuler-Harms, 2000: 155).[11]

In 1987 the *Direktorenkonferenz der Landesmedienanstalten* (DLM) was set up in order to further co-operation among the various *Landesmedienanstalten* (Donsbach & Mathes, 2000: 506). The intention was to co-ordinate the supervision of channels throughout the Federal Republic and to make sure that they comply with the provisions of the broadcasting treaty. In 1994, the *Arbeitsgemeinschaft der Landesmedienanstalten* (ALM) was founded as a co-ordination body. Besides this, there are the so-called *Gemeinsame Stellen* for youth protection, programming and advertising.

Most *Länder* went for a system in which a private broadcasting system is operated by a private company. Two *Länder* deviate from that pattern. North Rhine-Westphalia has a two-tier model, in which programming is carried out by a company with a pluralistic structure, strictly separated from a private company which operates the business.

---

[10] The Berlin *Landesmedienanstalt* is rather small, with 7 members (Kepplinger, 2000: 126) appointed by the Berlin House of Representatives. In Hamburg and Mecklenburg-Vorpommern too the supervisory bodies are relatively small, but they do have a representative composition (Schuler-Harms, 2000: 154).

[11] The first open channels on television were started up in Ludwigshafen, Dortmund and Berlin. In radio, Berlin, Hamburg and the *Land* Saarland played a pioneering role. By 1999 there were more than 70 open channels. Nine open channels only transmit radio shows, seven are in charge of radio as well as television broadcasts, the other only television broadcasts (Walendy, 1993: 309; Breunig, 1998: 236–237; Willems, 1999: 24–28).

Bavaria's constitution forbids private broadcasting, so that an alternative model of a public broadcasting system was devised, in which private operators can broadcast their programs under the umbrella of the *Bayerische Landeszentrale für neue Medien* (BLM) (Held & Schulz, 1999: 111–113; Ricker, 2000: 266; Schuler-Harms, 2000: 154).

There are also a number of models aiming to safeguard philosophical and political diversity. A system with *inner pluralism* applies in Bremen, Hamburg, North Rhine-Westphalia and Schleswig-Holstein, whereas the other *Länder* deem the situation to be acceptable if the overall programs of the private organizations in their respective areas are ideologically balanced (Schuler-Harms, 1998: 148).

The legal provisions applying to private radio operations show major differences from one *Land* to another. Most *Länder* give licenses to radio stations which cover their territory completely. Bavaria, Baden-Württemberg, Lower Saxony and North Rhine-Westphalia also accept local as well as regional stations (Van Eyghen, 1996: 36; Schuler-Harms, 2000: 153).

3.2 Development

Germany's commercial channels originated in a number of pilot projects for cable distribution.[12] The Ludwigshafen pilot project was started up on January 1, 1984, and also provided for the possibility of private-sector radio and television broadcasts. In the pilot project of Ludwigshafen, the *Programmgesellschaft für Kabel- und Satellitenrundfunk* (PKS) was in charge of the entertainment broadcasts and the *Aktuell Presse Fernsehen* (APF), founded at the end of February 1984 by 165 newspaper publishers, provided the actual news broadcasts. These two initiatives gave rise to the channel *SAT. 1* on January 1, 1985. On January 2, 1984, *RTL plus* started a German broadcast from Luxembourg, that could originally only be received in Saarland, Rhineland-Palatinate and in parts of North Rhine-Westphalia. RTL plus was renamed *RTL* in November 1992 (Chronik, 1994: 49–52; Hickethier, 1998: 426–427).[13] Among the first commercial stations we also find *musicbox*, a video-clip channel which had been part of the Ludwigshafen project from the very beginning, and *Eureka* (news and magazines, Ribbens, 1993: 45, 54). In 1988 musicbox was renamed *Tele 5*, and in 1989 Eureka was converted into *Pro 7* (*Pro Sieben* since October 1994, Süddeutsche Zeitung, 1994, 25 October). They were both conceived as fully-fledged channels (*Vollprogramme*) (Hiegemann, 1992: 46, 48; Matzen, 1996: 193; Donsbach & Mathes, 2000: 507).

A new phase of expansion began in 1992–93. Six new channels were set up: *RTL2*, which presents a full complement of programs for a young and active audience, and five

---

[12] In 1978 the prime ministers of the *Länder* decided to set up pilot projects for cable networks in four towns: Berlin, Mannheim-Ludwigshafen, Munich and Dortmund (Donsbach & Mathes, 2000: 500).

[13] Some sources (Internationales Handbuch für Hörfunk und Fernsehen, 1996: 143; http://www. novell.de/presse/success/sat.1.htm mention January, 1984 as the starting date of Sat.1. RTL plus moved its main seat to Cologne an the end of 1987 (Chronik, 1994: 60; Hickethier, 1998b: 427).

channels for specific target-groups, viz., *Der Kabelkanal* (today called *Kabel1*, with mainly serials, feature films and game shows for a target audience of 6-to-39-year-olds), *n-tv* (news), *VOX* (information)[14], *VIVA* (music, target audience 14-to-29-year-olds) and *Deutsches Sportfernsehen* (DSF), which evolved from Tele 5.

Yet another spate of new channels were launched in 1995–96; they were largely targeted at specific audiences: *VIVA 2* (music, for 25-to-49-year-olds), *Super RTL* (serials, feature films, Disney cartoons, music shows for families with children), *VH 1* (music and lifestyle video clips, for 25-to-49-year-olds), *Nickelodeon* (feature films and animated films for children between the ages of 9 and 14), *tm3* (a women's channel), *Wetter & Reise TV*[15], *Home Order Television* (*H.O.T.*, teleshopping), *Onyx TV* (music programs for 30-to-55-year-olds). (Internationales Handbuch für Hörfunk und Fernsehen, 1996: B136-B148; Breunig, 1996: 196–197). At the end of 1996, the American home-shopping channel *QVC* started its German broadcasts and the German branch of *Bloomberg TV*, a channel for economic news, was launched in August 1998 (Matzen, 1997: 128; Matzen, 1999: 328). In February 1991 the *Premiere* pay-channel was launched.[16] All in all, in 1998 there were 17 supraregional German private channels in the Federal Republic. In addition, there were 32 regional and local channels (Hickethier, 1998a: 204). Finally, the cable networks also present a number of foreign channels: *CNN, Euronews, Eurosport, MTV Europe, NBC, TRT, TV Polonia, TV 5 Europe*.

3.3 Ownership and Cross-Ownership

SAT. 1 used to be controlled by media mogul Leo Kirch (43%) as well as Axel Springer Verlag (40%). Kirch increased his share to 59% through a takeover of publisher Holtzbrink's interest (15%) as well as the former Ravensburger Filme + TV GmbH (1%) (Röper, 1999: 367, 377). At the end of June 2000, it was announced that SAT. 1, Pro Sieben, Kabel1 and the news channel *N24*, founded by Pro Sieben in January 2000, would merge, to become *ProSiebenSat. 1 Media AG*. Springer would still participate in the partnership with 11.5%, the KirchMedia KGaA with 52.5%. The remaining shares would be divided between different shareholders. The Rewe trade concern, which owned 41.6% of ProSieben, would exchange this stake for a 6% interest in KirchMedia KGaA. In addition to his stake in ProSiebenSat. 1Media AG Leo Kirch holds 100% of

---

[14] Vox was restructured, and developed into a *Vollprogramm,* which at the moment focuses on entertainment (Breunig, 1996: 196).

[15] On January 29, 1998 Wetterkanal stopped broadcasting; Nickelodeon did so on May 31, 1997 (Matzen, 1999: 328).

[16] The precursor of Premiere was the *Teleclub* pay-channel, launched in Hannover on November 1, 1986, and which was also distributed on cable in Oldenburg from late October 1988 on. The Teleclub project was developed by the Bertelsmann concern, Axel Springer Verlag, and Leo Kirch's Beta-Taurus group (Van Hoorde, 1993: 27, 29; Chronik, 1994: 56, 62).

DSF and of the Premiere pay channel (Röper, 2001: 12; Frankfurter Rundschau, 2001, January 12).

The second large broadcasting group is RTL-Group. CLT-Ufa, a Bertelsmann daughter company, owns 89% of the shares of RTL, 34% of RTL2, 50% of Super RTL and 99.7% of Vox (Daten, 2000: 27; Frankfurter Rundschau, 2000, March 23; Frankfurter Rundschau, 2000, May 12).

Private broadcasting tycoons also enjoy a strong position in other sectors of the media. Kirch has a 40.1% stake in Axel Springer Verlag and is Europe's number one as far as the ownership of rights to films and serials is concerned. Springer and CLT/Ufa participate in many private radio stations (Seufert, 2000: 174; Röper, 2001: 7, 11, 18).

Table 2. *Share Ownership of Private Television Channels in October 2000 (in %)*

SAT.1	ProSiebenSAT.1 Media AG (Kirch)	100.0
RTL	CLT/Ufa	89.0
	BW TV und Film Beteiligungs GmbH (Bertelsmann + Westdeutsche Allgemeine Zeitung (WAZ)	11.0
Pro Sieben	ProSiebenSAT.1 Media AG (Kirch)	100.0
DSF	KirchMedia GmbH & Co. KgaA	100.0
RTL 2	CLT/Ufa	34.0
	Bauer Verlag	32.0
	Tele München (Dr. Kloiber)	32.0
	Burda Verlag	1.0
	Frankfurter Allgemeine Zeitung	1.0
n-tv	CNN Turner Broadcasting (Time Warner) & Time Warner Entertainment	49.8
		28.5
	GWF Gesellschaft für Wirtschaftsfernsehen mbH (Holtzbrinck)	18.9
	Nixdorf family	1.6
	Verlag Norman Rentrop	0.8
	Karl-Ulrich Kuhlo	0.3
	Own shares	0.2
	Deutsche Fernsehnachrichten Agentur	
VOX	CLT-Ufa	99.7[17]
	DCTP	0.3
Kabel 1	ProSiebenSAT.1 Media AG (Kirch)	100.0
Super RTL	CLT/Ufa	50.0
	Disney Television (Germany) Inc.	50.0

Sources: Daten, 2000: 27 (situation November 2000); Frankfurter Rundschau, 2000, May 12; http://www.kirchmedia.deu/neu/de/pub/kirchmedia/unternehmen/index.htm; http://www.rtl2.de/2131.html (for recent changes).

A striking feature of channels catering for specific audiences is that a growing number of foreign media groups, particularly American and British, are trying to corner part of the German television market. Walt Disney holds 50% of Super RTL, CNN Turner Broadcasting and Time Warner Entertainment Germany 49.8% of n-tv (Daten, 2000: 27). In

---

[17] In March 2000, CLT-Ufa took over the shares of Murdoch and Canal Plus withdrew in May.

December 1999, Murdoch sold his 49.9% participation in VOX, but at the same time took a 24% stake in KirchPayTV KGaA (Frankfurter Rundschau, 2000, January 29; Frankfurter Rundschau, 2000, May 12).

Local newspaper publishers have very big stakes in private radio stations, which means there is a danger of duopolies emerging (Donsbach & Mathes, 2000: 510–511). In the same area of private radio broadcasting, moreover, big press concerns such as Holtzbrinck (AVE), WAZ and Burda play a major role (Seufert, 2000: 174; Röper, 2001: 20, 25, 29).

IV　The Present Situation

4.1 Revenue and Expenditure

The public broadcasting organizations are mainly funded through license fees and advertising revenue. Whereas revenue from licenses keeps rising all the time, ARD's advertising revenue began to fall from 1989 on, at first slowly, but subsequently at an alarming rate. This is a development which did not affect ZDF until a few years later, but between 1992 and 1993 ZDF's advertising revenue was virtually halved, and the drop continued in 1994. Since 1995, the advertising revenues of ARD as well as ZDF stabilized between €150 and 180 million each year (ARD-Jahrbücher, 1996–1999; ZDF-Jahrbücher, 1996–1999).

Table 3. *Evolution of Revenue from License Fees and Advertising (Public Channels)*

	ARD				ZDF			
	License Rev. (in € million)	%	Advert. (in € million)	%	License Rev. (in € million)	%	Advert. (in € million)	%
1988	1,848.4	70.7	495.8	19.0	450.3	54.5	317.1	38.4
1989	1,884.2	71.7	477.6	18.2	458.5	53.3	340.4	39.5
1990	2,210.1	75.1	405.8	13.9	530.6	54.2	357.0	36.5
1991	2,285.4	75.7	382.4	12.7	544.4	54.1	360.1	35.8
1992	3,424.2	80.6	318.0	7.5	690.3	59.3	361.2	31.0
1993	3,580.5	79.6	283.7	6.3	722.5	60.2	188.4	15.7
1994	3,693.7	80.9	185.8	4.1	745.4	70.0	168.2	15.8
1995	3,751.7	82.7	168.7	3.7	792.1	72.2	172.9	15.7
1996	3,799.6	81.8	192.5	4.2	802.8	71.9	174.1	15.6
1997	4,282.2	83.0	168.1	3.3	1,150.8	77.7	154.1	10.4
1998	4,350.9	82.6	178.0	3.4	1,164.7	77.7	155.9	10.4

Sources: ARD-Jahrbücher, 1989–1999, ZDF-Jahrbücher, 1989–1999 and our own calculations

In 1988 more than 85% of expenditure on advertising in broadcasting went to the public corporations (Ridder, 1989: 310). In 1991 the ratio was about fifty-fifty (Storck, 1993: 201 and our own calculations), and in 1993 the private channels accounted for more than three-quarters of advertising expenditure in broadcasting (Debus, 1994: 291). In 1994 the situation had become even more serious: a mere 16% of the money spent on broadcasting advertising went to the public corporations (Debus, 1995: 249). In 1999 the ratio was 11.3% for the public organizations against 88.7% for the private channels (Heffler, 2000: 234 and our own calculations).

The chief cause of this decline is the overwhelming TV advertising market share that private companies have cornered. In 1988 the three private television operators then in existence accounted for a net advertising turnover of € 132,0 million, against € 805,8 million for ARD and ZDF together (Ridder, 1989: 310). In 1991 for the first time, advertising revenue was higher for private channels than for public corporations (Storck, 1992: 162). In 1995 89.8% of net revenue from television advertising went to private channels, leaving a mere 10.2% for the public corporations (Heffler, 1996: 289). In 1999 the ratio was 92% for the private channels against 8% for the public corporations (Heffler, 2000: 234 and our own calculations).

In the field of radio the change is less striking, although the share of public stations fell from 85.5% in 1988 (Ridder, 1989: 310), to 49.9% in 1993, to 36.6% in 1995 and to 32% in 1999 (Heffler, 1996: 289; Heffler, 2000: 234). Needless to say, this has led to a major change in the structure of the public corporations' disposable income. In 1988, for instance, ARD's advertising revenue stood at 19% of the channel's overall income, but in 1994 that share had dropped to a mere 4.1% (ARD-Jahrbuch, 1995: 200)[18] and in 1998, this share had dropped to 3.4% (ARD-Jahrbuch, 1999: 198). The figures for ZDF were 38.4% in 1988, 15.8% in 1994 and 10.4% in 1998 (ZDF-Jahrbuch, 1989: 192; ZDF-Jahrbuch, 1995: 236; ZDF-Jahrbuch, 1999: 289 and our own calculations). For ZDF, the ratio between revenue from viewing fees and from advertising had always been about 60 to 40, but in 1994 it stood at 82 to 18 (ZDF-Jahrbuch, 1995: 244) and in 1998 at 88.2 to 11.8 (ZDF-Jahrbuch, 1999: 295). For ARD, the ratio shifted from 78.8 against 21.2 in 1988 to 95.2 against 4.8 in 1994 and to 96.1 against 3.9 in 1998 (ARD-Jahrbuch, 1995: 200; ARD-Jahrbuch, 1999: 198 and our own calculations).

Expenditure is on the rise, both with public and with private channels, but percentage-wise the rise is the most marked in the commercial channels.[19] A large part of the overall increase in expenditure can be attributed to the fight for the acquisition of the rights to screen feature films, serials and sporting events, a fight in which the private channels

---

[18] The 1995 ARD-Jahrbuch calculations are based on the figures quoted in the 1989 ARD-Jahrbuch but do not take account of the fact that the 1990 ARD-Jahrbuch used other percentages. In several places, the ARD yearbooks change percentages or figures. The calculations in the present article use the most recent data.

[19] Until 1995 it was hardly possible to obtain an adequate picture of the expenditures of the private channels. The first study which outlines a relatively differentiated image of the economic situation of the private channels reproduces the situation of 1995–96 and appeared in 1997 (Seufert, 1998: 153–154).

constantly strive to outbid both the other private channels and the public channels (Seufert, 1996: 115). The costs of the public corporations continue to be higher than those of commercial channels because the latter spend a much smaller share of their budgets on productions of their own (Seufert, 2000: 162, 171), which allows them to keep their human resource costs lower as well. In the past, ARD used to spend about 40% of its expenditure on human resources, but this share began to fall in 1992 owing to budget cuts and rationalization efforts. In 1999, the staff costs amounted to 31.5% of the total expenses (ARD-Jahrbuch, 2000: 213). ZDF's human resource costs have fluctuated in recent years between 22.9% (1989) and 25.2% (1992). In 1998 the commercial television channels' human resource costs stood at 9% (Seufert, 2000: 171).

Table 4. *Evolution of Revenue from Advertising (Private Television Channels, net turnover, exclusive of production costs, in €million)*

	1988	1991	1995	1996	1997	1998	1999
RTL	63.7	516.8	1,002.2	1,048.7	1,144.3	1,196.4	1,244.5
SAT 1	59.0	410.2	830.2	846.1	849.3	909.1	943.8
Tele 5/DSF	9.2	21.7	35.8	51.1	63.9	74.6	97.0
Pro Sieben	-	84.4	682.0	746.2	807.8	827.8	848.2
Kabel 1	-	-	77.2	105.8	134.5	161.6	194.3
n-tv	-	-	57.8	n.a.	n.a.	n.a	n.a
VOX	-	-	n.a.	n.a.	n.a.	152.4	165.9
RTL 2	-	-	166.9	206.5	208.1	213.2	227.0
Super RTL	-	-	-	27.9	52.6	63.4	83.3

Sources: Ridder (1989: 310); Daten (1993: 20); Daten (1999: 19); Heffler (2000: 234)

Table 5. *Evolution of License Fees (monthly, in €)*

	Listening Fees	**Viewing Fees**	**Total**
1953-1969	1.0	2.6	3.6
1970-1973	1.3	3.1	4.4
1974-1978	1.5	3.8	5.3
1979-1983	1.9	4.7	6.6
1983-1987	2.6	5.7	8.3
1988-1989	2.6	5.8	8.4
1990-1991	3.1	6.6	9.7
1992-1996	4.2	8.0	12.2[20]
1997-2000	4.8	9.6	14.4
2001-	5.3	10.8	16.1[21]

Sources: Daten (2000: 9) (€ 100 = DEM 196)

---

[20] In the new Länder only from January 1, 1995.

[21] In June 2000, the Prime Ministers of the Länder approved of an increase of 1.7 from 2001 onwards (Frankfurter Allgemeine Zeitung, June 16, 2000).

As a result of the growing success of commercial broadcasting, the advertising revenue of the public corporations has fallen drastically. The latter have for years campaigned for the removal of legal restrictions on television advertising (viz. a maximum of 20 minutes per day, before 8:00 p.m.), but so far there have been no changes. Another means for safeguarding the funding of the public corporations is to raise the license fees, but for this a political decision is required.

In February 1994 the Federal Constitutional Court gave an important ruling concerning these fees. The Court found that the fee-setting procedure adopted up to that time was in violation of the Constitution since the presence in the KEF of a number of representatives of the *Länder* governments and the fact that the ultimate decision rested with the prime ministers of the *Länder*, meant that the freedom of broadcasting was not adequately safeguarded. The representatives of the *Länder* governments have since been replaced with independent experts and a new procedure has been adopted. The public corporations now determine their financial requirements based on their programming; the KEF, in its new composition, examines if the amounts asked for comply with the principles of efficiency and economy, and gives its opinion. Finally, the *Länder* governments or parliaments decide on any raise in the fees. The corporations may challenge the decision in court (Frankfurter Rundschau, 1994, February 23; Chronik, 1994: 218; Hesse, 1995: 179–84; Hesse, 1999: 180–186; Schuler-Harms, 2000: 156).

4.2 Programming

The public corporations are responsible for the basic supply, so that their television broadcasts offer a full range of programs, with news, entertainment as well as culture. Contrary to what the theory of convergence might lead us to expect, the share of news and educational programs on public channels has not declined. Between 1985 and 1999 the share of these programs in ARD's overall scheduling even went from 38 to 44.6%, and from 34 to 45.7% in ZDF. On RTL the share of news and educational programs varied from 13% in 1985 to 25% in 1988 and to 23.2% in 1999; in SAT. 1 from 18% in 1985 to 26% in 1988 and from 13.9% in 1995 to 19.2% in 1999. Although Pro Sieben professes to have a full program, its share of news items used to be very low (between 3 and 6%). However from 1995 it was on the increase, even reaching 13.3% in 1999 (Krüger, 1996: 421; Krüger, 1999: 325; Krüger, 2000: 280).

Entertainment – both fiction and non-fiction – on ARD increased slightly between 1985 and 1995, from 40 to 41.4%, but dropped again from 1996 on (35.8% in 1999). On ZDF entertainment remained virtually constant, most of the time between 35 and 38%. With the exception of RTL (49.1%) the percentages on the major commercial channels were higher than 50% in 1999: SAT. 1 54.9%, Pro Sieben 58.8%. Worth noting is the fact that RTL substantially increased its share of non-fiction entertainment: from 7% in 1991 to 17.4% in 1995 and to 21.5% in 1999. Non-fiction entertainment used to be very low with SAT. 1 (between 0 and 6% between 1985 and 1992), but in the last few years the percentage increased from 9.6% (1993) tot 19.3% in 1999. On Pro Sieben the share of fiction dropped from 80% in 1989 to 43.5% in 1999 (Krüger, 1996: 421; Krüger, 2000: 280).

Smaller commercial channels schedule fiction and advertising to the virtual exclusion of anything else. In 1994 the share of fiction on VOX, RTL2 and Kabel1 was between 60 and 76% (Krüger, 1995: 195). RTL2 and Kabel1 offer almost no news programs and documentaries; VOX, with 17%, is an exception.[22]

All in all, then, the structure of programming on the public channels is fairly stable, and as far as news and cultural programs are concerned, the public corporations are clearly ahead of the game (Krüger, 2000: 280). Moreover, they continue to be very active as producers. ARD and ZDF play an important role, especially in the field of television drama and fiction television films (Zimmer, 1998: 8). Besides this, the public channels support the German movie production too. Out of 30 German movies which are produced annually in co-operation with television, more than 90% appear in co-operation with the public channels.

In contrast with the public corporations, the commercial channels have implemented rapid changes in the structure of their programming, and their focus shifts regularly. In the course of the day, however, they do adopt a fairly fixed schedule, with serials which recur day after day. Most of the time these serials are repeat showings of American and British serials which were broadcast on the public channels several years ago. In 1992 RTL plus launched its own daily soap *Gute Zeiten, schlechte Zeiten*. ARD reacted with *Marienhof* (Mohr & O'Donnell, 1996: 34, 49). In 1992–93 RTL and SAT. 1 began making their own television films, and Pro Sieben did so from 1994 on. Consequently, if there is any convergence in television broadcasting, it could be argued that it is the commercial channels which have adapted, at least in certain areas, to the public channels.

The feature films which are broadcast by RTL and SAT. 1 are chiefly American and German entertainment pictures. On weekends the two major private channels used to show erotic films as well, at least until 1994–95, when interest in these items appeared to be waning. In primetime on weekends, it is mainly bestsellers which are scheduled. RTL2 especially broadcasts lower quality movies from RTL's vaults. Inside the Kirch group, synergy effects were pursued too: for example, both Pro Sieben and Kabel1 bought movie packages in the USA (Focus, January 3, 2000).

The newscasts of the commercial stations tend to become infotainment (Krüger, 1998: 325). Magazines whose content is politically and culturally more difficult are broadcast in so-called 'window' programs, for which the responsibility is not assumed by RTL or SAT. 1, but which are made by separate producer companies who have their own license. In recent years, the big private channels broadcast mainly talk shows focusing on aggressive confrontation and intimate personal problems (Hickethier, 1996: 153–154; Die Zeit, 1996, October 11; Hickethier, 2000: 218). From 1992 reality shows were scheduled during the evening hours. In the mid-1990's interest for these de-

---

[22] This is undoubtedly because VOX was initially conceived as a news channel.

creased, but competition over this format was re-ignited by the success of reality soap *Big Brother* on RTL2.

In radio too there are very clear-cut differences between public and commercial channels. ARD's stations have a wide range of news, entertainment and cultural programs. The share of music broadcasts increased from 55.0% in 1981 to 63.4% in 1997. As for spoken programs political news broadcasts gained ground at the expense of educational and cultural programs (Hickethier, 2000: 211).

A feature of the changing media scene since the early 1980's is that the various channels of the *Länder* corporations are becoming increasingly differentiated. The first channels usually present mixed fare for a slightly older audience. The second channels were, and often still are, cultural programs.[23] The third channels were originally service-oriented (BR 3, HR 3), but today they are often background programs in which easy listening music and spoken items alternate. The 1980's saw the emergence of fourth and fifth programs, which target specific audiences. Thus *BR5* and *InfoRadio* (SFB/ORB) provide news items; *MDR Sputnik, Fritz* (ORB/SFB) *NDR-Joy Radio* and *Eins live* (WDR) cater for a young audience. SFB has had a *MultiKulti* program since September 1994; it targets the ethnic minorities in Berlin and its environs, but also aims to establish contacts between the native Germans and other cultures (Gerhards, Klingler & Milde, 1998: 572; Hickethier, 2000: 211–212).

The commercial radio stations actually have only two types of programs: background programs, chiefly with music, and programs for specific audiences. The stations' own editorial contribution is usually small, with the bulk of programming coming from external sources (Hickethier, 2000: 213).

4.3 Audience Shares

A comparison of ratings shows that between 1987 and 1995 public TV stations went from enjoying near-monopoly to outsider status. In 1987 ARD's first and third channels together with ZDF enjoyed a market share of 94% (Kiefer, 1994: 122–123). By 1992 this share had dropped to 51.1%. In 1993 commercial channel RTL achieved for the first time a market share larger than that of any of the public corporations. In 1995 the shares of the public corporations had dropped to 39%. In 1998, ARD's first channel became market leader for a short while due to the live broadcast of a number of big sport events (like the Soccer World Championship in France). In 1999, RTL regained market leadership and the three public chains had a market share of 39.9%. A striking phenomenon in this context is the growing success of ARD's Third Programs. As for the smaller commercial channels, they have managed to enlarge their market share in recent years (Darschin & Frank, 1994: 99; Darschin & Frank, 1996: 176; Darschin, 1999: 155; Darschin & Kayser, 2000: 147).

---

[23] In some cases it is the third (NDR 3, SFB 3, WDR 3) or the fourth channel (BR 4) which is the cultural channel. See Hickethier (1996: 150); ARD-Jahrbuch (1995: 227). WDR transformed its first channel into a youth channel in April 1995 (Frankfurter Rundschau, September 5, 1996).

Table 6. *Evolution of Television Market Shares*

Year[24]	1987	1992	1993	1994	1995	1996	1997	1998	1999
ARD 1	42.2	21.7	17.0	16.3	14.6	14.8	14.7	15.4	14.2
ZDF	40.9	21.3	18.0	17.0	14.7	14.4	13.4	13.6	13.2
ARD 3	5.3	8.1	7.9	8.9	9.7	10.1	11.6	12.3	12.5
SAT 1	1.5	13.2	14.4	14.9	14.7	13.2	12.8	11.8	10.8
RTL(+)	1.3	16.9	18.9	17.5	17.6	17.0	16.1	15.1	14.8
Pro 7	-	6.7	9.2	9.4	9.9	9.5	9.4	8.7	8.4
Tele 5/DSF	-	3.3	1.3	1.2	1.3	1.1	1.2	1.1	1.3
RTL 2	-	-	2.6	3.8	4.6	4.5	4.0	3.8	4.0
Kabel 1	-	-	1.6	2.0	3.0	3.6	3.8	4.4	5.4
n-tv	-	-	-	0.3	0.3	0.3	0.5	0.6	n.a.
VOX	-	-	1.3	2.0	2.6	3.0	3.0	2.8	2.8
Super RTL	-	-	-	-	1.1	2.1	2.3	2.9	2.8
tm3	-	-	-	-	-	-	0.3	0.6	1.0
3sat	-	-	-	1.0	0.9	0.9	0.9	0.9	0.9
Arte	-	-	-	0.2	0.2	0.3	0.3	0.3	0.3
Eurosport	-	-	-	1.2	1.2	1.2	1.1	1.1	1.1
Kinderkanal	-	-	-	-	-	-	0.6	0.9	1.3

Sources: Daten (1989: 72); Daten (1993: 76); Darschin & Frank (1994: 99); Darschin & Frank (1996: 176); Darschin & Kayser (2000: 147); ZDF-Jahrbuch (1996: 217); ZDF-Jahrbuch (1997: 218); ZDF-Jahrbuch (1998: 214); ZDF-Jahrbuch (1999: 251).

In the Eastern *Länder* RTL and SAT. 1 enjoyed a stronger position than the public channels until 1997. This is still the case with RTL, but since 1998, ARD 3 managed to push SAT. 1 off its second position in the eastern *Länder*. In Western Germany, ARD 1 regained the position of market leader in 1997 (Darschin & Kayser, 2000: 147–148).

The public channels continue to be the primary sources of information. In 1999, 68% of viewing time spent on news went to public channels, and only 32% to commercial channels. Conversely, 60% of the time spent on entertainment went to the private channels and only 40% to the public channels (Darschin & Kayser, 2000: 152, 154). Although the public corporations have lost ground in radio broadcasting, they remain market leaders. Yet their share fell from 82% in 1988–89 to 55.3% in 1999 and to 52% in 2000 (ARD-Jahrbuch, 1999: 212, 419; Frankfurter Rundschau, July 6, 2000).

---

[24] 1988–1991: adults older than 14, only West Germany; 1992–1994: viewers older than 6; 1995–1999: viewers older than 3.

Table 7. *Evolution of Radio Market Shares*[25]

Year[26]	Public Stations	Private Stations
1988/89	82.0	18.0
1989/90	79.0	21.0
1991	72.2	26.5
1992	69.8	29.0
1993	65.7	34.3
1994	60.1	39.9
1995	59.3	40.1
1996	58.6	41.4
1997	58.2	41.8
1998	56.6	43.4
1999	55.3	44.7
2000	52.0	48.0

Sources: ARD-Jahrbuch (1989: 182); ARD-Jahrbuch (1990: 193); Keller & Klingler (1996: 445); ARD-Jahrbuch (1998: 413); ARD-Jahrbuch (1999: 212, 419); Frankfurter Rundschau (2000, July 6) and our own calculations.

4.4 The Future of Public Broadcasting Service[27]

4.4.1 Public Service Under Fire

Even in the past, Germany's public broadcasting corporations were criticized. The amount of red tape and the wasteful policies of the public channels were denounced, and quite often they (especially ARD) were blamed for being too left-wing.

In August 1992, the CDU launched a ten-point-program demanding that ARD and ZDF stop broadcasting breakfast shows. The number of existing radio stations were to be cut, existing culture-oriented TV stations Eins Plus, 3sat and Arte were to merge, and the public channels were not to broadcast advertising any more (Frankfurter Rundschau, August 22, 1992).

Although it had been argued at the time that competition from the private sector would raise the quality of the public channels, some politicians, among whom Wolfgang Schäuble, the then leader of the parliamentary party of CDU/CSU, now reversed that argument: the public corporations' programming was viewed as not different enough from that of the commercial channels, which led to the question whether the public corporations were still entitled to revenue from license fees (Frankfurter Rundschau, January 6, 1993; Süddeutsche Zeitung, January 28, 1993).

---

[25] Deviations from 100% are due to rounding off and to inclusion or exclusion of other stations, e.g., foreign and military stations.

[26] 1988–1991: only West Germany.

[27] This aspect is exhaustively dealt with by De Geetere, 1999: 41–75.

In late 1994 and early 1995 a full-scale attack was launched against ARD. In a January 1995 memorandum, Bavaria and Saxony's conservative prime ministers Stoiber and Biedenkopf argued that ARD's first program should be discontinued. The proposal meant that only ZDF television would still broadcast for the whole of the Federal Republic and that the regional third channels would be upgraded. Furthermore, the two prime ministers contended that a structural reform of ARD was an absolute necessity. The 11 *Land* corporations were to be reduced to a maximum of 6 or 7. That would also make the *Finanzausgleich* superfluous, as the remaining corporations would all be of about the same size. The two politicians even threatened to regionalize the fees for receiving-sets, i.e., the various *Länder* would then be in a position to levy different fees, another measure which would mean the end of the *Finanzausgleich* (Frankfurter Rundschau, January 31, 1995; Die Zeit, February 10, 1995). The threat to ARD's first program has since been lifted. The first step in ARD's restructuring was the merger of SWF and SDR into SWR in 1997.

While in 1993 conservative politicians had tried to undermine the public service's mixed financing (radio and TV license fees as well as advertising), they turned to a new line of reasoning in October 1996, contending that as the private channels were contributing more and more to the basic supply of programs, the public channels could no longer be entitled to constitutional privileges, for example with regard to funding. Since it is inconceivable that the private channels should be financed from license fees, they should be given a monopoly on advertising, and the mixed funding of the public channels ought to be abolished. Furthermore, the conservative government coalition of the time argued that the private channels had begun to resemble the written press more and more due to the emergence of target-group channels and pay-channels, so that they had an individual right to the freedom of broadcasting, which meant that broadcasting licenses ought to be abolished (Frankfurter Rundschau, October 14, 1996; Stock, 1997: 149–150).

Conservative politicians are not the only cause of the rough time had by the public service in recent years: commercial broadcasters did much to complicate the life of ARD and ZDF. Using arguments from a controversial study by media specialist Klaus Merten, they sided in 1993 with CDU politician Schäuble to accuse the public channels of not fulfilling their duty of *Grundversorgung* (basic supply of programs) (Frankfurter Rundschau, January 26, 1993).

When the public broadcasters got permission, through the 1996 state treaty, to start two target group channels, their commercial rivals lodged a complaint with EU commissioner for competition policy Karel van Miert. They argued that the financing of the new channels through radio and TV license fees was in violation of EU policy concerning state support, and that co-operation between ARD and ZDF was illegal. The complaint was thrown out in February 1999, however (Michel, 1998: 120–121; Matzen, 1998: 135; Matzen & Herzog, 2000: 316; De Coninck, 2000: 28–29). The commercial broadcasters persisted, issuing in November 1997 a document (*Medienordnung 2000 plus*) which argued that not only did the public service no longer have a monopoly on *Grundversorgung*, but that commercial channels could quite adequately present the public with a balanced program supply. Moreover, they contended that ARD and ZDF should give up advertising and that license fees should be replaced by a cultural levy to be paid by all households (Frankfurter Rundschau, November 28, 1997).

4.4.2 Structural Changes Within the ARD

Defenders of the public broadcasters knew that the structure of the ARD would be different after 2000. The main problem lay with the system for the redistribution of financial resources (*Finanzausgleich*) and the future of the small channels (SFB, RB, SR). The 1996 state treaty provided that the *Finanzausgleich* treaty could be terminated by the individual *Länder* on December 31, 2000. After more than two years of discussion and various proposals from ARD, the prime ministers came to an agreement about a new regulation of the *Finanzausgleich* in November 1999. From January 1, 2001 onwards, the amount of €95 million was cut to €82 million, and, by the end of 2005, would be reduced to 1% of ARD's share in the TV and radio license fees.

V The Future

It goes without saying that the recent technical innovations have not gone unnoticed in the Federal Republic. Digitization and data compression have spurred a convergence in electronic communication services, so that the issue of what constitutes 'broadcasting' becomes even more acute. Private broadcasters and providers of new services as well as deregulation advocates want the concept of broadcasting to be defined as narrowly as possible. On the other hand, the *Länder* and the public broadcasters favor an all-embracing interpretation. In any case, there is a clear need for a number of concepts to be defined anew (Schuler-Harms, 1998: 133, 142).

In 1996 a dispute arose between the *Länder* and the central government over jurisdiction regarding multimedia applications (Frankfurter Rundschau, June 15, 1996). In mid-1996 they agreed that the *Länder* would be competent for all services targeting the community as a whole (pay-television, pay-per-view, electronic press, video-on-demand, etc.). The federal authorities would deal with those services which consumers can use on an individual basis (Schuler-Harms, 1998: 138; Held & Schulz, 1999: 79). In early 1997 the *Länder* negotiated a treaty (*Mediendienste-Staatsvertrag*) on such services as teleshopping addressing the public directly, teletext, video-on-demand, on-line services, etc. By mid-June of the same year the *Bundestag* had passed new legislation regarding the information and communications field (*Informations- und Kommunikationdienstegesetz*). This stipulates that no authorization or application is required in the case of communication services for individual use. Examples include various online services: telebanking, Internet connection offers, teleshopping in electronically accessible interactive databanks, etc. The state treaty as well as the federal law came into force on August 1, 1997 (Matzen, 1998: 136; Schuler-Harms, 1998: 138; ARD-Jahrbuch, 1998: 132, 141).

Although *Deutsche Telekom* had a pilot project (*Show Case Berlin*) up and running in February 1995 (Frankfurter Rundschau, March 1, 1995), the first real digital platform was not launched before the end of July 1996. This was apparently due to disagreements on technical standards for digital television. Uncertainty about impending mergers between media concerns added to the confusion[28].

On August 3, 1995, Deutsche Telekom, Bertelsmann, CLT, ARD, ZDF, RTL and Canal Plus had entered into a provisional agreement on the distribution of the shares of a *Multimedia Betriebsgesellschaft* (MMBG). The goal was to design a common decoder for the so-called set top box (which converts digital signals into analogue signals for display on an analogue TV set, and which decodes Pay-TV encoded signals).

At the end of August 1995, in connection with the *Internationale Funkausstellung* (IFA), a prototype of the MMBG-decoder, the *mediabox*, was presented. At the same time, the *Beta-Technik* corporation (a subsidiary of the Kirch group) presented its own decoder, the *d-box*. Attempts to come to a common solution to the decoder problem with Kirch, failed.

Initially it looked as if Bertelsmann and Murdoch would co-operate, with the Australian tycoon taking a stake in Premiere. In the end Murdoch chose Kirch, buying 49% of the shares of *DF 1*, the first German platform for digital television, which was launched by Kirch on July 28, 1996. For a monthly subscription of € 10, viewers had access to a package of 20 channels specializing in feature films and specifically targeted programs.

Towards the end of July it was announced that Bertelsmann was also seeking an alliance with Kirch, for the sake of the latter's dominant position in the program market. At the time the decoder dispute seemed to have petered out. Kirch and Bertelsmann would develop a decoder together and Bertelsmann would broadcast its digital programs (*Club RTL* and Premiere) via DF1 (Matzen, 1997: 120). However, after protests from other MMGB partners, Bertelsmann changed its mind. In September 1996 Deutsche Telekom withdrew from MMBG, alleging that the program supply on offer by other partners was too small. The withdrawal meant the end of MMBG. As a result Bertelsmann shelved its plans for digital television and declared that in future it would focus on *free TV* and on Premiere (Matzen, 1997: 120, 127). Pro Sieben had announced at the end of July that it was going ahead with its plans for digital television as of November 16, 1996, but shelved the project in September (Matzen, 1997: 120).

After Murdoch had withdrawn from DF 1 (March 1997), Kirch and CLT-Ufa joined forces. At the end of August 1997, CLT-Ufa and Kirch announced that DF 1 would be liquidated and its program supply integrated into the common pay-TV channel Premiere. In 1998, however, the European Commission forbade the planned co-operation between Kirch, Bertelsmann and Deutsche Telekom in the field of digital television, as it would have resulted in total control over the digital TV market by these companies.

At the end of March 1999, it was announced that Kirch had taken over a majority stake in Premiere. Shareholder Canal Plus withdrew completely and CLT-Ufa reduced

---

[28] For a detailed history of digital television in Germany, see Vandenhende, 1999: 34–75.

its participation to 5%. Practically at the same time, it was announced that the digital television activities of Premiere and DF 1 would be pooled. After the changes in the property structure of Premiere were approved by the German regulatory authorities, Premiere and DF 1 merged on October 1, 1999, becoming *Premiere World* (Matzen & Herzog, 2000: 319, 325). Viewers have access to four 'worlds' (*Movie World*, *Sports World*, *Family World* and *Gala World*) for a monthly subscription ranging from € 10 to 28, depending on the number of channels. For a special fee, Premiere World offers additional channels such as *Classics* (various music styles), *Seasons* (documentaries) and *Blue Channel* (erotic movies). A pay-per-view system allows access to an additional supply of material, including erotic movies (Breunig, 2000: 385–388).

Public broadcasters ARD and ZDF presented their digital projects in August 1997. In addition to simultaneous digital broadcast of all of ARD programming, *ARD Digital* also had three special offers. The programs of the first channel were broadcast in a changing sequence via *ARD MuXx* between 8:00 p.m. (currently 3:00 p.m.) and 1:00 a.m. *ARD Extra* offers a comprehensive news coverage, while *ARD Festival* broadcasts ARD serials and television movies (Reiter, 1997: 410–414; Albrecht, 1997: 415–417; Breunig, 2000: 380). ZDF started *ZDF.vision*, which broadcasts programs from ZDF, 3sat, Der Kinderkanal, DeutschlandRadio Berlin, Deutschlandfunk, from a number of 'guest' channels: ORF.SAT, EuroNews and EUROSPORT, as well as *ZDF.info* (advice and services), *ZDF.doku* (reports and documentaries) and *ZDF Theaterkanal*. *ZDF.vision* also offers *ZDF.digitext*, the digital version of the analogue teletext (Emmelius, 1999: 219–222; Breunig, 2000: 380, 384–385). ARD and ZDF's digital packages, launched on an experimental basis in 1997, were officially sanctioned in 1999 by a new state treaty which came into force on April 1, 2000 (Eberle, 1999: 66; Staatsvertrag, 2000: 9).

Commercial broadcasters RTL, MTV and Onyx are currently planning free digital TV packages, while *MSGMediaServices* (MSG), a subsidiary of Deutsche Telekom AG, has a digital platform which is partly accessible by payment. Foreign corporations such as the Dutch *United Pan-Europe Communications* (UPC) have also been trying to access the German market (Breunig, 2000: 389–391).

The question remains whether digital (pay-)television will be as successful as operators expect. DF 1 had been hoping for 3 million subscribers by the year 2000. In October 1999, at the start of Premiere World, it only had 365.000. Premiere had set itself a target of 2.7 million subscribers by 2000. In September 2000, the actual figure was 1.6 million. All together (analogue and digital spread), pay-channel subscribers total 2.2 million (Breunig, 2000: 391–393).

After the establishment of the *Nationale Plattform DAB* (1990, later called *DAB-Plattform e.V*), the *Länder* prime ministers decided to introduce digital radio (DAB) on an experimental basis, on March 24, 1993. In 1995 the first DAB pilot projects were started up in Baden-Württemberg, Berlin-Brandenburg and Bavaria. Saxony, Thuringia and Saarland followed suit in 1996, and other pilot projects were initiated in North Rhine-Westphalia, Hesse and Saxony-Anhalt in 1997. It was expected that 1997 would see DAB's official launch, but problems with frequency allocation, management, and financing delayed the move to early April 1999 (Laveyne, 1999: 46, 51, 57, 113–114, 121).

All public broadcasters are present on the Internet. 85% of the commercial radio stations have an on-line offer. ARD ('Tagesschau'), ZDF ('heute'), SAT. 1 ('SAT. 1 Nachrichten') and RTL ('RTL News', 'Guten Abend RTL') offer on-line news as well. The public radio stations let anyone interested download news broadcasts as text or audio files. Private radio channels often stick to newswire material and infotainment (Neuberger, 2000: 105).

It is clear that the broadcasting scene in the Federal republic is constantly changing, so much so that it is hard to predict what the situation will be like in the near future. And the decisive elements in this evolution are political as well as technological.

References

Albrecht, M. (1997). ARD-digital: Vernetzen statt Versparten. Das digitale Programm-bouquet der ARD, *Media Perspektiven* 8: 415–417.

ARD-Jahrbücher (1989–2000). Hamburg: Hans-Bredow-Institut.

Breunig, C. (1996). Zwischen Standortpolitik und Vielfaltsziel. Zulassung neuer Fern-sehanbieter durch die Landesmedienanstalten und Folgen für die Kabeleinspeisung, *Media Perspektiven* 4: 195–208.

Breunig, C. (1998). Offene Fernseh- und Hörfunkkanäle in Deutschland. Strukturen, Programme und Publikum der Bürgermedien, *Media Perspektiven* 5: 236–249.

Breunig, C. (2000). Programmbouquets im digitalen Fernsehen. Marktübersicht, In-halte und Akzeptanz von digitalem Free-TV und Pay-TV in Deutschland, *Media Perspektiven* 9: 378–394.

Chronik des Hörfunks und Fernsehens in Deutschland (1994). In Hans-Bredow-Institut (ed.), *Internationales Handbuch für Hörfunk und Fernsehen 1994/95* (pp. 1–87). Baden-Baden/Hamburg: Nomos.

Darschin, W. (1999). Tendenzen im Zuschauerverhalten. Fernsehgewohnheiten und Programmbewertung, *Media Perspektiven* 4: 154–166.

Darschin, W. & Frank, B. (1994). Tendenzen im Zuschauerverhalten. Fernsehgewohn-heiten und Programmbewertungen 1993, *Media Perspektiven* 3: 98–110.

Darschin, W. & Frank, B. (1998). Tendenzen im Zuschauerverhalten. Fernsehgewohn-heiten und Programmbewertung 1997, *Media Perspektiven* 4: 154–166.

Darschin, W. & Kayser, S. (2000). Tendenzen im Zuschauerverhalten. Fernsehgewohn-heiten und Programmbewertungen 1999, *Media Perspektiven* 4: 146–158.

Daten zur Mediensituation in Deutschland. (1989–2000). Frankfurt a. M.: Media Perspektiven.

Debus, M. (1994). Segmentierung der Zielgruppen. Der Werbemarkt 1993, *Media Perspektiven* 6: 286–296.

Debus, M. (1995). Anhaltende Dominanz der Fernsehwerbung. Der Werbemarkt 1994, *Media Perspektiven* 6: 246–257.

De Coninck, N. (2000). *Neue öffentlich-rechtliche Spartensender in der Bundesrepublik: Der Kinderkanal und der Ereignis- und Dokumentationskanal Phoenix. Entstehungsgeschichte und erste Erfahrungen.* Ghent: Mercator Hogeschool (Unpublished Master's Degree Thesis).

De Geetere T. (1999). *Probleme der öffentlich-rechtlichen Rundfunkanstalten in der Bundesrepublik Deutschland seit der Einführung des kommerziellen Fernsehens.* Ghent: Mercator Hogeschool (Unpublished Master's Degree Thesis).

Der Spiegel (1995–2000). Several Issues.

Der Vertrag zur deutschen Einheit (1990). Frankfurt a. M.: insel taschenbuch.

Deutsche Welle. Available at [http://www.dwelle.de/dw/Welcome.html].

Die Zeit (1995–2000). Several Issues.

Donsbach, W. & Mathes, R. (2000). Rundfunk. In E. Noelle-Neumann, W. Schulz & J. Wilke (eds.), *Fischer Lexikon Publizistik Massenkommunikation* (pp. 475–518). Frankfurt a. M.: Fischer Taschenbuch Verlag.

Dritter Staatsvertrag zur Änderung rundfunkrechtlicher Staatsverträge (Dritter Rundfunkänderungsstaatsvertrag) (1996), *Media Perspektiven Dokumentation* I: 1–34.

Eberle, C.-E. (1999). ZDF.vision. Das ZDF-Programmbouquet und seine Rechtsgrundlagen, *ZDF-Jahrbuch 1999:* 64–66.

Emmelius, S. (1999). ZDF.vision – Die Zukunft sichern, *ZDF-Jahrbuch 1999:* 218–222.

Focus (2000). Several Issues.

Frankfurter Allgemeine Zeitung (2000). Several Issues.

Frankfurter Rundschau (1992–2001). Several Issues.

Frei, N. (1983). Hörfunk und Fernsehen. In W. Benz (ed.), *Die Bundesrepublik Deutschland* 3: *Kultur* (pp. 319–357). Frankfurt a. M.: Fischer Taschenbuch Verlag.

Gerhards, M., Klingler, W. & Milde, J. (1998). Jugendmedium Radio. Die Rolle des Hörfunks bei Jugendlichen im Kontext von Multimedia, *Media Perspektiven* 11: 570–577.

Hans-Bredow-Institut (ed.) (1994). *Internationales Handbuch für Hörfunk und Fernsehen 1994/95*. Baden-Baden/Hamburg: Nomos.

Hans-Bredow-Institut (ed.) (1996). *Internationales Handbuch für Hörfunk und Fernsehen 1996/97*. Baden-Baden/Hamburg: Nomos.

Hans-Bredow-Institut (ed.) (1998). *Internationales Handbuch für Hörfunk und Fernsehen 1998/99*. Baden-Baden/Hamburg: Nomos.

Hans-Bredow-Institut (ed.) (2000). *Internationales Handbuch für Hörfunk und Fernsehen 2000/2001*. Baden-Baden: Nomos.

Heffler, M. (1996). Moderates Wachstum und konsolidierte Marktanteile der klassischen Werbeträger. Der Werbemarkt 1995, *Media Perspektiven* 6: 286–293.

Heffler, M. (2000). Der Werbemarkt 1999. Radiowerbung mit deutlichem Umsatzplus, *Media Perspektiven* 6: 230–239.

Held, T. & Schulz, W. (1999). Überblick über die Gesetzgebung für elektronische Medien von 1994 bis 1998: Aufbau auf bestehenden Regelungsstrukturen, *Rundfunk und Fernsehen* 1: 78–117.

Hesse, A. (1995). Ausgewählte Rechtsprechung mit grundsätzlicher Bedeutung für die Rundfunkordnung in der Bundesrepublik Deutschland, *Rundfunk und Fernsehen* 2: 178–204.

Hesse, A. (1999). *Rundfunkrecht*. Muenchen: Vahlen (2nd edition).

Hickethier, K. (1996). Rundfunkprogramme in Deutschland. In Hans-Bredow-Institut (ed.), *Internationales Handbuch für Hörfunk und Fernsehen 1996/97* (pp. 147–158). Baden-Baden/Hamburg: Nomos.

Hickethier, K. (2000). Rundfunkprogramme in Deutschland. In Hans-Bredow-Institut (ed.), *Internationales Handbuch für Hörfunk und Fernsehen 2000/2001* (pp. 208–222). Baden-Baden: Nomos.

Hickethier, K. u. Mitarb. v. Peter Hoff (1998). *Geschichte des deutschen Fernsehens*. Stuttgart/Weimar: Metzler.

Hiegemann, S. (1992). Die Entwicklung des Mediensystems in der Bundesrepublik. In Bundeszentrale für politische Bildung (ed.), *Privat-kommerzieller Rundfunk in*

Deutschland. Entwicklungen, Forderungen, Regelungen, Folgen (pp. 31–88). Bonn: Bundeszentrale für politische Bildung.

Holzweißig, G. (1989). *Massenmedien in der DDR*. Berlin: Verlag Gebr. Holzapfel (2nd edition).

Keller, M. & Klingler, W. (1996). Jugendwellen gewinnen junge Hörerschaften. Media Analyse 1996, *Media Perspektiven* 8: 441–450.

Kepplinger, H.M. (2000). Kommunikationspolitik. In E. Noelle-Neumann, W. Schulz & J. Wilke (eds.), *Fischer Lexikon Publizistik Massenkommunikation* (pp. 116–139). Frankfurt a. M.: Fischer Taschenbuch Verlag.

Kiefer, M.-L. (1994). Mediennutzung in der Bundesrepublik. In Hans-Bredow-Institut (ed.), *Internationales Handbuch für Hörfunk und Fernsehen 1994/95* (pp. 116–131). Baden-Baden/Hamburg: Nomos.

Kirchmedia. Available at [http://www.kirchmedia.de/neu/de/pub/kirchmedia/unterneh men/basics/firmenstruktur.htm].

Krüger, U.M. (1995). Programmprofile kleinerer öffentlich-rechtlicher und privater Sender. Programmanalyse von 3sat, Arte, RTL2 und VOX, *Media Perspektiven* 5: 194–209.

Krüger, U.M. (1996). Tendenzen in den Programmen der großen Fernsehsender 1985–1995, *Media Perspektiven* 8: 418–440.

Krüger, U.M. (1998). Modernisierung bei stabilen Programmstrukturen. Programmanalyse 1997: ARD, ZDF, RTL, SAT. 1 und ProSieben im Vergleich, *Media Perspektiven* 7: 314–330.

Krüger, U.M. (1999). Stabile Programmstrukturen trotz besonderer Fernsehereignisse. Programmanalyse 1998: ARD, ZDF, RTL, SAT. 1 und ProSieben im Vergleich, *Media Perspektiven* 7: 322–339.

Krüger, U.M. (2000). Unterschiedliches Informationsverständnis im öffentlich-rechtlichen und privaten Fernsehen. Programmanalyse 1999: ARD, ZDF, RTL, SAT. 1 und ProSieben im Vergleich, *Media Perspektiven* 7: 278–296.

Kübler, F. (1999). Medienkonzentrationskontrolle im Streit. Komplexe Randbedingungen und aktuelle Konflikte, *Media Perspektiven* 7: 379–385.

Laveyne, E. (1999). *Digital Audio Broadcasting (DAB) in der Bundesrepublik Deutschland*. Ghent, Mercator Hogeschool (Unpublished Master's Degree Thesis).

Matzen, C. (1996). Chronik des Hörfunks und Fernsehens in Deutschland. In Hans-Bredow-Institut (ed.), *Internationales Handbuch für Hörfunk und Fernsehen 1996/97* (pp. 183–229). Baden-Baden/Hamburg: Nomos.

Matzen, C. (1997). Chronik der Rundfunkentwicklung 1996, *Rundfunk und Fernsehen* 1: 117–128.

Matzen, C. (1998). Chronik der Rundfunkentwicklung 1997, *Rundfunk und Fernsehen* 1: 135–142.

Matzen, C. (1999). Chronik der Rundfunkentwicklung 1998, *Rundfunk und Fernsehen* 2: 319–329.

Matzen, C. & Herzog, A. (2000). Chronik der Rundfunkentwicklung in Deutschland 1999, *Medien & Kommunikationswissenschaft* 2: 316–325.

Meyn, H. (1999). *Massenmedien in Deutschland.* Konstanz: UVK Medien.

Michel, E.-M. (1998). Grünbücher, Richtlinien und Mitteilungen. Rundfunkentwicklung unter dem Einfluß europäischer Regelungen, *ARD-Jahrbuch 1998*: 119–127.

Mohr, P. & O'Donnell, H. (1996). The rise and rise of soap operas in Europe. In *Alliances and Alignments. Communications in the New Europe, The Scottish Communication Association, Journal 2* (pp. 34–70). Edinburgh.

Neuberger, C. (2000). Massenmedien im Internet 1999. Angebote, Strategien, neue Informationsmärkte, *Media Perspektiven* 3: 102–109.

Noelle-Neumann, E., Schulz, W. & Wilke, J. (eds.) (2000). *Fischer Lexikon Publizistik Massenkommunikation.* Frankfurt a. M.: Fischer Taschenbuch Verlag.

Reiter, U. (1997). Die Strategie der ARD im digitalen Zeitalter. Ziel der Integration aller in die neue Informationsgesellschaft, *Media Perspektiven* 8: 410–414.

Ribbens, L. (1993). *Das Privatfernsehen in der Bundesrepublik Deutschland und in Flandern. Eine vergleichende Untersuchung.* Ghent: Provinciale Hogeschool voor Vertalers en Tolken (Unpublished Master's Degree Thesis).

Ricker, R. (2000). Medienrecht. In E. Noelle-Neumann, W. Schulz & J. Wilke (eds.), *Fischer Lexikon Publizistik Massenkommunikation* (pp. 244–267). Frankfurt a. M.: Fischer Taschenbuch Verlag.

Ridder, C.-M. (1989). Werbemarkt 1988. Bewegung innerhalb stabiler Strukturen, *Media Perspektiven* 6: 305–312.

Röper, H. (1999). Formationen deutscher Medienmultis 1998/99. Entwicklungen und Strategien der größten deutschen Medienunternehmen, *Media Perspektiven* 7: 345–378.

Röper, H. (2001). Formationen deutscher Medienmultis 1999/2000. Entwicklung und Strategien der größten deutschen Medienunternehmen, *Media Perspektiven* 1: 2–30.

RTL2. Available at [http://www.rtl2.de/2131.html].

Rundfunkrecht. Staatsverträge der Länder, Landesrundfunkgesetze, Landesmediengesetze, Bundesrundfunkgesetz (1990). München: Deutscher Taschenbuch Verlag.

Schuler-Harms, M. (1996). Das Rundfunksystem der Bundesrepublik Deutschland. In Hans-Bredow-Institut (ed.), *Internationales Handbuch für Hörfunk und Fernsehen 1996/97* (pp. 83–100). Baden-Baden/Hamburg: Nomos.

Schuler-Harms, M. (1998). Das Rundfunksystem der Bundesrepublik Deutschland. In Hans-Bredow-Institut (ed.), *Internationales Handbuch für Hörfunk und Fernsehen 1998/99* (pp. 133–151). Baden-Baden/Hamburg: Nomos.

Schuler-Harms, M. (2000). Das Rundfunksystem der Bundesrepublik Deutschland. In Hans-Bredow-Institut (ed.), *Internationales Handbuch für Hörfunk und Fernsehen 2000/2001* (pp. 139–159). Baden-Baden: Nomos.

Seufert, W. (1996). Wirtschaftliche Aspekte von Hörfunk und Fernsehen. In Hans-Bredow-Institut (ed.), *Internationales Handbuch für Hörfunk und Fernsehen 1996/97* (pp. 101–117). Baden-Baden/Hamburg: Nomos.

Seufert, W. (1998). Wirtschaftliche Aspekte von Hörfunk und Fernsehen. In Hans-Bredow-Institut (ed.), *Internationales Handbuch für Hörfunk und Fernsehen 1998/99* (pp. 152–168). Baden-Baden/Hamburg: Nomos.

Seufert, W. (2000). Wirtschaftliche Aspekte von Hörfunk und Fernsehen. In Hans-Bredow-Institut (ed.), *Internationales Handbuch für Hörfunk und Fernsehen 2000/2001* (pp. 160–178). Baden-Baden: Nomos.

Staatsvertrag über den Rundfunk im vereinten Deutschland (1991), *Rundfunk und Fernsehen* 4: 556–600.

Staatsvertrag über den Rundfunk im vereinten Deutschland in der Fassung des vierten Rundfunkänderungsstaatsvertrags (2000), *Media Perspektiven Dokumentation* I: 1–32.

Stock, M. (1997). Medienpolitik auf neuen Wegen – weg vom Grundgesetz? Das duale Rundfunksystem nach der staatsvertraglichen Neuregelung (1996), *Rundfunk und Fernsehen* 2: 141–172.

Storck, M. (1992). Werbefernsehboom – ein Geschäft für die Privatsender. Der Werbemarkt 1991, *Media Perspektiven* 3: 158–171.

Storck, M. (1993). Verschiebung der intermedialen Gewichte. Der Werbemarkt 1992, *Media Perspektiven* 5: 198–210.

Stuiber, H.-W. (1998). *Medien in Deutschland, 2: Rundfunk.* Konstanz: IVK Medien.

Süddeutsche Zeitung (1993–2000). Several Issues.

Vandenhende, D. (1999). *Digitales Fernsehen in der Bundesrepublik Deutschland.* Ghent: Mercator Hogeschool (Unpublished Master's Degree Thesis).

Van Eyghen, M. (1996). *Der private Hörfunk in den neuen Bundesländern.* Ghent: Mercator Hogeschool (Unpublished Master's Degree Thesis).

Van Hoorde S. (1993). *Pay-TV in der Bundesrepublik Deutschland und in Belgien. Eine vergleichende Untersuchung.* Ghent: Provinciale Hogeschool voor Vertalers en Tolken (Unpublished Master's Degree Thesis).

Walendy, E. (1993). Offene Kanäle in Deutschland – ein Überblick. Rechtsrahmen und Entwicklungsstand, *Media Perspektiven* 7: 306–316.

Wilke, J. (2000). Medien DDR. In E. Noelle-Neumann, W. Schulz & J. Wilke (eds.), *Fischer Lexikon Publizistik Massenkommunikation* (pp. 219–244). Frankfurt a. M.: Fischer Taschenbuch Verlag.

Willems, L. (1999). *Offene Kanäle in der Bundesrepublik.* Ghent: Mercator Hogeschool (Unpublished Master's Degree Thesis).

Witt, C. (1992). Der Staatsvertrag über den Rundfunk im vereinten Deutschland. Ein Markstein für Bestand und Entwicklung des öffentlich-rechtlichen Rundfunks?, *Media Perspektiven* 1: 24–28.

ZDF-Jahrbücher (1989–1999). Mainz: Zweites Deutsches Fernsehen.

Zimmer, J. (1998). Auftrieb für fiktionale Fernsehproduktion in Deutschland. Aufwendungen des Fernsehens für Leistungen der Filmwirtschaft 1995–96, *Media Perspektiven* 1: 2–14.

Italy

by Carlo Sorrentino

I   Historical Background

The history of the Italian media can be summed up in three words: education, participation, and market. In fact, these three objectives, in this order, characterized the pro-
ductive and cultural logic of the Italian media, with consequences affecting both content
and the political and economic factors that always go hand in hand with media development.

After a long period during which the media's educational function prevailed, the
1970's were characterized by a participative ideal which caught on mostly as a political
and cultural hope; finally, in the last twenty years, the stress has shifted on to the market – a change which was made possible by the advent of a commercial television group,
Silvio Berlusconi's Fininvest, which boosted the traditionally weak advertising market
and led to an unprecedented level of economic competition, one which had been un-
known even in the other media.

We shall now try to analyze how these three ways of seeing the media system originated and developed over the years. The pedagogical and educational logic of the system is a direct consequence of the ways in which modern journalism was born in Italy
with national unity in 1860. It seems legitimate to trace the origin of this event back to
the forming of a national state, since most of the daily papers published today were
founded just at that time. The ideal leading to the publication of such newspapers was of
a political nature – the desire of some notables committed to the cause of Italian unity
(called *Risorgimento*) to provide themselves with a means of forging public opinion and
through which they might state clearly the value of national unity and promote a
national identity. The purpose was not so much to inform, but rather to spread the ideals
of the Risorgimento.

In addition to this political interest there was an elitist view dominating matters related to information – which could hardly have been otherwise, given the country's extremely low literacy rate (10%). The combination of a political agenda and elitism led to
a strong focus on education.

This constant persisted in time because in Italy the industrial revolution of the late
nineteenth and early twentieth centuries had a very weak impact. Literacy remained
scarce, which did little to favor the growth of the information market. While many
newspapers disappeared, those remaining changed hands and were gradually acquired
by major industrial groups intent on establishing good relations with the political establishment: the focus on politics persisted.

The focus on politics served to reinforce the media's educational purpose, viewed as
an ideal instrument to forge consensus – a perspective which was retained by Fascism in

its two decades of rule. Given its dictatorial nature, such a government was obviously bound to revel in a view of the media as a consensus building tool.

This outlook persisted even beyond the Liberation, which was accomplished on April 25, 1945 by the Allies with the help of the *Resistenza* – Italian partisans harassing the Germans and the small number of Fascist supporters which had retreated to Northern Lombardia in the so-called Italian Social Republic of Salò. In this respect, we may find it interesting to observe the clash between the allied forces and the representatives of the partisans (which had formed the CLN, the Committee for National Liberation) about the slant which should be given to the information system. The market-oriented idea of the Allies contrasted with the political and educational view of the CLN. While just after the unification the media had been viewed as a tool to further unionist ideal, with the advent of the Republic the aim was now to promote the democratic ideals. The media were now supposed to guide this process by supporting the action of the political forces.

This relationship between politics and information is a long-lasting factor in the history of the Italian media (Sorrentino, 1995), as we can observe in the careers of the most important media men, who in many cases became journalists after having been part of the *Resistenza* and played some political role (Bechelloni & Buonanno, 1981). It was in this context that radio became successful and that television was born on January 3, 1954. RAI rose in 1944 from the ashes of URI, which had been created in 1924 and had changed its name to EIAR in 1927. The radio and television state corporation was even more subject to politics than print media since it was created by law as a state monopoly. However, the advent of television – and later its success – was a blow to the relationship between the political-cultural establishment and the media system.

In fact, until then the low literacy rate had hindered the development of a print media market; public opinion was still being forged through traditional socializing and politically biased channels: parish churches for the Catholic culture providing grass-roots support for the leading Christian-Democratic party (DC), and the so-called *case del popolo* (*houses of the people*) – popular clubs and meeting places for the socialist subculture, which in post-war years would be dominated by the Italian Communist Party (PCI) and the Marxist doctrine. At the same time village and small town squares and taverns were still effective as a force shaping social life. Even the urbanization process and the intense migratory boom of those years (coinciding, of course, with industrial development and the resulting economic boom) never fully deprived them of their function as social cementing agents. Unlike their counterparts in other countries, the media were never the main socializing agent towards industrial modernity.

It was in this scenario of marginality of the media system – itself hardly aware of the extraordinary social changes befalling the country in those years – that television was born and became popular. In addition to the advantage of being easily accessible even to an illiterate or newly educated population, one may usefully wonder whether one of the factors for the rapid success of this medium did not lie in its power of reaffirming those community values that are central to the Italian reality, given its nature as a collective medium. In fact, as many historical accounts of this event remind us, viewing usually took place in taverns (Bechelloni, 1997), clubs, or movie theaters, where films were interrupted to show major sports events or the first popular television quiz show, *Lascia o raddoppia* (*Double or Quits*) hosted by Mike Bongiorno, a young Italo-American who himself represented the American origin of the medium. The American myth – as we shall see – would be as ever-present in the national imagination as it would be opposed by the political and cultural elites (Gundle, 1995).

Unlike what happened in other countries, where the advent of television followed the industrialization process which had brought mass literacy and widespread reading, in Italy the rise of television coincided with the industrial boom, preceded mass schooling and replaced reading, which never caught on. This different chronological development would be enough to highlight the great political and cultural importance of this medium.

The political establishment was not slow in grasping the implications of this state of affairs and television's resulting potential. Of course the advantage was all on the side of the relative majority party, the DC, that favored the appointment of Ettore Bernabei as executive director of the public corporation. Bernabei was a journalist and a politician, and the former secretary of then Christian Democratic leader Amintore Fanfani.

Bernabei was director-general of RAI from 1961, when the second television channel was created, until 1975, the year of a major reform of the public radio and television system. His tenure was characterized by the growing strength of the radio and television system, but always in strict contiguity with politics. At the same time, the reference to Catholic culture was a fundamental aspect of TV programming under Bernabei.

With regard to programming, the two channels followed a rigid weekly schedule made of fixed programs by genre: Monday movie, Wednesday sports, Thursday game show, and Saturday entertainment show. While the first channel was after a large popular audience, the second had a more elitist outlook. Broadcasting time was limited, starting in the afternoon with children's programs, followed by a strong emphasis on prime-time.

The economic aspect of the television phenomenon, and of the media phenomenon at large, appeared to be secondary. RAI was operating as a monopoly and was mostly funded through license fees paid by TV set owners; in addition there was advertising revenue, although it was limited by law to a level meant to protect the print media, which were never particularly prosperous, and which had everything to fear from television competition.

Economic competition was almost insignificant in a media system which was still weak and where most publishers were large steel and iron, car, oil, and textile industrial groups maintaining unprofitable publishing businesses for the sake of securing the benevolence of political circles. The most obvious indicator of the scarce economic weight of the media phenomenon at the time is the persistent marginality of advertising – the financial heart and soul of any media system.

Although Italy in the 1960's and 1970's could be regarded as an industrially advanced country given the extraordinary economic performance called *miracolo italiano*, investment levels in the advertising sector were comparable to those found in underdeveloped countries. The reason for this was the cozy relationship between the political establishment and the major economic players owning the media, and it found its legitimization in the positions voiced by the cultural elites. On the one hand, the political parties did not dislike having the media in a state of economic dependence because in this way they could better control them with promises of public funding and tax and legal advantages[1]; on the other hand, the large economic groups had no interest in developing the advertising market since this would have been an implicit acknowledgment of rising competition in their markets, where they usually enjoyed a convenient situation of oligopoly[2]. These interests found their legitimization in a cultural atmosphere in which the strength of the Catholic and Marxist cultures produced a basic hostility towards the consumerist logic substantiating capitalistic market societies, and whose most distinct expression is advertising.

II   Information and Participation: The Myth of the 1970's and the Birth of Private Broadcasting

The educational model began showing problems between the late 1960's and the early 1970's. This was certainly brought about by the events of 1968. It no accident that the arrival of private individuals in the management of radio and television spaces was defined with the adjective *libero* (free): *radio libere, televisioni libere*. The stress on free expression confirms the shift from an educational to a participative dimension of information. The freedom of expression theme went hand in hand with the dynamism apparent in the early 1970's in left-wing journalism and in some sectors of the periodical press; this was the time when so-called *advocacy journalism* was introduced in Italy. New topics and new social subjects were being covered; there was a rising awareness of the social ferment in the country, which politically produced a shift to the left, with political and electoral successes for the PCI.

This generated a long-lasting tendency to think of information as of an opportunity for participation. Worth a mention in this respect is the debate about the advent of commercial television, in which the economic side of the problem was neglected for the sake of a reflection on media diffusion and ownership. Still, it was just in those years that the economic aspect emerged in its dramatic relevance owing to a colossal rise in costs which was not paralleled by a matching revenue increase.

A participative and decentralized logic seems perfectly suited to cable television, and in fact some such experiments were made, like the one promoted by the Emilia-Romagna regional council, which entrusted a team of experts with a feasibility study to cable the major cities in the region. However, these experiments were stopped by new postal regulations outlawing cable television – a controversial decision which brought

---

[1] After a long procedure, the law on publishing was passed as late as 1981.
[2] Suffice it to say that until the advent of commercial television in the second half of the 1970's, RAI did not accept advertising campaigns from car manufacturers, probably in order to favor FIAT.

about the fall of the government (Richeri, 1996). Although in 1974 the Constitutional Court authorized cable television channels on a local basis, the following year the RAI reform act (law no. 103 of April 1975) limited this possibility to the operation of single channel networks, which deprived cable of it economic and technological potential as a multiplier of television channels: it is absurd to think of cable for one channel only.

Behind the participative logic we can detect a growing relevance of the information system, whose growth was a source of concern for the political establishment. It is no accident that this tendency developed just as a large group such as Rizzoli entered the field of television broadcasting, while all other major publishing groups started considering with growing interest the possibility of entering the world of television.

The relationship between politics and the media system was changing, and the former uniformity of purpose between the political establishment and the information system was being replaced by tight control on the part of the political establishment. This may be the one crucial element needed to understand all law-making initiatives on the matter, from the above-mentioned episode of cable TV to the 1981 law on publishing, but also – as we shall see – to explain the lack of such initiatives in the field of radio and television from the mid-1970's until 1990. This legislative gap strengthened the weight of restrictive political interference and negotiation.

In 1975 the RAI reform act was passed. Control over the public radio and television system passed on from the government to Parliament. The third television channel was created. The value of cultural and information pluralism was especially safeguarded.

There was a differentiation between the channels and their news departments; while the former were in charge of scheduling, the latter concentrated on news. RAI 3 joined the two existing channels, RAI 1 and RAI 2; it was specifically meant to offer regional programming in an effort to meet the participative requirements set out by the new regional, political and administrative level (which had come into force in 1970)[3]. Soon, however, RAI 3 turned out to be no more than a third channel with an editorial line inspired by the opposition – namely the Communist Party, which in this way joined in the so-called *carving out* practice which had already linked RAI 1 to the majority party (the Christian Democratic Party) and RAI 2 to the Socialist Party.

The regional logic also inspired the creation of a private television system. In fact, in the early 1970's some *pioneers of the ether* had carried out the first commercial radio and television experiments – illegally, since they infringed on the legal radio and television monopoly. However, in July 1976 a ruling by the Constitutional Court acknowledged the right of broadcasting on a local basis, permitting the existence of private radio and, most of all, private television: in a media system which had never known a local dimension, private broadcasting started with just such a territorial scope.

Soon, however, it became clear that the regional dimension could not be successful. The inadequate means of small broadcasters meant that they could never dream of challenging the RAI colossus, with its three television and as many radio channels, with its

---

[3] The regional administrative level was envisioned by the 1948 Constitution, but had not been implemented before.

more than 15,000 employees and its regular source of income in the form of license fees.

As a result major publishing groups soon entered the fray: Rizzoli, Mondadori, and Rusconi attempted to develop national networks. Soon, however, these companies came to realize the difficulty of *making* television, a very different business from the one they already controlled. As a consequence commercial television would come to mean the *Fininvest* group owned by Silvio Berlusconi, who in 1980 transformed his local television holdings into the Canale 5 network, and who in 1984 already owned three channels, after acquiring Rusconi's Italia 1 and Mondadori's Rete 4, both on the verge of bankruptcy.

The success of the Fininvest group could be summed up in the link between advertising services and television programming, which is implemented with originality, audacity and determination. Unlike the publishers, who considered the *television challenge* as belonging to an adjoining field, in other words to a market roughly similar to their traditional *turf* (book publishing), Berlusconi – who came from the building industry – thought of himself only as a television publisher.

Perhaps for the first time in Italy the media world was seen from a strictly economic point of view. The Fininvest group, like RAI, was both producer and distributor of television programs, and it managed the advertising market by means of its own agency, Publitalia 80. Fininvest's advertising revenue went from €6.46 million in 1980 to €454.48 million in 1984. The whole Italian media system benefited from the enormous growth in advertising investment: from RAI, which chose to challenge Fininvest in the field of commercial television, to the print media, which could finally solve their chronic deficit problem.

The RAI-Fininvest duopoly was based on a legislative loophole, as it was obvious that the commercial group was not acting any longer on a local basis, but managed to overcome formal clauses with stratagems approaching illegality and by broadcasting pre-recorded programs exclusively. This structural weakness forced Fininvest to cultivate the benevolence of the political establishment, by tying itself to Socialist Party leader Bettino Craxi, who was prime minister in the early 1980's.

As we have already seen, the political establishment found it convenient to keep the television system in a legally ambivalent situation. In such a way, it could control both the public channels – which were subject to parliamentary control by law, and heedful of political balances by custom – and the only major private group – which was anxious not to fall out with those who, on account of the loophole which made its existence possible, might wipe it out any day.

Not before 1990 was a comprehensive radio and television act passed – a law which became popularly known as the *Mammì law* after the then Minister of Postal and Telecommunication Services. The purpose of the Mammì law was to outline a legislative framework which would accommodate the changes in the system brought about by commercial television. The law came fourteen years after the Constitutional Court ruling that freed up the air waves and long after the birth of the Fininvest group, but was criticized for merely *reflecting* the existing situation. Under the law each television publishing group was authorized to own three networks, or 25% of the twelve television networks licensed to broadcast nation-wide. This limit would be repealed in December 1994 by a ruling of the Constitutional Court declaring it unconstitutional. There has been no change in this situation since despite the creation of a parliamentary committee during the last legislature, the so-called *Commissione Napolitano*.

Although unanimously praised in the beginning, the Mammì law soon became the object of criticism because it was considered incapable of controlling such phenomena as the internationalization of markets, technological development, the variety of new uses, and most of all an ever-widening television offer.

Notable was the persistence of what seems a characteristic specific to the Italian media system: a confused legislative context which is hardly able to regulate so strategic a field – economically, politically, and culturally – and to adequately face the challenges presented by global competition in the telecommunications and multimedia markets. A major reason for such a confusion is the difficult balance between the fear of media power – which led to highly restrictive legislation – and the need to formulate rules that are flexible enough to be of some use in an ever-changing field.

This situation and attendant climate of controversy are made even worse by the lack of a controlling authority. The only existing body is the *Garante dell'Editoria* (guarantor for publishing), created by the 1981 law which reformed publishing, and whose powers the Mammì law extended to radio and television for matters such as anti-trust initiatives, programming and advertising. While the creation of a regulatory authority is still considered vital, while the need for it was made more urgent by Silvio Berlusconi's presence in the political arena, and while various proposals have been made on the subject, to date there is still no such institution. A law was passed creating regulatory bodies for the civil service and setting out some general principles, but the definition of their operating modes was left to the authors of a new law which is expected to come into force in 1997.

III   The Turning Point of the 1980's

The explosion of the advertising market (facilitated by the aggressiveness of commercial television), the lowering of costs made possible by the new technologies, and the very late implementation of the law reforming the publishing sector – which in a few years earned publishers some € 516.46 million – are the main factors behind the birth of a media market in Italy. This all happened, however, as late as in the early 1980's. Producing information and media contents may be a profitable business. But such had never been the case in Italy.

The emergence of this market redefined the relations between the economic and political spheres. There never was a marked rift, and in fact there is still a close relationship (which sometimes can be both perverse and obscure) between politics and information, but the diversity of purposes did take a more definite shape.

We may identify several levels to observe this diversity of purposes. First of all, the power of the economic sphere grew stronger, and this happened as part of a more complex process of economic globalization leading the major companies to consider expanding internationally. Second, there is the strength of the large business groups that own the media, a consequence of the profit-making opportunities born of the brand new media market. Finally, the diversification and broadening of the media system produced by the market has placed this system – and therefore also the information world – in a position of unprecedented social relevance.

The media logic became the privileged viewpoint from which to observe and narrate reality. This does not mean that the media hold a centrality which translates *ipso facto* into influence, but rather that they have a diffusive power which cannot be disregarded. The sources of information cannot avoid being exposed to the media, and must identify competitive methods to match the information requirements of the media. Even the political establishment is subject to the need of being able to negotiate its own access to the media on the basis of its ability to produce news-stirring events.

One can note an emerging and still relative independence of the media which is changing the fiduciary pact between them and politicians. There is still an element of that mutual trust which comes from shared backgrounds – it is no coincidence that journalists are often former politicians – and from the myriad instances of cronyism and equivocal relationships; but this trust is increasingly turning into wariness.

IV   Local Broadcasting

Beyond the RAI-Fininvest duopoly, the Italian radio and television market has been traditionally characterized by local fragmentation. Under the Mammì law there were 714 governmental licenses for TV broadcasting at the end of 1995, with many applications still awaiting processing.

Table 1. *Local Networks – Earnings for 1998*

Earnings, in €	# of networks
0 to 250,000	127
250,000 to 500,000	58
500,000 to 1 million	50
1 million to 1.5 million	28
1.5 million to 2.5 million	17
Over 2.5 million	14

At the end of fiscal 1998 only 307 of the remaining 439 local networks presented balanced accounts – in other words more than 100 networks were in deep financial trouble. Among existing networks only 49 have a capital larger than €516,000; on the other hand, 76 networks were able to cover with their net capital 50% of their activities and investments. These 307 networks mostly derive their earnings from advertising (91%, or €210.62 million – see table 1). In recent years things have appeared to be settling down, with the main 100 networks posting improved performance.

Although in such a fragmented market it is impossible to ascertain the exact scale of advertising investment, we can say with certainty that average annual revenue per television station is lower than €413,000, and that as a consequence these broadcasters are forced to survive in very precarious conditions, which means that they can hardly be expected to meet high professional standards. This also makes it impossible to gather precise data regarding ratings for local television channels, since the strong territorial fragmentation of the audience areas hinders meaningful measurements[4]. Only in few instances does the program supply approach professionalism. By law, every channel must broadcast news, but hardly ever are such news well packaged. For the rest, production is very poor and limited to soccer programs, talk shows on current events and subjects of regional interest, or teleshopping. As a last resort, these stations use old fiction, worn-out films, and TV serial re-runs.

Table 2. *Advertising Investment in Italy by Medium (Market Ratio) – 1989–1999*

	1989	1990	1991	1992	1993	1994	1995	1996	1997	1998	1999
Newspapers	23.9	24.6	24.0	23.5	22.7	22.9	22.8	21.1	21.3	20.7	21.8
Periodicals	19.2	17.9	16.9	16.4	15.5	14.5	14.2	15.6	16.4	16.8	15.4
Print media total	**43.1**	**42.5**	**40.9**	**39.9**	**38.2**	**37.4**	**37.0**	**36.7**	**37.7**	**37,5**	**37.2**
RAI TV	13.9	13.9	14.3	14.7	15.0	16.1	15.9	18.7	18.7	18.2	18.3
National commercial TV	30.7	31.5	32.7	33.6	35.3	35.3	35.3	34.4	34.1	35,1	35.1
Local commercial TV	2.5	2.3	2.4	2.5	2.6	2.6	2.6	1.9	1.3	1.1	1.1
Foreign TV	1.2	1.3	1.5	1.6	1.6	1.6	1.6	1.1	1.4	1.3	1.2
Television total	**48.2**	**49.0**	**50.9**	**52.4**	**54.5**	**55.6**	**55.5**	**56.1**	**55.5**	**55.7**	**55.7**
RAI radio	1.4	1.4	1.4	1.3	1.3	1.3	1.5	1,7	1,7	1.7	1.6
Commercial radios	2.0	1.9	1.9	1.9	2.0	2.0	2.5	1,7	1.8	2.1	2.6
Radio total	**3.4**	**3.3**	**3.3**	**3.2**	**3.3**	**3.3**	**4.0**	**3,4**	**3.5**	**3.8**	**4.2**
Cinema	0.2	0.2	0.2	0.2	0.2	0.2	0.2	0.3	0.2	0.2	0.2
Other	5.0	4.9	4.7	4.3	3.8	3.4	3.3	3.5	3.1	2.8	2.7
Grand total	**100**	**100**	**100**	**100**	**100**	**100**	**100**	**100**	**100**	**100**	**100**

This fragmentation becomes even more evident in the case of radio (no less than 3,993 broadcasting licenses). Even if we purge these data and only take into account the sources which broadcast regularly, we are still dealing with some 2,500 stations: almost one third of the 8,400 stations enumerated in 1991 (Carat, 1992). Among this multitude,

---

[4] These surveys are conducted by Auditel, a research institute which builds ratings on a national scale using audiometry technology, and by other research institutes on small samples of very limited significance.

however, there are only ten commercial radio stations broadcasting on a national scale, plus six syndicated broadcasters which interconnect at certain times of the day to transmit a national or multi-regional program. Only 52 stations have a turnover exceeding € 362,000. Unlike what happened with television, there is no such thing as concentration here. Most stations are situated at the fringes of the market, while the rest broadcast mostly music and programs aimed at young listeners. On the other hand, the three RAI radio stations (which share between them one-third of the total daily ratings) are aimed at a more educated and adult audience (Menduni, 1996).

The presence of two large television groups – RAI (public) and Fininvest (private) – each with three general interest networks, has determined the investment of considerable economic resources in the advertising market owing to terms that were particularly advantageous for advertisers. As a result investment increasingly concentrated on the television medium, which currently absorbs over half of the total resources, to the detriment of the print media (table 2).

The massive presence of advertising on television translates as a glut of commercials which has often resulted in the violation of the limit fixed by the 'Television Without Frontiers' Directive: in Italy the tolerated limit is now 18% hourly and 15% daily. As a consequence, sponsors' promotional messages were inserted within programs as a successful subterfuge to overcome this limit, but the trick was defeated by new norms which assimilated such sponsors' messages to commercials proper in the calculation of the advertising ratio.

Initially the central position of television in the advertising market was part and parcel of a buoyant business climate, so that it also benefited the other media, including the print media. But this changed with the recession of the nineties. In 1993, for the first time in twenty years, there was a drop in advertising revenue. The complaints which periodically come from the FIEG (Italian Federation of Newspaper Publishers) are becoming increasingly bitter. But even the two television groups must face growing economic difficulties. For each of the two groups, managing three general interest television networks with round-the-clock programming is a very difficult economic proposition.

New rigor is needed in the management of all the channels. RAI has taken action on an accounting level. Personnel has been reduced by 7% (from 12,713 to 11,809 individuals); more careful management results in a better use of the production potential. As for Fininvest[5], it has cut general costs by 16.9% and reduced – although not significantly – its personnel. At the same time, it has lowered its commissions for advertising agents and distributors in order to raise its net earnings. But most of all it has lowered its production costs by 25.1%. Program genres which have suffered most from this cost reduction drive are those requiring a higher initial investment, such as fiction, whose production budget has been halved.

---

[5] In 1996, as part of a general reorganization of the holding company (which operates in the television, advertising, retail, and insurance markets), the name of Fininvest's television arm was changed to Mediaset.

After the roaring 1980's and their advertising explosion and geometric progression of costs (Ortoleva, 1995; Menduni, 1996), the emphasis is now on offering advertising packages at reduced prices. Over the last few years interest for advertising has flared again, mostly because of renewed investments in services as well as investments by consumer electronics suppliers and telephone companies following the end of Telecom's monopoly. In the last five years a general increase of investments of about 23% has been recorded, with a forecast 15% increase for the next years (this can be explained by Italy's low advertising investment to GDP ratio, the lowest in Europe – see table 3).

Table 3. *Advertising Investment to GDP Ratio*

Country	Population (x 000)	%	GDP in € (billions)	%	Adv. in US$ (billions)	%	Inv. to GDP ratio
Europe	375,000	100	10,282	100	104,086	100	
France	58,877	15.7	1,584	15.4	12,490	12.0	78
Germany	82,250	21.9	2,360	22.9	26,249	25.2	110
Italy	56,970	15.2	1,282	12.5	8,473	8.1	65
Spain	39,371	10.5	607	5.9	6,099	5.9	100
Great Britain	59,172	15.8	1,575	15.3	22,236	21.4	140
Others	78,360	20.9	2,872	27.9	28,529	27.4	98

An analysis of the genres on offer (table 4) shows a clear prevalence of information and culture on the public channels (41.1% as compared to Mediaset's 23.1%), while Mediaset offers more varied programming in the fields of fiction (33.5% vs. RAI's 12.5%) and entertainment (19.3% vs. RAI's 14.1%). The 1993–95 data show the stability of such trends, except for film programming, which in 1993 was stronger on RAI (21.8%

Table 4. *Ratings by Television Genres and Program Supply on RAI and Mediaset* 1993–1995

	1993				1994				1995			
	RAI		Mediaset		RAI		Mediaset		RAI		Mediaset	
Genres	Ra-ting	Offer	Ra-ting	Offer	Ra-ting	Offer	Ra-ting	Offer	Ra-ting	Offer	Ra-ting	Offer
News/culture	35.1	37.5	15.9	21.2	35.0	34.7	20.5	23.6	35.1	41.1	19.7	23.1
Entertain-ment	21.5	13.6	29.8	23.5	19.6	14.0	23.5	21.3	22.7	14.1	25.6	19.3
Movies	15.1	21.8	20.0	13.7	14.7	17.5	19.5	12.2	13.2	13.7	19.9	15.1
Sports	9.8	8.8	3.8	2.8	12.2	8.1	3.5	2.4	9.5	6.7	4.0	2.0
Fiction	14.3	12.3	21.5	32.5	13.6	13.3	21.9	34.2	13.1	12.5	21.4	33.5
Cartoons/ Comedy	1.8	3.0	4.5	6.2	2.5	3.6	4.8	6.3	4.0	3.4	4.9	7.0
Other	2.4	3.0	4.5	0.1	2.4	8.8	4.3	-	2.5	8.4	4.5	-
Total	100	100	100	100	100	100	100	100	100	100	100	100

vs. Mediaset's 13.7%), but which in 1995 saw Mediaset prevail with 15.1% (RAI: 13.7%).

Ratings for the past five years (table 5) clearly show the fierce RAI-Mediaset competition which has completely crushed the other TV channels, whose audiences keep falling.

Table 5. *Daytime Ratings by Television Channel*

	RAI 1	RAI 2	RAI 3	RAI (total)	Canale 5	Italia 1	Rete 4	Media-set (total)	Others	Total
1991	21.48	19.13	8.84	49.45	16.35	11.06	10.55	37.96	12.59	100
1992	18.96	18.27	8.95	46.18	19.56	11.78	11.70	43.04	10.78	100
1993	18.13	17.74	9.34	45.21	20.53	12.48	11.74	44.75	10.04	100
1994	19.91	16.39	10.09	46.39	20.26	12.57	10.76	43.59	10.02	100
1995	22.76	15.50	9.67	47.93	21.21	12.07	9.49	42.77	9.30	100
1996	23.98	14.81	10.96	49.75	22.28	11.59	8.32	42.19	8.06	100
1997	22.84	15.90	9.37	48.11	21.86	10.53	9.26	41.65	10.24	100
1998	22.88	15.84	9.33	48.05	20.74	11.25	9.57	41.56	10.39	100
1999	22.30	16.00	9.00	47.3	21.20	11.30	10.40	42.90	9.80	100
2000	22.90	14.80	9.30	47.0	22.5	11.20	10.10	43.80	9.20	100

In the first three years of the decade, the RAI-Mediaset supremacy resulted in a narrowed divide between the two competitors: in fact the 1993 data show a balanced situation (RAI: 45.21% – Mediaset: 44.75%) in daytime ratings; but afterwards RAI continued to gain ground.

Before analyzing the data for each individual channel, we must stress that the three public networks have never pursued a strategy of channel differentiation on a target audience basis, but that they have privileged a specific political and cultural flavor: RAI 1 (the *flagship* channel – Catholic), RAI 2 (secular/Socialist), and RAI 3 (Communist/post-Communist). This differentiation is even more easily detectable in the news departments of the three channels.

On the other hand, the three Mediaset networks have always been target-oriented: Canale 5 has a more general target, Italia 1 tries to attract young people, and Rete 4 targets a female audience with its intensive programming of *telenovelas* and soap operas (with its nightly programming grid an exception since it caters to movies enthusiasts). As table 3 shows, RAI's declining ratings in the early nineties as well as their later upturn follow exactly the pattern of its first channel, while RAI 2 shows a progressive fall of about one percent yearly. Regarding Mediaset it is worth stressing, on the other hand, the slow but steady growth of Canale 5, the regularity of Italia 1, and the decline of Rete 4, which has become even more pronounced in recent times.

Even if we choose to concentrate on primetime (table 6), we observe a slight but steady growth in RAI's ratings, mirrored by a slow decline in the ratings both of Mediaset and of the other television channels.

Table 6. *Primetime (8.30–10.30 p.m.) Ratings by Television Channel*

	RAI 1	RAI 2	RAI 3	RAI (total)	Canale 5	Italia 1	Rete 4	Media-set (total)	Others	Total
1991	22.28	15.70	10.17	48.15	19.74	11.69	10.09	41.52	10.33	100
1992	20.70	15.92	10.67	47.29	19.96	11.97	11.44	43.37	9.34	100
1993	20.51	15.73	11.74	47.98	19.66	13.04	11.13	43.83	8.19	100
1994	21.43	15.10	11.78	48.31	20.39	13.37	9.72	43.48	8.21	100
1995	23.85	14.28	10.91	49.04	22.26	12.29	8.81	43.36	7.60	100
1996	23.27	14.77	9.89	47.93	21.53	12.06	9.01	42.60	9.47	100
1997	23.82	15.68	9.44	48.94	22.17	11.06	8.35	41.58	9.48	100
1998	24.28	15.30	9.23	48.81	21.38	12.00	8.34	41.72	9.47	100
1999	24.70	15.20	9.60	49.5	21.30	12.00	8.30	41.60	8.90	100
2000	25.10	14.20	10.00	49.3	22.50	11.70	7.90	42.10	8.60	100

Average daily viewing figures are on the rise. Between 1997 and 1999 an increase of 9 minutes per year was recorded in Italy: from 207 minutes in 1997 to 216 in 1998, and finally to 225 minutes in 1999. The Italians come in second for viewing time (behind the Hungarians, with 232 minutes in 1999) and the Italian average is higher than the European one (199 minutes).

Till the late 1990's the most significant products were mainly imported from the USA (more than 50% for Mediaset and about 1/3 of RAI's overall programming). In the new millennium the trend seems to be reversing: Italian production is now thriving, making Italy one of the few European countries – with Great Britain – where foreign products account only for a small part of the whole programming grid. Of course this process has been encouraged by the Strasbourg decisions to protect national and European production. First of all it is the result of a new awareness of Italian production's success both in the area of entertainment and in that of fiction. Nevertheless, despite last year's significant improvements, high costs remain a serious problem for Italy's fiction industry.

The production of two hours of primetime Italian fiction costs about €620,000, as compared to €310,000 for an American production. Half an hour of sitcom produced entirely by an Italian TV network costs between €67,000 and €77,000, while it cost €7,750–10,330 to purchase an equivalent American production. Rather than setting limits which inevitably end up being infringed, governing authorities should ensure that the audiovisual industry reinvests in production, possibly through such incentives as tax cuts.

These costs explain why production mostly focuses on entertainment (71% of the national production in 1999, as compared to 29% for fiction production), which is rather surprising in light of the situation in other countries (in the USA entertainment makes up only 6% of TV programming, while in Germany fiction accounts for 61%).

Growing competition in the radio and television market has also boosted the research market. In the past few years radio and television marketing has grown considerably, which would have been unthinkable under a monopoly system. The war for audiences requires a much more sophisticated definition of programming schedules, as well as more careful program production.

At the same time, the area of proper scientific research is becoming more refined. We can mention a few research areas which are characterized by more careful attention to the social and territorial contexts of the communication processes, and by an attempt to explore national characteristics in the relationship between media and society (Wolf, 1995). Starting from a qualitative analysis of the audience and availing themselves of ethnographic approaches, these studies explore the complexity of the communication interactions which are at the basis of media use, seen as one of the many interaction modes of an individual (Mancini, 1991; Casetti, 1995).

Similarly, political communication has developed as a consequence of the deep and traumatic transformations in the Italian political establishment. In particular, the establishment of a majority voting system has fostered the personalization of politics, thus magnifying a characteristic which is typical of the media and encouraging, as a consequence, a media orientation of electoral campaigns. This process has marked a further step towards the emancipation of the media system (Mancini & Mazzoleni, 1995; Livolsi & Volli, 1995, 1997; Morcellini, 1995, 1996).

There is also renewed attention to the world of information; here the analysis is based on more articulate paradigms, in which the examination of the professional and news making cultures is considered in the light of the different negotiation forms among the various social agents presented by market logic and technological innovations (Bechelloni, 1995; Sorrentino, 1995).

For the first time keen attention is being paid to the production of television fiction, in accordance with the birth of national producing. In this respect, the observatory on television fiction (which Milly Buonanno has been heading for more than ten years) has been trying to identify in the imagery of television fiction the distinctive cipher of the Italian culture's universe of symbols and values.

V   Today's Television

Following the crisis of the past few years which forced broadcasters to reduce their debt, the Italian media market has now been in an impasse for some time, while are being developed a body of rules as well as a better understanding of the changes both in the advertising market and in the media system's technological developments and structure.

RAI's programming has in the past few years lost its distinguishing characteristics as a public service broadcaster in its costly attempt to compete with private channels, while the political upheavals of the 1990's rocked those political pillars which – however questionable – had long supported the corporation. Since July 1993, RAI had four different boards of directors and seven managing directors. Nevertheless, after recovering from its major period of economic crisis, RAI was able to earmark €387 million for technological innovation in its 1994–96 budget. The company closed its 1997 operating year with a net profit of €870 million. However, this overhaul does not make it any less arduous to meet both the goal of production diversification (which requires heavy investments in technology) and that of competition with commercial TV and theme-based channels in securing the exorbitantly-priced rights to major sports events (Menduni, 1998).

Advertising makes up a significant part of RAI's earnings (from 36 to 41% between 1996 and 2000). This obviously has an influence on production processes, which become increasingly similar to those of commercial TV. Nevertheless, a study recently pointed out that 74% of the Italian population believe in the specificity of public TV which should lead to an improvement of the quality of the offered product, even if it means a loss of audience (Zaccone, Teodosi, Medolago Albani, 2000).

Accordingly, the debate on RAI's privatization has been heating up: this process would be the offshoot of a popular referendum held in 1998 on this subject. The debate now focuses on the following issues: how should RAI be privatized, how many – and then which one(s) – of the three RAI channels should be privatized, and how long would the privatization process take? Italy's politicians have no interest in privatizing RAI, unlike the main publishing and telecommunications groups. The parties of the center and left-wing coalition would like to maintain control over public TV in order to limit the 'TV power' of their main political opponent, Forza Italia leader and television tycoon Silvio Berlusconi.

Prime Minister Berlusconi assures that he won't privatize RAI. This political strategy is meant to ward off charges that he would be in a position to make laws in a field where he has huge personal interests. He would thus be able to maintain a status quo which is clearly in favor of the main commercial TV group – his own Mediaset. As regards initiatives about new communication media, RAI has focused more on digital and pay-TV than on the Internet. RAI brought out three non-pay-per-view digital channels, then provided ten specialty channels to Telepiù, one of Italy's two digital satellite platforms. Recently RAI created Rai.net, which is entirely dedicated to the Internet.

Mediaset remains the only true commercial television group. After financial consolidation and with its stock now being traded on several exchanges, the group (which relies heavily on advertising revenue) has benefited from the advertising boom noted in Italy over the past two years, with an increase of about 10% in yearly sales. Economic consolidation is an absolutely necessary condition for Berlusconi's group if it is to enter the process of diversification required by the new law regulating the television sector (no. 249 of July 31, 1997). This law makes it illegal for any private television broadcasting entity to possess more than two national television networks and more than one encrypted one; it also makes it impossible for any single entity earn over 30% of its revenue from the radio and TV sector. This ceiling is lowered to 20% in the case of co-ownership between radio and TV and printed media. Hence, Mediaset will have to transfer its third network on to satellite. At the same time, its competitor, RAI, must completely remove one of its three national networks from the advertising market.

These provisions explain Mediaset's renewed interest in the European television market: further investments in Spain's Telecinco (whose sales are growing), but above all entry into the telecommunications sector through an interest in Albacom (a fixed telephone company) and participation in an alliance of corporations that attempted to obtain a license to become the third national supplier of cellular phone services. This competition was then won by Wind-ENEL (the Italian electrical power monopoly, which is being privatized). Mediaset has also an interest in one of the five societies which will manage the next cellular telephone generation through UMTS. Then Mediaset created its own Internet portal, 'Jumpy.'

The second group of Italian TV stations are expanding very slowly. This network belongs to movie producer Cecchi Gori and includes two national channels (TMC and TMC2) as well as a regional television station located in Florence (Channel 10). Though they have been part for a few years now of the Italian Auditel system that measures share of audience, the two stations together never capture more than a 5% share of viewers. There has been a lot of talk of Cecchi Gori getting out of the television market and selling off his enterprise to a big foreign media group. Most commonly mentioned has been Murdoch, an Australian tycoon with an intense interest in the Italian market but who has found it difficult to penetrate it. Murdoch has had talks with Cecchi Gori; he is in perennial negotiations with Mediaset – in fact in 1998 he seemed to be a hair's breadth away from acquiring a majority interest. Above all Murdoch had signed an pre-agreement with Stream, Telecom Italia's pay-TV channel, but that was wrecked by a government decree which prevented a single broadcaster from purchasing the rights to live broadcasts of all of the A league team soccer matches.

Having lost his hopes in a Murdoch takeover, Cecchi Gori applied to Telecom – the main Italian telecommunications company, which was public until a few years ago and enjoyed a complete monopoly in fixed telephony. After its privatization Telecom was taken over by the Olivetti group following the largest bid the Italian market had ever known. Telecom took over Cecchi Gori's television company through one company controlled by Telecom itself (SEAT), but the Authority for Italian telecommunications stopped the acquisition because Telecom remains in a situation of monopoly with respect to fixed telephony and cannot therefore be allowed to venture into cable TV. This is a highly controversial stand and the deal is currently dormant, even though Telecom's shareholder (Colaninno) had enough interest in the TV group to strike an agreement with those international partners that allow a minor participation in Telecom's shareholding.

As regards pay-TV, after years of exclusive domination by Telepiù (now owned by French group Canal Plus), Italy – just like the other major European countries – has now two competing operators. The second one is Stream, a company spawned in 1993 by Telecom, which at the time held the telephone system monopoly. After years of very slow growth owing to the extremely varied offerings of the regular television system, pay-TV subscriptions have begun to increase markedly in the last two years. The reason is to be found prevalently in the fact that pay-TV offers digitized images and soccer games on a pay-per-view basis. In fact, Telepiù (Tele+) and Stream share the broadcasting rights for the games of Italy's major teams. In the year 2000 Telepiù's and Stream's subscribers virtually reached the two million mark.

There are about one million Tele+ subscribers, with a 1,000% increase in viewers making the switch to digital – that is they went from 50,000 to 500,000 in one single year (1997–1998). We can therefore state that the pay-TV market, far from being geared to an elite segment, is becoming a mass market in its own right. If growth levels continue to hover below projections made several years ago, it is because consumers have yet to reach the high level of technological sophistication needed to deal with more interactive and dynamic devices, and because they remain somewhat intimidated by the rapid rate of technological change, with its attendant dangers of choosing pieces of equipment that may become obsolete in a month or so. Things are bound to change with the advent of the multicrypt standard and the new generation of set-top boxes (which allow for the definition of a universal digital television system).

At the threshold of the third millennium, the keywords are diversification and internationalization. Alliances, mergers and acquisitions follow one upon another at a relentless pace. This means that the Italian media system now finds itself in uncharted territory, having always been sheltered from the threat of foreign operators before.

A national approach to communication seems ever more difficult to pursue in this era of convergence within the telecommunications system, where the boundaries between sectors are increasingly blurred and the size of investments in the new sectors require supranational synergy.In facing this situation, Italy is characterized by the specifics below:

- An overabundance of non-pay-per-view TV offers
- A monopoly shared by the two main TV entities
- A prime focus on TV on the part of advertisers, and one greater than in any other European country
- A gradual increase in the cost of national and European audiovisual products which has encouraged self-production
- A lack of broadcasting facilities as alternative solutions to terrestrial links. Cable is virtually nonexistent, while satellite remains under-developed.

In other words, analog transmission and generalist TV will remain pillars of the Italian media system for many years to come. There are also perspectives of innovation which are even clearer also thanks to the general awareness that the universally opened national TV is now passing through a phase of maturity.

The most remarkable news has to do with content. The digital revolution has meant increases in transmission capacity, channel efficiency, and quantity and quality of services, which opens up untold perspectives. This results in the gradual convergence of the telecommunications, information, and media worlds, as evidenced by recent corporate alliances. Leading telecommunications company Telecom has acquired through one of its subsidiaries one of Italy's largest Internet access providers (Virgilio), and we have seen that it is now trying to acquire Cecchi Gori's TV group, TMC. Mediaset has entered the Internet world through Jumpy; major publishing houses such as HDP, Espresso, or Monti-Riffeser made the same choice and all now have a presence on the web.

The possibilities created by technology contribute to the development of new products and services. The Internet is the most significant platform for such experiments: companies use it to offer communications products and services which are only apparently in contrast with its innovative character, such as web radio or web phone. An extremely original convergence of contents is the possibility of receiving telecommunications services on a TV set and television services on a PC. And of course, all this has an influence on economic aspects. Still to come is a market convergence (audiovisual services, telecommunications, Internet, etc.) which will revolutionize societal structures, an advance indication of which is the above-mentioned recent mergers. These will be factors of vertical integration resulting in the creation of new industrial groups able to manage the various phases on an autonomous basis, from content production to final distribution (cf. the Vivendi-Universale and AOL-Time Warner mergers abroad, and the Telecom-Seat-TMC merger in Italy).

It is no wonder then that new companies are constantly appearing. A lot of managers from the main Italian networks are striking out as independent TV production companies and content providers focusing on multichannel products. These initiatives are in fact often funded by the very telecommunications and information companies that will be – thanks to their considerable economic resources – the main actors of the upcoming TV-telephone-Internet convergence. Their activity is also simplified by better relationships with the final client, gradually reached through years of intense marketing activity, especially in the area of cellular telephones (in 1999 the number of cellular telephone subscribers exceeded that of fixed telephone subscribers). With more than 32 million subscribers Italy is without a doubt the largest European market and the third largest worldwide.

It will be interesting to observe the changes taking place in the production process. New content providers will become established alongside more traditional broadcasters. These newcomers are soccer teams, race-tracks, publishers of specialized magazines, producers of videos for discotheques, etc. and they have in common the fact that they own the rights to images that can support new channels (in December 1999, the first TV channel belonging to a soccer team went on the air: the Milan Channel). But there are also multichannel producers with their own program libraries who will supply the owners of the two existing platforms as well as future specialty channels.

For this reason it is necessary to look at future perspectives taking into account the development of access technologies to digital products and services. In recent years Italy partly made up for lost time in comparison with the other European countries. As table 7 shows, the presence of personal computers (PC's) in Italian households doubled in the last five years, reaching 26.6%. As for peripherals (such as CD-ROM drives and modems, respectively used in 18.9% and 8.6% of Italian households) the growth is even more evident.

Most dramatic has been the growth in the CD-ROM market, which went from €49 million in 1995 to €243 million in 2000, and is expected to increase by 15% in

2001. Thanks to the introduction in early 1999 of free Internet access through providers, Internet use is increasing as well. Unfortunately, the high telephone prices are an obstacle, even though they have been declining with the end of Telecom's monopoly. As of June 30, 2000 there were 122 telephone services suppliers, 90 of which were authorized to operate in fixed telephony while six of them offered services for residential subscribers. Prices have fallen by 20% in the last four years. The introduction of the *Freenet* model resulted in a 150% increase between 1998 and 1999 (3,200,000 to 8,200,000 subscribers, or 14% of the population). Expansion perspectives are very encouraging, but we are still lagging far behind other European countries (21% on average). The Italian school system recently tried to boost computer literacy, one of the main factors of rapid development in the USA and in other European countries.

Table 7. *Diffusion of Electronic Media and ICT Services in Italian Households*

Electronic Media/Services	1995	1996	1997	1998	1999
Personal computer	13.6	17.3	21.5	23.7	26.6
2 or 3 PC's	-	0.6	0.9	1.5	1.8
Printer	9.3	11.6	15.6	17.0	20.0
Scanner	-	-	1.3	2.8	5.9
CD-ROM drive	1.7	6.0	11.2	14.3	18.9
Modem	1.6	2.8	5.6	6.7	8.6
Internet	0.3	0.8	2.0	2.7	4.9

The number of ISDN-based Internet users has been on the increase as well. In 1997 there were 900,000 of them, while in 1999 the figure had jumped to 3,200,000 subscribers. Another interesting indicator is the sums invested for advertising purposes on the Web; these went from €1.5 million in 1997 to €31 million in 2000, this last figure being expected to double in 2001. The corporate strategy of choice is to create Internet portals that need to offer a wide variety of organized contents. Users prefer portals whose logo is easily and immediately identified and which make it possible to be immediately and continually up-to-date about contents. The most visited Italian Internet portals include those belonging to the main international groups (such as Microsoft or Yahoo), or those belonging to telecommunications companies such as Tiscali or Seat. The main publishing groups have set up Internet portals too, while radio and TV companies have been keeping a low profile in this field, even though there are signs that this may be changing. After a period of immobility, advertising again shows a great expansive capability. General advertising investments in the last five years have increased by 23.2 %. The results are particularly positive for TV (+25.5%) and for radio (+31.5%). Forecasts are positive too. In future use of services will be paid directly by the users mostly through some digital platform, which is bound to change the nature and intensity of competition (Autorità per le garanzie nelle comunicazioni, 2000).

The analog phase still prevails, however, and will continue to do so for years; it is characterized by a substantial lack of physical resources (terrestrial frequencies) and is based on the predominance of very few companies. On the other hand we must be prepared to face the impact of digital technology. Market internationalization is one of the first results of this process. Among networks, Mediaset is looking to expand in Germany, Spain, and Great Britain. For the first time foreign companies (Disney, Discovery, Universal, Bloomberg, etc.) are entering the Italian TV market, while those already present become stronger. Canal Plus/Telepiù, Italy's largest pay-TV provider, has sales of about €516,000. At the same time telecommunications companies enter the editorial content market: Telecom, with its pay-TV subsidiary Stream as well as the recently purchased TMC. Another example is power company ENEL, which is going to be privatized and which owns a major telephone company (Wind); it began by purchasing part of Telepiù (for a short time), then behaved with great caution, looking with particular interest at the unending talk concerning the privatization of RAI. Also, Canal Plus has established connections with Vodafone, which controls two major Italian telephone companies: Omnitel and Infostrada.

The market is becoming more and more complex: suffice it to say that direct expenses on the part of households as well as changes in the time spent using them will be significant for those products which are more and more multilevel. This will even result in changes in the legal structure, making it more difficult to identify leading actors. In Italy there is a heated debate concerning the need to monitor compliance to the anti-concentration provisions of the act on TV which came into force in 1997. The development of these innovations is hindered by uncertainty of prospects from the point of view of the final client. The most evident case in Italy is the never-ending discussions between the two pay-TV suppliers (Telepiù and Stream) about the compatibility of their set-top boxes. While the Authority has made such compatibility compulsory on penalty of heavy sanctions, we still have in Italy two conflicting standards and harmonization is not expected before the Summer of 2001. Market growth necessarily hinges on availability to potential users of the equipment needed to take advantage of all the services offered by the market. The behavior of these two suppliers did little to encourage viewers to invest in their products. On the one hand number one telecommunications company (and former telephone monopoly holder) Telecom appeared caught in great contradictions as regards cable: it had initially planned huge investments in connection with the Internet, then changed its mind. Users were unwilling to invest in satellite reception equipment because it would make cable connection impossible. On the other hand, a variety of traditional TV offers persist, especially as regards successful pay-TV products such as recent and successful movies or sporting events – especially soccer. Unsurprisingly last years' significant increase in pay-TV subscribers is related to two events: the acquisition of TV rights directly from soccer teams and their equal distribution between the two networks, as well as the incredible success of the first truly popular multilevel TV program, 'Big Brother.' This was broadcast 24 hours a day and prompted a sudden rise in Stream's subscribers. Mediaset's portal (Jumpy) also gained a lot of subscribers because it continually gave a lot of information about the program.

Of course all companies have a keen interest in the growth of digital platforms. Experts foresee that the impasse will be overcome both thanks to the opening up of the Italian media system and to the possibility of using digital terrestrial platforms which could within a few years provide better economic and technical conditions to fledging channels and interactive services. It should be pointed out that in the last few months initiatives regarding cable in many metropolitan areas and middle-sized towns have been announced by companies that have felt encouraged by the deregulation of telecommunications and the availability of broadband services that can offer telephone and TV services as well. When this happens, Italy will be in step with the trend ongoing in other European countries, where pay-TV subscriptions, while representing only 9.5% of TV revenues in 1995, will make up for about 30% in 2002 (Ioppolo & Pilati, 1999). Among the various types of services that pay channels can supply, the strongest request will probably be for near-video-on-demand while video-on-demand and all interactive services will increase much more slowly. The cause for this lies in the above-mentioned technological difficulties as well as the need to create more familiarity and ease with the upcoming, richer and more complex relationship with the TV set.

As far as radio is concerned, we can foresee a future in which the numbers of listeners will steadily increase. In the 1990's the number of daily listeners went up by about 8 million (Menduni, 1999), which is explanation enough of a notable increase in radio advertising (+31.5% in the last five years), since the radio is able to offer an audience of young listeners with a good educational background and an above average income, exactly the profile sought out by potential advertisers. Although there is still a myriad of local stations, much more than in the field of television, we do note a rising trend in syndication, with about ten stations having quite significant ratings and business volumes, though nothing comes close to threatening the record held by RAI, which has three national radio stations, a satellite channel and an isofrequency channel giving traffic reports. These data are tantalizing to a few publishing groups, who are falling over themselves to gain a foothold in the sector: the Espresso-La Repubblica Group, which has bought several radio stations, or the Sole-24 Ore Publishing Group, owned by the Italian Confederation of Industrialists (Confindustria), which publishes Italy's major economic newspaper and has been producing Radio 24 now for several months.

We thus find ourselves on the brink of significant change. What has been called the digital revolution in the big media will change the whole structure of the media system along with the ways we use it. Consumers will have at their fingertips sundry alternative uses of the media thanks to multimedia technology. Television will never be the same again, and this will bring about deep changes in the social significance of the media and their use.

References

Autorità per le garanzie nelle comunicazioni (1999). *Relazione annuale sull'attività svolta*, Presidenza del Consiglio dei ministri.

Autorità per le garanzie nelle comunicazioni (2000). *Relazione annuale sull'attività svolta*, Presidenza del Consiglio dei ministri.

Bechelloni, G. & Buonanno, M. (1981). Un quotidiano di partito sui generis: L'Unità, *Problemi dell'informazione* 2.

Bechelloni, G. (1995). *Giornalismo o postgiornalismo*. Naples: Liguori.

Bechelloni, G. (1997). Italian television. In H. Newcomb (ed.), *Encyclopedia of Television*. Chicago, IL: Fitzroy Dearborn.

Buonanno, M. (1991). *Il reale è immaginario*. Rome: RAI, VQPT (Verifica Qualitativa Programmi Trasmessi) 104.

Buonanno, M. (1992). *Sceneggiare la cronaca*. Rome: RAI, VQPT 111.

Buonanno, M. (1993). *Non è la stessa storia*. Rome: RAI, VQPT 117.

Buonanno, M. (1994a). *Il bardo sonnacchioso*. Rome: RAI, VQPT 122.

Buonanno, M. (1994b). E' arrivata la serialità. Rome: RAI, VQPT 126.

Buonanno, M. (1996). *Ciak! Si gira*. Rome: RAI, VQPT 140.

Carat (1992). *European Radio Minibook*. Paris.

Casetti, F. (1995). *L'ospite fisso. Televisione e mass media nelle famiglie italiane*. Milan: Ed. San Paolo.

Gundle, S. (1995). *I comunisti italiani tra Hollywood e Mosca. La sfida della cultura di massa*. Florence: Giunti

Ioppolo D. & Pilati A. (1999). *Il supermercato delle immagini*, Milan: Sperling & Kupfer

Livolsi, M. & Volli, U. (1995) (eds.). *La comunicazione politica fra prima e seconda Repubblica*. Milan: F. Angeli.

Livolsi, M. & Volli, U. (1997) (eds.). *Il televoto*. Milan: F. Angeli.

Mancini, P. (1991). *Guardando il telegiornale. Per un'etnografia del consumo televisivo*. Turin: Nuova ERI.

Mancini, P. & Mazzoleni, G. (1995) (eds.). *I media scendono in campo*. Rome: RAI, VQPT 132.

Menduni, E. (1996). Radiofonia. In E. Pucci (ed.), *L'industria della comunicazione in Italia*. II Rapporto IEM, Milan: Guerini e Associati.

Menduni, E. (1998). Televisione e radio. In E. Pucci (ed.), *L'industria della comunicazione in Italia*. IV Rapporto IEM, Milan: Guerini e Associati

Morcellini, M. (Ed) (1996). *Elezioni di TV*. Genoa: Costa & Nolan.

Morcellini, M. (1996). La TV dell'incertezza, *Problemi dell'informazione* 3.

Ortoleva, P. (1995). *Un ventennio a colori*. Florence: Giunti.

Richeri, B. (1996). Verso le reti a larga banda. In E. Pucci (ed.), *L'industria della comunicazione in Italia*. Milan: Guerini e Associati.

Sorrentino, C. (1995). *I percorsi della notizia. La stampa italiana fra politica e mercato*. Bologna: Baskerville.

Wolf, M. (1995). Come si è sviluppata la ricerca sui media, *Problemi dell'informazione* 4.

Zaccone Teodosi A. & Medolago Albani F. (2000). *Con lo Stato e con il mercato?* Milan: Mondadori.

United Kingdom

by Tomas Coppens and John Downey

Public service broadcasting in the United Kingdom is often cited as the basis for many similar broadcasting systems around the world. Yet in many ways it is different from those systems which are claimed to be modeled after the BBC. Competition was introduced in the British television market as early as the 1950's, while other public broadcasters continued to enjoy a monopoly position until the end of the 1980's. While competition has made PSB into an evolving concept with commercial broadcasters obliged to fulfil certain public service functions, the notion of PSB has not changed as dramatically in Britain as in many other countries. Britain's public service idea, although copied many times, still remains quite unique.

I   A History of British Broadcasting (1922–1996)

The first broadcasting company was set up in Britain in the 1920's by radio manufacturers hoping to boost sales of receivers by enticing consumers with programs. The privately owned British Broadcasting Company went on the air in 1922; it was granted a monopoly by the Postmaster-General and funded by a Post Office license fee, payable by anyone who owned a receiver. At the head of the company was Lord John Reith, the 'architect of public service broadcasting in Britain' (Cain, 1992: 10). Reith has been described as a man who "promoted a service designed for the 'betterment of the masses,' which perhaps could be more unkindly viewed as a form of forced cultural assimilation to the values and attitudes of the British upper middle class" (Alvarado, Locksley & Paskin, 1992: 296). Soon the government started to see the potential of this new medium and in 1927 it made the BBC into a public corporation, controlled by a Board of Governors whose members were appointed by the government.

The BBC started experimenting with television as early as 1929. The Selsdon Committee[1] granted the corporation a monopoly for television broadcasts as well. The BBC started regular television broadcasts in 1936. During World War II, however, the television service was canceled and the BBC concentrated on radio. Radio played an important role in the war not only by opposing Goebbels's propaganda machine with its V-Campaign broadcasts but also, more generally, through seeking to foster a British *imaginary community* of common interest and destiny, papering over class and regional antagonisms in particular, in the face of a common enemy.

The importance of the BBC in nation building and the consensus generated during the war meant that the BBC, in the aftermath of the war, seemed untouchable – it be-

---

[1] A parliamentary committee named after its chairman, Lord Selsdon.

came a cherished national symbol. Viewers and listeners were proud of their *Auntie Beeb* and paid their license fee without complaining much.

The public service idea was at its high point during that period. Public service broadcasting in Britain meant a centralized, national broadcasting service which should be available to all at a relatively small cost, and should preserve the social and cultural traditions of the nation. This concept lost some of its tone when competition was allowed. Before such an important decision was made, however, a special Parliamentary Committee was installed to advise the government. This procedure was followed for every crucial broadcasting policy decision.

The *Beveridge Committee Report* found that the BBC's monopoly should remain intact but the Conservative Party, suspicious of the political role of the BBC since the 1927 General Strike, did not agree. Its leader, Winston Churchill, often accused the BBC of being 'biased to the left' (Davis, 1976: 15) and was encouraged by television manufacturers, potential advertisers, and Tory back-benchers to allow a commercial broadcaster. The supposed left-wing or anti-British bias of the BBC became a perennial lament of the right in Britain and this issue has become itself a 'media event' in times of national crisis such as the Falklands War in 1982 and the Gulf War in 1991, when elements of the Conservative Party felt that the BBC did not beat the drum loudly enough, if at all. These periods demonstrate the ideological contradictions inherent in an organization at once a *national* institution – a fundamentally controversial concept – and committed to the principles of *objective* journalism. By the time the Conservatives regained power, in 1951, they were determined to reform the media landscape and introduce commercial television in the UK. The 1954 *Television Act* formed the legal basis for the new commercial service by setting up *the Independent Television Authority* (ITA), a public licensing body. The ITA had to make sure that the new commercial network could work independently and granted 15 regional licenses to as many production companies which formed the Independent Television Network (ITV), a state-regulated network with a public service role as well as being profit-orientated. ITV started broadcasting in September 1955.

In 1962 the government decided to authorize the creation of a third television station. Both broadcasters wanted an additional channel, but the *Pilkington Committee* decided that the BBC would get the extra channel. The Corporation argued that a second network would provide a more balanced mix of programs with a popular BBC 1 and a culturally innovating BBC 2 directed at specialist minority audiences. This plan was very well received by the Committee, which also argued that "commercial television had not sufficiently proved itself" (Alvarado, Locksley & Paskin, 1992: 299), and BBC 2 went on the air two years later. Such a decision was indicative of the recognition of the diversity to be found within the *nation* and the strength of the public service ethos in the public sphere. A culturally paternalistic consensus viewed the commercialization of *culture* with a good deal of suspicion.

With a new Conservative government in 1970 the ITA insisted again on an additional network, but the Heath government was not inclined to grant the ITA's wish. However, it did allow commercial radio stations on a local level. As a result of the 1972 *Sound*

Broadcasting Act the ITA was replaced by the *Independent Broadcasting Authority* (IBA), controlling both television and the new commercial radio stations, the *Independent Local Radios*. Nation-wide commercial radio, however, was still not permitted.

When a fourth network became possible the *Annan Committee*, which published its report in 1977, supported the idea of a TV network in the hands of a new body, the *Open Broadcasting Authority*. The idea was dropped when the Labor government was replaced by the first Thatcher government in 1979. The fourth network was, instead, allocated to the *Channel Four Television Company Ltd*. The 1980 Broadcasting Bill gave this new channel a special mission, one of culture, innovation and special attention to ethnic minorities. ITV held the monopoly on advertising revenue by selling both its own advertising time and that of the newly launched Channel Four.

The establishment of a commercial competitor to BBC 2, emphasizing the provision of *quality* television to a variety of niche audiences, was a key step in the ideological legitimization – achieved through a compromise between economic and public service imperatives – of commercial broadcasting in the UK. The critical and financial success of Channel Four has contributed to a general questioning of the role of the BBC and the maintenance of the license fee in the UK.

The 1980's also saw the first non-terrestrial channels, when Rupert Murdoch launched four Sky channels on the Astra satellite in 1989. A year later competition emerged in the form of technologically superior BSB, which distributed its channels by cable in March 1990 and by satellite one month later. Both services were financially vulnerable and merged in November 1990 to become BSkyB, Britain's largest satellite broadcaster; this provides an interesting case study of the relative importance of markets and technology in media development. The development of technology was set back by market imperatives.

The breakdown of the social democratic consensus in Britain in the 1970's and 1980's and the rebirth of consumer culture together with the Thatcher government's determination to *beat back* state interference in economic, social and cultural life led to a broad debate on the future of the BBC and the concept of public service in the UK. The *Peacock Committee* examined the possibility of turning the BBC into a subscription channel by abandoning the license fee but nothing came of this. However, while the proposals of the Peacock Committee were not adopted entirely, the 1990 *Broadcasting Act* was influenced by the committee's extreme neo-liberal agenda. The Act introduced a number of far-reaching changes:

- the financial structure of Channel Four was revised;
- another commercial terrestrial channel was agreed: Channel Five (launched in 1997);
- a new franchise system was introduced, whereby the license is allocated to the highest bidder;
- national commercial radio stations were permitted;
- the functions of the IBA were split between the *Independent Television Commission* (*ITC*) and the *Radio Authority* (*RA*).

The new Act was a definite turning point in British broadcasting. ITV companies could no longer afford to broadcast programs that did not attract large audiences as a consequence of the loss of financial security provided by the monopoly on advertising. The government, however, did foresee the possible dangers of populist programming and a profit-maximizing agenda and countered by enforcing a new taxation scheme with several disincentives.

The British broadcasting system is now one that can be characterized as competitive, with three commercial terrestrial television channels with a variety of public service obligations battling it out for advertising revenue, a number of cable and satellite channels, and a public broadcaster that has evolved, through its alliance with Pearson (an international media company), into a tough player on the international media market. The Act introduced national commercial radio and further deregulated the radio market.

Many commentators thought the end of public service broadcasting was nigh. Sparks (1995: 339) concluded that "the economic and regulatory conditions which made British television a PSB system have been eroded." Others like Scannell (1996: 24) were more optimistic: "PSB has not simply held its ground through the flurry of parliamentary inquiries, reports, green and white papers, and Broadcasting Acts of the last ten years, it has emerged from this process stronger and more secure, in some respect, than it was before the process began."

The BBC in recent years has undergone a profound identity crisis, seeking both to compete with commercial stations in terms of audience share and to provide the public with programming that is not readily available commercially. To do both is difficult (there is a perceived inverse relationship between innovation and audience share) and both are necessary in order to secure the position of public service in the UK. If audience share falls significantly, then the universal license fee is bound to come once more into question since many viewers would, in effect, be paying for a service that they do not use. If the BBC fails to produce innovative programming, then its special status is called into question as its service would not differ substantially from that of commercial companies. This has led to the development of different strategies for the different areas of the BBC program supply depending on market circumstances.

II   Current Situation

The current situation of Britain's public and commercial broadcasting services is a complex one. There are five terrestrial national television channels, eight national radio stations (five BBC stations and three commercial ones), close to 300 local radio stations (about 250 commercial stations and 40 BBC stations), about 250 satellite stations, close to a 100 cable services, and several digital terrestrial and satellite services.

The largest British broadcaster is the BBC. Its radio service includes five national radio stations, nine regional radio services in Northern Ireland, Wales and Scotland, about 40 local radio stations, and the famous World Service with a global weekly audience of 150 million listeners in more than 40 languages.

Radio 1 is a mixed-genre music station aimed at a young, mainstream audience. Once the most popular of British stations, it rapidly lost listeners with the arrival of national commercial radio stations in the mid-90's, but has recovered somewhat recently as a result of a rebranding exercise to distinguish the station musically from its commercial competitors. While this led to initial problems with loss of listeners as the station changed its programming (or rather its DJ's), the only viable future for Radio 1 would appear to be one where the station is critically acclaimed. After initial skepticism, this rebranding has won critical plaudits and perhaps offers a model that BBC Television might adopt further down the digital road. Radio 2 is the light-entertainment channel, Radio 3 the cultural channel, and Radio 4 the speech-based information channel. The newest addition to the BBC family is Radio 5 Live, launched in 1994 as a replacement for Radio 5 which only existed for four years. Radio 5 Live has specialized, very successfully, in live sports and live news coverage.

Table 1. *Radio Listening Shares (1993–1999, in %)*

Station	Sept. 93	Sept. 94	Sept. 95	Sept. 96	Sept. 97	Sept. 98	Sept. 99
BBC Radio 1	19.6	11.8	11.8	12.5	10.1	10.5	10.6
BBC Radio 2	12.7	12.9	11.8	12.3	13.0	13.6	12.2
BBC Radio 3	1.4	1.1	1.1	1.4	1.1	1.3	1.2
BBC Radio 4	10.0	10.5	10.3	10.5	11.2	9.2	10.6
BBC Radio 5 Live	2.0	2.4	3.0	3.2	3.4	3.6	4.2
BBC Local/Regional	10.4	9.9	9.7	8.9	8.8	9.6	11.4
All BBC	**56.1**	**48.6**	**47.8**	**48.9**	**47.5**	**47.8**	**50.3**
Atlantic 252[2]	3.0	4.3	3.5	2.9	2.5	1.5	0.9
Classic FM	2.4	2.8	2.9	3.3	3.0	3.4	4.1
Talk Radio UK	-	-	1.7	1.8	2.0	1.7	1.5
Virgin Radio	2.1	3.6	3.3	2.5	2.2	2.7	2.2
Commercial Local/Regional	33.6	38.2	38.7	38.3	40.4	40.5	39.2
All commercial	**41.1**	**49.0**	**50.1**	**48.8**	**47.5**	**49.9**	**47.8**

Source: Radio Joint Audience Research (Rajar)

For the first time in British media history the share of commercial radio stations exceeded in 1995 that of the BBC, which was mostly due to the arrival of national commercial stations. The 1990 Broadcasting Act, inspired by the Peacock Committee's Green Paper, allows three *Independent National Radios*. The Radio Authority started allocating the licenses for these three new services in 1991. The license for the light-classical station was given to Classic FM, now owned by the GWR radio group, after the highest bidder withdrew for financial reasons. Classic FM started its programs in 1992

---

[2] An Irish-based radio station targeting the British audience.

and became quite successful. Its attempts to conquer overseas radio markets have met with less success and are the main reason why Time-Warner chose to sell it off to GWR. The license for the commercial pop-rock station was awarded to a joint venture associating Virgin, the owner of a record company and an airline, and former ITV franchisee TV-AM. The station started broadcasting in 1993 under the name Virgin Radio but has changed owners since then. The third license, for a speech-based station, was allocated to Talk Radio, a consortium with Canadian group CanWest, Media Ventures International and Hambros Bank. Talk Radio started broadcasting in 1995 and has been sold as well, first to CLT-UFA and later to TalkCo. None of the three national, commercial radio stations remained in the hands of the original owner. Other commercial channels include some 250 Independent Local Radios (ILR), 15 cable radio services, 19 satellite radio services, and 48 temporary Restricted Service Licensees (RA, 2000).

The British television market is also highly competitive, and increasingly so. The main broadcaster remains the BBC with a market share of about 40%. The biggest part of that share is generated by BBC 1, the more popular channel, which mostly competes with ITV. BBC 2 is a more cultural, innovating channel, and is thus a close competitor for Channel Four. Though still the biggest channel, ITV has lost a big part of its share of the audience (and advertising) market in the last few years. Ten years ago ITV had a 45% share. The other large, popular channel, BBC One, has also experienced a decline of its share of about 10% in ten years time. Of course, competition has intensified since then, with the launching of one satellite channel after another and the new terrestrial Channel Five, but the two smaller terrestrial channels seem to have coped very well. In ten years the respective shares of BBC 2 and Channel Four have stabilized, or even grown in the case of the latter. This presumably has to do with the character of many satellite and cable channels, which places them in direct competition with ITV and BBC One, as well as the tastes of satellite and cable TV users.

Table 2. *Television Audience Shares (in %)*

Television Station	1990	1995	1996	1997	1998	Jan 99	July 99	Jan 00
BBC 1	37.0	32.0	33.5	30.8	29.5	28.7	28.8	28.6
BBC 2	10.0	11.0	11.5	11.6	11.3	11.0	10.7	10.7
Total BBC	**47.0**	**43.0**	**45.0**	**42.4**	**40.8**	**39.7**	**39.5**	**39.2**
ITV	44.0	37.0	35.1	32.9	31.7	33.0	29.9	30.1
Channel 4	9.0	11.0	10.7	10.6	10.3	10.2	10.9	10.7
Channel 5	-	-	-	2.3	4.3	4.5	5.7	5.3
Total Commercial Terrestrial	**53.0**	**48.0**	**45.8**	**45.8**	**46.3**	**47.7**	**46.4**	**46.1**
Others (cable/satellite)	-	**9.0**	**10.1**	**11.8**	**12.9**	**12.6**	**14.1**	**14.6**

Source: Broadcasters Audience Research Board

The biggest blow to ITV's audience share has been the 1990 Broadcasting Act giving Channel Four full responsibility for its own advertising. Channel Four put on more popular programs, without abandoning its mission, and managed to gain in both audience and advertising share, causing ITV to rethink its strategy. The new strategy of the main commercial channel consist of even more popular programs, soaps, game shows, and so on, but this has yet to prove successful. ITV's share was even more at risk with the arrival of the new terrestrial channel which was launched in March 1997 (Channel Five). This general-interest channel hoped to gain a 5% market share by the end of 1997. While Channel Five didn't achieve this goal until 1999, ITV saw its share drop to around 30%.

The share of non-terrestrial broadcasting – lightly regulated satellite and cable television funded mainly by private subscription and advertising – has grown to about 15%, the biggest part of which is generated by the ten BSkyB channels. As the penetration of satellite receivers continues to increase (currently over 4 million British households), so too do the shares of satellite channels. BSkyB has a range of different channels, such as general-interest channel Sky One as well as several specialist channels (Sky Movies, Sky News, Sky Sports, etc.).

Cable television was long an unsuccessful proposition, but in the last few years cable penetration has grown considerably. More than 3.3 million homes now watch television over broad-band cable – about 25% of the 12 million British homes that have access to cable – while the number of cable services has soared (almost a hundred).

Table 3. *Cable and Satellite Development 1992–2000 (number of homes)*

Period	Satellite	Cable
January 1992	1,893,000	409,000
January 1993	2,387,000	625,000
January 1994	2,754,000	744,000
January 1995	3,060,000	973,000
January 1996	3,542,000	1,399,000
January 1997	3,804,000	1,845,000
January 1998	4,117,000	2,471,000
January 1999	4,114,000	2,911,000
January 2000	4,196,000	3,352,000

Source: Broadcasters Audience Research Board

III   Organization and Financing

The legal basis of the BBC is a *Royal Charter*, which was renewed for the sixth time in 1996, guaranteeing the existence of the Corporation until the year 2006. The BBC's mission is one of information, education and entertainment. It is supervised by a government appointed *Board of Governors*, but day-to-day management is in the hands of a *Board of Management*, headed by a Director-General (Greg Dyke since November 1999). This structure has created some conflicts, since it pits the BBC Governors – usually selected on the basis of political allegiance – against the professional managers, who are often internally recruited. The BBC is a huge organization, with

21,000 employees offering both radio and television services to the nation. The BBC is centrally organized in terms of management but there has been in recent years greater use of production bases outside of London. The *London Television Center* is the heart of the Corporation, which results in a certain amount of criticism: "As seen from other parts of the United Kingdom, the BBC is persistently biased towards the South-East of England, has a metropolitan attitude that regards the rest of the country as culturally inferior to the culture of the metropolis, and systematically misunderstands and marginalizes the cultural interests of Scotland, Wales and Northern Ireland" (Scannell, 1996: 27). Therefore, the BBC has committed itself to strengthening the position of its local production centers in Bristol, Birmingham and Manchester and in the three regions of Northern Ireland, Wales and Scotland. In 1996 only 29.5% of network programming was commissioned outside London and the Southeast (BBC, 1996: 38). Of course financial considerations also come into play in decisions about outsourcing production.

ITV has a very different structure. It is a network formed by 15 regional and two national private television companies. The licenses are awarded auction-style by the ITC, but the highest bidder does not always win since there is a so-called *quality threshold* which many candidates fail to clear. The two national licensees are GMTV, which provides breakfast television, and Teletext, which replaced Oracle as the commercial Teletext provider. The 15 regional companies make programs (mainly news) which are broadcast only in their region and programs which are aired nationally, for example during primetime. The national programs of the smaller companies, such as Border Television or Channel TV, are very limited in terms of both output and resources. The bigger companies make most of the programs intended for national broadcasting. The government Communications White Paper, published in December 2000, foresees a relaxation of restrictions on mergers of ITV companies to strengthen their position in domestic and international markets and in the development of digital TV. This may have implications, however, for the regional diversity of TV in the UK.

Channel Four and Channel Five are a network which consists of only one body. The former does not, however, make its own programs. One of the main motives for creating Channel Four was to stimulate the British television industry. Thus the government prohibited Channel Four from making its own programs. The channel is forced to commission its programs from independent producers or ITV franchisees. The other terrestrial channels are also required to commission at least 25% of their programming from independent production companies. The BBC commissions 29% of its television output from independent producers; for ITV this figure is 31%, for Channel Four it is 76%, and for Channel Five, 85%.

The public and commercial channels also differ greatly in financing. The BBC enjoys a guaranteed income (at least until 2006) while ITV, Channel Four and Channel Five rely on advertising to generate revenue.

The BBC is a public corporation funded mainly by a yearly collected license fee. Its World Service is funded by a special grant paid by the Foreign Office. Over 22 million households pay a license fee (€ 54.5 for a black-and-white television set and € 164.2 for a color set). A new license fee settlement guarantees an income growth with above-inflation increases to the license fee. An additional digital fee paid by subscribers to digital services was proposed in order to generate extra funds for the Corporation, but was rejected in March 2000 by Chris Smith, the Secretary of State for Culture, Media and Sport. This amount largely goes to the BBC, which collects the fee itself, but it is also used to fund other public bodies like the ITC, the Radio Authority or the Welsh Channel Authority. The license fee is of vital importance to the public broadcaster, since in 1993 more than 86% of its income was funded by the license fee (this figure dropped to 78% in 1997). Other income sources include the sale of television programs (books, magazines, videotapes, and audiocassettes) and, increasingly, merchan-dising. This generates about 15% of the BBC's income.

Table 4. *BBC Home Services License Fee Income and Operating Expenditure*

Year	License Fee (in € million)	Operating Expenditure (in € million)
1989-90	2,011	1,843
1990-91	2,251	2,051
1991-92	2,415	2,370
1992-93	2,597	2,496
1993-94	2,737	2,599
1994-95	2,846	2,669
1995-96	2,958	2,856
1996-97	3,112	3,103
1997-98	3,267	3,320
1998-99	3,542	3,515
1999-00	3,714	3,780

Source: BBC (100 = £61.5)

During the Thatcher years the BBC could no longer take its license fee income for granted and was threatened with the loss of this vital financial resource, which forced it to reorganize and find new income sources, such as international activities. The Conservative government, still unhappy about presumed left-wing leanings, started to question the license fee and suggested other funding mechanisms such as advertising or subscription. The whole public service ethos of the BBC was challenged by the threat of commercialization. The need to be profitable would inevitably clash with the ideology of universal service provision. Some even went as far as suggesting that *Auntie Beeb* should be privatized. These plans forced the BBC to strive to save money. John Birt, the director-general as of 1992, soon found himself making plans to drastically cut costs through massive layoffs (4,000 jobs in four years) and new cost-saving schemes such as *Producer Choice*, in which the producer has the option of working with BBC staff and equipment or with external means, whichever is cheapest; this effectively established an internal market. In the end the BBC's financing system was not drastically altered by the new Royal Charter. However, with the adoption of internal market principles Birt managed to sneak in a dose of Thatcherism. Goodwin (1993: 500) comments that "the impression is left that one of the key reasons that the Tories have opted for 'Steady as she goes' on the BBC is that the corporation itself is already steering a course which conforms with Tory political objectives." The BBC also made cuts to its famous World Service, the most international of all radio stations, with its weekly audience of 150 million on all continents. Due to cuts in the Grant-in-Aid (currently € 276 million) the BBC was forced to reduce its services by, for example, discontinuing its French service for Europe.

Continuing insecurity about the license fee has made the Corporation aware of its financial vulnerability and its dependence on the government, and led it into a search for alternative income sources. Although in the end the new 1996 Royal Charter sustained the license fee as the income source for the BBC, the latter hoped to generate a fifth of its income from alternative means by the year 2000, a rather optimistic view. The main alternative income provider is *BBC Worldwide*, the department responsible for the international and commercial activities of the BBC. It was launched in 1994, integrating BBC World Service Television, World Service Radio and BBC Enterprises. BBC Worldwide Limited generated an additional income of € 133 million in 1999/2000, the largest part of which is accounted for by television sales and subscription and advertising revenues from the BBC's commercial channels. Online shopping and computer games as spin-offs of successful television programs are the latest additions to BBC Worldwide. Another BBC commercial subsidiary is *BBC Resources Limited*, which provides facilities and other program resources to internal and external services.

The main income source for the commercial television stations is, of course, advertising. There is some sponsoring, but this is only marginal in comparison with other countries.

Table 5. *Terrestrial Television Advertising Revenue (in €million)*

	1992	1993	1994	1995	1996	1997	1998	1999
ITV	2,411	2,374	2,554	2,700	2,814	2,843	3,023	3,145
Channel 4	393	532	634	723	793	827	897	957
S4C	5	6	10	13	13	15	15	15
Channel 5							230	303
Total	2,809	2,912	3,198	3,436	3,620	3,685	4,165	4,420

Source: ITC

World Service cutbacks coincide with the build-up of the BBC's international, profit-seeking cooperation with Pearson. It appears that the ethos of public service stops at the UK's borders. This is indicative of a substantial ideological shift within the BBC. Although on many occasions the BBC World Service might justifiably be accused of 'media imperialism,' of still believing in the 'white man's burden,' some journalists have sought to challenge this hegemonic position from within. Capitalism now appears to be far more important than colonialism and this might result in the total suppression of already marginal voices of resistance. For this reason, the debate about the future of the

World Service is interesting in that one can observe an uneasy alliance of right and left in opposition to the cutbacks, a 'negative consensus' based on radically different attitudes towards colonialism.

Each of the ITV licensees generates its own income within its area. But the advertising business has not been kind to ITV. Its share of the terrestrial television advertising market has dropped from 85% in 1991 to 66% six years later, thus landing many of the franchisees into trouble. "The 1990 Act was designed in the middle of a boom in advertising revenue but came into force in the middle of a recession which had a severe effect on advertising. As a consequence, some of the financial projections upon which bids for franchises were made turned out to be too optimistic" (Sparks, 1995: 330). The prospects for ITV companies are not very bright, bearing in mind the creation of new competitor Channel Five and the increasing popularity of Channel Four among advertisers (which provides them with an affluent professional audience).

Channel Four's financing mechanism has drastically changed as a result of the 1990 Broadcasting Act. Before the Act the channel was only indirectly funded by advertising. The ITV licensees funded the channel and in return gained the right to sell Channel Four's advertising time, each in its own region. This system was devised to guarantee the autonomy of Channel Four and to preserve its distinctive character. Since January 1993, however, Channel Four has been responsible for generating its own income by selling advertising time. But if Channel Four's advertising revenue share is under 14%, its income has to be supplemented by the ITV companies. If the channel exceeds the 14% threshold it has to donate 50% of its surplus to the commercial companies. Because the latter has been the case since the new mechanism was introduced, Channel Four has been forced to pay large amounts of money to the ITV franchisees (up to € 125 million in 1996).

Channel Four launched a vigorous campaign against the new financial scheme with moderate success. The 1996 Broadcasting Act alters the mechanism slightly. Channel Four no longer automatically needs to pay 50% of its surplus to ITV. Starting in 1998, the government was to decide each year which percentage of the surplus should be handed over. Even though this change was meant to work to the advantage of Channel Four, the station was not too happy about it as it created an unwelcome dependency on the goodwill of the government. In the end this financial flow was stopped and Channel Four made its last payment (€ 107 million) to ITV in 1999. There have been many acrimonious encounters between the poorer ITV companies and Channel Four over this issue as the poorer companies depend on Channel Four's money for survival. Channel Four was even being accused of pandering to a popular market by increasing the number of US programs in order to raise audience share. This should disabuse anyone of the notion that there is a clear line of demarcation in the UK's broadcasting duopoly between public service, on the one side, and commercial interests, on the other, for here we have commercial stations arguing about who best serves the public interest in order to deserve increased resources. Indeed, one would be hard pressed to see a clear distinction on the basis of channel programming. In the long run, this trend must be worrying for the BBC since it makes it unclear why its special status should continue. This suggests that, if the BBC is to survive in the face of increasing competition, it needs to change its identity.

The new Channel Five was seen as another major threat to ITV's income, although many commentators questioned the viability of the latest terrestrial channel. Its license has, for example, been described as a license to lose money. The expansion of the advertising market is not endless (although the percentage of GDP spent on advertising is much lower in the UK and the rest of Europe generally than in the US), but the biggest problem was the huge capital investments Channel Five had to undertake even before it started broadcasting. All British videotape recorders had to be retuned due to disturbances caused by the Channel Five signal, which set the channel back some € 113 million. Even then the channel only reached about half of the British households (80% by the end of 1997). The financial problems attendant to the launch of a new station had caused many candidates to withdraw their bids and led to a second licensing round in 1995 after no viable candidates entered in 1992. Out of four candidates, Channel Five Broadcasting, a consortium made up of United Broadcasting and Entertainment, Pearson, and the Luxembourg-based CLT-UFA, was chosen as the new channel's franchisee, with a € 36 million bid. Initial pessimism about the viability of Channel Five has quietly faded as the station slowly found its place in the viewers' and advertisers' markets.

Commercial radio is mainly funded by advertising. As might be expected, since the launch of three independent national radio stations, the radio advertising market has been growing the fastest, although it is still relatively small compared to television, newspapers and magazines. By 1998 radio had cornered close to 5% of the advertising market.

Direct-to-home satellite services started in 1989. Before that satellite channels relied on cable to reach British audiences. Cable and satellite channels are mainly funded through subscription fees. Satellite, cable and digital revenue (advertising, sponsorship and subscription) have been growing considerably in the last few years.

Table 6. *Satellite, Cable and Digital Revenue (in €million)*[3]

1991	1992	1993	1994	1995	1996	1997	1998	1999
227	496	764	1,117	1,595	2,167	2,783	3,235	3,476

Source: ITC

IV   Anti-Trust and Cross-Ownership Laws

The 1990 Broadcasting Act includes several restrictions on holding commercial television and radio licenses. Non-EEC nationals, bodies having political connections, religious bodies, advertising agencies and public broadcasting bodies like the BBC and the Welsh Authority cannot be granted a license for both commercial television and radio.

---

[3] Advertising revenue, sponsorship and subscription income. Excludes revenue from overseas audiences.

More important are the restrictions imposed to prevent accumulations of interests. One person or group may only control two regional ITV licenses or one national ITV license although it is likely that such restrictions will be lifted in the future given the contents of the 2000 Communications White Paper. Furthermore, ownership of radio licenses is restricted to one in the case of a national service and twenty in the case of a regional service. The 1990 Broadcasting Act was an act of deregulation since, prior to 1990, companies could hold only 1 regional license. Holders of two regional or one national ITV license or the Channel Five license may not have more than a 20% interest in any corporate body which holds a license to provide a service falling within either of the two other categories. A similar restriction limits cross-ownership of television and radio licenses. A license holder may not have a stake of over 20% in a license to provide a different service. The same goes for owners of a satellite service license. They may not own more than 20% of a terrestrial service. Finally, the Act also sets limits on controlling interests in both newspapers and licensed services. The owner of a national or local newspaper may only have a 20% stake in a television or radio service. Furthermore owners of a national newspaper may not have a stake above 5% if they already have a 5% stake in another license. The same applies for license holders – they may not have more than a 20% interest in a national or local newspaper and they may participate in no more than two national newspaper corporations provided both stakes do not exceed the 5% rule. Again, it is likely that rules governing cross-media ownership will be relaxed in the future in favor of regulations that calculate the total voice (i.e., all media taken cumulatively) controlled by corporations. This significant shift is foreseen in the 2000 Communications White Paper.

The Conservative government led by John Major did not stop there, however, and further deregulated the broadcasting market. Following the *Green Paper on Media Ownership* the Department of National Heritage (which gained responsibility for the media only a few years ago), introduced a new Bill in 1995 and this was subsequently enacted in slightly amended form in 1996. This Act has and will continue to have a major impact on the British media landscape. It aims to strengthen the position of the British entertainment industry in the global media market. Increased deregulation at lower levels has led to a spate of takeovers, mergers and joint ventures. The most critical reaction to the Act has come from media tycoon Rupert Murdoch since greater restrictions have been effectively placed on companies already dominant in the media market. Murdoch's company, News Corp, was restricted in its desire to gain a firmer grip on British broadcasting by newspaper owners who control more than 20% of the market being forbidden to participate in regional or national Channel Three or Channel Five, or a national or local radio station. Others can participate freely and can control up to 15% of the television or radio market. Under this rule Murdoch's News Corp has a 37% newspaper market share, and the Mirror Group, a 26% cross-media ownership in Britain (Doyle, 1996). Similarly, broadcasters who have a share of over 15% in the radio or television market may not have an interest in newspapers. Other major changes include a new maximum of owning 35 local radio licenses instead of 20 and the reservation of exclusive rights for eight major sports events for terrestrial television. The most important change, however, is the new concentration policy concerning terrestrial broadcasting. ITV production companies are no longer limited to a maximum of two regional licenses, but can now control up to 15% of the total television audience market. Since ITV has a share of about 30 to 35%, this means that a single company can own up to five or six licenses and that the whole ITV network could fall into the hands of three major groups, such as Granada, Carlton, or United Broadcasting and Entertainment. A deal was already made that could create one of Britain's most powerful entertainment groups, even before the Bill was passed. United News and Media and the MAI group merged in 1996 to create United Broadcasting and Entertainment, a corporation which owns newspapers (Daily Express, Sunday Express, Daily Star), several magazines, three ITV licenses (Meridian, Anglia, and HTV), and an important stake in the new Channel Five.

It seems clear, then, that while the main political parties are suspicious of allowing one or two huge concerns to dominate the UK's national media landscape, there is a trend towards the creation of much larger media enterprises with interests in a number of different media. The intention is partly to strengthen the position of UK media in both domestic and international markets and to facilitate more equitable competition between News Corp, the Mirror Group, and the rest.

V   Media Economics: Local/Global Media Moguls

The United Kingdom has a long tradition of media moguls and today the world's major media players are very active in British broadcasting. Rupert Murdoch owns a range of satellite channels under the name of BSkyB and Pearson has a stake in the international and commercial activities of the BBC. In addition, new faces have emerged over the last few years, due to continuous liberalization of cross-ownership and media concentration rules. United Broadcasting and Entertainment, Granada, and Carlton are already a household name in their own country and are seeking a place in the international market.

Rupert Murdoch is one of the biggest names in global media economics today, owning a vast amount of newspapers and television stations in a variety of countries. In 1997 his News Corp was the second largest multimedia company in the world, with a turnover of €14,240 million, almost 60% of which comes from its audiovisual interests (European Audiovisual Observatory, 1999). Murdoch's interest in British broadcasting is at the moment limited to 40% of BSkyB, the major satellite broadcaster. The Sky channels were launched in 1988 and merged two years later with their financially troubled competitor, British Satellite Broadcasting, in which Pearson had a stake, to form BSkyB, which now has an audience of about 5 million and made a €172 million profit in 1995. Murdoch's attempts to win a share in terrestrial broadcasting have been as yet unsuccessful. The 1996 Broadcasting Act prohibits Murdoch from obtaining a stake in regional or national Channel Three or Channel Five terrestrial television, since he controls more than 20% of the newspaper market with The Times, The Sunday Times, The Sun, and News of the World.

Pearson is best known for its stakes in the financial press, but has become an increasingly important force in broadcasting. Even before Pearson became a major player in British broadcasting, the company was 20th in the list of top multimedia companies with sales of €2,058 million in 1993 (European Audiovisual Observatory, 1994). Then the Pearson group acquired British company Thames TV, a former ITV member and now the largest independent producer, and Australian television company Grundig. In addition to its stake in BSkyB (which it recently sold to Vivendi) Pearson has become very active in terrestrial broadcasting, with stakes in the ITV company Yorkshire Television as well as the latest terrestrial station, Channel Five. Through Thames Television Pearson had a share in satellite channels UK Gold and UK Living (which were sold in 1997 to Flextech), joining forces with the BBC. This led to a major, €49 million deal in 1994 between Pearson and the public broadcaster, resulting in the launch of news channel BBC World, which can be viewed by close to 170 million homes all over the world, and entertainment channel BBC Prime, which is only available in Europe and sub-Saharan Africa.

The continuing trend towards less stringent anti-trust and cross-ownership rules have permitted new media moguls to emerge, especially among the ITV companies. The 1990 Broadcasting Act changed the procedure for ITV licensing, awarding the license to the highest bidder. Many of the smaller companies became financially very vulnerable after the licensing round, while the bigger companies were anxious to raise their interest in commercial television. After a number of takeovers three major groups now control the ITV network with two major licenses each. In addition, they all have stakes in other ITV franchisees. The 1996 Broadcasting Act allows even further takeovers, any company can control up to 15% of the total television market, which means it can control almost half of ITV's audience. The following concerns have thus emerged as major players in the field of UK media:

- In 1996, television group MAI merged with Lord Stevens's United News and Media which controls 13% of the newspaper market. Under its new name United Broadcasting and Entertainment, this is one of the largest entertainment groups in the country. It holds the ITV license for the South-Eastern region of England and the Anglia license, thus controlling Eastern England, with the exception of the London area. With the take-over of HTV the number of licensees under United control went up to three, giving United a share of about 7% of the television market. United Broadcasting and Entertainment also has a stake in Channel Five. In 1997 the company was 29th on the list of top European audiovisual companies with a total yearly turnover of €3.2 billion, of which €637 million is generated by the company's audiovisual activities (European Audiovisual Observatory, 1999).

- Michael Green's media company Carlton Communications obtained the license for London (weekdays), outbidding Thames Television, one of the pillars of ITV. After taking over Central (Central England) and Westcountry (Western England) it now controls about 9% of the television market. The company also owns a cable entertainment network, SelecTV, now renamed Carlton Select. With a turnover of €3.2 billion Carlton is the 19th largest audiovisual company in the world, the 7th largest in Europe (European Audiovisual Observatory, 1999).

- Granada Media Group is the media arm of a hotel and leisure giant. It has long been the licensee for the North West region of England and later obtained LWT (London Weekend Television), Yorkshire Television and Tyne Tees Television, thus controlling 4 ITV licensees – over 10% of the television market. Granada Vision is a division that explores the market for new channels, both in the UK and overseas. With BSkyB it formed Granada Sky Broadcasting which launched three new satellite services in October 1996. On the list of top audiovisual companies Granada can be found at number 38 (17th in Europe) with a turnover of €7.4 billion (European Audiovisual Observatory, 1999).
- The Scottish Media Group is Scotland's leading media group; its main shareholders are cable operator Flextech and the Mirror Group. The Scottish Media Group has an interest in regional newspapers and controls the two Scottish ITV franchisees, Grampian and STV.

Continuous rumors about impending mergers (United Broadcasting and Entertainment + Carlton; Granada + Scottish Media Group) indicate that further concentration within ITV is very likely.

Channel Four is another big name in the world's audiovisual market. According to the European Audiovisual Observatory (1999) the broadcaster is the 46th largest audiovisual company in the world (21st in Europe), with a turnover of €1000 million in 1997.

The biggest name in British broadcasting remains, however, the British Broadcasting Corporation. The BBC is also a major international radio and television player. In 1997 it was nineteenth on the list of the world's top multimedia companies and the fourth largest European audiovisual company (turnover of €4.8 billion). Furthermore, it remains Europe's main exporter of programs (European Audiovisual Observatory, 1999). In 1995 it launched BBC World, an international news channel which broadcasts 24 hours a day, and BBC Prime, an entertainment channel. Two years later the Corporation closed a deal with Flextech, which is controlled by American cable giant TCI, and launched several thematic pay-TV channels under the name UKTV: UK Arena (art), UK Style (life-style), and UK Horizons (nature). A deal with the Discovery Channel strengthened the BBC's position in the United States. Discovery distributes BBC America (a best-of channel) to 11 million American homes. The Corporation is also making a name for itself in the area of digital broadcasting with six digital television channels (BBC Choice, BBC Knowledge, BBC News 24, BBC Parliament, BBC One Widescreen, and BBC Two Widescreen) as well as a digital news 'Teletext' service (BBC Text). Its Web site (BBC Online) consists of one million pages and is the most used non-portal site outside the US.

The British radio market also has its own moguls. Some of the biggest international media groups invest in British radio, such as Time-Warner (Classic FM), Virgin (Virgin

Radio) and CanWest (Talk Radio). The major radio broadcaster after the BBC, however, is local radio station group GWR which also recently took over the leading national commercial radio station Classic FM, which has an audience of about 4.6 million in the UK. Classic FM has met with some success broadcasting to other European countries such as the Netherlands. GWR has 32 local licenses with a total audience of over 14 million and owns Prospect, New Zealand's largest commercial radio group. In 1997, however, GWR was forced by the Radio Authority to sell off some licenses since its audience share had grown to 17.6%, which is well over the 15% limit.

VI Media Content

From the beginnings of independent television, in the early 1950's, until 1990, broadcasters had to comply with the 86/14 rule, which stated that at least 86% of programming in evening peak time has to be of British origin. Outside peak time the required percentage was 70%. This rule survived until 1990. Now British television channels are required to broadcast a minimum of 51% of programs of European origin, although loopholes in the previous 'Television without Frontiers' Directive (1989) have been taken advantage of by broadcasters.

The terrestrial channels mostly comply with these quota. Two thirds of BBC 1 and 2's program supply originate in the EU, while for commercial broadcasters the figures range from 70% (ITV) to 65% (Channel Four) to 53% (Channel Five). Although American products are broadcast and some are very successful, a high percentage of peak time programs are homemade and even more successful. BBC 1 has a new UK made output in peak time of 83%, against 60% for BBC 2.77% for ITV and 56% for Channel Four, giving the BBC an overall percentage of 72% of new UK made productions in peak time, while terrestrial commercial television has 67% (BBC, 1996). Taking into account the fact that repeats of UK made programs are not included and that both BBC 2 and Channel Four broadcast a large amount of European programs, there is absolutely no question of a complete Americanization of British television. Out of all fiction programs aired on British television, only a marginal percentage is US made. For the public broadcaster the figures are 17.2% (BBC 1) and 14.2% (BBC 2), while for the private channels the percentage is 17.5% (ITV), 26.2% (C4) and 19.3% (C5) (European Audiovisual Observatory, 1999). It is worth noting, however, that Channel Four's British content output has declined over the past year and that there is a definite increase in American programs on that station. But US made programs are not so much of a threat for national culture in the UK as elsewhere since both countries share the same language.

British media legislation does not set out quotas of categories of programs which should be broadcast. The government mostly leaves content up to the BBC and the Independent Television Commission (ITC), trusting them to make sure that programming is varied. Only Channel Four is legally obliged to provide at least four hours of news, four hours of current affairs and seven hours of educational programming per week; in general, however, there are only a few obligations about religious programs and Party Political Broadcasts. As we have seen before, a lack of a precise policy is not at all a sign for uniform and mostly populist programming. The BBC and ITV set their own (high) standards.

The government does, however, enforce rules of taste and decency. There is, for example, the so-called 9:00 p.m. 'watershed'; "after this time, it is assumed that progressively more adult material may be shown and it is assumed that parents may reasonably be expected to share responsibility for what their children are permitted to see" (Alvarado, Locksley & Paskin, 1992: 305). There are, additionally, a number of organizations which make sure that the broadcasters comply with legislation and which can take action if they do not. One of them is the Broadcasting Standards Council (BSC) whose main task is to assess the quality of programs and, more specifically, police the portrayal of sex and violence. The Broadcasting Complaints Commission (BCC) deals with any complaints from individuals or groups about unfair treatment or invasion of privacy. Besides these two bodies the Welsh Fourth Channel Authority, Radio Authority, ITC and BBC Program Complaints Unit have a similar task. A parliamentary commission suggested a merger between BSC and BCC to integrate similar tasks into one body. Blumler (1995: 369) also suggests a single body. "The duties proposed for such a body include: handling complaints from viewers; monitoring programming and scheduling trends as television channels proliferate and compete for audiences; and serving as a forum for regularly raising and debating issues of broadcasting development, policy and adequacy of service over a wide field." The 1996 Broadcasting Act created a new statutory body for standards and fairness in UK broadcasting: the Broadcasting Standards Commission. Its three main tasks are to produce guidelines relating to standards and fairness, to monitor, research and report on such issues, and to adjudicate on complaints. There are thirteen Commissioners, who are appointed by the Secretary of State for Culture, Media and Sport.

Although British media content is of a high standard and certain developments witnessed in other countries have yet to find their way fully to the UK, there is some concern about a decline in programming and scheduling standards. Kilborn (1996: 142), for example, speaks of the "tabloid-ization of factual programming." The new financing mechanism of Channel Four has led to the raising of a number of concerns in recent years. In its early years the station was widely praised by many authors. "It has not just added quantity to our television mix, or indeed quality. More importantly, it has brought variety and diversity (...), freshness and vitality" (Whitney, 1985: 3). Now, however, several authors have expressed their concerns about the road currently being traveled by Channel Four. Kilborn (1996: 144) claims that "even Channel Four, which since its inception has been particularly committed to the documentary, may no longer be the Eldorado it once appeared to be, now that market place pressures are beginning to exert their influence." Dunne (1994: 45) states that "in order to continue producing programs that honor the remit, Channel Four is using more populist programming to subsidize their 'worthier' efforts." The Independent Television Commission noticed some decline in quality as well, reprimanding the channel for "lack of taste and decency" in The Word in 1994 and for broadcasting too many repeats. The channel does however maintain its distinctive character as Dunne (1994: 46) admits: "The channel's new direction is, in the main, financial, its programming remains innovative and, to a great extent, faithful to the altruistic ideals of 1982."

Table 7. *Network Output Analysis BBC 1*

	1993/94	1994/95	1995/96	1996/97	1997/98[4]	1998/99
Informative[5]	38.9	43.6	40.6	38.1	65.2	63.8
Narrative[6]	25.3	26.6	27.0	27.8	4.7	5.7
Entertainment	7.8	7.9	8.3	9.1	11.6	10.7
Sport	10.0	10.2	8.3	12.3	8.9	8.9
Children	13.0	11.7	11.6	9.5	8.0	7.2
Other[7]	5.0	5.0	4.2	3.2	1.6	3.7

Source: BBC

Table 8. *Network Output Analysis BBC 2*

	1993/94	1994/95	1995/96	1996/97	1997/98	1998/99
Informative	47.6	46.7	49.3	49.6	66.8	66.9
Narrative	22.8	22.2	19.1	17.2	1.6	1.2
Entertainment	3.7	4.8	4.8	4.6	7.6	6.7
Sport	14.8	12.7	12.2	10.9	12.8	14.1
Children	3.7	5.8	6.2	8.8	6.6	6.8
Other	7.5	7.8	8.4	8.9	4.6	4.3

Source: BBC

Table 9. *Network Output Analysis ITV*

	1992	1993	1994	1995	1996	1997	1998	1999
Informative	32.2	32.7	30.7	32.1	34.0	36.1	38.8	41.7
Narrative	35.7	34.0	34.9	34.5	34.5	33.9	30.3	27.6
Entertainment	18.4	15.4	16.0	16.6	16.2	14.5	11.9	10.5
Sport	5.7	5.9	6.3	5.6	4.5	5.2	8.2	8.9
Children	7.9	9.6	9.0	8.7	8.6	7.9	8.3	8.9
Other	0.0	2.4	3.1	2.5	2.2	2.4	2.5	2.4

Source: ITC

---

[4] Since 1997/1998 the BBC no longer takes acquired programs into account in its network output analysis, which explains the strong decline in narrative programs.

[5] Including news and current affairs, factual programs, arts and religion, documentaries, education (incl. Open University), parliamentary broadcasting and weather.

[6] Including drama, feature films and teleseries.

[7] Including presentation and continuity.

Table 10. *Network Output Analysis Channel Four*

	1992	1993	1994	1995	1996	1997	1998	1999
Informative	35.4	29.6	32.1	32.6	31.3	32.5	31.2	33.4
Narrative	28.3	24.9	25.9	29.5	33.2	30.1	30.7	26.1
Entertainment	18.6	20.9	21.6	20.7	18.5	18.6	16.9	21.0
Sport	7.8	9.2	8.6	9.2	9.2	10.0	9.9	10.0
Children	9.8	13.6	11.1	7.4	7.3	8.4	11.0	9.2
Other	0.1	1.8	0.7	0.0	0.5	0.4	0.3	0.3

Source: ITC

Table 11. *Network Output Analysis – Channel Five*

	1997	1998	1999
Informative	25.6	24.0	25.9
Narrative	36.9	39.6	39.2
Entertainment	14.3	11.4	9.8
Sport	13.8	14.1	14.6
Children	9.4	10.9	10.5
Other	0.0	0.0	0.0

Source: ITC

VII   The Future of British Broadcasting

As in many other countries almost all broadcasters see their future in digital broadcasting. The digital revolution raises high hopes with some authors. Clemens (1996: 7) predicts a British media landscape "where consumer demand can be identified and personally targeted via huge computerized database, where telecoms can link consumers anywhere in the world and where the supply of information is limited only by what can be provided 'economically', that is at a price consumers are prepared to pay." Authors have different opinions about the potential impact of digital subscription and pay-per-view channels on the existing national PSB channels. Clemens (1996) again predicts that specialist channels will be very successful with advertisers, enabling them to buy the best movies, sport, music, or even news.

British audiences seem to be adjusting quickly to the digital revolution. The number of subscribers has been boosted by vigorous competition between the two main commercial digital broadcasters: Sky Digital (satellite) and ONdigital (terrestrial), which resulted in the giving away of set-top boxes for free. By the end of 1999 16% of British homes were already receiving digital television, provided either by the BBC or by one of the commercial broadcasters. Sky Digital launched in October 1998 had 3.6 million subscribers by June 30 2000 and expected 5 million by calendar year end. Ondigital launched in November 1998 had 774,000 subscribers by June 30, 2000 and expected 1 million by calendar year end. The various cable operators had 400,000 subscribers by

June 30, 2000. Twenty percent of UK households received digital TV as of June 30, 2000.

This unexpectedly fast take-up prompted the government to announce that the process of switching over completely from analogue to digital television could commence as early as 2006 and could be finished by 2010, at which point analogue television would cease to exist, provided 95% of the population have access to digital equipment at that time. As might be expected, the government is keen to benefit financially from the sale of the spectrum previously allocated to terrestrial analogue television.

The first project was that of Rupert Murdoch's BSkyB, which launched its digital satellite package in October 1998 with 140 channels. One year later Sky Digital announced 1.8 million people had subscribed to the digital package, which was well above its own expectations.

The 1996 Broadcasting Act contains a number of provisions about digital terrestrial television. The Act proposed to establish six multiplexes with at least three channels each. The BBC was allocated the multiplex with the largest coverage. The other five multiplexes were to be awarded by the ITC although two of these were legally reserved for ITV and Channel Four (for this purpose they have set up a joint venture called Digital 3 & 4), while Channel Five and S4C (the Welsh equivalent of Channel Four) got the other multiplex (allocated to S4C Digital Network). The remaining three multiplexes were awarded by the ITC to British Digital Broadcasting (BDB) in 1997. BDB later changed its name into ONdigital and launched its services in November 1998. ONdigital is a joint venture of Granada Media Group and Carlton Communications. BskyB was involved as well, but pulled out following objections expressed by the ITC. After the operating licenses, eighteen content licenses were allocated to a wide range of licensees (including some of the major ITV franchisees as well as BSkyB). These licensees can cover a number of services on the different multiplexes. They must contract with the multiplex operators for a place on the platform (ITC, 2000).

The *Radio Authority* has granted one license for Digital Audio Broadcasting (DAB) so far. *Digital One*, controlled by the largest commercial radio group (GWR), received this license in October 1998 and offers the three national, commercial channels and some other new radio services. Some local digital radio licenses have been awarded as well.

Cable broadcasting has not been very successful so far and is likely to suffer in future with increased competition from both satellite and digital terrestrial channels. Nearly 3.3 million homes now subscribe to cable television. Cable operators, many of which are of American origin, all offer up to 45 channels to their subscribers, for a total of almost 100 cable television channels and 15 cable radio channels. Some of these cable channels could justifiably be described as 'original and innovative,' such as Live TV, owned by the Mirror Group, with its programs *Topless Darts* or *Fate and Fortune*, a fortune telling show. Only after cable telephone services started to appear did cable become moderately successful; still, the much touted 'multimedia' services have not really been implemented by cable operators. ITC's Jon Davey comments "cable operators are firmly in the fairly traditional business of distributing television channels and providing a telephone service (…). There is little that can be seen as innovative" (Davey, 1996: 5).

VIII Public Service in the Age of Digital Services

The seemingly inevitable drift towards an essentially commercial digital broadcast system raises the question of the future of public service broadcasting in Britain, particularly, but not solely, the license-fee funded BBC. The Labour Party has traditionally sought to defend public service broadcasting, or at least the idea of public service broadcasting, from its right-wing critics while seeking to open the doors of the BBC to voices that might be more supportive of the social democratic political project. With the 'modernization' of the Labour Party in the UK and the election of a Labour Government in 1997 the debate has shifted grounds somewhat. The Labour Government now seems more supportive of the ambitions of commercial media for both straightforwardly electoral reasons and for reasons to do with wealth creation (the 'information' revolution is often presented as the motor of economic change). All this points to a regulatory light touch while doing enough to keep public service ticking over to appease the government's traditional social democratic supporters and to correct 'market failure.'

Chris Smith in his speech to the Royal Television Society in October 1998 reaffirmed the principles of public service in the changed multi-channel environment. It is worth listing the elements that define the role of the BBC according to the present government. The BBC should:

5. be a benchmark for quality;
1. provide something for everyone, making the good popular and the popular good;
2. inform, educate, entertain, expanding people's horizons with new and innovative programming;
3. operate efficiently and effectively and provide value for money;
4. stimulate, support and reflect the diversity of cultural activity in the UK, acting as a cultural voice for the nation.

For Smith, the BBC should be the social glue or cement of the nation, it should bring people together in front of the electronic hearth. The BBC has just about retained audience share in recent years. The ITV companies have lost market share to cable, satellite and other terrestrial channels. This may, however, have something to do with social class of cable and satellite subscribers and their previous viewing habits. The greater penetration of digital services in the next few years might lead to a declining BBC market share and the rise of niche programming and channels on digital format. However, the BBC's reach appears secure. In times of crisis or catastrophe, it arguably can still fulfil its adhesive function.

It would be fair to say that public service broadcasters do not quite know how to respond to the threat of losing market share. It is seen as crucial for their survival that the universal license fee remains intact. However, it is uncertain whether public service broadcasters can maintain their audience-share in a multi-channel environment. BBC 1, the major general channel, now has an audience share of about 28%, while BBC 2 has a share of about 10%. As Brian Winston points out, in such circumstances it is wise of the BBC to place emphasis on the inevitability of its declining audience-share in this new environment. This lesson is not lost on John Birt, the former BBC Director General, who sought to justify the BBC in terms of reach rather than audience-share (currently about 92% of the UK population tune in for at least three minutes per week to BBC broadcasts). Evidence from the USA, however, where there has been a multi-channel environment for a number of years, suggests that the large networks do not suffer that badly. Consequently, if the BBC only loses a few percentage points, it looks as though it has been performing well when, in fact, it has more to do with viewing habits formed over many years of monopoly. That said, the BBC does appear to be sitting uncomfortably on the horns of a dilemma. If it competes with popular commercial channels, it does not appear as though viewers are really getting anything more from their license fee. If it concentrates on providing programs that for commercial reasons cannot be found on private TV, it will have a relatively small audience share. In such circumstances, the majority of viewers might feel as though they are not getting their money's worth. The strategy of the BBC so far (and one that is mirrored by most public service broadcasters) is to compete with popular private television in terms of programming while also attempting to provide programs which, while they might not be commercially viable, are justified in terms of some 'public good' which accrues from their transmission, the 'Heineken' approach of reaching parts that commercial broadcasters do not wish to reach. This strategy is not *entirely* wrong. John Keane argues that "public service media should certainly serve minorities and circulate knowledge and culture, and stimulate criticism and experimentation, even slapping the face of public taste as often as possible. But they must do more than that. Public service media should build on the 'decommodifying' achievements of the original public sphere model, *all the while acknowledging that it has now slipped into a profound and irreversible crisis*" [emphasis added] (1991: 126). This is a recognition of the undesirability of creating a challenging public service that challenges only a small percentage of the population. Such a move would effectively deliver the large majority of the audience to the private sector. Any change must be gradual and cumulative. We disagree with Keane's belief that the decline of the public sphere is irreversible. Epistemological certainty about the present is tenuous at best, and future developments are anybody's guess. The problem is that public service is responding to the new digital environment along commercial and not democratic lines. This in itself is indicative of a sea change that has occurred in EU societies since the mid-1970's. It is here that pressure must be brought to bear in order that these potentials may be exploited for the benefit of democratic culture and politics.

This traditional conception of the nation-building function of the BBC is matched with a Reithian approach to cultural value. The distinctions between high and low culture have certainly not broken down in the Department of Culture, Media and Sport (DCMS). The good is likely to be unpopular, so this line of reasoning goes, because of the inadequacies, the lack of taste, of the people and so the BBC must strive to educate their taste. Smith goes on the say that it is to be expected that the BBC will lose audience share in the future but that does not cast its future into doubt as long as it can remain true to its traditional ethos: "What it needs most to retain public confidence is to continue to be true to its distinctive public service ethos and program range… That way, it will continue to sustain near universal reach and its near universal public respect" (1998). This is shorthand for the BBC retaining its distinctiveness i.e. no advertising, no subscriptions and for not succumbing to the temptations of other broadcasters in the search of market share. The implication is that the BBC is becoming too similar to commercial broadcasters in its attempt to maintain market share and by doing so places its future at risk.

One of the key decisions that Smith or his successor is faced with is the date of analogue switch-off. Commercial broadcasters are pushing for an early switch-off date in order to encourage consumers to switch as soon as possible. National Economic Research Associates (NERA) and Smith Systems Engineering delivered a report to DCMS and the Radio Communications Agency in January 1998 on the costs and possible timing of switch-over and switch-off. Basing their predictions on the history of color television, they forecast that it will take until 2013 to reach either 90% (lower forecast) or 100% (higher forecast) digital penetration of the broadcasting market. Take-up, they argue, will be gradual because based on the replacement of sets which they believe will remain constant at a new one every eight years. Consequently, the net costs to households is relatively small, roughly € 1.6–3.2 billion. They also point to the economic advantages of early switch-off to the state in terms of the revenue generated by the auction of the spectrum currently used by analogue television for mobile communications. They conclude that, while switch-off is unfeasible within five years, it is possible on a 10 to 15 year time scale. This means that switch-off will likely take place in the early years of the 2006 BBC Charter and raises the question of how the migration of the BBC to a digital environment is to be funded from now until then. Consequently, Smith set up an Independent Review Panel – chaired by Goldman Sachs chief economist Gavyn Davies, a former advisor to the 1974–79 Wilson and Callaghan governments and a friend of new Labour – with a view to inquiring into the future funding of the BBC. The panel reported in July 1999.

As Brian Winston pointed out some years ago and as the Davies Panel quickly recognized, the funding of the BBC is obviously dependent on the role one sees it playing in society at large: "the question of the license fee is whether or not the concept of public service broadcasting is a viable one for the twenty-first century. That is the central issue of the real agenda" (1994: 31).

The Davies Panel Report clearly belongs to the current trend of seeing little or no contradiction in a mixed economy of broadcasting where public and private sectors apparently complement each other. The argument against the BBC having commercial interests is seen by the Panel purely in terms of old-fashioned elitism, part of the British disease of disdain for the profit motive. They praise, therefore, the developments that have taken place in the last fifteen years or so in the BBC such as the introduction of Producer Choice and BBC Worldwide. The BBC "was snooty about the need to generate commercial revenues" (1999: 7). But no longer.

The BBC's share of revenue accruing to broadcasters has fallen quite rapidly between 1993 and 1998 from 42% to 31% while market share has declined slightly, from 43% to 41% (1999: 48). However, predicted revenue shares are expected to decline at a slightly faster rate owing to the deal struck as part of the 1996 Charter, which allowed for real income increases in the early years in order to pave the way for the switch-over to digital broadcasting but allowed for no subsequent, real income growth from license fees. If the conditions of the 1996 Charter were to be adhered to, BBC revenue would increase in real terms by about 0.45% per annum between 1998 and 2008, as opposed to 7% in the private sector. Another factor that needs taking into account is the predicted 'super-inflation' in the costs of talent and programming rights because of increased competition (if diversity will accompany digital television, why is the price of talent and programs escalating?).

To make up ground the BBC asked the government for an extra €972 million per annum in order to deliver more digital services and compete for talent and programs. The intention is to develop BBC Choice into a fully-fledged third channel aimed at the younger citizen and expand education and World Wide Web (WWW) provision (this dovetails nicely with new Labour's knowledge economy, information society, etc., rhetoric). The Davies Panel recommends that an extra €243–324 million per annum be given to the BBC and expects the BBC to generate around €162 million per annum through savings and commercial activities (primarily through halving the number of employees of the Broadcasting Center, which currently accounts for 3% of the BBC's budget, making more profit from BBC Worldwide, and selling off part of BBC Resources). This would give the BBC a real income growth of 3.5% per annum until 2006 (1999: 55).

The extra €243–324 million is to be raised through charging digital viewers an additional license fee of, on average, €2.54 per month. The actual figure will of course depend on the number of digital households – the fee will decrease in later years as their numbers increase. The Panel rejected the idea that there should be an across-the-board increase to the license fee for both analogue and digital as this would appear unfair to analogue-equipped households who cannot receive the digital services. The precedence of differential charging, the Panel argues, was established for TV licenses and then for the switch-over from monochrome to color TV.

The two most interesting issues raised in the report pertain to the importance of online activities with respect to future notions of public service and the scope of BBC activities. In its search for ways in which the BBC could raise revenue, the Panel even considered the possibility of privatizing the highly successful BBC On-line operation (which received around 100 million hits per month in 1999). While this is suggested for non-UK on-line services, privatization of the UK sites is rejected as the Panel sees such work as becoming central to the role of the BBC in the future. Although this is not mentioned in the report, the on-line services allow for a different kind of relationship between institution and citizen. Rather than simply supply the finished product, as it were, the BBC can play an enabling role, providing a platform that allows citizens to communicate with one another. This issue is flagged up with a view to a future review of broadcast legislation: "Perhaps also the government should look at whether to require Internet access in the basic packages of services offered by the three digital platforms [i.e., terrestrial, cable and satellite] after the analogue signal is switched over" (1999: 79). Internet access as a universal service obligation would undoubtedly be a step in the right direction.

The Panel also stumbled across the perennial questions concerning the nature of public service and its purpose. Panel members seem to think they know what public service broadcasting is when they see it, but are not convinced that BBC employees can do the same. Thus, clearer criteria and performance criteria are requested. Once a blueprint becomes available, they should adhere to it more closely: "The Board of Governors should insist on clearer criteria for what the BBC is doing and continue to shift its focus towards its distinctive strengths" (1999: 35). The problem with this pared down vision of the BBC is its conservatism. Rather we should ask: what role could the BBC play in developing a participatory public culture? This would necessitate finding new strengths rather than simply playing to old ones.

The Davies Panel's muted defense of public service broadcasting was considered much too bold by the House of Commons Culture, Media and Sport Select Committee, chaired by Gerald Kaufmann, when it reported in December 1999. The Select Committee Report quite rightly points out that introducing differential charging at this point in time would lend support to the argument that paying should be related to viewing. While private broadcasters have opposed the introduction of what they call a 'digital poll tax' because it would slow digital take-up, those that take the long view must be rubbing their hands. If the BBC loses both share and reach in the coming years, the universality of the license fee is sure to be brought into question. The Select Committee suggests that the digital supplement would also not be fair as it would affect the poorer digital households more than the richer ones. The Select Committee does not recommend an alternative because they are skeptical about the BBC's request for more funding and the most likely solution – an increase in everyone's fee – does not seem fair. But all this confusion and dissent on the BBC's funding, which focuses upon universality and fairness (the ability to pay), may open the door for a more radical approach: funding which is not in effect based on a regressive tax and which establishes public service as a right and not a privilege.

The money already spent by the BBC on digital channels – particularly the €88 million on News 24 – has been, according to the Select Committee, largely wasted, and they see no evidence of the BBC becoming a leading player in the provision of digital services either now or in the future. Increased BBC revenue should come from an increase in commercial activities rather than from license payers. Their report picks up on the most progressive of the Davies Panel's suggestions concerning BBC Online and suggests the reverse. The BBC should cash in on the success of Online by transferring it to BBC Worldwide and exploit its commercial potential to the full. The report's implicit vision of public service, in other words, is one of a safety net.

The DCMS responded to the Select Committee report in March 2000. It agreed with the Select Committee critique of the Davies Panel's idea of introducing a digital supplement to the license fee for digital households, and increased the license fee for all TV households by 1.5% above inflation for the period April 2000-April 2006/7 (the date of the next Charter). This will give the BBC a € 317 million per annum real increase in revenue. This relatively generous settlement was justified owing to a faster than expected take-up of digital TV, with obvious implications for the timing of switch-over from analogue to digital. In return for increased funding the BBC was expected to achieve efficiency gains and to submit without too much debate to a different regulatory environment. The 2000 Communications White Paper suggests that a unified media and telecommunications regulator will be established (OFCOM) to which the BBC will be accountable in terms of fulfilling its public service remit.

Greg Dyke, the new Director-General of the BBC, began work on a blueprint for the future of the BBC in 1999. By the summer of 2000 he and his team were ready to go public on what they thought the BBC should look like in the age of digital TV. The first shot was fired by Mark Thompson, Director of BBC Television, in a speech at the Banff Festival in Canada on June 12. According to Thompson, public service TV must change considerably to meet the challenges laid down by the digital environment. The new environment means that the BBC will be open to much fiercer competition for viewers from both international (notably from the USA) and domestic competitors. Based on initial research with users of the Electronic Program Guide (EPG) – the electronic navigational tool for digital viewers – Thompson argues that viewers will increasingly focus on individual programs and genres rather than on mixed genre channels. The idea of 'hammocking' is dying, if not already dead. This idea was one of the tactics of public service broadcasting from early on where audiences for less popular, 'more serious' programs could be enhanced by putting them next to popular programs in the schedule. With remote controls now almost an extension of their bodies, viewers think nothing of switching channels many times in an hour, and this habit will become even more second-nature with the advent of the EPG and multi-channel environments. The only way of maintaining some 'audience flow,' according to Thompson, is to have specialist channels i.e., move towards a publishing model of broadcasting. Audiences will increasingly make up their own schedules using the EPG and TiVO, a home storage device allowing for recording up to 30 hours of TV on a hard disk (the contents of which can be displayed on the EPG). Thompson points to initial audience research from the US which shows that households with a TiVO were watching the majority of their TV off the box rather than 'live' after a few weeks.

It was left to Thompson's boss, Dyke, to flesh out the implications of this reading of viewer behavior in the digital age in the MacTaggart lecture at the Guardian Edinburgh International Television Festival in late August 2000. The BBC will offer seven television services on the five channels that it has on its digital terrestrial multiplex:

1. BBC One will be "more engaging, more exciting, more gripping" than before through relegating some current affairs, documentaries, religion and the arts to BBC 2 and replacing them with *hard-hitting* popular programming. The emphasis here is on grouping together programs with high audience ratings – comedy, mainstream sport, popular drama, high-budget factual programs.
2. BBC Two will, after analogue switch-off, focus on intelligent factual programs, key leisure and lifestyle programs, thoughtful analysis, creatively ambitious drama and comedy, and specialist sports.
3. BBC Three will offer comedy, drama, music, arts and education programs aimed at a young audience. The target age range (although not stated in the lecture) is somewhere between 13 and 30.
4. BBC Four will be 'unashamedly intellectual' providing programs for an older, middle class highly educated audience.
5. BBC News 24 will be a 24 hour rolling news service.
6. Daytime Children's TV for preschoolers.
7. Daytime Children's TV for children aged 6 to 13.

What exists at the moment in the public sphere, therefore, are brief sketches of the proposed services. On the basis of these two speeches, a number of concerns can be raised. First, it is unclear how public service television is to provide the social cement of the nation (as Smith and Dyke want it to do) when the model proposed is based on the accepted fact of a highly fragmented audience. Service specialization will surely serve to cement this fragmentation rather than unify the nation. For those less concerned with nation-building, the prospects of sharing a common democratic culture are also retarded by the niche service approach. Second, there is no word about on-line developments. The most progressive part of the Davies Panel report seems to have been ignored and we are left with a situation where poor people pay the same license fee as rich people with the license fee being used to develop a very useful and highly regarded on-line service that poor people have less access to because they cannot afford computers and internet connections at home. It is difficult to know what is meant by universal service (constantly hailed as a key public service value) in this regard or, indeed, natural justice. Third, there remains a very worrying lack of clarity about what public service is. What emerges from Thompson's speech in particular is a tired, confused postmodern cultural relativism-cum-populism rather than a coherent set of cultural, ethical and political values:

> "But the trouble is that the whole question of what is and what isn't valuable in broadcasting, or in the arts or any other aspect of culture is itself up for debate. There's certainly a vociferous lobby who believe that what you could term traditional elite culture is the one true religion and that it's the duty of public service broadcasters to defend it to the death. But for other cultural arbiters, and it must be said probably for a large majority of the viewing public, elite culture is just one more niche, and one which appeals to a diminishing minority" (Thompson, 2000: 6).

Without wishing to mount a blanket defense of 'elite culture' it does seem that what matters here are numbers rather than values because it is all a matter of opinion anyway. The defenders of public service, therefore, are failing to talk about what the values of public service broadcasting ought to be. Cultural values may be up for debate but this debate has certainly not made a great contribution to the recent development of media policy in the UK and this does not bode well for the future of either public service broadcasting or the promotion of a more democratic public culture.

IX   What Price the Future?

With the birth of the fifth terrestrial channel, the launch of digital satellite and terrestrial television, digital audio broadcasting, and further experimentation with video-on-demand and the fast growing Internet (one in three British homes is connected to the Net), the British media landscape promises to become increasingly complex.

It is therefore perhaps unwise to attempt to predict the future of the electronic media in the UK. Having said that, the influence of BSkyB is very likely to increase dramatically over the next decade. Not only does BSkyB have access to vast library stocks (essential in a multi-channel environment) but it also has led the way in developing the set-top boxes necessary to receive digital television.

The multi-channel environment and the plethora of niche channels also make it likely that the BBC's identity crisis will continue. Given the radically different economic, social, cultural, and media context it is difficult to see the BBC being able to continue to fulfill the function that Lord Reith assigned it in the 1920's. Technological progress together with the heterogeneous nature of British society has put paid to the goal of creating a unified national community. For the BBC to survive more or less in its present form it needs to come up with answers to a question that it has struggled with over the last decade or so: what does it do that is different from and better than commercial programming? Only if credible answers are provided will its privileged position be secure.

References

Alvarado, M., Locksley, G. & Paskin, S. (1992). Great Britain. In A. Silj (ed.), *The New Television in Europe* (pp. 295–333). London: John Libbey.

Bell, N. (1994). Travels with my aunt, *Cable and Satellite Europe* 128: 18–22.

Blumler, J. (1995). United Kingdom. In Bertelsmann Foundation & European Institute for the Media (eds.), *Television Requires Responsibility. Volume 2: International Studies* (pp. 335–390). Gütersloh: Bertelsmann Foundation Publishers.

British Broadcasting Corporation (1996). *Annual Report and Accounts*. London: BBC.

British Broadcasting Corporation (2000). *Annual Report and Accounts 1999/2000*. London: BBC.

Broadcasting Act (1990). *Broadcasting Act 1990: Chapter 42*. London: HMSO.

Cain, J. (1992). *The BBC: 70 Years of Broadcasting*. London: BBC.

Clemens, J. (1996). Database marketing and the future of public service, *Intermedia* 24(2): 6–9.

Cormack, M. (1993). Problems of minority language broadcasting: Gaelic in Scotland, *European Journal of Communication* 8(1): 101–117.

Cormack, M. (1995). United Kingdom: more centralization than meets the eye. In M. de Moragas Spá & C. Garitaonindía (eds.), *Decentralization in the Global Era. Television in the Regions, Nationalities and Small Countries of the European Union* (pp. 203–214). London: John Libbey.

Davis, A. (1976). *Television. The First Forty Years. A History of Television in Britain*. London: Independent Television Publications.

Davey, J. (1996). Growing underground, *Spectrum* 22: 4–5.

Davies Panel Report on Future Funding of BBC (1999). Available at [www.culture.gov.uk/creative/bbcreport.html].

Doyle, G. (1996). Deregulierung für den Medienmarkt. Neue Regelungen für Medienkonzentration und digitalen terrestrischen Rundfunk in Großbritannien, *Media Perspektiven* 3: 164–170.

Dunne, A. (1994). The future of Channel Four after the Broadcasting Act 1990, *Irish Communications Review* 4: 41–47.

Dyke, G. (2000). *MacTaggart Lecture*.
Available at [www.bbc.co.uk/info/news/news264.htm].

European Audiovisual Observatory (1994). *Statistical Yearbook. Cinema, Television, Video and New Media in Europe. Edition 1994–1995*. Strasbourg: Council of Europe.

European Audiovisual Observatory (1999). *Statistical Yearbook '99. Film, television, video and new media in Europe*. Strasbourg: Council of Europe.

Evans, B.T. (1995). United Kingdom. In L. Schaffer Gross (ed.), *The International World of Electronic Media* (pp. 99–122). San Francisco: McGraw-Hill.

Goodwin, P. (1992). Did the ITC save British public service broadcasting?, *Media, Culture and Society* 14(4): 653–661.

Goodwin, P. (1993). The future of the BBC, *Media, Culture and Society* 15(3): 497–502.

Gordon, J. (1994). Twenty-one years of independent radio. In A. Millwood Hargrave (ed.), *Radio and Audience Attitudes* (pp. 33–39). London: John Libbey.

Government Response to Davies Panel Report (2000). Available at [www.culture.gov.uk/creative/govresbbc.html].

Hearst, S. (1992). Broadcasting Regulation in Britain. In J. Blumler (ed.), *Television and the Public Interest. Vulnerable Values in West European Broadcasting* (pp. 61–78). London: Sage Publications.

Independent Television Commission (1996). *Annual Report & Accounts 1995. Licensing and Regulating Commercial Television.* London: ITC.

Independent Television Commission (2000). *Annual Report and Accounts 1999. Licensing and regulating commercial television.* London: ITC.

Keane, J. (1991). *The Media and Democracy.* Cambridge: Polity Press.

Kilborn, R. (1996). New contexts for documentary production in Britain, *Media, Culture and Society* 18(1): 141–150.

Lambert, S. (1982). *Channel Four. Television with a Difference?* London: British Film Institute.

O'Drisceoil, F. (1995). Scots Gaelic and Welsh language broadcasting in the cultural context: a comparative analysis, *Irish Communications Review* 5: 49–56.

Radio Authority (1996). *Annual Report and Financial Statements for the Year ended 31 December 1995.* London: Radio Authority.

Scannell, P. (1996). Britain: public service broadcasting, from national culture to multiculturalism. In M. Raboy (ed.), *Public Broadcasting for the 21ˢᵗ century* (pp. 23–41). London: John Libbey.

Scholes, M. (1997). Digital applications review, *The Bulletin* 14(1): 24–25.

Sparks, C. (1995). The future of public service broadcasting in Britain, *Critical Studies in Mass Communication* 12: 325–341.

Starks, M. (1996). Public service philosophy and the dangers of fragmentation, *Intermedia* 24(2): 16–19.

Thompson, M. (2000) *BANFF Lecture*.
Available at [www.bbc.co.uk/info/news/news245.htm].

Tonge, G. (1996). The individual in the 2005 domestic environment, *Intermedia* 24(2): 10–12.

Towler, B. (1996). Rating the ratings system, *Spectrum* 21: 12–13.

Whitney, J. (1985). The state of industry, *Airwaves* 1: 3.

Winston, B. (1994). Public service in the 'New Broadcasting Age'. In S. Hood (ed.), *Behind the Screens: The Structure of British Broadcasting in the 1990's* (pp. 20–42). London: Lawrence and Wishart.

Russia

by Hedwig De Smaele and Sergej A. Romashko

The Soviet Union had a centralized, monopolistic, State-owned media system under Party control, whose programming entirely consisted of propaganda. Societal changes led Russia to introduce a dual system, with State and private broadcasters operating along one another. The *Federal Service for Television and Radio Broadcasting* was established in December 1993 as the licensing agency of both State and non-State broadcasters. In July 1999 it was replaced by a new *Ministry for Press, Television and Radio Broadcasting, and Mass Communications*. A bill on broadcasting was prepared but, after several years, it still has not been made into law.

In the absence of such a law, broadcasting is regulated indirectly by multiple other laws (law on the mass media, law on advertising, law on information, etc.) and mostly by presidential decrees. Radio and television are still largely dependent (financially and organizationally) on the government, while corporate control (especially Russian banks) over the media is growing. The notion of public service television remains alien. ORT, the first and most popular channel, is a public broadcaster in name only, as it is partly owned by the State and by private shareholders. RTR and *Kultura* are State-owned nationwide broadcasters. Another 90 State broadcasters operate locally. Independent broadcasters are generally local stations; NTV can be considered nationwide, and Moscow-based TV6 broadcasts to large portions of the country. The growth of private channels has gone hand in hand with the development of the advertising market, the introduction of systematic audience research, and the commercialization of the media content.

I Broadcasting in the Soviet Union

1.1 Functions of the Mass Media

The Soviet theory of the mass media was based on Marxist ideology. The mass media were ideologically committed to the Party and the working class. They fulfilled for the State the hegemonic functions of dominance, ideological homogenization of the audience and reproduction of the existing social order (Jakubowicz, 1995: 127). Vladimir I. Lenin (1870–1924) summarized the functions of the press into the role of a collective "propagandist, agitator and organizer." His views on the press were applied to broadcasting and the mass media in general. The latter were used primarily to inform and educate, not to entertain. But even *information* tended to be *education* or even *re-education*. *Partisanship* was regarded as the most important principle in broadcasting, and this meant close ties between the medium and the Party. In Soviet eyes partisanship was not in contradiction with concern for *objectivity* and *truthfulness*.

1.2 Structure and Control

During the Soviet Era the mass media were dependent on both the State and the Communist Party of the Soviet Union (CPSU). Although radio and television belonged nominally to the State, it was the CPSU that controlled its content and regulated its activities through numerous resolutions and directives. Like nearly all other aspects of life in the Soviet Union (including the economy, culture and science), broadcasting bore the stamp of the CPSU.[1]

The State monopoly on television and radio was absolute. The authority in charge of radio and television broadcasting was "the USSR State Committee for Television and Radio Broadcasting," or *Gosteleradio*. The chairman of Gosteleradio was a member of the government of the USSR and a member of the Central Committee of the CPSU. Gosteleradio was divided into Central Television, Central Radio and External Radio Services. The Ministry of Communications was in charge of the technical aspects of broadcasting. All means of communication (including broadcasting facilities) were considered State property (Article 11 of the Constitution of the USSR). Radio and television were financially totally dependent on the State budget. From 1922 to 1962 a system of user fees existed, but this was abolished and replaced with a tax on the purchase of new television and radio sets.

Glavlit, the official State censorship institution, was established in 1922 to prevent the disclosure of "military secrets" and all kinds of information "not to be made public" or branded "anti-Soviet agitation." Ideological purity was the key issue in censoring the programs.[2] The government thus instated as a pre-publication *political* censorship, in turn leading to *self-censorship* and to the banning of any critical journalism. Political censorship was also achieved through the organs of the Communist Party of the Soviet Union. Media *policy* was the monopoly of the CPSU (Politburo), with *Agitprop*, the Department for Agitation and Propaganda, as the main controlling unit. All radio and television editors had to be party members and were educated, trained and selected by the Party. Through the system of appointments the Party gained administrative control over broadcasting.

√Another way of controlling the media was to limit access to information sources, both for media workers and individuals.√The media were almost entirely committed to the materials provided by official news agency TASS and the semi-official APN-Novos-

---

[1] According to article 6 of the Constitution of the USSR, the Communist Party of the Soviet Union is "the leading and guiding force of Soviet Society and the nucleus of its political system, of all State organizations and public organizations. The CPSU exists for the people and serves the people. The Communist Party, armed with Marxism-Leninism, determines the general perspectives of the development of society and the course of the home and foreign policy of the USSR, directs the great constructive work of the Soviet people, and imparts a planned, systematic and theoretically substantiated character to their struggle for the victory of Communism."

[2] Article 39 of the Constitution and articles 70 and 190-1 of the Criminal Code criminalized "anti-soviet" activity. Article 50 of the Constitution limited press freedom "in accordance with the interests of the people and in order to strenghten and develop the Socialist system."

ti. The Soviet media system was a closed system, strongly isolated from foreign influence. Examples of barriers to the international information flow were the jamming of foreign radio stations and the strictly limited and controlled import of foreign newspapers and books.

1.3 Programming

The choice of programming was determined by the function of the mass media, namely propaganda and agitation rather than information and entertainment. Programs were not geared to audience interest but reflected the Party's views and interest. Radio and television mostly carried stories about political and economic *achievements* in the Socialist camp, and contrasted this with the *decadence* (unemployment, strikes, terrorism) of the Western countries. Cultural programs (literature, music, folk arts) received a lot of attention as well.[3] Pure entertainment (light music, variety shows, games, soap operas) was neglected. Films had to be ideologically correct in the same way as information programs.

The various power struggles at the top influenced the media and their programming. The *Krushchev Era* (1953–64) was one of temporarily liberalization, known as *"thaw."* A restoration of openness (e.g., stopping the jamming of foreign radio stations) and more vivid information (e.g., the modern radio station *Mayak* with music and news flashes around the clock) characterized the media. The Union republics enjoyed relative independence in determining their own programs. In contrast the *Brezhnev years* (1965–1985) became known as a period of *"stagnation."* Under Sergei Lapin as chairman of the State Committee for Radio and Television (1970s), extreme centralization of radio and television throughout the Soviet Union was implemented. The main newscast *Vremya* (Time), introduced in 1968, was transmitted at 9:00 p.m. on all channels and distributed to all time zones. No concurrent broadcasting of the domestic productions of the republics was allowed. As a result the audience of the newscast was as high as 80% of the adult population (Mickiewicz, 1988: 8). Central programming was made possible by the advent of satellite technology. From 1965, the Soviet Union invested in expensive communication satellites which enabled the distribution of programs made centrally in Moscow in the whole Soviet Union. Thanks to satellite technology 98% of the population could receive at least one television program, 94% at least two, 49% at least three, and 18% at least four (Lutz, 1996: 73).

The division of television channels was established during Lapin's term. In the seventies the central television had four channels. *Program One* was the all-Union basic channel. It transmitted news and current affairs programs as well as entertain-

---

[3] According to article 27 of the Constitution of the USSR "the State concerns itself with protecting, augmenting and making extensive use of society's cultural wealth for the moral and aesthetic education of the Soviet people, for raising their cultural level. In the USSR development of the professional, amateur and popular arts is encouraged in every way."

ment, drama and movies intended for large audiences. The program was made in Moscow and relayed by satellite (13.5 hours daily). *Program Two* (1956) was directed to Moscow and its environs and specialized in documentaries and culture (4.5 hours daily). *Program Three* (1964) emphasized education and popular science. It was seen on the European side of the country (12.4 hours of daily transmissions). *Program Four* (1967) was directed at industrial centers and the six republics on the European side. This channel had plenty of sports and drama (daily average of 5.5 hours). In 1982 *Program Two* became an all-Union channel as well, but it failed to develop its own identity. The first channel was considered the most important (15 hours daily) while the second channel carried less important stories and reruns of the first channel, as well as a limited amount of local programs (13 hours in total). *Program Three* was the Moscow channel (5 hours daily) and *Program Four* the educational channel (4 hours daily). The St. Petersburg channel (*Channel Five*) was available in Moscow and European Russia as well.

Before World War II the Soviet Union had only one central radio channel. A second one began operating in 1946, and a third one in 1947. In the 1970's, radio channels were as follows: *Program One,* an all-Union channel, similar to the first program on television, with news, current affairs, culture, sports (20 hours daily). *Radio Mayak* (1964), an all-Union channel with music and news flashes every half hour (24 hours a day). *Program Three* with educational programs, classical music and literature for the whole Union (18 hours). *Program Four* was directed at the Moscow area, with classical music and literature (9 hours). The Soviet Union also operated an external broadcasting service, *Radio Moscow International.*

II   Broadcasting during Glasnost (1985–1991)

In 1985 a new period opened in the history of the Soviet Union. M.S. Gorbachev, the youngest General Secretary since Stalin, implemented *perestroika* or the restructuring of the Soviet economy, and *glasnost,* or the opening to information. This double-barreled effort represented a sweeping change in the USSR's communications and information policy. Gorbachev's intent was not to change the Socialist system, but to improve it. The economy had to be reorganized, society modernized. Glasnost was seen as an instrument for exposing obstacles to reform and for making the people more supportive of his efforts. Glasnost was directed and controlled from the top of the power hierarchy with Gorbachev himself as a competent user of the media. But as the mass media themselves changed, became more diverse and independent, they slipped out of the Party's control. A new *glasnost* developed from the bottom up.

2.1 Programming Changes

The programming profile became more diverse. The mass media were encouraged to report more events and more fairly, with increased speed and topicality. Criticism and self-criticism were stimulated. Glasnost was applied to the present (economic failures, crime, corruption; sensitive ideological themes such as dissidence, ethnic issues and religion) as well as to the past (demythologizing of Stalin, increased treatment of the blank spots in history). One clear indicator of glasnost was the appearance of live broadcasts, starting in 1987. For the first time, citizens were able to watch uncensored programs, to receive information that was not imposed from above, to hear personal views from journalists and forces, opposing the government and the CPSU. In June 1988 the 19th Congress of the CPSU was broadcast live. Live broadcasts of the sessions of the Congress of the Members of Parliament and the Supreme Soviet in 1989 and 1990 attracted huge audiences.

Audience participation grew. There had long been in the Soviet Union a tradition of writing letters to the editorial offices of newspapers and broadcasting organizations. From 1985 to 1989 the annual number of letters received by the Central Television rose from one million to two (Paasilinna, 1995: 147). Other means of feedback became possible: participation in the program via the telephone, street interviews, debates. A new kind of audience relationship was created. Daily TV broadcast hours were increased by four hours, principally adding to morning (breakfast television) and night time schedules (Ganley, 1996: 72). Hard-hitting current affairs programs such as *Vzglyad* (View), *Pyatoye Koleso* (The Fifth Wheel) and *600 Sekund* (600 Seconds) became highly popular. Among the other new programs were youth programs, music programs and an increasing amount of foreign programs (especially American series).

2.2 Structural Changes

The move to a deregulated mass communications system took place in the summer of 1990. On June 12 the Supreme Soviet passed the "Law on the Press and other Mass Media" which banned censorship and freed the media (Article 1).[4] Every organization, political party, group or individual (over the age of eighteen) had the right to establish a mass medium. A monopoly position was not allowed (Article 7). Every registered media

---

[4] The mechanism of censorship was never completely abolished, however. In August 1990 GLAVLIT was wound up, but immediately replaced by the *Main Administration for the Protection of State Secrets (GUOT)*. In September 1991 President Yeltsin signed an edict about "measures for the defense of press freedom in the RSFSR," creating the "State Inspectorate to Protect the Freedom of the Press and Mass Information" within the Ministry of Press and Mass Information, with the mandate to petition government, founders and editors of publications as well as television and radio stations whenever violations of the law are noted. This amounted to a restoration of censorship. The only difference between the new edict and Glavlit's 70 year old censorship practices was the fact that the new law would permit censorship after rather than before publication.

organ had the right to operate, but registration was mandatory (Article 8). The authorities were no longer allowed to interfere in journalistic work. A mass medium's activity could only be stopped by its founder or a court of law. The law organized the relationships of the media and the Party, State, financiers, journalists and citizens. It was the first law in the history of the Soviet Union that guaranteed a right to information for the mass media and, indirectly, the population at large.

But even before this law came into force (August 1), president Gorbachev passed a decree (July 14, 1990) "on the democratization and development of television and radio broadcasting in the USSR." Rather than complementing the above-mentioned Press Law, the decree was a step backward. Radio and television were described as *stabilizers of society*, preserving the judicial order and the interests of the State. It was stated that radio and television had to be independent "from political and public organizations" but "turning the State television and radio institution into an instrument of propaganda of the personal views of its employees" could not be permitted either. The dominance of the Party was replaced by dominance of the government. Journalists had to be slapped back into line. The decree can be considered a reaction to political unrest in Eastern Europe and the Soviet Union. By mid-1990 13 of the 15 Soviet republics, including the Russian Federation, had proclaimed their national sovereignty. In February 1990 the CPSU lost its monopoly position by revoking Article 6 of the Constitution.

Another presidential decree (February 8, 1991) transformed Gosteleradio into the "All-Union Television and Radio Company," to which the power and assets of its predecessor were divested. The radio and television for the whole Union such as the Moscow and Leningrad *Teleradio* committees and the external services were under direct control of the Company. An all-Union Television and Radio Council was established for the coordination (e.g., agreements on frequencies and foreign contacts) between the *TV/ Radio* committees of the republics, having detached themselves from the central organ.

III   Broadcasting Regulation in the Russian Federation

When the Commonwealth of Independent States (CIS) was formed[5], all of the laws of the Soviet Union were declared invalid, including the first Law on the Press. A new *Russian Federation Law on the Mass Media* was adopted on December 27, 1991 and went into force on February 8, 1992. The new law was much more detailed and had more regulatory aims than the previous law. The Russian law re-emphasized the inadmissibility of censorship (Article 3) and guaranteed unlimited (except by existing legislation) freedom to seek, obtain, produce and disseminate information; to found, own, use and

---

[5] By December 25, 1991 when M.S. Gorbachev officially stepped down, the USSR had broken down into 15 sovereign States. The Commonwealth of Independent States was formed to unite several of the newly independent States – with the exception of the Baltic republics as well as (initially) Georgia. With 148 million inhabitants on 76% of the territory of the former Soviet Union, the Russian Federation is by far the CIS's most important State.

manage media outlets; to prepare, acquire, and operate technical devices and equipment, raw goods and materials intended for the production and distribution of mass media products (Article 1). The main thrusts of the law are also included in the new *Russian Constitution*, adopted by national referendum on December 12, 1993. Everyone has a right to freedom of speech and free dissemination of thoughts and ideas, and a right to seek, obtain and freely transmit, disseminate and produce information. Freedom of the press is guaranteed. Censorship is banned (Article 29).

The Russian law on the mass media also provided the skeletal framework for the issuance, regulation and annulment of television and radio broadcast licenses. So, not only did television and radio broadcasting corporations require *registration* as media organizations with the Russian Press and Information Committee, they must also obtain a *license* as a broadcaster. According to Article 30 of the law, broadcast licensing is to be done by the Federal Commission for Television and Radio Broadcasting, whose formation and operation are to be established by a specific *law on broadcasting* of the Russian Federation. Nine years later, Russia is still lacking a broadcasting law.[6] In the absence of a law, broadcasting is under the direct control of the Federation President and broadcasting activities are primarily regulated by means of presidential decrees and government orders. Orders and decrees succeed one another at a rapid rate, thus causing an unstable and uncertain situation where arbitrariness can flourish.

The presidential decree of December 22, 1993 and a prime ministerial directive of November 1, 1994 established the *Federal Service of Russia for Television and Radio Broadcasting*. This remained the licensing agency for both State and non-State broadcasters until July 1999.[7] The government order of December 7, 1994, "On Licensing Television Broadcasting, Radio Broadcasting and Operating on the Television and Radio Communications Systems in the Russian Federation" replaced earlier orders on licensing[8] and required a second license. In addition to the broadcast license, issued by

---

[6] A bill was passed on first reading by the State Duma (Lower House of Parliament) on October 26, 1994. Although the Duma gave its final approval on the draft, it was vetoed by President Yeltsin and rejected by the Federation Council (Upper House of Parliament) in April 1996. A new project was proposed in 1997 but rejected by the Duma in May 2000. In the meantime, the draft had undergone some changes in volume and scope, growing from 56 articles in 1994 (the *Ignatiev draft*, as proposed by Mikhaïl Poltoranin's Mass Media Committee of the State Duma) over 70 articles in 1997 (State Duma of February 18, 1997), then shrinking back to only 46 articles in its December 3, 1998 version.

[7] After the virtual defeat of *Russia's Choice* in the 1993 elections, the Yeltsin government dissolved the Information Ministry of the Russian Federation and split its previous management and regulatory functions between two non-ministerial level organizations: (1) The Federal Service for Television and Radio Broadcasting (FSTR) and (2) The *Press Committee of the Russian Federation (Roskompechat)*. In addition, a special *Arbitration Tribunal*, established to resolve media disputes and monitor press coverage of the 1993 elections, was formalized as a part of the president's administration, and renamed the *Presidential Judicial Chamber on Information Disputes* (December 31, 1993).

[8] The new regulations required the holder of any license, issued between August 1, 1993 and December 7, 1994 to be revised accoring to new FSTR terms.

the Federal Service, broadcasters had to obtain a frequency license issued by the Ministry of Communications (*Minsvyazi*), which allocated them a specific frequency and a number of broadcasting hours. Frequency and broadcast licenses were granted for up to five years, after which they had to be renewed. Licenses remain with the recipient and are not transferable.

The Federal Service for Television and Radio (FSTR) had other responsibilities alongside licensing. It was responsible for disbursing government funding to the State broadcasters, and also had responsibilities regarding the transmission arrangements for State broadcasters. Further, it coordinated the activity of national and regional State television and radio broadcasting organizations, assisted in ensuring a modicum of objectivity in the national and international reporting of Russia's political, economic, social and cultural life, and conducted a unified State policy when deciding production, technical and financial matters in the area of television and radio broadcasting (BBC, 1996: 4).

On July 6, 1999 President Yeltsin signed a decree establishing anew a *Ministry for Press, Television and Radio Broadcasting and Mass Communications* which was to absorb the State Press Committee and the Federal Service for Television and Radio. The press ministry is headed by Mikhail Lesin, who until then was the first deputy chairman of the All-Russian State Television and Radio Company (RTR) and who worked for Yeltsin's election campaign in 1996. The press ministry is in charge, among other things, of developing and implementing State policy on the mass media, mass communications and advertising, as well as controlling the use of broadcast frequencies and upgrading technology. Lesin denied rumors that the new ministry had anything to do with the campaigns for the elections of the State Duma (1999) and the presidency (2000).

Table 1. *General TV Data*

Total population (1999)	146,693,000
Number of households	45,300,000
Number of TV households	44,800,000
Penetration of television	99%
Penetration of color TV's	89%
Penetration of VCR's	25%

Source: Länderanalysen der Frankfurter Allgemeinen Zeitung GmbH Informationsdienste, February 1995; Russian Research, June 1995.

IV   Overview of Broadcasting Organizations in the Russian Federation

The draft broadcasting law of 1994 recognized only three types of television and radio companies: *governmental* companies (owned by government organs), *public* companies (co-owned by government organs as well as other legal entities and citizens) and *private* companies (owned by citizens and/or legal entities, not including governmental organs). The draft law of February 18, 1997 distinguishes between *commercial* and *non-commercial* television and radio companies. Four types of non-commercial companies are considered: *governmental* (owned by government organs of the Russian Federation), *municipal* (owned by local government organs), *public* (owned by non-commercial organizations, including government organs) and *other* non-commercial companies. Governmental and public broadcasting organizations are considered "cultural organizations" (Article 22).

Table 2. *TV Landscape: National Terrestrial Channels (2001)*

Channel	Nature	Technical Penetration	Program Supply	Revenue Sources
ORT	public (49% State, 51% private)	99%	general-interest	State/advertising
RTR	governmental	96%	general-interest	State/advertising
Kultura	governmental	75%	cultural	State
TV Center	municipal	35% (Moscow)	general-interest	Moscow city/advertising
NTV	private	60%	general-interest	advertising
TV6 Moscow	private	60%	general-interest	advertising

4.1 The Main State Broadcasters (Governmental and Public)

4.1.1 Ostankino/ORT

When the Soviet Union was abolished, the Russian Federation took over most of the structures and institutions from the ex-Soviet Union. One of the first acts of the new government was Yeltsin's signing of a decree (December 27, 1991) providing for Russian jurisdiction over the central television system. The *"All-Union State TV and Radio Company"* (*Gosteleradio*) was transformed into the *"Russian State TV and Radio Company Ostankino."* The system stayed State-owned, State-funded and State-controlled. Moreover, Ostankino remained a broadcasting organization that had to serve not only Russia, but the whole Commonwealth of Independent States. Its programs were transmitted on *Channel 1* of the Russian television system which reaches 99% of the population of the CIS (about 220 million viewers). Channel 1's broadcasts are available in five versions (one for European Russia and four time-shifted versions, Orbita 1 to 4, for areas further East).[9]

On November 30, 1994, Yeltsin signed a decree giving control of broadcasting on Channel 1 to a new organization – *Russian Public TV* (ORT)[10] as of April 1, 1995, 51% of ORT's shares are federal property. The remaining 49% are owned by a number of private shareholders, including numerous banks. This partial privatization was explained by the intolerable financial situation Ostankino found itself in due to huge transmission costs and a bloated payroll (total staff of about 10,000 in early 1995, see Lutz, 1996: 70).

According to the draft broadcasting law, ORT is a *public* television company. According to western standards however, ORT cannot be called *public* since it serves a narrow group of financial and political interests. The chairman of ORT is appointed by the President. Six out of eleven members of the board of directors (1998) are representatives of the government. Although ORT has some popular programs (entertainment, games and series), in its news bulletins it is seen as dull and unswervingly loyal to the government and president (the *president's television*, see Omri Daily Digest, October 7, 1996). Because of its biased coverage, the State Duma and the Federation Council (the Russian Parliament) passed several laws to nullify the creation of ORT – but all of these were vetoed by President Yeltsin.[11]

In addition to its television work (Channel 1), Ostankino traditionally operated four nationwide radio stations: *Radio-1*, the mainly speech-based, traditional *First Program*; *Radio Mayak*, the music and news station, *Radio Yunost*, the youth-oriented station (music and information), and *Radio Orfey*, the classical music station. Due to huge budget problems, in August 1997 *Radio-1* was liquidated while *Mayak* and *Yunost* were merged into one station under the name *Mayak*.

---

[9] In the beginning there were some plans for the creation of an "interstate television channel," shared (and paid for) by all CIS members, and not only by the Russian Federation. This project came to nothing, and the *Mir* (World/Peace) *Interstate TV and Radio Company* was set up in October 1992 as an attempt to maintain some sort of broadcasting system encompassing the whole of the former Soviet Union. The programs MIR produced, were transmitted by other companies, mainly the First Channel, Ostankino. Lack of both money and political will meant that MIR's activities have been largely ignored: six hours of its programs were being transmitted weekly by Channel 1 in 1993, a figure that was down to only three hours in 1995 (Lutz, 1996: 64). In 1997 the MIR broadcasts were shut down completely.

[10] *Ostankino* became a production company for ORT, but the latter uses programs from other sources as well.

[11] In 1995 the Duma twice passed laws to nullify the creation of ORT. However, President Yeltsin vetoed the laws and in November 1995 the Constitutional Court refused to hear an appeal from Duma members on this matter. In July and October 1996 the Duma passed non-binding resolutions calling for the renationalization of ORT. See *Omri Daily Digest*, April 6, June 8, November 6, May 16, July 18, October 7, 1996.

4.1.2 All-Russian State TV and Radio Company (VGTRK or RTR)

The *Vserossiyskaya Gosudarstvennaya Teleradiokompaniya*, often referred to as RTR (Russian Television and Radio), was formed in 1990 in a move to give the Russian Federation (at that time the Russian Republic) its own voice, independent of the Soviet channels.[12] In December 1990 *Radio Rossiya* or Radio Russia was launched and in May 1991 *Rossiyskoye Televidenie* or Russian Television started to broadcast 6 hours of programming on the *Second Channel*. After the August coup, RTR took over the whole second channel. The Second Channel can be received by 96% of the population of the former Soviet Union; it has a potential audience of 200 million viewers. It is the second most widely seen channel and the only alternative to ORT in many parts. In the Baltic and other CIS states, however, RTR is partially or completely pre-empted by national (local) governments, which have been using the frequency for their own purposes. Like ORT, it is available in five versions (one for European Russia and four time-shifted versions, Dubl 1 to 4, for areas further East).[13]

The All-Russian State TV and Radio Company is a governmental company. Its activities are financed by the Russian government and by advertising. The chairperson is appointed by the President. Created as an opposition channel, in contrast to the central television, the *Russian Television* became a government channel as well. In September 1996, *RTR Teleset* (Russian Radio and TV Network) was launched. The project encompasses two satellite channels: one for sports and one for movies, *Meteor-Kino*.

Until September 1996 VGTRK also operated the educational station *Russian Universities TV*, which shared *Channel 4* with the independent television station NTV. *Universities TV* had the use of the channel in the morning and the afternoon, and NTV in the evening. Since autumn 1996 NTV has been running a full-time program on the fourth channel. Russian Universities TV disappeared, and with it most of the country's educational television. In 1997 however the concept of educational television was partly reintroduced with the establishment of Kanal Kultura.

VGTRK operates two radio stations:
* *Radio Rossii* (Radio Russia) began broadcasting in December 1990. It broadcasts about 22 hours a day, mainly information programs. It is reported to be the most listened to station in the country, with a 19.5% market share (March, 1999).

---

[12] By mid-1990, 13 of the 15 Soviet republics had proclaimed their national sovereignty. The Russian Federation was one of them (June 12, 1990). Each republic and each large city took control of its own stations, which left the Federation out in the cold as it did not have channels of its own: the institutions of the Russian Federation had always coincided with those of the Soviet Union. So, one of its first resolutions, the Supreme Soviet of the Federation provided for the creation of independent mass media in the republic. It took an open confrontation between Soviet Union President Gorbachev and Russian Federation President Yeltsin for this to become fact.

[13] There have been discussions about switching the first and second channel between ORT and RTR. RTR is arguing that, because it is fully State-owned, it has more rights to the use of the main broadcasting network than the only 51% State-owned ORT.

- *Golos Rossii* (The Voice of Russia) is a short-wave external service, the legal successor to Radio Moscow International. In 1996 it broadcast worldwide in 32 different languages for a total of 539 hours per week. This is down from 66 languages and 1,638 hours per week in 1991 (Omri Daily Digest, July 24, 1996). The station is totally dependent on the State budget.

4.1.3 Kanal Kultura (VGTRK)

On August 25, 1997 President Yeltsin signed a decree awarding State-owned RTR the right to operate a new nationwide television network, showing primarily cultural and educational programs. Both channels, Kultura and RTR, receive joint financing from the State budget. In contrast with RTR, Kultura is not allowed to run commercial advertising – a requirement that is no longer complied with. The head of Kultura is appointed and dismissed by the President (as is the chairman of RTR).

The new channel started broadcasting on November 1, 1997 using a frequency formerly used by St. Petersburg *Channel 5*. Its potential audience consists of 100 million people in the European part of Russia; its real audience is negligible. In the city of St. Petersburg and in Leningrad, Kultura's programs are broadcast for only a few hours a day, leaving room for the regional broadcaster, the *Petersburg Television and Radio Company*. During Gorbachev's glasnost period the St. Petersburg (Leningrad) channel was considered radical democratic, with controversial programs such as *600 sekund* and *Pyatoye Koleso*. Now, it seems to have lost its earlier spirit. Its audience ratings are low, although its potential audience is about 70 million people.

4.1.4 TV Center

The third channel with a potential audience of 35 million viewers in the Moscow region was shared until 1997 by the city channel MTK TV *(Moskovskaya Telekompaniya)* and the commercial station *2x2*, the latter occupying the channel during the evening prime time period (18:00–23:00). Both were replaced by a new channel from June 9, 1997 onwards: *TV Center*, an initiative from Moscow Mayor Yuri Luzhkov and heavily sponsored by the Moscow city authorities. The government of Moscow city owns 67% of the shares with the other 33% in the hands of private investors. TV Center reaches a potential audience of 60 million people, not only in Moscow but also in other cities of Russia, Azerbaijan, Kazakhstan, Kyrgyzstan, Uzbekistan, Belarus, Latvia, Lithuania, Estonia and Ukraine through the network of affiliated regional stations. Two satellite channels are planned as part of the *TV Center* consortium: *Meteor-Kino* and *Meteor-Sport*. The launch of the station was widely seen as linked to Yuri Luzhkov's presidential aspirations.

4.2 Private Broadcasters

Although estimates vary, the number of non-governmental television stations in Russia falls somewhere between 500 and 750. According to the Federal Television and Radio Service, 1,987 broadcast licenses were granted between 1992 and 1998 (1,138 for television and 851 for radio). State broadcasting amounts for about 10% of the total number of licenses issued (*Post-Soviet Media Law & Policy Newsletter*, 15 February 1999: 36). These numbers are not conclusive, however, because some stations have been granted broadcasting licenses but never used them, while others never received licenses but broadcast anyway. This is especially true of cable operators. Part of the variation in estimates hinges on different definitions used of a television station. If only licensed terrestrial broadcasters with exclusive access to a channel are counted as stations, the number will be closer to 500. However, in many cities, two or more broadcast licenses were issued for a single frequency, with different companies licensed to use certain hours of the day or certain days of the week. Many of these broadcasters call themselves stations and are viewed as such by the FSTR, even though they may only broadcast a few hours a week (Internews, 1997; EAO, 1999: 365).

4.2.1 Radio

The investment costs needed for private television slowed down an immediate introduction of commercial television. In the beginning only private radio stations were established. Most of them were joint ventures, set up with the help of foreign companies. Most of them had only a limited broadcasting area and were broadcasting for only a couple of hours per day. The government's influence continued to be strong for the simple reason that it controlled the technical access to the airwaves and doled out the licenses. According to A. Mayofis, a board member of NVS (Independent Broadcasting System), foreign investment can help Russian media avoid being dragged into politics (Media Developments, April 1996). Russian law still does not limit foreign media ownership but the uncertain political situation in Russia prevents foreign investors from becoming involved in media projects in Russia.

French-Russian joint ventures seemed to be successful. *Radio Rossii-Nostalgie*, set up in 1990 by *Gosteleradio* (later RTR) and French radio station *Radio Nostalgie*, broadcasts 24 hours a day (mostly French) music and news every half hour. French-Russian station *Europa Plus* has been on the air 22 hours a day since 1990 with an all-round program, in Moscow and a number of other Russian cities. A third French-Russian initiative, *M-Radio*, has been broadcasting mixed programming 24 hours a day since 1990 as well. *Echo Moskvy* (Echo from Moscow) was the first completely Russian independent radio when it started broadcasting in August 1990. The station was established by the Municipality of Moscow, the faculty of Journalism of the Moscow State University, *Ogonyok*'s editorial board and the radio association within the Ministry of Communications. *Echo Moskvy* became well known during the August 1991 putsch, because it successfully maintained its independent voice. *Echo Moskvy* broadcasts 24 hours a day, mainly information (science, culture, sport, talk shows, etc.) and music. Its programming is financed by advertising alone.[14]

Russkoye Radio started broadcasting in August 1995 as an FM station in Moscow. According to ComCon2 audience surveys *Russkoye Radio* has become the fourth most popular station in Moscow in less than one year, with an audience estimated at 593,000 listeners or about 9% of the potential Moscow audience (Media Developments 17, September 1996), and up to 13.9% in 1999 (ComCon 2). Its chosen broadcast format is exclusively Russian music, ranging from parlor songs of the early 1900's to "Techno." In addition, the station broadcasts 24 hours a day in 14 other cities. Its funding comes from advertising.

FM radio is the most dynamic part of the Russian broadcasting structure, due to the lower costs involved as compared with TV, and also to its flexibility and close contact with the audience. Dozens of stations are operating in the main Russian cities, mostly in Moscow and St. Petersburg. FM radio is even going transregional or transnational through transmission of its programs to the other cities. An example is Radio 101 in Moscow, now available in more than ten Russian cities as well as Kazakhstan. The benefits of joint ventures in this field, symptomatic of the first years of the new era are now virtually irrelevant. While private radio is flourishing, State-owned radio broadcasting is gradually dying. The radio stations have been forced to significantly reduce their air time after severe cuts in federal subsidies. Commercial radio will not be able to fill the gap, because huge transmission costs preclude any profits in broadcasting to small towns and villages (Omri Daily Digest, 21 February 1997).

4.2.2 Independent Television NTV (Nezavisimoye Televideniye)

NTV started broadcasting as a news-oriented station in October 1993. From January 1994 NTV was able to broadcast eight hours a day during prime time (18:00–24:00) on the *Fourth Channel*, which it shared with *Universities TV*. The Fourth Channel reaches about 60 million viewers in European Russia. By the end of 1994 NTV's programs were relayed by the *Gorizont* satellite as well so it reached 100 million viewers in Russia, Kazakhstan, Ukraine, Belarus and the Baltic States. NTV became a success story, reportedly self-financing after little more than one year, with excellent nightly news programs (*Segodniya*) and the weekly current affairs program *Itogi*. The controlling share of NTV (77%) was held by *Most Bank* chairman Vladimir Gusinskiy; the NTV staff owned the rest. Gusinskiy supported and was supported by Moscow mayor Yuri Luzhkov but the NTV network became known for its sharp criticism of official politics, particularly its bold coverage of the Chechnya conflict (1994–1996).

---

[14] March 1999 market shares for these channels: Europa-Plus – 9.8%, M-Radio – 1% and Ekho Moskvy – 6.3%. The share of Radio Nostalgie was less than 1%.

After some years, however, its news coverage appeared to be less independent and more pro-government. In 1996 NTV executive director Igor Malashenko joined Yeltsin's campaign committee and the network strongly supported Yeltsin's 1996 re-election effort. In June 1996 *Gazprom* (the gas monopoly, with close ties to the government) acquired about 30% of NTV, raising questions about the objectivity of the station's news programs as well. The relationship between the authorities and NTV became friendlier, resulting in Yeltsin signing a decree on September 20, 1996, giving NTV the right to broadcast 24 hours a day on Russia's fourth television channel. NTV had frequently expressed its wish to broadcast around the clock.[15] Another presidential decree (January 21, 1998) awarded NTV the status of 'All-Russia Television and Radio broadcasting organization' which guaranteed that NTV would enjoy equal rates for transmission services as ORT and RTR.[16] Program supply did not change dramatically because of extended broadcasting hours. Information remained a priority, with news updates several times a day and a longer 10:00 p.m. news program.

In September 1996, NTV launched a package of five satellite channels, *NTV Plus*, devoted to sports, Russian films, foreign films, children's programs, and music. As of 1997 the NTV Plus network boasted an audience of some 30,000 households in Moscow, St. Petersburg, and Yekaterinburg, and up to 150,000 in 1999. In 1997, *NTV International* was created to distribute NTV broadcasts to foreign countries such as Israel. The NTV holding (December 1997) includes distribution company *NTV Kino*, production company *NTV Profit*, design company *NTV Design*, as well as regional television network *TNT Telenetwork* and radio station *Ekho Moskvy* (since 1995).

The relationship between NTV and the Presidency soured with the transfer of power from Boris Yeltsin to Vladimir Putin in March 2000. President Putin wanted to restore the authority of the State above the growing authority of so-called oligarchs such as Vladimir Gusinskiy (NTV) and Boris Berezovskiy (ORT). NTV's failure to pay back a number of public loans was seen as a golden opportunity to take action against Gusinskiy's media empire. In exchange for NTV's debts, Gazprom (the partially State-owned oil company) acquired a substantial amount of shares of the Media MOST media outlets, including NTV. According to NTV spokespersons, the attacks on Gusinskiy and his media endangered press freedom in Russia. Gusinskiy however, had shown very little concern for press freedom. "Like the other oligarchs, he only comes to life when his own interests are directly at risk" writes *Moscow Times* analyst Robert Coalson (2000). Time will show whether the new ownership structure of NTV affects its programming.

---

[15] The presidential decree bypassed the FSTR and Minsvyazi licensing procedure. NTV received not only broadcasting rights but also the frequency license and the transmitter and relay network.
[16] "All-Russia television and radio broadcasting organizations" are defined as media outlets that broadcast in more than half of the Russian regions. The decree names RTR, ORT, NTV and Radio Mayak, directing the government to charge them equal rates for transmission services. The decree is seen as a victory for NTV which, pursuant to an agreement with the Communications Ministry, has paid government rates for its transmissions since January 1996. The Duma passed a resolution urging the government to charge NTV and other non-State television and radio companies higher rates for the use of transmission facilities. The presidential decree of January 1998, however, confirms NTV's privileged status.

Figure 1. *Media Imperium of Vladimir Gusinskiy*

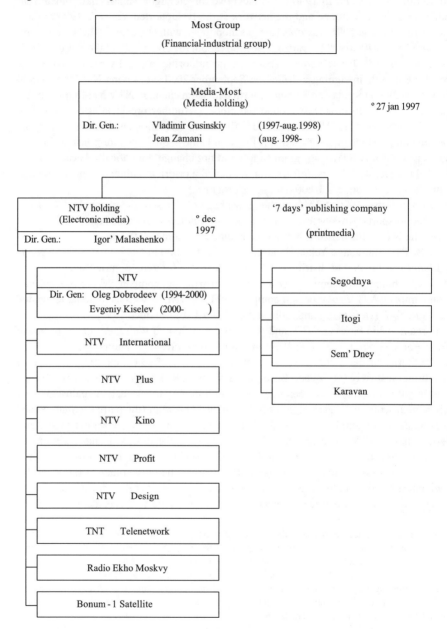

4.2.3 TV6 Moskva

TV6 Moskva was established in January 1993 as a Russian-American joint venture between Moscow Independent Broadcasting Corporation and Turner Broadcasting Systems, owned by media magnate Ted Turner. Its programs were entertainment-oriented (movies); the station did not produce its own news programs, but used CNN news bulletins. After Turner pulled out in 1994, the station became wholly Russian-owned, with Eduard Sagalayev and Boris Berezovskiy each holding 37% of the shares, while Lukoil held 15% and the Moscow government Committee on Science and Technology held 10%. In June 1999 Sagalaev sold Berezovskiy a large, undisclosed, chunk of his shares. Sagalaev now owns less than 10% of the shares while Berezovskiy and entities close to his LogoVAZ car dealership now own more than 60% of the channel.

TV6 is one of the more successful non-governmental stations. From five hours of daily broadcast in 1993, reaching a potential audience of 500,000 viewers in Moscow, the station grew to 20 hours a day for 100 million viewers in 252 cities in Russia, Ukraine, Kazakhstan, Uzbekistan, Kyrgyzstan, Moldova and the Baltic states. Over six years of growth, the programming changed substantially. In 1993 the daily schedule was made up of two movies – one Russian and one American – and a CNN news block. Today original programming such as talk shows, entertainment, information, humor and sports takes about 50% of the total air time. In 1996 in a joint effort with TSN news agency, TV6 launched daily news blocks. The same year saw the start of a weekly political news show, "Observer." Movies remain a priority.

4.2.4 Other Channels

Russia's national broadcasting landscape is characterized by hundreds of small-scale initiatives. While local television channels in Moscow (e.g., *Kanal 31*) and St-Petersburg (e.g., *Russkoe Video, TV3*) capture reasonably large audiences, for many other channels networking is the only viable solution. Cooperation – based on a partnership between regional/local stations – suits the local stations, since most of them are unable to fill their airtime with their own material. Cooperating preserves them from charges of video piracy and allows them to legitimately fill airtime with popular shows. As for the Moscow channels, partnerships with regional stations enable them to enlarge their audience nationwide. Both NTV and TV-6 distribute their programming nationwide via affiliated stations. In addition, Media MOST launched regional network TNT on January 1, 1998. Other major networks include AST (Association of Satellite Tele-broadcasting, launched in 1995 by the Moscow commercial channel *2x2*), STS (Network of Television Stations, launched by the American company Storyfirst in October 1996), and REN-TV/NVS. REN-TV started its activities in 1991 as a private production company and launched a television station in Moscow in 1996 (Channel 49). NVS (Independent Broadcasting System) was created as a commercial program purchasing cooperative in mid-1994. Since then it has grown into a proper national network with over

70 affiliate stations in Russia, excluding Moscow. In May 1996 NVS began distributing its program by satellite as well, purchasing time on a Gorizont satellite. Since January 1, 1997 the cooperation with REN-TV has provided NVS with a foothold in Moscow (good for attracting advertisers), including production capabilities and a program archive.

4.2.5 Cable and satellite

Russia's switch-over to cable and satellite television allows broadcasters to break out of the limits imposed by local transmitters and relay stations around the country. Nevertheless most satellite networks still depend on cable (RTR) or even relay stations (REN-TV, AST) for distribution. NTV Plus is purely satellite based, on the other hand: viewers pick up its signal directly from a dish. One of the problems for NTV Plus is the competition of the foreign satellite companies (such as CNN, NBC, BBC, RTL), whose programs are not only reproduced but also partly translated for Russian audiences.

There are several hundreds of private cable networks in Russia. Most of them operate very locally and serve only a few apartment buildings, by connecting a VCR player to the so-called "collective antenna systems." The first cable network was NIKA TV, established in Moscow in October 1990. Many of these stations have already gone under or developed into larger entities, offering access to multiple cable and satellite channels. *Kosmos-TV* is by now the leading cable and satellite network (but it only reaches wealthy Russians, due to high subscription rates), offering a range of foreign channels and a Russian movie channel. Cable stations provide entertainment only, often movies from pirated video cassettes. According to a ComCon2 survey, 15% of the residents of provincial cities watch a local cable network. Most of them are between 25 and 40, a key target group for advertisers (Chernykh, 1996: 21).

As the Russian government imposed high taxes on video libraries and video clubs, while classifying cable networks as "mass information media," and exempting them from taxes, capital started to flow from the video business to cable. Factors that can hinder the development of cable are the relatively high cost of wiring a city for cable and the ongoing development of direct satellite broadcasting. Moreover, people in Russia are not used to paying for a connection. On the other hand, cable television can carry much more than a single television signal. That, plus the limited number of broadcast television channels and the absence of any significant investment in the telephone infrastructure for many years, has led some to suggest that cities in the CIS will in future be re-wired to provide better telephone service, as well as dozens of television channels, including pay-per-view channels (Media Developments, April 1996).

Tables 3 and 4 show the market shares of the main channels for total programming time as well as prime time (1994–1998). Russian Public Television (ORT) is still the most popular television channel, especially in daytime hours. Russian Television (RTR) comes in second during daytime, but is outstripped by NTV in the evening. NTV's programming is far more popular in Moscow and the North-West of European Russia than

Table 3. *Market Shares of the Main Channels – Urban Population (1994–1998)*

	1994	1995	1996	1997	1998
ORT	53	56,9	53	51	41
RTR	21	16	17	14	18
Russ.Univ./NTV	5	5,7	8	12	16
Peterburg/Kultura	4	5,3	3	1	1
TV-6 Moskva	2	2,8	3	4	4
2x2/MTK/TV Center	4	3,3	3	1	1
AST	-	-	-	1	0
STS	-	-	-	3	3
REN-TV	-	-	-	1	2
Video	-	-	-	1	3
Others*	11	9,9	13	10	10

(in %, 15 years and + till 1995, 11 years and + since 1996)
* mainly regional and local channels

Table 4. *Market Shares of the Main Channels in Primetime (18:00 – 22:00 p.m.) Urban*
       Population (1994–1998) (in %, 15 years and + till 1995, 11 years and + since
       1996)

	1994	1995	1996	1997	1998
ORT	46	47,7	51	52	40
RTR	27	24,9	18	13	15
Russ.Univ./NTV	6	8,7	9	12	18
Peterburg/Kultura	3	3,8	3	1	1
TV-6 Moskva	5	2,8	3	3	3
2x2/MTK/TV Center	2	0,7	1	1	1
AST	-	-	-	0	0
STS	-	-	-	3	4
REN-TV	-	-	-	1	2
Video	-	-	-	1	2
Others*	12	11,4	15	12	13

* mainly regional and local channels
Source: Russian Research Ltd. – RTR/GEAR-Eurodata TV (EAO, 1999: 365).

Table 5. *Market Shares of the Main Channels, Nationwide and in Moscow (July 1997)*

	National	Moscow
ORT	48	35,9
RTR	14,3	12,9
NTV	13,3	24,9
Peterburg	1	0,4
TV-6 Moskva	3,10	24,9
TV Center	-	1
STS	2	10
Others	18,4	12,9

Source: DBM&B in *Marketing Russia* 1 (4) December 1997: 36.

anywhere else in Russia (see Table 5). Local independent stations are becoming increasingly popular, but as market research firms combine the ratings of the various local stations into a single aggregate figure, these findings only show that the local stations as a whole have viewership.

V   Financing of Broadcasting Organizations

State broadcasting organizations have two sources of income: government subsidies and advertising (sponsorship) revenue. There are no license fees charged to radio and television set owners. The 1996 federal budget allocated about € 489 million to television and radio broadcasting. However, the government has difficulties in actually meeting its budgetary previsions. Public channel ORT claims not to have received State money since 1995. Cuts in air time and staff as well as programming changes were not sufficient to counter the burden of debts and the threat of bankruptcy. On December 28, 1998 President Yeltsin signed a decree on "Measures of State Support for ORT," granting the television station a credit line of up to € 106 million, but at the cost of increased governmental pressure on the channel.

A major problem for broadcasting organizations is the cost of signal distribution. The system of satellites, transmitters, and other facilities needed to transmit signals over Russia's vast territory is still largely in the hands of the Russian Ministry of Communications. State broadcasters do not own or control these facilities themselves. It was estimated that some 70–80% of State broadcasters' expenditures went to the Communications Ministry for signal distribution. The State broadcasters' debt for non-payment of transmission costs was estimated to be a total of € 27 billion by November 1, 1995. In December 1995 the government put the Federal Service for Television and Radio Broadcasting in charge of the radio and TV transmission issue. It gave such transmissions "federal supply status" and allocated € 754 million to the Ministry of Communications to restore transmissions (BBC, 1996: 4–5).[17] Approximately 70% of all independent TV broadcasters use transmitters, relay links, and towers owned and operated by the Ministry of Communications, while many of those who own their own transmitters have installed them at government transmission facilities.

After a two and a half years struggle the law "On State Support for the Mass Media and Book Publishing in the Russian Federation" was adopted on October 18, 1995 and came into force on January 1, 1996. This statute established a range of taxation, foreign currency retention, and customs privileges for the mass media, such as the abolition of import duties on audiovisual equipment, as well as lower postal, telegraph and tele-

---

[17] Due to non-payment of transmission costs, RTR, ORT, and the State-owned radio stations have been switched off, temporarily or permanently, in some regions and CIS states. The availability of these Russian-language broadcasting sources has become a political issue in the republics, especially in regions heavily populated by Russians, where inhabitants want to maintain ties to Russian culture.

phone communications services rates and a system of State grants for certain types of broadcast programming.

In the advertising market State and private broadcasters are in competition. Estimated advertising spending on Russian television totaled €489 million in 1995 and €635 million in 1996 and 1997.[18] The August 1998 economic crisis caused a sharp decline in advertising expenditures, which hit television hard. Most of the funds spent on television advertising are foreign-based (Procter & Gamble, Masterfoods, Unilever, etc.). The advertising market is highly monopolized. The business of marketing television advertising time to advertising agencies was for years in the hands of two companies: *Premier SV* and its close ally, *Video International*. Sergei Lisovsky's *Premier SV* was the sole media broker for State channel ORT Russian Public Television, Moscow's MTK channel, and the St. Petersburg's channel, until the agency was ousted from the market after the 1998 crisis. *Video International* represented most of the remainder: the national channel RTR, and NTV Independent Television. The only crack in this wall around Russian television advertising sales was TV6, which sold partly through Video International but also has its own media sales operation. There are plans for a new advertising agency founded by TV6 together with ORT, Boris Berezovskiy's LogoVAZ and the American company News Corporation, one of the structures in media magnate Rupert Murdoch's information empire. The whole media sales industry came under scrutiny after the March 1, 1995 murder of V. Listyev, a journalist who was about to take over as head of ORT. Listyev had indicated he would make a priority of dealing with ORT's corrupt advertising department and announced a moratorium on advertising until the situation was sorted out. He was promptly killed after that.[19] Meanwhile, Lisovsky was named general director of *ORT Reklama* (the sole sales agent for ORT airtime) and *Premier SV* became the sole media broker for *ORT Reklama* (April 1996).

On June 14, 1995 the first "Russian Federation Advertising Law" was adopted by the State Duma. According to this law advertising may not exceed 25% of broadcasting volume in 24 hours (Article 11). In radio and television programs, advertising breaks are allowed: in no children's and religious broadcasts; in educational broadcasts, no more than once in 15 minutes and for no more than 45 seconds; in radio plays and feature

---

[18] Estimates vary widely. According to NAKS SV (see Wendlandt, 1996) the 1995 figure is 489 million, while Kagan's estimate is 448 million, with other estimates ranging from 691 million to 1 billion. For 1996 Kagan gives a figure of 649 million, while other estimates reach the 1 billion mark. Total spending for 1997 was between 568 and 589 million according to Gubanov (2000: 21). It costs about $ 1 to reach 1,000 viewers in Russia, as compared to $ 15 in the US (Moscow Times, March 4, 1997).

[19] Ostankino had no centralized revenue collection service. All business negotiations were conducted by the studios, or even individual program makers who usually charged advertisers 2–4 times above official rates. Reports from Moscow indicated that Ostankino generated a 5.4 million income out of commercials under its standard rate scale, plus an additional 32.3 million under an unofficial rate scale, the latter sum being skimmed off by corrupt operators and politicians. Listyev announced he would eliminate all advertising until a new, centralized system was set up (see Hilliard, 1996: 100; Pankin, 1993; Wendlandt, 1996).

films, not without the consent of the owners of rights; in live broadcasts, if not per schedule required by the Russian Federation Act on the *Rules of Presenting the Activity of the Organs of State Power in the State Mass Media*[20]; no more than twice in broadcasts running for less than 15 minutes; no more than twice in other broadcasts running from between 15 to 60 minutes (Article 11). Advertising must be readily recognizable (Article 5). The law guarantees protection from unfair competition in the sphere of advertising and the prevention and curtailment of improper (misleading, unethical, false, subliminal) advertising (Articles 6–10). Advertising for alcoholic drinks, tobacco products, medicines, and weapons is limited (Article 16). Advertising for alcohol and tobacco products in radio and television broadcasts is not allowed during daytime hours (7:00 a.m.–10:00 p.m.) nor in broadcasts for minors. Advertising may not target minors directly or use images of persons under the age of 35 years of age; it may not show a person smoking or drinking (Article 16–1). In 1996 advertising for alcohol and tobacco products on both radio and television was banned completely. Sponsorship is considered a legal form of advertising but hidden advertising or *commercial reporting* as it is called in Russian, is forbidden. Media organizations are not permitted to take payments for placing advertising in the guise of international, editorial or authored material (Article 5). Although forbidden, *commercial reporting* is widespread among both State and non-State, national and local broadcasters.

Table 6. *Advertising Expenditure – Market Shares by Major Types (1996)*
Total = € 1,157 million

Media	Market Share (in %)
TV	18.6
Radio	4.7
Press	46.9
Outdoor (street, subway, etc.)	9.5
Direct mail	3.0
Others	17.0

Source: *Marketing Russia* 1 (2) May–June 1997: 29.

VI   Media Economics (Local Media Moguls)

The only concrete piece of anti-monopoly regulation in Russia is a stipulation in a December 7, 1994 decree concerning the licensing procedure of broadcasters: a legal entity cannot obtain a license for more than two channels in one region if the coverage areas of the companies overlap in full or by more than two thirds. The successive versions of the draft Russian law on radio and television broadcasting included anti-mon-

---

[20] On January 13, 1995, President Yeltsin promulgated a bill entitled "On Rules of Presenting the Activity of the Organs of State Power in the State Mass Media," which includes duties imposed on State-owned media to disseminate reports by various officials and government agencies.

opoly guarantees and so did the numerous proposals "on the introduction of amendments and additions to the federal law on Mass Media." The main thrust of these proposals was to limit the concentration of newspapers, radio stations, and television channels in the hands of any one given legal entity or private person. The law also proposed to do away with the notion of the mass media *founder* who cannot be held accountable for anything. This was to be replaced with the concept of an *owner* that would be responsible for the fate of a television or radio channel or a print publication, most probably materially. The bill also prohibited the owner of a medium from undertaking any commercial activity aside from broadcasting or publishing. None of these proposals has become law.

So goes the theory... Meanwhile multi-sector integrated media companies have emerged. The *Moskovskiye novosty* newspaper company, after facing economic problems in the weekly publication market, looked for other profitable media sectors and made investments in radio. *Kommersant* Publishing House is an example of a horizontally integrated media company which produces related products. *Kommersant* publishes several financial publications, magazines for the financial elite, owns news, advertising and photo agencies, and other companies. A third type of media companies secure their position through multi-sector integration: media and insurance companies, banks, travel agencies, trade companies. Since the mid-90's there has been a trend toward growing corporate control over the media, and growing integration between big business and the media. In particular Russian banks have been steadily increasing their investments into the media business. By building financial media empires, Russian's financial elites find a way into politics, thus suggesting a Russian model for the concept of media moguls (Vartanova, 1996: 8).

The Most group, owned by Vladimir Gusinskiy, has its main activities in banking and real estate, but also controls commercial television channel *NTV* (51%), the satellite network NTV Plus, and the regional network TNT. It controls the *7 Dnei* publishing company which publishes the *Segodniya* newspaper, the weekly newsmagazine *Itogi,* and the television weekly *7 Dnei*. The Most Group also sponsors the radio station *Echo Moskvy*. In order to control these media activities, a new holding company was established in January 1997: *Media Most*. Vladimir Gusinskiy resigned as Most Bank president and Most group general director to become executive director of *Media Most*. Media Most acquired all the Most group shares held in the above-mentioned media outlets. Seventy percent of the shares of Media Most belong to Gusinskiy personally.

Giant Russian financial conglomerate Menatep Group, which includes *Menatep Bank*, Russia's 11 th largest bank, and a wide range of holdings in Russian industrial companies, has a stake in ORT (Russian public television) and recently bought a minority stake into the *Independent Media Publishing* company. *Independent Media Publishing* publishes the Russian editions of magazines such as *Playboy, Cosmopolitan, Good Housekeeping,* as well as a number of popular English language publications (*Moscow Times, St. Petersburg Times*), and owns *Skate*, a financial information and Internet publishing company. In order to control its media activities Menatep Bank established the

Rosprom media holding. *Oneximbank/Rosbank*, which is part of the *Interros* financial-industrial group, is mainly active in the field of regional and print media (*Izvestiya, Komsomolskaya Pravda*) but also has an interest in *Radio Evropa Plus*, a French-Russian radio station. The Stolichny Savings Bank has a 5% stake in the ORT broadcaster. Stolichny Bank chairman Aleksandr Smolenskiy was chosen to head a new consortium of commercial banks called ORT-KB. Together these banks now hold 38% of the shares of the 51% State-owned network.

Another main player in the media field is Gazprom, Russia's gas monopolist and the other main shareholder of NTV (30%, recently increased to 49%). Gazprom also has an undisclosed stake in RTR, a stake in satellite network AST as well as one in several print publications (*Trud* among others). In order to control its media activities Gazprom established the Gazprom Media holding in December 1997. The LogoVAZ corporation, owned by Boris Berezovskiy, is one of the largest private shareholders of public Russian television network ORT (LogoVAZ: 11% and LogoVAZ-owned *Obiedinenniy-Bank*: 8%) as well as TV6 (60%). LogoVAZ has also invested in *Nezavisimaya Gazeta, Novye Izvestiya* and the *Ogonyok* and *Matador* news magazines. In July 1999 Berezovskiy purchased the controlling stake of the prestigious newspaper *Kommersant*. LU-Koil has a 15% stake in TV6, a 75% stake in the Moscow-based regional network REN TV/NVS and a 49% stake in *Izvestiya*.

Two major media empires can be distinguished: those of Vladimir Gusinskiy and of Boris Berezovskiy, although there is a noticeable difference between the two. While Gusinkiy established a real press, television and information concern, following a specific strategy, Berezovskiy's activities in this area are diverse, loosely structured and inspired by people and opportunities more than by a clear policy (Katsjkaeva, 1997). Both moguls had close ties with the Yeltsin government. Both Berezovskiy's and Gusinskiy's media clans supported Yeltsin in the presidential election campaign (June 1996), and both were rewarded: Gusinskiy's NTV channel got the daytime slot on the fourth channel and Berezovskiy was appointed to the position of deputy to the secretary of the Security Council of Russia. Their privileged position came to an end with the transfer of power to new President Vladimir Putin in May 2000.

VII   Media Content

In the Soviet Union domestic production was dominant, complemented by programming from other Socialist countries. Western programming was very limited because of ideological reasons. The broadcasting organizations of Central and Eastern Europe were united in the *International Radio and Television Organization* (OIRT), the counterpart of the Western *European Broadcasting Union* (EBU). The *Intervision* program exchange enabled broadcasters from the Eastern European bloc to exchange programs, including news and sports, practically without the need to pay for the rights, based on the principle of reciprocity.

On January 1, 1993 the OIRT was dissolved and united with the EBU. *Intervision,* the news exchange operated by OIRT, was integrated into the *Eurovision* news exchange. A single European audiovisual market was formed. According to Fabris the trend in common market thinking in the EC Directive on Transfrontier Television (1989) was already going on beyond the borders of the EU member states. European products are defined (Article 6) in such a way that other European countries (non-EU members, but members of the Council of Europe) have equal footing. Even co-productions between EU-member countries and other countries – such as Russian-German co-productions – fall under this definition. This offers a number of opportunities for Eastern European media production (Fabris, 1995: 230).

Joining the global communications network after being isolated for 70 years is not without its dangers. Cultural imperialism is a threat felt by many in Russia as they observe indigenous cultural traditions being eroded (McNair, 1994: 130). There is a clear overload of American programs. Russian broadcasters have only limited resources for domestic production; the airing of foreign programming is often cheaper. Russia's ability to resist what may be perceived as economic and cultural imperialism will depend on how successfully it can generate indigenous production of sufficient quality to retain the interest of audiences. "Both the viewers and the professionals have already understood this, that there is a need for more Russian programs in Russia" (Kira Proshutinskaya, ATV's chief editor, cited in Meek, 1995). The initial fascination of the late eighties and early nineties for Western, especially American films and series, has faded away. Russian films from the sixties to the eighties now enjoy equal popularity. The television schedules in Russia are changing in the direction of domestically produced programs. Whereas in the Soviet Union all domestic programming came from government companies or film studios, programming now comes from a variety of sources as independent commercial production companies (REN-TV, VID, ATV, etc.) have emerged. Local production is concentrated on the genres of information, entertainment, and talk show programming. Series and drama are still dominated by Western programming, as Russian production companies are just beginning to enter this genre.

Russia does not yet have a set percentage of locally produced programming. According to *Mayofis,* a board member of NVS, introduction of local content laws would be even counterproductive because there simply are not enough Russian producers able to provide such programming as viewers would want to watch (Media Developments, April 1996). The 1997 draft Russian law on radio and television broadcasting does include under Article 9 some provisions regarding the protection of domestic radio and television production: two thirds of the daily broadcasting time of a governmental or public broadcasting company, excluding news, education, sports, and popular scientific programs, must be domestically produced. In this definition, domestically produced programs are those whose production process is controlled by Russian legal entities or citizens. In the more recent draft of December 1998, however, this stipulation is not included.

Governmental and public television and radio companies are required to provide a universal (general-interest) programming scheme, offering a variety of information, sports, educational, cultural, and entertainment programs (Articles 23–4, 29–4). Additional requirements are included in the draft law regarding the development of Russian culture and education. Governmental and public broadcasting organizations must set aside time for the popularization of Russian cultural treasures and cultural achievements and the heritage of the peoples of the Russian Federation (Articles 23–5, 29–5). On December 20, 1995 the Russian government passed a resolution on the creation of a State fund for television and radio programs (*Gosteleradiofond*), in accordance with a decree by President Yeltsin. The principal function of the fund consists in selecting, forming and storing programs aired on television or radio as part of the cultural heritage of Russia's peoples. The fund will also carry out research in the storage, search and restoration of television and radio programs of cultural value.

Table 7. *Top 10 Recurrent Programs on ORT/Adults 18+*
(At least two broadcasts between January and April 1995 for the Top 10 recurrent programs)

Title	Country of Origin	Genre	Average Starting Time	Audience (in %)	Market Share (in %)
Field of Wonders	Russian	Game	19:50	39.6	60
Wild Rose	Mexican	Series	19:30	34.0	65
Beaumonde	Russian	Entertainment	19:00	30.6	62
KVN-95	Russian	Game	20:00	30.2	49
Prime Time	Russian	Entertainment	19:00	26.5	55
The fifth corner	Russian	Series	19:50	25.6	46
Weather forecast	Russian	Others	19:45	23.5	49
Theme	Russian	Entertainment	19:55	22.8	38
US	Russian	Entertainment	19:55	21.7	37
Time (Vremya)	Russian	News	21:00	21.7	36

Source: Russian Research, January-April 1995.

Additional requirements are also included in order to protect children and minors. Erotic programs, for example, are restricted to early morning hours (1:00 a.m. to 5:00 a.m.) (Article 16). Strikingly, Article 29–5/7 of the draft law stipulates that public television and radio companies must "use the results of sociological investigations for meeting the various information needs and respecting the tastes and interests of television viewers and radio listeners." In the Soviet Union programming was not geared to audience interest. Entertainment was neglected. In today's Russia commercialization has forced broadcasters to focus on audience maximization.[21] The result has been a rapid

---

[21] Surveys show however that Russian viewers are not particularly satisfied with the quantity and quality of existing television programming. A mid-1996 ComCon2 survey shows that 70% of the

downmarket move in the content and style of many Russian media. Series and soap, sensationalism, erotic programs, game shows, superficiality in information characterize the commercial strategy of appealing to the lowest common denominator in order to attract the largest audiences. Teleshopping is a relatively new plague on all channels, except the first. In general, programming on all channels is somewhat similar. By way of illustration we display the Top 10 of recurrent programs on the main channels ORT and RTR. The top slots in popular programs are dominated by the lighter albeit homemade genres of entertainment, series and games. News reviews (especially *Vesti* on RTR and *Vremya* on ORT) are the only information programs that can be considered popular. Analytical programs are far less popular. On the whole, as compared with data collected over 1987–90, the television audience of the 1990's has lost much of its interest for politics. Instead it shows more interest in series and entertainment (Postfactum, 1993: 15).

Table 8. *Top 10 Recurrent Programs on RTR/Adults 18+*
(At least two broadcasts between January and April 1995 for the Top 10 recurrent programs)

Title	Country of Origin	Genre	Average Starting Time	Audience (in %)	Market Share (in %)
Santa Barbara	American	series	20:35	26.2	41
Details	Russian	news	20:25	22.6	39
News (Vesti)	Russian	news	20:00	21.8	36
Celebration every day	Russian	children progr.	20:25	21.4	34
Film poster	Russian	magazine	20:35	19.9	36
Edera	Italian	series	14:20	18.7	65
At Ksyusha's	Russian	entertainment	20:25	14.6	28
Gentlemen show	Russian	entertainment	22:25	13.5	30
Small town	Russian	entertainment	21:30	13.5	27
Film director in my own right	Russian	entertainment	21:30	13.5	28

Source: Russian Research, January-April 1995.

respondents would like to see more television programs and channels than are currently available (PSML&P, November 1996: 20).

VIII Telecommunications

While the former Soviet Union developed an elaborate broadcasting system, telecommunications did not enjoy a high priority in the national investment plans. This was partly due to the Marxist-Leninist view of material production as being the only source of economic growth and welfare while services were seen as unproductive. Another important factor was the ruling class's wish to control information flow. Individualized telecommunications were seen as a threat. And indeed, modern telecommunications technology makes it more difficult for governments the world over to censor information. Furthermore, Western nations imposed tight export restrictions for 'sensitive' technology and curtailed the East's ability to buy advanced communications technology from the West. Nowadays there is a growing perception that economic efficiency, particularly market-oriented reforms, requires a more extensive and more open, less centrally controlled telecommunications infrastructure (Bauer, 1994: 258). Existing networks have to be expanded and upgraded in order to meet business and academic data transmission demands. Digital equipment and packet-switched networks have to be installed. This replacement process is being done by various major European and US equipment manufacturers. Arranging transfer of military technology to civilian uses could accelerate the digitization of civilian networks in the former Soviet Union.

Itar-Tass reported about 1.9 million Internet users in Russia as of June 1999. Three years before only about 500,000 people used e-mail and about 50,000 people used the *World Wide Web* regularly in Russia, according to a report by Russian firm *Rusinfoil*. Russians are the most frequent visitors to Russian sites, making up 28% of the users, with Americans coming in second (25%). Sixty percent of the information available is in Russian, with the balance in English (Orttung, Omri daily digest, November 12, 1996). Almost all Russian language newspapers, such as *Izvestiya, Nezavisimaya Gazeta, Kommersant-Daily Express, Chas Pik* and *Segodniya* have electronic editions on the Web. Recently a wide variety of regional newspapers have also started to make their contents available on the Internet. A Russian-language electronic mailing list, intended to foster the flow of information between journalists and media organizations (RJOUR-L) was launched on May 20, 1996. In Moscow a center offering free instruction to non-commercial organizations and the mass media on how to create their own WWW home pages has been established as part of efforts to expand usage of the Internet. Both initiatives are funded by foreign (American) organizations. Internet-related activities have become a hot item in the last few years, especially since the end of 1996, but there have been no Internet versions of broadcast programs yet. Many non-governmental television stations now use e-mail for communication with advertisers and production companies as well as for communication among affiliates. Some programs are giving their e-mail address for hearer/viewer recall. Another telecommunications gateway is the cooperation between television programs and computer/telecommunications companies. Such programs mostly focus on advertising and teleshopping. A case in point is *Virtual'nyj kiosk*, daily (except on Sundays) on the 2x2 channel: 12 minutes of advertising and shopping for hardware and software, including Internet access.

IX   Conclusion

The transformation of the Russian media occurred within the general framework of *perestroika* and the ongoing economic, political and social turmoil of Russian society. The Soviet Union had a centralized, monopolistic, State-owned media system under Party control, whose programming consisted entirely of propaganda. Societal changes led Russia to introduce a dual system, compatible with European standards, with public/ State and private broadcasters, operating along one another. The media monopoly is no more. New relationships are springing up between the media and the consumers of media contents.

After a first stage of enthusiastic awakening to the new media freedoms (the *glasnost* era), came disillusionment. Media corporations faced huge financial problems. The process of drafting media laws slowed down. The struggle among different political groups to get control over broadcasting grew again. Russia's mass media are still largely dependent on the government as well as political and financial, oligarchic groups (financial and organizational dependence), which translates as direct and indirect pressure. Their only alternative to State control seems to be commercialization, while the notion of public service television remains alien. Continued political involvement of the media slows down the professionalization and transformation of the journalistic community into an autonomous professional group dedicated to a public service ideal.

The development of the media roughly corresponds to the political and economic development of society. The only place where a free and democratic media system can emerge and thrive is a stable democracy in an open society with a stable, multi-party system. It must be based on a broad consensus in matters political and economic, and there must be economic growth within a market economy (Jakubowicz, 1995: 130). As long as Russia does not have a normal working economy nor a genuine civil society, it cannot have free and democratic media.

References

Androunas, E. (1991). The struggle for control over Soviet television, *Journal of Communication* 41 (2): 185–200.

BBC (1996). The BBC's guide to Russian broadcasting, *Post-Soviet Media Law & Policy Newsletter* 27/28: 4–7.

Bauer, J.M. & Straubhaar, J.D. (1994). Telecommunications in Central and Eastern Europe. In C. Steinfield, J.M. Bauer & L. Caby (eds.), *Telecommunications in Transition. Policies, Services and Technologies in the European Community* (pp. 255–271). London: Sage Publications.

Bystrytski, A. & Djaguinova, E. (1995). Scénarios pour l'audiovisuel russe, *Diffusion UER*, Winter: 11–14.

Chernykh, A. & Grocott, J. (1996). Russian networks race for the sky, *Post-Soviet Media Law & Policy Newsletter* 33/34: 20–23.

Coalson, R. (2000). Media watch: uniting to protect media, *The Moscow Times* 19 May. Available at [http://www.moscowtimes.ru/19-May-2000/stories/story40.html]

European Audiovisual Observatory (EAO) (1999). *Statistical Yearbook 1999. Film, television, video and new media in Europe.* Straatsburg: European Audiovisual Observatory.

Fabris, H.H. (1995). Westification? In D.L. Paletz, K. Jakubowicz & P. Novosel (eds.), *Glasnost and After. Media and Change in Central and Eastern Europe* (pp. 221–231). Cresskill, New Jersey: Hampton Press.

Ganley, G.D. (1996). *Unglued Empire: The Soviet Experience with Communications Technologies.* Norwood, New Jersey: Ablex Publishing Corporation.

Gubanov, A. (2000). Televidenie: gody 1990–2000, *Sreda* 6–7 (June–July): 19–22.

Gulyaev, M. (1996). Media as contested power in post-glasnost Russia, *Post-Soviet Media Law & Policy Newsletter* 29: 12–16.

Internews (1997). *A Survey of Russian Television.* Moscow, April 1997. Available at [http://www.internews.ras.ru/report/tv/index.html]

Jakubowicz, K. (1995). Media within and without the State: Press freedom in Eastern Europe, *Journal of Communication* 45 (4): 125–139.

Katsjkaeva, A. (1997). Televidenie i novaja rossijskaja oligarchija (Television and the new Russian oligarchy). *Zakonodatelstvo i praktika sredstv massovoj informatsii* (The Russian Version of *Post-Soviet Media Law & Policy Newsletter* 30 (2). Available at [http://www.internews.ras.ru/ZiP/31/file.html].

Lazutkin, V. (1996). Lazutkin assesses State of Russian television, *Post-Soviet Media Law & Policy Newsletter* 33/34: 12–14.

Lutz, P.M. & Jankowski, J. (1996). Zur Situation des Rundfunks in der Gemeinschaft Unabhängiger Staaten (GUS). In *Internationales Handbuch für Hörfunk und Fernsehen 96/97* (C1, pp. 64–74). Hans-Bredow-Institut. Baden-Baden/Hamburg: Nomos.

McNair, B. (1994). Media in Post-Soviet Russia: An overview, *European Journal of Communication* 9 (2): 115–135.

Meek, J. (1995, March 19). Red eyes at night in Russia, *The Guardian:* 9.

Mickiewicz, E.P. (1988). *Split Signals. Television and Politics in the Soviet Union.* New York: Oxford University Press.

Paasilinna, R. (1995). *Glasnost and Soviet television. A Study of the Soviet Mass Media and Its Role in Society from 1985–1991.* Research Report 5. Audience Research YLE (Finnish Broadcasting Company).

Pankin, A. (1993). Russian media on the way to independence, *The Bulletin* 10 (3): 13–14.

Pietkiewicz, B. (1996). TV music – an Eastern European view, *Diffusion EBU*, Summer: 18–21.

Postfactum News Agency (1993). *Mass Media Audience.* Moscow/St. Petersburg.

Price M.E. (1995). Law, force and the Russian media, *Cardozo Arts & Entertainment Law Journal* 13 (3): 795–846.

TV International (1998). Backed by Russian media giant, NTV aims high in volatile market, *TV International* 6 (6): 10–11.

Richter, A.G. (1995). The Russian press after perestroika, *Canadian Journal of Communication* 20 (1): 7–23.

Vartanova, E. (1996). Corporate transformation of the Russian media, *Post-Soviet Media Law & Policy Newsletter* 32: 5–8.

Wendlandt, A. (1996). Cartel of 2 calls the shots in Russia's media market, *St. Petersburg Times* 2, July 9.

Canada

by David Taras and Ruth Klinkhammer

I   Introduction

The Canadian media system was shaken by enormous changes in 2000. Indeed the geological plates on which it has rested for the past twenty years have shifted dramatically. What we are seeing in effect is a transition from an older media model in which broadcasters focused only on broadcasting, and newspaper owners were only concerned with newspapers – to a new system in which multi-platform media groups dominate the landscape. In essence, Canadian media conglomerates have adopted what can be described as the AOL-Time Warner model. The first major step towards this new world was taken in early 2000, when telephone and satellite giant Bell Canada Enterprises (BCE) bought Canada's largest TV broadcaster, the CTV television group, for Cdn$ 3.2 Billion. In September 2000, BCE made a bid to acquire *The Globe and Mail*, one of Canada's two national newspapers and long considered *the kingdom and the power* of the newspaper industry in Canada. In August, television mogul, Israel Asper, the owner of CanWest Global, acquired Conrad Black's Canadian newspaper empire for Cdn$ 3.5 billion. Black's holdings included a new national newspaper, the *National Post* (although Black will retain a 50% stake in the paper for at least another five years), 13 of the country's largest dailies and 136 smaller papers.

Convergence has become the new watchword as media executives have spoken almost mantra like about the possibilities inherent in the new business model. Leonard Asper, president and CEO of CanWest Global told an audience in Winnipeg in January, 2001 that "In the future, journalists will wake up, write a story for the Web, write a column, take their cameras, cover an event and do a report for TV and file a video clip for the Web. What we have really acquired is a quantum leap in the product we offer advertisers and a massive, creative content-generation machine"(Zerbisias). Even as they are furiously integrating, leveraging and cross-promoting their many media holdings, they are also gambling that the Internet will become a main gateway, a principal portal, for television broadcasting, newspaper publication and radio listening. Hence both BCE and CanWest Global are in the process of reinforcing their presence on the Web through Sympatico.ca (BCE) and Canada.com (CanWest Global) among other sites, and are furiously integrating, leveraging and cross-promoting their many media holdings.

In another dramatic move, Quebecor Inc., owner of Canada's other large newspaper chain, The Sun newspapers, and the Internet portal Canoe.ca., purchased TVA, Quebec's largest private broadcaster and Videotron, which controls the cable market in Quebec. Quebecor, which also owns a stable of printing plants, is one of the largest printers in the world. Other media players have also succumbed to the temptations of convergence. Rogers Communication, Canada's largest cable company and a major force in cell-phones, video distribution, and the magazine industry bought major league base-ball's Toronto Blue Jays and is attempting to acquire CTV Sports Net, a cable channel that is now up for sale.

During the 1990's the Canadian media skyline could be described as a series of low level buildings with the publicly financed Canadian Broadcasting Corporation (CBC) and Radio-Canada, its French language counterpart, looming a little larger than the rest. Today, three immense skyscrapers dominate the horizon. BCE, Global and Quebecor all tower over a much smaller and more run down CBC.

Even as these giant conglomerates were reshaping the Canadian media environment, Canadian broadcasting was being transformed in various other ways. Since the mid-1990's Canada has been in the midst of a cable and satellite revolution that has given most Canadians access to close to 70 channels. In the fall of 2000, the Canadian Radio-Television and Telecommunications Commission (CRTC), the regulator of the information highway in Canada, licensed close to 300 new digital pay and specialty services. Although cable operators will be obligated to carry only a select number of these new channels, and will only offer the other new services if they attract audiences, the al-ready dense forest of cable channels will soon get even denser. With access to a TV uni-verse where there will be a channel to match almost every conceivable interest, lifestyle, viewpoint and hobby, Canadians will soon be living in the age of 'micro-niched' or 'Me' television. The audience share for speciality and premium channels mushroomed from 18% in 1997 to 24% in 2000 and is likely to increase even further (Universal Com-munications Management, 2001: 23).

While the main line private broadcasters own much of the prime real estate on cable TV, using cable services to recycle and cross-promote their TV programming, the pro-liferation of cable channels has spawned important new experiments. For instance, there is now an Aboriginal Television Network and a network devoted to the needs of older Canadians. And in what's been called a major breakthrough in media convergence, Can-ada's first Internet TV station began broadcasting in January 2001. The station, www.U8TV.com, is devoted exclusively to the lives of eight young Canadians living in a Toronto loft. Cameras broadcast live action from the loft 24 hours a day, 7 days a week and each evening three hours of highlights are shown on the Life Network specialty channel.

As a result of these changes, the CBC – Radio-Canada, once at the center of the Ca-nadian media system finds itself increasingly on the periphery. Several rounds of deep budget cuts, the refusal by regulators to allow it to mount new cable services and the steady erosion in the size of its audience, now threaten its long-term survival. Although it still remains the largest journalistic organization in the country and has the capacity to set the national news agenda, its ability to fulfil its mandate under current budgetary conditions has become all but impossible.

The CBC has responded to these challenges by conducting yet another of what has become a long series of 'visioning' and 're-engineering' exercises. The corporation's new President, Robert Rabinovitch, a man with extensive government and private sector experience, unveiled a new corporate plan in July 2000. Rabinovitch moved decisively on a number of fronts. The president's strategy was to refocus the corporation so that it adhered more closely a purer model of public broadcasting. The effect, he hoped, would be to challenge or more accurately perhaps to shame the government into making a renewed financial commitment to the CBC.

What was most shocking perhaps was Rabinovitch's candor. He told a parliamentary committee that if the CBC were a public corporation it would file for bankruptcy (Rabinovitch, 2000: 1–4). He then announced plans to completely 'Canadianize' the CBC's prime time schedule, bolster news and information programming as the primary focus, deepen its commitment to children's programming and special events and beef up its already considerable investment on the Web. This also meant that the public broadcaster would retreat from program areas in which it could no longer compete. Rabinovitch also announced that the corporation would slowly wean itself off of its reliance on corporate advertising. In a dramatic step, the CBC pulled advertising from the first half-hour of its flagship news program, *The National*.

This chapter will review the history of the Canadian media system with particular emphasis on the role of public broadcasting. The chapter will focus on the CBC's mandate, the development of Canadian content requirements and on the public broadcaster's often uncomfortable and troubled relationship with its political masters. The rise of private broadcasters, the growth of cable, the relationship of Canadian audiences to American media and the challenges presented by the emergence of new technologies and of the new multiplatform media conglomerates will also be described.

II   The CBC and the History of the Canadian Broadcasting System

The decision to establish a publicly financed Canadian Broadcasting Corporation emerged because of a number of factors. The most telling reality was that by the mid 1920's American broadcasters had already set up shop in Canada and the vast majority of Canadians who had radios were listening to US programs. While the Canadian government may have been slow to realize the potential that radio would have as a force for nation building, the specter of an American dominated system galvanized it into action. The choice facing Canadians was perhaps best expressed by an early supporter of public broadcasting, Graham Spry, who argued that Canadians had to choose between "the state or the United States." Either the government intervened to establish a publicly financed broadcasting system that would be in Spry's words "a single, glowing spirit of nationality" or Canadian broadcasting would simply become an adjunct to the American commercial system (Nash, 1994: 85).

A number of other factors weighed heavily on the decision to establish a public broadcaster. Canada's great distances and sparse population made it unlikely that private broadcasters could serve the needs of the country as a whole. They were likely to set up stations only in the large cities such as Toronto or Montreal where profits were assured. More to the point was that during the fierce ideological battles of the 1930's, left-leaning politicians, including leading members of Prime Minister Mackenzie King's government, feared that the airwaves would be dominated by a business elite that would have little interest in seeing broadcasting as a 'public trust.'

Another factor was that many Canadians still had strong emotional and cultural ties to Britain and saw the British connection as a way of counterbalancing US influence. The existence of the publicly financed British Broadcasting Corporation provided a compelling alternative to the US commercial model and it had the 'glow' of respectability that came from being what for many Canadians was still the 'mother' country.

The Canadian Broadcasting Corporation was established in 1936 after the failure of a first experiment, the Canadian Radio Broadcasting Commission (CRBC) that had been created in 1932. It is interesting to note that the federal government had been prevented from moving into broadcasting earlier because several provincial governments had argued in the courts that broadcasting was predominantly a provincial rather than federal matter. Since provincial governments had jurisdiction over education and the federal government controlled commerce, it was not immediately apparent whose claims would prevail in the courts. Only in 1932, after the Judicial Committee of the Privy Council (in Britain) ruled in its favor, could the federal government proceed with its first broadcasting act.

That act laid the foundations for the broadcasting system that exists today. First, the Canadian broadcasting system would include a mix of public and private broadcasters. While the publicly financed CRBC, and later the CBC, would be the principal broadcaster and regulator, private broadcasters were allowed to gain a foothold alongside the public system. Second, the new corporation would be a public rather than a state run enterprise. While the network was financed in part by a grant from Parliament, an excise tax on the sale of radio sets ensured a steady flow of revenue from radio listeners. In 1936, guidelines were put in place to ensure that an arms-length relationship existed between the CBC and the politicians that it had to report on. News reports, for instance, were to be read in a neutral sounding tone and be strictly non-partisan.

Broadcasters soon had to face the great Canadian dilemma of having to provide equal but very different services in both English and French. Although there were early attempts to establish a single system that alternated between English- and French-language broadcasts, these experiments collapsed almost immediately. In 1934, the decision was taken to create what in effect are two distinct broadcasting systems. So while the CBC and Radio Canada share the same mandate and corporate structure they have become two distinct entities serving very different audiences.

In the aftermath of the Second World War the basic philosophy and features of the Canadian broadcasting system became more clearly defined. The crucial Royal Commission on National Development in the Arts, Letters and Sciences (Massey Commission) of 1949 and the Royal Commission on Broadcasting (Fowler Commission) of 1955, further reinforced the view that the federal government should play the dominant role in ensuring the survival of Canadian culture. The logic behind the policy was perhaps best expressed by the Fowler Commission report:

"The choice is between a Canadian state-controlled system with some flow of programs east and west across Canada, with some Canadian content and the development of a Canadian sense of identity, at a substantial public cost, and a privately owned system which the forces of economics will necessarily make predominantly dependent on imported American radio and television programs" (Royal Commission, 1957: 10).

The Commission insisted that broadcasting could not be seen only as a commercial venture.

"(…) if the less costly method is always chosen, is it is possible to have a Canadian nation at all? The Canadian answer, irrespective of party or race, has been uniformly the same for nearly a century. We are prepared, by measures of assistance, financial aid and a conscious stimulation to compensate for our disabilities of geography, sparse populations and vast distances, and we have accepted this as a legitimate role of the government in Canada" (Royal Commission, 1957: 9).

But the challenges presented by the arrival of television broadcasting in Canada in 1952 were of a different order of magnitude, on a different scale, than had been the case with radio. Most important perhaps was that hundreds of thousands of Canadians living close to the border, were receiving American TV signals and had developed a firm loyalty to US network television even before the arrival of Canadian TV. As was the case with radio, American television preceded Canadian television in Canada. Television, however, was and is a much more powerful and pervasive cultural instrument than radio and the job of creating a vigorous alternative to American programming proved to be a far more costly and arduous task. The realities of a particularly Canadian predicament soon became evident; Canadian television would be in a minority position within Canada.

The costs of maintaining a television system that reached across a vast country proved to be a major undertaking. The old financial regime based on an excise tax on the purchase of TV sets and an annual grant from Parliament soon crumbled under the weight of building a TV system that had to compete with the American networks. Inevitably the government gave into temptation. The excise tax was dropped and advertising became a part of the revenue mix. While the CBC still depends on a grant from Parliament for over 60% of its revenue, Cdn$ 764 million in 2000, it has become increasingly dependent on TV advertising. Ads brought in Cdn$ 504 million in 2000 (CBC Annual Report, 1999–2000).

The Broadcasting Acts of 1968 and then 1991 provide the basic architecture of the Canadian broadcasting system. The system's bricks and mortar are the sweeping mandate given to the Canadian Broadcasting Corporation and the role given to the CRTC to administer the Canadian content provisions that govern the awarding and renewal of radio and TV licenses. Under the provisions of the Broadcasting Act of 1991, the CBC is to be the main supplier of Canadian programming and the broadcaster of record, the chronicler of the country's public affairs and cultural life. Its programming is expected to be uniquely Canadian and to "contribute to shared national consciousness and identity." The broadcaster must reflect regional and linguistic differences as well as the country's multicultural and multiracial makeup. According to the CBC's corporate plan for the period 2000–2005: "The CBC's mission is simple – to tell Canadian stories, to provide Canadians with relevant news and information, to support and contribute to Canada's rich cultural capital and to build bridges between communities and regions and to bring the 'best of the World' to Canadians" (CBC Corporate Plan, 2000:1).

This means in effect that the corporation is the frontline broadcaster at all of the important events in the life of the country. It must be there to broadcast Canada Day Celebrations on July 1st, Remembrance Day ceremonies, the opening of Parliament, the Budget address, the Governor General's Speech from the Throne, federal and provincial elections, state funerals and federal-provincial conferences among other events. The problem of course is that these programs are often costly to produce in that they displace programs that might be more attractive to advertisers. In addition, the broadcaster is expected to serve as the primary window for original Canadian dramas and films, produce regional newscasts and documentaries and provide a rich menu of sports programming.

As presently constituted the CBC consists of a phalanx of networks and services including the main English- and French-language TV channels, Radio One (AM) and Radio Two (FM) in both languages, and Newsworld and the *Réseau de l'information*, which are 24-hour all-news networks available on cable. The corporation also maintains a northern service that broadcasts in a variety of aboriginal languages, and Radio Canada International, a radio service that broadcasts overseas. The CBC has also made a sizeable investment in its main web site – cbc.ca – and a host of other network and program sites.

There is a wide, some would say a yawning, gap between the CBC's mandate and the budget with which it has had to operate. The corporation has long since reached the point where it can no longer pretend to be all things to all people. It has been forced to vacate entire areas of the TV schedule and become a niche broadcaster that specializes in only certain formats – news, documentaries, children's television, ensemble comedy and sports. Many of its major shows, including its banner news program *The National*, are broadcast several times each night and the same episodes of hit shows are repeated several times a week. In the age of what Dan Schiller calls 'digital capitalism,' with huge multi-tiered media corporations and an explosion in cable and Internet services, the CBC seems to be based on an older model and a previous era (Schiller, 2000). Yet despite its many wounds, the corporation can still produce a big canvas documentary series such as *Canada: A People's History*, a 30 hour, Cdn$ 25 million extravaganza covering some 12,000 years of Canadian life which aired in the fall of 2000.

The CBC's decline can be attributed to a number of factors. First, the draconian budget cuts imposed on the corporation beginning in the mid-1980's have never been restored. The public broadcaster has effectively been downsized by an estimated 50% over the last 15 years. While the corporation was an easy target for budget cutters when virtually all government spending was being drastically reduced in the early 1990's, there seemed to be a special zealousness where the CBC was concerned. Some observers believe that the long standing antagonism between the public broadcaster and the political leaders, that its often criticized in its news reports and parodied in its comedy skits, has been at the root of many of the CBC's troubles. Prime Ministers from John Diefenbaker (1957–63) to Pierre Trudeau (1968–79, 1980–84), from Brian Mulroney (1984–93) to Jean Chrétien (1993-) have all complained bitterly about the treatment that they have received from CBC reporters (Taras, 1999). The break point has usually been over the CBC's coverage of national unity issues. Prime Ministers were especially concerned when CBC reporters would place the federal government's constitutional polices under an intense and often critical scrutiny or give valuable air time to separatist politicians.

Pierre Trudeau probably went the furthest when he suggested what might happen if the CBC didn't play the government's tune: "We will put a lid on the place (…) we will close up the shop. Let them not think we won't do it. If need be, we can produce programs, and if not, we will show people Chinese or Japanese vases instead of the nonsense they dish out. That would be of some cultural benefit" (Nash, 1994: 391). But it was Brian Mulroney, who hamstrung the CBC's Board of Directors with political appointees and would often phone the then CBC Chairman, Patrick Watson, with comments that ranged from "angry protestations to subtle suggestions," who initiated the first round of drastic budget cuts (Taras, 1999: 137).

This slow bleeding of the corporation in budgetary terms meant that the CBC lacked the resources to expand aggressively into the new cable frontier when the first flurry of cable licenses were being granted in the late 1980's and early 1990's. While the CBC was given two valuable franchises – Newsworld and RDI – private broadcasters were given the most lucrative and valuable pieces of cable real estate. The direction, the entire tilt, of the Canadian broadcasting system might have been different had the CBC been allowed to develop five or six cable services in areas that were decisive to its mandate. Instead private broadcasters were given licenses in areas such as religious, children's, ethnic, cultural, comedy, sports and business television that were once the CBC's exclusive preserve.

Canadian content requirements are another key ingredient of Canadian broadcasting policy. 'CanCon' rules are currently structured according to a points system that rewards broadcasters for airing programs that have Canadians in key production, acting and technical roles. Canadian content requirements for radio were recently raised from 30% to 35% of overall programming. Canadian music, defined again by the nationality of the principal singer and musicians as well as other key production personnel, must constitute 35% of all music played between 6 a.m. and 6 p.m. Monday to Friday. Sixty-five percent of all music played on French-language radio stations must be in the French language. The basic rule on TV is that at least 60% of all programming during the broadcast day must qualify as Canadian. In 1999, the CRTC raised the ante on private broadcasters by insisting that they air at least 8 hours per week of 'priority' Canadian programming during the lucrative primetime schedule – 7:00 p.m. to 11:00 p.m. Programs that meet CanCon requirements also qualify for a host of government subsidies and tax incentives.

Critics argue that the problem with Canadian content regulations is that they are aimed at job creation rather than cultural production. Points are awarded according to the citizenship of the principal actors, singers or producers. They are not based on whether programs or songs tell Canadian stories or address Canadian themes. The dilemma was perhaps best expressed in an editorial in the *Ottawa Citizen* that complained that:

> "When Canadian singer Alannah Miles crooned about Mississippi and that 'slow Southern style' in 'Black Velvet,' CanCon gave it the Maple Leaf seal of approval. Ditto for Amanda Marshall's 'Birmingham' (that's Alabama for anyone who hasn't been south of Windsor). All sorts of country artists singing in fake Nashville drawls score, too, because they have Canuck passports tucked into their cowboy boots. In fact, very few Canadian recording artists actually make clear references to things Canadian because they know the real prize, the American market, won't know what to make of them" (Stanbury, 1998: 55).

So while the intention of the Broadcasting Act of 1991 is to preserve a strong Canadian presence through the mandate given to the CBC and through the enforcement of Can-Con provisions, the act has to some degree become toothless – a paper tiger. The advent of new multimedia empires, the arrival of new technologies that blur the lines between conventional and other forms of broadcasting, and the slow but steady erosion of the CBC have stripped the act of much of its meaning and authority.

The Heritage Committee of the House of Commons will begin hearings in fall 2001 on the future of Canadian broadcasting. Among the issues on the table will be whether the Broadcasting Act needs to be revised, funding arrangements for the CBC and the challenges of media convergence.

III   Private Television and the Americanization of Canadian TV

The Canadian television system can perhaps best be seen as resembling a geological formation with many different layers of rock and sediment. While the CBC can still be seen as providing a basic bedrock of Canadian and public affairs programming, a number of provincial governments also have their own educational channels. Radio-Quebec, TV Ontario and the Knowledge Network in British Columbia offer programs that serve provincial needs and are integrated to some degree with the educational systems in those provinces. Much like the CBC, provincial broadcasters have had to endure sharp budget cuts and a frenzy of criticism about their role and utility from right-wing politicians bent on privatization. Indeed, as part of the wave of privatization that took place under the Klein government, Alberta's Access network was sold to private broadcasters in the mid-1990's.

The two largest players in the TV game in Canada are the private networks. As figure 1 shows, CTV and TVA hold the largest share of the national television audience in terms of station groups. Licensed in 1961, CTV began as an uncomfortable alliance among the owners of largely independent broadcasting stations across the country. For almost three decades, the network was essentially a co-operative that brought ownership groups together for the purpose of buying top rated Hollywood shows, from which they garnered the lion's share of their profits, and producing a small number of Canadian news and dramatic programs. By the time that ownership was finally consolidated under giant BCE in 2000, CTV had become a valuable TV property. The network consists of 25 conventional stations, many of which dominate their local markets, and a phalanx of valuable cable services including The Sports Network, a 24 hour news headline service, CTV Newsnet, the Outdoor Life Network, The Comedy Network, Talk TV, and History Television. Its nightly newscast, the *CTV National News*, rivals CBC's flagship news show, *The National*, in terms of both audience numbers and prestige, and its *Canada AM* morning show dominates breakfast hour programming.

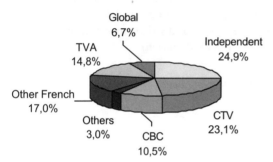

Figure 1. *National Audience Shares Across Canadian Conventional Channels 1999* *(All persons 2+)* Data: Nielsen Media Research – Source: Canadian Media Directors' Council

Can West Global is in some ways the new kid on the block. In 1974, the CRTC licensed Global TV as an independent station in Winnipeg, Manitoba and later as a regional network based in Southern Ontario. After years of slowly and steadily buying and then linking 15 stations across the country, owner Israel Asper was finally able to turn Global into a national network in 2000. Global had also moved into cable controlling Prime TV, a cable service for older Canadians, and a chunk of ROBTv – the Report on Business cable channel. Just as Asper was fulfilling his long cherished dream of building Canada's third national network, he chose to pounce again. In a dramatic move, Global bought Conrad Black's very substantial Canadian newspaper holdings. It should also be noted that Global has expanded overseas gaining important footholds in New Zealand (TV3, TV4) Australia (Network 10), Ireland (TV3) and in Northern Ireland (Ulster Television).

The growth of the private networks has been aided by the CRTC's curious policy of 'Canadianization by Americanization.' The logic behind the policy is that only by becoming profitable could Canadian broadcasters produce high quality Canadian programming and that the only way to become profitable was to air big ticket Hollywood shows. While CTV and Global have made considerable efforts to produce front line Canadian shows, their profits depend heavily on airing US shows. It is far more economical to go to Hollywood and buy popular programs 'off the shelf,' than to produce top quality Canadian shows from scratch. Hollywood programs have recognized stars, are promoted heavily in the American media and are attractive to advertisers. Investing in Canadian programs involves considerable risk; up-front development costs are considerable and because of the small size of the Canadian market most shows need to be sold in the United States and overseas in order to be profitable. It is hardly a secret that American programming made the big difference for CTV in 2000. Its big money winners were *Who Wants to be a Millionaire*, which attracted over 3 million viewers per show, *ER* which drew an audience of 2.4 million viewers, and such shows as *Law & Order, Ally McBeal* and *The West Wing* which also garnered large audience numbers (CTV Annual Report, 1999). The daytime schedule was sprinkled with American soap operas and talk shows. Canadian dramas such as *Cold Squad*, *Power Play* and *The City* were clustered, some would say confined or ghettoized, in the Friday night schedule.

According to the CRTC, in 1999, 95% of Global's primetime audience watched American shows. The number for CTV was 88% (Simpson).

Table 1. *Top 10 Specials in the 1999–2000 Viewing Season (Age 18+)*

Network Specials	In 000s
Survivor Season Finale	5,338
Academy Awards	4,791
Superbowl	3,678
Academy Pre-Show	3,310
Golden Globe Awards	2,766
Grammy Awards	2,598
Grey Cup Game '99	2,190
Emmy Awards	1,965
Anne . . . Green Gables 3	1,862
American Music Awards	1,831

Source: Television Bureau of Canada
Data: Nielsen Media Research

Table 1 indicates the extent of the problem most starkly. The breakdowns presented in figure 1 do not highlight the large number of Canadians watching American shows on Canadian conventional networks and Canadian specialty channels. But as table 1 demonstrates, the top drawing special in spring 2000 was the season finale of the American reality TV show *Survivor* which boasted a Canadian audience of over 5,000,000. Of the top 10 specials listed, only the Grey Cup football championship and the Anne of Green Gables special were Canadian events. Even hockey, that once vaunted bastion of popular interest and passion, no longer draws the numbers it once did. Nielsen ratings show that in the first three weeks of May 2001 more people tuned in to watch *ER*, the *West Wing* and *Law and Order* than they did Canadian teams competing in Stanley Cup playoff games (Nielsen Media Research, 2001).

It should also be pointed out that Canadian production is fuelled by a bountiful array of government policies and subsidies. The Federal government, in partnership with the cable industry, contributes to a broadcasting fund that helps finance new productions. Through Telefilm Canada, Ottawa backstops new ventures by staking out an equity position and both the federal and provincial governments provide generous tax breaks to attract both domestic and foreign TV and film production. Most important perhaps is the CRTC's policy on simultaneous substitution. This policy allows American TV signals to be blocked when Canadian and American networks are airing the same programs during the same time period. If Global and CBS, for instance, air the hit series *Friends* at the same time, then the US signal is deleted. This gives Canadian advertisers exclusive access to large audiences and lures advertising dollars to Canadians stations. According to one estimate 'simulcasting' brings in over Cdn$ 100 million to Canadian broadcasters annually.

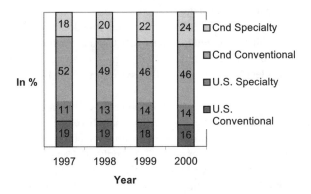

Figure 2. *Audience Share of Tuning – 2000 (Adults 18+)*
Source: Universal Communications Management
Data: Nielsen Media Research

As mentioned earlier, the Canadian broadcasting system also includes a smorgasbord of cable services. A number of cable channels have after difficult beginnings gained their sea legs to the point where they are now stable and even lucrative ventures. The Sports Network and Youth Television have become mainstays of Canadian television and in 1999–2000 commanded audience shares of 3.7% and 3.2% respectively. The problem for Canadian nationalists is that the CRTC has ruled that for every two Canadian cable channels that have been licensed, cable operators can include one American channel in their line-ups. This means that the giants of US cable TV – CNN, the Learning Channel,

Arts & Entertainment, CNBC, WTBS etc. – have become a major part of the Canadian television landscape. The effect, of course, is to further erode and diminish audiences for Canadian programming. A layer of pay-per-view channels, which offer showings of recent movies as well as a smattering of WWF wrestling specials, are also available on cable.

As figure 2 shows, there was some good news for Canadian networks last year. Canadian conventional television broadcasting networks, including the CBC, CTV, and Global, maintained their audience share in the year 2000 while Canadian specialty networks increased their share slightly. But the trend line is unmistakable.

The steady pull of audiences away from Canadian content may continue as more specialty channels are granted licenses. In the spring of 2000, the CRTC received 446 applications for Category 1 and 2 pay and specialty digital services and approved 289 licenses. There were 16 English and 5 French licenses awarded under Category 1. These services, which must be carried by cable operators, have stricter CanCon quotas. Category 2 licence holders will have to negotiate with cable companies to have their channels carried. Not all viewers will be able to access these new digital channels. There are only 2 million homes in Canada with digital service, compared to 7.5 million on regular cable systems. It is expected that the country's major broadcasters, who were the primary beneficiaries of both category 1 and 2 licenses, will begin major marketing campaigns to push Canadian cable users toward digitization.

Further fragmenting the market are Canada's two domestic satellite direct-to-home services – BCE's Express Vu and Shaw Communications' Star Choice. Each of these services has approximately 100,000 subscribers. A small army of approximately 250,000 Canadians subscribe to 'illegal' American satellite systems such as DirecTV, EchoStar and C-Band.

The greatest dilemma facing Canadian television is the powerful and relentless invasion of television signals from the United States. While Canadians have become used to being, in Pierre Trudeau's memorable description, "in bed with an elephant," it is still true that "the elephant's every move is a cause for concern." Not only are Canadians exposed to a great deal of US programming on Canadian TV but Canadian viewers are also part of the markets of US border stations. Signals from Boston, New York State, Detroit, and Seattle among other locations splash across the border and are part of the mix of alternatives available to Canadians. There is also, in some instances, a pull in the other direction. Viewers in smaller US border cities such as Buffalo or Spokane fall within the commercial and media orbits of larger Canadian cities such as Toronto or Calgary.

This cross-border relationship is laced with complexities. Although provisions of the Income Tax Act discourage Canadian corporations from advertising in foreign media, advertising dollars invariably leak across the border. For many Canadian companies the prospect of reaching Canadian viewers by advertising on US stations – especially during late night talk shows that draw large Canadian audiences – is too tempting to pass up. Having a border that is so porous has also created a myriad of legal and regulatory problems. For instance, when courts in Ontario ordered a publication ban during a particularly grizzly murder trial, media outlets in Buffalo gleefully reported all of the horrifying details.

IV   Conclusion: The Rise of the Super Conglomerates

The rise of the new super conglomerates poses important new questions for those concerned about media concentration. On one level, these new conglomerates bring obvious benefits. Companies such as BCE and Global have the resources to create first rate Canadian TV programming that can compete against Hollywood in ways that were previously impossible. Not only do they have the financial weight that is necessary but they have the capacity to promote and leverage their products across a wide spectrum of other media. These conglomerates can also play a crucial nation-building role on another level. BCE and Quebecor are Montreal based companies that are headed by French-Canadians. We may be witnessing the creation of a single Canadian media system that can more fully integrate and bring unity to the country.

But not everybody is so certain that this new era of convergence will be positive. Quebecor, CanWest Global and Rogers Communication are saddled with heavy debts as a result of pursuing their convergence strategy and it is not clear that they can effectively integrate the various parts of their media empires in the ways that that will be lucrative. As one writer warned: "(...) many of Canada's largest advertisers will simply not be attracted to an offer of coupling their advertising on, say, CTV's *Who Wants To Be A Millionaire* with ads in *The Globe and Mail*" (Gray).

There are also concerns that Canada has entered a new era of cross media ownership in which in quite a number of cities a single corporation owns both the major newspaper and the major TV station. In Vancouver, for instance, Global now owns two TV stations as well as both major newspapers. Critics are worried that citizens will be bombarded by a single set of ideas and commercial messages and have no other outlets for gaining the information that they need about the life of their communities. The CBC, which used to act as a kind of media life insurance policy because it could offset the power of commercial media by providing different and more thorough coverage of public affairs, is now a diminished force. It is unlikely to regain its old position on center stage without a wholesale reform and reworking of Canadian media policy.

Others contend that Canadians now have so many media options, that there is such a kaleidoscope of choices on cable, satellite and on the Internet, that the old concerns about media concentration are no longer as valid. And that it is precisely for these reasons that the country needs large conglomerates capable of maintaining a strong Canadian presence and identity in the new media age. Whether such super conglomerates will be able to deliver the quality and variety of media that a country such as Canada needs remains to be seen.

References

Canadian Broadcasting Corporation. (2000). *Annual Report 1999–2000*.

Canadian Broadcasting Corporation. (2000). *Entering the New Millennium: Summary of the Corporate Plan 2000–2005*.

Canadian Media Directors' Council (2000–2001). *CMDC Media Digest*. Toronto: Marketing Magazine.

CTV Inc. (1999). *Annual Report 1999*.

Gray, J. (2001). Convergence. *Canadian Business*, May 14: 34.

Nash, K. (1994). *The Microphone Wars: A History of Triumph and Betrayal at the CBC*. Toronto: McClelland & Steward.

Nielsen Media Research (2001, May 7, 14, 21). *National: Top Programs*. Available at

[http://www.nielsenmedia.ca].

Rabinovitch, R. (2000). *Opening Remarks to the Standing Committee on Canadian Heritage*.

Royal Commission on Broadcasting Report (1957). Ottawa: Queen's Printer.

Simpson, J. (2001) Just another brave new prime time, *The Globe and Mail*, March 5: A11.

Stanbury, W.T. (1998). Canadian content regulations: The intrusive state at work, *Fraser Forum*, August.

Taras, D. (1999). *Power & Betrayal in the Canadian Media*. Peterborough, Ontario: Broadview Press.

Television Bureau of Canada (2000–2001) *TVBasics 2000–2001*. Toronto: Television Bureau of Canada. Availabe at [http://www.tvb.ca].

Universal Communications Management (2001, March) *Media Mix*. Toronto.

Zerbisias, A. (2001) Ready or not: CRTC takes on media convergence, *Toronto Star*, May 4. Available at [www.thestar.com].

United States of America

by David Ostroff

The US electronic media system is large and highly complex. There are more than 10,500 commercial radio stations, and almost 1,300 commercial television stations. There are also more than 2,000 non-commercial radio stations and almost 400 non-commercial television stations. More than 2,300 low power television stations also broadcast. About 67% of the 100 million homes subscribe to cable television. Some 15 million homes receive programming directly by satellite or microwave-based *wireless cable*.

Commercial television stations can choose to affiliate with one of six national networks, while more than 150 'basic' (primarily ad-supported) television services are delivered by multi-channel providers. About fifty pay channels and pay-per-view services are available to cable and satellite subscribers. There is also a non-commercial television service supported by government subsidies, and underwriting by corporations and individuals.

Radio is even more complex. Since the rise of television radio has been primarily a local medium. However, much of the programming, such as recorded music, is from centralized sources. As with television a national non-commercial radio service is available to affiliated stations.

The average household has the television on for more than 7 hours per day; the average adult male watches almost 4 hours per day and the average adult female watches more than 4 ½ hours per day. Teenagers watch almost 3 hours per day, and children more than 3 hours per day. Commercial broadcasting is a significant component of the US economy. Almost $68 billion was spent buying airtime in the electronic media in 1999.

Table 1. *US Electronic Media Advertising Expenditures 1999* (in $million)*

National Broadcast Television Networks	13,961
Broadcast Television Stations	23,180
Syndication	2,870
Cable Networks	7,500
Cable Systems	2,929
National Radio Networks	880**
Radio Stations	13,591**

*Source: TVB
**Source: RAB

Broadcasting, cable television and the other services are regulated by the federal government, but cable television systems are also regulated in part by municipal or other local governments. Telephone companies, which have been authorized to offer video services, are regulated by the Federal government and by the individual state governments.

In this chapter we will describe the legal/regulatory system within which the US electronic media operate. Then, we will assess the structure and dynamics of the media industries. We will also examine the impact that digital technologies are having on the electronic media.

I   Regulatory Structure

The regulatory structure of the US electronic media are examined from two perspectives: the relevant laws, and the regulatory agencies.

1.1 Laws Affecting the Electronic Media

All laws in the United States devolve from the Constitution. Article I, Section 8 of the Constitution gives the Federal Government authority to regulate commerce between and among the states. A series of court decisions have established that broadcasting is 'interstate' commerce, even if the signal remains within the boundaries of a single state. Other court decisions have extended Federal authority to cable television.

Another important influence is the First Amendment to the Constitution. The law prohibits any government entity from interfering with the rights of individuals or corporations to express their opinions. In practical terms, the government is prohibited from directly censoring program content. While the government can impose sanctions for violating certain rules, the decision to carry any specific program is left to the broadcasters. Further, the government cannot require that any specific content be presented. The First Amendment specifies freedom of speech and of the press. While court decisions have expanded First Amendment rights to newer media, those rights have not been as expansive as for the older print media. As one example, if a broadcaster gives or sells time to a political candidate, the opponents must be given an opportunity to by an equal amount of time, at the same rate. No such requirement exists for the print media.

The first law to address modern broadcasting was the Radio Act of 1927. It established the 'public trustee' system, in which private enterprises are licensed to operate broadcast stations for the benefit of the public. A Federal Radio Commission was created to supervise the regulation of broadcasting. In 1934 a new Communications Act was made law. It consolidated all communications regulation under one Federal Communications Commission (FCC). The Radio Act was transferred almost intact into the new law, which also includes provisions dealing with telephone, point-to-point wireless radio and other technologies. The Communications Act remains the primary law affecting electronic media, although it has been amended a number of times in the years since 1934. For example, in 1967 the Act was amended to authorize and create a non-commercial 'public broadcasting' system, and in 1984 federal authority over cable television was established. Most recently, the Telecommunications Act of 1996 made significant changes in the law, especially regarding telephone and cable.

Many other laws impact the electronic media. The US Criminal Code outlaws the use of broadcasting media to commit fraud; the broadcasting of gambling information (with the exception of government-sponsored lotteries); and the over-the air broadcast of *indecent* content. The Communications Act and the political campaign laws place a number of requirements on operators of the electronic media: if a candidate for public office is given or sold time on a station or cable channel, the opponent(s) must receive equal opportunities for free or purchased time (there are exemptions for legitimate news programs). All candidates must also be allowed to buy advertising time at the lowest rate charged by the media outlet to any advertiser. The Federal Trade Commission Act applies to advertising, including those commercials appearing in broadcasts.

One law, the Administration Procedures Act, mandates uniform procedures that all Federal agencies, including the FCC, must follow in formal rule-making. For example, the FCC must publicly announce its proposed actions, allow sufficient time to receive public comments from any interested party, and once a decision has been reached, explain the reasoning behind its actions.

As do all government agencies, the Federal Communications Commission issues Rules and Regulations. These expand upon the more general statements or requirements of the Communications Act. As one example, the Act contains a paragraph requiring broadcasters to maintain logs of their program activities. FCC Rules and Regulations specify the details of what must be included in those logs, how long they must be kept in the station's files, etc. These details fill several pages of the FCC Rules and Regulations.

1.2 Institutions with Regulatory Authority

The United States government is composed of three branches with 'separate but equal' powers. In other words, while each branch plays a different role in media policy making, none has legal superiority over the others. An 'independent regulatory agency,' the Federal Communications Commission has day-to-day authority over the electronic media.

Congress

Congress is composed of two bodies. Members of the House of Representatives are elected for two year-terms from districts based on population. The Senate is composed of two members from each state; Senators serve for six year terms. Congress most directly influences the electronic media by writing or amending laws. Bills relating to the electronic media can originate in either house, and each house must separately pass the law. Each house usually passes somewhat different bills, so a conference committee meets to reconcile the bills; each house must then vote to accept the new version. If the president refuses to sign the bill (vetoes it), a 2/3 vote of each house can overturn the veto. The only override of a veto during the administration of President George Bush, in

1992, involved amendments to the Communication Act increasing the government's authority to regulate cable television subscription charges.

Congress has direct oversight authority over the actions of the Federal Communications Commission, and controls the FCC's budget. For example, the Congress might reduce the Commission's budget to carry out certain activities, while expanding it in a different area. Or, it might direct the FCC to take specific actions such as placing greater priority on enforcing some rules than others. Many Congressional priorities are expressed during hearings, where Commissioners are summoned to testify about particular issues. While Congress cannot require a particular action, without going through the lengthy steps needed to pass a law, these hearings allow members of Congress to make their positions known to the commissioners.

Congress may also require the FCC to collect certain data and report it to Congress. The 1996 Telecommunication Act contained a number of such provisions, such as requiring the FCC to report annually on the amount and nature of competition in the television/video industry.

Each house has a standing subcommittee of its respective Commerce Committee which most directly involves itself in telecommunication matters. The committee chair, representing the majority party in that house, and the most senior committee member from the minority party exert a great deal of influence over the activities of the subcommittee. Their relative abilities, status, and influence with other members can significantly affect legislation.

While the President nominates the members of the FCC and designates its chair, the Senate must approve the nominations. Presidents wish to have a smooth confirmation process, so there is usually consultation between the Executive and Legislative branches about potential commissioners. Influential members of Congress may recommend nominees, who are sometimes staff members, or important constituents. The Senate has, on rare occasions, rejected a Presidential nominee.

Executive Branch

As mentioned, the President nominates the members of the Federal Communications Commission and designates one to be the Chair; presumably the Chair will share the President's philosophy of government. Once confirmed by the Senate all Commissioners may serve to the end of their term; neither the President nor Congress can remove a commissioner unless he or she is convicted of a crime. The administration is able to make its position known to Commissioners through lobbying and formal involvement in the rule-making process.

Presidents have also exercised influence on the media industries through the moral or political power of their office. The National Telecommunications and Information Agency, part of the Department of Commerce, provides technical advice to the President. It also administers grants made to public (non-commercial) stations, and manages spectrum which has been allocated for non-military government use. Other executive agencies, such as the Departments of Justice, Defense, Transportation, and State may also be involved in some aspects of policy-making.

Judiciary

The Federal Courts have jurisdiction over the actions of the other two branches and agencies such as the FCC. However, the courts may not initiate actions but only act on appeals by affected parties. Court decisions are based on the conformity of actions or laws to superior laws. In other words, any act of Congress or the Executive must conform to the requirements of the Constitution or relevant laws. Actions by the FCC must conform to its own rules, the Communication Act, other laws (such as the Administrative Practices Act), and the Constitution. As with other government agencies, the FCC's decisions can also be appealed to the courts on the grounds that the commission failed to follow required procedures. In these situations the court may tell the FCC to reconsider an issue, but the actual decision may ultimately be upheld in the courts.

The Federal Communication Commission (FCC)

The FCC is responsible for the day-to-day regulation of the telecommunication industries. It is an 'independent regulatory agency,' which means that neither the executive nor the legislative branch completely control its actions. The members are appointed by the President, but must be approved by the Senate. The President also designates one member to be chair of the FCC. The FCC is headed by five commissioners, no more than three of whom can belong to the same political party (normally, then, a president will appoint three members of his party, and the chair will be a member of that party). Further limiting the direct power of either branch, FCC commissioners serve five year renewable terms. In theory at least some commissioners will serve beyond a single presidential term. While some commissioners do serve out their terms, many resign early, allowing a president to appoint most or all of the commissioners.

Commissioners have typically been appointed on the basis of political connections rather than expertise in telecommunication issues. Most have been lawyers. These politically-appointed commissioners sit at the top of a bureaucracy of about 2,000 which actually makes most of the day-to-day decisions. Decisions about the award of licenses and changes in the FCC's rules and regulations must be approved by the commissioners, but staff recommendations are usually followed in these cases. There are seven bureaus: Common Carrier; Enforcement; Wireless Telecommunication; Mass Media; Consumer Information; International; and Cable Services. The Office of Plans and Policies engages in long-range system planning, while the Office of Workplace Diversity and the Office of Communications Business Opportunities have the goal of increasing the participation of women and minority group members in the media industries. Other offices provide a variety of staff functions, such as engineering, and legal advice.

1.3 The Structure and Philosophies of the US Media System

The US broadcasting system is based on a *public trustee* model. Organizations, primarily businesses supported by advertising, are licensed by the government to operate stations in "the public interest, convenience, and necessity" (Communications Act of

1934). A smaller, non-commercial service also operates. Broadcasters pay no fee for the license they receive (other than for the administrative costs entailed in granting the license), although such fees have been considered by Congress. For many years the license term was seven years for radio stations and five for television. The Telecommunications Act of 1996 changed the license length; each renewed or new license will be for eight years. If the FCC finds a licensee has failed to serve the public interest, it may choose to not renew the license, and make it available to new applicants; it can renew the license for a shorter term, and licensees can be fined for violating FCC Rules and Regulations. Complaints against broadcasters can come from the public (including other broadcasters) or by the FCC staff (staff complaints usually involve violations of the technical rules, such as broadcasting with too high a power). Licensees are allowed to sell ('transfer') their license, with the FCC's approval. Because of their limited number licenses are valuable. A radio station in a major city like Los Angeles might be sold for $100 million, and even in a smaller city like Kansas City, Missouri, recently sold for $8 million. During the first ten months of 1999 sixty television licenses were sold, with a total sales price of more than $2,630 million.

Localism has been one of the fundamental principles of US electronic media policy since the 1920's (Ostroff, 1982). This obligation can be seen in a number of requirements. The broadcaster is required to serve the needs of the local community to which the station has been licensed, demonstrating that it presents programs that address 'issues of local importance.'

Requests for new stations are made to the FCC. Petitioners must demonstrate that their proposed station will not cause technical interference to existing broadcasts. The petitioner must also demonstrate the technical, financial, and operational ability to operate the station. The FCC may select a competing applicant for the station, regardless of who originally asked for the channel to be assigned to the community.

Stations are required to maintain a 'public file,' containing copies of specified reports. These files must be made available to any member of the public during normal operating hours.

Low Power Television service has existed since 1982. In 2000 there were about 2,300 of these stations, which have a signal that covers about 10 square miles. They are licensed to local community groups, businesses, schools and universities, and religious organizations. They can be commercial or non-commercial.

In 1999 the FCC launched an inquiry into whether to authorize a new radio service, Low Power FM (LPFM). These stations, which would have a signal covering only a few square miles, would be owned by local people. Significant opposition to the plan came from both commercial and noncommercial radio broadcasters, who argued the new service would create interference for their stations (the law does not allow them to argue against the service on the grounds of unwanted competition). Broadcasters won support from some influential members of Congress, and restrictions were placed on the frequency allocations for LPFM. However, by the end of 2000, more than 250 stations had been authorized to proceed with the licensing process, and additional authorizations were to be announced by the FCC (FCC, 2000).

While locally-oriented service remains one of the stated goals of US broadcasting policy, the economic realities of program production work against a completely local service. In the case of television, local programming is usually limited to news programs at various times of the day, one or two local public affairs programs (usually on Sundays), and some sports. Local organizations may be able to publicize events or themselves in free 'public service announcements.' Radio is more variable. While some stations maintain a strong local identity through news, public affairs or sports programming, other stations simply retransmit complete program services delivered by national networks.

Regional broadcasting in both radio and television is generally limited to news and sports. For example, the Florida Radio News network provides stories to affiliated stations from its headquarters in the state capital, Tallahassee, and occasionally from affiliates in other cities. Most university and professional sports teams create radio or television networks of stations to broadcast their games to listeners in their region. In the case of the major professional sports, the networks often regionalize their broadcasts, televising a game of interest to people in one part of the US, and a different game to another part of the US.

In the 1920's broadcasters created networks to act as centralized program distributors (the networks also own and operate stations in major cities; ownership rules, discussed below, limit the number of stations that can actually be owned by the network corporations). Stations not owned by the networks enter into contractual 'affiliation agreements' allowing them to carry the network programs. Each of the major broadcast television networks has about 210 affiliates. Federal regulation of electronic media is predicated on physical use of the spectrum. Therefore, networks, which are program creators and distributors, are not licensed. However, indirect regulatory control is exerted through the affiliates. Rather than a law prohibiting a network from doing something, the law will state, "No licensee may affiliate with a network that (...)."

The three 'major' broadcast television networks trace their roots to the 1920's, although they have undergone ownership changes since then. The National Broadcasting Company (NBC), owned by General Electric, is the oldest of the networks. The Columbia Broadcasting Company (CBS) also operates a radio network. In 1999 the company was purchased from Westinghouse by Viacom, a media conglomerate which owns such properties as Paramount Studios, the Blockbuster chain of video rental stores, and the UPN Network. As of March, 2000, the future of UPN is in doubt. The law prohibits ownership of more than one broadcast television network, and Viacom has yet to find a buyer for the network. Viacom is the second largest media conglomerate in the United States (behind America Online-Time Warner). The American Broadcasting Company (ABC), which also owns and operates radio stations and radio networks, is owned by the Disney Corporation. All three have extensive holdings in cable program networks.

In the late 1980's Rupert Murdoch created the Fox Network. Fox is not yet a full-service network, offering about 15 hours per week of primetime programming (compared to more than 20 by the major networks), and has yet to begin a regular news operation. Two smaller networks, United Paramount Network (UPN) and Warner Brothers

Network (WB) began operation in the mid-1990's. At this time each provides only a few hours per week of programming, compared to the three 'majors' which provide programming throughout the day and night, as well as morning and nightly news programs.

The Pax network, composed largely of stations in the weaker UHF band began in the late 1990's. It has attempted to offer programs deemed suitable for family viewing. As of this writing, however, NBC has purchased a minority stake in Pax, which includes managerial control of the network.

Technological developments have altered the electronic media systems in the United States. In the mid-1980's 90% of all television viewers watched what were then three major networks during primetime (8:00 p.m. to 11:00 p.m.). Today, that number is less than 45%. The remainder watch the Fox, WB, and UPN Networks, cable-delivered networks, independent stations, and public television.

Table 2. *Primetime Audience Shares*

Network	Primetime Average Share
PBS*	4
Commercial**	
ABC	14
CBS	14
NBC	13
Fox	10
UPN	4
WB	4
Ad-supported Cable Networks (Combined)***	38

(Table shows estimated general viewing levels for comparison purposes. Total exceeds 100% due to rounding error, and different time frames for broadcast and cable)
*1997 (PBS, 1997)
**2000–2001 Season to Date (September-March) (Nielsen Media Research, 2001)
***2000 calendar year estimate (Reynolds, 2001)

Beginning in the early 1970's, and continuing until the mid-1990's, the broadcast networks could not own the rights to the programs they provided to their affiliates. Instead, they leased those rights (usually to show a program twice) from producers, which are usually major Hollywood film studios. After the network rights expire the program owners secure additional revenue by selling the rights to repeat the program episodes to stations around the United States and to broadcast services outside the US. These restrictions have been partially lifted, but there are still caps on how much of its programs a network can own. With the exception of news, documentaries, and most sports, then, for many years the networks largely served as packagers, promoters, and distributors of programs, rather than as program creators.

The restrictions were limited in the mid-1990's because of the competition from cable and satellite networks. The result has been vertical integration of broadcast networks with production organizations; Fox and its Fox Studios, Viacom with CBS, etc., and Paramount Pictures, and Disney, with its Disney and Touchstone providing content to ABC, epitomize this change. The organizations are also increasingly sharing resources among their various services. For example, Viacom's MTV produced the opening and halftime musical entertainment portions of CBS' telecast of the 2001 Super Bowl, the championship game of professional American football.

Most broadcast outlets are supported by advertising. However, the more accurate description is that broadcasting in the US is *advertiser-driven*. Program decisions are built around the needs of advertisers. Advertising is targeted to reach desired consumer groups, and programs are selected which will attract the most desired groups. Elaborate promotional and scheduling strategies are used to attract a desired target group in the competition with other broadcasters. Since evidence suggests that audiences 'flow' from one program to the one that follows, program 'blocks' are crafted for each 'daypart' to encourage audiences to stay with a television channel. For example, from 8:00–10:00 p.m., a network might schedule four half-hour situation comedies considered especially attractive to women. Viewers will presumably begin watching at 8:00 p.m., and stay with the similar programs presented all evening by that outlet. Competing outlets will either try to attract the same type of audience with similar (presumably 'better') programs, or to 'counterprogram' by attempting to attract a different type of audience. The group most desired by advertisers is women, aged 18–49, who purchase most consumer products. While certain advertisers may wish to reach other audiences (men, for example), programs for these audiences are scheduled less often (for example, sporting events, which attract a male audience, are found primarily on weekends).

The networks earn their money by selling advertising time to national advertisers. To reach the national audiences the network must combine the separate audiences of its 'affiliates.' In return for access to the affiliate's audience, the network not only provides programs at no cost to its affiliates, but also pays them 'compensation.' Affiliates are also able to sell advertising time to local advertisers before or during network-delivered programs. Networks have limited power in their dealings with their 'affiliates.' Contracts are for three years, and affiliate changes can – and do – occur at the behest of either party. No affiliate can be required to carry any program from its network. Stations sometimes pre-empt a network program to carry an event of local interest (such as a sporting event) or because station management does not believe the network's program is appropriate for its local audience. Sometimes a station will permanently or temporarily change the time of a program's broadcast from that intended by the network. However, too many pre-emptions or schedule changes is a reason why networks sometimes change affiliates.

Changes in the broadcast industry created by new technologies, and by reduced audience shares are straining the traditional network-affiliate relationships. In some cases networks are demanding payments from some affiliates, or are denying compensation for some popular, expensive programs. The multicasting allowed by digital television has led at least one station to affiliate with more than one network. There have been formal complaints by affiliate organizations to the FCC and to Congress.

Table 3. *Fiction Program in Primetime 1999*

Broadcast Networks	Number of Hours/22 Primetime Hours
ABC	15.5
CBS	18.5
NBC	16.5
Fox	13 (15 hours/week)

Selected Cable Networks	
Arts & Entertainment	7
Discovery	0
Lifetime	20
TNT	19
USA	19

Not all television stations are affiliated with a network. 'Independent' stations buy most of their programs from syndicators. A few may produce some of their own programs. Affiliates of WB and UPN are, for the most part, independent stations, receiving network programs for a few hours a week.

Syndicated programs include original programming, such as 'Baywatch,' talk shows, and game shows, and 'off-network' programs. Off-network programs have previously aired on one of the broadcast networks and the old episodes are now sold to individual stations. While most off-network programs have aired within the past few years on a network, some popular programs from the 1960's and 1970's still appear in reruns.

Radio in the United States is highly fractionated. Stations attempt to offer programs that will attract very well defined demographic or psychographic groups. Demographically-based niche-program formats are the rule; most such formats are based on music. Few stations provide more than one format.

The development of communication satellites brought about a rebirth in networked radio programming. Some networks provide brief hourly news bulletins, special events, or sporting events. Other networks provide complete music programming (local announcements are inserted live or, more commonly, in pre-programmed tape inserts). In recent years networks providing national 'talk' programs have achieved success. In some cases these networks provide 24-hours per day of programming. Affiliates may carry some or all of these national programs.

There are few programming requirements for broadcasters. Broadcasters must demonstrate that their overall programming serves the public interest convenience, or necessity. Thus, most stations provide regular or periodic news, public affairs (usually on Sundays), or religious programs. The First Amendment severely limits the extent to which programming rules can be imposed by the government. Broadcast television stations are required to provide at least three hours of programming each week addressing the educational needs of children. Any person who is the subject of a 'personal attack' in a broadcast must be given an opportunity to respond. As mentioned, above, a number of rules pertain to programs or commercials pertaining to political candidates.

1.4 Public Broadcasting

While commercial services are dominant, the US also has a smaller non-commercial 'public broadcasting' system. FM channels between 88.1 and 90.1 MHz are reserved for non-commercial radio service. A channel, usually in the less desirable UHF band, is reserved for non-commercial television stations in most markets.

Audiences for public television generally mirror those of the commercial broadcasters, although viewing patterns for public television programming do not parallel those of commercial programming; most public television audience members view selectively. Nonetheless, in the late-1990's, 90 million viewers watched public television in an average week. The average household watched public television just under 3 hours a week. Primetime audiences for public television, while smaller than those for commercial broadcast television, were typically higher than for cable networks offering similar programs (PBS, 1999).

In its first decade, the 1950's, what was then called educational broadcasting struggled for funding and public acceptance. In a February 1967 report the Carnegie Commission on Educational Television urged creation of a Corporation for Public Television to receive and disburse government and private funds and improve programming. Under the urging of then-President Lyndon Johnson, Congress passed the Public Broadcasting Act of 1967. The Act changed the name of the non-commercial service from *educational* to *public* broadcasting, and created a Corporation for Public Broadcasting (CPB).

The Public Broadcasting Act prohibited CPB from owning or operating network service, so in 1969, the Corporation created the Public Broadcasting Service (PBS) to provide the interconnection for television programming. PBS did not create programming; it distributed programming funded and created by others. In 1973, PBS was reconstituted as a station-owned membership organization. CPB created National Public Radio (NPR) in 1970. NPR was to provide programming, as well as interconnection service. NPR began live network operations in May, 1971.

Most non-commercial stations are owned by non-profit organizations. Beyond this generalization, it is difficult to categorize types of ownership. PBS and NPR affiliates tend to be licensed to state educational broadcasting commissions, to colleges and universities, to broad-based non-profit community corporations, and to local school boards and systems. Non-commercial radio stations that are not affiliated with NPR are even more diverse – universities, community corporations, school boards, churches, religious groups, seminaries, high schools, college student government associations, cities, counties, and youth clubs.

Serious problems persist for public broadcasting. The stations jealously guard their own programming power against influence from CPB, NPR, and PBS. A second problem is political meddling. The Carnegie Commission had recommended that the Corporation be funded by a tax on television sets rather than having to depend entirely on Congressional appropriations. To avoid controversy and to get the Public Broadcasting Act passed, this tax was not part of the legislative package. As the commission foresaw, there has been political interference in programming policies both from members of Congress and from the executive branch. A third problem involves money. Public broadcasting needed funding that continued for longer than one year. This would allow long-range planning and operational stability. Congress began multi-year appropriations for CPB in 1975, but attached conditions to the appropriations.

Overall, public broadcasting gets about half its money from taxes. But only about 16% of that tax money comes from the federal government. Public broadcasting's tax revenues also come from state governments, tax-supported colleges and universities, local governments, federal government grants and contracts. The other half comes from subscribers, businesses and foundations which underwrite program costs, auction participants, private colleges and universities, and other sources. In actual dollars, public broadcasting operates on a relatively minuscule budget. PBS' annual programming and production budget would not quite cover expenses for three hours of programming per day for three months on one commercial television network.

Table 4. *Program Budgets (in $)*

PBS FY 1996 Production, Acquisition, Promotion and Distribution Budget	314,000,000 *
Average per-episode fee paid by commercial networks for television series (1998-99)** 30 minute Situation Comedy 60 minute Drama	856, 471 1,490,595
Average per-episode fee paid for 30 minute situation comedy, "Friends" (NBC)**	3,250,000
Average per-episode fee paid by commercial networks for 1 hour news magazine, Dateline NBC (NBC)**	680,000
Amount Paid by ABC for two showings of the theatrical movie, "Mission Impossible" ***	20,000,000
Cable Television Networks Overall Program Investment (1999)	8,000,000,000****

*(PBS, Annual Report 2000)
**(NATPE, 1999)
***(Levin, 1996)
****(NCTA 2001)

Congress specifies how CPB should spend its federal appropriation. Only a small portion may go to CPB's operating expense. The majority goes to television and radio at a ratio of about three-to-one. For each medium, most of the money must go for community service grants (CSG) used to pay the costs of locally-produced programming; the remainder to national programming. The station may spend the money almost any way it wishes. It uses a portion for programming. The National Endowment for the Arts (NEA), the National Endowment for the Humanities (NEH), and the US Department of Education provide additional federal funds for programming at both national and local levels. The NTIA administers the Public Telecommunication Facilities Program which makes facilities grants for local stations. Facilities grants are used to purchase equipment or meet other infrastructure needs. PBS derives about a quarter of its funding from CPB. This pays for management and the satellite relay interconnection. The rest comes from the dues PBS charges its member stations, from interest income, and from its program library and other services. The dues of NPR's member stations provide more than 60% of NPR's operating budget. Stations derive funds from listeners, businesses in their communities, and grants from the Corporation for Public Broadcasting. NPR also seeks grants and underwriting from corporations, foundations, associations, and individuals.

Battles over funding accelerated in the mid-1990's. Efforts to restrain government spending made public broadcasting a target. Some in Congress opposed spending federal money on cultural activities. They argued that public broadcasting reflected a biased political viewpoint, and primarily served an upper middle class elite which did not need a subsidized broadcast service. In reality, public broadcasting's audience is demographically similar to the public at large. Many advocates of eliminating federal funding for public broadcasting said that support was no longer needed. First, they argued that public broadcasting had not capitalized on other funding sources, such as program sales or merchandising products based on such popular programs as 'Sesame Street.' A second argument was that cable-delivered services such as Arts & Entertainment, Discovery, Nickelodeon and The Learning Channel provided sufficient children's, documentary, cultural and educational programming.

When the Republicans won control of both houses of Congress in 1994 their leadership spoke of phasing out federal funding for public broadcasting. After extensive lobbying by the stations and the Clinton Administration, the original funding levels were reduced, but not eliminated. For example, the allocation for FY 1996 was originally to be $312 million; it was reduced to $275 million. Funding for 1998, 1999, and 2000 was set at $250 million per year.

1.5 Cable Television

There are about 10,500 cable systems. The largest has about 1 million subscribers, while the smallest may serve only a few dozen homes. The industry is dominated by multiple system operators (MSOs). While there are more than 50 such MSOs, the largest ten serve about 90% of US cable subscribers. The largest AT&T, will control access to 40% of the US households, pending completion of its purchase of MediaOne. The second largest MSO, Time Warner, serves about 10% of the US households. Unlike broadcasting, there are no limits on the number of cable systems any one entity can own. While the FCC had limited subscriber holdings to no more than 30% of all multichannel subscribers, a court decision in March 2001 said the limitation was beyond the authority of the FCC. A continuing trend has been 'regional clustering' of systems, so that an MSO can achieve operational efficiencies. More than half of cable subscribers are served by systems in such clusters. About 70% of cable subscribers have access to 54 or more channels.

There are more than 200 program services available to cable systems and satellite broadcasting companies. Most of these services operate 24 hours a day. The majority, called 'basic' services, earn revenues through the sale of advertising time, and program carriage fees charged to cable systems. A few are 'pay' or 'premium' services, which charge subscribers a monthly fee of around $ 10.00 per month. They feature theatrical films and some original programs. The most popular services, such as all-sports ESPN, and all-news CNN, are carried by virtually every cable system. Other services are less widely carried. Viewing levels for even the most popular cable program services are far below those of the major broadcast networks. Most program services seek a niche audience attractive to particular advertisers. Some, such as Lifetime (women), Black Entertainment Television (African Americans), and Nickelodeon (children), seek to attract demographic groups. Others, such as ESPN (sports), CNN (news), and The History Channel seek subject-interested audiences. There are a few general interest services, such as USA Network and Turner Network Television.

The cable industry is marked by vertical integration between system operators and program suppliers. In 2000 one or more of the top five cable MSOs held an ownership interest in each of 99 national program services. The result is that these program services are given preference for channel carriage on AT&T systems. Until the Cable Act of 1992, these services also discriminated against non-cable multi-channel competitors, usually by charging them higher program fees than the cable operators. The Act required that all multi-channel services have equal access to program services.

Local governments and cable systems can negotiate for the carriage of one or more Public, Educational, or Government access channels. These 'PEG' channels provide additional opportunities for government bodies or individuals to reach the public. The nature of these PEG channels varies widely. Some cable systems have an electronic message board. In other cases channels are devoted to carrying live telecasts of meetings of government bodies, of locally-produced entertainment, or instructional programming produced by local universities or public schools. Some 'public access' channels are required by local franchise agreements to carry any program that does not otherwise violate the First Amendment. Sexually provocative programs and programs produced by such extremist organizations as the Ku Klux Klan and the American Nazi Party sometimes appear on these channels.

The cable television industry is structured differently than broadcasting. Cable television systems must receive a 'franchise' from a local governing body (usually the municipal government) because they use public 'rights of way' (streets, intersections, etc.) for their systems. While any organization which meets the terms of the franchise can build a cable television system, the economics of cable television make such 'overbuilds' by competing cable operators very rare. There is also some federal regulation of cable television. Aside from technical issues, these federal rules are designed to ensure that local broadcasters have access to cable distribution in their service area, and that subscription charges are not excessive.

'Must-carry' is a complex and controversial law. To ensure that local broadcast stations are available to cable subscribers, systems 'must carry' any full power local station which requests it (low power stations do not receive must carry protection). On the other hand, if a station believes a cable system will benefit from carrying its signal, the station may negotiate for its 'retransmission consent.' This might entail the system paying the station, or another arrangement, such as providing free time for promotional announcements. In 1997 the Supreme Court voted to uphold the rules. The Court's majority said the goal of maintaining the free over-the-air broadcast system was more important than the burden imposed on the cable systems by the rules.

1.6 Satellite Broadcasting

Because of the widespread availability of cable television, satellite to home broadcasting has been slower to develop in the United States than in many other countries. Beginning in the mid-1990's, digital satellite services, owned by Hughes Communications, a subsidiary of General Motors (DirecTV), Hubbard Communications (USSB), EchoStar (Dish Network) and Primestar (owned by a consortium of cable operators and program networks), began to make inroads into the cable audience. The Cable Act of 1992 allowed these services access to the cable program services, providing a supply of content. The services supplemented the existing networks with specialized pay-per-view movies, and subscription packages of professional league sporting events. Relatively low-cost ($ 100) receivers are sold through electronics stores, and large retail stores, increasing the availability to the consumer. About seven million homes subscribe to one of the services.

In 1997 Rupert Murdoch's News Corp, which had planned to offer an American Sky Broadcasting satellite service, but lacked access to high powered satellites, pursued a merger with EchoStar. The agreement fell apart after a few months, leaving North America outside of Murdoch's satellite empire, although reports persist of a possible merger with or purchase of one of the two US satellite services.

The satellite industry has undergone significant consolidation in the late 1990's. DirecTV bought out its quasi-partner, USSB, and the subscriber list of Primestar, which ceased operations. Thus, DirecTV and Dish Network remain as the two digital satellite services available to US subscribers. A third service, Sky Angel, uses transmits from transponders on an EchoStar satellite. It provides 'Christian' and family-oriented programming to about 1 million subscribers.

One impediment to the growth of satellite service had been restrictions on carriage of local television stations and their affiliated networks. In 1999 Congress passed the Satellite Home Viewer Improvement Act to amend the Copyright laws to allow such carriage, and agreements between the leading broadcasting trade association and the satellite services were later reached. Data have shown that in the small number of markets where such local stations are available on the satellite, subscription levels have increased (FCC, 2001).

1.7 National Anti-Trust and Cross-Ownership Initiatives

One means of assuring that a 'diversity of voices' will be heard through the broadcast media has been to impose ownership limitations on stations. Restrictions include concentration of ownership and cross-media ownership. Recent government actions have removed some restrictions, and there has been discussion of removing or loosening others. For many years no licensee could own more than seven AM radio stations, seven FM radio stations, and seven television stations. In the 1980's, the number of stations was high enough for the restrictions to be loosened. Limits were increased to 30 AM and 30 FM radio stations, and 12 television stations. Television station ownership was further restricted: a licensee's station could reach no more than 25% of the US population. The Telecommunications Act of 1996 changed the limits again. In the case of television there was no change in the number of stations, but the population cap was increased to 35%. Congress also directed the FCC to examine whether to remove the ownership limit.

Most broadcast regulation in the US is based on 'markets.' These are defined in some cases by the US Bureau of the Census, which identifies metropolitan areas, or by the 'Designated Market Areas' identified by the research company, A.C. Nielsen. There are 210 television DMAs, ranging from New York (with 6.8 million households) to Glendive, Montana (3,900 households).

In the case of radio, national ownership limits were generally eliminated. Thus, the 1999 merger of two radio conglomerates led to a corporation, Clear Channel Communications which will own more than 800 stations after divesting itself of some of the stations. Instead of national limits the FCC imposed local limitations on market concentration with the number of stations in the market as the determining factor.

Table 5. *Restrictions on Radio Ownership*

# of Stations in Market	Maximum # to be Owned	Maximum # in Same Service
45 or more	8	5
30-44	7	4
15-29	6	4
14 or less	5 or no more than 50%	3

However, ownership restrictions do not completely limit concentration in radio. Local Marketing Agreements (LMAs) allow a licensee to manage stations in a market other than those it owns. Restrictions apply only to ownership of broadcast stations. There is no restriction on the number of cable television systems any one entity may own, nor are there restrictions on the reach of networks or syndicated programs. Through their owned and affiliated stations each of the major broadcast networks reach about 98% of the population; popular syndicated programs reach more than 90% of the population.

Cross-media ownership restrictions also exist, although many of these may be reduced or eliminated in the future. Current prohibitions include:

- Newspaper/broadcast station in the same market (existing combinations were allowed to remain when the law was imposed in the 1970's).
- One-to-a-market rule (licensees may own television stations or radio stations, but not both). The 1996 law relaxed this restriction in the largest fifty markets. Ownership of two television station in the same market if at least eight separately-owned stations remain in the market.
- Newspaper/cable system in the same market.
- Broadcast station/cable system in the same market.

The 1996 Telecommunications Act eliminated previous restrictions on the cross-ownership of a broadcast network and a cable television system. As noted, telephone/cable system cross-ownership restrictions were also relaxed. The most significant actions regarding media concentration have occurred with the recent mergers of major media conglomerates. The media conglomerate, Viacom, purchased CBS; the Walt Disney Corporation purchased Capital Cities Broadcasting, owners of the ABC Networks, and media giant Time Warner purchased Turner Broadcasting. The policy goal appears to be to allow the creation of large global media conglomerates able to compete with each other and other international entities such as Rupert Murdoch's News Corporation.

II   The Future: Convergence between Broadcasting and Telecommunications

The Telecommunications Act of 1996 removed entry barriers between the telephone and cable businesses. The new law allowed telephone companies to provide video delivery services within their service areas. While there were restrictions on the extent to which telephone companies could control their local video markets, within weeks of the law's passage, Denver-based US West purchased Continental Cable, then the third largest MSO with 4.2 million subscribers. The purchase, for $10.8 billion, included Continental's share of programming services including a part of Turner Broadcasting System, and equity in the Primestar satellite service. In 1999 the company, renamed MediaOne, was purchased by the largest cable operator, AT&T, which is also the largest long-distance telephone company in the US.

2.1 Telephone Company Entry into Video Delivery

The private sector operates the US telephone system. Regulation is under the authority of both the Federal government and the respective state governments. For more than 100 years one company, American Telephone and Telegraph (AT&T) dominated the telephone industry, offering both local and long-distance service, equipment manufacture, and research. Other 'independent' telephone companies, such as General Telephone and Electronics (GTE) and United Telephone, operated in some parts of the country. AT&T's growth was periodically challenged by the government. In 1956 AT&T agreed to stay out of such businesses as cable and broadcast television and computer services. In 1984, the Department of Justice forced AT&T to divest itself of its seven regional Bell operating companies, or *RBOCs* (the 'Baby Bells'). Under the antitrust laws, the supervision of the break-up came under the authority of the Federal District Courts. In recent years mergers have reduced the number of RBOCs to five. AT&T remained primarily as a long-distance service provider.

In 1988 the court gave the RBOCs permission to establish videotex gateways. The telephone companies also wished to expand into video delivery. RBOCs invested in cable systems outside their service areas and lobbied for unrestricted ownership. They also developed digital compression technologies for video transmission over copper telephone lines. Advocates of marketplace regulation urged further freedom for RBOCs. But the telephone companies earned huge revenues: each of the five RBOCs have higher annual revenues than the entire cable television industry. Newspaper publishers, cable operators, and broadcasters feared that the RBOCs would use their overwhelming financial resources to crush or control existing newspaper and television media. The first two groups fought telephone company entry into their businesses. Television broadcasters also worried that they would have to pay for telephone company carriage of station signals.

In 1992 the FCC declared that telephone companies could transmit 'video dialtone' signals over their systems, but could not own the programming. In 1994 the FCC granted authority to the RBOC, Bell Atlantic, to offer video dialtone services, and later authorized other RBOCs and the independent telephone company GTE to begin video dialtone trials. Some RBOCs bought existing cable systems, while others, such as US West, invested in such media giants as Time Warner (it later divested its holdings). Some telephone companies sought expertise in the video business by investing in cable television systems outside the United States. Bell Atlantic created Bell Atlantic Video Services, and began testing an interactive video-on-demand service. A group of telephone companies, including several RBOCs and independent GTE; and Disney, created Americast. The telephone companies were to handle technical and marketing functions, while Disney would license programming to the venture, and act as a liaison to other program suppliers. Later the partners dissolved the company without rolling out a commercial service.

The costs and technical complexities of offering these services, and the rise of the World Wide Web have led to the cessation of most of these video trials. The most notable exception has been the 1998 purchase of the largest cable operator, TCI by AT&T, which is using the cable infrastructure to allow it to offer internet and telephone services.

The new law created a concept called the *open video system* (OVS). OVS systems would operate more like common carriers than cable systems. They are expected to provide channels to program providers on a non-discriminatory basis. OVS operators may provide their own programming on their channels as long as channel capacity exceeds demands from other programmers. The open video system is also subject to must-carry and retransmission consent requirements, and franchise-area requirements for public, educational and government access (PEG) channels (Emeritz et al., 1996). As of early 2001 the FCC had authorized 25 OVS operators in 50 areas. However, there are only about 60,000 subscribers, and the largest operator, RCN has announced that it will stop its expansion because of a tight credit market (FCC, 2001).

Operators can choose, instead, to act as traditional cable systems, and comply with local and federal cable rules. However, telephone companies are limited to a 10% financial interest in cable systems in their service area, and may not participate in system management. The Telecommunications Act also redefined and reiterated the concept of 'universal service.' Historically, US policies regarding broadcasting, telephone, and other telecommunications services have sought to ensure that as much of the population receive those services as possible. This universal service philosophy was first espoused by AT&T in the early 1900's. Ensuring that everyone has telecommunication services serves public safety and public information goals, and the interests of a monopoly provider which can spread the costs among its customers. Universal service is less attractive in a competitive market. The new law mandated that the FCC develop mechanisms to ensure that services would be provided to as many people as possible. Schools, health care providers and libraries received special attention. Schools and libraries would receive some services at discounted rates, rural health facilities would receive telecommunication services at rates comparable to those charged in urban areas.

2.2 National Information Infrastructure

In 1993 the Clinton Administration unveiled its strategy to weave all of the communication elements into one interconnected 'information superhighway.' Like the Interstate Highway system built during the 1950's and 1960's, the *National Information Infrastructure,* or NII, was expected to remake the US' cultural and economic foundations. The NII was described as "a wide and ever-expanding range of equipment including cameras, scanners, keyboards, telephones, fax machines, computers, compact disks, video and audio tape, cable, wire, satellites, optical fiber transmission lines, microwave nets, switches, televisions, monitors, printers, and much more" (National Institute for Standards, 1996).

Other elements included 'information,' such as video programs, business databases and library archives; 'applications and software' to allow access and use of the information; and 'network standards and transmission codes' to allow interconnection and interoperation between networks; and people to create information, develop applications and services, build facilities and train others. Although the Interstate Highway System was built largely with federal tax monies, the economic and political realities of the 1990's meant that much of the NII would be built and operated by the private sector. The federal government's role was to facilitate and encourage cooperation among the competing industries, coordinating standards, and providing funding for demonstration projects. The NII was seen as part of a larger Global Information Infrastructure. The US National Information Infrastructure and the European Union's Information Society are similar initiatives.

Much of the development of the NII has played out against the development of the Internet. Growing out of a 1960's Department of Defense project to safeguard communications in event of nuclear war, the ARPAnet soon spread to research universities. Eventually it came under the authority of the National Science Federation as the Internet spread to the wider public. By the late 1990's the federal government had moved out of direct supervision of the Internet, with control passing to the regulated private sector telecommunications industry.

Individual access to the Internet is available through a number of avenues. Of course most universities and other educational institutions provide free access to students and staff. Commercial Internet Service Providers (ISPs) range from national companies, such as America On Line, to small local firms. Monthly service charges are about $ 20 per month; there is no charge for local telephone calls in the United States. Web-site hosting is typically available for $ 30 per month. Web sites have become so commonplace that most companies include their web address in print and broadcast advertisements.

The internet is also being used in ways that may create alternative means of distribution of multimedia content. the television network NBC created MSNBC, a television service available to many cable and satellite subscribers, with an accompanying web site. Disney, which owns such services as the ABC television network, the all-sports ESPN, and the Disney Channel, has created a web site that serves as a portal to program clips, special features, and supplemental program material.

Of course, any new technology brings with it new (and not so new) issues. Those concerned about children's access to sexually-explicit material have been particularly vocal. The 1996 Telecommunication Act contained a provision, The Communications Decency Act (CDA) which would impose significant penalties on ISPs which carried such material. However, the CDA was ruled by the Supreme Court to be a violation of the First Amendment. While some efforts have been made to create new legislation, most efforts now revolve around developing filtering software.

Copyright issues have also been prominent in policy deliberations related to the Internet. Of course, these issues have an international context, as well, and efforts in this area have met with only limited success. The development of the MP3 standard and such hardware as the Rio playback device have created concerns among music publishers interested in protecting the value of their properties. The rise and subsequent legal demise of Napster is well-known to most internet users.

A potentially important issue is whether broadband operators (primarily cable television) can limit subscribers' access to internet service providers. AT&T has tried to limit its cable subscribers to its own service, @Home. Competing services, such as America On Line (AOL), complained that they were being shut out by a monopoly provider. The FCC declared support for AT&T's argument that it needed such control to 'grow' its new and unproven service. AOL responded by merging with Time Warner, the second largest operator of cable systems, giving it access to many cable homes regardless of whether it could eventually reach an accommodation with AT&T.

As is the case elsewhere in the world, the telephone companies and the cable companies are competing for delivery of internet services to subscribers. The cable industry with its digital capacity, and telephones with DSL have yet to reach a climax in their battle. In the meantime, in some parts of the United States another competitor, electric utility companies, have also begun to offer internet access.

The issue of taxation of Internet-based commerce has the potential for a significant Federal-States battle. The primary source of revenue for the Federal government is income taxes. States and localities rely more heavily on sales taxes, but collecting these taxes on an enterprise outside of any state's borders is difficult if not impossible. Thus far, Congress and the Executive Branch have resisted efforts by the states to allow them to collect sales taxes on Internet-based commerce.

Some concerns have been raised about the use of internet services among various socio-economic groups. The so-called 'digital divide' between the poor and more economically advantaged groups was an issue of particular interest to the FCC during the Clinton Administration, but the issue is considered less pressing by the FCC under the chairmanship of an appointee of President Bush.

2.3 Digital Terrestrial Broadcasting

In the late eighties the Commerce and Defense departments as well as the electronics industry pushed for development of a US high definition television standard. *Advanced Television* (ATV) would replace the existing National Television Standards Committee (NTSC) system in place for the last fifty years. More than twenty proposals were submitted, but all had important weaknesses. The applicants were encouraged to propose a *best of the best* standard combining elements of all of the proposals. After months of negotiation, a *grand alliance* was announced, composed of American and European entities. In 1990 General Instrument proposed a digital approach.

As the *grand alliance* developed digital HDTV technology, two important developments occurred. In 1994 the *grand alliance* reported that its system could carry multiple data streams. In effect, a broadcaster might have as many as many as four 'channels' to offer. Then, in early 1995 the FCC encouraged the committee to consider scanning formats for 'standard definition television' (SDTV) that would also be available in the proposed digital standard. In other words, a digital signal could be transmitted, creating a picture with less resolution than high definition.

Ultimately, implementing an advanced broadcast television system would rely on the availability of receivers. No broadcaster would stop broadcasting in NTSC if viewers could not receive ATV signals. The FCC proposed that broadcasters be given a second, UHF, channel for ATV transmission. The station would broadcast the current NTSC standard signal on one of its channels, and ATV on the other. After a transition period, during which manufacturers would stop making NTSC receivers, the first channel would be returned to the public for reallocation through the government. In the Telecommunications Act of 1996 Congress instructed the FCC to go forward with its allocation plan. Two political issues quickly arose. Some members of Congress suggested that broadcasters should pay for the additional channel. Broadcasters opposed the idea of a spectrum fee, and further proposed that they should be allowed to keep both channels. The spectrum fee will not be imposed, but the FCC has reiterated that it will reclaim one channel after the transition for use by other communication services.

In 1997 the FCC issued its rules for the new digital television service. The 'big four' network affiliates in the ten largest markets (which serve about 30% of the TV households in the US) were to begin digital transmissions by May 1999. Those affiliates in the remaining top 30 markets would begin as of November 1999; at that point digital signals reached about 53% of US television households (although few had the receiving equipment to view the programs). All commercial stations must offer digital services by 2002, and public television stations by 2003. NTSC service is to end in 2006, although in any market in which fewer than 85% of viewers have digital receiver stations may continue dual analog and digital broadcasts. During the transition the stations are not required to provide identical programming on their analog and digital channels, nor is there a requirement that transmissions be in High Definition TV (Federal Communications Commission, 1997). Stations that 'multicast' must offer at least one 'free' channel and must pay a special tax on revenues earned from pay television channels. As of early 2001, 183 stations in 62 markets were transmitting a digital signal during at least part of the day.

Some broadcasters have complained about the timetable for digital conversion, and many others have argued that they should be allowed to keep their second channel. However, members of Congress have maintained a firm position that the second channel will be turned back to the FCC for reallocation to other services, and that the digital conversion must continue at a rapid pace. The FCC is also considering requiring at least some sets be equipped to receive digital signals in order to accelerate the acceptance of the new service.

One issue that remains unsettled is whether cable television systems will be required to carry the additional digital channels under the must-carry rules. Although broadcasters have argued that they should, thus far the statements from current and former FCC members have sided with the cable industry. Still unresolved, however is whether a cable system will be able to alter or delete additional material or interactive services transmitted as part of a broadcast digital signal.

PBS has been the most aggressive US broadcast organization in promoting digital services. PBS expects to offer multicast services, including a new children's channel, and enhanced services, with embedded information supplementing program content that can be downloaded into a computer for later retrieval.

An unanswered question is whether broadcasters will use the digital spectrum for High Definition transmissions (as originally intended by the government) or multicasting. Many observers suggest that multicasting will prove more profitable. However, competition could spur broadcasters to transmit in high definition. Cable operators and digital satellite services have channel capacity to allow transmission in high definition without additional transmission expenses, although they might have to eliminate some existing channels to free up bandwidth for simulcasting during the transition period. Program services which rely heavily on motion pictures would be able to convert to a high definition format relatively quickly. If consumers consider the HDTV picture to be an incentive for watching one channel over another, broadcasters would have little choice but to convert to HDTV broadcasts.

The change to digital services means that broadcasters have to purchase new production equipment. Consumers will have to buy new receivers, VCR's, camcorders, or converter equipment. While stations in major cities will be able to absorb these costs (estimated at $3 million or more), alarms have been raised by stations in smaller cities, for whom the estimated cost of digital conversion exceeds their annual profit. The federal government has created a fund to help public television stations pay for their conversion.

Digital services are also about to begin for radio listeners. In 2001 the first of two authorized national satellite-delivered radio services were to begin offering 100 channels of music and talk/news programs. These *digital audio radio services (DARS)* are intended largely for the automobile listener (which make up the bulk of the typical radio audience). Both Ford and General Motors have announced plans to offer the receiving equipment as options in their automobiles.

Terrestrial radio broadcasters, too, have begun a move towards digital transmissions. A consortium led by CBS Radio has conducted technical experiments showing digital transmissions can be made simultaneously with analog broadcasts on the existing assigned channels. Thus, a smooth transition to a complete digital radio service would be possible without the additional spectrum required for the introduction of digital television. The radio consortium has petitioned the FCC to accept the system, beginning the process that will probably lead to terrestrial digital radio broadcasting in the next few years. A merger between the CBS-led consortium and a competing group, forming a company called iBiquity, will help to accelerate the process.

Many cable television systems have upgraded to digital services, usually combining coaxial cable distribution to the home, with optical fiber linking neighborhood nodes with the cable headend (a system called 'HFC' Hybrid Fiber-Coax). These digital systems are delivering more than 175 channels, allowing them to compete with high capacity satellite services. More than 10 million cable households received digital services at the end of 2000 (National Cable Television Association).

References

Communications Act of 1934, 47 U.S.C 303.

Current Briefing (1997). Looking Back at the Audiences of Public Broadcasting. *Available at [http://www.current.org/pb/pbaud1.html]*.

Emeritz, R., Tobias, J., Berthot, K.S., Dolan, K.C. & Eisenstadt, M.M. (1996). *The Telecommunications Act of 1996: Law and Legislative History*. Bethesda, MD: Pike and Fischer, Inc.

FCC (2000). Mass Media Bureau, Policy and Rules Division, *FCC Authorizes New LPFM Service*. Available at [http://www.FCC.gov/mmb/asd/lowpwr.html].

FCC (2001). *Annual Assessment of the Status of Competition in the Market for the Delivery of Video Programming*.

Levin, G. (1996). Hit films form pricey platform, *Variety*, June 3.

National Cable Television Association (2000). *Cable Television 2000*.

National Cable Television Association (2001). *Cable Television Industry Overview 2000*.

National Institute for Standards (1996). *What is the NII?* Available at [http://nii.nist.gov/nii/whatnii.html].

NATPE (2000). *TV Trends Online*. Available at [http://www.natpe.com/resources].

NATPE (1999). *License Fees for Top 20 Network Primetime Series*. Available at [http://www.natpe.com/resources].

Nielsen, A.C. (1996). *PBS National Audience Report*. Schaumburg, IL: Nielsen.

Ostroff, D. (1982). *Bathtub Gin, Flappers, and 400 Mhz: FCC Policy Towards Cable TV as a Reflection of the 1920s*, Paper presented at the annual meeting of the Society of the History of Technology, Philadelphia, PA.

PBS (2000). *The PBS Annual Report*. Available at [http://www.pbs.org/insidepbs/annualreport/activities.html].

PBS (1999). *Inside PBS*. Available at [http://www.pbs.org/insidepbs].

Reynolds, M. (2001). *USA, Nick Top Ratings*, Cable World. Available at [http://www.telecomclick.com].

Smith, F.L., Meeske, M. & Wright, J.W. II (1995). *Electronic Media and Government: the Regulation of Wireless and Wired Mass Communication in the United States*. White Plains, N.Y.: Longman Publishers.

Television Bureau of Advertising (2000). *Estimated Annual U.S. Advertising Expenditures 1998–1999*. Available at [http://www.tvb.org/tvfacts/trends/advolume/ 1998_1999.html].

Documentation Section
Legal Information on Public Television Channels in the European Union

I   Extracts from the Treaty of Amsterdam (Articles 86, 87, 88, and Amsterdam Protocol)

Amsterdam Treaty (Article 86): Services of General Economic Interests

1. In the case of public undertakings and undertakings to which Member States grant special or exclusive rights, Member States shall neither enact nor maintain in force any measure contrary to the rules contained in this Treaty, in particular to those rules provided for in Article 12 and Articles 81 to 89.
2. Undertakings entrusted with the operation of services of general economic interest or having the character of a revenue-producing monopoly shall be subject to the rules contained in this Treaty, in particular to the rules on competition, insofar as the application of such rules does not obstruct the performance, in law or in fact, of the particular tasks assigned to them. The development of trade must not be affected to such an extent as would be contrary to the interests of the Community.
3. The Commission shall ensure the application of the provisions of this Article and shall, where necessary, address appropriate directives or decisions to Member States.

Amsterdam Treaty (Article 87, ex Article 92): Aids Granted by States

1. Save as otherwise provided in this Treaty, any aid granted by a Member State or through State resources in any form whatsoever which distorts or threatens to distort competition by favoring certain undertakings or the production of certain goods shall, insofar as it affects trade between Member States, be incompatible with the common market.
2. The following shall be compatible with the common market:
   (a) aid having a social character, granted to individual consumers, provided that such aid is granted without discrimination related to the origin of the products concerned;
   (b) aid to make good the damage caused by natural disasters or exceptional occurrences;
   (c) aid granted to the economy of certain areas of the Federal Republic of Germany affected by the division of Germany, insofar as such aid is required in order to compensate for the economic disadvantages caused by that division.
3. The following may be considered to be compatible with the common market:
   (a) aid to promote the economic development of areas where the standard of living is abnormally low or where there is serious underemployment;

(b) aid to promote the execution of an important project of common European interest or to remedy a serious disturbance in the economy of a Member State;

(c) aid to facilitate the development of certain economic activities or of certain economic areas, where such aid does not adversely affect trading conditions to an extent contrary to the common interest;

(d) aid to promote culture and heritage conservation where such aid does not affect trading conditions and competition in the Community to an extent that is contrary to the common interest;

(e) such other categories of aid as may be specified by decision of the Council acting by a qualified majority on a proposal from the Commission.

Amsterdam Treaty (Article 88 – ex Article 93): Aids Granted by States

1. The Commission shall, in cooperation with Member States, keep under constant review all systems of aid existing in those States. It shall propose to the latter any appropriate measures required by the progressive development or by the functioning of the common market.

2. If, after giving notice to the parties concerned to submit their comments, the Commission finds that aid granted by a State or through State resources is not compatible with the common market having regard to Article 87, or that such aid is being misused, it shall decide that the State concerned shall abolish or alter such aid within a period of time to be determined by the Commission. If the State concerned does not comply with this decision within the prescribed time, the Commission or any other interested State may, in derogation from the provisions of Articles 226 and 227, refer the matter to the Court of Justice directly. On application by a Member State, the Council may, acting unanimously, decide that aid which that State is granting or intends to grant shall be considered to be compatible with the common market, in derogation from the provisions of Article 87 or from the regulations provided for in Article 89, if such a decision is justified by exceptional circumstances. If, as regards the aid in question, the Commission has already initiated the procedure provided for in the first subparagraph of this paragraph, the fact that the State concerned has made its application to the Council shall have the effect of suspending that procedure until the Council has made its attitude known. If, however, the Council has not made its attitude known within three months of the said application being made, the Commission shall give its decision on the case.

3. The Commission shall be informed, in sufficient time to enable it to submit its comments, of any plans to grant or alter aid. If it considers that any such plan is not compatible with the common market having regard to Article 87, it shall without delay initiate the procedure provided for in paragraph 2. The Member State concerned shall not put its proposed measures into effect until this procedure has resulted in a final decision.

Amsterdam Treaty (Article 151 – ex Article 128)

1. The Community shall contribute to the flowering of the cultures of the Member States, while respecting their national and regional diversity and at the same time bringing the common cultural heritage to the fore.
2. Action by the Community shall be aimed at encouraging cooperation between Member States and, if necessary, supporting and supplementing their action in the following areas:
   • improvement of the knowledge and dissemination of the culture and history of the European peoples;
   • conservation and safeguarding of cultural heritage of European significance;
   • non-commercial cultural exchanges;
   • artistic and literary creation, including in the audiovisual sector.
3. The Community and the Member States shall foster cooperation with third countries and the competent international organizations in the sphere of culture, in particular the Council of Europe.
4. The Community shall take cultural aspects into account in its action under other provisions of this Treaty, in particular in order to respect and to promote the diversity of its cultures.
5. In order to contribute to the achievement of the objectives referred to in this Article, the Council:
   • acting in accordance with the procedure referred to in Article 251 and after consulting the Committee of the Regions, shall adopt incentive measures, excluding any harmonization of the laws and regulations of the Member States. The Council shall act unanimously throughout the procedure referred to in Article 251;
   • acting unanimously on a proposal from the Commission, shall adopt recommendations.

Amsterdam Protocol on the System of Public Broadcasting in the Member States

The High Contracting Parties,
Considering that the system of public broadcasting in the Member States is directly related to the democratic, social and cultural needs of each society and to the need to preserve media pluralism;
Have agreed upon the following interpretative provisions, which shall be annexed to the Treaty establishing the European Community.
The provisions of the Treaty establishing the European Community shall be without prejudice to the competence of Member States to provide for the funding of public service broadcasting insofar as such funding is granted to broadcasting organizations for the fulfilment of the public service remit as conferred, defined and organized by each

Member State, and insofar as such funding does not affect trading conditions and competition in the Community to an extent which would be contrary to the common interest, while the realization of the remit of that public service shall be taken into account.

II   Extract from the Commission's Communication of 26 September 1996 on "The Services of General Interest in Europe"

51. In most Member States, television and radio have a general interest dimension, despite the structural and technological changes affecting these markets. The general interest considerations basically concern the content of broadcasts, being linked to moral and democratic values, such as pluralism, information ethics and protection of the individual. The way these general interest considerations are catered for varies considerably from one country and region to another, particularly as regards how they are funded.

52. The main piece of the Community legislation directly relating to this sector is the so-called "Television Without Frontiers" Directive of 1989, which provides the legal framework to guarantee freedom of movement for television programs by co-ordinating the national rules which might have raised legal obstacles to free movement. The coordinated areas are rules applying to promotion of the production and distribution of television programs, advertising and sponsorship, the protection of minors and the right of reply. The Member States must ensure freedom to receive programs and must not hinder the retransmission of programs broadcast from other Member States for reasons relating to the coordinated areas. The European Parliament and the Council are currently in the process of revising the directive to clarify and adapt the present rules.

53. In addition, the rules on competition provide a safeguard against the abuse of dominant positions and, via the merger control arrangements, prevent the development of oligopolistic and monopolistic market structures.

III   Resolution of the Council and of the Representatives of the Governments of the Member States, Meeting within the Council of 25 January 1999 concerning Public Broadcasting Services

The Council of the European Union and the Representatives of the Governments of the Member States of the European Community, meeting within the council,

A. referring to the Council's discussion on public service broadcasting;
B. considering the fact that public service broadcasting, in view of its cultural, social and democratic functions which it discharges for the common good, has a vital significance for ensuring democracy, pluralism, social cohesion, cultural and linguistic diversity;
C. stressing that the increased diversification of the programs on offer in the new media environment reinforces the importance of the comprehensive mission of public service broadcasters;
D. recalling the affirmation of competence of the Member States concerning remit and funding set out in the Protocol on the system of public broadcasting in the Member States to the Treaty of Amsterdam;

Note And Reaffirm That:

1. the Amsterdam protocol confirms that it is the unanimous will of the Member States to stress the role of public service broadcasting;
2. thus the provisions of the Treaty establishing the European Community shall be without prejudice to the competence of Member States to provide for the funding of public service broadcasting insofar as such funding is granted to broadcasting organizations for the fulfilment of the public service remit as conferred, defined and organized by each Member State, and insofar as such funding does not affect trading conditions and competition in the Community to an extent which would be contrary to the common interest, while the realization of the remit of that public service shall be taken into account;
3. the fulfilment of the public service broadcasting's mission must continue to benefit from technological progress;
4. broad public access, without discrimination and on the basis of equal opportunities, to various channels and services is a necessary precondition for fulfilling the special obligation of public service broadcasting;
5. according to the definition of the public service remit by the Member States, public service broadcasting has an important role in bringing to the public the benefits of the new audiovisual and information services and the new technologies;
6. the ability of public service broadcasting to offer quality programming and services to the public must be maintained and enhanced, including the development and diversification of activities in the digital age;
7. public service broadcasting must be able to continue to provide a wide range of programming in accordance with its remit as defined by the Member States in order to address society as a whole; in this context it is legitimate for public service broadcasting to seek to reach wide audiences.

About the Authors

Frédéric Antoine is Professor at the Department of Communication, University of Louvain (UCL), Louvain-la-Neuve, Belgium. E-mail: antoine@reci.ucl.ac.be

Daniel Biltereyst is Associate Professor at the Department of Communication Studies, University of Ghent, Belgium. E-mail: daniel.biltereyst@rug.ac.be

Susan Bink was a Junior Researcher at the Department of Communication, University of Nijmegen, The Netherlands until July 2001. She is currently a researcher at STOA (Stichting Omroep Allochtonen) in Utrecht, The Netherlands. E-mail: subink@stoa.nl

Valérie Castille is a doctoral researcher at the Department of Communication Studies, University of Ghent, Belgium. E-mail: valerie.castille@rug.ac.be

Patrizia Cincera is a PhD student at the Department of Media, Information and Telecommunication Studies, Free University of Brussels, Belgium.
E-mail: pcincera@ulb.ac.be

Tomas Coppens is a Teaching and Research Assistant at the Department of Communication Studies, University of Ghent, Belgium. E-mail: tomas.coppens@rug.ac.be

Leen d'Haenens is Associate Professor at the Department of Communication, University of Nijmegen, The Netherlands. E-mail: l.dhaenens@maw.kun.nl

Hedwig De Smaele is a post-doctoral researcher at the Department of Communication Studies, University of Ghent, Belgium. E-mail: hedwig.desmaele@rug.ac.be

John Downey is Lecturer in Communication and Media Studies at the Department of Social Sciences at Loughborough University, United Kingdom.
E-mail: J.W.Downey@lboro.ac.uk

Ruth Klinkhammer is Project Manager, Media-Supreme Court Research Project, University of Calgary. E-mail: rlklinkh @ucalgary.ca

David Ostroff is Professor of Journalism and Communications at the University of Florida, Gainesville, USA. E-mail: dostroff@jou.ufl.edu

Caroline Pauwels is Assistant Professor at the Department of Communication, Free University of Brussels, Belgium. E-mail: cpauwels@vub.ac.be

Ib Poulsen is Professor at the Danish University of Education, Copenhagen, Denmark. E-mail: ibp@dpu.dpu.dk

Serge Regourd is Professor at the Faculty of Business and Social Administration, Université Toulouse 1, France. E-mail: serge.regourd@univ_tlse1.fr

Sergej A. Romashko is Professor at the Free Russian-German Institute of Journalism, Moscow State University, Russia. E-mail: sergejromashko@aha.ru

Guido Ros holds a Ph.D. in Communication Science and is Professor at the Department of Applied Language, Mercator College, Ghent, Belgium.
E-mail: guido.ros@yucom.be

Frieda Saeys is Professor at the Department of Communication Studies, University of Ghent, Belgium. E-mail: frieda.saeys@rug.ac.be

David Taras is Professor at the Department of Communication and Associate Dean of the Faculty of Social Sciences, University of Calgary, Canada.
E-mail: dtaras@ucalgary.ca

Henrik Søndergaard is Associate Professor at the Department of Film and Media Studies, University of Copenhagen, Denmark. E-mail: henrik.sondergaard@uni-c.dk

Carlo Sorrentino is Researcher, Sociology of Cultural Processes, at the *Cesare Alfieri* Faculty of Political Science, University of Florence, Italy.
E-mail: sorrentino@dispo.unifi.it

Kees van der Haak was Endowed Professor at the Deparment of Communication, University of Nijmegen, The Netherlands until October 2000. He is now retired.

Leo van Snippenburg is Professor at the Department of Communication, University of Nijmegen, The Netherlands. E-mail: l.vansnippenburg@maw.kun.nl.